Washed with Sun

Landscape and the Making of White South Africa

WASHED WITH SUN

JEREMY FOSTER

University of Pittsburgh Press

Published by the University of Pittsburgh Press, Pittsburgh, Pa., 15260

Library of Congress Cataloging-in-Publication Data

Foster, Jeremy (Jeremy A.), 1955-
   Washed with sun : landscape and the making of white South Africa / Jeremy Foster.
     p.   cm.
   Includes bibliographical references and index.
   ISBN-13: 978-0-8229-4332-7 (cloth : alk. paper)
   ISBN-10: 0-8229-4332-8 (cloth : alk. paper)
   ISBN-13: 978-0-8229-5958-8 (pbk. : alk. paper)
   ISBN-10: 0-8229-5958-5 (pbk. : alk. paper)
   1. South Africa—In art. 2. Landscape in art. 3. Arts and society—South Africa—History—20th century. 4. Landscape—Psychological aspects. 5. Whites—Race identity—South Africa. I. Title.
   NX653.S66F67 2008
   700.968--dc22   2007049532

CONTENTS

List of Illustrations   vii

Acknowledgments   xi

1. Introduction: Landscape, Character, and Analogical Imagination   1

2. From Imperialism to Nationalism:
   South Africanism and the Politics of White Nationhood   14

3. Visual Representation, Discursive Landscape, and "A Simple Life
   in a Genial Climate"   45

4. Between Corporeality and Representation:
   Theoretical and Methodological Excursus   80

5. Baden-Powell and the Siege of Mafeking:
   The Enactment of Mythical Place   91

6. John Buchan's *Hesperides*:
   The Aesthetics of Improvement on the Highveld   119

7. Prospect, Materiality, and the Horizons of Potentiality on
   Parktown Ridge   144

8. Mrs. Everard's Lonely Career:
   The Komati Valley and the Depiction of Nostalgic Displacement   178

   Color plates follow page 192

9. Modernity, Memory, and the South African Railways:
   The Iconography of Emptiness   200

10. The Life and Afterlife of a Contrapuntal Subjectivity   238

Notes   263

Bibliography   307

Index   327

ILLUSTRATIONS

The British Isles and part of British South Africa to the same scale   *xvi*

Burning a Boer farm house   *20*

Aerial view of Norval's Pont Concentration Camp, ca. 1901   *21*

Alfred Milner with the Kindergarten at Sunnyside   *22*

"Information for passengers by the Castle Royal Mail Packets Company, Ltd."   *24*

Expansion of British South Africa, 1806 to 1906   *25*

View of Union Buildings, Pretoria   *28*

Statue of Cecil John Rhodes, 1907   *41*

The Smuts and Phillips families in front of Vergelegen   *42*

Inauguration ceremony, Delville Wood, Longueval, France, October 1926   *43*

Cape Dutch outbuilding restored as Sir Lionel Phillips's library   *46*

View of National Gallery, Gardens, Cape Town   *55*

Road to the Berg River, near Paarl   *57*

Cemetery near Franschoek   *57*

Distant view of the farm Rome   *59*

Uitvlugt werf and track, Land van Waveren   *59*

View in Kirstenbosch Botanical Gardens with Skeleton Gorge behind   *62*

Aerial view of Delville Wood Memorial, Longueval, France, 1930s   *64*

Chapman's Peak Drive, 1920s   *65*

False Bay coast at St. James, near Cape Town   *65*

Panorama of the veld near Potchefstroom   *68–69*

Early hunting trophies, Sabie Game Reserve   *70*

Car pont crossing, Kruger National Park   *70*

Polo meet, Frankfort, Orange Free State, 1920s   *74*

Calisthenics on the beach, Port Elizabeth   *74*

Cecil Rhodes on back *stoep* at Groote Schuur, ca. 1893   *76*

Jan Smuts hiking with Prince George, Table Mountain, 1934   *78*

British soldiers drinking from a stream in the veld   *92*

South African War Boer field map   *96*

Ellis's Corner fortification, during siege of Mafeking   *97*

Baden-Powell on hotel roof during siege, looking through binoculars   *100*

War correspondents waiting for Lord Roberts to enter Kroonstad   *103*

Baden-Powell's bird's-eye sketch of Mafeking beseiged   *104*

"Old Acquaintances": Baden-Powell stalking another scout   *106*

"Worcesters charging a kopje"   *109*

"Eventide—when the smoke of battle clears"   *109*

"Lord Roberts' Irresistibles on the way to Pretoria"   *109*

Military life: view of small camp on the veld   *111*

Military life: Lt. Key, East Yorks, prepares his ablutions   *111*

Military life: base-camp on the veld   *112*

Military life: field cannon, soldiers, and horses on the veld   *112*

The City's Own in Action near Pretoria, C. E. Fripp   *115*

Haenertsburg, Woodbush, Soutpansberg District, 1890s   *120*

Panoramic view of burnt farmhouse   *123*

"Transvaal: Eastern Section"   *133*

"The Edge of Beyond": Eastern Transvaal Escarpment   *135*

Escarpment near Harrismith   *141*

Lady Dalrymple receiving visitors on the steps at Glenshiel   *145*

Panoramic view of Johannesburg, 1889   *146*

Grocott & Sherry's plan of Johannesburg and suburbs, 1898   *147*

Alan Yates, view from Northwards, Parktown, 1920s   *150*

View looking West along Parktown Ridge, 1905   *153*

View of Parktown Ridge from Jan Smuts Avenue, after 1922   *154*

"Rhodes Over Africa," Kidger Tucker   *155*

Inauguration ceremony, Rhodes Memorial, Cape Town, 1912   *156*

View of the Union Buildings, Pretoria, from Meintjies Koppie   *161*

Cloister at Villa Arcadia   *162*

North-facing loggia at Villa Arcadia   *163*

Pilrig and the Stone House newly completed, early 1900s   *165*

The Stone House, entrance view   *166*

Timewell, stonework detail   *167*

Ednam, garden with pergola and a mixture of nonnative and native plants   *170*

The Stone House with mature garden   *171*

Glenshiel garden with mixed plantings   *171*

Gardens at Government House, Pretoria, looking toward the veld   *173*

Timewell, view through front door toward Magaliesberg   *175*

Voorkamer, South Africa House, London   *176*

"The Huts," Riviera, Killarney   *177*

Map of upper Komati River valley   *182*

Campfire scene in the Sabie Game Reserve   *201*

Elevations, Cape Town–Hutchinson section of the SAR   *207*

Kaaimans River bridge construction   *208*

"Entrance to the Karoo" (railway with figures)   *209*

View from summit of Hex River Pass   *210*

Advertising South Africa in Great Britain   *213*

"Union Limited in Tulbagh Kloof"   *215*

"A Passenger Train Crossing the Karoo"   *216*

"Mountain, Wood & Stream," scene on the Groote River   *217*

Blaauwberg Strand, Cape Town   *219*

A Karoo farm   *220*

Hermanus   *220*

Near Oudtshoorn   *221*

Kaaimans River in the 1920s   *221*

Wilderness lagoon in the 1920s   *222*

Swartberg Pass   *222*

Transkei, general view   *223*

God's Window, near Graskop, Transvaal   *223*

View of Drakensberg (Giant's Castle)   *224*

First train entering Selati game reserve, 1912   *225*

Rest camp in Kruger National Park, with ranger in foreground   *226*

Kruger National Park, 1932   *226*

Curios by the train, Victoria Falls station   *227*

African women and South African Railways train, Transkei   *228*

"Zulu Types," 1920   *229*

Traditional ox-wagon on a country road   *230*

Farmhouse near Franschoek   *231*

Historic irrigation canal, Elsenburg, near Stellenbosch   *232*

"On the Rolling Highveld"   *233*

Landscape near Bethlehem, Orange Free State   *233*

View from window of moving train, Aangenaamvallei, Cape   *235*

"View from the stoep of retired civil servant, Robertson"   *243*

Man seated on rock, Pilgrim's Rest District   *245*

Outspan, Ermelo District   *247*

South Africa House, London, 1935   *249*

Springbok rampant, South Africa House, London, 1930s   *249*

Mining landscape south of Johannesburg, 1930s   *252*

Wagons across the veld; re-creation of the Great Trek, 1938   *253*

View west from the Union Buildings, Pretoria, toward the Magaliesberg   *257*

COLOR PLATES (follow page 192)

"Comparative Value of African Lands"

Zimbabwe Ruins at Midnight, E. S. Turner

In an Old Dutch Garden at the Cape, E. S. Turner

The Hex River Valley, R. Gwelo Goodman

A Farm on the Hills, Kuils River, Edward Roworth

The Paarl Church, R. Gwelo Goodman

Gems from a Floral Paradise

"Where Good Sport Is Followed by Good Appetite"

Climatological map of South Africa

Newspaper placard: Relief of Mafeking

Map showing military situation in South Africa on 31 December 1899

Physiographic map and cross-sections, Transvaal Colony, 1906

Eastern Highveld near Machadodorp today

"A deep sabbatical calm . . .": The South African Highveld

View of the escarpment from Buchan's "pernicious fever flats"

Summer in the Soutpansberg, George Smithard

Bosch en Dal, Herbert Baker

Villa Arcadia, view looking up steps

Peace of Winter, Bertha Everard

Komati River near Lekkerdraai

Panorama, upper Komati valley

Panorama, lower Komati valley

Sides of lower Komati valley, near Lekkerdraai

Bonnefoi store, ca. 1997

Twantwani, Bertha Everard

Baboon Valley, Bertha Everard

Looking towards Swaziland (also known as *Opal Valley*), Bertha Everard

Pale Hillside, Bertha Everard

Winter in the Transvaal, Bertha Everard

Spring, Eastern Transvaal, Bertha Everard

Winter in the Lowveld, Bertha Everard

Moon and Shadow, Bertha Everard

Trees and Trenches, Delville Wood, Bertha Everard

The New Furrow, Bertha Everard

Amajuba, J. H. Pierneef

From Sea Level to 6,000 Feet

Johannesburg Station concourse

Proposed new Johannesburg Station main entrance

"On the Stoep: A Golden Afternoon on a Fruit Farm in the Cape, W. Province"

"Christmas in South Africa"

LIST OF
ILLUSTRATIONS

ACKNOWLEDGMENTS

Even in the slow and painstaking world of writing and publication, this book has had an extraordinarily long and protracted history. It began at the University of London during the mid-1990s, and it is perhaps inevitable that its ideas and arguments are colored not only by my intellectual peers and mentors, but also the historic and geographical circumstances surrounding me at that time. I had just come from teaching design at the University of Pennsylvania, where Marcia Feuerstein, Denis Playdon, and Kate Wingert had triggered in me an abiding interest in the bodily construction of space; and Rita Barnard's passionate interest in all things South African and firm belief that "everyone has at least one book in them" had provided the crucial spur to taking the leap into this work. In 1994, fully democratic government was a few years old in South Africa, and the imagination-challenging project of reenvisioning and rebuilding the nation was very much on people's minds throughout the world. This was especially true in London, home to probably the largest, longest-established, and most visible community of the global South African diaspora, and one kept constantly in touch with South Africa through numerous flights every day.

The catalyst for all of this was Denis Cosgrove, who, along with the financial support of Royal Holloway College, paved the way for me to come to London to study full-time. Over the years, Denis proved to not only be a brilliant, generous, and supple mind but also an unendingly supportive supervisor and advocate, always ready to remind me of my goals when I flagged—a role that he has continued to fulfill ever since. Faculty and students at the Royal Holloway Department of Geography proved to be a supportive and challenging group of colleagues. These include Felix Driver, David Gilbert, David Simon, Dipti Bhagat, Ann Boddington, Orly Derzie, Jessica Dubow, Paul Kelsch, Luciana de Lima Martins, Jonathan Nix, Teresa Ploszajska, and Rebecca Preston. Regular seminars at the Institute for Historical Research and the Institute for Commonwealth Studies were an important part of my studies in London and were where I met numerous people who made helpful suggestions about my work, some of whom became good friends. These include Phil Crang, Pyrs Gruffudd, Peter Henshaw, Miles Ogborn, George Revill, James Ryan, and Hilary Sapire. Faculty at other British universities were also extremely generous in sharing their ideas, reading my work, and making constructive suggestions; they included Morag Bell, Paul Gough, David Matless, Catherine Nash, and Gordon Pirie, as well as John Noyes and Bill Schwartz, the two estimable readers of my final dissertation. Farther afield, Donald Kunze in the United States, Peter Bishop in Australia, and Sheila Hones in Japan performed the same task. I was also lucky to find in London people who helped me maintain vital theoretical connections to the design disciplines, such as Peter Beard at the Architectural Association and Gillian Darley of the Landscape Foundation. During my time in London, two friends in particular, Matilda Palmer and Jessica Dubow, served as a private Greek chorus, devoted and often fiercely critical commentators who constantly reminded me precisely what I was trying to say and why it was important to say it.

Both during my research and later when working on the book, many people in South Africa gave generously of their time and energy. Some were academics in a wide range of disciplines, who unstintingly helped me develop my ideas and introduced me to the intellectual ferment and unique debates that characterize academic life at the southern tip of the African continent today. These included Barnie Barnard, Clive van den Berg, Bannie Britz, David Bunn, Jane Carruthers, Nico Coetzee, Roger Fisher, Ora Joubert, Iain Low, Peter Merrington, and Susan Parnell. Others I met with while in South Africa furnished me with facts and insights not to be found in any book or archive, and which greatly enriched (and in some cases, transformed parts of) my work. These included Kathy Brookes at MuseumAfrica, Clive Chipkin, Eric Conradie at the Transnet Heritage Museum, Genevieve Faure at Vergelegen, Frieda Harmsen, J. L. Keene at the South African National Museum of Military History, Doug McMurtry at Brenthurst, John and Jill Moffett at Kirklington, Mauritz Naude at the National Cultural History Museum, Karel Schoeman at the South African Library, Jurgen Witt at the Tzaneen Historical Society, and my old and infinitely wise friend Els Greshoff. Thanks too are due to staff at the State Archives in Pretoria and the Cape and Free State Archives; the McGregor Museum in Kimberley; the Johannesburg Art Museum; the Johannesburg Public Library, and the Pretoria Art Museum. As the project turned into a full-length monograph and new challenges emerged, I discovered a whole new set of valuable allies. These include Gloria Kury, and Saul Dubow and Alan Lester at the University of Sussex, whose belief in my work and steady behind-the-scenes support for the project played a crucial role in sustaining my own focus during lengthy periods when a myriad of personal and professional circumstances tempted me to abandon it entirely. Finally, Peter Kracht, Devin Fromm, and Sara Lickey at the University of Pittsburgh Press all helped to pull the project together and transform it into this book.

Some of the material in the book has seen the light of day before, and I am grateful to several editors and publishers for permission to reuse, update, and expand on these earlier essays. Portions of chapter 5 first appeared in "John Buchan's *Hesperides*: Landscape Rhetoric and the Aesthetics of Bodily Experience on the South African Highveld, 1901–3," *Ecumene* 5, no. 3 (1998): 323–47; and parts of chapter 6 appear in "Landscape Phenomenology and the Imagination of a New South Africa on Parktown Ridge," *Journal of African Studies* 55, no. 2 (1996): 93–126. Chapter 8 draws on "'Land of Contrasts', or 'Home We Have Always Known'? The SAR&H Publicity Dept. and the Imaginary Geography of South African Nationhood, 1900–1930," *Journal of Southern*

African Studies 29, no. 3 (2003): 657–80; and "Capturing and Losing the Lie of the Land: Railway Photography and Colonial Nationalism in Early 20th Century South Africa," in *Picturing Place: Photography and the Geographical Imagination*, ed. J. Ryan and J. Schwartz, 141–61 (London: I. B. Tauris, 2003).

I am especially grateful to the Graham Foundation for the Advanced Studies in the Visual Arts, whose generous grant allowed me to include many photographs here, some never published before, from more than twenty archives in Britain and South Africa, and to photograph several works of art for which no reproducible imagery existed. For further financial assistance to cover the printing costs associated with these images, I would like to thank Dean Mohsen Mostafavi and the Cornell University College of Architecture, Art, and Planning. I was also lucky enough to find photographers of the caliber of Carla Crafford, Les Hammond, and John Robinson, who undertook this work for me efficiently and professionally. I also could never have gathered and coordinated the over one hundred images needed for the book without the assistance of many people in sourcing, reproduction, dispatching, and copyright administration. These included Eurika Deminey at the Transnet Heritage Foundation, Sharon Crampton at the Oliewenhuis Museum, Lawrence Makitla at the South African National Parks, Dirk Oegema at the Pretoria Art Museum, Candi Nel at the Johannesburg Art Gallery, Kate Abbott at the University of Witwatersrand William Cullen Library, Jill Addleson and Liana Turner at the Durban Art Gallery, Kathy Brookes at MuseumAfrica, Raelene Stefano at the Barrow Construction Company, Jo Pretorius at the National Archives in Pretoria, Marise Bronkhorst at the Cape Archives, Brendan Bell at the Tatham Art Museum, Enla Minnaar at the Department of Public Works, Teresa Watts at the National Army Museum, Andrew Gough at the British Library, Annelie Kriel and Maryna Fraser at Barloworld, and Alta Kriel at Groote Schuur. I am especially grateful to John Barrow Jr., Ivanonia Roworth Keet, James Stevenson-Hamilton, and Leonora Everard Haden, who, as descendants of those who commissioned or created photographs and paintings, gave me permission to use reproductions of these in the book. I also received invaluable practical advice and assistance on matters graphic and digital from Kris Flahive and Carol Slawson at Cornell.

Of no less importance are those in Britain, South Africa, and the United States who have, over the years, provided me with a home away from home conducive to research and writing. These include Brita Eikhoff, Matilda Palmer, Helen Lloyd, Jonathan Dinnewell and Ian Wylie in London; Sue Parnell and Owen Cranshaw, Michael and Susan Dall, Abre and Carla Crafford, Bannie and Alma Britz, Judy Loveday, Eileen Weinronk and Keith Coxon, David and Tarna Hilton-Barber, Anton and Bridget Krone, Kip and Val Anderson, Peter and Birte Voss, Clive Glazer and Clare Loveday, and Nick and Gill Grice in South Africa; and Pat and Pam Foster in the United States.

Finally, I must acknowledge the unfailing faith, patience, and forbearance of Gary Ferguson, who has lived through the ups and downs, not to mention the *longeurs*, of this project, sometimes close by and sometimes from afar, and without whose critical but loving support it would never have been completed. It is to him that it is dedicated.

Washed with Sun

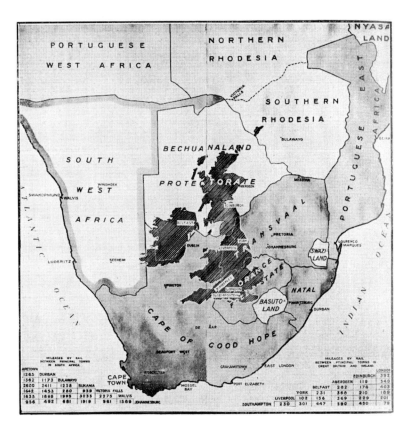

The British Isles and part of British South Africa to the same scale. *SAR & H Magazine* 4, 1924.

INTRODUCTION

Landscape, Character, and Analogical Imagination

> If historical writing is a continual dialectical warfare between past and present—a continual shaping and forcing of the configuration of the past so as to release from it the meanings it always had, but never dared to state out loud, the meanings that permeated it as an unbreathable atmosphere or shameful secret—then what entities and images will come first?
>
> —T. J. Clark, "Reservations of the Marvellous"

Over its short life, the nation of South Africa has become known for its turbulent political history as well as the distinctiveness of its landscapes, yet relatively little attention has been paid to how these two factors might have been connected. The emergence of a white society that called itself "South African" in the twentieth century has usually been ascribed to an intertwining of economics, class, and race, and the role of geographical factors in this process has largely been seen in instrumental terms, focusing on resource competition, the spatialization of ideology through segregationist legislation, and shifting attitudes toward nature.[1] While much has been written on land use, settlement patterns, property relations, and the influence of the frontier experience on the subsequent human-land relationships in the subcontinent,[2] the imaginaries and iconographies that underpinned this territorialization have only recently started to receive attention, more often from archaeologists, cultural historians, literary theorists, and architects than from geographers.[3] This is understandable. Because the politics of imperialism, nationalism, economic maximization, and racial difference have dominated South Africa's history over the last century, utilitarian rather than aesthetic analyses have often seemed more appropriate to thinking about relations between humans and the environment in the subcontinent. Yet it could be argued that a parallel version of this narrative of cultural formation might be traced, using hitherto overlooked processes that have to do with the imaginative appropriation of landscape, mediated by taken-for-granted cultural practices of observation and description. Such an account would be supported by the historical tendency, in many different countries, for the emergence of the "imagined community" of nation-hood to coincide with the emergence of a collective subjectivity toward a given territory, and for this to often occur when significant physical alterations of the national landscape are taking place.

The roots of Europeans' problematic relationship with the southern reaches of the African continent can be traced back to their encounter with it at the end of the fifteenth century. Unlike other parts of the world "discovered" in the early modern period, the African continent was never seen as an Eden. It belonged not to the New World but to the *ecumene* of the Old, of which it formed the farthest, most fearsome extremity.[4] Even before the early Portuguese explorers had physically set foot on land, they had, viewing it from offshore, given it a powerful and tragic identity as Adamastor, the mythical figure of Camoens's epic poem, *The Lusiads*. It fell to the Dutch, however, who colonized the region from 1652 until 1799, to test this premonition through actual settlement and further exploration. Neither the Dutch East India Company, which administered the Cape Colony as a victualing station, nor the prosperous population of a then-underpopulated Netherlands, saw the subcontinent's interior as having much to offer, though a few adventurous Dutch colonists did penetrate it as *trekboers*, hunters, and explorers.[5]

For the British, who assumed control of the Cape at the beginning of the nineteenth century, the region posed an equally awkward environmental conundrum. It was unlike overseas territories that had been discovered by imperialism elsewhere in the world: it was neither irremediably different and other, nor completely devoid of the familiar social relations of home.[6] The Cape was already populated by a mixture of indigenous inhabitants and colonists who spoke a European language but refused to act out the modes of life that might have been expected of them as Europeans. Conversely, these "uncivilized" peoples seemed at odds with the apparently fertile and benign environmental character of some parts of the subcontinent—a character persuasive enough to encourage the British government to actively promote further colonization in the 1820s and control the region's territory and inhabitants once these colonists had arrived.[7] Still, until 1850, the dominant focus of European trade, travel, and emigration continued to be the Orient or the New World, and Southern Africa remained a pastoral backwater, largely off the map as far as most potential emigrants and entrepreneurs were concerned. European geographical imaginaries only started to assume political and cultural significance in the region after 1860, when the discovery of mineral resources in the interior dramatically brought the subcontinent into contact with the world of mercantile capitalism. After 1880, though, the region was propelled out of its pastoral isolation by industrialization and transformed into an autonomous, modern society by the geopolitics of imperialism.

There is little doubt that the rapidity and lateness of South Africa's social transformation contributed to the racist cast of the society that subsequently grew up there, as well as the unusually reflexive relationship it developed with its geographical territory. During the twentieth century, the preoccupation with finding some kind of psychic accommodation with "the land" became a defining feature of white South African nationhood, an ever-present topic in art and literature, and a recurring anchor of identity both in the minds of those who controlled the land and those dispossessed and exiled from it.[8] One only needs to think of the work of modern South African authors as diverse as Nadine Gordimer, J. M. Coetzee, Andre Brink, and Doris Lessing (to name only the most obvious examples) to realize that, for those of European descent living in the subcontinent during the twentieth century, the native landscape constituted as inescapable and problematic an inheritance as the indigenous populations. One reason for this preoccupation has undoubtedly been the subcontinent's spectacular scenic environment. Over the centuries, few European visitors to Southern Africa have been prepared for the affective power of its landscapes; even those hostile to the prevailing political dispensation or unsusceptible to natural scenery have been surprised by seductiveness of the country's powerful sense of place. This remains true today, when the country has undergone radical political and social change and we are skeptical about notions of universal aesthetic appeal, but many individuals still describe South Africa as one of the most beautiful countries in the world.

Nevertheless, contemporary critical theory suggests that in tracing the roots of white South Africans' preoccupation with landscape, we need to move beyond the realm of pure aesthetics into less obvious and less ideologically charged processes of meaning-making. Today, no exploration of place and identity can ignore Foucault's and Said's arguments that political and economic ideologies are inextricably intertwined with the way individuals and collectivities appropriate space and, indeed, are integral to the radical transformation of received notions of space and place in the modern era.[9] Others, such as Peter Bishop, Denis Cosgrove, Stephen Daniels, James Duncan, Nicholas Green, Derek Gregory, Ann Hyde, David Lowenthal, David Matless, and Rob Shields have developed these ideas by looking at how spatial imaginaries are constructed, mediated, and disseminated through representational practices and discourses.[10] All of these authors emphasize that such practices and discourses simultaneously shape identities and subjectivities even at the same time as they transform geographical space into socially constructed, ideologically charged place. An important strand of this writing has been how these discourses use landscape to mediate the construction of the imagined communities of nationhood, especially in the context of the new and emergent colonial and postcolonial societies.[11]

Broadly speaking, this book follows this same intellectual tradition in its exploration of how landscape helped mediate the construction of the cultural identity that came to be known as "South African." Looking at the period of national formation from 1900 to 1930, it charts how the movement toward nationhood was facilitated by the cultural use of the subcontinent's terrain, mediating the tensions between nostalgia and modernity that were an integral part of this new country. Although I situate this appropriation of landscape within the political events and economic relations shaping early twentieth-century South African society, my primary concern is with culturally produced and circulated representations that were infused with unarticulated (and perhaps unarticulable) anxieties and desires. Looking at a period before the radically unequal power relations later characteristic of South African society had become fully entrenched, I am interested in the contingent ways Europeans living in the subcontinent during this period constructed a sense of themselves and their place in the world, not so much as rational schemers—economists, social scientists, and empirically-minded historians—but also as dreamers, storytellers, and fantasists, caught up in a "thick," lived-in world of experience and memory.[12] For this reason, the book is structured around a series of studies exploring how individual encounters with the subcontinent's terrain were transposed into a sense of collective identity through landscape representation. These studies are based on archival study and fieldwork undertaken in South Africa and the United Kingdom from 1995 to 1997.

As this approach suggests, the book has broader ambitions than simply recounting the history of how landscape and white identity became intertwined in South Africa. It also seeks to question the ways in which humanistic and historical geography have recently come to theorize the cultural use of landscape. While acknowledging the wealth of recent inquiry in geography and the other social sciences on landscape representation and cultural identities, I am also interested in incorporating ideas raised in art history, philosophy, literature, architecture, and landscape studies about the taken-for-granted imaginative exchanges that arise between people and the material world. Weaving through the following pages is a desire to draw into the discussion about landscape and identity the role of situated experiences and imaginaries and how these are mediated through observation, description, and interpretation. The book could therefore be seen as an attempt to stage a conversation between epistemologies that seldom acknowledge each other about the relationship between places and identity. It also attempts to recover something of the contingent, improvisational nature of the individual lives that are usually aggregated in hindsight as social history.

In part, this approach has been provoked by empirical evidence: during the early twentieth century, discussions of what a distinctly South African identity might be repeatedly invoked the importance of direct, lived experience of the subcontinent's landscapes. But this approach is also a response to the call for accounts of what colonization felt like on the ground in a particular place, the need for narratives that counter the empire of theoretical discourse that itself risks reinscribing the universalizing effects of historic imperialism. In this, though, I am not so much interested in taking up Said's notion of "traveling theory" as in trying to move beyond received ideas about South Africa as a somehow uniquely flawed society, in which questions of race and power have determined all forms of social and cultural production, and from which little else can be further learned.[13] This view fails to address the curious paradox that at the same time twentieth-century South Africa was a highly divided and unequal society, it was also, by certain cultural measures, and given its small size and marginal position relative to Western centers, an unusually productive one. The view of South Africa as a flawed society also skirts questions of how race and power might have been imaginatively legitimized and naturalized by everyday practices and experiences, and obscures how the often demonized ideas held by whites about space and place were embedded in and produced by profoundly modern and transnational networks of knowledge and discourse.

Thinking and writing in a transdisciplinary way is always risky, bringing with it the burden of establishing your intellectual credentials in discourses whose histories and canons are unfamiliar—sometimes to your readers, sometimes to yourself as author. It also brings the related dangers of simplifying and misunderstanding the complexities and nuances inherent in these discourses. We are all well acquainted with forays made by writers from different disciplines into critical theory that are embarrassingly naive, simplistically equating what can be seen and made with complex and historically rooted values and ideologies. We are also equally aware of critical accounts of human activities that require a degree of situational knowledge by those who have no firsthand experience of those activities, which flatten out that knowledge, and read instead like the work of "reasoners who frame deep mysteries, and then find them out."[14] If I fall into one of these two categories from time to time, I beg the reader's indulgence, in the cause of interdisciplinary dialogue.

But my approach is also profoundly rooted in my own experience and subjectivity. One cannot argue that landscape representation is grounded in the specifics of lived experience and cultural subjectivity without acknowledging one's own. This book is, after all, yet one more layer, albeit a highly abstruse one, in the ongoing representational discourse about South African landscape. Therefore, it has to be stated that the following exploration of the relationship between South African landscape and white identity is written by someone who is trained as an architect and landscape architect and is part of the largely invisible international diaspora of white South Africans who have left (but maintain ties with) the country over the last forty years. My training as someone who habitually works with material landscapes and how individuals and groups involuntarily respond to them will already have become implicit in my interest in lived, subjective experience of place. That I grew up in South Africa poses the possibility that my bias toward the material and the experiential is rooted in a nostalgia that seeks to recuperate a way of life in which such realities loomed large. Although I have lived outside of South Africa for more than two decades and no longer feel particularly exiled from the country, there may be some truth in this. On the other hand, this may be no bad thing. Nostalgia, as Peter Bishop reminds us, is a human emotion that is, at root, about the desire for a fundamental sense of belonging and "Being," a major part of which are the subjective, affective dimensions of human relations with place—in other words, precisely what this book is about.[15]

I raise these matters not only to declare my own authorial position, but also to introduce the theoretical questions and genealogies of thought that lie at the heart of this book, which are ultimately traceable to my own personal history and experience. At stake here is what the distinguished human geographer Yi-Fu Tuan calls one of Western philosophy's most perennial questions and a ubiquitous dimension of human experience: the relationship between surface and that which lies beyond or behind it, between sensory impression and intellectual understanding.[16] Even though I can posit a number of rational, intellectually derived, explanations why and how landscape was used to construct white cultural identity in South Africa, for me, at a certain level, these still seem like rationalizations after the fact. Growing up in South Africa, connections between landscape and identity always seemed, quite simply, given. My own fascination with the country's landscapes long predated any reflexive understanding of the political and cultural values that coursed through them, and this understanding does not capture the texture and depth of that connection.

Ideologies, of course, always feel like that. Constellations of ideas produced as part of historical processes, they are usually passed off as mere conventional wisdom or common sense. Without discounting such arguments, it still seems that the South African landscape somehow communicates in an unusually direct and wordless way to a wide array of people. Traveling around South Africa when I was growing up, I noticed that certain districts displayed a distinct quality, and how in some instances, this took on an animistic quality best described as a "mood."[17] This mood varied greatly, and was independent of whether the landscape was named, inhabited, or had any recorded history that I was aware of. Seemingly inhering in the experiential and (as I now know how to describe them) phenomenological qualities of the landscape, it resembled the character found in human individuals—infinitely nuanced and hard to describe, yet always distinctive. As with people, so with these naively given sections of geography, some seemed to welcome one into their aura while others made one feel profoundly uncomfortable. Certainly, it did not seem too far-fetched to personify some of these landscapes as threatening, joyful, austere, calm, contorted, exhilarating, or expansive.

On such naive intuitions are intellectually ambitious projects launched. I started wondering whether the affective power of the South African landscape was just something I personally imagined, or whether it was something that others discerned too. In other words, was it really there? I began to observe and ask others whether they experienced equally libidinal responses to the landscape, and found that while some did not, many did. For these individuals, as for me, this sense seemed to have little to do with personal histories and associations, nor did it derive from images they had seen or texts they had read about the landscape in question. This curiosity was deepened when I met people visiting South Africa, or even simply seeing photographs and films of it for the first time, who professed to experience some the same kinds of responses to the landscape. Increasingly, I wondered what there was about the South African landscape that affected people who came in contact with it and (possibly) transformed those who lived in it permanently. The possibility began to emerge in my mind this perceptual character was more than the straightforward projection of privileged, politically marginal white South Africans minds. This possibility seemed to be corroborated when I traveled outside the country and found that few landscapes I encountered—no matter how distinctive their scenic quality—seemed to evoke such a strong affective response in me.

The whole question of subjective response to landscape has of course, received a great deal of attention, through lenses that have ranged from the scientific and statistical, through the psychological, to the cultural and political.[18] My concern, however, is with the possibility that certain parts of the earth's surface can evoke powerful and *similar* intimations of something there, noumenal or otherwise, in different people. Although such topographical intimations are forgotten today, they played a central role in Western environmental imagination until the end of the eighteenth century and remained current up until the end of the nineteenth century. Most crucially for this study, though, this kind of hermeneutics was closely related to those operative in the other practical arts—such as architecture, theater, painting, and geography— that were the often-unacknowledged contributors to the so-called landscape idea.

Most ancient cultures subscribed to some version of the idea that the earth was a potentially fertile maternal figure that needed to be inseminated to bear fruit (hence, the inherently constructive basis of culture, which is closely related to the act of cultivation). From this evolved notions that certain sites were imbued with an agent or spirit that could either be nurtured or destroyed. Such sites were usually those untouched by human activity, where the spirit of the Mother Earth was manifested: singular trees or hills, unworked rocks, caves, rivers, and especially springs. This imaginary evolved into the classical concept of genius loci, imaginary figures that were associated with and characterized as particular places or locales in the landscape. Sometimes rendered as a "god," the genius loci mediated the sense that certain locales embodied a living presence that had to be respected and in some cases, appeased.[19] The discernment of an invisible (or not yet visible) presence, in need of recognition, enunciation, and possibly accommodation, remained a constant of the environmental imagination in classical societies, from the originary oracles and Hippocratic occult tokens of the ancient world to Vitruvian observational strategies for discerning propitious signs for inhabitation and the sophisticated translation of these at key Roman sacred places.[20] Even during the Renaissance flowering of humanism and retreat of pagan animism, ancient sacred presences of the earth continued to be invoked within and refracted by the geometric symbolism of that most cultivated of human artifacts, the garden.[21] Although notions of the environing natural world as an animate and meaningful "thou" increasingly gave way to the sense of it as an inert "it" after the Renaissance,[22] the irrational notion of significant natural presence continued to challenge human recognition and description during the Enlightenment, when the perceived relationship between appearances and content was radically rethought as a part of the general weakening of religious belief and the rise of scientific rationalism. The second half of the eighteenth century was a particularly crucial period when, under the influence of Montesquieu and Rousseau, there was a growing skepticism of a priori explanations and a strengthening belief that everything was subject to natural laws. It was precisely at this time that constructs of "type" and "character" first emerged as attempts to provide a rational framework for those sensations that had previously fallen within the realm of the mythical, the religious, and the interpretive. Closely related was the emergence of aesthetics, the attempt to develop a consequential science of appearances, which mediated the emergence of modern—that is, instrumental—representation, and the occlusion of an older poetic tradition of classical mimesis.[23]

These developments in environmental thought and aesthetics remain relevant today because they occurred as part of a general transition, in which centuries-old forms of perception became incorporated in the epistemologies of seeing, feeling, and thinking that we still inhabit. This transitional quality was exemplified by the Third Earl of Shaftesbury's influential ideas on nature and garden design. Shaftesbury wrote extensively about the genius of the place, arguing that "figures" (specific arrangements of physiography or plants) hid "form" (the inner native character, or "natural force," only available to the intuition and imagination).[24] Although they belonged to different orders of reality, figure and form were not unrelated: the former provided access to the latter, which constituted the genius of the place; again, the intellectual maneuver involves the play between surface and depth, and the problematization of what is really there. Crucially, Shaftesbury also argued for a more abstract notion, that of the "genius of the Nation," which was taken up and elaborated in Herder's idea that every culture had a unique "way of thinking, acting and communicating."[25] For all their intellectual rigor, Shaftesbury's theories were essentially a reworking of the construct of the notion of genius loci; they typify the Enlightenment project of reconciling feeling with rationalism. Shaftesbury's writings, themselves influenced by landscape theorists Pope, Addison, and Morris's discussions about the genius of place, would in turn become the basis for nineteenth century "natural theology," exemplified by the writings of Ruskin and the poetry of Hopkins.[26] While the idea of living environmental presence appears to die with these two thinkers, it became transposed into geographical environmental determinism and continues to manifest itself in contemporary constructs of deep ecology and the Gaia theory.[27]

Shaftesbury's was not the only Enlightenment attempt to translate the sense of "something there" in the environing world into rational, intellectual structures. Johann von Goethe's empirical observations of natural phenomena introduced another question that still haunts the Enlightenment project (and landscape studies) today: whether the laws that seemed to govern nature were *found* or *applied*. He addressed this conundrum by arguing that "[o]ne need not seek for something beyond the phenomena," that "they themselves are the lore," proposing that morphology, the study of form as a way of understanding the genesis of things, would reveal the systematic organization of this "lore."[28] In this way, Goethe's observations established the epistemological foundations for the use of landscape as the fundamental unit of geographical knowledge, most notably in the work of von Humboldt.[29] And it was surely a Goethean notion of morphology that underpinned the "naively given section of reality," the unit of regional landscape that the America cultural geographer Carl O. Sauer used as the natural mediation between the variability of the physical world and the systematization of analytical thought: "In the selection of the generic characteristics of landscape the geographer is guided only by his judgment that they are *characteristic* . . . [He] is . . . constantly exercising freedom of choice as to the materials he includes in his observations, [and] continually drawing inferences as to their relation."[30]

To the degree that all these modes of thinking about the environment are concerned with recognizing, identifying, and describing "something there," they are also concerned with questions of representation. A persistent question haunting all of them is that possibility that the relationship between observing subject and observed object is more than the former receiving the latter (what has sometimes been called "instrumental representation").[31] This question takes us back to a premodern (or poetic) understanding of representation, in which there is a more active exchange between human subject and material object, and the transference of meaning occurs through an imaginative act of completion on the part of the subject. This form of intellection is most potent when we are confronted by objects whose empirical inscrutability requires us to become active accomplices in their interpretation (as Lacan remarks, "to trap a human, one need only present the possibility that something is concealed").[32] Tracing such imaginative participation requires not so much a theory of *communication* as one of *reception*, an acknowledgement that meaning occurs at the site of the subject (reader, user, or audience) rather than being fully formed and present in the object.[33]

It is no coincidence then, that at precisely the same time as ancient intimations of genius loci were being transposed into the quasi-objective "genius of place," a parallel transposition from poetic to instrumental representation was occurring in architectural theory. David Leatherbarrow has argued that architectural meaning has always to some extent been rooted in an imaginative mutuality that arises between users and a building's situation, materials, and means of construction.[34] In this mutuality, a building's character stems from the way it simultaneously participates in being a building and a body.[35] This reciprocity is grounded in elaborations of the simple, but primal spatio-corporeal coordinates such as near/far, up/down, in/out, or left/right, which we learn growing up in the world. Donald Kunze deepens our understanding of this imaginary reciprocity between subject (person) and object (building or environment) when he argues that in architecture, the user "receives the building by identifying with it bodily."[36] This user is more than a "mechanical, biological client" of the building; the user identifies with its formation, thinking his or her way into its often inaccessible parts, and the building becomes an "analogue not just of *a* body but *of the receiver's* particular body." Thus, the identity of the user is "born for the first time, out of (the building's) constituent parts."[37] Intimations of character, then, are a consequence of an identificatory form of imagination.

The body implied by Leatherbarrow and Kunze is thus not the abstracted, idealized, or geometric body of the Renaissance—in other words, that of metric equivalence or figural resemblance—but an older one, "displaced [and] realized *through* displacement."[38] This displaced, poetic body was implicit in pre-Enlightenment treatises on building, which characterized architectural form according to proportion, conduct, and decorum, concepts that were expressed and understood through the gestural relationship of the parts.[39] As the meaning of these terms suggests, what was being referred to was a way of being rather than what something was; the character of a building inhered in the relational tension between its spaces and forms, the "display of details in context."[40] This way of conceptualizing architecture exploited the fact that every building, like every body, is fundamentally like others, while also always being slightly different: in size, in situation, in status, in function. It also reflected the phenomenological reality that the universal is only perceivable in the particular, and that the particular is only perceivable in relation to the universal. It is precisely this same hermeneutic that underpinned the emergence of "type," another construct through which Enlightenment thinking sought to rationalize and make replicable that which had previously been intuited and concealed.[41]

Enlightenment intimations about environmental morphology and genius of the nation, as well as notions of architectural character and type, would all seem to be rooted in this involuntary, displaced, poetic body. All imply an imaginative exchange between human subjects and material objects funded by recognition, literally *re*-cognition, more spontaneous and ubiquitous than recall, and deriving from the subconscious (or implicit) rather than conscious memory.[42] Recognition was central to Aristotle's notions of representation, which were most tellingly laid out in the *Poetics*.[43] For Aristotle, representation was motivated by the desire for knowledge, and its vehicle was mimesis. Too often defined as "imitation" or "resemblance," mimesis in its original sense was about the recognition of forms of evidence that are immanent but not (yet) objectified or given form. For Aristotle, the most explicit manifestation of mimesis occurred in drama. Unlike textual narrative, the unfolding of events on a stage achieves its effects through visible action, not explanation, description, or the recounting of objectively verifiable facts. Dramatic mimesis is never simply imitation; it is an autonomous, fictional *re*-presentation of lived experience whose plausibility rests on a situated synthesis of visible action: as much of this representation as possible unfolds through spatial movement and gesture. Similarly, knowledge about the character or identity of those who participate in this reconstruction arises from how they behave under circumstances, something that was recognizable to the audience as a way of being. Thus, the audience's intimations of character were tied to the knowledge they brought to the performance, and shaped by *their* sense of what was probable and necessary in the dramatic situation. Shared knowledge was the basis for both likely and unlikely action; the events of the plot could only be meaningful if they tapped into known structures of experience.

This digression into Aristotelian representation reveals that recognition of bodily displacement is much more than passive response to visual display. At once constructive and synthetic, reflective (drawing on what has already been experienced) and inventive (directed to the dawning of things), it exposes the underlying continuities between representation, memory, and imagination. The *Poetics* also suggests that the perception of the visible (*what* something is) cannot be separated from knowledge of that which is known but invisible at present (*how* something is). This is echoed by notions in art theory that an important part of the effects of painting are achieved through *metaphoric* appeals to subconscious and involuntary dimensions of bodily experience.[44] That such involuntary recognition has wider application than just dramatic representation is confirmed by the fact that both Kunze's and Leatherbarrow's arguments about architectural character draw heavily on Aristotle, and it is precisely the (re)cognition of life or action that triggers the participative mutuality between buildings and bodies.

The question arises whether this identificatory mutuality by which architectural forms are imbued with corporeal character can be extended to landscape. Does landscape, especially unimproved landscape, invite bodily displacement and the discovery of the self in it through the way its parts are composed and interrelated? Kunze himself introduces this doubt with his argument that the prime relational mode of bodily displacement is "frontality": to attend to something, to make sense of it, is to face it, bodily, mentally, and sensorially. "[W]e face what faces us, our senses are met fully by the images and sensation before us."[45] (This echoes observations made frequently by artists that they feel objects in the world are looking at or speaking to them.)[46] The implicit frontality of the bodily encounter with the world means that imaginative displacement acquires a sagittal or penetrative quality, perpendicular to the surface of the object, a prereflective intuition of an inward substance that mirrors that of the interrogative body-subject itself. "'Depth' . . . is less a Cartesian matter of quantitative extension and more an atmosphere or temperament that affects small objects and local events even more intensely than larger landscapes. Its discontinuities (horizons, shadows, *terrae incognitae*) infect our locale to the extent that we prefer objects (books, boxes, drawers, cabinets) as more adequate representatives of global order."[47]

This insistence on solidity and objecthood as prompts to the sagittal imagination casts into doubt whether such participatory imagination applies to landscapes, especially if we see landscape as cognate with space rather than form. Landscapes are neither objects nor bodies in the accepted sense of the world. They are never as bounded and solid as buildings, nor are they as clearly intended as human artifacts. Equally, their difference in scale from our bodies is of a quite different order of magnitude than buildings. Countering this, one could argue that every instance of topographical intimation in the long history of Western environmental imagination has involved a repertoire of forms that could be read in terms of life or action, in which there were distinctive topographical figures of the kind that, effectively, most readily engaged the senses that Kunze argues have the tightest grasp on spatial reality —vision and touch.[48] They included standing and rising figures (promontories, headlands, high points), discontinuities in the general terrain (clefts, caverns, folds), or particular moments in the broader landscapes where topographical elements converged and organized themselves into a characterful, quasi-corporeal lie of the land. This synecdochic figuration was, fundamentally, mimetic, an imaginative projection of ways of being (thus, often genius loci were gods who displayed *human* behavior distilled and exaggerated). It could also be argued that Shaftesbury's figures and forms were recognizable and legible to the degree that they participated in some bodily way of being, and that Goethe's sense of the morphological was rooted in the physical processes and interactions, another analogue of life or action through which material forms arise. Similarly, in Sauer's naively given section of reality, geographical character is figured not so much through fixity and replication as through recurring patterns and relationships between an array of phenomena (how things are).

Could affective feelings triggered by a landscape be a consequence of a prereflective, corporeal-mimetic recognition of life or action in its material constitution, rather than evidence of some kind of secret fixed or complete essence standing behind the object?[49] If so, exchanges between landscape formations and latent corporeal knowledge through participatory visual imagination would deepen the imbrication of human subjects and topographies, and make the act of recognition automatically and involuntarily an act of identification. In this involuntary but profoundly physical form of identification, material formations would become homologies for subjectivities (or, simply how one feels right now, here, in this situation). This possibility has been beautifully captured by Michael Pollan in his account of his search for a site for a small building in the New England landscape he owns:

> I realized that I wasn't just looking for a view, but for something more personal than that—a point of view. . . . Some spots . . . implied an oblique angle on the world, while others met it forthrightly. I could see that I was going to have to decide whether I was a person more at home in the shadows, or out in the sunny middle of things. . . . Some sites offered what seemed like the geographical correlative of shyness, others self-assertion. It was as though the landscape were asking me to declare myself, to say this place, not that one, suited me, in some sense *was* me.[50]

The fact that most people will recognize the simple commonplace truth of Pollan's topographical epiphany suggests that this participatory, bodily form of subjectivity remains accessible and meaningful today. It is precisely this identificatory kind of enmeshment of body-subject and topography that I believe was at work in my own responses toward the South African landscape, and which I believe inheres as a potential for many others in that same landscape. The question arises, though, whether this involuntary, participatory imagination is significant enough to shape the process whereby collectivities make use of their environments to forge a sense of identity. This generally is the fundamental question around which much of this book revolves.

Corporeal, participatory forms of environmental imagination implicit in the constructs of type and character have fallen out of favor today, as the ongoing post-Enlightenment rationalization (and disembodiment) of the human-environment relations continues. Recent theoretical-critical writing about landscape has turned its back on older, analogical forms of environmental imagination and focused instead on how culturally and socially produced processes, interacting with each other in and across space, condition not only *what* we perceive in the world but also *how* we construe it. Today, most discussion of the role of the poetic, displaced body in the affective signification of space is confined to the fields of dance, dramatic performance, film, architecture, and landscape design—all endeavors that have little to do with the ongoing fashioning of broad cultural identities and whose effects are geographical only in the most indirect sense. Ultimately, of course, the replete richness of any individual's experience of the material world is untranslatable, and objects can trigger a wide array of associations, meanings, and interpretations. Yet, as Pollan's experience (and my own, as a designer) suggests, it remains true that certain kinds of places, configurations, and situations do generate similar, albeit involuntary responses in most, if not all, people, and that these responses provide the raw material for the making of meaningful, imaginatively inhabitable places.

Reasserting the role of involuntary, participatory bodily imagination as a constitutive factor in the construction of cultural identities is not to retreat into environmental determinism; rather, it is simply to acknowledge the heterodox, multilayered means by which geographical space and place are appropriated and understood. It also recalls Tuan's enigmatic relationship between sensory impression and intellectual understanding. But to do this requires adopting an interpretive, hermeneutic approach, which focuses on meanings found in the world (rather than hovering around above it) as a consequence of lived experience. This means bracketing (but not excluding, as the next two chapters demonstrate) structuralist and semiotic theory, with its focus on the social constructedness of meaning, its preoccupation with political power and justice, and its propensity for reducing objects to signs. By invoking older, less socially determined, and more analogical ways of figuring the nexus between places, individuals, and identities, I am neither suggesting that these should be revived nor that they should be rejected. Rather I am interested in finding ways of integrating these dimensions of the geographical imagination within contemporary theories about cultural identities and representational discourse. I am not so much interested in recuperating Shaftesbury's "genius of the Nation" so much as exploring how some of its philosophical, anthropological, and psychoanalytical implications might play out in more contemporary cultural use of landscape.

Ultimately, though, the theoretical wager of this book is that commonplace descriptions and interpretations of geographical place might be read as unconscious interpretations of ourselves, both as autonomous subjects and characterful collectivities, and that this involuntary (and unthinking) characterization of the material world offers important insights into our imaginative interactions with that world. Both as a topic and a construct, character is undecidable and highly accessible (or

LANDSCAPE,
CHARACTER, AND
ANALOGICAL
IMAGINATION

recognizable). Because it describes *how* rather than *what* something is, it is an instinctively understood strand of what we call an identity. At the same time, and this is especially true if we reclaim an older, less personified version of the construct, it suggests the possibility of some kind of articulation between such apparently incommensurate phenomena as physical terrain and a disposition or way of being in the world. The construct of character also makes space for the kind of unmediated, contingent experiences and feelings that arise as an integral part of lived relations with place, and how these might become bound up with the workings of place description and interpretation. The topic of character reasserts the importance of the material and sensory particularities of places in shaping people's attachment to and identification with those places, even at the same time as it emphasizes that this attachment and identification itself is shaped by where and when it occurs. In two quite different senses, then, this book attempts to reclaim the South African landscape from the margins it has often been consigned to—those of the global imagination and those of critical discourse—and suggest that the subcontinent may demonstrate something important about how the geographical imagination works.

FROM IMPERIALISM TO NATIONALISM

South Africanism and the Politics of White Nationhood

> Waar wij spreken van "Afrikanders" meenen wij niet . . . Hollandsch sprekende
> of Englesch sprekende Zuid Afrikanen; maar hen die gevormd zijn en nog worden
> gevormd tot die bijzondere natie. [When we speak of "Afrikanders," we mean
> neither . . . Dutch- nor English-speaking South Africans, but those who have
> already become and are becoming a particular nation.]
>
> —*Die Volksblad*, 1875

> And so you see, the true Imperialist is also the best South African.
>
> —Lord Alfred Milner, 1905

Contemporary social theory questions the notion that identity is given, innate, or en-
dogenous, proposing instead that it arises as a result of conduct and practice. Within
this situationally constructed model, however, two alternative interpretations of identity are recognized.[1] The first sees identity as deriving from a sense of incompleteness
that leads to the desire for something missing; thus, lack defines a person or a place
because identity is known through difference.[2] The second construes identity as an
affirmative, active flux, something that arises through practice, cognate perhaps with
the quality or condition of being.[3] In this second definition, "identity" is very close to
"subjectivity," and the two terms are often (and confusingly) used interchangeably.
Like identity as a quality or condition of being, subjectivity is neither imprinted, nor
develops as a separate, internalized entity, but is formed through interaction with
an array of phenomena beyond the self, honed by living in the world, with others.[4]
Thus, although it usually refers to dimensions of human consciousness experienced
as private and individual, subjectivity cannot be formed in isolation: it arises largely
through (socially constructed) experience.[5]

There is probably no form of socially constructed identity that is more taken for
granted (and therefore culturally powerful) than that associated with living in a geographically bounded place or territory. The equation of place and identity is one that

few question: where you come from is assumed to say significant things about who you are. The strength of this equation seems to be proportionate to scale. So powerfully are geographical territory and nationhood intertwined in most people's minds that it is almost impossible to talk about national consciousness in isolation from the physical territory with which that consciousness identifies itself.[6] Shared subjectivity toward geographical space is one of the primary ways in which cultural groups come to imagine themselves as groups. Until recently, few people questioned the notion that the world is ineluctably divided into nations, organically grown entities that are collective answers to the "call of the blood." The psychic equation of collective identity and geographical space remains as appealing as ever, even as we move into a postcolonial and perhaps even postnationalist era.

History, however, shows that the relationship between geographic territories and those who inhabit them is far from given; it is neither a straightforward spatialization of a priori social and cultural values, nor an unproblematic, somehow natural source of those values. Such assumptions are the outgrowth of ideas that arose during the Enlightenment, when images of spaces and places started to be used to clarify imaginary identities that transcended older, more ambiguous cultural and ethnic markers. After the end of the eighteenth century, the notion of national territory became one of the chief means by which the abstract idea of "the nation" was conveyed to its putative subjects and its unique character rendered tangible. "Nations"—groups of people who believe themselves to share a common destiny—do not need to possess (or *be*) a state, but they frequently aspire to, because only states have sovereign power.[7] Such power is most clearly expressed through having space, that is, geographical territory deemed necessary for the security and vitality of the nation. This territory may be space actually inhabited by the nation, or space it does not occupy but which nevertheless helps define it. In general, though, nations seek to maximize control over this territory, first by establishing a consensus over its boundaries, and second by increasing internal cohesion, usually by diminishing regional variations within those boundaries (see color plate 1). The key agent here is the state, one of whose primary functions is to control and administer the nation's territory in a way that reinforces the cultural cohesion of its population and, recursively, that population's identification with the state. Thus, nation, territory, and state are rarely synonymous, and the relationship between them is complex, ambiguous, and symbiotic (something that is obscured by the erroneous belief that the nation and the state are the same, exemplified by the expression "nation-state").

Not being synonymous, the nation and the state seldom coevolve.[8] Apart from a few older societies that already existed in Western Europe before the end of the eighteenth century, most others inside and outside of Europe were the products of the spread of the nationalist ideological blueprint, which invents nations where they do not exist.[9] In some instances, where the nation-to-be had an imagined homeland rather than an already occupied territory—here, Zionism is the prime example—nationhood came first and had to find its appropriate state and territorial definition. In many cases, however, of which South Africa is one example, the state emerged before there was a nation (-to-be). In fact, most nations came about largely as the result of the creation of states; in most cases, the establishment of a state was the single strongest force in creating a people.[10]

15

Thus, although a nation cannot be conceived of without the specific territory that gives it roots and boundaries, it is essentially an artifice, the outcome of socially and politically constructed myths forged over time. While a number of different scenarios have been identified in this social construction of the nation, it is generally agreed that it is a process sociologically inseparable from the emergence of modern society, in which isolated, premodern communities and identities are dissolved and replaced by democracy, industrialization, advanced capitalism, and the emergence of a larger unitary society stratified by class.[11] The emergence of the nation-state thus coincides with the inclusion of the broad mass of population in civic society, and a shift from *Gemeinschaft* to *Gesellschaft* that creates the need for solidarity with and membership in the new, larger social structure.[12] This process of identity formation invariably brings with it a longing for national form that is answered by geographical space, which provides a means for welding together fragmented individual and group experience. Indeed, it is largely through the definition, control, and reification of territory that the nation's citizens become socialized as citizens. This occurs through a long, complex process that involves the manipulation and control of the environment, the molding and interpretation of social space, the definition and hardening of national boundaries, and the imaginative abstraction, inhabitation, and use of the nation's territory through cultural discourse. This is precisely what occurred in South Africa during the first three decades of the twentieth century.

The transformation of peoples without a sense of their own history into nations at the end of the nineteenth century was a result of fundamental shifts in philosophical, historical, and anthropological discourse earlier in the century; nationalism was the offspring of the Enlightenment and Romanticism. Before this, the nation's genius was seen to reside in a sophisticated, largely urban Zivilization, in which nature (human and otherwise) was implicitly ruled and shaped by cultivation.[13] Over the course of the nineteenth century, however, there arose an alternative to this civilizationist model of society, which sought to legitimize the nation-state in terms of regional or vernacular mores and traditions. The belief arose that all societies contained a core essence, or Kultur, that had to be discovered. This cultural essence was believed to derive from local geography, climate, and customs, and manifest itself in the collective use and transformation of such local natural phenomena. Toward the end of the nineteenth century, this so-called culturalist model of society, in which a heightened scrutiny of nature was mirrored by an increasing scrutiny of human nature, began to express itself in a number of different ways. In industrial nations, the growth of disciplines like archaeology, anthropology, and folklore and quasi-scientific geographical discourse emphasized the interconnectedness of climate, terrain, and racial character.[14] Among smaller imagined communities still struggling toward self-determination and territorial autonomy, like the Irish, the Catalans, and the Finns, this culturalist model manifested itself in the recovery and resuscitation of languages and other expressions of folk or peasant traditions like costume, dance, music, native crafts, and pagan heroes, as well as the emergence of architecture adapted from a number of indigenous sources.[15] Thus, while very few modern nations have ancient roots, most incorporate premodern elements within their cultural identity.[16]

Geographical territory defines national identity through two distinct hermeneutics: internally (how the national community is linked to the land); and externally (how the national community is delimited in relation to other groups). In the early years of South African existence, the country's hybrid, transitional political character as an autonomous nation-colony within a global empire, as well as its unresolved borders, meant that both these hermeneutics were simultaneously in play. Indeed, it could be argued that the unfolding discourse of South African nationhood exemplified to an unusual degree the way in which place-based identities arise in the modern era, both within and across geographical scales that may be both larger and smaller than the state. The resultant geographical identities are as often transnational as national. Nested within or overlapping each other, they may reference groups of countries as well as localities and regions within a given country. Thus, during the period of identity formation in South Africa, the country's national identity could not be understood separately from the larger-scale British imperial identity that both covered and divided its territory, and which was, in its own right, more than the sum of its constituent parts.

Implicit in such overlapping, multiscalar, place-based identity formation is the reality that no region or locale is ever perceived without some imaginary reference to others elsewhere. All political collectivities' identification with geographical territory involves weaving together, in a shared narrative, memories of often quite different geographical and historical scales. Needless to say, the memories referred to here are not the true records of past events, but a selective, socially constructed set of fragments from which identity is crafted and recrafted.[17] The transition from *Gemeinschaft* to *Gesellschaft* is effected precisely through the replacement of the preconscious, personal memory embedded in everyday life with socially constructed, collective memory, mediated by cultural representations stressing roots, boundaries, and belonging. Nations' claims to deep roots are made not only for geopolitical reasons, however, but also for reasons of collective security. The very idea of nationhood is impossible without the social use of memory. Nationhood is founded on a "narrative of descent" that isolates and reifies a variety of identity-forming principles (race, religion, language, cultural *moeurs*, continuity of inhabitation) that link the nation to a shared past in a shared territory.[18] Given the rapid economic and cultural transformations usually associated with the emergence of the modern nation-state, it is no accident that the land—apparently both unchanging and distinctive—looms large as an icon of continuity. During periods of rapid social change the land becomes an object of consolation to a wide range of individuals, partly because even as it changes and decays it is renewed, and partly because its life is longer than theirs.

This reification of the land as icon of nationhood is encouraged by the way most landscapes contain material traces of past activities that can be selectively used to justify a cultural group's activities in the present and the future.[19] Wherever history and mythology are used to construct a common past, landscape has the potential to stand for an imaginary shared space in which the great story of nationhood has unfolded, rendering it timeless and indisputable. (Hence there are very few countries whose anthems do not in some way celebrate the qualities of their geographical regions and environments, or whose national narratives do not single out ways of life rooted in such places.) In almost every country, the spread of collective memory was marked by the emergence of loci considered to be visible containers of the narrative that had given rise to the new national order, and which otherwise would have been lost from view.[20] This allegedly timeless pact between nation and nature is usually deemed to be especially evident in rural landscapes in remote parts of the national territory that remain untouched by industrial capitalism or rural mechanization (often precisely those regions left behind by those whose lives are most disrupted by the emergence of the modern nation-state). Consequently, prevailing responses to landscape at the historical moment when a nation achieves political and cultural autonomy (for example, the Netherlands in the seventeenth century, the United States in the nineteenth) tend to lay the groundwork for shared and enduring ideas about the relationship between a nation's culture and its landscape.

This seminal historical moment occurred later in Southern Africa than in many other parts of the world.[21] Because of this, the imperatives favoring the construction of an imagined nation and the placing of that nation in a bounded geographical territory were strong and were complicated by a number of unique factors. The country came into being as a state without a nation, without clearly defined borders, its polity fashioned from a demographic minority recently at war with itself and divided by that most fundamental badge of cultural identity, language. The new nation was moreover of a kind never been seen before: an independent, predominantly European society in Africa with strong ties to Britain.[22] And, as we shall see, the construction of a narrative of descent was further complicated by the fact that the only true peasantry could not be recognized, because they happened to belong to a different race from the dominant polity.

Polarization and Persuasion: The South African War and the Creation of Union

The story of place-based identity formation in twentieth century South Africa begins with the social, political, economic, and environmental factors that conditioned this process before, during, and after nationhood. At the end of the nineteenth century, the African subcontinent was divided into two British possessions—the Cape and Natal Colonies, which occupied the maritime littoral, and two Boer republics, the Zuid Afrikaansche Republiek (ZAR, South African Republic) and the Oranje Vrijstaat (Orange Free State), in the interior. This division followed the most basic of environmental differences, which are still evident today. Because of the almost continuous mountain ranges that divide the subcontinent's narrow coastal belts from an expansive, relatively flat interior, its southern and eastern margins receive the most precipitation, and only the eastern half of the interior receives adequate rainfall and has permanently flowing rivers.[23] In a part of the world where a perennial supply of water is rare, this had a lasting effect on population density and distribution. In the colonial period, most European settlement was confined to well-watered areas within a few days travel from the coast, close to the sea and the market economies to which the settlers owed their marginal existence. The annexation of these coastal margins by the British in the early nineteenth century, along with pressure from southward moving African tribes along the eastern seaboard, led to the departure from the Cape Colony of more than ten thousand Dutch-speaking farmers in the 1830s and 1840s. Unwilling to live under a British colonial administration after the repeal of slavery, these descendants of earlier Dutch, German, and French colonists under the Dutch East India Company made their "Great Trek" into the interior, where they established their two independent republics on the elevated grasslands that until then had been the home of Africans of Nguni descent.

This division of the subcontinent into a coastal littoral politically, economically, and culturally connected to Europe, and an isolated interior populated with widely dispersed, barely socialized subsistence farmers, both black and white, came to an abrupt end during the closing decades of the nineteenth century. The discovery of diamonds and then gold in the interior dramatically inverted the territorial value of the subcontinent to mercantile imperialism and expanded trade networks into the African interior after 1860. The resultant influx of foreign capital and personnel into the subcontinent (whose entire 1890 white population numbered only 600,000)[24] introduced powerful tensions between the tradition-bound governments of the Boer republics and the European immigrants who financed, owned, and ran the mining companies. These tensions were particularly acute in the South African Republic, where the richest goldfields lay. The discovery of gold coincided with a time when worldwide demand for the metal was critically in excess of prevailing supply and British imperialism was at its apogee.[25] Under the guise of protecting British expatriate interests, tensions in the Boer republics began to be exploited by imperialist politicians in London and the Cape from 1895 onward.

The resultant war between Britain and the Boer Republics, which broke out two months before the end of the century and lasted until early 1902, became, effectively, a civil war in which all those living in the subcontinent were forced to take sides. The South African War also dramatically called into question the aggressive strategies Britain had used to accumulate its empire, and proved to be a catalyst for a profound reevaluation of long-held notions of national identity and purpose in Britain.[26] However, the war's most crucial effect was to bring together in a powerful way the various social and economic forces present in the subcontinent at the end of the nineteenth century. No other event heightens the connections between history and geography—and hence, identity formation—like war, and the South African War was undoubtedly the single most important event shaping white society in the subcontinent during the next half-century. The conflict transformed the European geographical imagination of the region and helped bring about the politicization of the relationship between people and place. It also introduced notions of territoriality where there had previously mostly been notions of locality, and left a legacy of place- and space-based memories that would, indirectly and directly, be used to anchor and shape identities in the postwar period.

The mobility of labor and capital in the subcontinent during the 1880s and 1890s meant that before the war, many English-speaking whites had lived in the Boer republics, while many Dutch-speaking whites had lived in the British colonies of the Cape and Natal.[27] During the war, this loose relationship between people and place came to an end. British-subjects were evacuated from the Boer republics at the start of the war, and Boer sympathizers were placed under house arrest by the British forces in the border zones.[28] Captured Boer troops were incarcerated in prison camps, and in some cases deported overseas. Most significant, however, was Kitchener's policy after mid-1901 of rounding up and placing thousands of Boer women and children in concentration camps, ostensibly to prevent guerrillas still in the field from receiv-

Burning a Boer farm
house. MuseumAfrica
Photographic Collec-
tion file ref. 968.0447;
reproduced with
permission.

ing assistance, and to protect families whose menfolk had surrendered from being
driven from their farms by Boer forces.[29] Of the 18 percent of the tiny prewar Boer
population lost in the war, most died in these camps (some 28,000, of which nearly
80 percent were children).[30] For the Boers, a people whose way of life revolved around
autonomy on the land, the trauma of displacement from the land and loss of families
deepened as the war progressed.[31] Land belonging to imprisoned Boers was reclaimed
by African clans who argued that it had wrongfully been taken from them in previous decades.[32] After the war, still more Boers lost their farms through loan default,
either because they had been unable to work the land while they were imprisoned, or
because their stock, already diminished by the rinderpest epidemic of the 1890s, had
been destroyed or stolen. It is no surprise, then, that the war left a hatred of British
imperialism that would last decades among many Boers.

Among those who won, the war fostered imaginative connections between landscape and identity of a somewhat different, though equally potent, kind. When
peace was signed in May 1902, the two ex-Boer republics were transformed into the
Transvaal and Orange River Colonies, which, it was hoped, would in time be brought
into some kind of single political system with the older, self-governing colonies of
Cape and Natal. Whether this system would be federation or union was as yet un-
determined, but reconstruction was seen as playing a key role in bringing it about.
Reconstruction of these new Crown Colonies was overseen by Lord Alfred Milner,
since 1897 the governor of the Cape Colony and high commissioner for South Africa, and since the war, governor of the new colonies as well. Before the war, Milner
had spent much time at the Cape discussing the future of South Africa with Cecil
Rhodes, the multimillionaire mining magnate and imperialist prime minister of the
Cape Colony. Rhodes envisioned the postwar subcontinent transformed into a feder-

ated South Africa, a "union of civilized spirits mothered by Britannia, nursed and nurtured by the benevolent spirits of Europe."[33] His death shortly before the end of the war meant that it fell to Milner and his so-called Kindergarten of young, hand-picked, Oxford-educated administrators to implement this vision.[34]

In 1902, the Orange River and Transvaal Colonies were in chaos, and the task facing Milner was formidable. The results of the British "scorched earth" policies—burned farmhouses, machine-gunned stock, uprooted crops, and smashed orchards—were everywhere visible on both sides of the Vaal River, and thousands of Boer families needed to be reestablished on their farms.[35] There were few reliable maps of the region, only a jumble of hand-drawn deed diagrams of Boer farms, railway surveys, and military maps of strategic areas.[36] The Witwatersrand gold mines, the main motivation for the war and the region's sole economic resource, stood idle due to labor shortages and physical damage. Away from the Rand, only the railways, which during the war had been vital to British control and therefore were guarded by hundreds of blockhouses, were still in operation.

Milner's personal connections with a number of pro-imperial intellectuals at Oxford during the 1890s meant that he saw the reconstruction of the Crown Colonies as an opportunity to test a new kind of colonialism that could, at the proper time, be exported to the rest of South Africa and possibly to the rest of the British Empire.[37] As a result, the policies he and the Kindergarten developed for the new territories were shot through with the ideas then current in Britain about culture, society, and

environment. A key strand of this *mentalité* was a residual, overdetermined ruralism, whose historic origins can be traced to Britain's centuries-old history of landscape domestication, and the English aristocracy's eighteenth century withdrawal to country estates in response to early industrialization. By the late nineteenth century in Britain, these historic social phenomena became intertwined in a moral geography that romanticized the harmony between peasant life and the natural world and saw the most authentic expressions of culture arising from life on the land. This viewpoint, which I call "culturalist," located the nation's strength, stability, and identity in an unchanging, semifeudal, place-bound way of life characterized by custom and repetition rather than rootless, mobile trade.[38]

By 1900, this ruralist, anti-urban *mentalité* had almost become a defining feature of British society. The mid-Victorian period's promise of harmony—between religion and science, capital and labor, city and country, art and nature, aristocracy and democracy—had started to unravel, and the city was being demonized as a place of rampant capitalism, corruption, vice, vanity, ill health, and un-English cosmopolitanism.[39] After nearly a century of industrialization and urban growth, not only the mercantile establishment was perturbed by the cultural consequences of urbanization, but also Fabian socialists frustrated at their failure to alleviate urban poverty and degradation were increasingly embracing a nostalgic, pastoralist vision of how society might be transformed.[40] By the 1890s, this vision had led to the formation of many different guilds and preservation societies acting on behalf of ancient buildings, nature, customs, handicrafts, and folk songs, all of which emphasized the virtues of a settled rural existence against the vices of the city. This vision appealed especially to the growing urban bourgeoisie, who increasingly turned to rural life as a locus of privacy, sensation, and refreshment that counterbalanced stressful, upwardly mobile lives.[41] Sometimes, it also carried an implicit condemnation of Britain's supposedly feckless urban masses, concern over widespread agricultural depression and decline, and a generalized fin de siècle anxiety about continuing British imperial supremacy.

Insofar as they consciously thought about such matters, the ideal society envisaged by most Britons at this time combined the best qualities of both aristocracy and peasantry: a community of rural land*owners*, a "yeoman gentry" made up of educated, somehow classless individuals who would act as a bulwark against creeping urbanization and the spread of mass culture and revolution and would maintain patrician values of memory, continuity, and social order. In what was by this time the most industrialized society in the world, such ideas acquired an edge and a potency unequaled anywhere else. At home in Britain, they gave rise to the first garden suburbs, as well as the perception that the thinly settled, upland margins of Wales and Scotland were the home of people of outstanding hardiness, virtue, and probity. Abroad, it encouraged Britain to compete with other imperial nation-states to acquire overseas territories where resettled metropolitan masses could be regenerated through life on the land.

In South Africa, large tracts of the new Crown Colonies seemed admirably suited to the latter project. Although the acquisition of land for settlement had not been the main goal of the war, Milner and others in Britain perceived the project of reconstruction as a golden opportunity to establish a white man's country in Africa. Milner himself saw the bringing of peace to a region plagued by dissent and ignorance and the securing of the subcontinent as a loyalist British Dominion, as closely related goals, best achieved through the swift restoration of civil and economic life under an imperially minded administration. In Milner's exemplary vision of South Africa, not only the Boers but also the *uitlanders* had to be shown the contrast between the virtues of a British administration and the incompetencies of the superseded republican governments. He tackled the task of reconstruction across a broad front. He reorganized local and regional government along British lines, promoting industrial investment, and ensured that mines had adequate labor, but he also placed great emphasis on rural development.[42] A key strategy was attracting large numbers of enterprising young English-speaking emigrants to settle in rural areas, where it was hoped they would in time form a substantial farming class of loyalist smallholders. Particularly in the Transvaal, Milner believed that introducing English-speaking farmers in a pattern of "closer settlement" would, through a combination of cultural osmosis and a policy of Anglicization in education, help break down the prewar polarization between urban English entrepreneurs and rural Boer farmers and make the denizens of rural South Africa more friendly toward Britain. Because this policy was formulated when the war was still in progress, and the postwar political dispensation still uncertain, Milner hoped to attract emigrants from Britain and the other colonies as well as soldiers who had fought in the war, who could help combat ongoing Boer guerilla attacks and provide men for local militias once peace was declared.

The central fact behind Milner's emigration proposals, however, was that his vision of South Africa as a united "white man's country" loyal to the British Crown was only realizable if Africans remained politically disempowered and sufficient numbers of whites supported it through the ballot box.[43] This either meant that the defeated Boers had to be induced to support his vision, or substantial numbers of British immigrants had to be attracted to settle in South Africa. (Milner initially estimated

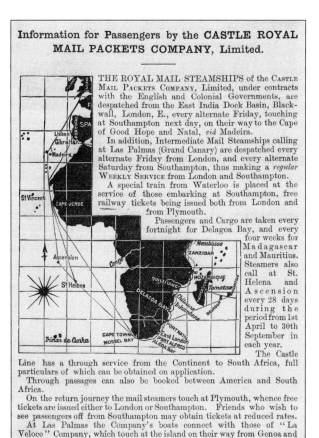

Information for Passengers by the **CASTLE ROYAL MAIL PACKETS COMPANY, Limited.**

THE ROYAL MAIL STEAMSHIPS of the CASTLE MAIL PACKETS COMPANY, Limited, under contracts with the English and Colonial Governments, are despatched from the East India Dock Basin, Blackwall, London, E., every alternate Friday, touching at Southampton next day, on their way to the Cape of Good Hope and Natal, *via* Madeira.

In addition, Intermediate Mail Steamships calling at Las Palmas (Grand Canary) are despatched every alternate Friday from London, and every alternate Saturday from Southampton, thus making a *regular* WEEKLY SERVICE from London and Southampton.

A special train from Waterloo is placed at the service of those embarking at Southampton, free railway tickets being issued both from London and from Plymouth.

Passengers and Cargo are taken every fortnight for Delagoa Bay, and every four weeks for Madagascar and Mauritius. Steamers also call at St. Helena and Ascension every 28 days during the period from 1st April to 30th September in each year.

The Castle Line has a through service from the Continent to South Africa, full particulars of which can be obtained on application.

Through passages can also be booked between America and South Africa.

On the return journey the mail steamers touch at Plymouth, whence free tickets are issued either to London or Southampton. Friends who wish to see passengers off from Southampton may obtain tickets at reduced rates.

At Las Palmas the Company's boats connect with those of "La Veloce" Company, which touch at the island on their way from Genoa and

"Information for passengers by the Castle Royal Mail Packets Company, Ltd." Union Castle Guide to South Africa, 1896–97. Author's collection.

that nearly 150,000 would be needed.)[44] Thus, Milner's policies astutely interwove political expediency and an almost Jeffersonian cultural idealism. They simultaneously masked the underlying agenda of Anglicization, assuaged metropolitan concerns that annexation of the ex-Boer republics had largely been driven by the greed of a cosmopolitan, profit-oriented, *urban* culture, and transposed contemporary ways of thinking about culture and nature to what was being seen as a new, quasi-British country. Milner's promotion of rural settlement was central to these policies. Without rural settlement, rootless urban industries like mining rather than agriculture would become the long-term backbone of the South African economic and hence cultural life; the land would remain largely undeveloped, leaving the region's economy overly dependent on mineral resources that might soon be exhausted.[45] Implicitly British rural emigration would not only promote scientific, progressive, and therefore surplus-producing agriculture, but also build a conservative yeoman gentry society that was both autochthonous and loyal to the British crown.

Apart from their social and ideological agendas, these plans for rural settlement mediated a significant change in geographical perception about South Africa. Predominant images of nineteenth-century agriculture in South Africa had been generally pessimistic, emphasizing the backwardness of farmers and the ecological fragility of the land. Compared to other parts of the world the British had colonized— Australia, New Zealand, Canada, and Argentina, for instance—South Africa seemed

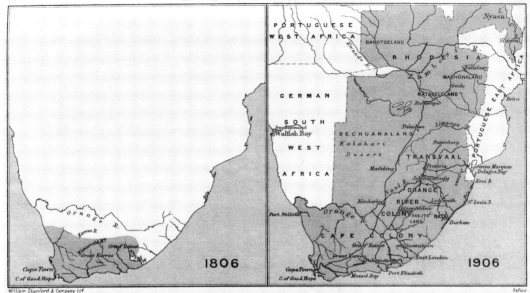

far less organized and technically developed, and it produced fewer exports. Milner's optimism owed as much to his lack of any real knowledge about the land's carrying capacity as it did to romantic visions of the subcontinent and overconfidence in what British administration and governance might achieve, when applied to the Boers' apparently hopelessly "unscientific" farming methods.[46] Hence, his assertion: "It is our duty and interest to preserve the Boer as a farmer; (but) it is neither our duty nor our interest to preserve him as a negligent landowner."[47] Milner's confidence in the region's agricultural prospects was reflected in the sponsored immigration schemes and Land Settlement Board he set up to provide loans and assistance to individuals considering taking up farming in South Africa. Milner also established an agricultural services department in the Transvaal to encourage new farming methods, veterinary research, and pest control, and he set in motion several major reconnaissance surveys to explore irrigation opportunities.[48] Africans who had reclaimed white farms were driven back into assigned tribal areas by the South African Constabulary (formed from British Army volunteers at the end of the war), and Boers whose farms were above a certain size were given assistance with restocking, fencing, boreholes, and seed.[49]

Milner's plans met with stiff opposition from a number of quarters. In South Africa, the Dutch argued that he wanted to swamp them with British emigrants, while urban and mining interests accused him of squandering money on agriculture. In Britain, liberals focused on the underlying political agenda behind the land settlement and, using the example of Ireland to show how disastrous a plantation policy could be, argued it would, if anything, exacerbate tensions in the region. The more imperially minded complained that not enough was being done to encourage settlement, while officials in Whitehall cast doubts over whether the policy was practical in a country where agricultural prospects were so unknown. Milner, who had little taste for diplomacy or public rhetoric, was forced to devote considerable time and energy

Expansion of British South Africa, 1806 to 1906. Archibald R. Colquhoun, *The Africander Land* (London: John Murray, 1906).

25

FROM
IMPERIALISM
TO
NATIONALISM

to promoting his ideas to the public, usually through the offices of his Kindergarten. As it turned out, his plans for reconstruction had barely begun to be implemented before he was replaced as high commissioner by Lord Selborne in 1906. This was closely followed by the return of a Liberal government in London, which conferred self-governing status on the Transvaal and Orange River Colonies the following year, long before Milner thought it would or should have.[50]

Nevertheless, Milner and members of his Kindergarten laid down enduring structures for the governance, economy, and ordering of social relations in the new country. Milner's Reconstruction articulated a conceptual blueprint for white South African society that had a lasting appeal for many English-speaking whites who, whether civilians, administrators, missionaries, scientists, artists, or hunters, all believed in the fundamental rightness of imperial objectives in South Africa.[51] This in itself was an important achievement at a time when both Britain and its colonies were seriously reconsidering the nature of their relationship with each other. When formulating his policies, Milner had been mindful that the recent events in South Africa had made white colonial populations elsewhere in the empire restive. (Some forty-nine thousand colonial troops from Australia, New Zealand, and Canada had fought alongside British troops in South Africa.) During the first decade of the twentieth century, although increasingly dependent on its colonies as trading partners, Britain also wanted to shift onto them some of the financial burdens of colonial administration and of safeguarding free trade through control of the seas.[52] Meanwhile, the colonies (or Dominions, as they became after 1907) increasingly aspired to become self-governing nations with their own economic infrastructures and control of their own social and political affairs.[53] Although the colonies were generally in favor of remaining part of a *cultural* "Greater Britain," the political, economic, diplomatic, and trade implications of achieving this simultaneously with greater independence from Britain were problematic. It was also unclear what kind of identity the populations living in these colonies would have under this future dispensation.

An influential document in addressing these questions was a 1905 book, *Studies in Colonial Nationalism*, by Richard Jebb, another imperialist with Oxford and Kindergarten connections.[54] After traveling throughout the empire immediately after the South African War, Jebb came to the conclusion that it needed to be revitalized as a "field of expanding loyalties." He proposed a New Imperialism that would generate devotion to Britain and the monarchy while encouraging the emergence of what he termed colonial self-respect. Divisive regional ethnic differences would be replaced by a "higher allegiance" to the civilized and democratic ideals of a Britannic Commonwealth.[55] Jebb argued that this would not only recognize colonial aspirations but also appease the more progressive (and traditionally anti-imperial) elements of metropolitan British society: liberty, not force, was to be the cement of this new, expanded empire.[56] He coined the term "colonial national" to describe the identity of these "English-speaking or English-influenced countries developing independent cultures" that would belong to this new imperial framework.[57] In Jebb's estimation, colonial nationalism seemed most likely to take hold in Canada and Australia and least likely in New Zealand and South Africa.[58]

Certainly, in South Africa, the ideal of colonial nationalism was ill-equipped to deal with realities like a large indigenous black population and a white population polarized by war.[59] Theoretically, the appeal of belonging to a powerful, transnational polity should have weakened the internal animosities among whites that had been created by the war. In practice, the response was much more mixed, especially after the Bambatha Rebellion in Natal in 1906, and after the Transvaal and Orange River Colonies gained self-government in 1907.[60] Colonial nationalism obviously appealed to the wealthy, educated white elite whose cultural, political, and economic power depended on the viability of the Rand goldmines, as well as settlers who had a personal interest in continuing strong imperial ties. Many whites in the old Boer republics, however, saw colonial nationalism as a Trojan horse for exploitative imperialism-as-usual. Among these whites, the South African War had left a deep distrust of the British that was deepened by the belief that they would thwart any laws that maintained or increased differences between themselves and the African population. Probably for this reason, educated, politically active Africans tended to put their faith in colonial nationalism; while it did not specifically guarantee them rights, it seemed more likely to offer them better prospects than a locally constructed political dispensation.[61]

Although Britain's main goal in annexing the Boer republics—political and economic control of the Rand mines—had been successfully achieved by 1910, the consolidation of the four colonies into a single new colonial national state proved more difficult, and the official passing of the South Africa Act in 1909 was uncertain until the last few months.[62] The successful passing of the act was due in part to the work of the Kindergarten and other disciples of Milner who had stayed on after he had returned to Britain.[63] Broadly, the members of this group subscribed to Milner's idea that fusing the four colonies would help destroy the political and geographical basis for separatist memory, but they set about achieving this in a more cautious and subtle manner than their mentor. Both before and after union, they worked to promote an imaginative vision of a unified South Africa that complemented the political one and put in place what they saw as the cultural underpinnings necessary for an autonomous white man's country.[64] They tirelessly lectured on the advantages of union and set up a "Closer Union" movement with chapters in many regions and its own monthly journal in which various topics of national interest were discussed. In the years before union, members of the Kindergarten also worked to establish the foundations of various ostensibly apolitical institutions that would in time play a significant role in the new nation's social and cultural life.[65] With their imperial perspective, the Kindergarten realized that, in the words of one eminent historian, "While Canadians or Australians or New Zealanders were born, South Africans had to be *made*."[66]

In the end, the Kindergarten's behind-the-scenes efforts combined with those of accomodationist Boer veterans, who were appreciative of the gains to be made from ties with Britain, and persuaded the majority of white South Africans that union was in their best interests. This consensus was only limited and temporary, however. The reconciliation achieved between Boer and British at the Peace of Vereniging had really only been a provisional one, and both sides remained determined to win the peace.[67] The South Africa Act was a compromise that glossed over these residual differences, and the new Union of South Africa came into existence in May 1910 with a divided polity and a political system that was in some ways tentative and incomplete. A racially exclusive, British-influenced parliamentary system was agreed upon, but

View of Union
Buildings, Pretoria,
completed 1912.
Transnet Heritage
Museum Library
Publications Colour-
Spread Collection;
reproduced with
permission.

apart from the entrenchment of a nonracial qualified franchise in the Cape, the new
constitution incorporated compromises on racial issues that would eventually lead
to the complete disenfranchisement of the African population. The South Africa
Act left open the possibility that the Union's four provinces might form part of a
still incomplete British-African imperial subsystem, which one day would include
the Rhodesias and the three protectorates of Basutoland, Swaziland, and Bechuanaland. The unresolved character of the new nation was reflected by the fact that it had
two nominally equal official languages, English and Dutch, and three capital cities:
Cape Town (legislative), Pretoria (administrative), and Bloemfontein (judicial). Its
first government was formed by the centrist white South African Party under Prime
Minister Louis Botha, an ex-Boer general who also received some support from
English-speaking whites.[68] Within a couple of years, this vision was given material
form in the twin towers of the new Union Buildings in Pretoria, intended to represent
the reconciliation and partnership between the two "white races" that made up the
new South Africa[69]

The Growth of the South African State and the Politics of White Nationhood

It was perhaps inevitable that a nation that came into existence under the hopeful
motto of "Unity is Strength/Eendracht Maakt Macht" would struggle to achieve
a clear national identity. Soon after union, two broad strands of political ideology
emerged that, although latent in the subcontinent before 1899, had been precipitated
by the war and are probably best understood as competing conceptualizations of a
modern nation that was both connected to and separate from a mother country. Over
the next two decades, these two ideological positions would vie for control in South
Africa, become entrenched in white party politics, and harden into increasingly di-
vergent constructions of national identity. Although these two ideologies sometimes
made political use of the same events and phenomena to present opposing points of

view, this contestation masked (and facilitated) a concurrent evolution of a shared, place-related vision of nationhood and identity.

The one construction of nationhood was that promoted by the state itself, which used a homogenizing political rhetoric of patriotism to erode ethnic, historic, and regional differences in pursuit of economic and bureaucratic efficiency and to promote a sense of a unified imagined community. In the other construction of nationhood, a sense of identity cultivated initially by a smaller group within the state in order to achieve self-determination became a form of nationalism that sought to remake the state according to its own cultural and ideological blueprint.[70] The discourse of South African nationhood and identity from 1910 to 1948 can be crudely described as a situation in which the former position initially had the upper hand, but was eventually eroded and overcome by the latter. Both political groupings were headed by an alliance of cultural activists who sought to promote their particular version of national identity through the creation of a narrative of descent that incorporated a set of supposedly unifying cultural values and ideas.

Each of these ideological positions manifested itself through a distinct geopolitical spatiality and definition of what constituted national territory.[71] Initially, the dominant position was occupied by a loyalist "Greater South African" subjectivity (effectively, the local expression of Jebb's colonial nationalism), which enthusiastically embraced both the imperial connection and the possibility of a larger, more culturally diverse geographic territory that included the other British territories in the subcontinent. This imagined Greater South Africa was part of a larger imagined territory, the British Empire, and the identity of its ideal citizen combined the best qualities of South Africa's two white "races." Because it promised continued links with Britain, this vision was understandably popular among English-speaking whites, as well as Britons who had visited the country themselves and been captivated by its potential.[72] Against this was opposed a "Little South African" subjectivity, which (somewhat grudgingly) accepted that the Union was part of the British Empire, but saw white South African identity as much more narrowly and exclusively defined, formulated around an emerging, explicitly indigenous white culture. The imagined territory of this group was much more limited and autonomous than that of Greater South Africa. A crucial difference between these two versions of white colonial national identity was that the former saw that some accommodation with the African population was inevitable, even if the exact date when this would take place was unspecified.

Given the political polarization around the issue after 1910, it would be easy to equate these two alternative visions of South African nationhood with language differences among the white population. The straightforward equation of language with nationhood is an easy one to make; language, along with race, is one of the most obvious badges of cultural identity. As we have seen, this belief had underpinned Milner's plans to Anglicize South Africa, and it would also become a central tenet of Afrikaner nationalist ideology. Historically, though, the notion that language was a key to identity only emerged as part of the discourse of identity formation that unfolded after union, which used language as a convenient signifier of differences that could have equally well been attributed to constructs of race, culture, ethnicity, and class.[73] Before the 1920s, when Afrikaans began to be more widely used, the term "Afrikaner" itself was seldom used, "Boer" or "Dutch" being more common,[74] and even this category included many emigrants of English (and especially Scottish) descent who had, after a couple of generations, adopted the language. (Until the end of the nineteenth century, "Afrikaner" was often used interchangeably with "Africander" to describe people of mixed race, who would later be called "Colored.")[75] Similarly, the appellation "English-speaking South African" (as opposed to "British overseas") barely existed in 1910, and only really came to define a distinct cultural identity in the early 1950s.[76] English-speaking inhabitants of the subcontinent rarely called themselves "South African" until after World War I; instead, they either identified themselves with metropolitan Britain or, as did many Afrikaners, with the part of South Africa in which they lived.[77] Even among these English-speaking white South Africans, there had always existed a diversity of allegiances to Britain. At the end of the nineteenth century, liberal-minded Anglo South Africans experienced Cecil John Rhodes's and Leander Starr Jameson's warmongering as deeply abhorrent betrayals, while others saw Britain as an interfering, "doddering old mother country."[78]

Until 1930, then, there prevailed in white South African society a more fluid relationship between language and identity, and consequently a looser definition of national identity, than that which later became associated with the country. Greater South African colonial nationalism in particular did not see any incompatibility between allegiance to the newly formed country *and* to the British Empire. It claimed to rise above political and language differences and to build a nation which drew on (rather than was defined and limited by) the imperial connection to realize a liberal and progressive future. Benefiting from this broadly inclusive Anglophone citizenship was an economically powerful minority of English-speaking whites who still unashamedly called Britain "Home," and for whom the idealism of colonial nationalism meant little. Although they lived some six thousand miles (and some three weeks of sea travel) from Britain, this minority felt a greater fealty and loyalty to the Crown than to the land of their birth. They expressed their identity through an essentially personal allegiance to the king, who embodied and bound the empire together, and whom they saw as guardian of their rights within South Africa.[79]

Nevertheless, a loyalist Greater South African identity initially appealed to a broad spectrum of whites because it was simultaneously engagingly idealistic and pragmatically vague. During the early twentieth century, South Africa was still very much a country of immigrants. From 1891 to 1904, the subcontinent's white population nearly doubled, and three-quarters of this growth was due to immigration. Many individuals who were to shape South African political and cultural life in the first half of the twentieth century arrived in the country between 1902 and 1905. Although a large proportion of these immigrants came from Britain, they also came from Europe, the United States, and other British colonies.[80] Like their predecessors in the second half of the nineteenth century, these non-British immigrants tended to learn English and subscribe to English (though not necessarily imperial) cultural values. Under these circumstances, Greater South African cultural identity invited the allegiance of colonial South Africans, as well as that of the more than 20 percent of the white population who had been born overseas.

The inclusivist vision of South African identity promoted by the Union's early governments was soon being challenged by "Little South African" cultural activists and intellectuals who, like their Greater South African counterparts, maintained ties to European coevals (in the Netherlands and Germany) and used a diverse range of cultural initiatives to raise political consciousness. In contrast to the other group's emphasis on material culture, Little South African initiatives were largely constructed around verbal culture, specifically the recognition of Afrikaans, a local demotic Dutch used as an everyday language by many non-Anglo South Africans (including many people of Khoisan and mixed-race descent). The First Afrikaans Language Movement had started in the Cape during the 1870s and received great support during the British annexation of the ZAR from 1877 to 1881, but had largely died out by the end of the century, because those who spoke the language were uninvolved in commerce and politics, which used either Dutch or English.[81] After 1902, however, the absorption of substantial populations from the former Boer republics in a single polity altered this unproblematic separation, and the recognition of Afrikaans became a rallying point for many who had been impoverished by the war as well as those affected by the closing of the hunting and farming frontiers.[82] Unlike the earlier Cape-Afrikaans movement, the Second Afrikaans Language Movement became a springboard for a wider cultural and political movement that increasingly revolved around republicanism.[83]

Two key events in 1913 acted as catalysts for this: the inauguration of the Vroue-monument, a shrine near Bloemfontein to the 26,000 Boer women and children who had died in the British concentration camps, and the speech made by General Barry Hertzog, another Boer veteran, to twelve thousand supporters at De Wildt, which sketched an alternative vision of South Africa's future that was as all-encompassing as its more imperially minded alternative. Even though he himself did not intend it as such, Hertzog's vision was taken as a rallying point by cultural activists who wanted to "build a nation from words": "Employing Afrikaans instead of increasingly obsolete Dutch, and defining it as a modern, white man's language, they sought to construct an Afrikaner nation which would fill Afrikaner churches, attend Afrikaner schools, and buy Afrikaner journals and books."[84] This literary-linguistic definition of South African national identity was first given institutional weight by the founding of organizations such as the Afrikaanse Taalgenootskap in 1905 and the Zuid-Afrikaansche Akademie voor Taal, Letteren en Kunst in 1909, and the establishment of the first South African literature prize, the Hertzog Prize, in 1914. The emergence of this language-based movement and its evolution into a full-fledged "Afrikaner" identity followed patterns in ethnic separatism elsewhere in the world. Awakened by a sense of relative economic disadvantage, it used programs of social regeneration and cultural resurgence to challenge the inevitability of assimilation promoted by the modern state.[85] Revolving around the development of a vernacular language, it was also underpinned by the secularization of knowledge and the rise of print technology.[86] Although the aftermath of the South African War offered a rich potential for exploitation along nationalistic lines, much of this only remained alive in folk memory and was not converted into writing until it suited the needs of the nationalist movement in the 1930s.[87]

An enormously influential figure in this process was the populist Gustav Preller, who from 1905 onward agitated for recognition of Afrikaans and helped establish a series of magazines aimed at increasing its usage among common people.[88] Preller understood the power of simple words and images to engage the collective memory of a dispersed, disempowered, and semieducated group and transform them into a single *volk*: every story, picture, or monument became a place where memories of the past could be (re)constructed and stored.[89] A number of journalists, ministers, and educationists took up Preller's ideas, and from 1914 onward, Afrikaans was gradually introduced into schools, and in 1918 it became a university subject. In the same year, the Broederbond, a clandestine organization to support Afrikaner cultural and economic interests, was established in the Transvaal. An Afrikaans publishing house, Nasionale Pers, was established to publish books and magazines that did not come from Britain (as virtually all English-language material did at this time).[90] The first Afrikaans poems—Eugene Marais's *Winternag* and Jan F. E. Celliers's *Die Vlakte*—had appeared a few years after the end of the South African War, and soon became touchstones of this new subjectivity, not only because of the language in which they were written but also because of the way they used that language to mediate a collective elegy for a lost life on the land.

However, it was not until 1925, when Afrikaans replaced Dutch as the Union's second official language, that it became possible to reach and mobilize the masses through writing in the language that many of them spoke. Before this, Afrikaner nationalism was still largely a populist movement and not yet a full-fledged political platform. Its primary constituency was an impoverished and sometimes illiterate underclass of displaced rural dwellers migrating to the cities, where they were susceptible to the rhetoric of intellectual activists like Preller who, finding themselves marginalized by the political establishment, rehabilitate themselves as demagogues.[91] At this time, there were a substantial number of non-English-speaking whites who still saw Afrikaans as a bastard, lower-class language, including the long-Anglicized old colonial Dutch families at the Cape.[92] In the Transvaal and Orange Free State, emigrants from Holland and the wealthier Hoog Hollands–speaking professionals and entrepreneurial classes that began to establish themselves after World War I continued to support Botha and Jan Smuts's centrist South African Party. For less-privileged whites of Dutch descent, however, nascent Afrikaner nationalism's combination of education, cultural uplift, and literature gave them a sense of heritage and a collective past and, by extension, a collective destiny.

This growing emphasis on language as the key badge of identity after 1914 posed a powerful, and in some ways unanswerable, challenge to proponents of a more inclusive colonial national (but ultimately Anglophone) construction of white nationhood. The apparent domination of English speakers in the professions, commerce, and government fanned feelings among politically and economically marginalized Dutch- and Afrikaans-speaking whites that their plight was the result of hegemonic British imperialism, and this strengthened the appeal of a nationalism mobilized around language difference and, increasingly, republicanism. This shift toward the reification of language as the primary signifier of identity placed an inclusive, nonethnic construction of national identity at a distinct disadvantage. If language is the primary medium whereby people imaginatively take hold of their lifeworld and assimilate it into their lives, then a language-based construction of identity worryingly undermined claims of English-speaking whites, even those who had lived in the subcontinent for generations, to be true South Africans.[93]

These crosscurrents of identity formation meant that the first fifteen years of the Union's existence were a prolonged struggle on the part of pro-Empire colonial national politicians to prevent the process of nation building from slipping into the hands of those who had a narrower, "tribal" definition of national identity. The Afrikaner National Party, formed by Hertzog and others who had broken away from Botha's South African Party in 1914, became the political instrument through which nascent Afrikaner aspirations were channeled. War in Europe, and the prospect of South African forces invading the territory of a former ZAR ally (German South West Africa) in 1915, prompted a rebellion by disaffected and disillusioned Boer *bittereinders* (hardliners) who denounced Botha and Smuts as traitors. Despite his own past as a Boer general, Botha put down this uprising with some force. Anti-British feeling among some Afrikaners was further inflamed when one of the uprising's leaders, Jopie Fourie, was tried and executed for treason.[94] The National Party attracted substantial support in the general election the following year, and it was not long before a small group of Afrikaner militants within the party were calling for a republic.

During World War I, the imperial government in London was anxious not to exacerbate these tensions, and it imposed no conscription on South Africa.[95] Nevertheless, some 146,000 whites did volunteer to fight, first in East Africa, then on the Western Front in France.[96] Although the Union contributed relative few men compared to the other more populous Dominions, its participation in the conflict had significant effects on South Africans' sense of nationhood, identity, and citizenship. At the same time, even though English-speaking South Africans heavily outnumbered Afrikaners in the Union's forces, the experience of fighting alongside each other helped foster a social closeness between officers and men and a common patriotism.[97] This was reinforced as the war progressed and the military situation worsened; the pre-1916 idiom of the war as a European "playing field" that had originally attracted many volunteers began to lose meaning, and gave way to the perception that South Africans were fighting for king and *country* rather than king and empire.[98] Meanwhile, back at home in South Africa, the war helped nurture anti-British republicanism among rural, Dutch, and Afrikaans-speaking whites, of whom more than half opposed the Union's war policy by 1917.[99] World War I produced similar divisions among black South Africans. Although most wanted little to do with this "white man's war," significant numbers were persuaded to serve in the South African Labour Corps in France, believing this would improve their standing as citizens after the war.[100] More than six hundred of these noncombatant South Africans lost their lives when the SS *Mendi* sank in the English Channel in 1917, the annual remembrance of which was used to rally support for black nationalist movements in the interwar period.[101]

During the war in Europe, import substitution and increased overseas demand for South African agricultural products brought about unprecedented expansion of the country's economy in areas other than its two primary industries, mining and agriculture. After the war, however, as Europe struggled to rebuild itself, the boom in South Africa collapsed, bringing a combination of inflation, unemployment exacerbated by the return of demobilized soldiers from Europe, and the spread of organized labor in the economically vital mine industry. News from Europe of the rise of Bolshevism, Irish secession, and the British General Strike encouraged similar political action in South Africa, where it was overlaid with racial dimensions. In 1922, industrial unrest spread along the Rand, and after nearly two months of civil anarchy, the Union government's attempts to bring order and declare martial law led to 230 lives lost and over 500 injured. The severe economic depression of 1921 and 1922 added to the numbers of rural Afrikaners already ruined by drought and indebtedness, and each year more of them joined the so-called second Great Trek to the urban areas that had begun after the South African War.[102] There, these impoverished migrants with little English found themselves in what felt like a foreign country. They not only encountered a dominant Anglo culture but came into direct competition for jobs (and sometimes housing, as in the Johannesburg neighborhoods like Fordsburg) with the Africans whom they had so recently known as dependents.

Although South Africa's participation in World War I had helped give shape to and strengthen white colonial national identity, the postwar years saw an even stronger growth of Afrikaner nationalism. Although Botha's death in 1919 had led to his replacement as prime minister by an equally powerful advocate of reconciliation, Jan Smuts, in 1924, Hertzog's Nationalists, in a coalition with the Labor Party, came to power on a wave of anti-imperialist and anti-business sentiment. This coalition, under the slogan "South Africa First," provided an outlet for the internationalist tendencies as well as the ethnically based grievances of poorer urban whites, and reflected a shift in the Union government's orientation from mining toward farming interests. The period of stability that followed was the result of improving economic conditions, but it also reflected a growing sense of a shared destiny between English and Afrikaner, largely due to Africans' refusal to accept their economic and political disenfranchisement by the white state. During the 1920s, this black resistance started to be channeled by the South African Natives National Council (founded in 1912 and the forerunner of the African National Congress) and the Industrial and Commercial Workers Union (founded in 1919). Racial fear of one form or another started to unite white South Africans and drive much new legislation.[103] This shift exemplified the complex ways in which race, class, and economics were becoming intertwined in South Africa and inscribed in the country's physical landscape.[104] Racial fears among whites stemmed in part from the increasing numbers of Africans in urban areas, who were there largely because of several pieces of legislation that effectively ended their economic independence and rural way of life. This legislation had started with the 1913 Land Act, often considered to be the equivalent of the Enclosures Act in eighteenth-century England.[105] This act had either driven Africans into remote, cramped reserves, which were supported by tribal leaders because they seemed to protect traditional ways of life, or into urban townships, where they provided cheap labor for the mines and other new industries. By the mid-1920s, nearly two-thirds of Africans lived in one of these two areas, leaving the remainder of country increasingly white.

Economic recovery after 1924 was strengthened by the interventionist strategies of the Hertzog-led Pact government, which, for all its populist rhetoric, built on the previous government's close links with big business and the *dirigiste* foundations laid by Milner's Reconstruction. The establishment of Eskom and Iscor in 1928, large parastatal corporations for the production of electricity and steel, jump-started domestic industrialization, while price support and control of various agricultural industries increased production, encouraged exports, and strengthened the Union's autonomy. The state-run South African Railways and Harbours (SAR&H) became the government's main instrument of economic development, and it was involved in a wide range of activities beyond its core activity of transporting goods and people. The SAR&H made the expansion of mining industry possible and was instrumental in encouraging the capitalization and mechanization of South African agriculture in the 1920s.[106] The expansion of the railways not only facilitated the flow of rural whites to the new industrial and economic heartland of the Witwatersrand, centered around the gold mines, but railways also became a primary source of employment for poor, uneducated whites.[107]

Concurrently, however, this ongoing industrialization and urbanization also gave rise to a progressive, urban intelligentsia that was self-consciously South African but retained strong intellectual ties to Europe. This new class of white South Africans was the natural outcome of the expanding mining-based economy. While the mines only made fortunes for a few dozen individuals, they drove an economic expansion that provided a variety of careers for working- and middle-class whites that would have been unimaginable in Europe. The better-educated soon found their way into the professions, the arts, some sectors of government and civil services, as well as colleges and the newly founded universities and research institutions.[108] The growth of modern scientific research within South Africa not only helped nurture the nation's growing sense of itself, but also helped educated white intellectuals justify their existence as Europeans in Africa, because it seemed to promise modern solutions to the subcontinent's many environmental and social problems.[109] The progressive, liberal values of this indigenous intelligentsia were bolstered by the many European-born and trained academics who staffed South Africa's new universities and colleges, as well the fact that many young white professional South Africans still apprenticed in Europe. The University of Witwatersrand, established with support from capitalist mining interests immediately after the war, attracted world-class faculty, such as the historian W. M. Macmillan, a regular contributor to the *Nation* and *New Statesman* in London, and anthropologist/physician Raymond Dart, who was to make epochal discoveries into the origins of man in the Taung quarries. Students at the new universities were an admixture of first-generation Jews, rural Afrikaners, and middle-class English (the offspring of wealthier white families still went to Oxbridge at this stage), an alliance that introduced a new, less imperial dimension to a white settler identity more inclined to question the superiority of European literature, culture, history, and politics.[110]

The geographical redistribution of South Africa's white population that had begun in the first two decades of the century accelerated during the 1920s. Nearly 18 percent of the Union's 1920 white population (an estimated 250,000) were uprooted from rural areas between 1890 and 1930, and by 1930, almost as many white South Africans lived in urban as in rural areas, and most of the country's wealth was being generated on the Rand. This population redistribution was as much a function of the push of rural change as it was of the cities' economic pull. By the 1920s, debates about the carrying capacity of remote *platteland* that had been going on since the turn of the century started to be resolved, and it became clear that rural ways of life and forms of agriculture practiced earlier were no longer sustainable.[111] After World War I, legislation that drove African tenantry off the land was complemented by government policies that concentrated the control of agricultural land in the hands of well-capitalized white farmers and encouraged improved management methods.[112] This intensified land use in rural South Africa further marginalized remaining squatter and migrant white farmers, who were dealt a further blow by the extended drought that lasted from 1922 to 1933.

Such utilitarian processes of establishing the carrying capacity of the land highlighted the shortage of geographical knowledge about the region and the urgent need for further substantive, state-sponsored research. Apart from some localized mapping for mining and military purposes undertaken before the South African War, remarkably little was known about South Africa's topography, vegetation, climate, and demography until the early 1920s.[113] During this decade, the first generation of South African geographers began to systematically accumulate data about the country's geology, soils, hydrology, botany, and climate, and to construct a more objective idea of what constituted normal environmental conditions. This growing geographical knowledge contributed to a growing sense of South Africa as a distinct society and revealed that the subcontinent had a unique and in some ways globally significant natural history. The Land Survey Act of 1927 initiated a systematic trigonometrical survey of the entire country that complemented the more established but still growing body of geological knowledge.[114] These two modern scientific practices combined to construct a "saturated knowledge" of the nation's territory that was at once vertical and horizontal and helped to foster ideas of South Africa's distinctiveness that seemed to be objective and apolitical.[115]

After 1924, Hertzog's consolidation of white domination by legislation proscribing African property ownership, labor, and movement was paralleled by legislation putting in place many of the symbolic props of a self-governing nationhood. In 1925, Afrikaans became the Union's second official language (previously it was Dutch); the following year, a new National Flag Act (replacing the Union Jack) and the National Parks Act were written into law and the country's first national park was established; and in 1928, the country's National Monuments Council was founded. Less obvious, though equally important in symbolic terms, was the development of local currency. As the country moved toward greater economic autonomy from Britain in 1920s, the first national paper money started introducing local symbols of national identity, notably images of indigenous wildlife, to supplement or replace heads of the British royal family. At a time when most large banks were British-owned, Afrikaners provided the major push for the introduction of a national currency.[116]

The historical coincidence of these various pieces of legislation with the emergence of relatively broad South African settler nationalism is no accident. The instrumental issues facing most modernizing societies are often useful vehicles for transcending ethnic separatism.[117] Although the government of the day was nominally Afrikaner, both the Flag and National Park Acts required the support of English speakers to pass. In most instances, this legislation also strengthened the state's role as a resource for the collective benefit of whites, and reinforced the definition of the national territory as a white man's country. By the end of the 1920s, although the exact composition of the nation was still a matter of dispute, there was a general consensus among whites about two fundamental principles: first, that South Africa would, for the foreseeable future at least, be an independent state within the Commonwealth, and second, that racial segregation between white and black would be upheld and entrenched.[118] It was around this time that the phrase "racial question" ceased to refer to tensions between English and Dutch/Afrikaans speakers, and began to be used to describe those between whites and nonwhites.

This strengthening of an internal sense of white national identity during the 1920s was bolstered by various external factors, including the clarification of the country's territorial boundaries, and international attention that invited white South Africans to see themselves through others' eyes. Popular awareness about South Africa in Britain stimulated by the South African War was intensified thirteen years later by the presence of South African troops in Europe, as well as Smuts's unprecedented inclusion in the Imperial War Cabinet.[119] After World War I, South Africa was mandated by the League of Nations to govern the former German South West Africa, while Rhodesians had decided in a 1923 referendum that they did not wish to become part of South Africa and instead became a separate, self-governing colony. British awareness of South Africa was further enhanced by the country's very visible participation in the Empire Exhibition at Wembley, as well as Hertzog's active role in the passing of the Balfour Declaration at the 1926 Imperial Conference, which confirmed the status of all the Dominions as autonomous communities within the empire.[120] This interest was further stimulated by the expansion of overseas tourism to South Africa during the 1920s. The SAR&H played a central role in this expansion, as well as promoting South Africa in Europe, the United States, and the empire as a country for settlement and investment. The SAR&H became an important agent in familiarizing overseas visitors with the landscapes of South Africa and also helped create South Africa's first national park in 1926.

Constructing Collective Memory, Promoting Patriotism

The middle of the 1920s was not only the historical moment when a broad white settler identity started to emerge, it was also a time when South Africanism, the broad cultural movement associated with the politics of a Greater South Africa, enjoyed its widest currency among whites. Although it evolved over its life span, loyalist South Africanism was grounded in the belief that differences between English speakers and Dutch or Afrikaans speakers could be "sublimated" to produce a common imperial South African ideal.[121] This was by no means a new idea. Notions of a hybrid, transethnic white settler identity had been circulating since self-government had been introduced at the Cape in 1872.[122] The Afrikaner Bond, the Cape-based cultural movement and political party made up of an older Dutch-speaking bourgeoisie, had been pro-imperial since its inception in the 1880s.[123] Loyalist South Africanism had, of course, also been latent in the rhetoric of "Closer Union," but it became a central tenet of the white, pro-imperial, colonial national state after 1910. This was no accident: as a form of national identity, South Africanism was patriotic rather than nationalistic. The ambiguity of patriotic allegiance was more adaptable to the cause of multivalent imperial unity than the idea of outright nationalism, which implied territorial limitations and an ultimate destiny of independence. Patriotism also glossed over ethnic and racial aspects of imperial ideology—the assumption that the empire was preeminently a union of people of *British* blood—and suggested that the persistence of older, place-based identities, rather than the imposition of a dominant, pan-imperial identity, might be the key to the empire's survival.[124]

The early Union governments' promotion of this form of cultural identity was supplemented by the cultural work of a coterie of white capitalists, philanthropists, and intellectuals with links to the Kindergarten and members of the British establishment, many of whom had come to South Africa before, during, or just after the South African War. This group was somewhat different from the more familiar (and notorious) Randlords, the two dozen or so self-made men who accumulated massive mining fortunes in South Africa, which they then used to buy the property and titles necessary to enter the highest echelons of British society.[125] As in other countries faced with the challenge of divisive ethnic nationalism, in South Africa a loose association of educated, upper-middle-class activists promoted a number of ostensibly apolitical initiatives designed to help a broad assortment of citizens imagine themselves as a unified group, situated in the historical time and geographic space of the new nation. Some of these same individuals continued to promote these cultural initiatives when this was no longer possible in mainstream political discourse. Although most members of this group were English-speaking, some were not. This reflected the underlying cultural idealism and commitment to reconciliation that was its founding premise, as well as the close personal ties that developed between those who dominated political and cultural life in a society as small as white South Africa was at this time.[126] This group of colonial cultural activists was supported by a small number of individuals with influence in political and publishing circles in London, who knew South Africa well and visited frequently. This group included most of the Kindergarten, as well as people like Rudyard Kipling, Violet Markham, and Fabian Ware, who came to prominence during the Edwardian period in Britain.

Of course, South Africanism also served a number of less selfless goals besides the promotion of an ameliorative white cultural identity. For some individuals, it was an attempt to overcome the gossamer-thin sense of connection they felt toward South Africa and a magnanimous gesture toward the country in which they had acquired their wealth and which many had come to love.[127] Others saw it as a way of securing patronage from and entry into the mercantile-political establishment. For others still, it was a way of tempering the hostility toward the perceived brashness and materialism of Randlord society that had emerged in South Africa and Britain and the anticapitalist tendencies that developed among the white working class on the Rand.[128]

We have already encountered the origins of patriotic South Africanism in the Kindergarten's various behind-the-scenes nation-building activities between the South African War and union. Its essentially discursive, imaginative nature was already evident in the *State*, the Kindergarten's monthly journal, edited by Phillip Kerr and Lionel Curtis, which was published from 1908 until 1912. In addition to promoting Closer Union, the *State* also published articles on settlement, immigration, literature, travel, agriculture, architecture, scenery, and art. As union became more certain, these articles were supplemented by pieces addressing the need for emblems of nationhood such as a national gallery and anthem, a national university, botanical gardens, the choice of capital cities, and the need for nature conservation. This was the first time many of these topics had been broached in South Africa, and these articles provided a foundation for a new self-image and understanding of a future national identity at a time when the nation of South Africa, properly speaking, did not yet exist.[129]

Given these beginnings, it is no surprise that the cultural rhetoric of patriotic South Africanism inherited the nostalgic pastoralist ideas about landscape and identity prevalent in late Victorian and Edwardian Britain as well as the idealism and future-oriented *dirigisme* of Milnerite Reconstruction. The latter started to become increasingly necessary after union, when Afrikaner nationalists started using appeals to language and memories of the South African War to fan the embers of emerging republicanism. After 1913, advocates of South Africanism began to realize that reconciliation between whites was all but incompatible with commemoration of the immediate past, which would have raked up questions of the war's course and consequences.[130] This inability to appeal to shared memory made South Africanism particularly hard to define or represent. Vague references in the *State* to the Boers as simple but assimilable people of the soil and the occasional publication of articles by Gustav Preller and C. J. Langenhoven (who would later write South Africa's national anthem) were soon revealed as inadequate. This need to negotiate the mnemonic minefield of the recent past meant that during the 1910s and 1920s the cultural rhetoric of South Africanism tended to dwell on the imaginary consolations and potentials mediated by material culture rather than on concrete facts and political realities.

The discursive construction of identity is always contingent on appeals to collective memory. This was especially true at the end of the nineteenth century in Europe, when transformations in social and economic life were challenging traditional ideas about cultural continuity and rejuvenating historical and museum culture.[131] This historical revivalism was also linked to the emerging nation-state's need to construct a narrative of descent that created a sense of membership in the larger, abstract imagined community of nationhood.[132] In South Africa, as in other colonial societies, constructing this narrative of descent was complicated by a number of different factors. First, in the colony, construction of the "imagined community" usually involves the creation of an entirely new collectivity, rather than the transformation and fusion of existing communities. This imagined community seldom, if ever, refers to indigenous, precolonial (and usually non-European) populations, but instead to European settlers who arrived at different times and usually share few identity-forming principles other than that they inhabit the same territory.[133] Furthermore, this narrative of descent necessarily draws on a brief history that is largely determined by the colonizing power and is invariably marked by regrettable episodes of brutal dispossession.[134]

All of these facts mean that the project of constructing a long, collective memory from a short, contested history almost always results in the exclusion of the nonsettler population from the "we" or "us" of the imagined nation. It also guarantees that as they evolve into modern nations, colonial societies tend to develop ambiguous attitudes to modernity.[135] For all their need to transcend history, colonial societies are also societies in which the future is contingent or unpredictable, and they have a strong psychic need to create a sense of sequence out of aleatory chaos.[136] Thus, although one would expect such new societies to reify development and technology as symbols of modernity and national progress, they are also often haunted by the loss of premodern experiences that characterized most of their history (see color plate 2). This ambivalence can be traced to the contradiction that lies at the very heart of constructed identities: to start over is to cut oneself off from the master narrative of history, the unspoken basis for authenticity and standing. This tension between impatience with the past and nostalgic longing for it is, if anything, heightened for intellectuals and cultural producers who travel between the metropole and the colony and for whom the narrative of descent needs to incorporate and make sense of two quite different histories.

It is no surprise that the first, top-down attempts to construct a patriotic colonial national culture in South Africa involved reinterpreting, classifying, and appropriating the past, but as in other dominions, this discourse also fostered the identity, esprit de corps, and self-confidence of an emerging white colonial elite, and saved some of the premodern practices, relations, and experiences that its growth was displacing.[137] Colonial national South Africanism attempted to fashion a narrative of descent that organized into an orderly progression and redeemed British conquest, control, and settlement of the subcontinent, and which romanticized violent or contested episodes of history.[138] The implied cultural values of this narrative were very much progressive, British ones that drew on the "the best that has been thought and said." At the same time, this narrative strove to provide an optimistic vision of the future, assimilating the Boers as white Africans and promoting a mutual admiration between colonial national white elite and what they perceived to be the African tribal aristocracy ruling over a contented peasantry.[139] For a number of decades, this romanticized view of Africans formed an integral and persuasive part of fundamentally racist assumptions and policies. It allowed members of the colonial national white elite to see themselves as paternal figures with a natural right to become involved in tribal legal and cultural affairs; it also allowed these whites to be perceived by conservative Africans as bulwarks against the designs of both more radical segregationists and the African intelligentsia.[140]

The cultural construction of this narrative of descent began before the South African War, at the Cape. A key figure was Cecil John Rhodes, who used the idea of a continuity of European settlement to legitimate his historicist cultural visions for the subcontinent and elide the more commercial and political ambitions of British imperialism. There is little doubt that the powerful afterlife enjoyed by Rhodes's vision and his own transformation into an inspirational figure for many colonial nationalists were mediated by the various memorials he caused to be constructed in South Africa, both before and after his death in 1902. As early as 1889, Rhodes had erected a statue of the Dutch founding father of white South Africa, Jan Van Riebeeck, in the center of Cape Town—setting a precedent for his own statue, which would be erected nearby in 1907, itself a pale precursor of the much larger and more famous memorial to him that was constructed on the slopes of Devils Peak and inaugurated in 1912.[141]

By this time, though, these kinds of historicist imaginaries had become part of loyalist South Africanist discourse through other means as well. In 1900, the Guild of Loyal Women had been founded at the Cape, primarily to identify graves and care for the cemeteries of both British and Boer war dead. This loyal unionist organization was involved not only in locating, marking, and maintaining all known graves but also in raising funds for *uitlander* refugees and Dutch women and children, and it

Statue of Cecil John Rhodes, 1907, Company Gardens, Cape Town. Cape Archives, file ref. R1569; reproduced with permission.

worked closely with overseas group such as the Daughters of the Empire in Canada and the Victoria League in Britain.[142] The year 1905 saw the founding of the National Society for the Preservation of Objects of Historic Interest and Natural Beauty in South Africa (later simply known as the "National Society") out of which the statutory National Monuments Council was to grow. This organization, which was modeled on the National Trust in Britain (founded in 1895), was soon complemented by the South African National Union, which promoted all aspects of national development, including indigenous arts, crafts, and industry.[143]

Equally influential was the literary and historical work of the first Cape Colonial archivist C. V. Leibrandt and historian Dr. George McCall Theal in the 1890s.[144] Although they sometimes offered competing interpretations of the past,[145] both writers glossed over contemporary differences among whites and emphasized a long, productive history of *white Protestant* cooperation, settlement, and culture at the Cape (thus potentially including Dutch, German, and French Huguenot, as well as English) (see color plate 3).[146] These ideas were given institutional form by publications such as the *Cape Monthly Magazine* and the formation of the Van Riebeeck Society in 1918. A recurring figure in popular histories at this time was Simon van der Stel, the Dutch governor at the Cape during the last part of the seventeenth century, who was held up by colonial nationalists as a historical antecedent of the cultivated, Protestant European-African identity they wished to promote. Theal's assertion that black people

The Smuts and Phillips families in front of Vergelegen. Barloworld Archives Phillips Collection file ref. #11, reproduced with permission.

arrived in Natal toward the end of the sixteenth century, and only settled on the Highveld in the eighteenth also helped undergird visions of South Africa as a white man's country by implying that black Africans had no more right to the land than Europeans.[147] Theal and Leibrandt provided the intellectual and historical ballast for the work of a largely Cape-based group of cultural producers that emerged at the turn of the century who sought to transcend the older, jingoistic colonial culture of overtly English churches and public buildings, ubiquitous statues of Queen Victoria, and private schools that were "little Englands on the veld."[148] This group of Anglophile South Africanists included, among others, the authors Alys Fane Trotter, Dorothea Fairbridge, and Percy Fitzpatrick; the architects Francis Masey, Franklin Kendall, and J. M. Solomon; and the artists George Smithard, Jan Juta, Edward Roworth, and Robert Gwelo Goodman.

Several key figures associated with the South Africanist movement were women. In South Africa, as in other colonial societies, women were expected to be not only mothers, homemakers, and educators but also promoters and guardians of cultural values. Like their male counterparts, these female cultural activists were well educated (often in Britain) and perpetuated a tradition set in the nineteenth century by the likes of Lady Anne Barnard and Lucy Duff Gordon, imperial women of means who commented on Cape society from a bifocal point of view.[149] In fact, Lady Ann Barnard was the subject of one of the many books by a central figure in the movement, Dorothea Fairbridge, who helped found both the Guild of Loyal Women and the National Society. Other key figures in colonial national cultural activism were Mrs. Marie Koopmans De Wet, an Anglo-Dutch dowager whose imposing townhouse in Cape Town, along with its contents dating from the turn of the nineteenth century, became South Africa's first cultural history museum in 1914; and Florence

Inauguration
ceremony, Delville
Wood, Longueval
France, October 1926.
Reproduced with
permission of South
African National
Museum of Military
History, Northern
Flagship Institute.

Phillips, the South African–born wife of Randlord Sir Lionel Phillips. Together, the
Phillipses formed the nexus of a network of patronage and taste-making that spread
into virtually every corner of cultural life. Both became ardent supporters of Botha
and Smuts when it became clear that the ex-Boer veterans were going to become politically dominant after 1906, and the couple used Lionel's money and influence to
support a wide range of initiatives.[150]

Florence Phillips was perhaps the ultimate cultural activist. A famous hostess
and patron of historians, writers, architects, and artists, she was sometimes called,
not entirely kindly, the "queen of Johannesburg." A founder of the National Society,
Florence started a furniture industry on their estates in the northern Transvaal and
commissioned Herbert Baker to design their house in Johannesburg. Florence Phillips also spent enormous amounts of her husband's money restoring the buildings
and gardens of Vergelegen, which had been the home of a famous governor of the
Cape from 1699 to 1709, Willem Adriaan van der Stel (Simon's son, known as "the
Rhodes of his day").[151] Florence Phillips was also a close friend and patron of Dorothea Fairbridge and shared horticultural interests with women like Ruby Boddam-
Whetham and Marion Cran, who, along with Fairbridge, wrote the first books on
South African gardens and gardening.[152] Both Florence and Lionel Phillips were
ardent nature conservationists, something that was reflected in the management of
their own properties and their commissioning of the first *The Flora of South Africa*
from the preeminent South African botanist Rudolf Marloth; this work ran to four
volumes and was published in 1913.

World War I was as important a catalyst in the unfolding discourse of colonial
nationalism as it had been in the realm of economic and politics. A sense of national

identity had already been hinted at before the war by the emergence in all the Dominions of national symbols such as the maple leaf and the wattle, but this sense gained potency during the conflict. The experience of fighting alongside their metropolitan counterparts, often under the authority of incompetent British officers, made many colonial soldiers feel that they had passed some crucial test, while at the same time highlighting differences between them and their metropolitan cousins.[153] The European battlefields became arenas in which prewar debates about the white Dominion's political and cultural future within the empire were rehearsed and tested, contact zones in which not only British, French, and German but also Canadian, Australian, New Zealander, and South African identities were forged and honed. Like their other Dominion counterparts, the South African Brigade developed a distinctive form of soldierly self-identification, under their newly created emblem of the vaulting Springbok.[154] The South Africans in Europe also saw themselves afresh, through the eyes of those among whom they moved: as white (*not* black, as some Europeans expected) men from Britain's Empire whose Dutch-Afrikaans vocabulary enabled them to communicate easily with Flemish speakers, but whose schooling in muscular Christianity, rugby, and classics also gave them a strong affinity with their British counterparts. Union soldiers played up this distinct Anglo-African identity, using South African cultural and verbal references, and idealizing the empty, hot, dusty landscapes of home in comparison to the devastated, waterlogged landscape of France.[155]

This process of differentiation continued in postwar calls from the Dominions for memorials that unambiguously commemorated their participation in the conflict. The (mostly) voluntary participation of Dominion soldiers in the war had epitomized the ideals of colonial nationalism, and although the Imperial War Graves Commission initially decreed there would be no national memorials, physical reminders of the Dominions, national efforts during the war were politically hard for Westminster to deny. For the Dominions, the World War I memorials were opportunities to give material, understandable form to the highly ambiguous, idealistic, transnational identity of colonial nationalism, and redeem the sacrifices made by tens of thousands of their citizens. Advocates of colonial national South Africanism embraced these opportunities for nation building with alacrity: a national war memorial was a unique chance to give symbolic form to and promote the transethnic cultural identity they sought to construct. The legend of the "Springboks on the Somme" was rooted in the notion that only a *nation* was worthy of the ultimate sacrifice of one's own life, and both English- and Afrikaans-speaking men had made that sacrifice in Europe.[156] The South African monument in France, which was inaugurated in October 1926, was one of the first Dominion memorials to be completed in Europe, probably because those responsible for its creation sensed that their position was threatened by the turning political tide in South Africa. Although it eventually received the approval of the Union government, which purchased the land on which it was built, the monument was initially the idea of South African politicians, financiers, and members of the British establishment with close connections to the Union and was paid for by public subscription.[157] Those who promoted and paid for the monument believed that the war had allowed South Africanism to take on a more distinctively national character while remaining subsumed within the wider British imperial context.

VISUAL REPRESENTATION, DISCURSIVE LANDSCAPE, AND "A SIMPLE LIFE IN A GENIAL CLIMATE"

> The landscape is not a pre-existing thing in itself. It is made into a landscape, that is, into a humanly meaningful space, by the living which takes place within it.
>
> —J. Hillis Miller, *Topographies*

Although there are numerous social, political, and economic reasons why territory carries so much weight in the construction of national identity, this agency is ultimately rooted in the origins of the so-called landscape idea, which emerged at the same time as that of the modern, reflexive individual. All landscape presupposes an observer; it is bound up with the act of framing and describing a discrete portion of the world through word or image. The landscape idea is most tellingly captured by the prospect, or perspectival view, usually taken from an elevated location, depicting a carefully selected part of the environment at a particular moment in time.[1] Seemingly universal and objective, the view privileges (and naturalizes) individual, subjective perception as the most legitimate way of interacting with the physical environment. It also exemplifies the empowered, modern Western gaze that distances, objectifies, and attempts to control people or territory perceived to be in some way other. The landscape view also mediates a sense of things being "in place"; it implies a primarily visual "scape" from which observers stand back, unobserved (see color plate 4). For many contemporary critics, the very construct of landscape belies an elitist, imposing/imposed way of seeing that emerged as part of mercantile urban capitalism in Western Europe as a point of view that suppresses the existence of those who are viewed or out of sight.[2]

It is precisely these ideological connotations that make landscape such an im-

portant phenomenon in the construction of modern nationhood and identity. The objectifying, idealizing nature of the landscape idea serves the state's political need to place the nation in a geographical territory. By emphasizing individual perception, it strengthens the relationship between a nation and its subjects: when looking at a national landscape, the spectator feels him- or herself to be a participant in the great collective drama.[3] Most crucially, though, landscape images construct modern nationhood and identity because they condition, and indeed form the currency of, popular discourse.[4] If the emergence of the modern nation requires the construction of a single imaginary social structure, then discourse is the essential vehicle of this unity. Discourse is the way people think and talk about the world according to where and who they are. In discourse, it is the languages and rules by which a particular group produces and communicates knowledge, as well as the material presence or weight of representation, rather than the originality of specific individuals' ideas, which is responsible for the development of shared mental constructs. The ability of cultural groups to imagine themselves as such through a shared disposition toward geographical space is largely dependent on discourses that, recursively, help define the boundaries of individual spatial knowledge and experience.

It is generally agreed that the most powerful vehicle in defining these boundaries is visual imagery of the shared territory. Smoothing out the world's inconsistencies, aberrations, and contradictions, and privileging that which is picturable over that which is not, such imagery offers a confirmation of nationhood through reproduction and circulation.[5] Rendering the national territory visible to all, landscape imagery mediates a shared spatial eidolon that mirrors the existential space of social practice and interaction. Images of the nation's landscape situate a country's citizens through a subtle process of familiarization and globalization, constructing an array of discursive places that stand for an imaginary territory, while simultaneously creating the audience/inhabitants of this imaged/imagined territory. (It is precisely readily reproducible representations that allow fractured or threatened polities to imagine themselves as a unitary nation.[6] Printing not only fixes meanings of words and images to a page, it helps fix the meaning of those words and images.) At the same time, landscape representation promotes the shared optic or structure of seeing that is latent in many forms of geographical imagination. The construct of landscape is always a *mediation* of environment and "posits a relation between a foreground actuality and background potentiality."[7] Thus, visual imagery not only plays an integral part in constructing what a culture or nation construes as landscape but also inscribes how a group conceives of a given terrain or locale. (This is why demonstrably superficial or untrue landscape stereotypes often have considerable power to mobilize political passions.)[8]

This discursive, imagistic placing of the nation within a specific geographical territory evolves recursively, gaining cultural currency over time. As a cultural group occupies and represents a given territory, a crucial transformation occurs: instead of the group defining the territory, the territory comes to define the group.[9] Moreover, what begins as a way of seeing and talking about a given territory or landscape often ends as a reconstruction of it. This reconstruction encompasses both the imaginative and the physical, as an emergent imaginary geography is given concrete expression by settlement, building, agriculture, infrastructural development, and eventually preservation. Over time, this dialectic between the imaginative and the concrete creates a "narrative of interaction" that binds nation to territory. Because the shared imaginary geography created by this narrative of interaction is grounded in social interactions with a constantly evolving physical world, it is in a state of constant evolution. Like ideas about national identity, it changes as people redefine their sense of self. Thus, like the landscape idea itself, this imaginary geography maps new cultural values onto a shifting material terrain, while simultaneously endowing practical actions with profoundly ideological implications. It is an essential part of the process whereby an intrinsically unknowable territory (nobody can be everywhere at once) is culturally occupied, spatialized, and invested with meaning.

The discursive construction of the imaginary geography of nationhood is seldom conscious or directed toward a specific goal, and it often evolves through a series of detours, false starts, and dead ends, all of which leave traces in the physical landscape. It arises out of a convergence between topographical specificity, political and cultural milieu, and the dominant modes of representation. Although reproducible visual imagery is its primary agent, the imaginary geography of nationhood can also be mediated by an array of other social practices that make use of the nation's territory. As I showed in chapter 1, these practices can range from agriculture, botany, geology, and mining to travel, paper money, and mountaineering; other possibilities include literature and even music. The underlying connection between the imaginary geography of nationhood and the making use of the nation's territory (itself part of the narrative of interaction) is reflected in the kinds of landscapes nations deem representative and worthy of protection. These vary from country to country, but on the whole, they tend to fall into two broad (and familiar) categories: rural landscapes, or *pays*, in which peasants appear to live in harmony with the land; and the wilderness minimally touched by civilization and modernity.

The first of these categories has its roots in the classical (and biblical) pastoral, an arcadian (that is, timeless) relationship between human society and nature created by a regular round of the *longue durée*. It implies generations wedded to the land through husbandry and expresses itself through modes of production, patterns of settlement, and folk culture that spring from the unceasing inhabitation of the same place or region. During the nineteenth century, when the modern nation-state emerged, this pastoral vision was taken up and reworked in the geographical notion of *genre de vie*, the way of life that ordinary people construct for themselves under certain ecological, technological, and social conditions.[10] It is, of course, precisely this culturalist construal of landscape and identity that underpinned the nostalgic pastoralism in fin de siècle Britain and informed Milnerite Reconstruction in postbellum South Africa. The second category, wilderness, is of more recent historical provenance. It emerged at the end of eighteenth century, when notions of the sublime, and then European Romanticism, encouraged the appreciation of landscapes previously considered terrifying, uninteresting, or even immoral because of their apparent uselessness for human purposes. The idea that wilderness might be an object of aesthetic regard was reinforced over the course of the nineteenth century by the emergence of nations with large tracts of unsettled or inaccessible territory, in which natural and geological landscapes devoid of human traces became reified as "natural monuments."[11] (The often-cited example of this is the United States, where, in the 1860 and 1870s, the fact that the newly accessible Rockies were older than Europe's oldest classical ruins underscored perceptions that the New World was somehow superior to the Old.)[12] This growing embrace of wilderness over the course of the nineteenth century fused two superficially unrelated imaginaries, which turn out to be different responses to modernity. Wild landscape not only refracted Romanticism's preoccupation with subjective unconsciousness and emphasis on the *élan vital* (life force) of raw nature over rational consciousness and civilization, it also provided a way of overcoming cultural resistance to the collectivization of consciousness necessary to establish the modern nation-state. (An example of this is early twentieth-century Switzerland, where the political elite sought to overcome the force of ethnolinguistic nationalism by proposing an overarching national identity grounded in the supposedly universally understandable character of the Alps.)[13]

Eric Kaufmann has proposed that two broad semiotics emerged in the nineteenth century concerning the connection between landscape and national identity.[14] The first, "nationalization of nature," describes the process whereby a nation establishes an imaginary homeland for itself by settling, naming, and historically associating itself with a particular territory. This imaginary, which Kaufmann argues was dominant in more established nations like Britain and France, emphasizes the imprint of a culture in the landscape and implies an encounter in which nature plays a relatively passive role. "Naturalization of the nation," by contrast, rather than exalting civilization and settled nature, reifies the primeval quality of untamed nature and stresses its (re)generative effects upon the nation's culture. In this semiotic, landscapes of identity become not working landscapes, but unimproved ones in which cultural essence is discerned through immersion and contemplation. In this imaginary, which Kaufmann associates with Switzerland and all the Scandinavian nations except Denmark, the nation comes to view itself as the offspring of its natural landscape (hence the Swiss conceptualization of the Alps as, alternately, a "defensive castle" and a "purifying force" for the nation). Whereas in the nationalization of nature the perceived direction of causation flows from culture to nature, in the naturalization of the nation the process is reversed: nature is understood to determine culture. This latter semiotic has tended to dominate in countries outside Western Europe where significant portions of the national territory were in a virgin state at the time of nationhood. It was especially potent in the United States, Canada, and the other Anglophone colonies like South Africa, something that Kaufmann attributes to a cultural inheritance highly attuned to nuances of nature.[15]

Maunu Häyrinen argues that as this discursively constructed imaginary geography of nationhood evolves, it passes through several phases and creates an array of landscapes or places considered typical and outstanding.[16] These landscapes and places tend to emerge at the same time as the geographic characteristics of the country are becoming understood through surveying and mapping. They become the subject of paintings, prints, photography, and literary descriptions, which render them as much cultural myths as physical landscapes or places. Like all cultural metaphors, these symbolic spaces may become degraded and forgotten over time. Many, however, survive and gain in cultural importance as they become increasingly historic and assimilated into a group of national icons that take on the character of clichés or stereotypes, known not only through self-consciously cultural media just mentioned, but also through educational curricula, ceremonial practices, and tourism. To acquire symbolic status, a landscape must usually be striking in itself and bear traces of past activity or some sign of its belonging to a region. Varying in scale from a single house to an entire region, these symbolic spaces are like works of art in that they draw their cultural value from the ability to accommodate a variety of different interpretations. Their cultural currency stems from a play between physical characteristics, the role ascribed to them in the nation's narrative of interaction, and their geographical position in the larger territory of the nation. Together, they constitute the shared imaginary geography of the nation, the building blocks of a unique territorial narrative, which mediate its social spatialization.[17]

Occasionally, a single symbolic landscape or region may come to stand for the many, a further abstraction of the imagined national territory Jouni Häkli calls a "discursive landscape."[18] Examples of this include the Australian Bush or Outback, the Canadian North, the United States' West (originally, New England), and Switzerland's Alps; all are as much imaginary place-myths as they are specific, delimitable territories. All of these mythical places have come to be used as a shorthand to describe a characterful, implicitly national landscape that is, in effect, everywhere and nowhere. This "synecdochic form of nationalism," which reflects the capacity for the idea of the region to support a nascent state of national consciousness and is especially evident during periods when there is little sense of social or geographical unity, is not confined to countries dominated by wild or unimproved landscape.[19] Even in countries where the landscape/identity semiotic is that of the nationalization of nature, one region—for example, "*la France profonde*" or "the Cotswolds"—can come to stand for the many, either because it is geographically located between other types, or because it gathers and distills in itself qualities of many of them.[20] Crucially, though, in every instance the emergence of symbolic landscapes is inseparable from the circulation of textual and visual imagery in a given society.

Landscape Painting and Ways of Seeing

Given these powerful connections between landscape representation and the discursive construction of national identity, it comes as no surprise that the period of national formation from 1900 to 1930 was also the heyday of landscape in South Africa. During these decades, a preoccupation with the native landscape was latent in many different forms of cultural production, and the geographical imagination—that is, a "sensitivity toward the significance of place, space, and landscape in the constitution and conduct of social life"—was a constant strand in cultural and political debates.[21] As we have seen, this preoccupation was partly a consequence of colonial nationalism's need to construct and "place" an imagined nation and of the belief that the apparently apolitical "land itself" was the ultimate source of cultural authenticity. But it was also facilitated by two key social phenomena that defined this period: the migration of some 250,000 whites from rural South Africa to the cities, and a dramatic increase in the number and availability of cheap, reproducible images of the country's landscape. As elsewhere, this led to the emergence of a number of discursive landscapes that constituted a shared cultural property, which needed to be protected if national identity was to flourish.

Because it is the most explicit manifestation of the urban, mercantile, visualist landscape idea, landscape painting is usually seen as one of the most important means of elevating the local and familiar to the national and significant, and linking nature to a national consciousness. It is largely through landscape painting that art becomes national or indigenous.[22] Although other forms of landscape representation are more dominant today, until the early twentieth century it was landscape painting that provided the best means of understanding the ongoing process whereby the subjectivity of the landscape view was translated into shared "ways of seeing" (and indeed, what Raymond Williams called "structures of feeling").[23] This mediation of ways of seeing landscape through painting is complex and elusive; it is not only a matter of artistic motifs, schools, styles, and influences, but is also bound up with patronage, reproduction, promotion, taste, and reception. Although a given society's way of seeing landscape may eventually reflect and be driven by the broad spectrum of working- and middle-class taste, this way of seeing usually originates among a minority for whom landscape is a cultural idea rather than a source of livelihood. This was true in South Africa, where, initially at least, a local way of seeing the landscape was shaped by individuals who made money from the rural landscape and liked to own pictures of it, but who seldom permanently inhabited it.

Broadly speaking, this evolution of a white South African way of seeing landscape followed patterns seen in other colonial societies, albeit with local nuances. This can be best understood by comparing South Africa to the British colony geographically most similar to it, Australia. Both were societies in which most of the white population lived in cities that clung to a relatively temperate, hospitable littoral. Both societies shared a settler spatiality formed by living between a vast, mostly arid and underpopulated hinterland, home of aboriginal people who, though "savage," had been there for centuries, and an ocean that served as a perpetual reminder of isolation from Europe.[24] In both countries, a distinctly local way of depicting the colonial landscape coevolved with a distinctly colonial cultural ethos that sought to both maintain continuities with and differentiate itself from the metropole. In both Australia and South Africa, the artistic appropriation of landscape as a prop of local identity *preceded* the emergence of an imagined community that saw itself as not-British, and indeed, along with growing knowledge of local geography, botany, and geology, could be said to have helped frame this idea.[25] Tellingly, painting continued to mediate a connection between landscape and identity in both countries long after it had ceased to do this in Europe. In both countries, this framing of the landscape as an icon of settler identity was performed by artists who had studied in Europe before emigrating to the colony, or who had been born in the colony but had studied overseas. Like the entrepreneurial, technical, and administrative peers with whom they often formed close social alliances, these artists helped shape the discursive landscapes of these new colonial societies by using skills and perceptions that were fundamentally metropolitan and were maintained by travel to and participation in cultural life in the metropole. These artists' encounter with the colonial landscape both drew on and problematized inherited metropolitan techniques and perceptions.

Beyond these broad similarities, landscape painting's role in mediating emerging cultural identity in Australia and South Africa diverged in significant ways. Australia's progression toward federation in 1901 was more gradual and peaceful than the accelerated formation of the South African state between 1899 and 1910, and its white settler society was not only much larger, but also more established, sophisticated, and homogeneous than South Africa's was at the time of nationhood. Several different parts of Australia had already been depicted, and some of the instruments of state patronage that usually foster links between artistic production and cultural identity—public commissions, competitions, galleries, schools—were already in place some twenty years before nationhood.[26] By comparison, substantial private patronage for South African landscape painting only really began to emerge around the same time as nationhood, and state support for the arts was largely absent until after World War I. This meant that the period of most intense artistic articulation between colony and metropole occurred earlier in Australia than in South Africa, when the cultural and political ties between the colony and metropole were stronger. The period of greatest artistic articulation between Australia and Britain also occurred when landscape itself was a central preoccupation in European art, at a time when earlier visions of landscape as a locus of improvement and contemplation coexisted and competed with more modern perceptions of it as something that could restore individual and social health in urban life. Both these strands of European landscape representation were already evident in Australian painting by the end of the nineteenth century, when Australians had begun to embrace a stylistically sophisticated and varied corpus of local landscape painting.

Although the equivalent period of national formation occurred only a couple of decades later in South Africa than Australia, a number of crucial artistic shifts took place in these decades. By the early 1900s, cultural relations between metropolitan center and colonial periphery were less asymmetrical, and landscape painting was no longer a locus of experimentation and innovation in European art. Another difference was that, initially at least, the group that could afford to buy paintings in South Africa—mostly capitalist mining bourgeoisie and Randlords—was quite small, had lived there for a short time, and displayed highly conventional tastes. In any case, most of the Randlords saw the purchase of paintings either as a capital investment or a way of securing personal social status in Britain (where they eventually settled), rather than as a way of contributing to South African cultural life.[27] As a result, the paintings they bought to display in their English townhouses and country estates were mostly academic Italian and Flemish Old Masters; if they did buy landscape paintings, they favored European subjects of historical character.

Lionel and Florence Phillips were a notably public-spirited exception to this rule of artistic patronage during the early 1900s. Florence may have personally believed that art galleries were an ideal way to edify and enlighten her white compatriots and remind them of their common cultural heritage, but she was able to act on this belief because her husband, virtually alone among his peers, understood how support for public works might mitigate public hatred for the Randlords.[28] Using funds her husband secured from his codirectors in London, Florence Phillips oversaw the funding and design of a new Johannesburg Art Gallery and worked closely with the renowned Anglo-Irish art collector Hugh Lane on the selection and purchase of what was the first comprehensive collection of public art in South Africa.[29] This collection was presented to the city of Johannesburg to mark the Union celebrations in 1910, six years before the new building, designed by Edwin Lutyens, was actually completed and inaugurated. Florence Phillips also orchestrated the establishment of a collection of seventeenth- and eighteenth-century paintings and Old Cape furniture that were donated to the city of Cape Town by another South African–born Randlord collector, Sir Max Michaelis. The Michaelis Collection epitomized the inclusivist invented tradition of colonial nationalism. It included both Flemish and English paintings and was installed in the Old Town House in Cape Town's historic Greenmarket Square, which dated from the days of the Dutch East India Company and was remodeled by Herbert Baker, based on The Hague's Mauritshuis. When it opened to the public in 1916, Smuts argued in true South Africanist spirit that it would remind "the Dutch population of the dominion the glories of their past civilization in the days when they first colonized South Africa, and by the representation of art in which the Dutch and English first met in spirit, symbolize the new Union."[30]

Despite her interest in protonationalist initiatives, the "cultural upliftment" of ordinary white South Africans, and personal support for many South African painters through purchases, commissions, and exhibits, Florence Phillips did not initially think paintings of the native landscape should be displayed alongside European works in the new Johannesburg Art Gallery. Implicitly, the only landscape paintings fit to hang on the gallery's walls were depictions of *European* landscape.[31] Phillips did, however, suggest that South African paintings might be grouped in a separate room for colonial art, and she proposed that a national portrait gallery might become the core of a future South African school of art.[32] (In the event, provision was only made to acquire South African works for the gallery in 1918.) Her ambivalence toward local painting probably stemmed from a number of factors. When she was involved with the Johannesburg collection, she had just returned from nine years in London and may have been mindful of European academic artistic conventions that not only considered landscape the lowest genre of painting but would have struggled to find recognizable aesthetic qualities in the South African landscape. Her lack of enthusiasm might also have had to do with the dearth of outstanding painters in South Africa before union. This did not mean there were no local landscape painters at this time, however. A handful of artists had been active at the Cape and in the Transvaal in the last decades of the nineteenth century, who depended almost entirely on private (as opposed to public) commissions for their income, and many artists made the landscape their subject.[33] This was not surprising: the region was still overwhelmingly rural, and, as in other colonies, landscape was what there was to paint (see color plate 5).

Notwithstanding Lady Phillips's myopia, a taste for landscape painting grew steadily among white South Africans, and by the 1920s, most of the country's best-known painters were primarily landscapists.[34] After 1905, the continually expanding mining economy began to create an indigenous (as opposed to émigré) urban white mercantile class whose members, unlike the Randlords, were as interested in developing local society as they were in accumulating wealth, and whose orientation toward the landscape was tied up with visions of South Africa as a white man's country with a real future.[35] Given the overt nation-building agenda of the Kindergarten mouthpiece, the *State*, it is no surprise to find that the magazine devoted considerable attention to the fine arts. Articles appeared on the relationship between painting and photography, on the Johannesburg Art Gallery collection, on the work being produced in different regions of South Africa, and on key artists.[36] In addition to promoting the fine arts as a badge of cultural maturity per se, the magazine frequently returned to the need for "an art which is the creature of its environment."[37] One commentator, writing in 1909 about one of South Africa's earliest large art exhibitions (the Winter Exhibition of the South African Society of Artists in Cape Town), observed that the region was still in a "pioneering period in matters relating to aesthetic existence," adding that landscape was a particularly appropriate subject in a country where recent history was "a sphere of controversy."[38] Hinting that even the landscape itself was not untainted by this controversy, this author argued that these paintings needed to capture "the very nature of the land," that is, "neither as a Romance Arcadia, nor as a mere portrayal of agricultural regions or mountain forms."[39] Other articles in the *State* dealt more specifically with the challenges of interpreting South African landscapes, the quality of local light and the particularities of local subjects.

The first generation South African painters included those who emigrated to the country—many of them between 1900 and 1914, in response to the growing mercantile class's appetite for art—as well as autochthonous South Africans who had studied overseas.[40] All subscribed in principle to the need for an art that was "the creature of its environment" and a primary expression of "national feeling."[41] Nevertheless, none of them were without inherited aesthetic values that conditioned what they depicted and how they depicted it. Even discounting the tastes of those who bought their work (and few could at this time), these artists did not simply sit down and paint what they saw, but proceeded by an interpretive process that Gombrich has called "schema and correction."[42] Painters start with a vocabulary of pictorial conventions onto which they graft the particular demands of the environment that they are trying to represent. Most early South African painters subscribed to a generalized academic naturalism that valorized likeness to life, atmosphere, and technical ability. For all the rhetoric of national distinctiveness (the South African Society of Artists, founded in 1902, made much of its *lack* of connection to the Royal Academy in London),[43] most early South African landscape paintings, today, look remarkably European in character. They depict nature as a realm of immersion and contemplation, using skills, techniques, and ways of seeing evolved in the gently lit, well-watered landscapes of Western Europe, whose main metaphorical charge derived from distinct seasonal change.

The Europeanness of these paintings was as much a matter of subject as it was one of style. The majority of South Africa's early artists lived and worked in the Western Cape, which resembled parts of Western Europe. They were drawn to subjects that were local equivalents of what they knew from their European studies, or in which local difference (color and light, say) was pleasurably discernible because it occurred in a scene that in other respects seemed European. Many of these early paintings suggest that it was only when it took on a melancholy, romantic aspect, under autumnal or twilight conditions, that the South African landscape could be considered as landscape at all. As one commentator described the challenges the local landscape posed to European ways of seeing: "We had no atmosphere. Everything was hard and clear. We had no trees and no rivers, and without trees and water it was impossible to make a beautiful landscape."[44] In retrospect, however, the South Africanness of these early landscape paintings is only indirectly apparent, a consequence of what they did *not* depict. There are no signs of contemporary northern hemisphere depictions of landscape as an intimate setting for refreshment, or a stage on which urban bourgeois subjects might construct an ideal self, and only very occasional examples of the rural worker posited as a therapeutic model for urban ills.

After union, experimentation with new and distinctive ways of depicting the South African landscape was limited by several factors. The country's few art schools were staffed by expatriates who were mostly British and extremely conservative. Although a number of arts organizations were established to nurture an indigenous school of painting, these organizations were highly provincial and offered conflicting visions of what such art might look like. Paintings that won recognition at their annual exhibitions were still largely quasi-European scenes that used a naturalistic palette and highly finished technique. There were few exhibitions to familiarize the public with new art, illustrated literature on art was almost nonexistent, reproductions were expensive and difficult to make, and color prints were extremely rare. Artists who tried to capture the unique qualities of the South African landscape were dispersed throughout the country, far from the cultural vitality of the Cape, and there were no art colonies where they could meet and work together.[45] Those who could afford to travel abroad found even dated European trends startlingly modern. (In 1920, not only Post-Impressionism but even Impressionism was unknown to most South Africans.)[46] Once they returned home, these artists found little public interest in even the relatively mild forms of modernism they had learned, and the financial

View of National
Gallery,Gardens, Cape
Town, with Delville
Wood Memorial
in foreground and
Devils Peak behind,
mid-1930s. Transnet
Heritage Museum
Library Photographic
Collection, neg.
#46341; reproduced
with permission.

temptations to pander to conservative popular taste were enormous.[47] This struggle to be modern and international in scope yet speak with an authentically local voice was a familiar one that artists shared with most other cultural producers in South Africa at this time, and it sometimes led to internal or external exile.[48]

This situation was reinforced by a general lack of public support for the arts. Although some cities had acquired public collections and galleries by the time of union, a National Gallery with a mandate to purchase significant local paintings was only opened in 1930, with an exhibition dedicated to South African painting. This institution had extremely limited funds, however, and had to rely on donations from wealthy patrons until the 1950s.[49] Although only a small proportion of the white population visited them, collections of highly finished pre-1870 European paintings such as those assembled for Johannesburg and Cape Town did shape local aesthetic expectations and ways of seeing. These collections also suggested that only those who had studied in overseas academies were likely to be good artists, and that art was meant to be valued and interpreted in terms of chronologically evolving national schools. These collections also reinforced the idea that art was a matter of technical skill and a verisimilitude to nature, and that experimentation with technique and style, even more than subject matter, was an affront to the status quo.[50]

The first (honorary) director of the South African National Gallery, Edward Roworth, was an emblematic figure in South African artistic circles before 1930. Also the first head of the country's first university art department, University of Cape Town's

Michaelis School of Art, Roworth was an omnipresent and powerful cultural figure, controlling selections of South African painting displayed at the Wembley Empire Exhibition in 1924 and the Imperial Exhibition in 1927. An Englishman who had arrived in South Africa in 1902, he remained, in the words of one critic, a "firebrand imperialist."[51] His own academic naturalist depictions of Cape Dutch farms and the Western Cape's rivers and mountains quickly found favor with the emerging merchant class. He was renowned for his staunch opposition to "modern" art and French "decadence" (it was probably this as much as anything else that secured him the National Gallery directorship), and in the first published commentary on South African art he bluntly asserted, "there is no such thing as a school of South African landscape painting."[52] As I will show in chapter 7, this was comprehensively disproven during the 1920s and 1930s.

From the Old Cape to Cult of the Veld: Naturalizing South African Nationhood

In this conservative cultural climate, modernism itself was often considered antithetical to national characteristics of art.[53] The typical South African landscape painted before around 1918—works by Edward Roworth, Jan Volschenk, Pieter Wenning, Hugo Naude, and Gwelo Goodman, for instance—was that of the coastal littoral, especially the Western Cape. Recurring subjects in many artists' work were the picturesque Cape Dutch buildings found within a radius of about two hundred miles of Cape Town. This style of architecture had flowered some seventy to eighty years earlier, when older, cruder Dutch colonial ways of building had been refined, formalized, and embellished by British Georgian architectural influences.[54] Not coincidentally for the colonial nationalists, the heyday of Cape Dutch architecture had also been a time when relations between the British colonial government and the older Dutch gentry at the Cape, many of whom were descended from seventeenth-century Huguenots, had been civil and constructive. These Cape Dutch buildings were either hidden in the valleys of the Western Cape and surrounded by vineyards, some of which dated from the eighteenth century, or they were tucked away in the older streets of Cape Town (the Koopmans De Wet house mentioned earlier was an unusually splendid and well-preserved example of these townhouses). These Cape Dutch buildings had largely been forgotten by the end of the nineteenth century, when many of them had been demolished or unrecognizably Victorianized. Equally significantly, the rich collections of seventeenth-, eighteenth-, and nineteenth-century Dutch, English, Cape, and Batavian furniture, porcelain, glass, silver, and copperware that had originally been such an important part of these houses' preindustrial, pre-Victorian interiors were starting to be dispersed and lost.

A significant factor in reviving interest in these buildings was the phylloxera epidemic that first broke out in South African vineyards in 1885. This had bankrupted many of the old Cape families who for generations had owned the wine farms on which these houses stood, and brought these properties into the hands of the urban, English-speaking, mercantile class.[55] It has been argued that the rediscovery of Cape Dutch architecture in late nineteenth-century South Africa was closely related to the historical revivalism prevalent in Europe at this time, which nurtured the idea that every nation had its own indigenous architectural tradition. No less a figure than Ruskin is recorded as having said that "the Cape farmers had invented perhaps

Road to the Berg River, near Paarl. Photograph by Arthur Elliot. Cape Archives, Elliot Collection #7712.

Cemetery near Franschoek. Photograph by Arthur Elliot. Cape Archives, Elliot Collection #3968.

the only new order of architecture . . . in some hundreds of years."[56] A more recent critical assessment of the Cape Dutch buildings is that they were simply "regional variants" of a worldwide "colonial vernacular" derived from eighteenth-century European prototypes.[57] Whatever its provenance, a revival of interest in this vernacular architectural revival became central to the processes whereby South Africanism used the invention of tradition to posit an imaginary colonial national identity (see color plate 6). These buildings became the touchstone for a movement in which architecture, history, bibliography, genealogy, archivism, handicrafts, and conservation all converged to facilitate the invention of a unique, indigenous heritage with which both white "races" could supposedly identify.

The cult of the Cape Dutch was set in motion in the 1890s by the editor of the *Cape Times*, Edmund Garrett, and artist and writer Alys Fane Trotter, who visited many of the old farms and made sketches of their buildings, which she later published in a history of the early colonial period.[58] Trotter's expeditions in turn inspired both the newly arrived English architect Herbert Baker and the magnate-politician Cecil John Rhodes, and thus laid the foundations of an intellectual bond and working relationship between the two men that would play an important role in shaping colonial national taste in general, and architecture in particular. Baker's Arts and Crafts training predisposed him toward the appreciation and preservation of vernacular building and material culture, but, as we shall see, he also used Cape Dutch architecture as a basis for a national style of architecture that spoke of the civilizing dimensions of imperialism inside South Africa and the reconciliatory ideals of colonial nationalism abroad.[59] He did this through building as well as lecturing and writing.[60] Once again, an important vehicle for this cultural work was the *State.* In addition to a series of articles on Cape Dutch architecture and antiques entitled "The Beginnings of Our Nation" by Baker's associate Masey, the *State* also published Baker's "The Architectural Needs of South Africa," the first article ever written on the subject, and a piece by another Baker associate discussing his new Union Buildings in Pretoria.[61] Another acquaintance of Trotter and a key figure in spreading the cult of the Cape Dutch was Dorothea Fairbridge, founder of the Guild of Loyal Women and National Society, born and based in the Cape but educated in England. A friend of Florence Phillips and Herbert Baker and an admirer of Rhodes and Milner, Fairbridge also began her public career writing articles on the old Cape houses for the *State.*[62] She became an expert on Cape history and a central figure in the network of Cape Edwardian artists and cultural enthusiasts; her illustrated books *Historic Houses of South Africa* (1922) and *Historic Farms of South Africa* (1931) became an essential part of most educated whites' libraries, as did her books on South African travel (*Along Cape Roads*, 1928) and gardening (*A Pilgrim's Way in South Africa*, 1928).

The cult of the Cape Dutch was further complemented by the work of photographers like Arthur Elliot, who made his name largely through his depictions of Cape Dutch buildings and their surroundings and contents. Elliot's photographs appeared in several large traveling exhibitions and associated publications, and they were also sold as prints and regularly reproduced in South African books (such as Fairbridge's), magazines, and newspapers.[63] Although he was not a professional photographer, Elliot's work perfectly captured the poetic interaction between strong African sunlight, mature European oaks, and simple whitewashed buildings, as well as the "delicate

Distant view of the farm Rome, with mountains behind. Photograph by Arthur Elliot. Cape Archives, Elliot Collection #5702.

59

Uitvlugt werf and track, Land van Waveren. Photograph by Arthur Elliot. Cape Archives, Elliot Collection #1018.

balance between picturesque dilapidation and unselfconscious prosperity" that was characteristic of Cape rural districts at this time.[64] These photographs, perhaps more than anything else, helped popularize the cult of the Cape Dutch among white South Africans. They inspired a form of idealized, nostalgic history in which the past was turned into "an object of tender regard . . . disarming historical judgment by the generalized pathos of looking at time past."[65] Elliot's importance as one of the first portrayers of a distinctly South African landscape was ironic, as he was an American who had come to South Africa in the late 1880s. Although he only photographed the Western Cape, Elliot was supported and patronized by all the Union's prime ministers of the period as well as many other public figures.[66]

Elliot's work, which encompassed not only buildings but also cultural artifacts and long-inhabited rural landscapes, suggests that the cult of the Cape Dutch was ultimately a celebration of the triumph of lasting settlement over token occupation of the land.[67] As Herbert Baker wrote, "the old homesteads . . . formed a living part of the harmony of the Cape landscape."[68] The cult of the Cape Dutch also gave symbolic form to reconciliation between Afrikaners and English-speaking whites and emphasized European, civilizationist values of age, elegance, benign settlement, "improvement," domestic economy, and connoisseurship.[69] Even more than it mediated a sense of place, the cult of the Cape Dutch naturalized a certain kind of discourse about history, cultural authenticity, and nationhood. Especially as mediated by Elliot's work, the cult of the Cape Dutch provided the new nation with a monument to its past that was in some respects more durable than the buildings themselves.[70] Because the cult of the Cape Dutch remained largely a badge of taste and identity for an educated colonial national minority, it failed to prevent the loss of many valuable buildings until the 1960s. Nevertheless, it proved useful in mediating the ongoing discourse of white South African cultural identity, sometimes in unpredictable ways. The influence of Baker's experience restoring Cape Dutch buildings on his subsequent work has already been noted. Less expected was how, immediately after World War I, the "timeless" Cape Dutch houses became potent symbols of the continuity, peace, and prosperity offered by the "white man's country" of South Africa, as compared to the chaos of Europe.[71] Similarly, a few years later we find University of the Witwatersrand's first architecture students using the simple, elemental qualities of Cape Dutch houses as inspiration for an indigenous version of internationalist modernism, when they made study trips to the Cape in the 1920s.[72] Perhaps the most bizarre echo of the cult of the Cape Dutch was the workers' village that the painter Gwelo Goodman designed for the Tongaat-Hulett Sugar Estates in the semitropical landscape of Natal in the mid-1930s, complete with replicas of many notable Cape public buildings.[73]

Like paintings of the Western Cape landscape, the cult of the Cape Dutch drew upon a bifocal geographical imagination. Caught between a European past and an African future, it posited a liminal discursive world that alternately mirrored and compensated for contemporary European experience. Both landscape painting and architectural conservation—the former visual and affective, the latter tectonic and historic—contributed to the emergence of the Old Cape as a founding discursive landscape of white South African imaginary geography; it became, in the usage of the day, the cradle where the new nation was born.[74] This foundational character was reinforced by the fact that, until the 1950s, everyone who traveled between South Africa and Europe had to pass through Cape Town and its hinterland. The Western Cape's long colonial history of Anglo-Dutch cooperation and quasi-European climate, physiography, and flora encouraged perceptions of it as a civilized European society unproblematically transplanted to a new country.[75] Lord and Lady Phillips's retirement to Vergelegen and their meticulous restoration of the estate and its buildings to something approaching their former glory epitomized how this form of invented tradition found a natural home in the Western Cape during the early twentieth century. By this time, the construction of the Old Cape as a cultivated African outpost of Europe had itself acquired a certain historic continuity in its own right. The Western Cape was the territorial heartland for an imaginary narrative of descent that extended uninterrupted from Jan van Riebeeck and the van der Stels through the loyalist Afrikaner cultural politics that emerged in the Cape Colony after self-government in 1854,[76] to the contemporary South Africanist politics of union. Because this discursive landscape venerated not just houses but also the cultural landscape and ways of life associated with it, it could be read as an expression of the nationalization of nature.

A similar double perspective was evident in another area of cultural production that made use of space and place to mediate a rhetoric of interaction and reconciliation: that surrounding the establishment of South Africa's national botanic garden, Kirstenbosch, in 1913. Like debates provoked by other forms of colonial science, that concerning botany simultaneously confirmed imperial ties and helped constitute an emergent national identity. By the end of the nineteenth century, many plants and animals had been brought to South Africa from Europe as well as from parts of the New World, and South Africa's natural and ecological history, like its cultural history, had become bound up in a web of imperial and intercolonial exchange.[77] From the outset, Kirstenbosch sought to differentiate itself from other imperial botanical gardens, which existed chiefly to collect and nurture specimens for Kew.[78] Instead, South Africa's botanical garden was intended to provide for the cultivation, display, and study of the flora of "the country in which it was situated," in other words, to become a landscape featuring unique and native rather than exotic specimens (see color plate 7).[79] Although the need for such a national botanical garden was justified in the usual utilitarian terms (and backed up by articles in early issues of the *State* and the *South African Association of Science Journal*),[80] it was also argued that scientific research per se was a sign of mature nationhood, and that exclusively indigenous plants and plant communities would somehow be uniquely expressive of South Africanness. The legislation establishing the national botanical garden was shepherded through Parliament, not without opposition, by Lionel Phillips, and Kirstenbosch was laid out in a north-facing bowl on the side of Table Mountain, originally part of Rhodes's Groote Schuur estate.

This linkage of indigenous flora to the project of nation building marked a shift in attitude toward the native landscape. Although an interest in floral preservation had been a hallmark of the Cape patriciate since the 1870s, most white South Africans were still indifferent toward African plants; as in other colonies, indigenous plants, people, and animals were overlooked and even despised until the closing of the frontier and the first stirrings of nationalism.[81] The insistence that the country's new bo-

View in Kirstenbosch
Botanical Gardens
with Skeleton Gorge
behind. Transnet
Heritage Museum
Library Photographic
Collection, neg.
#46822, reproduced
with permission.

tanical garden be devoted to native plants may, as Van Sittert has argued, have been symptomatic of the desire of established Cape botanists to reinvent themselves in the "argot of White nationalism," as the locus of political power shifted northward after 1910.[82] But this mobilization of national interest in native plant communities also created new opportunities to conceptualize and represent a unique place-based identity. The establishment of Kirstenbosch culminated three decades of intense botanizing in the Western Cape during which hundreds of new species were recorded and many thought to have died out were rediscovered. Like geological and trigonometric surveys of the 1920s and 1930s, this botanical activity imparted a sense of a natural fit between the nation's territory and European-imperial science and culture. Botanical activity also initiated another important cultural use of the Cape landscape. Many of the rarer endemic species were only found in inaccessible, unvisited parts of the Cape mountains, and the botanizing expeditions of the 1890s and early 1900s help encourage the rapid expansion of hiking and mountaineering as popular outdoor activities in their own right.[83]

But the Cape flora also posed intriguing questions about geographical origins and histories. That it differed from that found elsewhere in Southern Africa, which was adapted to a summer rainfall climate, was common knowledge. Less widely known until the early 1900s was how unique this flora was, not only in terms of its endemism and richness of species (90 percent of South Africa's indigenous plants originate in the Western Cape, even though it comprises less than 10 percent of the

"A SIMPLE
LIFE IN A
GENIAL
CLIMATE"

country's land area) but also its extreme antiquity. Trying to account for this unique botanical character, some proposed that the Cape Floral Kingdom (as it was formally named by Rudolf Marloth in 1908) had originated in Europe and been driven south by the last Ice Age. (This scenario was underscored by the fact that some Cape species had been successfully propagated, hybridized, and naturalized in Europe for nearly two centuries.)[84] Others, however, noted botanical affinities between the Cape flora and that of other coastal regions in the southern hemisphere, which suggested that Southern Africa had once been part of an ancient continent, Gondwanaland, that had subsequently broken up.[85] This ability for the Cape Floral Kingdom to articulate a geographical condition of "this, that and the other" contributed to visions of the Western Cape as a quasi-European south that was also somehow the cradle of the nation.[86]

An equally inventive dialectic between metropolitan, colonial, and imperial frames of signification arose in discourse surrounding South Africa's participation in World War I. The site chosen for the South African National Memorial was Delville Wood, site of a battle where some 2,400 South Africans were thought to have lost their lives in five days during the Battle of the Somme, and subsequently described as a piece of France "for ever part of Africa."[87] The Delville Wood Monument Committee, predictably, chose Herbert Baker as their project architect. By 1919, he had become South Africa's architect laureate and had been appointed by the War Graves Commission as one of the architects overseeing the design of all the war cemeteries. Unsurprisingly, Baker's design was a veritable kaleidoscope of invented tradition, drawing upon and intermingling European classicism and colonial African references. In a restored wood of native European trees, Baker planned allées of oaks grown from acorns collected from trees on Cape Dutch farms near Cape Town, themselves grown from acorns brought by French Huguenots at the end of the seventeenth century. The architectural elements of his design included pavilions based on Simon van der Stel's (Cape Dutch) Summer House on the slopes of Table Mountain in Cape Town,[88] a Great Arch through which passed an axis set up by the British cemetery outside the Wood, and a Voortrekker Cross located in its depths. The statue crowning this gateway was inspired by the story of the Twin Brethren, Castor and Pollux, who appeared in the sky to defend Rome, here intended to represent the "twin African nations" of English and Afrikaner, unified in the defense of European civilization.[89]

This recurring appropriation of various aspects of the Western Cape landscape as part of the colonial national narrative of descent did not mean that the discursive landscape of the Old Cape was unequivocal or uncontested. As always, social change and modernization were experienced and interpreted differently by people in different places and groups. Some of these cultural initiatives provoked debates similar to those that had occurred before union and refracted earlier regional and cultural differences, such as which of South Africa's cities should become the nation's capital, and where the national university, botanical garden, and observatory should be located. In Johannesburg there were complaints that the commission for the design of the National Art Gallery had been given to the Briton Lutyens rather than a local architect, and questions as to why the collection contained no local artist's work.[90] Similarly, Afrikaner nationalists were unconvinced by the supposed English and Dutch affinities conveyed by the Michaelis Collection, and queried why the collec-

Aerial view of Delville Wood Memorial, Longueval, France, 1930s. Reproduced with permission of South African National Museum of Military History, Northern Flagship Institute.

tion was located in Cape Town rather than Pretoria.[91] And although many professed the national character of Cape botany, it remained a largely imperial discipline, dominated by a Cape-based English-speaking elite with metropolitan connections until after World War II.[92] These kinds of tensions reveal that older regional affiliations remained alive in various guises long after union, and that a shared imaginative geography of nationhood took time to emerge in the minds of white South Africans. They also highlighted the constant (and sometimes productive) play between metropolitan, colonial, and imperial values that was part of the discourse of South Africanism. At the same time, however, such debates drew an ever-expanding array of places and landscapes into a shared narrative of interaction through which all whites came to identify with and to "place" themselves in the imagined nation of South Africa.

An alternate, and slightly more inventive, characterization of the Western Cape, and to some extent the rest of South Africa, which arose in the 1910s and 1920s was that of the region as quasi-Mediterranean.[93] Although a similar mapping was occurring at this time in other parts of the world that resembled Southern Europe, this imaginary developed unique connotations in South Africa.[94] In part, this was a simple matter of geography: the Western Cape lies at almost the same latitude south as Southern Europe lies north of the equator, has a equally rugged coastline, and possesses similar climate, topography, and vegetation. Also, almost alone in the world, the Western Cape is the only Mediterranean-like climate region outside of Europe that faces the sea southward.[95] But, as travel writing published during the 1910s and 1920s reveals, this view of the Cape was also driven by the emergence of popular tourism, which transposed a commonplace European geographical imaginary to the African littoral. Emphasis on similarities between the Cape and the classical world and descriptions

"A SIMPLE
LIFE IN A
GENIAL
CLIMATE"

Chapman's Peak Drive, 1920s. Cape Archives, Jeffreys Collection J3709; reproduced with permission.

65

False Bay coast at St. James, near Cape Town. Transnet Heritage Museum Library Photographic Collection, neg. #36429; reproduced with permission.

of Cape Town as a Naples or a Venice of the South Atlantic all alluded to a reliably sensual land that, if it was not home to the *dolce far niente*, was a place where the sun always shone, flowers always bloomed, and the pollution and straitlaced social mores of northern cities could be temporarily escaped.[96] The discursive landscape of the Cape as Mediterranean was grounded in a sense of history, although not so obviously as that of the Old Cape. The ubiquity of many old, picturesquely decaying buildings in the Western Cape captured the nostalgia for the passing of older, more "natural" civilizations, something that had always been implicit in northern Europeans' attraction to Italy since the Grand Tour and the literary pilgrimages of Byron and Goethe.[97] This imaginative elision is not as strange as it sounds, especially when one remembers that the history of Western tourism is in large part the history of travel to Italy.[98]

Although its cultural currency did not last very long, the Cape as Mediterranean was an important transitional discursive landscape, in that it attempted to imagine white South African society in "Zivilizationalist" terms, but also incorporated an expanded appreciation of the local terrain. To the extent that it was an inventive recasting of existing geography, the Cape as Mediterranean could also be seen as an evolution from the discursive landscape of the Old Cape: it not only emphasized the material culture of an already-achieved past, but also, as Peter Merrington has so eloquently argued, included strands of Greco-Roman antiquarianism, Etruscan and Minoan primitivism, and Egyptology, all of which had surfaced in pageantry and writing about South Africa at the time of union.[99] And although it originated in the Cape, the discursive landscape of the Cape as Mediterranean was not confined to the littoral. As we shall see, it also found expression in white-walled, tiled-roofed homes built by the Rand mining plutocracy in the wealthier suburbs of Johannesburg (Villa Arcadia, which Baker designed for the Phillipses, is a prime example), as well as along the Cape Riviera, which grew up along the mountainous, largely south-facing corniche of False Bay in the 1910s and 1920s.[100] The Cape as Mediterranean also manifested itself in a wide spectrum of writing about South Africa, ranging from novels through popular history and memoirs to gardening books, as well as paintings that played on the sensual and mythical associations of the Mediterranean world.

After World War I, a rather different discursive landscape started to emerge that was also generated by a dialectic between offshore memory and local topography, albeit one in which the latter played a more assertive role. This imaginary geography focused in particular on the qualities of the Highveld, the bare and spacious plateau covering the southern Transvaal, the eastern Orange Free State, and Basutoland (as they then were). This imaginary, which author Sarah Gertrude Millin, writing in the *State*, called the "cult of the veld," celebrated the vastness, emptiness, and desolation of the elevated interior, and was understandably more prevalent among whites living in the Orange Free State and Transvaal. The cult of the veld, which eventually became a central strand in white landscape subjectivity, initially captured the imagination of many writers, who struggled to describe its unique character. Although the following excerpts were written in the 1940s, both capture aspects of this understated, austere landscape's appeal:

> This last upland plain, resembling in its character the North American prairie, or the South American pampas, its monotony broken only by river valleys or those

zones of lesser altitude known as the Lowveld or Bushveld, the last refuge of the wildlife of untamed Africa, comprises by far the greatest part of the country. It is these invigorating plains, with their cloudless skies and dry crystalline air, together with the golden savannahs of the winter Bushveld, that men who have known their peace think of when they dream of Africa.[101]

This fascination is echoed by another visitor at more or less the same time:

> For [this] landscape, the most descriptive word is "expanse." So widely scattered are the farms on the *platteland* that they scarcely interrupt the sweep of the land-scape. . . . Because there is no inclement winter there are no large stock barns, merely sheds. Most of the farms are marked by groves of violet-trunked blue gums, the eucalyptus imported from Australia. After the heat of veld travel, the shade of these trees is like coming to an oasis. The air is filled with the noise of a thousand cooing doves.[102]

Once again, this kind of landscape reading first emerged in the public utterances and work of writers, artists, and intellectuals who, especially after World War I, strove to describe a distinctly South African national feeling or character that reflected natural rather than cultural phenomena. Painters in particular, for whom questions of representation and ways of seeing were always central, were particularly attuned to this idea; it was cognate with the problem of picturing an environment that did not conform to conventional associations and modes of representation. For those trained to engage the world in primarily visual terms, the best way to capture this local character was to focus on the unique and immanent phenomenal qualities of South African landscape—for instance, its "monotony, size and light"[103]—which, although not place-specific, were usually deemed to be especially strong in the interior.[104] It was ultimately within this essentially pictorial-visualist frame of signification, rather than a symbolic-iconographic one based on Bushmen and African art (as was briefly proposed by painters like Pierneef and Mayer in the early 1920s)[105] that an indigenous way of seeing would evolve over the next five decades.

Whatever its artistic ramifications, the emergence of the cult of the veld in the discourse of white identity also mediated an important cultural-geographical shift in white colonial nationalism. While it could be seen as a replay of the politics of union and continuing rivalry between the "imperial" Cape and "republican" Transvaal, the cult of the veld could also be seen as a more mature and less Anglophile expression of South Africanism. It offered a cultural alternative to the Transvaal's inheritance of jingoistic, urban-based politics and served as a compensation for the materialism of the city that sat at its heart, Johannesburg.[106] The cult of the veld could also be construed as a necessary "coming into the country," in which colonial national geographical imagination leapt the mountains of the coastal littoral and in-corporated the northern and eastern portions of the country—historically, the realm of Africans and Boers—into the imaginary "white man's land." Complementing the discursive landscape of the Old Cape, that of the veld mediated a growing social spatialization of the national territory to embrace *all* regions inhabited by white South Africans.[107] In these terms, at least, the cult of the veld could be seen as the logical playing out of the quasi-Jeffersonian implications of Milner's Reconstruction, and

Panorama of the veld near Potchefstroom. Transnet Heritage Museum Library Photographic Collection, negs. #25118 & 25119; reproduced with permission.

an expansion of territorial patriotism. This expansion of the imaginary geography of nationhood not only incorporated different kinds of landscapes, it also embraced different kinds of memories and associations. While the cult of the Old Cape stood for the imagined nation's historical and cultural roots, the cult of the veld stood for its future, mediating a belief in (re)generative effects of raw nature upon its emergent culture and identity. It was, in other words, a clear expression of the naturalization of the nation.

The growing sense after World War I that South Africanness might be better captured by the unspoiled nature of the interior than by the already-settled coastal littoral brought South Africa into line with most other colonial societies, where the symbolic landscapes of nationhood tended to be wild, or at least unimproved, rather than the *pays* inhabited by peasants. It is precisely empty landscapes, so evocative of exploration and adventure, which underpin narratives of descent that seek to perpetuate subjectivities forged on the frontier. The image of the empty, unimproved landscape also invited a whole array of cultural-discursive elisions, projections, and imputations about white South African society's right to exist in the subcontinent, not least of which was the erasure from the narrative of nationhood of the only possible candidates for the role of peasants, the indigenous population. This erasure, which happened in most former colonies, was not only a matter of appropriation and dispossession: in societies attempting to become modern Western nations, making indigenous populations the exclusive founders of the nation was simply not plausible

at this time.[108] Their omission was doubly necessary in early twentieth-century South Africa, however, because it was unclear which part of the indigenous population was the peasants—Boers or Africans. It is no surprise, then, that the place-myth of the empty landscape constitutes a more or less common theme in the following chapters

The growing focus in the 1920s on the empty, unimproved veld as icon of white nationhood also more accurately reflected the spatial qualities of the nation's territory. Before 1900, few travelers in South Africa's interior had failed to remark on its emptiness, and to this day, there are large tracts of the country where the sense of human inhabitation common in the northern hemisphere is absent; only an hour's travel from some urban centers brings you to places with little sign of human settlement.[109] This physical emptiness of the interior was matched in most early travelers' minds by the otherness of its vegetation and indigenous populations, and the utter wildness of the game that roamed across its vast plains. Some of these older European perceptions of the interior as a region of sport rather than agriculture and settlement were perpetuated in the cult of the veld. Just as the discovery and protection of the Cape Floral Kingdom had helped mediate the discursive landscape of the Old Cape, the preservation of the Bushveld and its fauna helped mediate that of the veld. Soon after the end of the South African War in 1902, members of the white elite on the Rand with an interest in conservation and veld management formed the Transvaal Game Protection Society. This group actively promoted the retention and expansion of the Sabie and Singwitsi game reserves, which Paul Kruger had created before the South

Early hunting trophies, Sabie Game Reserve. South African National Parks Stevenson-Hamilton Collection, file ref. M4-68; reproduced with permission of James Stevenson-Hamilton.

Car pont crossing, Kruger National Park. South African National Parks Stevenson-Hamilton Collection, file ref. M7-9; reproduced with permission of James Stevenson-Hamilton.

African War, a huge tract of land in the eastern Transvaal that would eventually be incorporated twenty-four years later into the Kruger National Park, South Africa's first.[110]

The creation of reserves like the Kruger National Park—in which Africans were strictly controlled, "nature" was maintained in as untouched a state as possible, and wild animals were encouraged to breed—posited a way of life that was unequivocally the offspring of its landscape. The erasure of indigenous human inhabitants in favor of indigenous fauna promoted white South Africans' untrammeled identification with wild animals, either through hunting or visual representation, as iconographic, surrogate projections of themselves.[111] Preserving the wilderness was to preserve, as an important strand of white identity, the "common love of nature and wild things," which as John Buchan had argued some twenty years earlier, touched "not upon politics or dogma but the primitive instincts of [all] humankind."[112] Transforming regions with little mining or agricultural value into wilderness preserves may have been expedient, but it recuperated a less disenchanted moment in the subcontinent's history[113] and allowed the continuation of hunting and other outdoor pursuits that were becoming important strands in South African white male identity.[114] This naturalization of South African male identity around outdoor life in "untamed nature" was strikingly captured by the 1907 adventure novel, *Jock of the Bushveld,* written by the ardent South Africanist (and friend of Milner) Percy Fitzpatrick. This account of turn-of-the-century Lowveld life was said to "breathe the very soul of the country" and be "full of sympathy with those whom 'wanderlust' drives forth into the silent places, . . . the fascinating regions of the mysterious veld."[115] *Jock of the Bushveld* was given to white South African boys for decades and became a much-read classic, and no doubt made a generation receptive to the establishment of the Kruger National Park, whose terrain it so evocatively describes.

Thus, in South Africa as in other countries, the creation of a national park was bound up with securing some imagined pure origin from which the nation was supposed to have carved itself out.[116] The notion that identity was somehow tied up with the conservation of indigenous nature, untouched by modernity, might have been the idea of a small group of white cultural activists, scientists, and politicians, but it would develop a broad popularity among white citizenry, in part because it posited an imaginary common ground for them, and in part because it provided a compelling centerpiece in a touristic image of South Africa. As in so much else, this ameliorative construction of white identity occurred at the expense of Africans' way of life. The Kruger National Park was established on economically marginal land populated by disenfranchised Africans, whose self-sufficient way of life on the land, already circumscribed everywhere else in South Africa, came to an end when the park was established.[117] Most Africans who had lived and hunted in the Sabie and Singwitsi reserves earlier were evicted; those allowed to remain did so as workers, trackers, and guides rather than farmers.[118] Notwithstanding its undoubted wildness, the Kruger National Park was in many respects a fantasy, enshrining olden-day ideas about nature that were no longer true, and by which South African society as a whole could no longer afford to live (see color plate 8).[119] Its synthetic South Africanness was reflected in the person after whom it was named, as well as the reuse of inherited African place-names to fabulate and romanticize a "savage" way of life in some ways cognate with the modern European idea of antiquity.[120]

Environmental Determinism and Traveling Subjectivity

This evolving discursive appropriation of South Africa's national territory cannot be distanced from the contemporaneous evolution in geographical knowledge. What is imagined is always contingent on what can be objectively proven and often flourishes in its absence. During the nineteenth century, when little was objectively known about the subcontinent, it had presented a conundrum for post-Enlightenment (and imperialist) geographical thought, which was preoccupied with the question of whether European bodies would flourish in a given overseas territory or degenerate and decline. Although the long-established colonial culture of the Cape and its hinterland encouraged perceptions of the region as a Cockaigne, during the first half of the nineteenth century, other parts of coastal littoral, like the Eastern Cape, contradicted received ideas about the relationship between landscape character and fitness for European settlement.[121] Similar questions were raised by the opening up of the interior by trade after 1860, when for a time, earlier visions of the interior as a realm of adventure and sport coexisted with the perception that certain elevated parts of the Karoo and the Orange River Colony might be ideal for Europeans recuperating from the ills of industrialization.[122] This identification of certain locations for medical tourism was not particularly scientific (being based on early nineteenth-century humoral theories of disease) and it did not necessarily mean that the subcontinent as a whole was considered suitable for permanent European settlement. At the end of the nineteenth century, when a quasi-scientific environmental determinism had become commonplace in both intellectual and popular discourse in Britain, some still cited the laziness of the uncivilized Boers as evidence of how Europeans might be corrupted by living in the subcontinent.[123]

As in much else, the South African War was instrumental in bringing these kinds of geographical perceptions of the subcontinent into white settler consciousness. Chapter 4 will explore how body-environment relations were thrown into high relief by the firsthand experience of soldiers and popular discourse about the war, both of which strengthened notions that a natural virility and bodily prowess was the inevitable inheritance of those who lived or would live in the subcontinent.[124] Although late nineteenth-century imperial geography had optimistically mapped the subcontinent as suitable for white settlement,[125] this question was only considered resolved in the 1920s, when a full generation of European settlers had lived out their lives in the high interior and South Africa's geology, climate, and flora had begun to be documented and better understood.[126] Because the first generation of geographers working in South Africa's universities and government departments responsible for this work were European-trained, they initially adopted a Eurocentric epistemology that emphasized the relationship between climate and fitness for inhabitation and development. As it was for their more famous anthropologist colleague Raymond Dart, so too for geographers such as Piet Serton at Stellenbosch University and John Wellington at the University of the Witwatersrand, research, writing, and teaching were colored in part by a need to make sense of whites' presence in South Africa.[127] This background of environmental determinism, being partly nurtured by social and political anxieties, was not necessarily diminished by greater scientific knowledge, and in fact it peaked as a strand of discourse in the 1920s.[128] It was subtly further inscribed by South Africa's early geographers' emphasis in their investigations on direct firsthand experience of the landscape, personal observation using field sketches and photographs, and discussion with informed local inhabitants.[129]

The early European-born geographers' environmentalist readings of South Africa were a more scientific equivalent of the imaginative discourses that naturalized the nation and evolved as the geographers themselves began to feel more at home.

As their knowledge of the subcontinent's interior became more detailed and it became clear that climate was not the sole factor determining whether South Africa was suitable for permanent settlement, they came to believe that in the end, whites "belonged" in the South African landscape (see color plate 9).[130] The resolution of such ostensibly geographical questions was, however, undergirded by historical narratives like Theal's and Leibrandt's, which marginalized African populations and played up the shared European roots of white South Africans. While acknowledging the divisions between the two white groups, these early geographers also pointed out the importance of a shared feeling among whites for the "call of the wide spaces, the charm of the simple life in a genial climate, the love of freedom and independence and the fascination of grappling with savage nature."[131] Here, earlier estimations of environmental suitability take on the quality of a preternatural serendipity.

The notion that South Africanness was bound up with "a simple life in a genial climate" found other expressions in the 1910s and 1920s. It was, as we have seen, latent in white artists' arguments about the landscape qualities of "monotony, size, and light" that needed to be captured by paintings that mediated national feeling. But a similar kind of rhetoric was also heard from the first generation of South African writers struggling to define South Africanism as something more than cultural inheritance or ethnic memory.[132] Some resorted to describing South Africanism as a way of being, "a sort of inspired bodily alertness . . . made up of vital energy derived from sunshine and distance."[133] Feelings (both physical and cerebral) of vitality and alertness were especially associated with life on the Highveld, where "the champagne atmosphere strings one up to feats of endurance, not without expense to the nervous system."[134] Crucially, it seemed, living in the South African landscape also imparted a particular spatiality: "Why do South Africans look beyond the things immediately below them? Why do their eyes have that far-seeing look? It is because they live in a country of long distances, great spaces filled with clear air."[135] This sensibility was not only a consequence of space and distance, but a particular way of encountering nature: "For all the furbelows of modernity, there is in South Africa an ever-present realization of nearness to life in the raw. . . . It is possible to lose touch with civilization almost at will; and even from the busiest of urban centres it is necessary to walk only a few miles in order to reach the veld."[136] "Be the veld open and straight, or be it broken . . . it typifies a certain freedom of human life, due to the long range, the big view, the open air." In this imaginary landscape, people are thinly dispersed, often alone; they can "call their souls their own. They live near nature, and they get some of its bigness into their beings."[137]

This equation of South Africanism with the inhabitation of a spacious, empty landscape carried two intertwined connotations. Because it almost by definition implied outdoor existence in an undomesticated terrain, it was a largely masculine notion of identity. (We have already seen how these overtones played out in wilderness preservation and the creation of a national park.) And, because bodily practice seemed to be so fundamental a cultural characteristic as to cut across political and ethnic allegiances, it was also useful in positing a kind of cultural solidarity between all white South Africans that was firmly rooted in the geographical particularity of the subcontinent. This discursive equation of a shared South Africanism with a reso-

Polo meet, Frankfort, Orange Free State, 1920s. Transnet Heritage Museum Library Photographic Collection, neg. #33469; reproduced with permission.

Calisthenics on the beach, Port Elizabeth. Transnet Heritage Museum Library Photographic Collection, neg. #43813; reproduced with permission.

lutely corporeal outdoor existence in an spacious, empty landscape was reinforced by the Union's participation in World War I. The South African soldiers' toughness, their emotive code of "craggy self-expression," and their "fighting-style that put a premium on stealth, patience, and high levels of individual initiative" were all cultural qualities thought to emerge in physical environments characterized by "long distances, and great spaces."[138] Tellingly, some of these qualities echoed the "martial masculinity" of the Boers, who were known for their improvisational unorthodoxy and mastery of the tactical retreat.[139] For other commentators, the South African troops' success in Europe stemmed from traits innate to those who grew up in spacious, empty landscapes, like artlessness and directness, a distrust of artificiality and pretense, and impatience with the inessential. In his history of the South Africans' participation in the war, John Buchan wrote: "A less boastful body of men never appeared in arms. . . . To talk to them after a hard-fought action was to hear a tale of quite ordinary and prosaic deeds, in which little credit was sought for themselves but much given to others. They had that gentle but inflexible pride which is too proud to make claims, and leaves the bare fact to be its trumpeter. I believe that to be a quality of South Africa."[140]

This enmeshment of outdoor life, masculinity, and South Africanism was especially appealing to Cecil John Rhodes and the circle that surrounded him, and there is a telling truth to the famous and much reproduced photograph that shows him sitting in solitary contemplation on the back step of Groote Schuur, a place from where he conducted many of his business and political affairs. The same idea also became inscribed in the scholarships set up in Rhodes's will. Although Rhodes intended these scholarships to allow young colonists from all over the Anglophone world to attend Oxford, the terms of the scholarship were clearly shaped by his own life experience in South Africa. He saw the scholarships as a means whereby Afrikaners could "become British,"[141] and literary and scholarly attainments eventually only comprised one-third of the weighting for eligibility.[142] Rhodes thought that "noble sport" and the code of "playing the game" would bring English and Afrikaner together and foster a common identity. Like other Anglophile colonial nationalists, he believed that "success in and fondness for manly sports" was a defining quality of white South African manhood.[143]

A rather more convincing and enduring example of this conjunction of outdoor existence with manly directness and an impatience with the inessential was Jan Christiaan Smuts. Smuts was both an exemplar of Anglophile, loyalist South Africanism and an emblematic cultural figure who continued to inspire many in Britain and South Africa even after his death in 1948. The scion of an old Cape Dutch family, he had grown up in the Transvaal Republic, where, after leaving to study law at Cambridge, he returned and became a brilliant young attorney. During the South African War he distinguished himself in the field as an accomplished commando leader, but afterward he came to believe that reconciliation between whites and South Africa's future as a modern, unified nation would be best achieved if it remained part of the British Empire. Even more than other Boer War leaders turned imperial statesmen like Louis Botha and Deneys Reitz, Smuts became a popular figure among the metropolitan establishment, an omni-talented philosopher-soldier welcomed everywhere from Westminster to the common rooms of Oxbridge, from London salons to the

homes of pacifist Quakers.[144] A familiar figure in Britain between the world wars, he was made vice-chancellor of Cambridge and an Allied commander in World War II and helped write the constitution of the United Nations.

It could be argued that Smuts's importance as an icon of loyalist South Africanism during the first half of the twentieth century stemmed from the fact that he represented an almost uncanny convergence of cultural allegiances. A Boer veteran won over to the cause of transnational imperialism, his vision of patriotism rose above narrow ideas of sovereignty and exclusive communal interests. He was an autochthonous South African with roots deeper than most Canadians or Australians who was nevertheless loyal to the Crown and Commonwealth.[145] But Smuts was also a powerful example of how colonial nationalism's expanded field of loyalties could be firmly rooted in a strong sense of place.[146] He was an international figure who nevertheless expressed his South Africanness through personal communion with nature rather than through ethnic badges or inheritances. His patriotism was rooted in a deep familiarity with and love for the "soil of Africa" rather than in any transcendental attachment to its *volk*, and he used the aesthetic clarity of the veld as a touchstone for pantheistic beliefs he regarded as relevant to all humankind.

An important part of Smuts's appeal was his unashamed attachment to the South African landscape. For many of his admirers, his character was defined by his regular ascents of Table Mountain when in Cape Town for Parliament, his penchant for camping out in the open, and the delight he took in the Virgilian simplicity of life on his farm at Irene outside Pretoria, which became a kind of shrine to him after his death.[147] His attachment to the soil was not only grounded in a deep aesthetic appreciation, it was also based on a thorough scientific knowledge; Smuts was not just an ardent mountain climber and conservationist, he was also an informed and active botanist with an encyclopedic knowledge of veld grasses, which he cultivated at Irene. Because his love of the soil was both practical as well as emotional, it was inclusive rather than exclusive. As Marks and Dubow have so eloquently argued, Smuts's way of engaging nature served as the basis of commonality and reconciliation, precisely because it was local, personal, solitary, and contemplative.

It is important to remember, however, the degree to which Smuts's disposition toward the South African landscape was grounded in a particular *subject*-position. As someone who traveled between cultures, Smuts enjoyed a uniquely double perspective on the world, one that saw "things in terms of what has been left behind *and* what is actual here and now."[148] Although often associated with landscape encounters characterized by domination and subordination, this traveling subjectivity not only imparts a malleable self-reflexivity, a tendency to see other places in a way that heightens awareness of one's own, but also a sense of having a better, perhaps more "universal" understanding of how things are.[149] Not unlike the émigré's vision of the entire world as a foreign land, in which present habits, expressions, or activities occur against the memory of these things in another environment, this traveling subjectivity encourages perceptions of both the immediate and the absent environment that are preternaturally vivid and reflexive because they always occur contrapuntally.[150] (The same double perspective was captured by the early twentieth-century imperial geographer Francis Younghusband's observation that people who always live in the same place are unable to see its full beauty.)[151] This contrapuntal awareness of place often coexists with an inability to feel truly at home in the world, and, perhaps, with an underlying and perpetual state of nostalgia. A recurring strand of émigré subjectivity is the desire to bring together the world of birth and the world of here and now, to frame the two halves of a life completely, without disruption and continuity.[152] Smuts was haunted by this tension all his life, and some have argued that his philosophy of holism was an attempt to transcend it.[153]

It could also be argued that Smuts's reflexive relationship to the land of his birth was the foundation of his underlying affinity with many educated metropolitan traveling subjects drawn to South Africa in the early decades of the twentieth century. Although the Cape had long functioned as a recuperation and retirement station for imperial officials who lived in less-salubrious parts of the empire,[154] immediately

77

"A SIMPLE
LIFE IN A
GENIAL
CLIMATE"

Jan Smuts hiking with Prince George, Table Mountain, February 1934. National Archives and Records Service of South Africa, file ref. SAB #8659; reproduced with permission.

after the war South Africa also attracted a number of restless, idealistic individuals concerned about how metropolitan society was evolving. For many who shuttled between Britain, other parts of the empire, and South Africa during the early twentieth century (of whom Rudyard Kipling was only the most famous), the tempered physicality of life in the subcontinent "actualized a kind of moral truth in its own right" and epitomized a lasting trope driving imperialism, that of "decay at the center and vitality at the margin."[155] It also seemed to offer the promise of a new subjectivity that "combined the realism of the man of action, the sensitivity of the artist, and the imagination of the creative dreamer."[156] South Africa's spare, sunstruck landscape was both a phenomenological equivalent of this utopian vision of culture and identity and a space in which to act it out.[157] This same contrapuntal subjectivity, which heightened awareness of the environment and promoted a wariness of easy contrasts between new and old, conservative and radical, nostalgic and modern, was readily absorbed by white colonial national South Africanists.[158] Although few were able to move as easily as Smuts, Fairbridge, Baker, and the Phillipses between the "life in the raw" of the veld and elevated social circles in Britain, many did travel, if not physically then imaginatively, between Britain and South Africa at this time, due to the long-standing networks of knowledge and ideas that linked the two countries and which were reinforced by metropolitan dominance of world publishing.[159]

Paradoxically, then, it could be argued that Smuts's importance as an icon of South Africanism during the first half of the twentieth century refracted the importance of traveling subjectivity in white identity during this period of national formation. This suggests that the imaginary geography of South African nationhood was rooted in

"A SIMPLE
LIFE IN A
GENIAL
CLIMATE"

the region's role as a contact zone, in which global networks of knowledge and local, resolutely corporeal experience were dramatically juxtaposed. It also suggests that the discursive appropriation of landscape as part of this identity was rooted in modes of life that played out at a number of different overlapping geographical scales. This multiscalar force field of geographical signification was as much a consequence of the geopolitics of New Imperialism and the unsettled nature of colonial national identity as it was of the dramatic social, economic, and political transformation of South African society from 1902 to 1930. But it also brought about a unique social spatialization that simultaneously posited an imagined national territory and mediated a way of inhabiting that territory. Stated differently, the narrative of interaction that bound the emerging nation of South Africa to its territory encompassed actions and memories that were not only collective, ideological, and social but also practical, autobiographical, and corporeal.

4

BETWEEN CORPOREALITY AND REPRESENTATION

Theoretical and Methodological Excursus

> Precisely because of its innate, calculated ambiguity, the landscape remains the only image in the world which is able to restore something of the structural opacity of "the real," and thus it is the most human and faithful, albeit least scientific, of concepts.
>
> —Franco Farinelli, "L'arguzia del paesaggio"

In early twentieth-century South Africa, the play between the cultural memory of the European metropole and local topographical experience initially gave rise to an imaginary geography founded on the nationalization of nature and emphasizing similarities between South Africa and Europe. Soon, this became overlaid by a more indigenous imaginary that drew upon autochthonous memory, emphasizing differences between the two countries and positing an identity based on the naturalization of the nation. Funding this evolution was the notion that a simple life in a genial climate and the bodily experience of inhabiting an empty, spacious landscape were the common and distinguishing qualities of South Africanness. This discursive use of landscape helped construct a sense of shared white identity at a time when overt appeals to conventional signifiers of identity were problematic, but it also helped erase the presence of a substantial other population, whose practical and imaginative relations with the same territory were poorly understood and ignored. At the same time, emphasis on the corporeal experience of landscape also mediated several ideological tropes that bound white, colonial national South Africa to fin de siècle Britain. It reflected the environmental determinist idea that British racial stock might be strengthened through physical labor on the land, and, refracting a condemnation of unhealthy, deadening urban life, gestured toward a recuperation of existence that many felt had been lost in Britain, where nature had become ancillary to human enterprise.

Nevertheless, this cultural preoccupation with a usually taken-for-granted aspect of existence was not entirely invented. A "simple life in a genial climate" *was*, arguably, the common denominator shared by many Europeans who lived in a region where the landscape was spacious, the climate was temperate, and labor inexpensive. This highlights the difficulty of separating ideology from practice in social groups' identification with geographical space, and of determining what kinds of evidence we can invoke in tracing this identification. As I have shown in chapter 2, the discursive effects of representation are implicit not only in the very construct of landscape but also in its social use to posit a collectivity bound to the physical territory of the nation. At the same time, all discursive use of landscape is grounded to some degree in habitual corporeal interaction with a material terrain and is, in the purest sense of the word, non-*sensical* without that interaction. (Even the Swiss use of Alpine landscape to symbolize national character in the early twentieth century was grounded in the very material facts that high mountains cover more than half of Switzerland, are constantly visible from most of its cities, and were, at the time, being experienced firsthand by increasing numbers of ordinary citizens.)[1] Material facts such as these are always in play in the social use of landscape. As Lefebvre insisted, collective space is fashioned and contested through a combination of imaginative, representational, *and* material practices.

As we have seen, broad cultural constructs like discursive landscapes both mark and compensate for citizens' physical distancing from the represented region or territory. Acting as screens and substitutes for direct engagement with the landscape, they obscure the transient and prereflective practices of making use that are an unspoken part of all forms of everyday inhabitation. Inherently shared (and sometimes collective), these practices are creative, improvisational, and situational.[2] They tend to go unnoticed in a culturalist understanding of the environment as a mere backdrop to the unconstrained ramifications of the human mind, and as a realm of raw sensory data with no intrinsic resistance, order, or logic. It is no accident that challenges to this kind of understanding have come primarily from anthropologists and archaeologists, whose work with non-Western cultures exposes them to forms of place-signification that involve acting, using, and doing, and reveals that the equation of meaning with visual appearance is a distinctly modern, Western habit.[3] Such non-visual, performative forms of place-signification cut across shared, intersubjective, and socially constructed meanings, as well as the subjective understandings that individuals bring to their encounters with the material world.[4] Some human geographers have responded to these arguments by calling for an alternative, nonrepresentational analysis of social space, generated through the actions and experience of individuals and groups as they "go along."[5] This recognizes the contingent, dialectical nature of place-signification—that we both make time and place and are made by them—and returns us to a definition of identity as an affirmative, active flux that is as likely to be grounded in habitual bodily practices unfolding in time and space as it is to be constructed through discourses and representation. While clearly owing something to notions of *genre de vie*, this practical or performative form of identity formation is not necessarily revealed by material landscapes or cultural artifacts. Instead, it is embedded in corporeal gestures, habits, orientations, reflexes, and memories that derive from the body set in motion and construct space as something that unfolds along the way, coming in and out of focus, constantly changing shape and taking on new meanings.[6]

The body in question here is not the "corpselike" body of poststructuralism.[7] It is neither (quite) the landscape as body (often feminized), inert before the probing (usually masculine) gaze,[8] nor its close relation, the recursive body as landscape sometimes seen in contemporary art.[9] Rather, it is the intentional body-subject of phenomenology: "the inherent capacity of the body to direct behaviours of the person intelligently, and thus function as a special kind of subject which expresses itself in a pre-conscious way usually described by such words as 'automatic', 'habitual', 'involuntary' and 'mechanical.'"[10] The most evolved example of this body-subject is Merleau-Ponty's, in which body and mind function as a unity, and internal (mental) subjectivity is integrated with external conduct via environmental undergoing. This resolutely carnal body-subject participates in an ongoing, habitual, and prereflective interaction with the world that is structured by the competencies of the body itself.[11] Bracketing both perceiving subject and perceived object, this body-world dialectic creates a continuity between the givenness of the body and the circumstantiality of the world; our perceptions of the physical world are "neither a passive registering nor an active imposing of a meaning." Thus, for Merleau-Ponty, to "sense" something is to coexist or "commune" with it, "to open oneself to it and make it one's own prior to any reflection or specifically personal act." This not only means that the "appearance of objects is always inseparable from a particular bodily attitude," but that space itself becomes a "perceptual field that is an invitation to action." Hence, his argument: "the thing is correlative to my body and, in more general terms, to my existence, of which my body is merely the stabilized structure."[12]

Merleau-Ponty's carnal body-subject's clearly informs Nigel Thrift's interactive concept of embodiment, which is always at the same time practical, dynamic, expressive, and involved with other objects.[13] It also recalls the displaced, poetic body, which I argue in my introduction is a key agent of architectural reception, as well as the recognition of "life or action" that I argue underpins genius loci. For Merleau-Ponty, however, space is not just the setting in which things are arranged but also the means whereby the position of things becomes possible.[14] It is through spac*ing*—in other words, through corporeal inhabitation of the world—that we orient ourselves and construct our geographical being. The body-subject geared to the world is also implied by Christian Norberg-Schulz's argument that the two most fundamental ways in which we establish an existential foothold in the world are orientation (knowing *where* we are) and identification (knowing *how* we are) in a certain place.[15] These hidden, existential connections between place and identity can be compared to the psychoanalytical construct of body image or body schema as the center of integration; there is no body separate from its (particular) domicile in space, and there is no space unrelated to the unconscious image of the perceiving self.[16] Following Merleau-Ponty, Norberg Schulz sees place identification as a consequence of an active, multisensory embrace of the world. Growing up in and being immersed in a particular landscape's sensory, spatial, and material qualities establishes a perceptual schema that determines future experiences and reactions.

This projective identification of bodies with environments is obviously situational and developmental.[17] Although it is registered through universal corporeal undergoing, it is locally determined and culturally conditioned (it happens some*where*). Norberg-Schulz argues that it is especially distinct when it occurs in natural (as opposed to man-made) environments, because these are inherently more diverse. Place-based identification arises within, and indeed creates, a horizon of experience that itself is conditioned by topographical practices and determines the world that is perceptually accessible to us. Thus, Nordic man identifies with and is especially attuned to nuances in fog, ice-cold wind, and the sounds snow makes underfoot, the Arab with the infinitely extended sandy desert, huge sky, and burning sun. Privileging such a bodily undergoing as a ground for subjectivity is of course deeply unfashionable, especially when tied to crude, premodern cultural stereotypes, but it is hard to dismiss the lived, tactile, kinesthetic bodily experience Norberg-Schulz describes and his formulation that "Jede Stimmung ist Übereinstimmung" (every character consists in a correspondence between inner and outer worlds).

All of this is contingent on the physically active body itself. The physical environment is largely unknowable without motility; it extends all around us, in every direction and beyond the horizon, an unequal match for our relatively weak and frontally oriented sight. Moreover, phenomenological sensation and knowledge derives from movement, not stasis. We cannot materially *know* an object except through approaching, circling, grasping, and penetrating its substantiality; all landscape experience is, to a degree, contingent on the disclosures that result from spatiotemporal bodily movement. This comprehension through movement and tactile appropriation is implicit in the temporal continuity of the body's preobjective and proprioceptive explorations, as is the knowledge they sustain, constituting habituation. Furthermore, as Leatherbarrow observes, both memory and expectation enter into this motor synthesis.[18] Thus, it is precisely the incompleteness of the landscape object—the way it reveals itself little by little over time, through motion—that reveals its actuality and makes it perceptually so rich and significatively so ambiguous.[19] The effects of proprioceptive exploration are not only contingent on *who* we are but also on what devices, if any, we use to extend our bodily motility.

The underlying connection between corporeal practice and perception is confirmed by the historical moment when landscape emerged as a construct in Western societies: more or less when local, limited, and practical relationships with the environment were transformed by increasing personal mobility, and ways of seeing were transformed by the introduction of new modes of surveying, recording, and representing it.[20] Early Enlightenment geographical commentaries such as those of Goethe and von Humboldt were implicitly those of peripatetic observers, whose ability to observe, compare, and classify was contingent on new opportunities for travel and hence new ways of encountering the earth's distances, obstacles, climates, geologies, and topographies.[21] This line of thinking can be extended to argue that a landscape is a formation that not only *looks* a particular way but also engenders a particular way of moving, a spatial choreography that is as characteristic and integral to its affective meaning as its visual appearance. This was recognized by C. L. L. Hirschfeld, an important Enlightenment garden theorist, who argued that movement in the landscape was the hidden link between the emotions and reason.[22] And we need look no further than that perennially enigmatic landscape sensibility, the Picturesque, to see how inchoate is this characterization performed by bodily practice. Although Picturesque landscape is conventionally discussed in terms of the arrangement of its visual elements, it could equally well be discussed in terms of the spatiotemporal experience of the body-subject (both physical and imaginative) set in motion among those elements and deeply encoded as kinesthetic memory within the body itself.[23]

This same body set in motion underpins anthropologist Tim Ingold's call for a naturalistic view of landscape that focuses on uses, technologies, seasonal cycles, and practices. Ingold distinguishes between landscape as visual impression (a series of retinal images or perceptions) and landscape as a form of continuously lived undergoing, organized through confrontation and collaboration. He construes the landscape experience as a "processual unfolding of a total field of relations that cuts across the emergent interface between organism and environment," and he argues that every landscape is always to some degree a "taskscape," a residuum of practice and labor over time.[24] His naturalistic analysis figures landscape as a resolutely material phenomenon that can only be (re)understood through corporeal use that is syntactical, gestural, and scalar and delineates its own field of operations and, in some cases, history. Thus, experience opens onto identity; the undergoing of the moving body-subject becomes in itself the stuff of connotation, a matrix of interactive signification that simultaneously calls territory and body-subject into being.[25] The landscape encounter becomes the ontological event of identity formation, a performance in which terrain and the (cultural) body-subject are conjointly characterized. All of this allows us to understand the full richness of Bachelard's enigmatic assertion that "Discoveries of poetic correspondences between self and material elements are not so much a question of intellectual abstractions from matter as discoveries of the self in matter."[26]

This spatiotemporal, corporeal identity formation is obviously strongest in situations of continuous inhabitation, though, as should be clear by now, this inhabitation operates on a number of different levels. Human groups may, in general, conform to the inert matter in which they live, but some environments also invite action through a temporal potentiality of future use.[27] (As Bergson argued, "The objects which surround the body reflect its *possible action* upon them.") This body potential that is both *in* and *of* the world is also to a degree both a subjectivity and an identity. It is mediated by particular ways of inhabiting particular topographies at particular moments in time and place.[28] Essentially heuristic, processual, and performative, body potential arguably fosters cultural assimilation over time: "the spirit of a society is *realized, transmitted* and *perceived* through the cultural objects . . . in the midst of which it lives. It is there that the deposit of its practical categories is built up, and these categories in turn suggest a way of being and thinking."[29] This is very similar to the involuntary responses that most people have to certain spatial situations and relationships, which designers draw upon in arranging and configuring the built environment.[30] Not coincidentally, body potential is also very close to "habitus," the term used by Bourdieu to describe that which links place and self. Buried within the self like an abiding possession, habitus is automatic, impersonal, and durable, a matrix of "predispositionality" rather than intentionality. Not to be confused with routine or habits, habitus serves as a figure of the between: between nature and culture, consciousness and the body, self and other, mechanism and teleology, determinism and freedom, even between memory and imagination.[31]

What binds these various conceptualizations of the relationship between geographical inhabitation and identity is their insistence that environments can never be reduced to images.[32] All of them attempt to recuperate the nonvisual, nondiscursive corporeality of making, doing, and use, and reassert the role of lived experience as an alternate to the apparent primacy of signs, symbols, and representational discourse.[33] Together, they breathe new life into the well-worn naturalistic tradition wherein place becomes a signifier of character and a metaphor for a state of mind[34] by reminding us that landscapes, "like persons, have biographies inasmuch as they are formed, used, and transformed in relation to practice."[35] They offer an enriched understanding of landscape as a lived-upon, topological field, a network of relationships and associations that weaves together what anthropologist Christopher Tilley calls somatic space (the space of habitual and unselfconscious action and sensory experience and bodily movement), perceptual space (the horizon of an individual's egocentric space, grounded in daily practice), existential space (lived space as constructed within the experience of individuals socialized within a group), and cognitive space (space that is the basis for reflection and theorization).[36]

This means that the cultural linkage of landscape and identity can never be completely reduced to a discursive setting in place and is probably better understood as a promiscuous process in which corporeal factors do not replace sociopolitical processes but become bound up with them.[37] On the one hand, this requires setting critical theory's focus on the sociopolitical, the discursive, and the intersubjective within longer histories of imaginary geographical connection and practice, and making space for the embodied, subjective encounter with the land itself. On the other hand, it requires opening up small-scale, phenomenologically rooted notions of space, place, and landscape to incorporate a stronger sense of relations within larger, discursively constructed worlds.[38] Overall, it requires moving our understanding of discursive landscape several degrees closer to background potentiality and further from foreground actuality.

This approach would seem to be especially helpful in making sense of the representation of colonial national South Africanism as a body-subjectivity always already engaged with the raw nature and a spacious, empty landscape. The characterization of South Africanness as an "inspired bodily alertness . . . (deriving) from sunshine and distance" relates simultaneously to Bergsonian ideas of body-subjectivity as a spatial dispositionality, metropolitan anxieties about racial decline, and fin de siècle dreams of recuperating a physical relationship with the world. Similarly, those who incorporate "some of (the veld's) bigness into their being" are, at the same time, Merleau-Pontian body-subjects *avant la lettre*, communing with and geared to the world, and newly autonomous white subjects confronting an empty, unimproved landscape. (A lifeworld where frequently the only voice one hears in the landscape is one's own is understandably a lifeworld in which people's relations with the land become more important than their relations with people in it.) Pushing this kind of analogous thinking to its limits, one could argue that Buchan's correlation of the "silent, mysterious veld" and the "gentle but inflexible pride [that] leaves the bare fact to be its trumpeter" itself posits a "correspondence between inner and outer world." All of these subjunctive statements, however, were fractional, subjective expressions of the broader imaginative exchange between humans and environment thought necessary to naturalize the nation. At the same time, however, these statements were based on encounters with the landscape that were culturally, ideologically, and technologically framed as well as grounded in specific biographies and corporeal experiences. Perceptions of the South African landscape's rawness and emptiness *were* culturally determined, but they were not so much conscious constructs as prereflective potentialities arising within the horizon of practico-material lived experience.

Tracing the multivalent narrative of interaction whereby the emerging nation of South Africa became bound to its territory during the early twentieth century is complicated by differences between the hermeneutics of cultural discourse and those at work in the corporeal encounter with the land. This tension—very similar to that between the social and intersubjective and the individual, subjective modes of geographical signification—is rooted in the paradox that space is both a socially constructed arrangement of divisions and territories *and* the ontic medium of such arrangements.[39] Conventional analyses of social spatialization founded on the practices and politics of geographical representation made after the event sit uncomfortably with the participatory, corporeal forms of landscape signification, which are largely transient.[40] Each landscape image or representation is also a translation, and not only because the transposition of lived experience inevitably entails a loss of some dimension of that experience. Different modes of representation reveal different (and sometimes hitherto unthought of) aspects of the world and lead to the atrophy and occlusion of others. The capacity of writing, painting, mapping, photography, and film each to interpret and construct geographical space in a particular way is amplified by each medium's particular propensity for reproduction, which affects how frequently and in what contexts the images and ideas it conveys are encountered. Thus, what landscape representations actually convey is contingent in part on the contexts in which they were produced and received and how these contexts were shaped by social, technological, and economic circumstance. We need to consider both the social background *and* the psychoperceptual connotations embedded in the representation; the histories of social relationships and ideologies *and* the encounter with individual images and works, in their own spaces.[41]

Conversely, because the exploration of the nonrepresentational must unavoidably be carried out by means of the representational, such explorations necessarily need to address the workings of representation itself, that is, hermeneutics.[42] This is because even if what happens when we look at landscapes *is* related to what happens when we look at images, and the iconographic power of images does dominate social construction in modern societies, landscape visualization can never be separated from the somatic, perceptual, existential, and cognitive dimensions of lived experience. It is only when our reading of what happens when landscapes are looked at (and represented) is open to this multivalency that we can begin to transcend the traditional body-mind dualism that divides thought, idea, sign, symbol, and language from emotion, disposition, instinct, passion, and desire.[43] This requires modifying our understanding of representation from the conventional conveyance of meaning to something akin to the philosophical construct of *metaxy,* that is, something that stands "between" and not "for" either the world or the viewer.[44] In this analysis, representations are construed as products of the imagination that, like discursive landscapes, are lodged in a conceptual space between the object and the viewer. This way of thinking about images displaces questions of origins, causality, functionality, even meaning from their privileged position, approaching them as screens, on (and *through*) which our imaginative constructions of the world are projected and worked out.[45]

Thus, place images are not so much constructors of, or surrogates for, shared imaginative geographies and identities as they are vehicles mediating their construction. (A familiar example of this is the way in which new modes of picturing landscape at first seem strange but with time and familiarity begin to look like true representations of what is there.) Landscape representation's role in the construction of imaginative geographies and identities is connotative, conditional, and contingent, drawing on and giving shape and meaning to unconfigured but vital lived experience. Even as we recall the capacity of representational discourse to shape ways of seeing and to loosen old responses and create new feelings, we also need to remember that an important part of a representation's meaning occurs at the site of the audience, where the representation is sometimes received and made use of in unpredictable ways. While this "making use of" includes the unique subjective exchanges that arise between individuals and specific representations, it also encompasses the oblique references to a shared experience of corporeal time-space, which underpins images' discursive appeal. Indeed, it could be argued that since the end of the nineteenth century, the desire to save or at least recuperate corporeal experience has always been a latent motive in landscape representation. The desire to re-enchant the world is, of course, doomed from the outset to a kind of failure, even when it succeeds as objective representation.[46] The ambiguous role of representation in simultaneously hiding and revealing different aspects of the world is something that I will return to frequently in the following chapters.

Approaching representations in this dialectical way highlights the subtle way action and memory are imbricated in and refracted by them. As we have repeatedly seen, spatiotemporal undergoing and inhabitation lie at the heart of territorial meaning; landscapes, in the first instance, disclose their meaning to a present and mobile body-subject driven by expectation and remembrance and open to sensation and experience. Similarly, the very construct of place fuses the corporeal, habitual dimensions of this encounter with ideas, constructs, and associations that may have little apparent relationship to the physical place (hence, the taken-for-granted way we place topics, stories, ideas, and rhetorical arguments, and narrate topography and space).[47] Any account that seeks to integrate the anthropological, naturalistic, and discursive dimensions of landscape must be sensitive to how the prelinguistic, corporeal potentialities of place both give rise to images, ideas, and constructs and evoke them.[48] It also needs to attend to how the foreground of perception and imagination evoked by the material landscape is always conditioned by a background of larger temporal and spatial field of relationships. As Tilley has argued, it is only when stories are rooted in specific locales—material reference points that can be visited, seen, and touched—that they acquire mythic value and historical relevance.[49]

At the same time, however, this dialectical relationship between the lived encounter and representation requires that we remain open to how representation can, reciprocally, construct landscape as affective, imaginatively inhabitable space. I have already discussed how every mode of representation has unique effects, and how some aspects of landscape only achieve visibility through representation.[50] There are also the expressive, connotative effects of individual representations that can best be described as "performative"; indeed, some have argued that there is never description without performance.[51] A performative, in Miller's definition, is "a contingent act in the human and social world that . . . makes something happen that was not predictable from the elements that were there to start with."[52] Performative utterances make themselves true by being uttered; they shape the world at the same time as they describe it. This notion of the performative is best captured by the construct of topography, a verifiable dimension of landscape that is never there already waiting to be described, but is made through the use of words or other signs.[53] Descriptions of places and landscape may become pretexts that enhance the encounter with the material terrain, imbuing it with a satisfying quality of corroboration, but this sense of corroboration is always grounded in the prereflective, practico-material schema of bodily subjectivity.

Paradoxically, this pretextual scripting of landscape is often most telling not in visual imagery, but in literary description. The practices of writing and reading of the text function as a continuation of the activities that characterized and "identified" the landscape or setting to begin with. (A fundamental example of this is what de Certeau calls "spatial stories," narratives that do not so much represent time or space, as found and authorize the practical and imaginative use of time and space.)[54] Texts about landscapes perform a kind of figurative mapping; they trace the movements and relationships that converge in an imaginary environment that, like a discursive landscape, is a synthesis of the actual terrain and the overlaid subjective meanings imposed on it by the author (or sometimes several generations of authors). Thus, for many people, Mississippi's character is inseparable from that evoked by Faulkner's Yoknapatawpha novels, Dorset's identity is bound up with Hardy's Wessex, and Paris has been irrevocably recast through the eyes of Balzac and Proust.[55] The affective charge mediated by such literary landscapes is of a different order than that framed by ideologically informed iconography, and it highlights the undecidable character of almost all places familiarized through representation, including those known through serious photography and film.

This multivalent theoretical approach that construes landscape as, simultaneously, an assemblage of material and cultural practices, a geographical space of representation, and a medium of cultural discourse informs the following account of place-based identity formation in early twentieth-century South Africa. I trace how white cultural identity and imaginary geography were jointly constructed through a play between corporeal landscape encounters and larger, socially constructed processes of signification. Instead of a comprehensive account of this process, I adopt a methodology of place-specific "soundings" into some of the multiple layers of geographical and cultural meaning-making at work in white South African society between 1902 and 1930. These soundings do not attempt to resolve the fundamental topographical aporia of "did you find that in the world, or did you make it up?" Instead, they focus on the promiscuous, constitutive dialectic between the bodily and the ideological dimensions of landscape and how these become intertwined and bodied forth in specific times and places. In each sounding, I consider how the texture of the original encounter with a particular locale was at once vividly personal and yet was also framed by larger fluxes of practice and signification. Each of the soundings explores the relationship between the subjectivity of specific protagonists, the practical and imaginative dimensions of the encounter, and the mediation of this experience through representation. My intention is to tease out the constitutive relationship between ideological subjectivity, taken-for-granted corporeal practices, and representation in translating this lived experience into intersubjective social spatialization.

My soundings are, of course, highly selective, but I hope they are representative. Their selection and definition was guided in part by the way South African territory was construed between 1900 and 1930, as well as the modes of landscape representation media that were dominant during this period. Each example attempts to understand the different levels at which the original landscape encounter worked simultaneously. All of them begin with the physical terrain in which the encounter originally unfolded. Material circumstances mattered, not only because they shaped the event space, but because they determined the somatic potentialities and perceptual horizons of the encounter. Figuring these material circumstances required visiting the places myself, something that was facilitated by the fact that most of them remain substantially unchanged. (Insights revealed by this fieldwork were, of course, bracketed by the knowledge that the subjectivities framing the original encounter were in some respects quite different from my own.) I then consider the circumstances of a specific person or persons at a specific point in their lives and how their landscape experience was shaped by existential and cognitive schema that pre-textually imbued the encounter with a particular set of associations and meanings.

All lived experience of places is conditioned by memories of other places, places that may be past, present, or future, real or encountered through hearsay and imagination, but are primarily those known in early life.[56] I have been interested in how certain individuals in early twentieth-century South Africa drew on this mnemonic conditioning to create a particular world image that others could participate in, and thereby helped construct a shared, imagined geography.[57] This process, whereby the individual subjective encounter was universalized, cannot be separated from how that encounter was mediated and (re)constructed through representation, however. Each study therefore also explores how a particular mode of landscape representation engaged and extended the original landscape encounter it made use of, and how this faciliated dissemination to a broader audience. I emphasize the kinds of landscape knowledge, memory, and experience privileged by each mode of representation, and how the place-meaning it helped construct was conditioned by the frequency with which it was reproduced and the contexts in which it was likely to be encountered. I also consider how the original encounter might sometimes have been conditioned by how, where, and for whom it would be represented, as well as some of the other ways in which the same landscape encounter or transformation might have been described and interpreted. (The most powerful discursive spatialization is often the result of multiple, intersecting representations.)[58]

Throughout, my theoretical wager is that the imaginatively displaced body-subject became a common agent linking physical terrain and imagined white character, and that in this play between topographical foreground and imaginative background, certain locales were construed as material homologies for a disposition that was at once cultural and corporeal. Although I treat my five case studies as discrete events, overlappings between them mean they could also be read as episodes in a broad, historically unfolding social spatialization, or as successive moments in the construction and elaboration of a shared imagined geography and identity. Together, they offer a glimpse of how, over time, the relationship of white South Africans with their national territory was constructed and reconstructed, as successive representations of a "simple life in a genial climate" started to become a new, discursive landscape of meaning.

BADEN-POWELL AND THE SIEGE OF MAFEKING

The Enactment of Mythical Place

> A man walks across this empty space whilst someone is watching him, and this is all that is needed for an act of theater to be engaged.
>
> —Peter Brook, *The Empty Space*

On the evening of May 18, 1900, London erupted into celebration. After months of defeat and humiliation, there was at last some good news about British forces in South Africa: Mafeking, a small colonial outpost on the border of the Boer Transvaal Republic, under siege virtually since the outbreak of war in early October, had been relieved (see color plate 10).[1] In fact, the news had been anticipated for several days, and the people of the city were well prepared to fill the streets in an orgy of rejoicing. Bells rang from church steeples, the Lord Mayor made an emotional speech outside Mansion House, effigies of President Kruger were burned, theater performances were interrupted for celebratory odes to be read from the stage, shop windows displayed images related to the siege, newspapers ran special editions printed in the colors of the Union Jack, and a generalized patriotic hysteria gripped the city for days.[2] The exuberance of these celebrations would prove to be unmatched even by those which marked the end of either World War, and led to the coining of a new word in the popular language of the day, "to maffick."[3] As one observer dryly commented: "[The British] are behaving as though they had beaten Napoleon."[4]

Today, this public hysteria seems wildly disproportionate to the military significance of the actual siege. The relief of Mafeking was by no means the first victory of the British forces in South Africa, nor is there any consensus whether, in the unfolding of the war, the siege was anything more than a relatively minor sideshow. Of no

British soldiers
drinking from a stream
in the veld. Museum-
Africa Photographic
Collection, file
ref. #968.04512;
reproduced with
permission.

intrinsic importance itself, the town in 1899 was "a very ordinary-looking place . . .
plumped down on the veld."[5] "An oasis of tin roofs and mud walls in the sandy wastes,
[it sat] where the Cape Colony, the Bechuanaland Protectorate and the Transvaal all
touched fingers on the flanks of the Kalahari desert."[6] The town was about half a mile
from the Barolong *stadt* (or tribal settlement) from which it took its name, where the
recently completed Cape-to-Bulawayo railway line crossed the Molopo River.[7] Mafeking had been garrisoned shortly after the outbreak of hostilities by forces raised in
Bulawayo and Bechuanaland, on the instructions of Lord Milner, the governor of the
Cape Colony and British high commissioner. Milner hoped that this would distract
Boer forces from what was (correctly) anticipated would be the main scene of fighting
farther east, until troop ships bringing reinforcements from Britain and the other
colonies could arrive at the Cape and Durban.[8] In this at least, the siege had been
effective, tying up nearly a fifth of the Boer forces in the field at this stage of the war.

Although more than eight hundred people died during the siege, militarily it was
a relatively unimportant affair, characterized by long periods of inactivity, and its
lifting was decidedly undramatic. The encircling Boer forces left in the night, and the
British relief column found no resistance when they finally reached the outpost. The
significance of the relief of Mafeking, then, seems to lie in some other frame of reference than the purely military. There is little doubt that the public hysteria provoked
by the lifting of the siege was partly an expression of salvaged national pride. In the
last decade of the nineteenth century, support for Britain's imperialistic adventures
was widespread and largely unquestioning: "might was right, England was strong,

92

BADEN-POWELL
AND THE
SIEGE OF
MAFEKING

what she had she held."[9] Most of British society shared a militaristic form of patriotism, imbued by imperialistic schools and churches, and shared public perceptions of the Boers as "ignorant, grasping and suspicious."[10] Although a liberal minority in Britain opposed the war, most of the middle classes accepted it as one forced upon Britain by the Boers' apparent acts of aggression. Some of the public hysteria over the siege may also have been due to the fact that the town had been the launching point of the Jameson Raid of 1895. This shabby and ill-fated expedition had revealed the imperialist designs of Rhodes and his metropolitan co-conspirators and set in motion the chain of increasingly belligerent exchanges between Britain and the Boer republics that led to war in October 1899.

But the first six months of war had also come as a resounding shock to a credo of military adventurism that had, until now, prevailed in virtually every campaign the British Army had initiated. Although the Boers' advances of the first months of the war had been checked, they were not easily repulsed. The battles of Colenso, Ladysmith, Spioenkop, and Magersfontein, and the protracted sieges at Kimberley and Mafeking, had dashed British expectations of a six-week war. They brought home the fact that Britain was dealing with far more than just another insubordinate society in ill-advised rebellion against the British Empire; its opponent was a nation that, though small, was well-organized and white. The so-called Black Week in mid-December 1899, when the British Army experienced a chain of stunning reversals and defeats at the hands of the Boers, silenced opposition to the war at home and convinced most Britons that attempts to stop the war should be made only once the Boers had been driven back into their territory. Although the eventual survival of the garrisons at Kimberley, Ladysmith, and Mafeking suggested that British pluck, courage, and endurance were no illusion, the early events of the war nevertheless sowed seeds of doubt about the superiority of British imperialism. The siege and relief of Mafeking occurred when metropolitan Britons were being forced to simultaneously question and violently defend imperial values (see color plate 11).[11]

This general uneasiness brought on by the war invites deeper readings of the siege of Mafeking as a polyvalent, mythical episode in which deep and contradictory ideas were glossed over and resolved.[12] Such a reading is tellingly supported by the fact that the siege had a hero, Colonel Robert Baden-Powell. As the commander of the troops in Mafeking, Baden-Powell was also the de facto representative of British government in the town during the siege, even though the adulation accorded him far exceeded that normally associated with this mundane title. Baden-Powell was the perfect example of being in the right place at the right time. Although he was already known to some in Britain at the start of the war, he was, by the end of the siege, renowned throughout the empire as the Hero of Mafeking, a title that he was to cultivate for the rest of his life. Shortly after the siege, and at the unheard of age of forty-three, he was promoted to the rank of major general. His distinctive slouch-hatted portrait, which had first appeared in shop windows during the celebrations, was subsequently reproduced on all manner of ephemera such as plates, matchboxes, biscuit tins, song sheets, and beer mugs.[13]

Nowadays Baden-Powell is better known as the founder of the Boy Scout movement. Started in 1908, the movement grew quickly to include branches in almost every English-speaking country, and in 1910 Baden-Powell resigned his army commission to devote his life to running it. From a membership that year of 100,000 boys, it doubled in size by the end of World War I, and by 1930 it had reached 420,000 members.[14] Baden-Powell's *Scouting for Boys,* published in the same year as the movement was inaugurated, became its handbook and probably the most widely read English-language tract of the twentieth century.[15] The Boy Scouts eventually expanded to include the Girl Guides and grew beyond its Anglophone base to become a worldwide movement: it is estimated that more than 500 million people all over the world had been exposed to Baden-Powell's ideals by 1980.[16] Although Baden-Powell maintained that scouting was not meant to be associated with religion or politics, the movement nevertheless helped promote many different strands of British imperialism, including constructions of race, class, gender, morality, military preparedness, personal conduct, and national health.[17] Seldom remembered today, though, is the way that Baden-Powell's fame as the first Boy Scout (for which he was knighted in 1929) was, both literally and figuratively, grounded in his experiences in Southern Africa.[18] None of Baden-Powell's own books about scouting, or indeed any biography of him, fail to mention that his idea for the movement grew out of his adventures in Africa.

The importance of Baden-Powell's South African experiences to his emergence as a global figure is revealed by the potent conflation of man and place in the public narrative of the siege of Mafeking, which rendered accessible normally hard-to-discern relationships between mythmaking and the geographical imagination. This accessibility was funded by the imaginative charge of the situated body—the individual, mobile, British, male body in the Southern African interior—coming to stand for the much more diffuse contest then sweeping the subcontinent. Although Baden-Powell's own actions were the most obvious aspect of this narrative, an equally important, if not so obvious, role was played by the landscape itself. In order to understand how this imaginative interpellation of place and identity occurred, we need to turn to the unfolding of the war that formed a backdrop to the siege.

Strategies, Tactics, and the Contestation of Practice

The initial successes of the Boers, which metropolitan Britons found so inexplicable, were partly attributable to differences between the way the two sides made use of the landscape in which they were fighting. Although the early battles of the war had unfolded along the foothills of the Drakensberg Escarpment, which form the marches between the Transvaal and the Natal, most of the rest of the war (of which the siege of Mafeking was a foretaste) took place on the high plateau that forms most of the South African interior. This was a landscape of vast distances and little topographical variation or even large trees; the only opportunities for visual prospects were occasional stony ridges or freestanding flat-topped hills known as kopjes (koppies).[19] In the northern Cape around Mafeking, the landscape starts to lift and roll and even these kopjes become rare. Here, where the semidesert thornveld of the Kalahari Desert slowly gives way to the shrub bushveld of the Highveld's westernmost extremities, the landscape is reduced to miles of pale grass, spotted with the dark tufts of camelthorn trees and overarched by the huge dome of the sky. More important even than its huge physical scale was the fact that it was a landscape that offered little in the way of topographical advantages to an army, or any of the traces of settlement and inhabitation Europeans soldiers were trained to use when engaging the enemy. The first European settlers in this region had been Boer pastoralists, who had only arrived in the middle of the nineteenth century and lived on huge isolated grazing farms far from the few small towns. Constrained by little other than sources of perennially available water, the usual syntax of human occupation was barely visible.

In this landscape, the Boer army was much better adapted and more effective. Although only a fraction of the British in size, and without uniforms, the Boers were both better armed and more mobile: 90 percent of the Boers were mounted, while only 15 percent of the British were.[20] Based on the peacetime commando system used to maintain law and order, the Boer army was essentially a citizen's army, in which strategy was more or less democratically decided.[21] Life on the veld had made the Boers excellent riders and remarkably accurate marksmen who used little ammunition, and their horses were acclimatized to South African conditions. Their normal way of life had also given them an exceptional ability to interpret the native topography. With access to few comprehensive maps other than old farm and mining surveys, they relied to a large extent on personal memory and hand-drawn field maps. As a result, the Boers operated best in fast-moving units that lived off the land (that is, what they could garner from farms belonging to sympathizers), avoided set battles, and ambushed the enemy in terrain that had been carefully reconnoitered in advance.[22]

Initially, the British forces were hopelessly outclassed. Commanded by authoritarian officers with little personal knowledge of the subcontinent, the ordinary soldiers were unprepared for fighting in a terrain without the normal cover. The British Army had more accurate maps than the Boers, but these were also extremely limited in coverage.[23] Even without the complicating factors of the harsh climate and inappropriate equipment, both the infantry regulars and the "steamroller artillery" were almost completely dependent on the railways to master the huge distances that were integral to warfare in the South African interior.[24] These two factors were in fact closely linked: the only parts of the interior that had been thoroughly mapped at this time were the borders with the Boer Republics and the corridors through which railway lines ran. These railways had been hastily constructed by the colonial Cape and Natal governments to link their ports to the previously remote interior after the discovery of minerals in the 1870s and 1880s, and their alignments followed political boundaries as much as the terrain or the most direct route.[25] The intimate connections between British imperialism and the railways were emphasized during the war, when the British Army's reliance on them meant that they had to be defended by numerous garrisons, such as the one stationed at Mafeking. This both tied up substantial numbers of troops, and drew enemy attacks: no major battle of the first part of the war was more than a few miles from a railway line. Fast-moving, independent Boer platoons familiar with the region soon realized that, in this expansive terrain, they simply had to attack trains and hard-to-repair stretches of railway in remote places to virtually cripple the British. This is well illustrated by maps of the early phases of the war, which trace Boer maneuvers in the hills of northern Natal as they weave a topographically inventive choreography around the stolidly engineered trajectory of the railway.

These two different ways of using the same landscape are cognate with de Certeau's dialectical conceptualization of human praxis into the strategic and the tactical. De

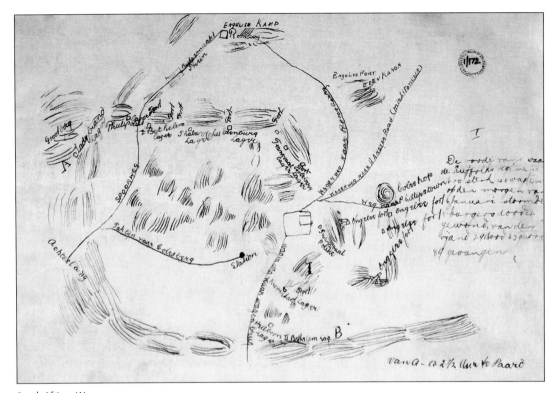

South African War
Boer field map.
Free State Archives,
Bloemfontein, file ref.
#1/172; reproduced
with permission.

Certeau saw strategic practice as "the calculus of force-relationships which becomes possible when a subject of will and power . . . can be isolated from an 'environment.'"[26] A strategy assumes a place that can serve as a basis for generating relations with an exterior distinct from it, and is the model for all political, economic, and scientific rationality. Tactics, on the other hand, are "a calculus which cannot count on a spatial or institutional localization. . . . The place of the tactic belongs to the other. A tactic insinuates itself into the other's place, fragmentarily, without taking it over in its entirety, without being able to keep it at a distance. It has at its disposal no base where it can capitalize on its advantages, prepare its expansions, and secure independence with respect to circumstances."[27] De Certeau saw tactics as "ruses" and "maneuvers," more about *ways* of being than *what* is used. Dispersed in time and space, tactics never achieve the triumph of space over time that is characteristic of strategies. They derive much of their power from the juxtaposition of the unexpected, the cunning creation of polymorphic situations. Like metaphor and wit, tactics throw the supposedly familiar and unchanging into new light. Despite their apparently subversive nature, tactical ways of operating are in fact endemic in the world, used by everybody in their daily routines, and ubiquitous in the plant and animal world.

In de Certeau's terms, the siege of Mafeking was a victory for tactical practices: it owed everything to inventive and diversionary tactics, and nothing to conventional military strength.[28] Baden-Powell oversaw a range of schemes designed to turn the unlikely resources he had on hand to advantage. He constructed a huge field gun by cobbling together various found objects and recommissioned, to surprisingly good effect, a ship's cannon dating from 1770, which had until then been used as a gate

BADEN-POWELL
AND THE
SIEGE OF
MAFEKING

post on a nearby farm. Dynamite bombs were devised from potted-meat tins, fuel was improvised by mixing cow dung and coal dust, and Africans were made to dig a large, complex network of defensive trenches that were never manned but misled the Boers about the size of the garrison. Other tactics were specifically directed at maintaining morale, largely through celebratory, even irreverent, reminders that the town was, after all, part of the empire on which "the sun never set." Using the local press, Baden-Powell published a local newspaper and stamps with his own head on them, and he participated in several insouciant exchanges with the besieging Boer commanders that revolved around possible cricket matches and dinners at the local hotel.[29] Although Baden-Powell downplayed this fact, Africans became increasingly active in defending the town and securing supplies during the last stages of the siege. Indeed, it has now become clear that the survival of the white garrison was largely made possible by the sacrifices of the Africans: although the British were in a weak position relative to the Boers, they still had unlimited power over the native population. Firewood was commandeered in vast quantities from the roofs of Africans' huts, and when food became scarce, rations to the Europeans were maintained by starving the Africans, many of whom died as a result.[30]

Scouting and the Transformation of Metropolitan Masculinity

The roots of these tactics are not hard to find. Baden-Powell had originally come to South Africa from India in 1895 to join the irregular troops left behind to monitor the situation in Matabeleland (later part of Rhodesia) after British regulars had brutally put down an insurrection by Shonas and Matabeles against white settlers. This

Bulawayo Field Force (BFF) was made up of a small group of men drawn from all over the empire who knew the African interior from firsthand experience as traders, scouts, prospectors, or ranchers. Beyond the reach of the niceties of parliamentary democracy, as well as normal army discipline,[31] the BFF's military practices were irregular in every sense of the word. To fight the immanent but hidden resistance to white settlement among the Africans, Baden-Powell developed a repertoire of guerrilla and counterguerrilla tactics, and used symbolic and real terror (such as the intermittent burning of villages and exemplary executions) to punish the Matabeles. He also sent back regular dispatches to the *Graphic* in London giving his version of the campaign, accompanied either by photographs taken with his own Eastman camera or his own easily reproducible line sketches.[32]

This use of his experiences to create a public narrative of his own deeds in Britain was helped by the fact that Matabeleland was the kind of region that engaged the geographical imagination of metropolitan Britain at the end of the nineteenth century. This was a time when frontiers were closing all over the world, and life in Europe seemed increasingly constrained and convention-ridden.[33] Regions opened up by Europeans overseas provided appealing worlds in which discipline and adventure, morality and escapism confronted each other.[34] These regions were especially appealing if they combined the familiar and the exotic. Barely touched by the constraining reach of European bourgeois society, Matabeleland boasted a rugged terrain as yet only partly settled by Europeans, a white man's climate as well as the promise of gold and land to ranch, and a brave, warrior-like native population.[35] Baden-Powell's perception that he was engaged in one of the last great adventures of empire was reinforced by the fact that one of the BFF's key men was an American scout, Frederick Burnham, a figure from whom Baden-Powell learned or borrowed many of the ideas he would later use during the siege at Mafeking.

Scouting had first come to prominence in North America during the eighteenth century, when both the British and the French armies had learned the skills of bushcraft, tracking, stalking, and ambush from Native Americans. By contrast to conventional military practice, which favored fighting in open terrain and the deployment of large formations of massed troops directed from vantage points that offered an overview of the unfolding battle,[36] the techniques of scouting emerged in the unmapped hilly and forested terrain of Eastern North America, and necessarily broke the military encounter into many smaller events that seldom occurred in the same location or within sight of each other. Scouting foreshadowed the techniques used in guerrilla warfare, literally "little wars."[37] Until the outbreak of the South African War, scouting was looked down on by European generals; reluctantly employed, it was carried out by irregular units who passed information back to the main army.

Thus, scouting practices were primarily associated with situations in which the maximization of tactical knowledge was likely to be more effective than the wielding of strategic power. A scout never properly engaged the enemy, even though he might be surrounded by them.[38] The original scout's survival depended on his ability to utilize the slightest physical evidence to find his way around in difficult country or to prevail over forces that were more powerful or outnumbered him. Scouting was a self-taught art, the result of individual practice in the lived present; almost by definition, it required the cultivation of personal, subjective qualities like pluck, alertness, and inventiveness. Unable to count on previous geographical description by others, scouts garnered their own knowledge of the region through almost obsessive forms of observation and memory.[39] European scouts were not above substituting personal observation over time with local field knowledge gleaned from the native population; they usually did this by accompanying their native informants on expeditions.[40] The lived encounter with the physical landscape remained the nexus of the scout's knowledge. This knowledge was inextricably intertwined with the topology of the events that gave rise to it in the first place: successful reading of the landscape involved not only heightened visual observation but also proprioceptive apprehension and kinesthetic memory of the landscape. Crucially, this attention to events and appearances was also reflexive: the scout's field skills included disguises and false signs to confuse opponents or throw them off his trail, or to create the impression that he commanded a stronger force than he did.

Just as the scout's subjectivity differed from that required by strategic power structures (which value methodical repetition and the willingness to submit to higher authority), the scout's knowledge of the landscape differed from that mediated by the conventional (and most strategic) form of geographical representation, the map. Ideally, the scout's knowledge arose in territorially peripheral spaces, regions that were, both literally and metaphorically, "just off the map" rather than ones where mapping and settlement made living by one's wits and senses redundant.[41] This difference is cognate with the difference between construing the world synoptically and construing it panoptically. The former is contingent on the imperatives of tactical bodily movement and memory; it is impossible without physical inhabitation of the landscape. The latter implies distantiation, resolution, order, and omniscience, a kind of strategic "all-seeing." Nevertheless, it is important to remember de Certeau's argument that the synoptical and panoptical visions of landscape are often, at a deeper level, interdependent. Although the scout's self-disciplined resourcefulness seemed to be antithetical to the powerful, depersonalized, and hierarchical practices of imperialism and occupation, it was, in a sense, facilitated by those practices.

Scouting as conceptualized by Baden-Powell was not only about changing practices but also about changing subjectivities. At the end of the nineteenth century, imperial Britain was at its greatest power and extent but its political establishment was also aware of the historical pattern of empires decaying from within. This was also a time when many among the establishment increasingly believed that national greatness lay in individual character—the ability to respond to shifting circumstance—rather than technology, natural resources, or population size.[42] The popularity of fictional accounts of American scouting in late nineteenth-century western Europe was closely related to anxieties about national character and preparedness and helped prepare the ground for Baden-Powell's books.[43] Although Baden-Powell maintained that scouting was simply meant to develop good citizenship (he argued that a scout's knowledge combined "the best of all art, science and sports"), his manuals also unashamedly set out to build character.[44] And, like others in Western industrialized countries, Baden-Powell believed that character was both a mental and physical phenomenon, best nurtured through unmediated contact with nature. In most European societies at this time, the healthy development of children was increasingly equated with free movement in the outdoors,[45] and civic and national pride was linked to a love of nature

Baden-Powell on hotel roof during siege, looking through binoculars. Historical Papers Collection, University of the Witwatersrand Library; Album 1559; reproduced with permission.

and physical resourcefulness (something that was especially evident in geographical education).[46] This faith in the character-building potential of nature became bound up with the imaginative geography of imperialism in adventure stories, popular at the time, of men living by their own rules and achieving much with slender means in untamed regions.[47] The subtext of these stories was that such experiences made individuals not only physically healthier but more in touch with their natural human instincts. Along with the unashamedly imperialist curricula in British schools at this time, these stories conveyed important ideas about how Europeans were expected to behave on the colonial margins, where limited material resources and freely available labor could easily lead to laziness, fatalism, and a general moral and intellectual lassitude.[48]

Traditional gender roles and identities, too, were seen to be threatened by the effects of industrial and urban environments. The ideal masculine identity was increasingly seen to derive from a closeness to nature, beyond the reach of the domestic, effeminate, and dissipated life of the home and the city, and isolated male communities in nature were particularly affirmative of manliness. These intertwined anxieties about masculinity and national character seemed to be powerfully confirmed by mobilization for the war in Britain, which revealed that only two-thirds of initial volunteers were fit enough for service, a figure that was even worse in urban areas.[49] Because military efficiency was perceived to be inseparable from the wider health, fitness, and morale of the nation, this apparent decline in the virility of Britain's men not only threatened national efficiency but also, by extension, imperial power.[50] The concern over the deterioration of the working classes (who formed the bulk of military recruits), and a general sense of a crisis of British masculinity generated by these figures was not helped by the physical puniness of British soldiers compared to their colonial counterparts, let alone the Boers themselves.[51] There was also little comfort in the fact that disease, not combat, turned out to be the primary cause of death among British soldiers in South Africa.[52]

While it is highly likely that Baden-Powell understood and played on these cultural anxieties and imaginaries in his accounts of his adventures in Matabeleland, he raised this kind of self-representation to a much higher level through his "sagacious lawlessness" at Mafeking.[53] His use of the siege as a founding narrative for the empirewide scouting movement inculcated a domesticated form of adventurous individualism that subtly reinforced the interdependence of the tactical and the strategic. Like adventure stories that were simultaneously made possible by and provided an escape from the constrained, regimented life in industrialized, urban Britain, Baden-Powell's practices at Mafeking were supported by the power and reach of imperialism, even at the same time as they seemed to subvert them.

Seeing and Being Seen: The Staging of Bodily Practice

Stories of adventure on the frontiers of the British Empire not only constructed an imaginary world that distracted from everyday life in Britain, they had another important function: they encouraged the metropolitan masses to identify with the otherwise invisible parts of the world into which their governments were pouring large quantities of money and men with little visible return. Nurturing and sustaining popular support for the empire in general, and the war in particular, were crucial goals for the British establishment and would have been impossible without the exponential growth of mass media at this time. Metropolitan interest in the South African War was proportionate to the enormous numbers of British soldiers involved, approaching half a million, but it was also encouraged by the development, in the decade before the war, of the means to bring news of contemporary events quickly and cheaply to an enormous audience.

In fact, the South African War coincided with the inauguration of a new phase in the development of mass media.[54] It was the first large war to have taken place since the emergence of cheap, mass circulation print media, and it probably contributed to their growth. Thanks to the 1870 Education Act, popular literacy had reached new levels in Britain.[55] Readership for newspapers like Lord Northcliffe's *Daily Mail*, which supported the war through an editorial policy of "explain, simplify, clarify," grew dramatically. Launched in 1895, it reached a circulation of almost one million by 1900.[56] Equally popular were magazines like the *Sketch*, the *Graphic*, and the *Illustrated London News*, whose rising circulation was thanks in part to the invention of modern reproduction techniques that made it possible to include many illustrations. The role of the jingoistic press in manufacturing popular support for the war was complemented by hyperpatriotic uses of the war in advertising, games, household ephemera, entertainment, and cinema, which was just starting to become popular in 1900 in the form of bioscopes shown in musicals halls. This heterogeneous and ubiquitous presence of the war as a spectacle in popular culture as much as anything else lent metropolitan patriotic fervor such an intensely theatrical quality. Mafficking crowds were, in effect, an extension of the music hall stage onto the streets; "in bursts of emotive, frenzy the working class experienced the entertainment of victory woven into national solidarity and impressive status."[57]

Another factor contributing to this heightened visibility of South Africa in Britain was the large numbers of war correspondents in the subcontinent at this time. The South African War was attended by the largest British and foreign press corps of any overseas campaign yet; the London *Times* alone had twenty-four correspondents in South Africa by the end of the war.[58] From British controlled ports, correspondents could quickly reach the interior by train and transmit their stories via telegraph back to British newspapers. (Rhodes is famously recorded as saying: "The railway line is my right hand, and the telegraph my voice.") These correspondents' accounts were the British public's chief source of information about the conflict, not only during the war but also after the peace, when they wrote many of the war's popular histories. The sheer size of the press corps meant that there was often fierce competition between correspondents for the news, and the exploits of reporters in securing their stories sometimes rivaled the actual events that they were reporting.[59] Dispatches written in the first person not only compensated for news that was not exclusive, they also contributed to the perception that the war was an adventure as much as a campaign.[60]

As the war progressed, the British Army itself played an increasingly active role in encouraging this situation. Lord Roberts, the commander in chief of forces in South Africa after 1900, himself cultivated a peculiarly modern relationship between the armed forces and the press corps, perhaps inspired by Baden-Powell's own manipulation of the coverage of the siege.[61] Even given the tenor of the campaign, Baden-Powell had an almost preternatural understanding of how metropolitan imaginings and the media supported each other. The tactics he used on the ground at Mafeking were consciously aimed at an audience much larger than either those trapped in the town or those who surrounded it, and, as in Matabeleland, he went to great lengths to ensure that news of these tactics got to this audience. Conscious of the fact that he had five war correspondents as well as a handful of the metropolitan establishment under his responsibility, Baden-Powell ensured that African runners managed to slip through enemy lines with dispatches in order to convey the story of the siege to the outside world. (His success in this regard was reflected on April 1 by a telegram from Queen Victoria, which read: "I continue watching with confidence and admiration the patient and resolute defense which is so gallantly maintained under your ever-resourceful command.")[62] After the war, he would continue to mine the story of the siege for a variety of moral lessons, with the numbers of Boer opponents becoming progressively greater over the years.[63]

There is little doubt that the excitement generated by the siege in Britain was encouraged by Baden-Powell's ongoing and highly reflexive reportage. This reportage was epitomized by a bird's-eye view he drew of Mafeking while the siege was still under way, and which appeared frequently in books after the war. Baden-Powell, a fluent artist who had been encouraged in nature study as a child and may have learned drawing from Ruskin, documented all phases of his life.[64] His sketch of the siege has an innocent and almost childlike simplicity about it, reminding one of the old-fashioned faraway, half-imaginary realms that appear inside the covers of any number of children's adventure books dating from this period. The drawing depicts the situation of the siege. Arrayed around the fringes of the settlement are Bechuanaland, Rhodesia, and the Transvaal, represented by words alone, while closer to the town itself, the Boer trenches appear as a continuous dotted line. The sketch's point

War correspondents waiting for Lord Roberts to enter Kroonstad. Reproduced courtesy of the Director, National Army Museum, London; Picture Library file ref. #1998-01-135-39.

of view combines the panoptical position of an imperial observer with a more synoptic vision encompassing the orderly grid of the European settlement and its cultural landmarks, the more formlessness of the Native *stadt*, and the apparently continuous ring of trenches that encircled them both.[65] The main axis of the sketch, the Cape-to-Matabeleland railway, lends it an unmistakably metropolitan orientation The viewer is placed south of the town, the direction from which British imperialism was making its way across Africa, and from which the relief column would come.[66]

Baden-Powell's sketch is reminiscent of chorography, a form of mapping that emerged during the Renaissance, that combined within one representation written historical and geographical narrative and graphic illustration.[67] Within the evolution of mapping, chorography marks a transition from the representation of imaginary worlds to the representation of measurable, verifiable ones, from the representation of place as characteristic topographical profile viewed from a particular point of view to representing it as a location within a continuum of known space viewed from an imaginary nowhere. Not accidentally, chorography emerged at a time when the world was seen as a theater, when "theater itself had the meaning not only of playhouse, but also a conspectus, a place, region or text in which phenomena are presented together for public understanding."[68] The underlying theatricality of Baden-Powell's sketch is

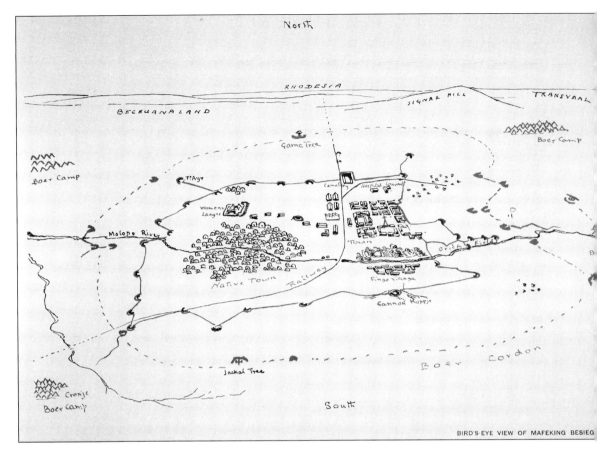

North

RHODESIA

BECHUANALAND   SIGNAL HILL   TRANSVAAL

                                                                              Boer Camp

Boer Camp   Game Tree

                    T'Ayr   Cemetery   Hospital (convent)
               Women's   P
               Laager

Malopo River   Town   British Field

                    Native Town   Railway   Fingo Village

                                              Cannon Koppje   B

                    Jackal Tree   Boer   Cordon

Cranje
Boer Camp   South

BIRD'S-EYE VIEW OF MAFEKING BESIEG

Baden-Powell's
bird's-eye sketch of
Mafeking beseiged.
R. S. Baden-Powell,
*Sketches in Mafeking and
East Africa* (London:
Smith, Elder & Co.,
1907). Reproduced
with permission of
the British Library,
London.

of a piece with the overall theatricality in the way the war was being experienced in metropolitan musical halls, melodramas, and bioscopes, as well as the carnivalesque manner in which the public greeted every British victory.[69] Baden-Powell's representation of the siege can be interpreted as grounded in the way theater has persistently been used throughout Western history as a medium representing abstract ideas.

As Aristotle recognized, an actor's most powerful tool for communicating abstract ideas is not verbal declamation, but action.[70] The gestural position of the body relative to space is an inchoate representation that goes before even the deployment of words. An actor's position relative to the audience—upstage, downstage, center stage—already conveys important information about the actor's internal state of mind and intentions. The meaning of relative position draws upon the fact that the body is always, potentially or actually, moving in time and/or space. The space to which we orient ourselves (where we are gazing, where we are about to move, or merely where we throw our mental attention) is always psychologically charged with meaning and intentionality.[71] The actor deploys this "moving-into" to construct the continuous narrative thread that binds and animates space and time; an audience learns little until the actor starts to move.[72] While this moving-into is based in the fundamental commonality of bodily praxis, it is the intensification of such praxis that distinguishes actor from audience and facilitates the appropriation and structuring of space as a stage. The most elemental version of this stage—that is, the one most readily created and destroyed—is the one that is negotiated through common agreement between the actor and the audience, that of the street performer.[73] This most basic form of the theater is the temporary appropriation of previously unstructured space through operations not overtly directed toward this appropriation. Wordless performance that selects and restructures one portion of continuous space as a stage can be likened to the (equally wordless) theater of tactical practice that delineates and structures a topography. Thus the stage/landscape emerges as part of purposeful action, while purposeful action's meaning is grounded in the way it makes use of where it takes place.

Theatrical performance is an event that seldom changes the physical context in which it takes place; the stage, like the landscape, is never the subject of the drama, but it is always a necessary adjunct to it. Dramatic meaning arises from complete and interactive situations (in which action makes use of space) rather than figures in context (static bodies en tableaux). Drama on a simple stage is solely conveyed through the deployment of the body, qualitatively different from drama on a conventional stage, where recognizable human artifacts (quite literally, "props") carry some of the burden of representation. Thus, in representational terms, bodily action and stage space are intertwined; in an audience's imagination, the stage is as much the product of the action as the actions are the product of the stage. Although the stage space remains physically unaltered by the action, it becomes charged with meaning through the audience's projective participation in the events that occur in that space.

All of this helps us to read Baden-Powell's chorographic sketch. The place depicted in it both situated the (tactical) practices he was so keen to convey to the outside world and emphasized the importance of the lessons he believed those practices embodied. The reduction of the context to signifiers like the river, the railway, and the distant hills, along with the decreasing physicality of drawing from the white town outward, simultaneously heightened the legibility of the garrison's actions, located those actions within imperial geographical space, and inscribed this place with the connotative meanings of the siege. In some respects, Baden-Powell's depiction of the town as concentrically *surrounded* (by enemy forces, then geopolitical territories, and finally, by an implied overseas audience) resembles the circus, the form of theater most closely related to the empty stage.[74] In the circus, scriptedness is diminished by both the heterogeneity and unpredictability of the action, and because the action is seen from all sides. Here, the drama encompasses not only the (scriptless) performance of the players, but also the reactions of the audience, who are always visible to each other. It is precisely this quality that separates mass entertainments (e.g., football matches) from conventional middle-class forms of spectacle (e.g., theater) that encourage the development of a critical distance between self and the action. The inventive, irregular tactics Baden-Powell used were, in conventional military terms, scriptless. At the same time, however, these actions and reactions of the garrison and the metropolitan audience complemented each other, conjointly refracting and constructing each other's performance.

We can see then that Baden-Powell's theatrical representation of the siege used the situation at Mafeking to transpose the scout's subjectivity into the discursive space of national consciousness in a multivalent way. The scout's knowledge, like all tactical knowledge, was, almost by definition, contingent and place-specific; it was situational

"Old Acquaintances":
Baden-Powell stalking
another scout.
R. S. Baden-Powell,
*Sketches in Mafeking and
East Africa* (London:
Smith, Elder & Co.,
1907); reproduced
with permission of
the British Library,
London.

OLD ACQUAINTANCES   35

WHEN SCOUT MEETS SCOUT

making use of context that varied according to the opportunities offered by that context. Moreover, the scout's terrain-reading skills were not meant only to ensure his
own unimpeded advance but to preempt his own detection, usually by giving his enemies misleading information. Even as he endeavored to remain invisible, the scout
constantly saw himself with another's eyes; an integral part of his subjectivity was a
heightened awareness of how his own actions might appear to others. Consequently,
the scout simultaneously became audience/spectator *and* actor; his actions in part
reciprocated those anticipated actions of the enemy, who was therefore rendered in
some way equal. (Baden-Powell recounts an episode in which he was stalking another
dark-faced enemy, who turned out to be one of his own men returning to the lines.)[75]
It is precisely this reciprocity of seeing and being seen that underpinned the underlying intersubjectivity between scout and enemy; as Baden-Powell loved to point out,
the highest accolade a scout could receive was to be recognized as an equal by autochthonous enemies with longer experience of the same terrain.[76]

Thus Baden-Powell's rendition of the story of Mafeking transformed the besieged
town into an imaginary theater of British imperialism by staging the siege as a play
of situated practice. Discursively engaging the Boers as well as the British public,
he transformed the Boers from protagonists into audience, subsidiary players, and
equals. Crucially, the forms of practice emphasized by this dramatization of the siege
were tactical ones previously considered unimportant to strategic imperialism but
they were common among his opponents. Appropriating these practices and making them his own, Baden-Powell engaged metropolitan imaginings and anxieties and
transformed himself into a match for his opponents, even though they, technically,
retained the military advantage.[77] Because these practices were deemed to grow out
of an inhabitant's knowledge of the region, this staging of the siege also rehearsed
how strategic imperial expansionism might be translated into tactical inhabitation
without loss of power or prestige.

Tactical Practice and Representation in a Terrain without Properties

De Certeau argues that the interdependence of the strategic and tactical is most tellingly demonstrated by the appropriation of urban space. Cities are complex physical
formations that are the result of many layers of political, economic, and institutional
jurisdiction and practice—in other words, what de Certeau calls the "proper" forma-

tions, over which individuals have little or no agency. Yet, he argues, it is precisely this realm of the already owned, mapped, built, and named that individuals use to construct, through tactical use, an affective and personally meaningful lifeworld that is uniquely their own. This appropriation of urban space—typically, through what de Certeau terms "walking in the city"—alternatively affirms, suspects, improvises, transgresses, and rejects, the physical world, without ever replacing (or even obscuring) it. Together, these individuals' inhabitations organize urban space and create a tacitly acknowledged subjective web of shared territories, horizons, and orientations. Paradoxically, this enunciative quality of inhabitation can only take place if the scaffolding of the "proper" is already in existence, even as the same proper formations render invisible the practices that underpin this enunciation.

At the end of the nineteenth century, most of the South African interior remained devoid of manifestations of the proper. Although not as quite as blank as Baden-Powell's sketch suggests, Mafeking was (and is) located in an almost featureless landscape. In 1899, it was just another locale in a subcontinent that held few specific associations or memories for imperial troops. It had few of the topographical features individuals turn to as a source of orientation in an unknown terrain, and it was not known through map names and symbols that can provide a substitute for such features. This topographical and historical emptiness was strengthened by the fact that this was a region in which distance and climate constantly undermined strategic military practices. The discrepancies between the daily experience of campaigning in this featureless terrain and the jingoistic and melodramatic representations of it in Britain were wryly vivid for most British soldier who actually spent time in South Africa. Many of these soldiers tried to capture what being in South Africa felt like to family and friends in Britain by means of postcards, letters, diaries and, later, memoirs. Rising literacy in Britain, along with new post office policies allowing postcards to contain a written message and British newspapers' practice of publishing local soldiers' letters all made this a war in which, to an unprecedented degree, individual voices and experiences were heard.[78] Negotiating between the strategy of the war that had brought them there and the tactics of personal experience, these personal accounts recorded a different way of being in this landscape that was as synoptical (representing movement through) as it was topographical (descriptive). Over the course of the war, these accounts constructed a web of inhabitation that systematically narrated the subcontinent in the minds of Britons at home.

Many of these accounts were like de Certeau's "spatial stories," homologous representations that allow a series of situated events to "coexist in a single description."[79] Through the sequentiality of narrative structure, spatial stories render time and space meaningful by giving them a relational structure.[80] Re-composing the material circumstances of the terrain into the typical, exemplary, anomalous, analogous, rare, accidental, or illegitimate places, spatial stories are an important means by which groups imagine the world as a legitimate theater for practical action.[81] Crucially, spatial stories go in procession, deriving from the past and preparing for the future, and thus incorporate both memory and imagination. The overarching spatial story that had prepared the way for all these individual soldiers' stories was, of course, that of imperialism: "Across the seas from the mother country were the daughter colonies establishing British forms of government, and beyond them, strange lands of outer darkness, places of disorder, and probably places of impurity. In time the Empire might claim these."[82]

Spatial stories can also be constructed by visual imagery. Up to this moment in history, pictorial representation had played a relatively insignificant role in warfare's construction of imaginatively charged geographical space. In part, this was due to technical limitations. Until the middle of the nineteenth century, reproducible images of war had tended to take the form of engravings made from the large, melodramatic paintings by war artists of key battles, sometimes reproduced as double-page spreads in magazines. This tradition of grand, artistically composed set-pieces, produced far from the action, themselves reminiscent of earlier academic European battle scenes, remained alive during the South African War in photographic form.[83] Photography had first been used to document the Crimean War and American Civil War, though images of these conflicts were essentially actionless: they either depicted the empty battlefields or the unmoving dead. Nevertheless, these images had nurtured popular interest in photography, which by the last decade of the century had become accessible to a much wider audience in Britain, thanks to the rapid evolution of cameras and the advent of cheap half-tone reproduction in illustrated magazines. During the South African War, images of the campaign in these popular magazines were supplemented by boxed sets of cards (often in stereoscopic pairs) depicting scenes from the war.[84] The South African War also marked the first uses of newsreels made in the field and aerial photographs for military purposes.[85]

Published photographs of the war were taken by official and commercial photographers, and apart from differences in uniforms and maybe setting, they were not that dissimilar from the stilted, melodramatic paintings of earlier wars and campaigns. Usually, the scenes they depicted were staged; the actual dead were hardly ever photographed, and images of casualties usually employed posed (living) figures. Like detailed studio portraits of the same era, these images were more concerned with recording *who* was there than how they were there, or even, in any real sense, where they were.[86] The dramatic gestures, postures, and facial expressions belong not so much to the actors/soldiers depicted, but to the story they supposedly illustrate; they contribute little to the characterization of the setting because these photographs represent neither real actions nor actual situations. The landscapes in these photographs are simply typical backdrops (as indeed they sometimes literally were) that creep into the corners of the frame; they are as immobilized and generic as the soldiers themselves.[87] These photographs are representations of the externally disciplined body-subject, trained in the predictable thoughts and responses British regular soldiers were supposed to carry with them wherever they went. In other words, these photographs captured imperialism's strategic and panoptic "calculus of force-relationships . . . isolated from an 'environment.'"[88] They also reflect the limits imposed by older photographic technology: official war photographers used fragile and cumbersome equipment whose range was far less than that of a rifle.[89]

The topographical muteness of these published photographs is especially striking when one compares them to another genre of photographs that emerged during the war: photographs depicting the same bodies and landscapes, but taken by private individuals. The South African War was the first war in which many ordinary soldiers had cameras. Kodak's introduction of celluloid film and portable cameras in the late

"Worcesters charging a kopje" (Underwood & Underwood stereo pair). National Archives and Records Service of South Africa, file ref. TAB 27996; reproduced with permission.

"Eventide—when the smoke of battle clears" (Underwood & Underwood stereo pair). National Archives and Records Service of South Africa, file ref. TAB 28039; reproduced with permission.

"Lord Roberts' Irresistibles on the way to Pretoria" (Underwood & Underwood stereo pair). National Archives and Records Service of South Africa, file ref. TAB 28243; reproduced with permission.

1880s had, along with the introduction of the inexpensive, foldable Brownie cameras a few years later, revolutionized photography, and many British troops brought these cameras with them to South Africa. A significant number of the troops came from the middle class, and most soldiers were no less keen photographers than other members of British society, knowing that the South African War would probably be the most significant experience of their lifetime.[90] Although they were not often published (at least, until recently), the thousands of amateur photographs taken by these soldiers today constitute the single biggest collection of images devoted to a single campaign in the National Army Museum in London. These photographs not only supplement those taken by official and professional photographers, they also convey an utterly different sense of how the unfamiliar landscape of the subcontinent was experienced and understood by individual British soldiers.

These photographs capture a completely different disposition from that in official photographs: that of active, situated individuals who are part of a self-sufficient community. Although occasionally posed, the amateur photographs mostly show soldiers caught in synoptic inhabitation, displaying expressions of fear, anticipation, boredom, distraction, self-consciousness, exhaustion, and amusement. Understandably, few depict actual military engagements. Instead of distant panoramas obscured by frozen, carefully composed foreground groups, we see individual soldiers who appear to have been dropped down into the veld in haphazard and unplanned ways. Tents, mess tables, horses, and tin baths stand around at some distance from each other, obeying no visible logic of location or use. Although the terrain is seldom pictured in its own right, it asserts itself, indirectly, as a powerful presence through its striking topographical blankness and lack of human artifacts. The apparent relationship between soldiers and this ever-present backdrop is, at once, active, situational, and unresolved; they are shown in various forms of dress and undress, displaying the incongruous (and distinctly aheroic) paleness of newly unclothed bodies.

These active, contingent, vulnerable, and resolutely civilian male bodies conveyed different connotations from the idealized, anonymous, and athletic figures of antiquity.[91] They were not only suggestive of scouting ideals of fresh air, physical exercise, and minimal clothing, they also allude to shifts in how men's bodies were being represented due to fin de siècle anxieties about gender and morality. At this time, muscular, athletic bodies were perceived as self-disciplined and purposeful—the opposite of effete, aesthetic male bodies whose character was revealed through their *covering*, that is, fashionable and self-conscious dress.[92] The figures in these photographs also remind us how bodies arrested in the midst of action can stand for dispositions and forms of praxis. Depictions of bodily movement and gesture have for centuries been a way of representing intangible, unconfigurable knowledge and were particularly common during the Renaissance, when theater was considered the central metaphor for the organization of worldly knowledge.[93] When amplified through reproduction, visual images of bodily action can create, compose, and inscribe with psychological character spaces that are far larger than that of the theatrical stage. Such staging is of course precisely what happened in these thousands of amateur photographs taken during the South African War, which convey a quite different theater of war to that framed by strategic practices of warfare guided by generals and maps and involving large formations of men.

MuseumAfrica, Johannesburg. PH2004-2448

Military life: view of
small camp on the
veld. MuseumAfrica
Photographic Collec-
tion, file ref. #968.049
(355.12); reproduced with
permission.

Military life: Lt. Key, East Yorks,
prepares his ablutions. MuseumAfrica
Photographic Collection, file ref.
#968.049 (355.12); reproduced with
permission.

Military life:
base-camp on the
veld. MuseumAfrica
Photographic
Collection, file
ref. #968.09566;
reproduced with
permission.

Military life: field
cannon, soldiers, and
horses on the veld.
MuseumAfrica Pho-
tographic collection,
file ref. #968.4450;
reproduced with
permission.

Here it is important to remember that neither the setting nor the male bodies in these images had ever been depicted before. The subject of these photographs was a landscape encounter devoid of any narrative other than the background one that gave rise to these soldiers being there. These photographs became highly charged representations because they initiated an implied subjective relationship to that setting. Unnamed and unpracticed, empty of artifacts and histories, the landscape they inaugurated was a situationally constructed stage. The active, individual, vulnerable bodies that inhabit it enacted and therefore initiated a new "spatial story" about the terrain in which they found themselves. In these arrested moments of situated action, then, the South African interior is composed as a topography that appears to have slipped out of conventional concatenations of landscape and practice and entered a new kind of *habitus*. While these photographs emphasized the solitariness of the individual male bodies they depicted, they compensated for this through the heightened sense of self-discipline and the personal resourcefulness they imply. The stark juxtaposition of human figures with the surrounding spatial emptiness, and the lack of obvious consonance between the terrain without properties and the individual soldiers emphasized their tactical, self-disciplined subjectivity and autonomy. Furthermore, these tactical, masculine bodies invited a sense of identification from people who had never been in the army or South Africa (that is, the British public), in a way that the strategic, externally disciplined bodies of official and published photographs never could. They also recuperated some of the rich life of the senses that seemed to be constricted by ongoing urbanization and industrialization.

These kinds of effects would have been reinforced by the fact that these were personal images, circulated through local networks of consumption, as opposed to the discursive, ubiquitous (seen by everyone, everywhere) official or professional photographs. These unofficial photographs performed very much the same kind of representation as the letters that soldiers in the field sent for publication in their hometown newspapers. The vulnerable, everyday corporeality refracted by these photographs suffused the landscape that was their setting, rendering it imaginatively accessible for the masses. Privately circulated in Britain, these snapshots would have been seen as part of the larger array of imperialistic representations, both textual and pictorial, of the war. Like Baden-Powell's sketch, only at a more modest, individual level, they offered a way for metropolitan Britons to imaginatively inhabit the subcontinent. Like the story of the siege, they helped organize space and time of the subcontinent's interior, and mediated a sense of genius loci. They created an accessible spatial story in which traditional forms of geographical imagination combined with very modern forms of discursive practice to shape perceptions about the newly visible region of South Africa. And, like Baden-Powell's sketch, these photographs refracted how a terrain empty of both historic narrative and artifact increased the visibility of human action and created a heightened sense of agency in the persons who inhabited it.

Seeing South Africa from Britain

It has been argued that the South African War transformed the subcontinent from the weakest link in the imperial chain into the strongest.[94] The war established a special relationship between the two countries that would last for half a century, a relationship that grew out of the fact that Britain's awareness of itself as a modern society was partly honed by events in South Africa. In 1901, almost one-half of the country's expenditure was devoted to fighting the war, and the income tax rate, last set in 1892, was doubled in 1902 to pay for this.[95] This was not only a matter of politics or economics. The effects of the war extended into every corner of British society and encouraged a critical mass of metropolitan Britons (four-fifths of whom belonged to the working class) to identify with South Africa as an imaginary space.[96] The scale of the military operation in the subcontinent was unprecedented: some 448,000 imperial troops, the vast majority of them British, were deployed to South Africa; over 75,000 of these men were invalided home sick or wounded, while another 22,000 died.[97] In Britain alone, the army made 242,000 new recruits between 1899 and 1902, and at some point during the war, nearly 15 percent of Britain's male population between the ages of eighteen and forty was in uniform.[98] Most of these men were irregulars who came from civilian life and returned to it when the war was over.

This penetration of the war into all classes of society between 1899 and 1902 created a temporary sense of *communitas* in Britain. *Communitas* is, appropriately, a theatrical term denoting the sense of community that arises in individuals participating in collective perception of the same event; the event ceases to be experienced as private, and becomes one experienced "as if through all eyes."[99] The exhaustive coverage in Britain of the war's progress, and ubiquitous references to it in popular culture, created new possibilities for popular memory and shaped a new audience in Britain with a capacity to see for the first time the imperial community of which they were supposedly a part.[100] The war offered members of the British working classes in particular a vision of themselves as active, valued members of a national community in which underlying inequalities and resentments were, temporarily at least, overlooked. The penetration of the war into metropolitan consciousness was not significantly altered by shifts in public opinion about the conflict. Despite the surrender of the two Boer capitals in mid-1900 and Kruger's escape into European exile, the war dragged on for another twenty months, during which Kitchener resorted to draconian measures such as farm burning and incarceration of Boer women and children to round up the remaining Boer commandos. These measures strengthened opposition to the war among liberals, feminists, and the labor movement in Britain as well as soldiers' public protests about the way the war was conducted in the field, and many antiwar demonstrations were held throughout 1901 and the first part of 1902. Despite this broad shift in public opinion and the decline of overt displays of patriotism, nobody could ignore a war that still employed nearly three hundred thousand soldiers.[101]

By 1902, then, the war had become a topic that engaged all Britain's citizens and turned South Africa into a geographical region that was at once other to, and yet constitutive of, the imaginary and emotional repertoire of the metropole.[102] In fact, as Bill Schwarz has argued, the subcontinent became a topic through which Britishness was, and would be, interpreted; for several decades afterward, policy toward South Africa would become a defining issue separating British conservatives and progressives.[103] This use of South Africa as a political bellwether grew out of the seeds of doubt the war sowed in Britain as well as the empire about the morality and sustainability of British imperialism. Provoking a great deal of soul-searching in Britain, the war not only "put the nation to the test" but turned South Africa into a space where important truths might be found.[104]

MAIN BOER POSITION

ADVANCED BOER POSITION

C. C. FRIPP.
JUNE 18 1900
— PRETORIA —

(from notes by Capt Edis . C.I.V)

This incorporation of South Africa into metropolitan consciousness after the war occurred in a number of different registers. The events of the war led to several important Royal commissions and enquiries examining Britain's military prepared-ness. Handbooks on field tactics published up to the outbreak of the World War I were heavily influenced by the British Army's experiences in South Africa and used fictional military battles staged in imaginary South African topography and military situations to make key tactical points.[105] Milner himself proposed turning postwar South Africa into a huge training camp for all imperial forces, with a garrison of over thirty thousand soldiers.[106] The authoritative *Times History of the War in South Africa*, published in 1905, whose readership was by no means confined to those with military interests, included more than one hundred maps at different scales and offered maps of several key engagements, showing how the ground held by each side shifted from hour to hour. These were complemented by panoramic topographical drawings by war artists showing the relative disposition of the two sides at key points in the battle. Many British soldiers, regular and irregular, became captivated by South Africa dur-ing their tour of duty and found it hard to settle back to a humdrum existence in Britain after the excitement and physicality of life on the veld. As one wrote after the end of the War, "I am very restive. . . . Oh, how I long for the good old trekking days; . . . this life seems so slow and dull and devoid of daily excitement."[107] Ex-soldiers from Britain and the other colonies made up a significant proportion of those who signed up for postwar immigration schemes to South Africa or who joined the various colo-nial administrations and militia.[108]

The tug of South Africa in Britain also affected many who had not participated in the war. Because many soldiers who lost their lives in the South African War were ir-regulars, their loss touched every level of British society, something that was evident in the dozens of Boer War memorials erected all over Britain. Names of South African places, towns, and battlefields that were etched into public consciousness as a result of reportage on the war became reinscribed in countless street names in Britain and elsewhere in the world. Equally important for a period were the pilgrimages many Britons made to South Africa to see the battlefields and the graves of the deceased. The first tours of the South African battlefields, run by Thomas Cook and using the same railway lines that had transported the British regiments during the hostilities, began even before peace was signed and initiated organized popular tourism to South Africa. Questions about how the dead imperial soldiers should be commemorated and who should be responsible for their far-flung graves were never satisfactorily re-solved, but they gave rise to colonial national cultural institutions such as the Guild of Loyal Women and the Victoria League, which would have an important influ-ence on the policies adopted by the Imperial War Graves Commission after World War I.[109]

This heightened awareness of South Africa in Britain was reinforced by the doz-ens of books and pamphlets about South Africa published during and after the war, many of which were the work of war correspondents. The knowledge of South Africa imparted by these publications was often exhaustive. A telling number of the writers drawn to South Africa by the war, such as Winston Churchill, Arthur Conan Doyle, Rudyard Kipling, Edgar Wallace, Erskine Childers, and John Buchan, went on to be-come respected figures in twentieth-century British politics and letters. This reflected the importance of the war as well as the easy transactions between fiction writing and popular journalism that prevailed at the time.[110] Even more than soldiers' experiences of the subcontinent (because they were mostly based on fleeting experiences of South Africa), this literature helped perpetuate a vision in metropolitan Britain of the subcontinent as a region of romance and adventure, in other words, "everything that actually existing England, destroyed by the mundane forces of unforgiving moder-nity, was not."[111] Although every individual had their own personal engagement with the war, the subject of their shared sense of *communitas* was as much South Africa as it was the fighting itself. Mediated through textual spatial stories and many different kinds of graphic images, the geographical space of subcontinent came into visibility as a result of the ebb and flow of the conflict across the region. Mostly played out on the Highveld, with excursions into the grasslands of Natal and in the final stages, the Karoo and the Northern Cape, the spatial story of the war introduced the metropoli-tan masses to a new discursive landscape, "the veldt" (veld) a terrain whose radical blankness welcomed a network of narratives and memories whose primary resonance was, paradoxically, six thousand miles away in Britain. In this spatial story, it was the emptiness and huge distances of South Africa as much as the human enemy that had put the British Army to the test.[112]

To the degree that Baden-Powell's staging of the siege of Mafeking posited how (strategic) imperialism might (tactically) reconfigure itself in South Africa, it became an important episode in mediating the special relationship that developed between Britain and South Africa after the war. Continually retold as a founding story of an empirewide Boy Scout movement, the story of the siege also helped establish South

Africa as part of that global imperium. The power of the Mafeking story was rooted in a form of synecdochic imagination much like that at work in *sacri monti*, elevated places throughout Europe appropriated by the religious imagination as metaphorical Jerusalems, which emerged during the medieval period. In South Africa, a cognate metaphorical fusion linked the reflexive imperial imaginaries and anxieties to an isolated settlement on the western marches of the Kalahari Desert. Bringing together somatic, existential, perceptual, and cognitive space in a single "very ordinary look-ing place," the story of the siege transformed Mafeking into a mythical place where the unknowable was transformed into the known, and disorderly lived reality was organized into an elemental story. This use of the desert settlement in the middle of nowhere not only epitomized the imaginative inscription of a hostile or indif-ferent world, it also enacted an exchange between the visible and the invisible that characterizes all places that embody myths and rituals. In such mythical places, the protagonist's disposition is transposed into spatial movement, an imaginative jour-ney into and *through* the depths of the place itself; "movement becomes linearized or dimensionally restricted, [and] the loss of freedom of movement is counterbalanced by a rupture in geometry, occurring in the symbolic center."[113]

We can see, then, how telling a depiction of the besieged town Baden-Powell's sketch was. Its rendition of Mafeking as a confined, circular space represented how the town became a symbolic center in which the loss of freedom of movement (due to the surrounding Boers) was counterbalanced by the transposition of the protagonist's disposition through an imaginative journey through the depths of the place itself (the result of Baden-Powell's sagacious lawlessness). This "rupture in geometry occurring in the symbolic center" was thus not only afforded by the siege but also necessary for it to gather and mediate the myriad individual spatial stories unfolding outside of it. Baden-Powell's sketch also captured how crucial were his own practices, which combined the ontological (body, space, time) and the cultural (vision, imagination, identity), to the emergence of Mafeking as a mythical place.

De Certeau's "tactical" is very close to the Greek *metis,* a way of being that includes creativity, inventiveness, and sleight of hand. *Metis* was originally associated with humans who had close connection to the gods, typically genius figures who existed "at the edge of both history and rational thought, and within heroic reach of the 'sublime' truths of the past."[114] Genius was thus associated with the irrationality (or one might say cunning inventiveness) of lovers, rhetoricians, prophets, and heroes, as well as the liminality of those who journey to and inhabit the edge of the known realm and are consequently identified with what was hidden.[115] Baden-Powell's narra-tive of the siege conveyed this *metis*-like character of the genius or hero in a number of ways. It distilled years of experience on the hidden margins of empire, it performed an emergent way of being that was rooted in irrational and cunning behavior and it was enacted by a liminal figure, the exception who proved the rule: a British Army officer, who thought and acted tactically at a time when strategic thought and action were proving to be disastrously inadequate.

Thus the Mafeking story epitomized the way places become appropriated as part of a densely contextual and cumulative cognitive weave. Like other mythical places, Baden-Powell's Mafeking conjured a wealth of rhetorical ideas and topics, including the redefinition of masculinity as an adjunct of a preindustrial setting; the characterization of the South African interior as a realm of self-disciplined, resourceful, and scriptless autodidacts; and the notion that this scriptless, masculine subjectivity was cognate with never being completely at home in the landscape. Above all, it mediated the idea that this subjectivity arose through the practical making use of the landscape rather than from birth, ethnicity, or cultural inheritance. These ideas and connotations in turn folded back to characterize the territory itself. Like the relationship between the contingent male bodies and empty veld in the soldiers' photographs, the relationship between Baden-Powell's tactical practices and the Western Kalahari was one that arises between actor and empty stage. "Mafeking" became a metaphorical place that focused metropolitan interest in Southern Africa, characterized the larger geographical setting, and offered a way of imaginatively inhabiting it.

The discursive place-myth of Mafeking thus helped stage ideas about the kind of society that might come into being in the region after the war and provided a way for potential British-born emigrants to construct a geographical identity in the subcontinent. The vision it afforded of South Africa—a realm of self-disciplined resourcefulness and bodily prowess, in which the dissipatory effects of both the modern metropolis and the colonial outpost could somehow be escaped—was primarily a masculine one, with little interest in domesticity and routinized urban culture.[116] The notion that the South African veld naturally gave rise to a democratic, masculine freemasonry laid the foundations for postwar reconciliation with the Boers, based on a grudging admiration for their bravery, inventiveness, and stamina during the war. At the same time, it also relegated the indigenous inhabitants to a shadowy existence, either as autochthons from whom one could learn the lie of the land or as subaltern workers who took care of the basic needs of life. This vision of European's future place in the subcontinent was encouraged not only by the strong ties with the metropole forged by the war, but also reinforced by administrators who were responsible for policies of postwar reconstruction and nation building.[117] Like Baden-Powell's scouting movement, the tactical appeal of this vision cut across narrow ideological allegiances.[118]

The siege of Mafeking, then, was not only an important episode in forging an idea of South Africa that transcended geographical scales and boundaries; it incorporated this idea into the British and imperial imagination. If the contestation between two forms of practice characterized by the war helped configure the region's previously unnarrated spaces into absences and presences, boundary areas, sacred places, and inhabitable districts, the Mafeking story served as a metonymy for this larger encounter. Rooted in the global spatial story of imperialism, the story of the siege mediated two interdependent aspects of its expansionist geographical imagination. Mafeking became a place of passage that connected things vertically *and* horizontally: it linked the geopolitical intensity of the periphery to the physical intensity of life there. At the same time, the story proposed a useful compensatory imaginary geography for the subcontinent. It narrated a convergence between landscape and a way of being, suggesting not only who but *how* the future denizens of this region might be.

JOHN BUCHAN'S *HESPERIDES*

The Aesthetics of Improvement on the Highveld

> The creation and use of landscapes . . . always emerges from biographical and
> place-specific historical and social contexts, at the same time that it contributes
> toward the uninterrupted becoming of biography and place.
>
> —Alan Pred, "Place as Historically Contingent Process"

In the southern hemisphere summer of 1902–3, the young Scottish lawyer John Buchan found himself in the opposite, albeit equally remote, corner of the Transvaal from Mafeking. The Woodbush was (and is) also a very different kind of landscape from the marches of the Kalahari: an area some seven hundred square miles in extent, located in northeastern Transvaal at the northernmost extremity of the great escarpment that runs down the eastern side of South Africa, it enjoys a mild, subtropical climate due to the upthrust of humid air moving in from the Indian Ocean three hundred miles to the east. The Woodbush derived its name from the dense native forests that had flourished there until the end of the nineteenth century, when they had been decimated by woodcutters. When Buchan visited, it was an undulating plateau of small streams winding through lush, aromatic meadows of grass, bracken, and tree ferns, with forests confined to the valleys and slopes leading down to the Lowveld below. Then only twenty-six years old, Buchan fell in love with the area, describing it as "an earthly paradise," and until his death nearly forty years later he remembered it as "the true Hesperides."[1] Indeed, so enchanted was he by the Woodbush that he determined he would one day return there to live: "In front I shall have a flower-garden, where every temperate and tropical blossom will appear, and in a sheltered hollow an orchard of deciduous trees, and an orange plantation. Highland cattle . . . will roam on the hillsides. My back windows will look down 4,000 feet on the tropics, my front on the long meadow vista with the Iron Crown mountain for the sun to set behind."[2]

119

Haenertsburg,
Woodbush,
Soutpansberg District,
1890s. MuseumAfrica
Photographic Collec-
tion file ref. HF Gros,
reproduced with
permission.

These intentions Buchan recorded in his four-hundred-page book, *The Africa Colony: Studies in Reconstruction*, nowadays a forgotten part of his substantial literary oeuvre, and published only a few months after he had returned to London.[3] *The Africa Colony* was based on Buchan's own experience in South Africa as part of Milner's Kindergarten. Buchan had come to South Africa at the end of 1901, when war was still being waged.[4] After working for a few months on improving conditions in the concentration camps, he became involved in administering the repatriation of Boers and attracting the British settlers who, it was believed, would be crucial to the region as a prosperous and loyal part of the empire after the war. As head of the Transvaal Colony's new Land Settlement Department, Buchan was responsible for drafting several ordinances and was required to travel throughout the region overseeing resettlement and surveying areas for new settlement. Buchan's travels through the Transvaal, following arduous (and sometimes dangerous) itineraries starting at the outermost railheads and passing through remote, sparsely settled districts, provided the basis for *The Africa Colony*.[5] Welcome escapes from sixteen-hour days at his desk in Johannesburg or Pretoria, these journeys allowed Buchan to get to know most parts of the Transvaal and its populations and took him to the western Transvaal, the Limpopo valley, the Highveld, and the Drakensberg Escarpment.

Buchan's involvement in Milner's Reconstruction is reflected in both the content of his book and the timing of its publication. *The Africa Colony* was intended to contribute to understanding in Britain about Milner's political and economic policies in South Africa and engage a wider audience in the historico-cultural connotations of the Reconstruction. Although there had been earlier English accounts of the *Zuid Afrikaansche Republiek*, these had been written when metropolitan interest in the region was largely confined either to the Witwatersrand gold mines or the opportunities it provided for hunting and adventure; none of these books had tried to provide a comprehensive overview of the region or seen it as a possible British colony.[6] *The Africa Colony* was one of the first book-length meditations on the future of the subcontinent. It was organized into three roughly equal sections that dealt with the subcontinent's history, present conditions in the Transvaal, and the region's future prospects as they appeared during the historically critical period of reconstruction.

Strikingly lyrical passages of landscape description permeate all sections of *The Africa Colony*, leading one to ask whether it was intended as a sober political document promoting New Imperialism or a piece of impressionistic travel writing. The answer to this question is probably "both": Buchan's narrative ushered in an entirely new phase of British imaginative inhabitation of the South African subcontinent, one that was the more or less inevitable consequence of the annexation of the Boer republics. *The Africa Colony* was aimed at encouraging colonial settlement and tempering metropolitan disquiet about the cost of governing and administering the colonies.[7] Like Baden-Powell's writings, Buchan's book drew on the metropolitan imaginary about the margins of the British Empire as regions of travel, adventure, and renewal. However, *The Africa Colony* deployed this imaginary in the service of peaceful settlement and development, focusing on the identity of the society that would emerge in the region rather than the military struggles required to secure it. As an extended attempt to apply fin de siècle ideas about culture, society, and environment to the project of imagining the future of postwar South Africa, *The Africa Colony* can be read as an attempt to recuperate the older conundrum of "fertile land, romantic spaces, and uncivilized peoples" in light of the dramatically changed geopolitical situation after the South African War. The underlying aestheticism of the account reflected Buchan's own personal circumstances at the time, as well as the view of the Kindergarten that "fused the common room of All Souls and the veld in a single psychic reality."[8]

Cultural Memory, Improvement, and the Imagination of a New Society

Although it was read by white South Africans, the primary audience of *The Africa Colony* was the mercantile and political establishment in metropolitan Britain. The book was written as "an intervention in high politics" for the small elite who effectively controlled the future of British South Africa; the some five hundred copies sold were intended "to mould public opinion and then virtually disappear from view."[9] Buchan was one of Milner's most eloquent spokesmen in countering the legions of opponents to Reconstruction in South Africa and Britain. He was not only an accomplished writer—Milner had hired him partly because of his pro-imperial writing for the *Spectator*—but he was personally responsible for one of the main tasks of the Reconstruction: land settlement in the two new Crown Colonies, which it was hoped would eventually be brought into some kind of political system with the existing self-governing colonies of Cape and Natal.

Buchan subscribed to the same broad set of ideas as Milner, which combined unashamedly political agendas with the "nostalgic pastoralist" optimism that agriculture would be the key to South Africa's future—optimism, it has to be said, that flew in the face of previous images of colonial rural society.[10] In *The Africa Colony*, however,

Buchan brought to these romantic ideas an added intensity and depth and explicitly linked them to imaginative nation building and identity formation. This was as much a consequence of his own background and experience as it was a defense of the policies Milner had asked him to implement. Although replete with political facts, economic statistics, and geographical descriptions, *The Africa Colony* was ultimately a work of literary and historical imagination.[11] The book is permeated by the belief that molding a national consciousness depended not only on strategic factors such as demographics, economics, and administration, but also on cultural factors such as memory, myth, and *genre de vie*.[12] Buchan was writing at a time when, as we have seen, the concept of national identity was a relatively recent, labile construction, bound up with the search for a "mythical pedigree for national difference."[13] Although the lack of large cities and an entrenched class system in the former Boer republics made them favorable territories for creating a new society, these lacks also made it difficult to conceptualize the identity of this society that was to be both connected to and yet apart from Britain. The question that haunts the entire book is "what sort of society would evolve in South Africa, now that all of it had been claimed for the empire?" As Buchan argues at one point, South Africa needs "a school of thought" that is "no tarnished European importation, but the natural spontaneous fruit of the land."[14]

Buchan pursued this question in a number of different registers, all of which engaged the geographical and historical imaginations. His predilection for poetical topographical description has already been mentioned; less obvious, but equally important, is the way this topographical writing is interpellated with factual discussions about subjects such as cattle breeding, irrigation, or demographics. For Buchan, the *land itself* was as authentic a source of prognostication about the suitability of the region for European settlement as statistics or facts. The passages of topographical description in the book were a serious attempt to imagine a nation and locate it in its imaginary landscape.[15] This is most explicit in the central section of the book, entitled "Notes of Travel" and devoted entirely to descriptions of unimproved, sparsely inhabited rural districts, mostly in the Transvaal Colony. Buchan barely mentions urban centers other than as points of departure ("on one side, there were the mining centres—cosmopolitan, money-making living at a strained pitch; on the other, this silent country"), and he finds the railways a decidedly alien presence.[16]

Buchan's perceptions of the Transvaal would have been undergirded by its visual appearance in 1901. Even discounting the devastation and depopulation wrought first by the rinderpest epidemic of the 1890s that killed over 90 percent of the cattle in the interior, and then by the war, settlement of the region had, at least in the sense that Buchan would have recognized, been insubstantial. Few people photographed the veld at the end of the nineteenth century, but when it does creep into the frame of images taken of emerging settlements, one is struck by the absence of even the most rudimentary signs of conventional rural inhabitation such as trees, windmills, fences, or even permanent roads.[17] Although most of the subcontinent's interior had been occupied and subdivided by Europeans for two or three generations by this time, they had physically inhabited only parts of it. Much of the land belonged to land speculators, mining companies, and absentee farmers.[18] At the turn of the century, well-established Boer farmers migrated seasonally between their *zaaiplaats* on the Highveld (for cultivation) and their *veeplaats* in bushveld (for grazing). Land that

had difficult physiography, an unhealthy climate, or lacked reliable water was often simply not taken up, nominally remaining state land but settled by otherwise dispossessed Africans or used by white farmers for hunting to supplement their incomes.[19] Even on permanently inhabited farms, the Boers practiced a form of agriculture that barely rose above subsistence level on properties where the physical boundaries were roughly established by eye and verbal agreement rather than theodolites and fences.[20] The Boers' main source of wealth was their cattle, which grazed on the native veld grasses; arable farming was confined to the cultivation of just enough grain, fruit, and vegetables to supply themselves and their dependents, or to fields around scattered African settlements.

The sketchiness and ambiguity of this land use would have been heightened for someone like Buchan, who was used to European notions that the right to ownership was conferred by the capacity for improvement. In some districts, he found it difficult to detect much difference between Boers' and Africans' way of life. Both appeared to work the land to the same degree, albeit with much less energy and application than a European farmer, and he observed that Africans were better at farming certain areas than whites. Even these perceptions of inhabitation and ownership were muddied by the complicated patterns of ownership and labor, in which the actual tilling of the land was seldom undertaken by the farmer-occupier himself, but by tenant farmers and sharecroppers who might be either white or black—a complex and semifeudal system that was already becoming environmentally unsustainable and would prove economically so in the postwar market economy.[21] Unlike many British in South Africa at this time, though, Buchan acknowledged the changes Africans and Boers had made in the land,[22] and having learned basics of Dutch and Afrikaans, he developed an empathy with the Boers (indeed, he was accused of being pro-Boer).

Buchan's sympathy with the Boers implied an inchoate belief in *genre de vie* as well as a classical idea about the relationship between agriculture and human culture, which equated tilling the land with virtue and sometimes saw cultivation of the land as a divine occupation. This did not, however, mean that he saw the Boers' coming displacement by British settlers as any less inevitable than the Africans' displacement by the Boers forty years earlier. Like his colleagues, Buchan subscribed to the historicist spatial story of ever-expanding imperialism and the belief that the land belonged to those who would make best use of it. And, like earlier British travelers in the subcontinent,[23] he also believed that neither the indigenous inhabitants nor the

Boers could be the natural custodians of an apparently temperate, fertile region like the Transvaal. In part, this belief was pragmatic: settlers of British extraction simply had a stronger claim to the land because they were more enterprising, had greater resources at their disposal, and would cultivate it more intensely.[24] However, unlike most of his colleagues, who wanted to pry the land from the Boers' "stubborn and wasteful grip," Buchan saw the Boers as "our forerunners," even though they "lived on the barest scale of existence, . . . without the aptitude or wealth to go farther." This allowed him to see the region not as virgin territory awaiting the plow, but as one already settled and in need of further development. Thus, in Buchan's imagination, the Boers were not so much hostile, primitive, hard-to-categorize "white Africans" as a positive omen for the future; their ruined farmhouses were not so much reminders of the recent war as confirmation that the land was already provisionally European. The Boers' ambiguous hold on the land rendered the region simultaneously European and yet empty, a combination of qualities that was not only powerfully appealing in itself, but also augured well for the society that would evolve there in the future: "Our colonial settlements have hitherto . . . fought a hard fight for livelihood, and in the process missed the finer formative influences of the land. . . . But here, as in the old Greek colonies, we begin . . . at certain high plane of life."[25]

Buchan's book could be read as just another example of the objectifying, self-effacing (usually white, usually male) gaze of the post-Enlightenment traveler and colonizer, supported by networks of European imperialist power.[26] Like other examples of that most Western mode of geographical representation, the book of travel description, *The Africa Colony* inscribed its author's subjectivity onto the region it described. Like that genre, it participated in discursive networks of knowledge—Said's "chain of references embedded in the library"[27]—which helped audiences at home, as well as travelers themselves, make sense of what is being seen and experienced. This inscription of the landscape was most obviously at work in the book's focus on the Highveld, which, like the peripheral places favored by the metropolitan geographical imagination, contained "elements of the recognizable world, recombined in a different order."[28] Like the upland margins of Britain, the Highveld was a terrain that in the early 1900s was especially green and lush, thanks to the high rainfall of the preceding decade. On the other hand, while this terrain appeared fertile and temperate, it had none of lowland Britain's intricate density, richness of incident and contrast, and absence of repetition. Buchan's description of the Highveld was also inescapably framed by British geography's mapping of the world's margins according to their suitability for European settlement. Late nineteenth-century maps rendered the interior of the Southern African continent especially desirable for settlement, because its high elevation suggested that it was healthy enough for continuous white inhabitation (see color plate 12).[29] This imaginary was implicit in Buchan's characterization of this "green open land" as a "tonic country where the inhabitants are rarely ill, and few doctors can make a living."[30] In fact, during the early twentieth century, before malaria and *ngana* had been brought under control in the Lowveld, this mapping was very real, and the Transvaal was still very much subdivided by elevation into areas that were described as "Healthy," "Unhealthy," and "Very Unhealthy" for Europeans.[31]

Buchan's teleological premonitions about the suitability of the South African interior for white settlement, and his certainty that the society that would grow out of this settlement would be shaped by the region's landscape, were profoundly deepened by another factor. Unlike most of the other colonial administrators who had grown up in southern lowland Britain, Buchan had grown up in Scotland. Although his family had lived in Glasgow and Edinburgh, Buchan had spent every summer either on his mother's family's farm near Peebles in the Borders, or in the northern Highlands.[32] As a result, he had developed a preternatural sensitivity to landscape in which topography and human history were inseparably intertwined ("my earliest recollections" he wrote in his memoirs, "are not of myself, but of my environment").[33] This encouraged him to see parts of rural South Africa as a kind of displaced rural Scotland; numerous passages in *The Africa Colony* dwell on similarities between the Scottish Borders and the South African Highveld in particular.

The rolling upland of the Highveld ranges between 4,500 and 6,500 feet in elevation and stretches for some 250 miles eastward from Johannesburg. Too dry and cold in winter to support forest, its characteristic vegetation is a variety of grasses; woody plants are rare except along watercourses or on rocky hills and mountain slopes.[34] Of this region Buchan writes: "The country, now that spring is here, is very beautiful—rather like the Scottish border, except that there are no burns, and the air and sunsets are perfectly amazing." He describes the Magaliesberg range north of Pretoria, forming one edge of the Highveld, as "a great range of jagged blue mountains which might be the Coolin's in the Western Isles of Scotland." He was drawn especially to the South Eastern Transvaal, "a country just like Scotland . . . [where] you ride up long green glens, with blue mountains at the top, and a fine full stream in the valley bottom." Throughout, Buchan resorts to colloquial Scottish terms such as "strath," "glen," and "sheep-walk" to emphasize the similarities between these two regions, where one looked out to a clear horizon, vegetated but treeless.[35]

These physical resemblances were reinforced by what seemed to Buchan to be historical parallels between Scotland and South Africa, and strong similarities of disposition—"tough, proud, and stubbornly independent"—between the Boers and the farmers he knew from his childhood.[36] In Buchan's reading of Scottish history, the Scots were no culturally or ethnically pure group themselves but had a long history of mixing between ethno-religious identities that had also been linked to the geographical divide between lowlands and uplands.[37] Buchan believed that the Scots' ability to forge a common identity despite differences in history, religion, and language was due to their shared experience of nature. This argument was of course grounded in the fundamental belief that "not religion, not language, not race, but place is the dominant feature of civilizations," and that culture ultimately derived from a "narrative of engagement" with the land.[38] Buchan found corroboration for such beliefs, as well as signs that they would determine the future character of South African society, in the many Scots emigrants he met while traveling in the Transvaal. Drawn from different parts of Scotland, these emigrants had been in South Africa for varying lengths of time. While most of them had lost their language, to Buchan they appeared to have retained many of their Scots cultural traits and values, even as they successfully assimilated into backcountry Boer society and acquired new locally grounded identities. Buchan seems to have believed that these emigrants had retained their Scottish character because they lived in a landscape that resembled the one from which they originated. This perception corroborated the notion, common in Britain at this time, that it was precisely the hardy peoples of the Celtic upland margins, like Wales and Scotland, who made the best colonists.

"A Thing Essentially Mysterious and Individual"

To reduce Buchan's encounter with the South African landscape to a straightforward imposition of metropolitan environmental stereotypes would be to overlook an important imaginative charge of his narrative. Many passages in *The Africa Colony* transcend straightforward landscape description and remind us that travel writing is always, to some degree, a struggle to save psychic resonance; it involves a balance between the recognition and recuperation of difference.[39] Buchan, by 1902, was a writer already well versed in the art of landscape description, and he described a landscape that, at least in its basic outline, would have been familiar to his readers from war photographs and engravings. ("Today every London shopboy knows what this wilderness of coarse green or brown grasses is like.")[40] Nevertheless, he frequently represents the South African interior as a terrain that eluded his descriptive powers (see color plate 13): "No natural feature was ever so hard to fully realize. One cannot think of a monotonous vastness, like the prairie, for it is everywhere broken up and varied. It is too great for an easy appreciation, as of an English landscape, too subtle and diverse for rhetorical generalities—a thing essentially mysterious and individual."[41] Elsewhere he contends, "No landscape is so masterful as the veld. Broken up into valleys, reclaimed in parts by man, showing fifty varieties of scene, it yet preserves one essential character . . . it is not created according to the scale of man. It will give him a home, but he will never alter its aspect."[42]

Trying to account for his struggle to find words to express his own powerful affective response to this landscape, Buchan points up the inadequacy of European modes of appreciation: "A modern is badly trained for appreciating certain kinds of scenery. Generations of poets and essayists have so stamped the 'pathetic fallacy' upon his soul that wherever he goes . . . he runs wild, looking for a human interest or historical memory. This is well enough in old settled lands, but on the veldt it is curiously inept."[43] Elsewhere he writes, "the veld has no memory. Men go and come, kingdoms fall and rise, but it remains austere, secluded, impenetrable, the still unravished bride of quietness."[44] He expressed similar sentiments years later in his memoirs, arguing that in South African, "one does not feel the malevolence of Nature . . . so much as its utter aloofness from human life"; it was a world "superbly impersonal" and "divinely inhuman."[45] These passing remarks, which simultaneously allude to a unique kind of landscape character and question conventions of landscape representation, are in fact key passages in *The Africa Colony*. Clearly moved by this landscape, which did not resemble any he had seen before, yet unable to account for why this should be so, Buchan does not gloss over this fact; indeed, he goes further, suggesting that not only are the environmental experiences afforded by the South African landscape beyond verbal description, but that such experiences might be better left unnamed, if not undescribed. Here, we seem to have moved beyond the Sublime into the realm of classical genius loci, and the Romantics' *élan vital*, which permeates both human unconscious and nature. (We also seem to be dealing with the "something looking back" that is neither man nor beast, which travelers sometimes sense in the *terra nullius* of the wilderness.)[46]

Buchan's account of his response to the Transvaal landscape raises multiple questions about how deeply embedded, ineffable experience is mediated through textual rhetoric. Any analysis of textual geographical description needs to recognize the way in which the structure of the generative experience and the modes of rhetoric enter into a dialogue with one other. The general organization and composition ("invention") of the text, as well as narrative mode and style ("eloquence") themselves are active in imparting a particular imaginative geography (which, arguably, encompasses both "disposition" and "memory").[47] These effects may be complemented by textual "displacements" (metaphors, analogies, and symbols) and "acts" (representations that do not so much name something as make it happen). These kinds of considerations are apposite, given that Buchan's intended audience was, for the most part, classically educated. Buchan's own Oxford education would have familiarized him with the tradition of rhetoric, which exploited the commonality between the practices of moving through and inhabiting space, and those of speaking and writing. But for him, the connections between travel and narrative would have been much less cerebral, the connections between action, place, and meaning something instinctively understood. During his childhood, divided between books and the outdoors, Buchan had developed a habit of identifying abstractions and arguments with particular localities and topographies. Bunyan's *The Pilgrim's Progress,* in particular, had been a formative influence, its plain narrative picturing "life as a pilgrimage over hill and dale, where surprising adventures lurked by the wayside, a hard road with now and then a long view to cheer the traveler."[48]

Even leaving aside these facts, there is good reason to think that *The Africa Colony* was intended as a geographic description that provided clues rather than answers and invited its audience to conspire with the work itself to realize its meaning. This would have flattered its educated audience, drawing on the capacity that prose and poetry ("articulated sounds existing in time") have for representing action,[49] and inviting an imaginative engagement on the part of the readers cognate with the author's own interrogative, corporeal encounter with the landscape. As we have seen, at the end of the century, the direct experience of nature had acquired a particular poignancy in metropolitan Britain, and Buchan was describing a region his readers had begun to see as suitable for cultural rejuvenation. His emphasis on the direct experience of the rural Transvaal also underscored his frequent calls in the book for a new settler culture that "bore the stamp of the soil," and cast the land itself as an active protagonist in the newly annexed territories narrative of descent—something that betrayed a profound belief in cultural identity based on the "naturalization of the nation."

Few of Buchan's urban readers would have engaged in the rural pursuits he knew as a boy, let alone the physical labor of working the soil; the nearest form of engagement with the land they would have known was the corporeality of travel, perhaps that of the excursive rambler or horseback rider, which has been called "so suggestive of unalienated labour."[50] The most effective (and *affective*, because it was only alluded to) way to invite such a reader's own imagination was, of course, indirectly, and the rhetorical invocation of firsthand travel experience occurs at several different levels in *The Africa Colony*. It is implicit not only in the ubiquitous descriptions of the terrain and its ineffable character, but also in the way the tripartite structure of the book places the bulk of that description as its centerpiece, as a touchstone for true prognosis (an imaginary future is most persuasively projected from an avowedly lived, affective present). The fact that each chapter in *The Africa Colony* is precisely dated highlights the influence of seasonal nuances of light, temperature, and precipitation on the impressions received and suggests that the loss of verisimilitude between actual experience and its textual retelling was minimal.[51] Similarly, Buchan seldom mentions the entourage that accompanied him on his tours of duty and casts himself as a solitary contemplative wanderer.[52]

Such facts only take one so far, though: one feels that for all its representational strategies, *The Africa Colony* describes what, for Buchan, was a genuinely powerful experience. He later wrote that his eighteen months in the subcontinent transformed his whole outlook on life, attributing this effect to "the land itself."[53] He described his feelings while traveling in the veld:

> I recovered an experience which I had not known since my childhood, moments, even hours, of intense exhilaration, when one seemed to be a part of a friendly universe. The cause no doubt was largely physical, for my long treks made me very fit in body, but not wholly, for I have had the same experiences much later in life when my health was far from perfect. . . . I seemed to acquire a wonderful clearness of mind, and to find harmony in discords and unity in diversity, but to find these things not as conclusions of thought, but in a sudden revelation, as in poetry or music.[54]

Buchan's association of this elevated subjective state with the word "poetry" is significant. As a published poet himself, he would have known how poetic invention—"bringing something into existence which did not previously exist"—is especially drawn to "that which resists the intelligence most successfully."[55] It draws on and encodes precognitive knowledge that is affective precisely *because* it lies just beyond consciousness. This knowledge is only accessible through metaphor; its existence is only proven by the intensity of subjective feelings which such metaphorical constructions elicit. I would argue that it was just such intimations of a "knowledge which does not know" that Buchan experienced in the Transvaal, and which he struggled to re-create for his readers in his topographical description. Questions of feeling and representation, surface appearance and sensed depth would have been especially pertinent for Buchan: as an intellectual with a strict religious upbringing, he was more aware than most of the way the collapse of natural theology had heightened the sense of numinous presence in the physical world.[56] Buchan's heightened attention to the inchoate character of the landscape, "a thing essentially mysterious and individual," which permeates *The Africa Colony*, can be directly linked to this disjunction between subjective experience and metaphysical belief.

Thus, we can see how, as both experience and representation, the landscape description in *The Africa Colony* was marked by Gilpin's observation that "half the beauty of a thing consists in the easiness of its introduction . . . the eye roving at large in search of objects cannot bear prescription . . . when it is apparent that the view is contrived, the effect is lost."[57] What initially seems to be a representational setting in place is in fact often a record of the temporally shaped ontologies of phenomenal experience. Buchan's recollection of the South African landscape as a terrain that alternately resisted intelligence and evoked feeling reminds one that even a reflexive ability to recognize (let alone frame and control) underlying similarities in the world is never free from the feelings of contingency that come with physically inhabiting it. Since the Enlightenment, there have been many travelers (Rousseau is one example) who were "more students than conquerors," for whom the arrival was ultimately less important than the actual journey, and whose identity was destabilized and transformed by the experience of this journey.[58] Paul Carter has argued that this alternate trope of travel is especially relevant in colonial situations, where the description of the terrain cannot be separated from the physical circumstances of the encounter with that terrain and the struggle to find convincing representational languages to describe it.[59] All of this suggests that if we are to fully understand the landscape encounter Buchan alludes to in *The Africa Colony*, we need to return to the dialectic between his own corporeal subjectivity and the topographical specificity of the landscape he was describing.

In chapter 3, I argue that "habitus," "body-schema," and "body-subjectivity" offer alternate ways of conceptualizing a corporeal communion between people and the environment that leads to identification with, and attachment to, place. This "knowledge that does not know" is also implicit in older poetic and rhetorical constructions of representation in which a substantial portion of meaning is imaginatively constructed, or completed, at the spatial and temporal site of reception, that is, the audience.[60] Simultaneously practical *and* imaginative, it is an introjection of the self into the organizational structure of the object through a kind of "body-world dialectic."[61] (It also strongly recalls Bachelard's statement that discoveries of "poetic correspondences between self and material elements are not so much a question of intellectual abstractions *from* matter as discoveries *of* the self in matter.") The body implied in this introjection is not an abstracted, idealized, or geometric body in (or coterminous with) the object, but an essentially gestural, proprioceptive body, realized through displacement.[62]

This suggests that the ineffable "felt presence" Buchan experienced in the Transvaal was based on prereflective comprehension of the relational aspects of landscape revealed to him as a traveling, corporeal subject, as much as it was on recognition of pretextual or personally familiar topographies. Buchan, who as a youth had himself "dreamed of a career of devastating bodily adventure," encouraged his readers to participate in his own synthetic imaginative processes through that commonest denominator of all, the sensing body.[63] Frequent references in the text to the raw materials of sensation—sight, sound, smell, movement—are reinforced by editorial interpellations: "Fine scenery is too often witnessed by men when living the common life of civilization . . . [b]ut on the veld there is bare living and hard riding, so that a man becomes thin and hard and very much alive, the dross of ease is purged away, and the body and mind regain the keen temper which is their birthright."[64] Describing the landscape in terms of its qualitative dimensions rather than in terms of recognizable figures sustained the rhetorical valorization of firsthand experience already implicit in the book's overall organization. It reinforced the idea of the Transvaal as a landscape best put together in the reader's imagination, and thus as a poetically charged whole that had not previously existed. This invocation of bodily movement and sensation had another important rhetorical resonance with Buchan's quest for an as yet unformed civilization of South Africa that would acquire the stamp of the soil:

it limned the idea that the subjectivity or way of being that arose in this landscape was one grounded in physical rather than cerebral life.

Buchan's persistent emphasis on bodily experience invites a closer scrutiny of his actual landscape encounter and how this might have been a product of the terrain through which he traveled. As we have seen, the bodily knowledge that does not know it plays a key role in rhetorical representation. It also lies at the heart of Merleau-Ponty's carnal body-subject, for whom the most "existential" dimension of phenomenological experience was *depth*, precisely because it is "neither a property of the object nor an intellectual construct."[65] Depth is of course the central problem of all landscape experience and representation—so much of it is beyond us—and it was clearly latent in Buchan's efforts to capture and convey the intensity of emotion he felt on the Highveld. The passages of firsthand experience in *The Africa Colony* describe landscape not so much as an inert, autonomous object as something called into being as a contingent, correlative of consciousness. Such landscape description opens onto a broader field of signification, which is embedded in the larger interior horizon of subjectivity, and may have no obvious connection to the immediate spatiotemporal encounter. Thus, his comments about the scale and monotony of the Highveld's spaces ("its vastness [is] always the dominant feature") and the absence of points of purchase for the eye (its "blind infinity") were both the product of a quite corporeal lack of orientation and articulation and the lack of strategic frames of geographical reference such as roads, towns, and accurate measures of distance.[66] Thus, Buchan observes: "It is nearly impossible to get a proper calculation of distance from country people in South Africa. They are accustomed to calculate in hours, which of course vary with every district according to the nature of the road and the quality of the transport."[67]

Physiographically, the Highveld is a region of long, gently tilting inclines, and its edges are as often simple escarpments as they are upstanding mountains. For all its extensiveness and apparent monotony, the portion of land visible from any particular point is, paradoxically, never very large (see color plate 14). As Buchan himself indicates, one feels oneself to be *on* rather than *in* the landscape, an undulating sea of grass in which distance is difficult to judge, and ever-moving clouds and their shadows are often the most distinctive features. This underlying placelessness was reinforced by the fact that in 1902, the Highveld was still largely devoid of settlement, stock, tillage, trees, and fences. Buchan was traveling through and describing a landscape that lacked enclosure, orientation, and articulation, with little other than the horizon that drew and held the eye: "One had the sensation of being somewhere on the roof of the world, for on every horizon but one the land sloped to a lower altitude, and even on the east the mountains seemed foreshortened, like the masts of a vessel just coming into sight at sea."[68] The unmediated dialogue between the two poles of the experiential world set up by the Highveld, inner self and outer horizon, was a fundamental one. As one author has written: "If one was asked which of all sights in nature is the most lastingly satisfying, would one not choose the horizon?"[69] This notion would have been potent for Buchan, who experienced his youth as the sequential, scalar unfolding of environmental horizons.[70] His childhood roaming of the Border hills had been driven by a sense of the "great back-country [that lay] just outside our narrow range; . . . if we could only cross a ridge or push beyond a turning in the road, our eyes would behold it." Now, on horseback, the open, treeless veld offered no frame of reference other than the edge of visibility—seemingly distant but surprisingly close, constantly shifting, always provocative. The horizon of the Highveld, like all horizons, unified the setting and forged the continuity of the experience of it.[71] Thus, Buchan's description of the region as "both strenuous and restful" was far more accurate than might at first seem apparent.[72]

Although vision is the sense that is best able to address depth's ambiguity, it is only one of several ways we are anchored in the world.[73] Each one of our senses constructs a different, but complementary, experience of the problematic of tension, orientation, and articulation inherent in depth. As we find out when one of them fails, all of the senses work in concert with each other, fluctuating in intensity and focus, and compensating for each other according to our situation and competence. Perhaps the most subliminal evidence of this is the proprioceptive knowledge engendered by movement of the body. Buchan's awareness of the horizon was not only a consequence of his elevated point of view on horseback, but of the distinctive autonomy and freedom that traveling by horse gave him; the self-guided motility that is key to the body's innate power of exploration is, if anything, sharpened for the rider with an unreliable map. The early twentieth-century Highveld offered as little impediment to the movement of the body as it did to the eye, and Buchan's itinerary was always somewhat contingent, at times made up as he went along. Distant hills that promised a good overview or the rare glint of water could be investigated without constraint. Traveling in this landscape privileged precisely the kind of situational, improvisational thinking that was a defining characteristic of fin de siècle masculinity. These kinesthetic circumstances of travel helped to figure the space of the Highveld as a distinctly "dramatic possibility of movement" that invited a more bodily, less abstract subjectivity.[74] In a situation in which movement was neither constrained nor repetitive, but reduced to its most elemental iteration, the pleasures of movement fell within the reach of reflexive consciousness. It is precisely movement that was more autonomous than that afforded by cart or train (the only other possibilities at this time) that underpins passages such as the following, which highlights the relational organization (character) of the terrain: "Climb to the top of the nearest ridge, and after a broad green valley there will be another ridge just the same: cross the mountains 50 miles off, and the country will repeat itself just as before. But this *sameness in outline* is combined with an *infinite variety in detail,* so that we readily take back our first complaint of monotony, and wonder at the intricate novelty of each vista."[75]

If the traveler's proprioceptive explorations establish a subliminal corporeal geography that counterpoints the sporadic glimpses of this and that afforded by sight, a similarly contrapuntal relationship develops between sound and sight. If sight "sets a world, as an object or series of objects, in front of the eyes," then sound *places* one in the world. The world of sound plays a key role in the encounter and memory of places; it is an event-world, while the world of vision is an object-world.[76] The world evoked by sound is "temporal, continually and perhaps unpredictably coming and going; . . . it generates a sense of life and is a special sensory key to interiority—unlike sight which presents surfaces." Buchan writes, "though the glen is quick with life, there is no sound: a deep Sabbatical calm broods over all things. The cry of the Kaffir driver from the road we have left breaks in with an almost startling violence on the quiet.

The tall reeds hush the stream's flow, the birds seem songless, even the hum of insects is curiously dim. There is nothing for the ear, but much for the eye."[77] In this passage he experientially places the reader in not just the space, but the lived time-space of the Highveld. He evokes a sound world that is less stark and more dreamlike than the world of sight, in which the only human voice one hears, sometimes for hours on end, is one's own.[78]

Intersensory play such as this, which verges on the synesthetic, does not supplement so much as augment our imaginary taking hold of the world. Textual evocation of the landscape as a multivalent field of sense stimuli simultaneously highlights the thinness of prior inhabitation and renders the landscape a living thing. In Buchan's account, the essentially visual "blind infinity of the veld" has its aural reciprocal in "this silent country," and when sound does break through, it is invested with a poignancy that comes from rarity: "the fall of water, rarest of South African sounds, tinkled like steel in the cold morning air."[79] This tension between the depth suggested by vision and that suggested by the other senses (the horizons of sight and sound—the invisible and silence—seldom coincide) characterized a landscape of scaleless foregrounds and hypnotic, intriguing horizons because it blurred the separation between interior subjectivity and exterior spatiality, making subjects reflexively aware of their every action and perception, a situation that might be likened to the "uncanny."[80] The multisensory depths of Buchan's account also address, rhetorically rather than explicitly, the core dilemma of a romantic ideology that strives for elemental or pristine experience: that once this elemental experience is achieved, it is destroyed. Resonant fragments of sensory data, rather than comprehensive topographical description, render the author's own journey less visible and encourage the reader to put a surrogate landscape experience together in their mind, *for themselves.* If the untouched can only be experienced by touching, then it is important to feel that one is the first to do so.[81]

Entering a Temenos: *Biography, Topography, and Aesthetic Feeling*

Although these fragments of sensory data cumulatively constructed a precognitive sense in the minds of the reader of what it would be like to journey across the Transvaal Highveld, Buchan's book was about more than simply corroborating fin de siècle metropolitan subjectivity through a rhetorical engagement of bodily experience on a high, open landscape on the margins of empire. It was, as we have seen, also an account of a profoundly emotional and transformative landscape encounter. As it turns out, this encounter was one that had considerable resonance for a generation and provided a template for emotive attachment to the subcontinent. Grasping how this occurred requires a return to the undivided body-subjectivity mediated by Buchan's book, and a consideration of how his response to the Highveld was shaped by private and personal subjectivity as much as phenomenal experience.

In his book about aesthetics, *Art as Experience*, John Dewey argued that the relationship between the unfolding of experience and emotional feeling is an intimate one.[82] Insisting that there is "no immaculate conception of meaning," Dewey argued that the ontological entrapment of human subjects in time meant that the present is always experienced as a kind of "doing and undergoing," and that the root of all meaning is "significant growth" of the psyche. The notion that subjective meaning

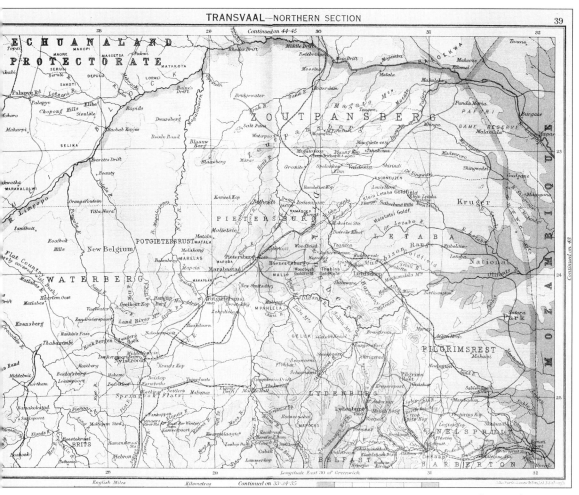

Continued on 44-45

Continued on 33-34-35

derives from a "process of articulation or growth" is crucial not only to Dewey's understanding of human communication and expression, but also to his understanding of aesthetic feeling, which he believed was a heightened form of experience. For Dewey, aesthetic feeling was never autonomous, "sheer emotional reaction," but a "dynamic resolution, a co-ordination and a harnessing of the tensions within experience," a "field-event incorporating horizons of feeling, the objects of sense, and the foci of consciousness."[85] Aesthetic feeling cannot be separated from the "total undergoing [that] binds the self and world," the grasping of "the present in terms of possibilities and histories" that is experience.[84] For Dewey, aesthetic feeling was, ultimately, the heterogeneous presence of sense; it was a latent possibility in all forms of human endeavor. Like Merleau-Ponty's "depth," it was simultaneously intellectual and emotional, encompassing all dimensions of being in the world.

Dewey's arguments suggest that the intensity of Buchan's encounter with the Transvaal landscape can be likened to an "undergoing" that was at once corporeal and biographical. Buchan was the ambitious and gifted son of an impecunious father, and while in the Transvaal, he was negotiating a decisive transition in his life. Like other provincial bourgeois who flocked to European capitals during the nineteenth

"Transvaal: Eastern Section." From *South and East African Year Book and Guide* (London: Sampson Low, Marston, and Co., 1926); Cornell University Library.

133

THE AESTHETICS
OF IMPROVEMENT
ON THE
HIGHVELD

century, he found the best escape from the limited horizons of home to be a career in the heart of the same culture that had consigned that home to provinciality in the first place. At the same time, however, this escape made Buchan acutely aware of the difference between his relatively impoverished but active, outdoor childhood and the emphasis on wealth and material possessions in metropolitan life. While his scholarship to Oxford had brought him some prominence in London and the Home Counties (as well as his invitation to South Africa to work for Milner), it had not eradicated his sense of being someone on the outside looking in at metropolitan society, who belonged to the upland margins from where the advanced pioneers of empire were conventionally thought to come. In 1902, his future was still unclear (he was even uncertain whether he would return to Britain), and he had not yet been accepted into the inner circle of the metropolitan establishment.[85]

We can best understand how pervasively this personal and private subjectivity (which was in fact shared by many in the colonies at this time) became intertwined with Buchan's experiential appropriation of the Transvaal landscape by returning to his description of the Woodbush. Although he visited the area many times, Buchan always felt he was "crossing the borders of a *temenos*, a place enchanted and consecrate."[86] This characterization of the Woodbush hints at the possibility for geographical forms, like other forms, to fuse and embody experience through imaginative displacement. Dewey believed that the emphasis we give to form in discussions of aesthetic phenomena reflects a need to integrate experience at a conscious level. He argued that "the aesthetic is a way of articulating experience so that it realizes expressive meaning and value."[87] Form develops its expressive charge by engaging precognitive knowledge about relationships within the thing itself, relationships that, because they are at base phenomenological, embody our own experiential "doings and undergoings" in the world, which otherwise have no obvious means of expression. As in Aristotelian representation, these relationships occur within the substance of the thing itself, the material and the space of which it is constituted: "Form is the energetic process of organizing material of experience into a consummatory event which does not transcend life but fully actualizes it. . . . It projects a teleology for the material which can only be realized through the material."[88]

In the Woodbush, Buchan found a geographical entity that, because of its small size (it could be crossed in under a day on horseback), constantly shifting play of clouds, fogs and mists, and distinct physiographic boundaries, was both subtly distinct from, yet also an integral part of the landscapes he had encountered elsewhere in the Transvaal. In 1902, it was also the end of the road north; from here, only native paths and animal tracks led off into the Lowveld.[89] Not unlike Buchan's childhood world in the Scottish Borders, the Woodbush gathered in a small geographical area several contrasting landscapes types, and encompassed "both the desert and the sown." At the same time, however, it was, for the Transvaal Highveld, an unusual place where one was afforded a long view: on all sides you could "journey to an edge and look down upon a wholly different land."[90] The appeal of the Woodbush was also rooted in the pleasures of high places, themselves rooted in the structure of the body itself. The congruence between elevation, vision, and human knowledge, first remarked upon by Petrarch on Mont Ventoux, is such a pervasive part of human appropriation of the world that it is easy to dismiss as banal.[91] In virtually every culture,

"The Edge of Beyond":
Eastern Transvaal
Escarpment. Museum-
Africa Photographic
Collection file ref.
#916.82; reproduced
with permission.

the capacity for humans to develop unfettered visual relations with objects separate and distant from themselves has been used in the selection and design of elevated sacred precincts and to encourage a contemplative relationship with the landscape.[92]

This effect was especially true on the eastern edge of this edenic upland, which overlooked the "pernicious fever flats" of the Lowveld, the semitropical savanna that stretched eastward from the foot of the Drakensberg Escarpment to the border with Portuguese East Africa (today Mozambique) and the Indian Ocean (see color plate 15). This created what Buchan calls "that most fascinating of all types of scenery, a garden on the edge of a wilderness."[93] The Woodbush was a landscape that articulated (or gave expression to) the entire horizon of experience that the previous fifteen months had given him. Within this doubly marginal geographical place, the rhetorically implied body-subject of his account found its most persuasive purchase: unlike in other parts of the placeless Highveld, in the Woodbush this body-subject did not have to rely on movement in order to realize the present in terms of possibilities and histories but was "consummated" by a topography that facilitated an imaginative dialogue between near and far. While the physical boundary of the Woodbush (the edge of the escarpment) was explicit, the imaginative boundary (the distant horizon) was not. The indeterminacy of this far horizon was both spatial and temporal; the "becoming place" it unified was simultaneously experiential *and* rhetorical: "As far as the eye could see, the faint blue line of the Rooi Rand, the Portuguese border, was just distinguishable from the sky, with the fingers of the little Lebombo breaking the thin line to the south. One forgot the weary miles of swamp and fever that lay between, and saw only a glorious sunlit plain, which might have been full of clear rivers and vineyards and white cities, instead of thorn and Kaffir huts and a few ugly mining shanties."[94]

Crucially, the unified presence of sense Buchan experienced here was the result of the juxtaposition of the familiar with the unfamiliar. Like the Highveld, albeit in a more intensified way, the Woodbush was a landscape that contained familiar elements recombined in an unfamiliar way. "From a cool fresh lawn you look over a hundred miles of nameless savagery. The first contrast which fascinates the traveler is between the common veld and the garden; but the deeper contrast, which is a perpetual delight to the dweller, is between his temperate home and the rude wilds beyond his park wall."[95] In the Woodbush, Buchan also found a geographical manifestation of the opportunities a "white man's country" offered for rejuvenating civilization by, bracingly, exposing it to "barbarism." As he remarks elsewhere, "It is much for a civilization to have its background—the Egyptian against the Ethiopian, Greek against Thracian, Rome against Gaul. It is also much for a race to have an outlook, a far horizon to which its fancy can turn. Even so strong men are knit and art preserved from domesticity."[96] Thus, Buchan uses the elevationally and climatically distinct place of the Woodbush to synecdochically represent his corporeal experience of the Highveld as a whole, and the cultural prognostications that resulted from that experience. The Woodbush serves as exemplary place not only for a future South African society that was "the fruit of the land," but also for the rejuvenation of metropolitan culture.

Tellingly, Buchan's terminology hints that the "perpetual delight" afforded by this place was contingent on it remaining somewhere that, environmentally and imaginatively, was (and was likely to remain) caught between Africa and Europe. The classical *temenos* was not only a demarcated space subject to rules of purity and reserved as a sanctuary, but it was also considered indispensable for small communities living among foreigners.[97] With hindsight, this form of geographical imagination, which assigns certain places to particular groups or cultures on the basis of some form of environmental suitability, hints at the patterning and differentiation of the South African territory that was to achieve its apotheosis under apartheid. At this time, however, it would probably be more accurate to say that it mediated a liminal subjectivity that did not seek complete control of the land, and indeed derived part of its charge from the continued contrast with that which it did not (yet?) control. This subjectivity was, of course, embodied in the "garden on the edge of wilderness" Buchan hoped to build there one day, but it was also implicit in the myth he invoked in describing the Woodbush. In classical literature, the Hesperides was a far-off place where heroes—liminal figures caught midway between the world of gods and men—were sent as part of their labors, to find and bring back to the center magical enigmas of nature.[98] Such a spatiotemporally unfolding trial by experience was exactly what Buchan had himself undergone in the Transvaal; the golden fruit he saw himself bringing back to metropolitan Britain through his writing was a revivified, and revivifying, relationship between self and the physical world. The trope of the explorer returning home, having undergone a transformative and irreversible experience, and bringing back an altered sensibility is an archetypal one, and it was one that allowed Buchan to integrate and render meaningful his life thus far.

The trajectory of the journey out and back from a known center has profound existential implications: movement of the subject not only animates and organizes the world but also, as de Certeau observed, inaugurates the subject itself.[99] It also implicitly underpins the literary trope of the journey, which, whether it is toward the future or the past, toward resolution or the unknown, always leads on to the image of

Paradise Lost or Regained.[100] Such literary figurations of place are endemic in fin de siècle metropolitan culture, which saw the world as divided into the timeless, rooted idyll of the rural and the ever-changing comopolitanism and opportunity of the city—a division that was a very real factor in Buchan's own life. Whether one reads Buchan's Hesperides as a Paradise Lost or a Paradise Regained (both are possible), a sense of movement that facilitates emergence permeates *The Africa Colony*. It is a narrative in which the experience of marginality, cognate with impotence and dispossession, is subtly transformed into an appreciation of the virtues of betweenness and becoming. The book suggests that it is precisely at the edges of things where the unknown and the known meet in unresolved conversation and new, more encompassing articulations of experience first become visible. Buchan's later statement that the "green summit against the unclouded blue above a populous friendly world" was for him one of the most primal environmental enchantments,[101] suggests that the experience of the austere, temperate grassland escarpment is cognate with a dramatic sense of incompleteness, symptomatic of what has been called the "neurasthenic and anxious" bourgeois self.[102] In the Transvaal in general, and the Woodbush in particular, Buchan first felt the productive aspect of the tension between urban center (the locale of rational governance, intellectual ideas, and personal autonomy) and natural periphery (the "kindly soothing pastoral" of his poetic imagination, which was grounded in his childhood).[103] Arguably, it was precisely the embrace and harmonization of this tension that underpinned his subsequent success as a member of the British imperial establishment, as well as many of his novels.[104]

Buchan's textual interrogation of the Transvaal landscape, then, was unconsciously entangled with his attempt to find an identity for himself. *The Africa Colony* exemplifies Tilley's observation that "personal and cultural identity is bound up with place; a topo-analysis is one exploring the creation of self-identity through place."[105] It can be read as a working out of identity through the act of writing, the description of an imaginary, yet-to-emerge world as a way of describing an imaginary, yet-to-emerge self. Buchan's situation at the time he wrote it gave rise to a profound identification with the condition of geographical liminality; the landscape he describes is best understood as not so much empty as incomplete or unfinished. Figured as an imaginary correlative of his own unfolding and incomplete subjectivity (bodily, personal, biographical), the region is rhetorical figured as a place that would function in much the same way for a more generalized subject, that of the metropolitan Briton. In *The Africa Colony*, newly annexed landscapes of the Transvaal Highveld were figured as a realm in which experiences, especially bodily ones impossible but yearned for in Britain, could be coordinated and harnessed.[106] The spaces of the Transvaal, liminal both in terms of their geographical location and their phenomenal qualities, could be incorporated, now that the region had become part of a Greater Britain within the imaginary horizon of a gray, crowded, blighted metropole.

From Nostalgic to Technological Pastoralism

This pervasive subjectivity of incompletion, cognate with the aesthetic "yearning for what is promised but never unveiled by beauty," was of course deeply embedded in, even perhaps, as Said has argued, an integral part of, imperialism.[107] Buchan's writings suggest that this aesthetic—what Schwarz has called the "colonial sublime"—

sprang from a subjectivity in which metropolitan anxieties about social change, the aspirations of middle-class second sons and nonmetropolitan Britons, and the often fleeting inhabitation of the landscape by "traveling subjects" were intertwined.[108] For Buchan and others who found themselves on the margins of the British Empire, the slippage between imperial expectations and daily life was neither surprising nor disagreeable. For these traveling subjects, the concatenation between personal situation and daily experience they found there brought about an inspiring sense of purpose and personal agency they would never have felt in Britain itself and encouraged an intensely poetic—in a fundamental sense of the word—geographical imagination. This reflexive sense of the power of landscape in turn reinforced the underlying idea that it was the colonies that would save the metropole from decadent materialism. In a new, more reciprocal kind of imperialism, the metropole would enrich "the rest of her culture and traditions" while "the spirit of the Dominions" would blow like a "strong wind freshening the stuffiness of old lands."[109] All of these biographical and existential imaginaries contributed to the sense of these young idealistic colonial administrators that a new kind of identity—one that was simultaneously autochthonous and still loyalist/imperial—would emerge in countries like South Africa.

For Buchan, these imaginaries were deepened by his Scottish upbringing: if the Scots could acquire a nested, bifocal identity that was simultaneously Scottish and British, the same might be possible for those who would live in an as yet unformed white South Africa. Because the values and cultural characteristics of this identity were, in the first instance, seen to derive from the experience of inhabiting the land, historic divisions between Boer and Briton living side by side in the same region would in time naturally fall away. As this reconciliation (in which most imperialists saw the Boers coming around to civilized, British values) was dependent on a corporeal relationship with the land itself, rural settlement became a central component in securing South Africa's long-term allegiance to Britain and the empire after the (inevitable) end to direct rule. Whether or not it was true, Buchan believed the Scots' adaptation to British sovereignty stemmed not from crude imposition of English culture and institutions on them, but a recognition of the cultural and material advantages that this allegiance brought, and he believed that in time the Boers would come to the same conclusion.[110] The underlying message of *The Africa Colony*, then, is that bluntly assimilationist policies of denationalization and Anglicization were not only unnecessary but counterproductive. Buchan believed that a common white identity could be forged without erasing older place- or region-based identities and that, in the long run, a nested, resolutely landscape-based sense of identity would be more likely to secure South Africa as part of the empire. Thus, at the same time as Buchan's participation in the larger project of imperialism heightened his reflexive sense of the Transvaal landscape's corporeality, his Scots background and the Transvaal's topographical character lent to his encounter with it aspects of a deeply affective return. A landscape more like Scotland would not have offered a sense of future possibility, while one less so would not have engaged his cultural and historical imagination.

Although Buchan never returned to the Woodbush after 1902 and *The Africa Colony* had a very limited circulation, his response to the South African landscapes was widely disseminated in his fictional writing. Internationally popular novels like *Prester John* and *Greenmantle*, seldom out of print since they were first published, elaborated many of the ideas about race, place, and identity first mooted in *The Africa Colony*. At a time when the colonies' appetite for literature was strong but most books and magazines were imported from the Britain,[111] Buchan's novels helped white colonial nationalist South Africans imagine themselves as part of a new society that grew out of its landscape.[112] For generations, these books also shaped perceptions of South Africa for millions all over the world. It could be argued, then, that *The Africa Colony* laid the foundations for an imaginative (and even perhaps mythical) inhabitation of the subcontinent that took on a life of its own and spread across time and space.[113] The fusion of the emotional and the associative with the topographical in Buchan's account posited a particular kind of subjectivity as native to the region. In his Scotland-based reading of the Transvaal landscape, a synecdochic form of nationalism occurs; the place of the Woodbush stands for the sensory world of the Highveld, while the illimitable Highveld stands for the whole of British South Africa. These nested Edens mediated a belief that white South Africans could forge a common identity without erasing old identities or forfeiting the imperial connection. There was thus far more to Buchan's emphasis on landscape as a defining feature of settler identity in South Africa than the need to defend Milner's settlement policies.[114]

While texts provide ways of seeing and speculating about places, they seldom determine the reconstruction of that place or the modes of life that evolve in them. Instead, perhaps, we should read Buchan's vision of the Highveld as a text that helped construct a decidedly utopian vision of the South African landscape by glossing over the contradictions between the romance of improvement and the hard realities of agriculture in South Africa. There is little doubt that the extraordinary resources that Milner devoted to rural resettlement were funded in part by such a vision. Within a year of the Peace of Vereniging, nearly 250,000 Boers had been resettled on the land and furnished with seed, building materials, livestock, horses, and mules, and large tracts of Crown and newly purchased land, mostly in the interior, had been set aside and prepared for immigrants.[115] Although Milner's rural utopia never came to pass—the war had destroyed much that reconstruction could never replace—strands of his vision did find echoes in South Africa during the early decades of the twentieth century, when romantic ideas about living on the land were as powerful as realities of under-capitalization, carrying capacity, land speculation, racial politics, and labor supply.[116]

Pragmatically speaking, Buchan's administrative labors bore little fruit. Few of the land settlement schemes he and his successors set up to attract small farmers survived beyond the end of the 1920s. As self-government became stronger, overseas interest in these settlement schemes diminished. It also soon became obvious that two hundred acres of land, which in Europe would have been generous, was insufficient in the South African interior, where semiarid conditions favored extensive pastoral rather than intensive arable farming. This was especially true in the Transvaal bushveld, where most new settlement actually occurred after 1906.[117] Other obstacles facing immigrant farmers were land values driven artificially high by large commercial companies engaged in speculation (often with an eye on mineral prospects), and the passing of the Native Land Areas Act, which greatly diminished rural tenantry and ended cooperative labor arrangements between small landowners. The only Milner settlers who survived were those who farmed in areas with access to irrigation schemes or railways (which raised the value of both land and crops), worked together to establish local cooperatives and creameries (a particular interest of Buchan's), or somehow managed to acquire more land. In reality, rural South Africa, instead of experiencing the white population growth and closer settlement that Milner had hoped for, started losing population in the 1920s. At the same time, the austere emptiness that had so appealed to Buchan and stimulated his cultural vision began to change as land use became more capital-intensive and historically complex and ambiguous patterns of land ownership became increasingly segregated, clarified, and entrenched.

In other respects, though, the imaginative charge of Buchan's literary vision remained alive for several decades, resurfacing in sometimes unexpected and ambiguous ways as part of the "cult of the veld." The apparently inevitable return to the six-thousand-acre farm long thought to be necessary for agriculture in South Africa favored individuals with access to large amounts of capital.[118] A significant number of rural landowners from the early 1900s onward were urbanites with capital acquired in mining, industry, law, or commerce, and until World War II, many remote, essentially uneconomical, farms on the Highveld were bought by members of the English-speaking urban mercantile class, who were able to make improvements on the land because they did not have to make ends meet by their farms alone.[119] On most of these farms, the form of agriculture practiced was as much about environmental and aesthetic improvement as it was about maximizing production and economic returns.[120] Although shrewd businessmen, these "cheque book" or gentleman farmers borrowed the British upper classes land ethos, itself based on a romantic view of history, in which large country properties were supported not by income from the land but by investment portfolios. This arrangement, which was contingent on low wages for large numbers of staff, came to an end in Britain after World War I but persisted much longer in South Africa.

Yet again, we encounter the example of Sir Lionel and Florence Phillips, who had firsthand experience of the English manorial existence during their exile in Britain from 1897 to 1906, when they poured huge amounts of money into their country estate, Tylney Hall, and actively supported rural life and traditions.[121] When they returned to South Africa, the Phillipses seemingly tried to call into being Buchan's own Hesperides, buying five farms in the Woodbush, where they set up a number of idealistic agricultural and industrial schemes and planted miles of oak avenues in the veld.[122] The Phillipses' preoccupation with the Woodbush also manifested itself in one of the three panels they commissioned for Herbert Baker's new Pretoria station in 1908, *Summer in the Soutpansberg*, which depicted the Woodbush (see color plate 16).[123] In one sense, this was not accidental: Buchan was a good friend of the Phillipses' and dedicated his famous 1910 novel, *Prester John: Adventures of David Crawford with a Lowveld & Escarpment Background*, to Sir Lionel. But the fascination with the "Berg," as the escarpment running down the east side of South Africa became known, which Buchan articulated in *The Africa Colony*, found many echoes among other colonial national gentleman farmers. Percy Fitzpatrick, the author of *Jock of the Bushveld* and a close friend of Milners, owned a farm in a similar topographical situation, on the edge of the escarpment, some two hundred miles to the south, near Harrismith.[124] Similarly topographically minded settlement schemes were set up by various philanthropic gentlemen in other elevated parts of the Southern Highveld,

THE AESTHETICS
OF IMPROVEMENT
ON THE
HIGHVELD

Escarpment near Harrismith. Transnet Heritage Museum Library Photographic Collection, neg. #31744; reproduced with permission.

including schemes of British Settlement of South Africa Ltd. in the Heilbron and Thaba Nchu districts, the Duke of Westminster's scheme near Clocolan, and Lord Lovat's scheme in Lindley district. Buchan's topocultural imaginary geography also surfaced in Smuts's vision of a Greater South Africa, which envisaged a temperate, highland backbone of white farms "served" by black lowlands, and in the touristic fascination with the passes and viewpoints all along the escarpment, captured by countless photographs in the 1920s and 1930s.[125]

For a time, these kinds of schemes and representations infused the Union's more temperate rural districts with a character that drew on at least a century of literary and artistic appropriation of the English rural landscape. This landscape tradition, with its constant undercurrent of improvement, cultivated a nuanced awareness of likeness, difference, and association in the selection and naming of properties, and went hand in hand with resolutely Picturesque forms of settlement and planting whose effects would last for decades. Many landowners quite consciously modeled their properties, imaginatively and physically, on the estates of the paternal landed gentry in Britain, with the homestead and its well-tended garden figured as a great house at the center of a picturesque ensemble of fields and workers housing.[126] (Here, quite tangibly, we see the playing out of Buchan's poetic idea of the garden on the edge of wild, the garden in bloom contrasted with the wilderness.) This borrowed landscape tradition also encouraged the emergence of discursive landscapes like the old Cape, the Cape Mediterranean, and the Highveld, as well as English-speaking white South Africans identification with districts construed as part of the Berg, such as the Eastern Orange Free State, the Natal Midlands, East Griqualand, and the Eastern Cape Borders.

Buchan's ideas about landscape, improvement, and white identity also survived in the guise of the technological pastoralism promoted by the Union governments after World War I, which perpetuated, through financial and scientific means, the earlier rebukes of idleness and wastage latent in Buchan's reading of South Africa's potential.[127] The Union Department of Agriculture worked to develop a shared progressive ethos of improvement with a small but influential group of Dutch, Afrikaner, and English-speaking farmers,[128] some of whom were acquaintances of Buchan and members of the colonial national urban establishment. After 1925, reflecting the new Nationalist government's shift in orientation from mining to farming interests, this entered a new phase, and the state began to use burgeoning gold revenues to offer white landowners significant increases in aid, and to intervene at all levels of production, marketing, and import control to raise prices of South African agricultural products. This technological pastoralism had more to do with reasons of state—creating national self-sufficiency, bolstering white rural society, and, eventually, safeguarding the imaginary *bodem* (soil or ground)[129] of Boer language and culture—than it had to do with economic logic or even South Africa's true agricultural potential.[130] Like Milner's Reconstruction, it was primarily directed at the high interior and the industrial heartland, rather than the longer-established, export-oriented coastal economies. Signs of this technological pastoralism in the landscape were fences, windbreaks, orchards, windmills, dams, irrigation schemes, dairies, grain elevators, railways, and tree plantations. This state support for white agriculture and rural society was tested to the limit by the extended drought in the late 1920s and early 1930s, as well as the Depression, which led to widespread rural poverty that would last for decades.[131] This, paradoxically, led to a revival of imaginative relations with the land of the kind that Buchan proposed: the family farm became a sacred icon of Afrikaner culture and political values, which emphasized the tilling of the soil as a "quasi-religious act in a *lebensraum* free from capitalistic relations, subject only to natural laws."[132]

Thus, while Milner's dream that a yeoman farming class would become the economic and cultural backbone of white South Africa never materialized, linkages between landscape, improvement, and white identity outlined in Buchan's book did become an important strand in white South African society. Because his early 1900s reading of the Highveld in *The Africa Colony* and the subsequent novels articulated a spectrum of rural landscape imaginaries recognizable by colonial national South Africans, it could also be said to have contributed to the emergence of the cult of the veld. At the same time, however, this projection of the unimproved veld as a key component of white imaginary geography contradicted another aspect of Buchan's original topoculturalist vision of South Africa's future, which was that the land available for black ownership should be increased rather than decreased. Buchan believed that grave dangers would attend an arrangement that forced Africans into a permanently inferior or subservient position, and that limited political rights should be guaranteed from the outset, and that the way must be left open to fuller rights in future.[133] Although the unevenness of capitalist development of land provided some havens and alternatives, as the twentieth century progressed, most Africans' access to land steadily diminished and whites' sense of entitlement to it increased. The encroachment of white farms was marked by an almost obsessive delimitation and control of the land and by disruption of Africans' traditional, communal, and seasonal use of pastures, marshlands, and river banks.[134] This disruption of long-standing patterns of land use invisible to most whites placed great stress on the land that Africans did have access to in the reserves and accelerated the flow of the African population off the land and into the cities.

PROSPECT, MATERIALITY, AND THE HORIZONS
OF POTENTIALITY ON PARKTOWN RIDGE

> The idea of nationality belongs to the realm of the imaginary rather than—or as
> well as—the real; it depends on ideas of what we might be rather than what we are.
> —Raphael Samuel, "Introduction," in *Patriotism*

Five years before the start of the South African War, the wife of the up-and-coming British mining magnate Lionel Phillips was riding out into the veld north of the mining settlement of Johannesburg. After climbing a gentle slope for about a mile, she found herself cut off from the noise and dust of the stamp batteries, on a narrow ridge that ran from east to west. Alone among the rocks, tall grasses, and occasional thorn trees, she saw below her a dramatic prospect of an open, empty grassland sweeping away to the north. Captivated by the sight, she returned home and persuaded her husband to build her a house there, which they called Hohenheim.[1] While possibly apocryphal, this story of how early Johannesburg's most desirable residential enclave came to exist is rooted in the city's morphology. In the 1890s, the original core of the town, centered on the farm Langlaagte, was expanding rapidly into the veld in the directions that offered the least impediment, east and west. This expansion followed the subterranean alignment of the main reef on which the city's wealth depended, and left untouched the high, undulating ridge that Florence Phillips had climbed and the veld to the north.

Johannesburg's transformation from a mining camp into a city coincided with the importation of a new form of urban development and emergence of the social and economic conditions necessary to implement it. An accident of topography naturalized this urban development and led to the emergence of a cultural place that, like

Mafeking and the Woodbush, helped gather, ground, and articulate an emerging white South African identity. Unlike the cultural places called into being by Baden-Powell and Buchan, however, which were primarily imaginative and discursive, in Johannesburg this place-making was as much physical as it was discursive. Built form both represents cultural intentions iconographically and initiates forms of practice and existence not entirely commensurate with those intentions. Always exceeding the intentions of their creators, buildings mediate their meanings through use as much as symbolism and representation. It is through such a play between intention, use, and symbolism that the residential enclave that grew up in Johannesburg at the turn of the century contributed to the growth and elaboration of colonial national South Africanism.

Unlike Cape Town, Johannesburg was never an outpost of the Old World, and its image of itself has always centered on its newness and tumultuous growth. In 1906, a mere twenty years after the discovery of gold, it was a town of one hundred thousand people, covering seventy-five square miles, with buildings rivaling those in London or Berlin and the full spectrum of human existence from incredible wealth to the most abject poverty. This sudden and exponential growth, which distinguishes Johannesburg from every other South African city, was the result of the discovery of gold in the mid-1880s, which had also been a major catalyst for the South African War and the annexation of the old Zuid Afrikaansche Republiek as a Crown Colony of the Transvaal. Although this annexation had been orchestrated by expansionist imperialists like Rhodes and Milner, in Johannesburg at least, the transfer to British administration ratified what was already an accomplished fact. Even in 1896, only 15 percent of the city's population were citizens of the ZAR, and from its very inception, it had been a town of recent immigrants (or *uitlanders*, as they were known) rather than Boers.[2] The huge influx of people attracted to the Witwatersrand in the 1880s

Panoramic view of
Johannesburg, 1889.
Cape Archives Jef-
freys Collection, file
ref. J2021; reproduced
with permission.

and 1890s came from all over the world as well as other parts of the subcontinent, and annexation simply consolidated the imperial capitalism that had shaped the city since its earliest days. Thus, from the outset, Johannesburg was the one city in South Africa where European imperialism's territorial acquisitiveness and economic exploitation was most explicitly realized.[3]

The creation of Parktown as an autonomous domain within the mushrooming city was closely linked to mercantile imperialism. It grew up on a large tract of land bought in 1892 by a group of émigré financiers and businessmen who hoped to find more gold reefs and speculate on the rapid growth of the town. Just north of the established city, the so-called Braamfontein Estate extended three miles from east to west and encompassed a series of elevated, stony ridges as well as a large sweep of veld immediately below. Until its purchase, the land had only been used for grazing and contained nothing but "veldgrass, a few proteas, kaffirplums and some thorn bushes in the rocky crevices."[4] When no gold was found on the land, the lower portions of the estate (some 1,400 acres) were given over to plantations to provide pit props for the mines, and the ridge was developed as a private leasehold township, which included the suburbs of Parktown and Westcliff (usually conflated as Parktown, or the Ridge). The layout of this township was radically different from that of the rest of the city: plots were a minimum of one acre in size, the street layout abandoned the quick and expedient grid used elsewhere in the city and responded to the natural contours and outcrops, and key sites were set aside for churches and schools.[5] Parktown functioned as a self-contained, fenced estate with its own bylaws until it was formally incorporated into the municipality of Johannesburg in 1901.

Because it was Johannesburg's first consciously planned residential quarter, at

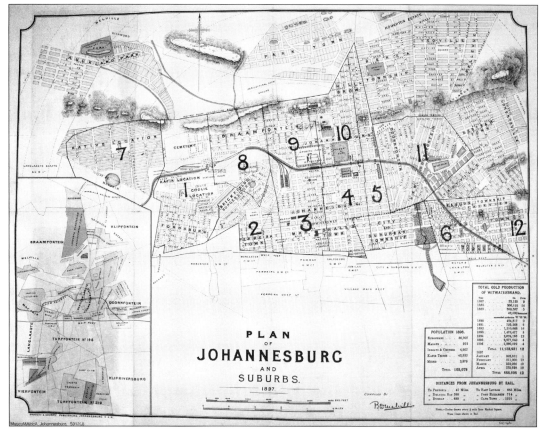

Grocott & Sherry's plan of Johannesburg and suburbs, 1898. MuseumAfrica/ Strange Collection, Johannesburg Public Library; reproduced with permission.

a time when new kinds of urbanism that integrated the city and nature were being sought in Britain, Parktown could be seen as a reflection of the garden city movement in Britain.[6] It is probably more accurate, however, to see it as a copy of the commuter enclaves then springing up in the Home Counties surrounding the national and imperial capital, London, which were, in many senses, the complete antithesis of the garden city, emphasizing architectural individualism, social competitiveness, and antitrade snobbery.[7] Parktown played a similar role in Johannesburg, introducing new class distinctions into a city previously only divided into black and white, and it laid the foundations for the city's social geography for the next eighty years.[8] At a time when incredible fortunes were being made very quickly, Parktown provided a domain in which the newly wealthy could distinguish themselves from their less successful neighbors.[9] English garden cities, the Surrey-Sussex stockbroker belt, and Parktown were all products of the same nostalgic pastoralist mentality, which, though antiurban, did not exclude ideas of urban improvement. In long-established European conurbations, naturalization of the urban environment could only be achieved through constructing suburbs and garden cities on the fringes and strategic upgrading of paving, lighting, sewerage, building codes, and parks in the centers.[10] Comprehensive urban planning was more readily implemented in the new colonial societies, and cities such as New Delhi, Salisbury, Canberra, and Johannesburg all experimented with forms of urbanism that articulated a locally distinctive intersection of nature and culture.[11]

147

PROSPECT,
MATERIALITY, AND
THE HORIZONS OF
POTENTIALITY ON
PARKTOWN RIDGE

The architectural implementation of this on Parktown Ridge only occurred after the Transvaal fell under British administration. At the outbreak of the South African War, few houses had been built on the north side of the Ridge, though the eucalyptus and fir trees that the Braamfontein company had planted in the veld below were well established.[12] Most *uitlanders* had hurriedly left Johannesburg at the outbreak of war in October 1899 to avoid internment, but they swiftly returned the following year, when the Union Jack was hoisted in the city.[13] Along with this return arrived Herbert Baker, an English architect who until then had lived and practiced in Cape Town and had become something of a court architect to Rhodes. Within months of his arrival in Johannesburg, Baker had built himself a house on the Ridge called the Stone House. This was a modest edifice, compared to most that would be built nearby during the following five years, a period when the future prospects of South Africa in general and the burgeoning gold-based economy of the Rand in particular seemed limitless.[14] By the time the Transvaal Colony was incorporated into the Union in 1910, the Ridge was largely built up with substantial mansions, the most significant of which were designed by Baker's practice.[15] In time, these were joined by churches and schools—again, largely designed by Baker—which later became some of the most prestigious in South Africa.

Lives Not Yet Lived and the Vision of the Veld

After the war, Johannesburg in general, and Parktown Ridge in particular, quickly became the home of South Africa's administrative and entrepreneurial elite. Captains of mining, industry, and the railways gravitated there after the war because Johannesburg was increasingly where South Africa's wealth was generated, while administrators and colonial officials chose to live there because they preferred the social, political, and natural climate of Johannesburg to that of Pretoria, where their official duties actually lay.[16] During the first few decades of the century, this community of capitalists, entrepreneurs, administrators, and politicians evolved into a distinct society, the men belonging to clubs in central Johannesburg modeled on those in St. James and Mayfair, and the wives devoting themselves to dinners, soirees, and fund-raising balls. Until 1906, the most powerful member of this so-called Parktown set was Milner himself, who during his short tenure in the Transvaal lived and conferred there with his Kindergarten in the house called Sunnyside. The Kindergarten formed an especially close-knit group within early Parktown society, and several of its members re-created the intellectual intimacy they had known at Oxford in the famous Moot House. Although Baker was not a member of the Kindergarten, he was close to many of them (he shared his new house with several of them while their own accommodation was readied for them) and like them, he was a young, talented, and highly educated Englishman caught up in the project of reconstructing the region. Like them, too, Baker enthusiastically embraced the outdoor life on the veld (he often joined others on their evening rides in the Sachsenwald with Milner), and, also like them, he translated this enthusiasm into a sustained public rhetoric in support of unification and nation building.

   The community of the wealthy and the educated that grew up on Parktown Ridge before and after union was, at the same time, close-knit and drawn from a wide range of social, ethnic, and cultural backgrounds. It included individuals who came from

148

PROSPECT,
MATERIALITY, AND
THE HORIZONS OF
POTENTIALITY ON
PARKTOWN RIDGE

older nouveaux riches parts of Johannesburg, others who had recently arrived from other parts of British South Africa, and those who had previously lived in the extended empire and Britain itself.[17] Some, like the Kindergarten and members of the English gentry and minor aristocracy, saw themselves as the British overseas, living in South Africa for an indeterminate but nevertheless finite period of time before they moved on to other parts of the empire, or back to Britain.[18] Others identified themselves as South Africans, either because they had been born there (families of Cape Dutch descent, for instance), or because they were emigrants who were grateful to the country that had allowed them to rise above their lowly origins. Parktown's inhabitants also included the German members of the Braamfontein Company's Board and the Jewish financiers who played such an important part in Johannesburg's development.[19]

The heterogeneous backgrounds of these individuals limited their allegiance to ethnic or geographical origins and gave them a vested interest in the capitalist expansionism of the British Empire; it also made them sympathetic toward a rhetoric of nation building that emphasized the region's future potential rather than its sectarian past. In the early 1900s, a South Africa that was part of a Britannic Commonwealth's "expanded field of loyalties" seemed to offer the best future even to the least imperially minded individuals. Almost all those who lived on Parktown Ridge were, in a sense, leading lives that had not yet been lived, oriented toward what was being, or would be, constructed. At the same time, however, they were caught up in the circuits of knowledge and ideas that linked South Africa to Britain and other parts of the empire, and they shared with those who lived in those countries the belief that the British Empire was an agent of civilization, improvement, and enlightenment. The Ridge thus became an important locale for translating New Imperialist ideals into colonial national ones and developing ideas about the future of South Africa. Many who lived there took to heart Rhodes's argument that it was "the duty of the wealthy in the raw, undeveloped country and cities of South Africa to build beautiful homes wherein to exercise the most excellent gift of hospitality [so that] strangers, pioneers and farmers could see and hear the best of the country and its people."[20] This in turn made the Ridge a natural destination for visiting minor royalty, aristocrats, and politicians, as well as writers, artists, and architects, who found ready patrons in the colonial gentry looking for ways to promote and disseminate their ideals of inclusive, loyalist South Africanist nationhood and reconciliation. Like others drawn to Johannesburg at this time, these writers, artists, and architects wanted to see for themselves this "white man's country," which had entered their consciousness as a result of the war and Milner's imagination-capturing project of Reconstruction. Some of these visitors were those familiar figures of imperialism, the privileged travelers of independent means whose social connections allowed them to undertake leisurely tours of a global network of embassies, government houses, plantations, and residencies. Others were South Africans who had studied in Europe and now divided their lives between the two worlds. Both groups acted as cultural go-betweens who represented the colonial national ideal to those in the metropole while recharging the Parktown set's project of reconciling imperialist ideology and national aspirations.

The epitome of the host-patron who made this whole nexus of cultural exchange and promotion operate was the same person who had "discovered" the Ridge in 1895,

Alan Yates, view
from Northwards,
Parktown, 1920s. From
Dorothea Fairbridge,
*A Pilgrim's Way in South
Africa* (London: Oxford
University Press, 1928),
pp. 72–73.

150

PROSPECT,
MATERIALITY, AND
THE HORIZONS OF
POTENTIALITY ON
PARKTOWN RIDGE

Florence Phillips. Although the Phillipses had decamped to Britain after his disastrous involvement in the Jameson Raid, they returned to the Transvaal at the behest of Wernher, Beit & Company's directors in 1907, to live in the palatial new Baker house the company built for them, Villa Arcadia, which was completed in 1909. Although never as wealthy as some of his codirectors, Lionel Phillips's fortune was sufficient to allow him and, more particularly, his wife, to become involved in virtually every aspect of colonial national cultural life.[21] Florence Phillips's cultural activism epitomized the peculiarly bifocal, traveling subjectivity that was shared by the Parktown set, as well as the aestheticized appreciation of the local that often resulted from this subjectivity. This tendency to see the local through metropolitan eyes was reinforced by the steady flow of British artists and writers to Parktown, for whom capturing and conveying the potential of South Africa to those who would never set foot inside the country was a constant concern.

An example of how they might have experienced and represented the Ridge occurs in Dorothea Fairbridge's *Pilgrim's Way in South Africa*.[22] Ostensibly an account of a tour Fairbridge made of the country in the 1920s, it is a carefully orchestrated narrative of places visited that was designed to promote a deeper understanding of and identification with the country. Fairbridge's book both outlines the emerging imaginary geography of colonial national South Africa and emphasizes Parktown's central position in it. The landscape of the subcontinent is rendered legible and meaningful by the journey as pilgrimage; the places visited and described in the narrative are cast as way chapels of a benevolent imperialism through their configuration within the overall trajectory of the journey's narrative. The book opens in Cape Town, which as we have seen, was the obvious point of departure for any description of the country at this time.[23] After a long railway journey up through the coastal mountain ranges and across the arid monotony of the Karoo interior, Fairbridge arrives in Johannesburg and is driven through the early morning streets to her friends' Baker-built house "perched on a ledge, overlooking charming houses and gardens."[24] Having reached this topographical and, in a sense, narrative high point in her journey, Fairbridge then turns, as it were, to look around her, expatiating on the various cultural and economic miracles that imperialism had wrought in the city.

At this point in the book, two photographs appear. Both are taken from inside one of Baker's Parktown houses, Northwards, and both use elements of the house's architecture and garden to frame the view of the landscape beyond. In these images, the corporeal journey up from the coast (and implicitly before that, the metropole) is extended by the mind's eye. In Fairbridge's narrative of the northward journey through African space, the Ridge, and the view from it, stages an ongoing imaginative journey into some undefined future. The Ridge is figured as a pivotal way chapel that both frames a disposition toward the subcontinent and hints at how those who lived on the Ridge incorporated the Transvaal landscape as part of their hybrid, inclusive, future-oriented subjectivity.

Topography, Cultural Horizon, and the View of Africa

In order to unpack the imaginative resonances of these views from Northwards, we need to first acknowledge that they were grounded in some very physical realities. Parktown Ridge was the tallest of a series of blunt quartzite ridges that formed the northern edge of central Johannesburg; while not very high in themselves, these ridges rose with striking clarity above the oceanic, illimitable grasslands that surrounded them. The highest points on the western Highveld, these ridges were, in the early 1900s, the only sign of the vast, wealth-bearing geologic formations that lay hidden beneath it.

That Johannesburg's most desirable residential enclave, like Buchan's imaginary Hesperides, came to be located on a high point in the landscape is no accident. The relationship between social power and topographical elevation has a long and probably universal history.[25] Ancient native Sotho-Tswana communities in South Africa had selected the summit or sides of kopjes and ridges for their Highveld encampments. Connection between social status and elevation are reinforced in places that are not only raised, but also level; the level, limited (and usually elevated) platform is a fundamental requirement for inhabitation, providing both the physical and conceptual foundations of "standing."[26] (It is also a matter of simple optics that level elevated platforms obscure the untidy circumstantiality of the middle distance and encourage an unmediated relationship between near and far.)[27] The elevated, level platform also implies orientation, another phenomenological inhabitational truth that combines pragmatic and existential knowledge. Orientation is a product of our frontally directed senses; it subliminally reveals what we consider most important and automatically configures the enhorizoning world. One of its oldest manifestations is the alignment of building sites with the transcendental place of the sun, bringing them into cosmically oriented space.[28] But orientation also has other, more practical connotations: "Approaching an unknown town, we tend to grasp its character and life through its topography, directing ourselves either toward or away from its center."[29] It is not surprising to find that those who had only recently arrived in the fifteen-year-old "unknown town" of Johannesburg, which was still finding its shape and order, mostly turned their backs on its noise, dust, and confusion and oriented themselves toward the veld and the African sun.[30]

The orientation of the Parktown houses may have been a pragmatic response to building on an elevated ridge on the boundary of a chaotic, dusty, clamorous city, but it became a crucial factor in construing the subcontinental landscape. A view implies not only a viewpoint, but also a frame. The northward view across the veld toward the horizon had little currency in the imaginary world of the city until these houses—named not only Northwards but also Hohenheim, The Chalet, Hilltop, and The View—were built and occupied. These houses simultaneously created the north of the veld, and the enclave of the Ridge as such. Period photographs show that until their gardens matured—a slow process on these rocky, exposed sites—the Parktown houses formed an undulating but single line along the front edge of the ridge, all more or less at the same elevation and facing in the same direction. Although they stood at some distance from each other, the size and massing of these houses made it as impossible for those who lived in them to be unaware of each other as it was for them to be unaware of the view to the north.

Thus, what started out as a pragmatic act of inhabitation set in motion the play of the larger geographical imagination. The view from the Ridge was, at the turn of the century, empty of human habitation; the featureless foreground of the plantation blended in the near distance with open Highveld in which, as we have seen, the concept of distance is ambiguous. For all its seductive expansiveness, the view from the Ridge was completely devoid of the Picturesque schema of field, grove, lane, gleaming river, and half-hidden roof that usually led European eyes to the horizon. Nor was there much evidence of ancient settlements or classical ruins, like those that had drawn the gaze of privileged nineteenth-century European travelers. This lack of the usual components of an imaginary painting was, however, replaced by something else; an extraordinarily complete emptiness. The landscape seen from the Ridge was intact and "unimproved"; not only close at hand and boundless, it was devoid of distinct signs of occupation.[31] The pleasure of contemplating this ambiguous distance was, as many of Johannesburg's early white residents noted, amplified by the extraordinary clarity of the "champagne-like" high-altitude air. Crucially, this seductive view was replicated in every northward-facing house on the Ridge, and, seen from within domestic space, was experienced as a space of private reverie. To

152

PROSPECT,
MATERIALITY, AND
THE HORIZONS OF
POTENTIALITY ON
PARKTOWN RIDGE

View looking west
along Parktown Ridge,
1905. MuseumAfrica
Photographic
Collection, file ref.
916.82; reproduced
with permission.

anyone who had grown up in a world where unspoiled nature was the preferred refuge from stressful urban life, the nearness of this unimproved expanse would have been powerful indeed. To those looking to the landscape for clues to their own identity or for a politically neutral phenomenon that embodied future potential it would also have been deeply corroborative.

The invitation to metaphorize this empty expanse was deepened by the nature of the horizon that terminated it: the Magaliesberg mountains some thirty-five miles away, which captured the imagination of virtually every visitor to the Ridge at this time, from Buchan onward.[32] The widespread fascination of the Magaliesberg, which marked where the temperate Highveld gave way to the more typically African bushveld, can be accounted for in two registers: what happened in front of it and what happened beyond it. Horizons stabilize us in space and, as we saw in chapter 5, provide the continuous spatial frame of reference that the fragmentary and episodic nature of sensory perception cannot. They are also where landscape is abstracted to its simplest expression—its outermost edge, seen as silhouette, or alternatively, as standing and rising figure.[33] Landscape as horizon is therefore landscape reduced to its most elemental as well as its most liminal expression. Both literally and imaginatively, the horizon is the termination of the visible and the beginning of the invisible. Standing and rising figures suggest connections between the realms of the physical and known (the inhabited earth), the imaginary (the invisible land beyond), and the transcendent (the sky).[34] And, because they represent landscape as object (not space), they facilitate the discernment of character. Thus, we find that the horizon seen from the Ridge was frequently characterized as archaic, primordial, and mysterious—in a word, "African."[35]

153

PROSPECT,
MATERIALITY, AND
THE HORIZONS OF
POTENTIALITY ON
PARKTOWN RIDGE

View of Parktown Ridge from Jan Smuts Avenue, after 1922. MuseumAfrica Photographic Collection, file ref. 916.82 JHB 2657; reproduced with permission.

This preoccupation with the horizon, already encountered in Buchan's description of the Highveld, harks back to the emergence of the landscape idea of Western culture in Renaissance Italy, when control of the hinterland by cities made fortified rural settlements unnecessary and there arose the possibility of countryside villas where those of high social standing could withdraw to recover from the fatigue and the obligations of urban life. The Renaissance Italian *villeggiatura* rejuvenated the classical ideal of rural life that was simultaneously linked to the town, and balanced the *vita contemplativa* and the *vita activa*. Along with this concatenation of urban culture and rural life there emerged the construction of the "three natures"—the highly manipulated first nature of the garden, the workaday second nature of cultivation, and the wildness of untamed third nature. Within this schema, wild, unimproved landscape was integrated as an essential part of a setting that included villa, garden, and working fields, usually in a single perspectival continuum.[36] While it was impossible to actually design this distant unimproved landscape (and indeed, it had by definition to not be designed), it *was* possible to give it agency and meaning through the way the house and its immediate surroundings were structured and oriented.[37] The distant, "wild" horizon, framed by the architecture of house and garden, became part of an intentional, orderly impression of infinity; it was always the natural horizon, not the physical perimeter of the estate, which formed the limit of the continuum that always included the three natures.

In postbellum South Africa, as in Renaissance Italy, this organization of the territory visible before the house into different "natures" helped render the unimproved landscape imaginatively inhabitable for an emerging urban mercantile class. At Parktown, Sachsenwald initially stood in as a somewhat undistinguished second nature, mediating between the foreground first nature of houses and gardens and the third nature of the empty veld stretching away to the African horizon of the Magaliesberg. This concatenation of the northward-stretching veld before the Ridge into

Kidger Tucker,
"Rhodes Over Africa."
MuseumAfrica
Photographic
Collection, file
ref. 920/Rhodes;
reproduced with
permission.

unimproved but accessible nature helped sustain a key strand of nostalgic pastoralist mentality especially pertinent to those who lived in Johannesburg: the fantasy that agriculture, rather than rootless mining, would be the backbone of South African society. This same concatenation of the "improved" and the "unimproved" through the directed view also mediated the ambivalent commingling of force and care that David Bunn argues underlies all imperialist governance.[38] It was of course precisely this kind of effect that Baker was referring to in his often-quoted opinion that the Union Buildings' location on Meintjies Kop in Pretoria would allow politicians to "lift their eyes up to the surrounding hills and the . . . splendour of the Highveld, from which they may gather inspiration and visions of greatness."[39]

The horizon is the dividing line between the visible and known and the invisible and imagined. In the early 1900s, the view from the Ridge did not terminate at the

155
PROSPECT,
MATERIALITY, AND
THE HORIZONS OF
POTENTIALITY ON
PARKTOWN RIDGE

Magaliesburg but extended over the horizon into the heart of the African continent. To understand the potency of this, one needs to consider the history of European colonization in the subcontinent. Until the annexation of the Transvaal, the most substantial British colony by far had been the Cape Colony, at the southern tip of the continent. The Cape was not just the natural starting point for any journey to South Africa, but it was also, implicitly, the point of origin for the vector of "illumination" that British imperialism would bring to Africa's dark interior. Thus, the view from the elevated platform of the Ridge not only aligned itself with the axis of Fairbridge's narrative but also with the general trajectory of European settlement, which by this time had been incorporated in Rhodes's imperial northward gaze from Cape Town, and his dream of a Cape-to-Cairo railway. This fantasy, never fully realized, was nevertheless rehearsed in death by Rhodes's funeral train, which wound its way from Cape Town to Bulawayo, and was echoed in the notional axes of the memorials to Rhodes in the Cape Town Company Gardens and on the slopes of Table Mountain, designed by Baker.[40] Rhodes's northbound imaginary may have been fed by intimations of the great mineral and agricultural potential still unrealized in the heart of Africa, but it also tapped into the self-consciously historicist underpinnings of the British Empire.[41]

The significance of this topographical, orientational convergence can only be fully plumbed by turning once again to the cultural milieu of those who wielded influence in the Transvaal at this time. The convictions of the Kindergarten were founded on their common educational background at Oxford, where all of them would have encountered the writings of John Ruskin, an enormously influential figure for educated Britons in the late Victorian period.[42] Ruskin's appeal to the imperial project lay in the fact that he not only addressed a huge range of topics—such as politics, economics, literature, natural history, art, and architecture—but also sought to integrate these topics in a single divinely ordered universe in which nature and culture were reconciled.[43] Ruskin's geographical imagination harked back to the roots of geography itself, the prescientific awareness of variation between regions, and found its quintessential expression in the region that was "essentially co-terminus with the Roman Empire."[44] This Mediterranean *axis mundi*, where Africa and Europe met and that Ruskin saw as "the meeting point of three great cultural streams, each originating in one of the broad climatic zones," was precisely the geographical region toward which the Ridge houses were oriented.[45]

Thus, the view from the windows of the Parktown house was not only a synecdoche for Rhodes's Cape-to-Cairo axis, it also mediated an array of Hegelian historical reciprocities that supported the idea of the Cape as quasi-Mediterranean.[46] The view northward from the Ridge was a prospect in the fullest sense of the word: at once profoundly geographical and historical, it was an orientation/disposition that conflated a number of seemingly unrelated ideas about time and space, culture and nature. It was, after all, the Mediterranean classical world that provided the intellectual warrant for New Imperialism, which in its most high-minded mood believed that it had inherited from the Greeks and Romans the burden of civilizing and settling the margins of the world. Like the ancient Greeks and Romans, the Kindergarten saw themselves as bringers of civilization to an unenlightened region. The Cape-to-Cairo trajectory, whose two ends Britain already controlled in 1900, powerfully confirmed this psychogeography: it led to the "cradle of civilization" clustered around the *mare nostrum* of the Mediterranean, which was also the cradle of imperialism. The prospect of the veld that the inhabitants of the Ridge discerned before them was not just African; it was also continuous with the cultural hearth of the Western civilization.

Herbert Baker and "An Architecture which Establishes a Nation"

Houses and gardens are usually thought of in scenographic terms (style), but they are also inventions that mediate our inhabitation of the world, both through the way they organize space and how they are made.[47] Houses and gardens are the most proximate, tangible portion of the spatial world we inhabit, where that world is most likely to be experienced through preconscious, participatory corporeal engagement—typically, through the roots of architectural construction: site, enclosure, and materials.[48] In Parktown, this engagement was most explicit in the houses designed by Herbert Baker. The Parktown houses varied greatly in style, ranging from Gothic, Renaissance, and Georgian to mock Tudor and Scottish baronial, and in this categorization, Baker's are usually labeled Arts and Crafts.[49] However, Baker's dozen or so houses on the Ridge cannot really be understood using such stylistic typologies. While they occupied sites similar to their neighbors and enjoyed the same "private continental view,"[50] they also made free use of different architectural vocabularies to embody and convey larger ideas about imperialism, national character, and the naturalization of white society.[51]

Baker emerged as an unofficial South African architect laureate during the first decade of the twentieth century, in part due to his talent as an architect, but also due to social connections.[52] His career had been launched shortly after his arrival at the Cape as a young man, in 1892, when he had been taken up by Rhodes. Rhodes in turn introduced him to Milner, who invited Baker to the Transvaal after Rhodes's death in 1901 to assist in postwar reconstruction.[53] Baker's reputation was also, in part, ascribable to the seriousness with which he sought to implement the ideas instilled in him by his education. He had trained in Britain at the height of the Arts and Crafts movement, which, under the influence of figures such as Morris and Ruskin, linked the practice of architecture to a number of progressive social agendas. Ruskin's copious writings on architecture were colored by a morally charged worldview that found signs of the divine in visible *form*: he believed that it was in the *apparent* qualities of nature that "symbolic truths about God and the goodness of the creation" were revealed.[54] Ruskin believed that forces of nature also shaped material culture over time, especially authentic vernacular architecture, which he saw as a key expression of human culture. His studies of rural buildings made from "the material(s) which Nature furnishes" attempted to capture moments when human inhabitation became a force of nature in its own right, adding "beauty and harmony to the landscape" (see color plate 17).[55]

In his advice to architects seeking to achieve beauty and harmony in their own work, Ruskin stressed the importance of direct, empirical observation of the geographical context: the "ideal might only be found by careful observation of unique examples in nature."[56] It is only after one has scrutinized many unique examples that the general and the specific emerge and the less obvious essential character of things reveals itself. Ruskin's favored vehicle of revelation was the kind of sketching that, as a form of engagement with nature, was more like that of a farmer or stonemason than that of a photographer or a traveler. He laid particular emphasis on understanding the manifestations of geology and climate—that is, the terrestrial and heavenly poles of the phenomenal world—as loci of a landscape's essential character. Thus, the rocks of a given region indexed characteristic forces of nature (that is, geological process as well as weathering) and revealed regionally differing interactions between these forces; in other words, climate and geology interacted to form topography. In architectural terms, these precepts translated into a preoccupation with questions of materiality and construction—what a building was made of, how it was put together, how it weathered in response to climate over time—rather than discussions about stylistic genres and vocabularies.

Although Baker and Schreiner's correspondence about Ruskin's supposed admiration of Cape Dutch architecture occurred years later, there is little doubt that Baker and Rhodes's friendship was strengthened by their common subscription to Ruskin's ideas.[57] Their first meeting grew out of Baker's efforts to preserve Cape Dutch buildings, in which the architect recognized much that his training had taught him to look for. These efforts were supported by Rhodes, both through his painstaking restoration of his own house, Groote Schuur, and through his preservation of many old Cape Dutch houses on the financially ruined wine farms he bought in the Western Cape. Forty years later, when he recalled working for Rhodes, three fundamentally Ruskinian topics dominated Baker's memoirs: topographical setting, climatic effects, and the craft of building.[58] In this account, we can see how the experience of working for Rhodes helped conflate Baker's own growing imperialist beliefs with a belief that the subcontinent's inherent nature would be a touchstone for the cultural character of a new South African society.[59] He links the phenomenological qualities of the landscape to the more serious and sweeping work of geopolitics, and uses them to justify ideas of settling and civilizing the subcontinent. He also approvingly records Rhodes's insistence that everything be made by local craftsmen from local materials, using techniques displaced by imported, prefabricated materials. The various commissions Baker undertook for Rhodes at the Cape were important not only in mediating the discursive landscape of the old Cape; they also established the imaginative rhetorical character for much of his later work. The vivid sensual and material qualities of the African landscape—its light and scale, scents and textures, climate and topography—were poetically engaged in a way that seemed to confirm the fitness of Europeans to appropriate and transform it.[60] His buildings projected an imaginary world eminently suitable for European inhabitation: healthful and physically empty, yet resonant with mythical and historic associations and receptive to the constructive hand of imperialism.

This dualistic architectural engagement with cultural imagination and material nature evolved considerably when Baker moved to the Transvaal. Initially reluctant to leave the Cape, once he had made his own northward journey to Johannesburg in 1901, Baker quickly recognized that here was a unique opportunity to create "a better and more permanent order of architecture . . . [an] architecture which establishes a nation."[61] Over the next decade, he had ample opportunity to do so: his architectural practices designed nearly three hundred houses and numerous significant public buildings in the Transvaal.[62] Writing what amounted to a personal manifesto in the *State*, several years after he arrived in the Transvaal, he argued that architecture needed to be distinctive and monumental, imperial and yet South African at the same time.[63] In the early 1900s, Johannesburg, unlike the Cape, had no local architectural tradition on which Baker could draw.[64] There were virtually no pre–gold rush structures, and the city's physical fabric was dominated by poorly constructed speculative buildings adorned with imported prefabricated elements. This uneven architectural fabric reflected the fact that the city had quite literally grown out of the bare veld in less than twenty years and had been subject to constant tensions between great surpluses of wealth and political instability.[65] It also reflected the fact that Johannesburg had come into being at precisely the time when the industrial nations were discovering lucrative markets in the colonies for their building components, which, despite haulage costs, could be sold more cheaply than similar items locally manufactured.[66] It was in this architectural Babel that Baker sought to develop a way of building that was less overtly expedient, ephemeral, and symbolically empty.

This search was overlaid with other concerns, however. Rhodes and Milner had chosen Baker as the architect most likely to give expression to the kind of postbellum society they hoped would evolve in South Africa, and in 1901, Rhodes sent him on an extensive, all-expenses-paid study tour of the Mediterranean. The tour's itinerary not only reflected the imaginative mapping of the Cape as Mediterranean, nascent at this time, but it also reflected Rhodes's desire that Baker acquaint himself with "classical architecture as a means of expressing imperialism."[67] In his *State* article, Baker echoed this idea, arguing that both the "timelessness" of imperialism and geoclimatic parallels between the two regions suggested that a new South African architecture should be rooted in the universality of Graeco-Roman classicism.[68] These arguments suggest that by 1909 Baker had abandoned his earlier Arts and Crafts ideals and the idea that a free adaptation of Cape Dutch architecture would suffice as a national

PROSPECT,
MATERIALITY, AND
THE HORIZONS OF
POTENTIALITY ON
PARKTOWN RIDGE

architecture. In this article, it is clear that Baker's exposure to the architecture of the classical world and his many commissions for large public buildings in the Transvaal had transformed his design philosophy. Thomas Metcalf has argued that by the time Baker left South Africa in 1913, he was interpreting Rhodes's and Milner's ideal of a politically engaged architecture not so much in terms of "architecture that established a nation" as an "architecture expressive of the ideals of the British Empire." According to Metcalf, this ambition required buildings that appealed simultaneously to a variety of different audiences and "testified to the continuous flow of . . . ideas among the various lands of (the) far-flung imperial system."[69] Although Baker did not use the same classical vocabulary for the Parktown houses as he did for the large Transvaal public buildings, these houses nevertheless participated in the same wide-ranging, traveling architectural vision.

That Baker's vision was about more than architectural style was confirmed by the fact that one of the most fundamental lessons he learned from his tour concerned siting. All over Italy, Sicily, and Greece, Baker was struck by the way finely proportioned and crafted buildings located in commanding positions in rugged, open landscapes enhanced the aesthetic qualities of both.[70] He adopted this strategy, with its gesture toward the Renaissance "three natures," for the Parktown houses and much of his other Highveld work, which culminated in the Union Buildings in Pretoria of 1910–12. The same fascination with juxtaposing civilization and wildness underpinned another Baker design strategy: the selection, where possible, of sites just below the ridge line. This left the slope immediately behind the building in its untouched native state and meant that the gardens became a series of walled terraces, creating an architectural platform for the building that dropped off dramatically to the veld below.[71] The underlying symmetry of the building plans imparted a sense of stability, autonomy, and orientation that stood against the unconfigured, unimproved third nature of the veld beyond. In time, the function of the building as threshold was reversed, as the wild below became built up and the ridge behind became preserved as a fragment of wildness.

Baker gained other insights in the Mediterranean that were closer to Ruskinian precepts about the relationship between forces of nature and culture.[72] Similarities of climate, topography, and vegetation between parts of South Africa, especially the Cape, and the Mediterranean region have already been noted. As we have seen, climate—especially when linked to elevation—had become a central strand of the European imaginative construal of the subcontinent, but it was also one of the "forces of nature" that Ruskin believed shaped regional and cultural character. Baker's own description of the Highveld was pure Ruskin. He made much of the "rarefied dry air" in Johannesburg, which "impelled all to live and work there at full throttle, [calling] forth the utmost that was in man for whatever purpose." Of the experience of living in Parktown, he wrote: "There, perched on high, 5,700 feet above the sea, we lived in the pure air from all the winds that blew, and above the frosts of winter that settled in the plains below. The almost daily thunderstorms in the summer months were formidable, but glorious to behold as they gradually dissolved and drifted away eastwards in the evenings with the glow of the setting sun upon the white dome-clouds fringed with the lightning flashes; the landscape was then seen through thin-spun veils of rain."[73]

160

PROSPECT,
MATERIALITY, AND
THE HORIZONS OF
POTENTIALITY ON
PARKTOWN RIDGE

View of the Union
Buildings, Pretoria,
from Meintjies Kop-
pie. Cape Archives,
Elliot Collection
#2690, reproduced
with permission.

This imaginative linkage of elevation, climate, and health powerfully influenced Rhodes's and Baker's shared faith that the subcontinent was a natural home for Europeans. Both men extolled the virtues of an active life and, to an extent, practiced the outdoor life that the subcontinent's climate made possible and that was to become enshrined as typically South African.[74] This way of life informed the climatically responsive design of Baker's Parktown houses, which were often quite simple in plan and usually only one (large) room deep. Laid out in wings and courtyards to make the most of the Highveld light and air, their spare, lofty rooms were the kind that in Victorian England would have felt gloomy and dark, but in South Africa became cool and elegant.[75] At the Cape, Baker had encountered the Dutch *stoep*, the raised platform at the front of the house, once characterized as "a covenant between the

161

PROSPECT,
MATERIALITY, AND
THE HORIZONS OF
POTENTIALITY ON
PARKTOWN RIDGE

Cloister at Villa
Arcadia. Barloworld
Archives Phillips
Collection, file ref.
#29; reproduced with
permission.

house and the sun." In his Transvaal houses, he transformed this feature through
the use of forms taken from the Mediterranean—the arcaded cloister, the loggia, the
pergola, and the walled terrace—demonstrating his own argument that "South Africa with its sunshine and limpid atmosphere must look to the South of Europe not to
the North for its architectural model."[76] Baker embedded these Mediterranean forms
in and around the house, creating what he called an architecture "of cool recess, of
void and spaces, and plain surfaces in deep shadow," in which one could retreat from
the sharp African sun while still enjoying the mild high-altitude temperatures.[77]

An aspect of Baker's Transvaal architecture less obviously related to climate was
its simplicity and modesty of decoration. Spareness, directness of expression, and
materials that "spoke for themselves" were of course central tenets of the Arts and
Crafts movement, but they also related to the way built form presented itself to the
eye in South Africa's "great spaces washed with sun."[78] Baker's quotation, in his
writing on South African architecture, of Wren's argument that one should design
"for the Observer's inhabitation and little for Pompe" may have been expedient,
given pragmatic constraints such as the limited availability and intractability of
local materials and skills, but it also demonstrated a suggestively participatory way
of imagining the connections between people and the places they inhabit.[79] This is
captured by his argument elsewhere that "[In South Africa] the landscape is so bare
in detail, and so vast and grand in its general features that the design and disposition of buildings must be conceived on a monumental scale to be in harmony with
the work of Nature."[80] At a fundamental level, Baker was expressing a need for some
kind of reciprocity between the formal qualities of the regional landscape—strong
simple masses that are only revealed by sharp contrasts of light and shadow—and

162

PROSPECT,
MATERIALITY, AND
THE HORIZONS OF
POTENTIALITY ON
PARKTOWN RIDGE

North-facing loggia at Villa Arcadia. Barloworld Archives Phillips Collection, file ref. #27; reproduced with permission.

those of the buildings constructed in it. But arguments that, in South Africa, the suppression of decorative detail would give "qualities of stability that . . . suit our big landscape" also derived from the deeply empirical and phenomenological knowledge of the craftsman profoundly in touch with the thing he creates, aware that certain materials, forms, and ways of making work better *in situ* than others.[81] To a degree, these kinds of arguments also echoed Buchan's elision of the "austere and mysterious veld" and the "gentle but inflexible pride which is too proud to make claims, and leaves the bare fact to be its trumpeter."[82]

Baker's interest in the nature of materials and the ways they are crafted was undoubtedly deepened by his study tour. In his Mediterranean travels, Baker encountered an architecture that was linked by an underlying technological continuity. Every building type—from the lowliest (and most recent) vernacular peasant house to the

163

PROSPECT,
MATERIALITY, AND
THE HORIZONS OF
POTENTIALITY ON
PARKTOWN RIDGE

monumental (and ancient) stone and marble edifices of the Acropolis and Forum—had its place within this continuity that made legible the nuances of use, status, and site. Continuity was achieved not only through the use of a consistent palette of locally found materials (and the augmentation of this consistency through weathering) but also through traditional ways of making. A continuous, adaptable architectural vocabulary based on local materials might have been a de facto characteristic of historic and vernacular building, but, as Baker intuited, in a newly annexed region without any vernacular to speak of, it could also be invented in new buildings to imply history, vernacular tradition, and hence, cultural belonging. It is ultimately through making—through material practice—that ideas (and cultures) become part of the world.

On moving to the Transvaal, Baker began tirelessly championing the development and use of local materials and became a staunch supporter of Florence Phillips's National Union, whose emphasis on local crafts is now largely forgotten as a strand of colonial national rhetoric. The Phillipses, following Ruskin and Morris, believed that well-designed and well-made objects had a beneficial effect on those who came into contact with them, and that "exemplary form" would in itself be a form of cultural uplift in a city like Johannesburg (the "Manchester of South Africa"), dominated as it was by mining, manufacturing, and the accumulation of wealth. They set up various cottage industries on their Woodbush estates that used local materials, and Florence argued for the inclusion of an Arts and Crafts collection in the planned Johannesburg Art Gallery and promised funding for an attached school of applied design (as opposed to fine arts), if this came about.[83] Local crafts and materials were essential in supplanting the "cheap bricks and thin iron" and eclectic mixture of imported styles and materials typical of the impermanent Rand architecture.[84] They were also necessary to cultivate skill, know-how, and the sense of the local. Craft helps construct identity because it always, simultaneously, constructs understanding of the physical world. In human artifacts, there are, properly speaking, no "natural" materials, only materials appropriated by humans from nature: all materials need to be worked in order to be extracted and made ready for use.[85] Hence, material's nature—and therefore its meaning as a quasi-subject—cannot be separated from the knowledge and techniques required to bring it into use, knowledge that is, in the end, also cultural.

All of this is implicit in the connections between unalienated labor, cultural authenticity, and natural aesthetics that Baker's architectural philosophy borrowed from Ruskin. While it is no surprise that Baker's large public buildings used carefully crafted local sandstone in a free classical style that recalled Palladio and Wren, the domestic equivalent of this in the Parktown houses had to be worked out *in situ*. While some of these houses were built from brick, Baker persuaded other more idealistic (and wealthier) clients to follow his own example and build in native stone, intentionally and expensively quarried from the same piece of land on which the house stood.[86] Baker's emphasis in his memoirs on these stone houses suggests that, along with the Union Buildings, he considered them to be the closest approximation of what he hoped to achieve in the Transvaal. Quarrying the same Ridge on which the Parktown houses were built grasped it in a directly physical way as an inhabited fragment of the larger regional landscape and brought the terrain's life in seasonal (and geologic) time under scrutiny.[87] Working the site in this way transcended visual appropriation; nature was transformed from something conceptual, ubiquitous, and distant

Pilrig and the Stone House newly completed, early 1900s, without gardens. Barrow Construction Company Photographic Collection, reproduced with permission.

into something close at hand and full of "necessary accidents."[88] The Ridge—and by extension, the larger Highveld landscape—became animated and known through tectonic appropriation and manipulation.

The transformative process whereby physical labor constitutively constructs knowledge about nature also constructs ideas about society. Baker's use of native stone may have seemed well-suited to houses situated on isolated, rocky sites (as the Parktown houses were), but it required skills not readily available in Johannesburg: Baker had to import stonemasons from England.[89] These houses, which "grew harmoniously out of the foundations of the ochreous, lichen-stained rocks" (and which were much imitated by others), helped naturalize a new colonial national country as part of a larger imperial social and technological order.[90] On one hand, they posited some kind of continuity between South Africanism and a long line of preindustrial societies deemed to be its forerunners.[91] On the other hand, these houses also demonstrated that it was precisely the transformative power of technique that lay at the heart of and justified imperialism's self-appointed civilizing role in Africa.[92] It was *European* skill, cultivated over the centuries, that would allow the unproductive and archaic African terrain to bloom and reveal its full potential. Thus, the stone-built houses rendered both the terrain *and* the European presence in it meaningful and comprehensible. That African stone, subjected to European expertise, yielded a workable building material not only demonstrated an underlying will to order in the landscape but also created new kinds of (practical) knowledge and identity that were simultaneously European and South African.[93]

In fact, the distinctive, simple, hammer-dressed stonework of Baker's houses was

The Stone House,
entrance view.
Barrow Construction
Company Photo-
graphic Collection,
reproduced with
permission.

a result of the discovery that the Parktown quartzite, while durable and close to hand, was also extremely hard to work.[94] The hierarchical modulation of cut, dressed, and semifinished stonework in Baker's Parktown houses and gardens expressed the potential nature of quartzite kopje stone itself.[95] It also conveyed a sense of a settled European identity coaxed out of the rock and the sometimes primitive care with which that identity was forced to fashion its new traditions.[96] Nor did the juxtaposition of imported timber (for woodwork, cabinetry, and furnishings) and locally derived stone necessarily detract from this effect. Indeed, it reinforced the notion that the larger landscape of South Africa was fundamentally a geological one, of earth and rocks rather than vegetation, and hence timeless, durable, and unchanging—precisely the qualities that a newly established society aspired to.[97] In the same way that the location and growth of the sprawling city itself was rendered inevitable by the reefs of gold that lay beneath its surface, the Parktown houses were rendered natural by the quarrying and transformation of their sites.[98] As objects that were simultaneously material and cultural because they embodied technique and labor, these rock-built houses were not dissimilar from the mine dumps then rising outside the city, which eventually came to be seen as emblematic icons of Johannesburg itself.

Nature, Nativism, and the Gardens of Rainless Winters

The incorporation of immanent natural forces of climate (through sensory effects and plan layout) and geology (through craft and construction) in Baker's Parktown

166

PROSPECT,
MATERIALITY, AND
THE HORIZONS OF
POTENTIALITY ON
PARKTOWN RIDGE

Timewell, stonework detail. Barrow Construction Company Photographic Collection, reproduced with permission.

houses becomes hard to isolate from the more overtly ideological questions of style and how the houses sat in the larger landscape. The vertical reciprocity with the landscape, achieved through material and sensual appropriation of local conditions, intersected with a horizontal reciprocity that engaged not only the limitless spaces of Africa but also the larger global imperialist spatiality of mobility, potentiality, and improvement. The Parktown gardens were crucial in connecting the rocky African platform, reconstituted in stone-built symmetry, with the private, continental view. Gardens are by their very nature ephemeral—not only always changing, but also easily lost—and very few of the original Parktown gardens survive today. Nevertheless, as we have seen, the garden played a key role in concatenating the Renaissance villa and the wilderness, and we know that in all his projects, Baker conceived buildings and gardens as part of a single schema. As in his houses, so in his gardens: Baker's designs were the exceptions that proved the rule of surrounding artificiality and eclecticism. From the limited documentation available, it seems that Baker's gardens eschewed the Victorian "gardenesque" that prevailed elsewhere on the Ridge and used a naturalistic formalism that posited a more constructive relationship between culture and nature, bringing garden and veld into a dialogue with each other.

This attention to the gardens was not unexpected. The colonial nationalist narrative of descent located the origins of white settlement in the planting of a garden (the Dutch East India Company's garden in Cape Town), and the Guild of Loyal Women had been founded primarily to sustain memory through the cultivation and beautification of grave sites.[99] Moreover, at the turn of the century, garden design had become a central topic in the culturalist discourse of nostalgic pastoralism in Britain, and it was inevitable that the making of gardens in colonial national South Africa would take on significant ideological overtones as well. Landscape design had already played a role in the construction of English (and British) cultural identity for nearly one hundred years before William Robinson's campaign to reform English gardening began in the 1860s, carrying ideological freight that included ideas of evolutionism, social reform, nationalism, the back-to-the-land movement, and even anti-imperialism.[100] In *The Wild Garden*, first published in 1871, Robinson mourned the loss of English ties to nature and the rural countryside and promoted use of wild and native plants, which "followed nature, the sole source of all design." Writing at a time when arable land was being rapidly converted into parklike country estates for the urban elite, Robinson expanded the repertoire of the garden to incorporate commonplace features of the rural landscape like ditches, hedgerows, and bogs, and he used planting that imitated the patterns of unimproved nature to disguise the transition from garden proper to the surrounding landscape. Denigrating formal planting, Robinson strove after an appearance of uncultivated, self-maintaining nature that concealed both neglect *and* care. Crucially, this quasi-Virgilian ideal required the resuscitation of old English plants, especially those associated with cottage and medieval gardens, and restrictions on the use of exotic and nonnative plants, except in specialized gardens reflecting different soil and microclimatic needs. Robinson saw the "wild garden" as a panacea for both the individual and the nation perceived to be suffering from the effects of industrial capitalism.[101] By the turn of the century, his theories had been embraced by the more progressive-minded gardeners like Gertrude Jekyll, whom Baker had worked with at Groote Schuur and knew through his connection with Lutyens.

Applying the Robinsonian equation of wildness with Englishness in Britain's overseas colonies was problematic. In the colonies, the native plants were never English, garden making was almost always bound up with sentimental memories of "home," the frame for the garden was not the rural English landscape, and the climate was often quite different.[102] At the same time, the horticultural arts were probably one of the most tellingly European ways white settlers could "hold the land for civilization."[103] In early twentieth-century South Africa, such contradictions between cultural memory, nativism, and improvement were further complicated by ambivalent attitudes toward the native landscape. Although indigenous flowers had first appeared for sale on the streets of Cape Town in the 1880s, and an interest in native plants was becom-

168

PROSPECT,
MATERIALITY, AND
THE HORIZONS OF
POTENTIALITY ON
PARKTOWN RIDGE

ing a hallmark of an educated white elite by the turn of the century, these plants were not horticulturally grown for several decades.[104] An appreciation of native plants was also not the same thing as wanting to live surrounded by the unimproved, native landscape. In the early 1900s, only an educated minority appreciated the Highveld's austerity, mystery, and "monotony."[105]

For many white South Africans, this landscape was still defined by its lack of seasonal change and ready poetic associations. Unlike in Europe, where trees were abundant, or parts of Australia, Canada, and the United States, where trees were cleared to make way for settlement, place making in South Africa could seldom rely on the foil of natural woodland. Early South African horticultural writers saw acclimating and planting nonnative trees as an essential part of European settlement, especially on farms, where trees helped differentiate the home site from miles of "bare veld."[106] Like European settlers elsewhere, white South Africans generally construed tree planting as partaking in an old semipagan tradition of forests as primal birthplaces of nations.[107] Many saw the progress of civilization in South Africa as inseparable from "the extended use of trees and shrubs [that made] the home and its precincts beautiful, [especially as] the country and the climate respond so well and under so many different conditions."[108] Almost by definition, this precluded the use of native trees and plants, with their stark, "queer" habits and dull colors.

The Highveld's lack of attractive, fast-growing indigenous trees meant that settlement was closely followed by experiments to find nonnative species that would flourish and survive there.[109] Some of these species, such as eucalyptus, poplar, cypress, wattles, willow, casuarina, tamarind, and jacaranda, not only survived but grew better than in their homelands, and by 1900, some had become so ubiquitous in the rural and urban environment that they were considered native by those with no botanical knowledge.[110] This process was already well advanced at the Cape, where nonnative trees and garden plants had been imported since the seventeenth century, mostly from Europe, which had a similar winter-rainfall climate. Indeed, some of these European cultivars thrived so well at the Cape that they survived there long after they had died out in Europe.[111] There is little doubt that the success at the Cape of plants like the (English) oak and the (Mediterranean) cluster pine and stone pine contributed significantly to perceptions of the Cape as a long-settled, quasi-European region and heightened its perceptual difference from parts of the country where a quite different palette of trees flourished, which originated in non-European, summer-rainfall regions of South America, Asia, and Australia.

As we saw in chapter 2, contradictions between cultural memory, nativism, and improvement accompanied the establishment of South Africa's first botanical garden in 1913, when the uniqueness (and vulnerability) of indigenous flora was beginning to be understood and harnessed to the politics of nation building. These tensions manifested themselves in a different way on the early twentieth-century Rand, where the earlier pristine emptiness of the veld was being encroached upon by the maturing eucalyptus trees of the Sachsenwald, isolated pockets of suburban development, and the continuous avenue of wattles (planted in 1910) that stretched northward along the Johannesburg-Pretoria Road. These same tensions and contradictions were also evident in the handful of Parktown gardens, often those of Baker's clients, which tried to embrace a Robinsonian integration of the local and the wild and promote a less-

Ednam, garden with pergola and a mixture of nonnative and native plants. Barrow Construction Company Photographic Collection, reproduced with permission.

alienated relationship with the native landscape. These Highveld gardens were milestones, perhaps even more so than those at the Cape, in the development of what Fairbridge called an art of gardening that combined "the climate and flowers of South Africa with the accumulated wisdom . . . which has made English gardens the loveliest in the world [to produce effects] beyond our dreams."[112] Like the rock-built houses they surrounded, the making of these gardens involved a reconstitution of the landscape that was visually self-effacing. The blasting out of the native rock, the importation of tons of soil, and the construction of extensive stone retaining walls, terraces, and pergolas was combined with native plants and rock gardens to create a seamless integration of house with its Ridge-top setting.[113]

Again, Florence Phillips, with her wealth and cultural activism, was in the vanguard. An ardent exponent of native flora, Florence Phillips was a central figure in the promotion of the conservation, protection, documentation, and cultivation of native flora as part of a broad cultural rhetoric of South Africanism. It is no surprise to find that Phillips's garden at Villa Arcadia became one in which the play between imperial Englishness and South African nativism was most active, and it soon became famous, admiringly referred to by authors and frequently opened to visitors (see color plate 18).[114] In establishing her second garden in Johannesburg, Phillips worked closely with Baker, and although few records survive of their partnership, there is little doubt that she influenced his work on other Parktown gardens. Northwards, Villa Arcadia, and Glenshiel, three of Baker's significant Parktown houses, also treated their rocky sites in a way that has been described as "deference to nature while conquering it."[115] These sites did not present an uncomplicated sequential transition from the man-made house to the wild of the unimproved veld. At Northwards, natural outcrops protruded

The Stone House with mature garden. Barrow Construction Company Photographic Collection, reproduced with permission.

171

Glenshiel garden with mixed plantings. Barrow Construction Company Photographic Collection, reproduced with permission.

through the architecture of walls and broad stairways, and the relationship between house and site was established by the broad viewing terrace seen in the foreground of the photographs in Fairbridge's book. At Villa Arcadia, too, although the house was quasi-Mediterranean in style, civilization and wildness are dramatically juxtaposed. As at the Union Buildings, the transition between the veld behind the house and the house itself is made by the court, whose opposing walls are made of native rock and man-made architecture.[116]

All the Parktown gardens exploited the abundant labor available on the Rand to overcome the challenges of gardening in the "land of rainless winter" (Fairbridge's description) and create verdant lawns and luxurious masses of English flowers that recalled the well-kept gardens of home. If they did employ native plantings as part of their cultivated garden, these were usually relegated to the lower slopes and outer margins. At Baker houses like Villa Arcadia, Glenshiel, Ednam, and Northwards, however, native plants were brought into the heart of the garden, close to the house. Complementing Baker's architectural use of the "accommodating sandstone of the Transvaal," the formal Italian rose and herb gardens at Villa Arcadia were interspersed with the plants of the veld and bush. Other parts of the twenty-six-acre property were given over to aloes, cacti, euphorbia, mesembryanthemum, and native trees—which the Phillipses collected in the veld and on their Woodbush estate—to create a bird sanctuary. At a time when horticultural novelties usually meant imported exotics, this use of veld plants alongside familiar denizens of the English flower garden implicitly raised native plants to equivalent aesthetic status and provided a natural expression of the fusion between these two worlds. These parts of the Baker gardens fitted the one category of horticultural "impurity" Robinson approved of, and that he saw as augmenting rather than working against nature: the garden determined by "meeting the wants" of the plants that might come from different parts of the world, in which new but fundamentally natural (that is, ecological) groupings were made.[117] Especially before introduced trees came to dominate the Ridge and screen the houses from each other, these native plants of the veld would have also mediated between the garden and the rugged native landscape that terminated the view—an effect that was especially powerful at Government House, another elevated, north-facing Baker house forty miles away in Pretoria.

Like his rock-built houses, Baker's gardens gave physical expression to a nexus between the wild African veld and the nostalgic associations and comforting domesticity of English memory, and spoke simultaneously of imperial connections and national distinctiveness. To the degree that these gardens became the most important component connecting and separating the Parktown houses to and from the veld, the far-seeing continental view from the houses was increasingly haunted by the ambiguously competing associations of paradise and degeneration.

The Veld Prospect and the Limits of Potential

On Parktown Ridge during the early twentieth century, an array of cultural phenomena and practices—gardens and buildings, views and craft, topography and travel, nature and culture—converged to nurture a new kind of identity. Fusing in one locale somatic, perceptual, existential, and cognitive space, the Ridge functioned in the larger South African context as a concentrated modification of territory that

Gardens at Government House, Pretoria, looking toward the veld. Transnet Heritage Museum Library Photographic Collection, neg. #46655; reproduced with permission.

engaged circuits of collective memory.[118] This fusion lent the Ridge the qualities of a visionary solution, a situation in which projections of the imagination (imaginative intentionality) and naturally occurring events or objects become closely aligned.[119] Topographical positions that afforded continental views suggested an orderly hierarchy of nature; building sites provided the means for their own transformation;[120] and native and the nonnative (people, plants, and architecture) flourished alongside each other.

Although there were places in Britain at this time that created similar topographical effects,[121] the Ridge's capacity to mediate a sense of reciprocity between "imaginative intentionality" and "naturally occurring event" was of a different order. On the Ridge, close-at-hand material engagement of the African landscape was complemented by the seductive view of that same landscape's emptiness and potentiality. Life in the Ridge houses brought together, within a single horizon of experience, unmediated sensual relations with nature and untrammeled access to it. Put differently, it yoked together what philosopher Edward Casey calls the two fundamental (and interdependent) ways of being in the world, "here-ness" and "there-ness."[122] As in Buchan's Woodbush, a nexus between these two fundamental poles of desire in a single locale provided a profoundly reflexive, poetic sense of inhabitation. Poised between the city and the veld, the Ridge afforded a prospect, in all senses of the word— simultaneously a vantage point on, an opinion about, and a manifestation of the landscape of colonial national South Africanism.[123]

This provisional reconciliation between the corporeal and the ideological was a product of a traveling subjectivity, which is neither implicated nor powerless (and in fact is sometimes powerful precisely because it is not implicated). Central to imperial thinking and latent in colonial national identity, this subjectivity is also cognate with the unresolved juxtapositions typical of metaphoric situations. A heightened sense of agency characteristic of traveling subjectivity thrives on the persistence of the conditions of becoming, and the landscape "prospect" afforded by the Ridge was contingent upon an absence of substantive experience of the African terrain. Sustained by the vision of members of the metropolitan establishment who visited the enclave, the residents of Parktown could imagine an all-encompassing disposition toward the landscape as a metaphorical correlative of their own identity. From the Ridge, a "natural" continuity between the visionary and the material, the universal and the particular, not to mention the future and the past, seemed gratifyingly, if fleetingly, possible in the early decades of the century.

One can best understand this by returning to the photographs in Fairbridge's book. Taken in the 1920s, these images were probably commissioned by Baker, and seem intended to capture an experience that was, in fact, hard to achieve at the time.[124] They manipulate the point of view from the Ridge so as to re-create a spatial relationship that Baker might have hoped to achieve two decades earlier. The continuity between the distant landscape and the architectural platform on which the photographer (and, therefore, the viewer) stands reaches for, rather than establishes, a sense of belonging and connection.[125] (Where a vertical opening has no threshold, as in these photographs, the link between the experiencing subject and landscape becomes especially strong.) At the same time, however, the terrain framed in these images seems curiously insubstantial and ephemeral. The foreground of house and garden obscures most of the landscape below, and the Highveld has been effectively reduced to the restless sky and the sharp line of the northern horizon. The contrast between foreground and background is that of reassuring solidity and tantalizing evanescence. Like the roughly worked quartzite stone of which the houses were built and the native plants that coexisted with English domestic plants in their gardens, the sense of place represented in these Ridge houses manifested both the labor necessary to bring them into being, and the incompleteness of that labor. The power of these images is metaphorical, rooted in the fact that imaginative interpretation of the material world occurs aphoristically, through a conjoining of the dissimilar without resolution.[126] They retrospectively capture the way the early twentieth-century Parktown Ridge had been both a physical place *and* an imaginary place, a domain in which the underlying contradictions between *arriviste*, "civilizing" imperialism and the romance of the illimitable veld coexisted, unchallenged, in a dialectical relationship. It was precisely this incompleteness and contingency that travelers, writers, artists, and other cultural commentators found so compelling.

Such visionary metaphorical conjunctions are, by definition, fleeting; their affective power is grounded in historical circumstances and tends to diminish over time, either because they persist and become taken for granted, or because the material objects and dialectical relationships they refer to fade from view. Prospects such as those from Parktown Ridge, lying as they do at the intersection of time and space, are stalked by change. By the 1920s, the middle ground of the Sachsenwald[127] and

the open veld had been infiltrated by suburban development that blended almost imperceptibly with the maturing gardens of the Ridge, and the clear concatenation of the three natures had vanished. Baker's photographer sensed that the imaginative arc between civilized foreground and the sublime limitlessness of the horizon was in fact no longer visible without careful positioning of the camera. By this time too, the *mentalité* of those who lived on the Ridge had also changed. Many of the original inhabitants had either left South Africa or become embroiled in the mundane challenges of governing a country in which emergent Afrikaner nationalism was challenging the ideals of colonial nationalism. Although the Ridge may have hidden the growing shantytowns of dissatisfied white and black labor to the south, it could not screen its inhabitants from the political demands emerging there, nor the sounds of unrest. Thus, not only the landscape before the Ridge, but also the ideological underpin-

175

PROSPECT,
MATERIALITY, AND
THE HORIZONS OF
POTENTIALITY ON
PARKTOWN RIDGE

nings that gave it poignancy slowly dissipated. The metaphoric viewpoint the Ridge afforded finally disappeared in the 1960s, when the enclave's integrity was destroyed by the construction of several large Nationalist government institutions and a major highway.

After Baker: The Emergence of a National Architecture?

What of Baker's "architecture which established a nation"? Like Buchan's prognostications about rural settlement, Baker's vision played out in unpredictable ways, realized as much in the breach as the observance. Baker's office became the preeminent architectural practice in South Africa until World War I and was responsible for an extraordinary proportion of the significant building projects undertaken during this period. Although the first South African school of architecture was established at the University of the Witwatersrand immediately after World War I, Baker's ideas influenced the development the country's architecture for several decades after he left to work in India and Britain in 1912.[128] The ubiquity of his work, as well as its material and aesthetic qualities and its high moral earnestness, appealed to the inherently conservative nature of white settler society, and by the 1920s, Baker had become an important cultural figure, much feted on his occasional visits to South Africa. Baker's influence was extended by the fact that many of the most gifted younger generation of architects worked in his various practices in South Africa and Britain some of them won the prestigious architectural prize named for him, which awarded them a year in the epicenter of Graeco-Roman classicism, Rome. All of these factors combined to encourage the use of a debased, hybrid, classical-cum-Cape Dutch style as a default South African architectural vocabulary until the 1930s. (Baker's work at Rhodes House at Oxford in 1931, and South Africa House in London in 1933, when his powers were declining, reinforced the national connotations of this kind of architecture.)[129] Even Gordon Leith, one of the most talented interwar South African architects and a vociferous proponent of a national style of architecture, did not diverge very much from Baker's design principles.[130]

As in the world of fine arts, in architecture local forms of expression continued to be influenced by current European ideas. Since the earliest days, South African archi-

"The Huts,"
Riviera, Killarney
(Leith & Partners).
Barrow Construction
Company photo-
graphic collection;
reproduced with
permission.

tects had either studied or worked (and often both) in Britain, and these professional links were further reinforced once architecture became an academic subject.[131] The traveling subjectivity in the architectural profession was reinforced by World War I, which also brought about a significant increase in the appreciation and evolution of regional expressions of architecture, in South Africa as in other combatant nations. Several of those who would dominate South African architecture from the 1920s onward had fought in Europe and the Middle East between 1914 and 1918, and they returned to South Africa with firsthand experience of many different landscapes and architectures as well as with renewed appreciation of local conditions and aesthetic inheritances.

Toward the end of the 1920s, there was increasing interest in a less colonial and more national style of architecture.[132] Although this movement quickly diverged into two or three different streams, all were in a sense inspired by Baker's arguments that a plain, unadorned architecture rooted in the fundamentals of good building rather than overt "style or prejudice" had an important role to play in building a coherent national self-image.[133] This reading of Baker's architecture came from Rex Martienssen, the leader of a small group of progressive young Transvaal architects with links to the University of the Witwatersrand, who tried in the 1930s to develop a frankly modernist style of architecture that drew on the internationalist theories of Le Corbusier. Others, like the Afrikaner Gerard Moerdijk, saw a uniquely South African architecture evolving along similar lines to the national romanticism that had flourished in different northern European countries since 1895. As in other areas of cultural life at this time, this discourse about a uniquely South African architecture refracted the continually evolving relationship between Britain and South Africa, with sometimes surprising consequences. It was to be expected that the increasingly nationalist artist Jan Hendrik Pierneef, in his crusade for an "egte Afrikaanse boustyl" (authentic Afrikaans architectural style) in the Afrikaner magazine *Die Boerevrou*, would reject Baker's architecture as the "building style of the enemy," but not that he would also dismiss Cape Dutch architecture as "un-Afrikaans." This reveals just how thoroughly the Old Cape, one of the foundations of Baker's work, had become associated with colonial national South Africanism by the early 1930s.

177
PROSPECT,
MATERIALITY, AND
THE HORIZONS OF
POTENTIALITY ON
PARKTOWN RIDGE

MRS. EVERARD'S LONELY CAREER

The Komati Valley and the Depiction of Nostalgic Displacement

> Though . . . "double exile" status does seem to heighten an awareness of spatial
> aspects of emotional states, to some extent everyone is an "exile" sometimes. In
> the case of those constructed in whatever form of the feminine, therefore defined
> as off-center, there are too many situations in which they must struggle to think in
> language which is not designed for them, searching in their dreams for the space
> which will fit them, yearning for a space in which to dwell comfortably.
>
> —Pamela Shurmer-Smith, "Cixous' Space: Sensuous Space in Women's Writing"

In December 1927, Bertha Everard wrote from the Transvaal to her older sister in
Europe: "I have decided never to show any more pictures anywhere in Africa. I get
such ridiculous notices, and it is such a terrible expense sending about. No one even
likes my best work and the other is so stale now."[1] The despairing tone of this letter was understandable. Seventeen years before, Everard's large landscape painting
Mid-winter on the Komati had been awarded the Gold Medal in Painting at the first
exhibition of the National Union of South African Arts and Crafts in Johannesburg,
organized by Florence Phillips to celebrate the declaration of union.[2] Although she
was virtually unknown at the time, one critic described Everard's paintings as "pictures of the veld so true, so vivid in their burning brilliance that judges, critics and
public have one opinion of them. . . . [S]he has caught the heat and atmosphere and
brilliance of South Africa in a marvellous manner."[3] Although Everard continued
to paint the same landscape, and exhibited her work frequently, few of these later
paintings evoked much critical enthusiasm within South Africa, and fewer still were
sold.[4] It was more often than not in London or Paris that this later work received ac-
colades matching those first made in Johannesburg. Indeed, her work was deemed of
sufficient quality in London to warrant inclusion in an exhibition alongside the likes
of Monet, Manet, Matisse, and Cezanne. It was not until the 1930s, when Everard had
virtually given up painting, that local opinion began to be more receptive to her work,

and only in the 1960s was she finally recognized as one of the finest interpreters of the South African landscape.

As work of undoubted quality, painted during the heyday of landscape in white South Africa, Everard's oeuvre raises provocative questions about the relationship between landscape painting and the construction of national identity, and reminds us that such relationships are seldom straightforward. When she was writing her letter in 1927, Everard was no doubt well aware of another innovative South African landscape painter who was receiving national recognition: Jan Hendrik Pierneef. A few years younger than Everard, and also working in a style that challenged the dominant artistic taste, Pierneef was becoming popular among the South African white establishment in the 1920s. His career was launched by the commission of twenty-eight large landscape murals for the main concourse of the new Johannesburg railway station, which opened in 1930.[5] Within ten years, Pierneef would become a revered "painter of the nation," commissioned to paint many different nationally significant projects, a popular and influential speaker on all aspects of the arts, and the first artist to receive the medal of the Suid Afrikaanse Akademie for Wetenskap en Kuns (South African Academy of Science and Arts).[6] Pierneef's success suggests that the business of mediating a shared imaginary geography is more than simply a matter of subject, artistic quality, or style. It is also determined by many other factors, such as how the paintings resonate within cultural practices and structures of seeing immanent in a given society, as well as the social structures and networks that determine how paintings are exhibited, reproduced, and discussed.

Despite Everard's lack of initial recognition, her work offers useful insights into the relationship between landscape painting and the white South African geographical imagination. Like most artists, Everard had a heightened sensitivity to the physical world around her. Her sensitivity derived from a unique perspective on that world: as a woman farmer with a comprehensive working knowledge of one part of rural South Africa, Everard was not only eminently suited to create an "art that grew from the soil" and that contributed to the construction of white South African identity, but there is good reason to think that she aspired to do so. The scale and emotive content (if not the subject matter) of much of her work was of the kind usually destined for display in galleries and museums and interpretation by critics and connoisseurs (notwithstanding her self-deprecating protestations). Everard also always preferred selling her paintings to public galleries or large institutions rather than to private collectors.[7]

Everard's lack of public recognition cannot, of course, be separated from the visual and cultural economies that supported landscape painting in early twentieth-century South Africa, which were limited by an absence of public support for the arts and the conservative tastes of the country's early art patrons. Although these patrons saw landscape as an appropriate subject of indigenous art, they demanded little of painting other than that it be a romantic or naturalistic depiction of what they could already see around them, preferably the landscape of the old Cape. During the 1920s, however, this conservative hegemony began to weaken. The Rand's growth as an economic as well as cultural and intellectual center led to rivalry between Cape Town and Johannesburg for leadership in the arts and encouraged a new interest in paintings that did not depict the Cape landscape. Lone voices began to promote not only

Impressionism and Post-Impressionism, but also the Fauvism of Van Gogh, Gauguin, and others. Artists like Maggie Laubser and Irma Stern brought an explicitly Expressionist style directly from Germany to South Africa in the early 1920s, and an autonomous, albeit short-lived, South African Institute of Art, intended to promote a national school of art, held its first national conference in 1925. Public acceptance of locally based modernism did not occur until the mid-1930s, however, when a new South African Academy of Art in Johannesburg was established with close links to the modern architectural movement based at the University of the Witwatersrand.[8]

Although they had little contact with each other, both Pierneef and Everard were part of this emerging generation of artists seeking to move beyond academic-naturalistic depictions of the Western Cape and find ways of depicting the broader South African landscape. Both adapted contemporary European artistic ideas for their work, and both were primarily landscapists concerned with finding ways to capture the character of the Transvaal, in particular. To this degree, both could be seen as participating in the imaginary project of naturalizing the nation and contributing to the cult of the veld. Despite these similarities, Everard's and Pierneef's work diverged considerably in character and effect, due to differences in their training as well as their personal circumstances, which inculcated quite different subjective attitudes toward landscape in general and to motif in particular.

Everard was trained in Impressionism, a school of painting that, although considered avant-garde in its day, built on long-standing traditions in European painting, including the notion that landscape uniquely embodied the relationship between the man-made and the natural, wildness and cultivation. Impressionism was particularly concerned with testing how the disruptions, inconsistencies, and contradictions modern life brought about in the landscape could be depicted without destroying this unique relationship.[9] It also attempted to grasp the revisioning of space and matter that occurred at the end of the nineteenth century, when the traditional view of space as "an inert void in which objects existed" gave way to the conception of it as "active and full."[10] This new spatiality placed especial emphasis on the relationship between artist and subject: background took on a positive, active function of equal importance with the subject or motif and demanded the full attention of the artist.[11]

The relationship between viewer and landscape subject became a persistent problematic in Everard's work. She followed European artistic trends avidly, chiefly through art journals, albeit in an era before color reproduction, though she did see some contemporary work firsthand when she visited Europe in 1911. Her interest in new ideas in art can be traced in her correspondence with her sister (also an artist), which often touches on the arguments of a group of painters then emerging in France who were questioning the principles of Impressionism. Although Everard did not fully embrace these revisionist ideas until she visited Europe again in the 1920s, her work was nevertheless deemed good enough to exhibit alongside French avant-garde painters in London long before this. Ultimately, though, Everard's work does not fit tidily into discussions of painting as a teleologically unfolding sequence of schools, traditions, and influences. Her approach to landscape painting was driven as much by her evolving personal response to the world she inhabited as it was by the desire to find an indigenous expression of contemporary European artistic theories.

Cultural and geographical distance from the metropole and the self-consciously nationalist discourse in emerging nations place unusual burdens on artists striving to be international in scope yet to speak with a local voice. To describe a colonial artist's work as "indigenous" and "authentic" can be tantamount to calling it either "of national significance" or "of no international significance whatsoever," depending on who is doing the characterizing. Others argue that colonial artists are never as provincial as when they are ignoring the particularities of local experience and following metropolitan models too slavishly. The question of significance is further complicated if the colonial artists see their primary audience as those living in the metropole and tailor their subject matter, style, and vision accordingly. While this is a matter about which no satisfactory conclusions can be drawn, it is obvious that discussing colonial art in terms of schools, traditions, and influences obscures the uniquely inventive, synthetic nature of colonial praxis and the colonial artists' struggle to find a new and convincing language for representing this experience in their chosen medium. Paul Carter has proposed that, instead of dismissing colonial artists' use of metropolitan techniques or styles as an inability to see, it might be more helpful to construe this as a local way of constructing a way of seeing, a provisional strategy for understanding unfamiliar subjects, which may lead to moments of invention or coincidence.[12]

At the same time, it is important to remember that even provisional, experimental depictions of spaces and places never depicted before, once painted, have the potential to become highly charged representations that disseminate implied subjective relationships with that landscape. As Cosgrove has argued, the landscape image—fundamentally, one individual's view of the world at a given moment in time, when the arrangement of the constituent forms is pleasing, uplifting, or in some way linked to their psychological state—tends to mediate a universally, or paradigmatic, validity for that state; in other words, claiming for it the status of reality.[13] It is therefore to Everard's personal subjectivity as an artist, her psychological state, that we turn first in our consideration of the discursive effects of her paintings.

A Woman's Place in a White Man's Country

Although she appears to have had few close ties with the proponents of colonial nationalism, Everard's own life, and lifeworld, exemplified many of its ideals.[14] Although born in the Natal Colony, Bertha King grew up in England. After studying music in Vienna, she returned to England to study art in 1893, and over the next few years she attended various art schools in London before spending two years living and painting in Cornwall.[15] In 1898, at the age of twenty-nine, she became an art teacher and, a few months after the end of the South African War, immigrated to the Transvaal Colony, brought by one of Milner's immigration schemes to teach in Pretoria. While spending her first holidays in the Carolina district, a remote corner of the Highveld known for its stark beauty and bracing climate, she met Charles Everard, then a forty-nine-year-old bachelor. An Englishman by birth, Charles had lived in the ZAR since the 1880s and owned a successful trading store at a place called Bonnefoi.[16] Bertha and Charles became engaged and married in mid-1903. Upon moving to Bonnefoi, Bertha set about designing and building them a proper homestead. Over the next few years, she also gave birth to three children, the last being born in 1909, the same year that she painted *Peace of Winter* (see color plate 19).

During the following decades, numerous enterprises other than painting com-

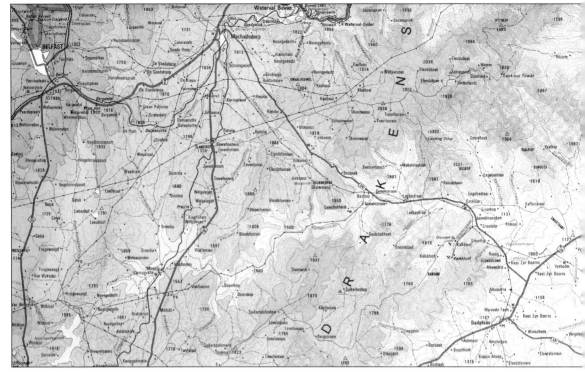

Map of upper Komati River valley. South African Government Printer, 1:250,000 series; #2530; reproduced with permission of Chief Directorate, Surveys and Mapping; w3sli.wcapegov.za.

peted for Everard's time. Apart from running a large household in a remote area and educating her three children at home, she persuaded her husband to buy a series of farms, which she developed herself. Everard's involvement with these farms was not merely supervisory (a difficult enough role for a white woman); diaries and letters record how she herself labored alongside her African workers plowing, fencing, dipping cattle, digging irrigation furrows, and building roads.[17] The most important of these farms was Lekkerdraai, which straddled a sinuous stretch of the Komati River about 60 kilometers from Bonnefoi and some 400 meters lower in elevation. From 1911 onward, this was used as a winter grazing farm and a retreat for Everard and her children, where many of her paintings were done. More farms were acquired in the late 1920s, which she ran with assistance from her by-then grown-up children.[18] Everard was also a devout Christian, passionately involved with missionary work among the Africans of the district, and for many years she ran a school for farm workers' children. She designed and built a small chapel at Bonnefoi and trained a succession of African catechists to serve in it. Everard also oversaw the design, construction, and furnishing of a new Anglican church in the nearby town of Carolina and erected a huge wooden cross on the hills above Lekkerdraai, where it was a regional landmark for many years.[19] Despite these many activities, Everard still defined herself as an artist and viewed her surroundings primarily through an artist's eyes.[20]

The landscape Everard encountered in 1902 was the same austere Transvaal Highveld that so entranced Buchan in the same year.[21] The armature of her world, though, was not the liminal *temenos* of the Woodbush, but the Komati, a perennial river, rare in South Africa, which rises in the Highveld and flows down to the Lowveld and the Indian Ocean some three hundred kilometers to the east (see color plate 20). Bonnefoi

MRS.
EVERARD'S
LONELY
CAREER

overlooks a shallow bowl on the Komati's upper reaches and owed its existence to a convergence of old wagon routes about a mile from a permanent stone bridge across the river. Bonnefoi was thus situated on the edge of the Highveld plateau. To the west, its empty vastness stretched for hundreds of kilometers toward Johannesburg, to the east lay the great Drakensberg Escarpment and the Lowveld. Here, the Komati carves a deep valley into the landscape as it descends some thousand feet in twenty miles, providing the route for the old wagon road that Everard took every winter from Bonnefoi to Lekkerdraai (see color plates 21, 22, and 23). Unlike the escarpment to the north and south, though, which is unbroken and dramatic, the "Berg" to the east of Bonnefoi is carved by rivers and streams into a series of undulating valleys and low passes, surrounded by restless, high horizons and peaks with ancient African names. Thus, Everard's world spanned both the "delightful monotony" of the Highveld and the more complex, dramatic topography of the Berg. Like the Woodbush (or indeed Parktown), this region encouraged a sense of inhabiting a frontier of civilization. Although hardly typical Highveld, the Komati valley was contiguous with the Highveld's oceanic grasslands, a territory in which the problems of depicting monotony, size, and light remained pertinent. This particular part of the Berg had also never been subjected to the composing eye of the painter (or indeed, photographer) before Everard's arrival.

Although she had servants, Everard's opportunities to paint were limited by her many different responsibilities. Probably because of these many responsibilities she was subject to frequent bouts of ill health, self-doubt, and depression. She traveled frequently to other parts of South Africa, especially after 1919, when her children left the farm to go to school in Bloemfontein and Cape Town. From 1922 to 1926 she left South Africa altogether, living and traveling in Europe with her sister and overseeing the education of her two daughters, who followed in her footsteps to study music, art, and agriculture. During these four years, first in England and then in France and Italy, Everard became intensely involved in contemporary European artistic culture, visiting exhibitions of new work to learn more about the latest theories and experimenting with them in her own paintings. After her return to South Africa, she traveled less but continued her energetic involvement in teaching, farming, and building.[22] Her painting also became increasingly sporadic; although she lived on Bonnefoi until her death in 1965, her last recorded work dates from about 1936, when she was 63, and she spent the last part of her life farming and raising horses.

Bertha Everard's life, which encompassed the cultural intensity of the centers of European culture and a Highveld outpost so isolated it only received electricity in the 1980s, gave her a very particular perspective on South African life and landscape. Her constant contact with Europe encouraged her to see South Africa both in terms of what she had left behind and what was actually there in front of her. Like Smuts, her perception of the veld was conditioned by an intimate, direct knowledge of its climate, soil, and vegetation, and like him, she viewed it in quasi-religious terms. As an educated, English-speaking, female Milner settler, though, living in an upland rural area, Everard's life was also structured by the roles assigned to women in the white man's country of colonial South Africa. In South Africa, as elsewhere, new imperialism gave women special responsibility, as mothers, homemakers, and educators, for implanting and domesticating British civilization, especially in temperate rural districts like the eastern Highveld, where European women and children were expected to thrive.[23] Such healthful regions, it was thought, provided numerous opportunities for outdoor life and physical exercise, and the ideal imperial homemaker was one who devoted her time and energy to an array of activities outside the house and in the community.[24]

The actual lifeworld of educated English-speaking settler women living like Everard on the Highveld in the 1910s, 1920s, and 1930s bore only a passing resemblance to the tightly knit rural society envisaged by proponents of Milnerite Closer Settlement. Even without the dwindling of immigration, the shift to extensive, capital-intensive nonarable farming and the increasing concentration of agricultural land in the hands of a few whites, who derived their wealth from nonagricultural sources, meant that rural districts were thinly populated.[25] Although never wealthy, the Everards were caught up in these transformations: most of their income derived from Charles's store at Bonnefoi (see color plate 24), and the additional farms were bought largely for purposes of prospecting for gold and platinum. (One of the reasons Bertha needed to work so hard was to make them profitable once their lack of mineral potential had been discovered in the 1930s.) As a woman and a homemaker, though, Everard's perspective on the Highveld would probably have been less concerned with capital and land accumulation than with the practical and social aspects of daily life.

Some sense of what these were is provided by another educated English-speaking woman living on the Highveld at this time, Madeline Alston, in her book *From the Heart of the Veld*.[26] Alternately inspirational and disciplinary, Alston's sentiments closely echo those in Everard's own letters and were probably widely shared.[27] Alston depicts the Highveld as a lifeworld in which the practical, imaginative, and perceptual were inextricably intertwined, largely due to the effects of distance. Long journeys, usually slow and arduous, were a central feature of life, and socializing was difficult. Women in particular were thrown onto their own resources; the distances separating farms brought both loneliness and lack of intellectual stimulation. The effects of this isolation were not all negative, however. Being forced to travel had a "broadening influence on the mind"; "movement and intelligence" were interdependent.[28] Isolation from peers, combined with perceptions of African and Boer neighbors as irremediably other, also lent ordinary objects heightened interest ("on the veld, a house is a landmark as well as a home"),[29] and prosaic cultural practices, habits and traditions an overdetermined poignancy. Living on the veld afforded a "joy in work which industrialism had killed" and a sense of autonomy and self-sufficiency that was contrasted with the helplessness of metropolitan counterparts, trapped as they were by "time-wasting social duties," "unnatural convention," and "formality."[30] In Alston's book, we see how the contrapuntal lifeworld of white colonial national settlers was heightened for women, whose lives were almost exclusively centered on the home: "the veld reveals that the intellect as well as the body is strengthened, not weakened, by the performance of domestic tasks."[31]

Alston describes a domestic perspective on the frontier of civilization, shaped by the resistances of time and space. For white settler women like Everard, living on the veld was at once exhilarating and incarcerating.[32] Makers simultaneously of "home" and "Home," these women inhabited a lifeworld in which there was little to counter the imaginative juxtaposition of remembered, distant places and physical engagement with an unspoiled environment. These two poles—England, the "multitudinous, throbbing" outside world of "ideas and discussion and the life of a community," with its tradition, beauty, and history held in perpetual focus via a three-week mail; and the spartan, self-sufficient, confined yet spacious world of the veld—played off and fed each other.[33] Tellingly, Alston never favors either of these poles as home: the "broadening influence" of travel is weighed against the "sense of social responsibility . . . [of] home-loving people"; similarly, while "change may suggest ideas . . . rapid locomotion [may] dissipate ideas by too much change."[34] In this irresolution, we see the peculiar spatiality called into being by colonial nationalism, which reconfigured the relationship between local and the imperial in such a way that London and the Home Counties felt closer to the veld than Johannesburg or Cape Town. The landscape of the Highveld farm was apprehended with the sort of intensity and clarity normally associated with displacement and homelessness. Thus, an innately liminal identity went hand in hand with, and perhaps fostered, an equally strong sense of belonging to the particular district in which they lived.

The Painter's Subjectivity and the Effects of Painting

Most of what we know of Everard's life and work suggests that she too inhabited a contrapuntal subjectivity that combined feelings of betweenness with a heightened attachment to the local.[35] A restless, intense person with an ambivalent attitude toward domesticity in all its forms, Everard constantly looked to Europe for intellectual stimulation, yet was deeply involved with her own family and farms.[36] She had little taste for public life or South African cities and often fled to Lekkerdraai to escape the constant flow of visitors to Bonnefoi. She traveled extensively but never learned to drive (though, like Virginia Woolf, she loved cars because they allowed her to escape the world), and she was happiest riding a horse across the veld.[37] In some respects, her itinerancy recalls that of a whole generation of colonial women who felt most comfortable on a ship on the high seas, a space between countries, removed from the structures generated by work, home, extended kinship, and politics.[38] All of this poses questions about how this subjectivity, or psychological state, might have become embedded in her paintings, questions that are especially interesting when we recall how, particularly at the turn of the twentieth century, landscape painting functioned as "a paradigmatic site of individual experience."[39]

The history of European landscape painting is generally told as a story of the disappearance of the figure and the erasure of narrative legibility in favor of the pure icon of nature.[40] Over the course of the nineteenth century, the subjectivity mediated by landscape painting increasingly became that of freedom of movement in an open countryside, uninhibited by landowners.[41] By the turn of the twentieth century, this progressive erasure of an implied relationship between land and owner had reached a point where the central issue in landscape representation was the relationship of the spectator to that which the picture shows—or to that which was conceived as picturable.[42] The disappearance of an obvious narrative and motif (captured by the question "what are we looking at?") raised the question of how the relationship between notional viewer and landscape—the means by which individuals identify with the depicted landscape—was to be figured. The significance of the disappearance of an explicit subject-object relationship in European landscape painting is revealed by tracing its manifestation in colonial landscape paintings. Jonathan Bordo has observed that initially, colonial landscape paintings included a witnessing human figure, which captured the crucial historical moment when the before of the landscape as wilderness was posited by a "sighting as testimony."[43] This single, mediating figure, however, threatened to contaminate the landscape *as* wilderness, and by the end of the nineteenth century, it started to disappear from paintings, until all that was left was the wilderness itself.[44] In these later paintings, Bordo argues, the erasure of both human traces and figural witnesses made the landscape both inviting and reassuring: inviting because the empty land apparently belonged to no one, reassuring because its aestheticizing distance froze time.

By this time in Europe, though, it had become evident that the responses elicited by paintings transcended mere acts of (re)cognition and were better described in terms of effects and effectiveness. Distinguishing a painting's noncognitive from its cognitive content meant attending not only to what it depicted and how it was painted, but also to how these two aspects of the painting supported or contradicted each other. Charles Harrison associates the effects (that is, noncognitive content) of painting with irreducibly metaphoric appeals to bodily experience; it is primarily in the automatism and involuntariness of these effects that we find "the signs of the body's resistance to ideology."[45] Thus, "it is precisely at those moments when distinctions between the technical and the metaphoric become hardest to sustain that the effects of landscape are most vivid, and the legacies of landscape most pertinent."[46] Harrison's arguments not only underscore discussions in chapter 3 about the need to approach images as screens on and through which constructions of the world are projected and worked out; they also reflect how any painter engages the phenomenal world. Even true-to-life paintings do not merely record the scene; the painter works and reworks the painting until she has recreated the essence of the view in front of and around her. Simplifying, distorting, or emphasizing certain relationships, the painter adds, rejects, or rearranges elements intuitively felt to add eidetic power to the picture.[47] This intuitive, noncognitive process is not about the transference of a preconceived design directly to the canvas or paper; rather, it is *found* there, as part of the process of mark making, itself driven by the painter's "unenvisagable vision."[48] If all landscapes are constructs that hover between foreground actuality and background potentiality, then the artist lays siege to her own noncognitive background potentiality, shaped by her subjectivity, through the marks on canvas or paper used to represent the foreground actuality.[49]

This means that landscape paintings can be read both *inward* (as representations that encourage the viewer to enter into an imaginary bodily relationship with the landscape) and *outward* (as problems of appearance in which the painter's subjectivity is revealed by what aspects of the landscape are deemed significant). Although artists' subjects are never unlimited, the choices artists make invite us to see how the world appears to them. In this, painters are like other people who express preferences for particular kinds of topographies or views, only they tend to see these *through* representation: a painter's notion of what constitutes a good subject will be partly conditioned by how such subjects challenge or flatter his skills.[50] Because painters' subjective construal of the world is always contaminated by a painterly way of seeing the world, their oeuvre simultaneously records *and* mediates their evolving subjectivity toward, and knowledge about, that world. This construal is of course ongoing and developmental. Like the process of setting down psychic roots in a new country, it involves reordering the imagination, imprinting new images, and fusing these with deep impulses and values, until they become part of the inner climate of the mind.[51]

Such a contingent, ongoing search for a way of seeing—less a capturing and putting down than a discovery and working out—informed Everard's painting of the Komati valley landscape. Although she borrowed contemporary European ways of seeing and representing, she did so in order to negotiate the tension between the foreground actuality and background potentiality engendered by her life on the Highveld. This was no small matter. If the Western concept of landscape is something to be seen, not touched, and the act of painting frames it through a set of predictable conventions, then the alienation mediated by these conventions will be heightened for a painter who also physically works the land.[52] (Hence, Ingold's rhetorical question: "If to dwell means to live in the world, and if representation entails taking one *out* of it, then how can one represent *dwelling?*")[53] The problematic nature of these artistic conventions would have been further heightened for a woman who "tended to see landscape in relation to domestic spaces and networks of interaction."[54] Both anecdotal evidence and the paintings themselves suggest that Everard struggled constantly to express what she felt about the landscape before her, to work out the painterly equivalents to her psychological state.[55] Painting was never simply a recreational activity for her, and the imperative to paint haunted her constantly. Between 1909 and 1922, she painted some thirty works, many of them her best, even though she had little time, painting left her physically and emotionally drained, and it provoked regular bouts of self-criticism.[56] Painting, it seems, along with farming, allowed Everard to overcome her ambivalent sense of belonging in the Transvaal and to escape, if only temporarily, the overdetermined domesticity that was her lot.

This suggests that Everard's work was an ongoing negotiation of the contrapuntal relationship between the here and now of the intimately known veld and the remembered world of ideas, tradition, beauty, and history.[57] Alternatively, we might say that her oeuvre can be read as a series of representational investigations through which she made a place for herself in early twentieth-century rural South Africa. Although Everard seldom dated her paintings, like Constable's they can still be read as chapters in a complex autobiography in which ideological structures became embedded in formalistic, artistic expression as personal subjectivity.[58] Unpacking this evolving vision of the Transvaal landscape shaped by both cognitive factors (personal ambition, artistic theories and skills, exigencies of time and space) and noncognitive ones (cultural beliefs, religious feeling, somatic experience, farmer's knowledge) requires teasing out the interplay of effectiveness and effects in her paintings. All evolved considerably, even as she continued to depict the same part of the eastern Transvaal.

Motif, Point of View, and the Embodiment of Memory

As we have seen, a figurative painting's point of view not only selects a motif but posits a relationship between notional viewer and the landscape. Even more than motif, this implied relationship between viewer and landscape lies at the heart of landscape painting's effectiveness. It is through this relationship that existential space and place are transformed into visual image and an arrangement of forms in response to a particular psychological state is posited as real. It is here that we need to begin our exploration of the representational and connotative qualities of Everard's work.

At the turn of the twentieth century, the tiny settlement of Bonnefoi constituted an important place in the otherwise empty landscape of the Eastern Highveld. To someone like Everard, unused to a landscape so lacking in articulation and orientation, the track from the nearest railway station and the tall, twenty-year-old eucalyptus trees that framed the front of her husband's store were significant features in this landscape (see color plate 24), and it is no surprise that these were her first subjects. The paintings she executed between 1902 and 1906 do not so much depict a view as a point of view.[59] A house as landmark, an avenue, or a junction of tracks were logical subjects for an artist developing her sense of the visibility and order of the surrounding space. Everard's point of view soon changed, however, and was increasingly directed outward, away from the store and the homestead, into the spaces of the veld. After she completed *Midwinter on the Komati* and *Peace of Winter* (color plate 19) in 1909 (both depicting a bend in the Komati on the Highveld floodplains not far from Bonnefoi), Everard seldom depicted the domestic, everyday world of Bonnefoi again, turning instead to the landscape of the Komati valley. In this, she not only turned her back, literally and figuratively, on the domestic realm, once her children were no longer infants, but she also reenacted the same classic pastoral move that had brought her first from Britain to South Africa, and then from Pretoria to Bonnefoi—withdrawing from the world to begin life anew in an unspoiled landscape. Mostly, these later paintings depicted the Berg landscape between the Highveld and the Lowveld. Although their subjects were chosen from a wide range of possibilities on the Everards' farms and elsewhere, they tended to fall into one of two genres: the valley prospect, which offered sweeping views from the brow of the escarpment or one of its promontories, and the veld fragment paintings, smaller works depicting more intimate passages in the landscape, located in the less dramatic, smaller side valleys.[60]

Usually looking eastward, the valley prospect paintings all depict a valley or extensive stretch of country from an elevated position. *Asbestos Hills* (ca. 1911), *Moonrise* (ca. 1913), *Green Hills* (mid-1910s), *Evening Voluntary* (ca. 1917), *Twantwani* (ca. 1916) (see color plate 25), *Land of Luthany* (ca. 1917), *Baboon Valley* (ca. 1917) (see color plate 26), and *Looking towards Swaziland* (also called *Opal Valley*, 1921) (see color plate 27) all carry a strangely compelling and enigmatic charge. Conventional landscape elements that help concatenate viewing subject and landscape in European painting are absent. There are virtually no signs of current or past human occupancy (shelters, dwellings, paths, smoke rising from fires), and the subject of the painting is unclear. (Thus, one reviewer, commenting on one of these valley prospect paintings, admired the way the eye was drawn to the "considerable reward" of the horizon, but wondered whether this was "sufficient to atone for the feeling of emptiness which marks the commencement of the journey.")[61] While these prospects of large empty spaces terminating in dramatic horizons *could* be read as representations of the Sublime, with its connotations of "awe, wildness, greatness, boundlessness," and feelings of "engulfment and inspiring strangeness," this would have been unlikely in someone who lived in and worked this landscape.[62] It is probably more useful to read the emptiness of these paintings in terms of the ambiguous relationship between viewing subject and landscape posited by other paintings that depicted the colonial landscape as wilderness. Bordo argues that these pictures were an important part of the discursive apparatus whereby territory was constituted as wilderness, because they enacted a kind of spacing between an inherited terrain saturated with indigenous knowledge and memory and the project of appropriation, which imagined the land as thinly populated or not populated at all.[63]

Arguments that an interplay of witnessing and erasure in colonial paintings allowed them to mediate a sense of the landscape as a perpetual "unresolved site of memory" are especially pertinent to Everard's later paintings. Although the Komati valley was a remote district in which human occupation was ambiguous because large tracts were unused for many months of the year, it is hard to believe that it was quite as devoid of human habitation as Everard depicts it. Although human figures do appear in some earlier paintings (for instance, *Pale Hillside* [see color plate 28] and *Spring, Eastern Transvaal* [see color plate 30]), they are unimportant parts of the composition, and they disappear in later paintings. It could also be argued that Everard's perception of the district as a realm of solitary and contemplative reverie required that it be empty of human settlement precisely in order to engage several different kinds of landscape memory simultaneously. The fact that her paintings were always of identifiable topographical features not only mediated a detailed knowledge of the district and an acute awareness of its landscape character, but also a respect for their local meanings. The appeal of the Komati valley had something to do with the fact that it resembled northwest England, where Everard had grown up.[64] But Everard's fascination with this landscape was also undoubtedly enhanced by the fact that it represented an intersection between personal associations and the cultural memory of colonial nationalism. For much of the year, the Komati valley resembled the kind of terrain that engaged the metropolitan geographical imagination the most—a landscape that recombined, in a different way, in a remote region just off the map, elements of recognizable worlds.[65] Like Buchan's Woodbush, Everard's Komati valley was a bigger, emptier version of the upland margins of metropolitan Britain, a landscape where the horizons were high, vegetated, and treeless, and the signature environmental image was "the green summit against unclouded blue."[66]

This fusion between personal and cultural memory was reflected in the care she devoted to finding points of view in this physical and imagined upland. As she traveled through the Carolina district, Everard was able, like Cézanne on Mont Sainte-Victoire, to find locations in which the arrangement of the landscape's constituent forms somehow matched an inner psychological state.[67] The disposition bodied forth in most of her paintings recalls what Peter Bishop has called the "pastoral body," a somatic identity that is contemplative, undramatic, and antiheroic, modest in scale and dimension, and characterized by gentle, irregular movement. For Bishop, the pastoral is connoted by indirection and obliqueness, the illusion that the natural world does not require human intervention in order to sustain it, or that at the very least, responds willingly to human intelligence and labor. (This pastoral is of course as much a subjectivity as a subject.) Bishop argues that this subjectivity is also at root nostalgic—both in the sense of the desire to return home and in the sense of the desire to experience a fundamental sense of belonging. This pastoral, nostalgic subjectivity is not only implicit in the valley prospect paintings' iconographic emptiness, but also in the way they cast the Komati valley as a hidden valley, a geographical island where threatened values could lie low and be preserved from modernity and change.[68] For a European-educated painter working in early twentieth-century South Africa like Everard, the escape offered by the hidden, empty valleys of the escarpment landscape was complex: it was, at the same time, a retreat from an industrialized, urbanized Europe and a retreat from the philistine provincialism of rural, colonial life. For a woman trying to balance personal and domestic responsibilities, the hidden valley became a space of free movement and untrammeled reverie. These multifarious strands of topographical subjectivity are usefully tied together by Bishop's association of valley views with a Jungian descent into the realm of myth and renewal.[69] He argues that the hidden valley mediates a subjectivity characterized by purity, continuity, and depth of memory and guards against one that is about horizontality, confusion, and ambiguity about identity.

The interpretation of Everard's pre-1922 paintings as a metaphorical descent into memory, belonging, and pastoral identity is supported by the fact that at the same time as she was painting prospects *of* these hidden valleys, she was painting a series of views *in* them. This corpus of veld-fragment paintings was the product of the quite literal, annual descent she made into this world every year. They reveal a complementary topography that, according to Bunn, "allegorized, as desire and anticipation, as a series of staging points" the journey she and her family made from Bonnefoi to Lekkerdraai each winter.[70] Like the valley prospect paintings, the subject of these views is ambiguous. Often without any discernible motif, they are spaces in which the mind is encouraged to wander. Unlike the larger paintings, though, they are less about regional topography and more about the material constitution of the land itself. Instead of personal and cultural memory, paintings like *The Krantz* (ca. 1909), *Pale Hillside* (painted sometime between 1911 and 1916) (see color plate 28), *Winter in the Transvaal* (ca. 1916) (see color plate 29), and *Winter in the Lowveld* (ca. 1916) (see color plate 31) capture Everard's growing firsthand knowledge of the landscape as a text with its own syntax and signifying potential. All Highveld farmers are attuned to the complex interactions between slope, orientation, and hydrology that subtly differentiate one place from another.[71] To a painter with a heightened sense of the local, such barely visible modulations would have become full of interest and significance. Like the valley prospect paintings, which distilled and represented the larger lie of the land, only at a much smaller scale, the veld fragment paintings bodied forth telling moments in a constantly shifting topography.[72]

Once again, though, the relationship between notional viewer and landscape was an important factor. In the veld fragment paintings, the point of view was one of embeddedness, even disorientation in the terrain, which was reinforced by Everard's occasional use of circular format. In all of the paintings, a high skyline conveys a sense of retreat and submersion in the landscape. Yet precisely because the landscape fills the frame, it presents itself as an object, but is caught as if in a sidelong glance, momentarily, at the edge of the field of vision. This oblique, indirect, glancing disposition is most suggestively conveyed in paintings like *Winter in the Transvaal* (color plate 29) and its summer equivalent *Masimoni Vale*, as well as *Moon and Shadow* (see color plate 32), *Morning Tree*, and *Wag-'n-bietjies*, all of which depict isolated indigenous thorn trees rising out of a sea of grass. These individual, mysterious trees could be interpreted as synecdochic genius loci figures. They are, however, also strongly reminiscent of the solitary trees seen in contemporaneous paintings by the Canadian Group of Seven, which, replacing the witnessing human figure found in earlier colonial landscapes, acted as stand-ins for the ambivalent re-sighting of colonial wilderness.[73] According to Bordo, the solitary trees in these paintings elide the difference between the picturesque (which is witnessed) and the sublime (which is unwitnessed).[74] They serve as traces of a subjectivity attracted by the wilderness, yet aware of its own likely complicity in destroying it. The inscription of the viewing subject in the figural witness of the tree facilitates the dissolution of colonizing presence, visually positing the landscape as unpopulated and "unspoiled" and hiding the cultural memory that gave rise to this "pure" vision.[75] Thus, in these veld fragment paintings of isolated trees, the Komati valley is figured as a landscape in which "progress" is paradoxically registered through the nullification of human presence and inhabitation—precisely the (impossible) elision that nurtured nostalgic pastoral visions of the subcontinent.

Technique, Appearance, and the Underlying Order of Things

We can see then that, despite their apparent lack of recognizable human interest, Everard's paintings of the Berg as empty veld were in fact active and full of meaning. The implied spatial relationship between viewing subject and landscape object may have been the primary vehicle of this effect, but this was complemented by technique, the translation into marks on canvas of the constituent forms that confronted the painter. South African artists' preoccupation with the subcontinent's monotony, size, and light may, like the unwitnessed wilderness, have been an enabling fiction that facilitated the "othering" of the South African interior, but it also alluded to very real difficulties painters experienced when depicting a terrain with an absence of clear motifs, few intermediate reference points (human or natural), and a limited range of color.[76] While Everard's confinement to the Komati valley and the escarpment partly obviated the first of these problems, the other two remained.

As we have seen, Everard had been trained in a school of painting that held that the nature of appearances was traceable to accidents of light and atmosphere observed firsthand. Impressionist painters argued that perception at the fringes of consciousness was closer to the actual optical sensation people receive than the laboriously refined images of reality they were accustomed to seeing on canvas. They sought to make the phenomena of light and color explicit and tactile; pigment and brushstroke replaced nontactile convention as communicators of meaning. By paying such close attention to the coming into being of appearances, however, it subverted the certainties of naturalistic, agreed-upon likeness, and reintroduced a sense of contingency, mystery, and wonder to the visible world. During the decades when Everard was most active, there was growing criticism of the way Impressionism's evocative, painterly marks reduced the motif to a shimmering surface and occluded the substantiality of the underlying order of things.[77] It was precisely the retrieval of this underlying order that drove the search for ways of painting that used a more analytical, optically constructed vocabulary. Post-Impressionism attempted to retain Impressionism's sophisticated attention to effects of light and color but reclaim the solidity and structure of the world it seemed to have banished. Everard was familiar with these debates through the writings of the English artist-critics Clive Bell and Roger Fry, who from

1910 onward promoted Cézanne's search for ways to communicate solidity as well as surface appearance by emphasizing the underlying structure of space and form.[78]

It is easy to see how negotiating this tension between contingent appearances and the underlying order of things would have been important to Everard. Although she experimented with an academic naturalist style before 1910, probably for commercial reasons, after this her painting became increasingly impressionistic, composed of color fragments, a multitude of short and variegated strokes applied either with brush or palette knife. In later paintings such as *Looking towards Swaziland* (see color plate 27), it is true, colors become less realistic and increasingly pure, and marks become ever larger and simpler and suggestive of the dynamics of spatial movement and recession. The paintings' understated, enigmatic motifs are filtered through this very physical exploration and become imbued with character through the way the marks that stand for them are formed, layered, mixed, and superimposed. Still, Everard never really abandoned "the anchorage of the recognizable subject." Her paintings were always of identifiable places, usually painted *en plein air*, and until the mid-1920s, she never embraced analytical or abstract Post-Impressionism.[79] This reluctance was telling, given that such modes of representation, which are more about space and structure than color and light, seemed especially suited to the depiction of South African landscape (an opinion that seemed to be supported by Pierneef's work).[80]

No doubt, Everard's slowness to adopt Post-Impressionist techniques was related to the conservatism and isolation of the South African art world. But we also need to remember that Everard's representation of this landscape was not just about optical truth; it was also about trying to represent the feelings triggered by this terrain, a nature of appearances cognate with her disposition toward it. Her representation of the appearances of the Komati valley cannot be separated from the challenge of remaking, through marks on canvas, how this grassland world took on form for her as "traveling subject," woman, painter, and farmer. This involved a sustained exploration of the relationship between appearances and an underlying order of things that was deeply personal, associational, and multivalent.

In the first instance, Everard's cleaving to the nature of appearances in this landscape cannot be separated from the fact that this was a terrain in which, paradoxically, surface dominated. As a farmer, she would have been highly attuned to the subtle shifts wrought by season, weather, and topography, which are really the only form of change, and therefore life, in these monotonous, austere grasslands. Impressionistic strokes of individual color, "flicker[ing] through the controlled tonality of the surface, and enliven[ing] it like the wind which moves through the mountain grass," represent the play of light and texture on the veld.[81] This is particularly true in the veld fragment paintings, which were synecdochic moments that refracted the larger topography of which they were part and captured how this was "received in moments, glances and accidental detours, kinesthetically unfolding through rambling and habitual encounters over time."[82] But this simultaneous assertion *and* fragmentation of the veld's surface appearance in the same paintings may also have been a representational strategy that expressed a subjectivity that always saw what had been left behind and what was actually present at the same time. As Bishop has pointed out, the phrase "seeing things as they really are" is not as simple as it sounds. Apparently

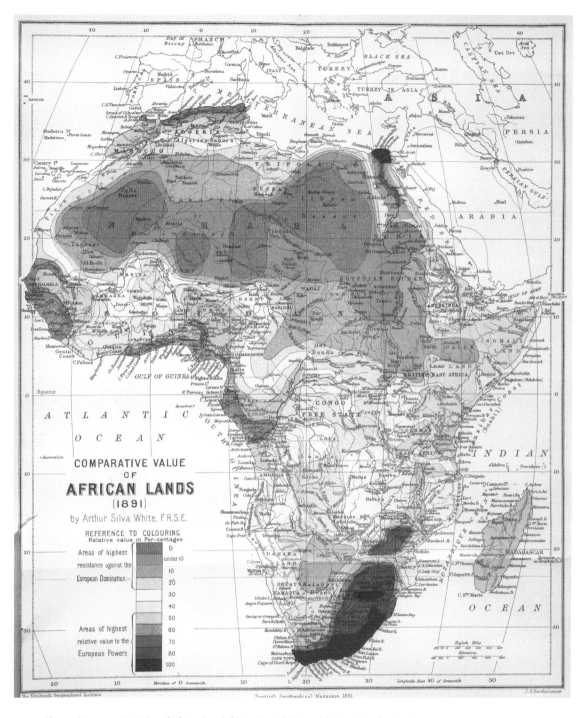

Plate 1. "Comparative Value of African Lands." From *Scottish Geographic Magazine* vol. 7 (1891); reproduced with permission of British Library, London.

Plate 2. E. S. Turner, *Zimbabwe Ruins at Midnight*. Transnet Heritage Museum Library Publications Colour-Spread Collection; reproduced with permission.

Plate 3. E. S. Turner, *In an Old Dutch Garden at the Cape: A Vision of Bygone Days in South Africa.* From *Illustrated London News*, 2 November 1929; Transnet Heritage Museum Library Publications Colour-Spread Collection; reproduced with permission.

Plate 4. *(above)* R. Gwelo Goodman, *The Hex River Valley*, watercolor, 1920s. Frontispiece, Dorothea Fairbridge, *A Pilgrim's Way in South Africa* (London: Oxford University Press, 1928).

Plate 5. *(opposite, top)* Edward Roworth, *A Farm on the Hills, Kuils River*, ca. 1907. Durban Art Gallery; reproduced with permission of Ivanonia Roworth Keet.

Plate 6. *(opposite, bottom)* R. Gwelo Goodman, *The Paarl Church*, ca. 1920. From Dorothea Fairbridge, *Historic Houses of South Africa* (London: Oxford University Press; Cape Town: Maskew Miller, 1922).

A WILD FLOWER FROM THE CAPE, WHICH HAS 200 MORE SPECIES THAN ALL ENGLAND : LEUCADENDRON GRANDIFLORUM.

FROM A DISTRICT ONLY SURPASSED BY HONG-KONG IN ITS WEALTH OF BLOSSOM OROTHAMNUS ZEYHERI, A WILD FLOWER OF THE CAPE.

Plate 7. *Gems from a Floral Paradise.* From *Illustrated London News*, 20 March 1926. Transnet Heritage Museum Library Publications Colour-Spread Collection; reproduced with permission.

Plate 8. "Where Good Sport Is Followed by Good Appetite." From *The Sketch,* 9 March 1927. Transnet Heritage Museum Library Publications Colour-Spread Collection; reproduced with permission.

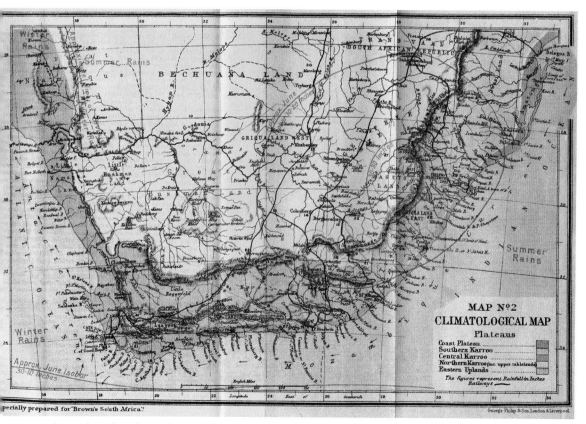

Plate 9. Climatological map of South Africa. From *Union Castle Guide to South Africa,* 1896–97, author's collection.

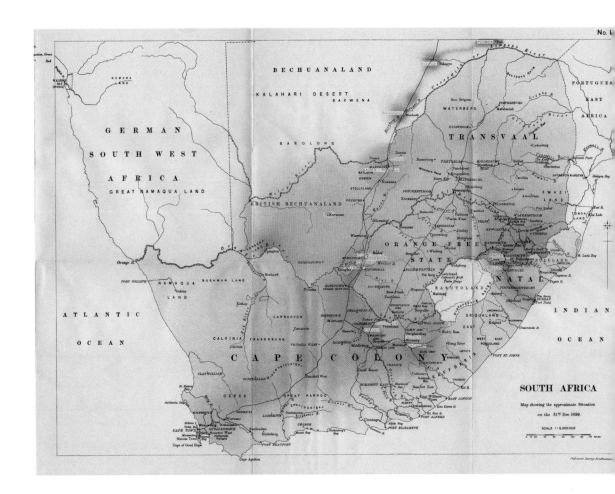

Plate 10. *(left)* Newspaper placard: Relief of Mafeking. Reproduced courtesy of the Director, National Army Museum, London; Picture Library file ref. #1994-12-122-1.

Plate 11. *(above)* Map showing military situation in South Africa on 31 December 1899. *The Times History of the War in South Africa, 1899–1902*, edited by L. S. Amery, vol. 1, p. 17 (London: Sampson Low, Marston, and Co., 1900–1909); Cornell University Library.

Plate 12. (opposite, top) Physiographic map and cross-sections, Transvaal Colony in 1906. Royal Geographical Society Map Library.

Plate 13. *(opposite bottom)* Eastern Highveld near Machadodorp today. Photograph by author.

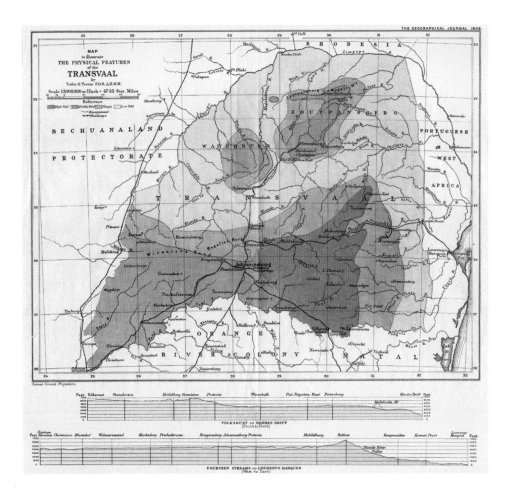

MAP
to illustrate
THE PHYSICAL FEATURES
of the
TRANSVAAL
by
Tudor G. Trevor F.G.S. A.R.S.M.
Scale 1:3000,000 or 1 Inch = 47.35 Stat. Miles

Plate 14. "A deep sabbatical calm . . .": The South African Highveld. Photograph by author.

Plate 15. View of the escarpment from Buchan's "pernicious fever flats," near Letsitele. Photograph by the author.

Plate 16. *Summer in the Soutpansberg*, mural painted by George Smithard for the Pretoria Railway Station, 1912. Transnet Heritage Museum Library; reproduced with permission.

Plate 17. *(above)* Herbert Baker, *Bosch en Dal*, Cape Town, watercolor. Groote Schuur Collection / South African Dept. of Public Works; reproduced with permission (photograph by Les Hammond).

Plate 18. *(left)* Villa Arcadia, view looking up steps. From Dorothea Fairbridge, *Gardens of South Africa* (London: A. & C. Black, 1924); author's collection.

Plate 19. *(above)* Bertha Everard, *Peace of Winter*, ca. 1909 (close facsimile of *Mid-winter on the Komati*). Johannesburg Art Gallery; reproduced with permission of Leonora Everard Haden.

Plate 20. *(right)* Komati River near Lekker-draai. Photograph by author, ca. 1997.

Plate 21. Panorama, upper Komati valley, ca. 1997. Photograph by the author.

Plate 22. Panorama, lower Komati valley, ca. 1997. Photograph by the author.

Plate 23. *(above)* Sides of lower Komati valley, near Lekkerdraai, ca. 1997. Photograph by the author.

Plate 24. *(left)* Bonnefoi store, ca. 1997. Photograph by the author.

Plate 25. Bertha Everard, *Twantwani*, ca. 1916. Tatham Art Gallery, Pietermaritzburg; reproduced with permission of Leonora Everard Haden (photograph by J. Robinson).

Plate 26. Bertha Everard, *Baboon Valley*, ca. 1917. Tatham Art Gallery, Pietermaritzburg; reproduced with permission of Leonora Everard Haden (photograph by J. Robinson).

Plate 27. Bertha Everard, *Looking towards Swaziland*, ca. 1921 (also known as *Opal Valley*). Pretoria Art Museum, reproduced with permission of Leonora Everard Haden (photograph by Carla Crafford).

Plate 28.
Bertha Everard, *Pale Hillside*. L. Haden Collection, reproduced with permission (photograph by J. Robinson).

Plate 29.
Bertha Everard, *Winter in the Transvaal*, ca. 1916. Government House, Pretoria; reproduced with permission of Leonora Everard Haden (Photograph by Carla Crafford).

Plate 30. *(above, left)* Bertha Everard, *Spring, Eastern Transvaal*, ca. 1916. Durban Art Gallery, reproduced with permission of Leonora Everard Haden.

Plate 31. *(above, right)* Bertha Everard, *Winter in the Lowveld*, ca. 1915. Oliewenhuis Art Museum, Bloemfontein, reproduced with permission of Leonora Everard Haden.

Plate 32. *(left)* Bertha Everard, *Moon and Shadow*, n.d. Pretoria Art Museum, reproduced with permission of Leonora Everard Haden (photograph by Carla Crafford).

Plate 33. *(opposite, top)* Bertha Everard, *Trees and Trenches, Delville Wood*, ca. 1926. Pretoria Art Museum, reproduced with permission of Leonora Everard Haden (photograph by Carla Crafford).

Plate 34. *(opposite, bottom)* Bertha Everard, *The New Furrow*, ca. 1930. Pretoria Art Museum, reproduced with permission of Leonora Everard Haden (photograph by Carla Crafford).

Plate 35. J. H. Pierneef, *Amajuba*, ca. 1930 (Johannesburg station panel). Transnet Heritage Museum Library, reproduced with permission.

Plate 36. *From Sea Level to 6,000 Feet. Illustrated London News*, 14 January 1928. Transnet Heritage Museum Library Publications Colour-Spread Collection; reproduced with permission.

Plate 37. Johannesburg Station concourse. *Illustrated London News*, 8 September 1934. Transnet Heritage Museum Library Publications Colour-Spread Collection; reproduced with permission.

Plate 38. Proposed new Johannesburg Station main entrance. Transnet Heritage Museum Library; reproduced with permission.

Plate 39. "On the Stoep: A Golden Afternoon on a Fruit Farm in the Cape, W. Province, Overlooking a Lovely Valley with a Rampart of Mountains Beyond." From *Illustrated London News*, 20 March 1926. Transnet Heritage Museum Library Publications Colour-Spread Collection; reproduced with permission.

Plate 40. "Christmas in South Africa." Transnet Heritage Museum Library Publications Colour-Spread Collection; reproduced with permission.

indirect, oblique marks that explore the painterly nature of appearances can, in fact, be accurate representations of an underlying order of things that combines "affirmation and wonder alongside . . . melancholy and impermanence."[83]

Living in and farming this land year after year would certainly have familiarized Everard with a number of other relationships between appearances and the underlying order of things that could be mediated through marks on canvas. The first of these is captured by Isabel Hofmeyr's observation that European colonial farming was founded on imaginary relations with the soil quite different from those of indigenous African pastoralists. Using quite visceral resonances of plowing deeply to justify its appropriation of the land, progressive European husbandry saw itself as making the soil thick through the addition of manure and fertilizer, in contrast to the Africans' thin, bodiless "scratching."[84] The landscape Everard inhabited, worked, and painted, however, was one that resisted this imaginary of plowing deeply; the Komati valley was better suited to infrequent pasturage than to frequent and intensive cultivation. Under these circumstances, it could be argued, the intense working of the surface of the painting became a form of substitute labor that thickened the surface of the (depicted) land, allowing the painter-subject to inhabit the landscape while permitting her to descend into the nostalgic, pastoral associations conjured by its empty, unpopulated topography.

Another way in which the relationship between appearances and the underlying order of things played out in Everard's work was in her attempts to capture the effects of specific times of day or year. Although she was often too busy to paint during daylight hours, a noteworthy number of her paintings depicted the landscape when it was undergoing a visual transformation: at dawn, at dusk, at night, at the onset of a storm, in the midst of a veld-fire, or during moonrise.[85] While it is a truism that landscapes are usually most expressive at the ends of the day (and capturing mood or atmosphere had been an important aspiration for landscape painting since Whistler's experiments in the 1880s), this is particularly true in South Africa, where the landscape's lack of spatial complexity and bleached colors are transformed when the sun is at a low angle at sunrise or sunset.[86] It is also useful to remember the phenomenological reality that transient light of dusk or dawn removes weight from the sky and lends weight to things, and consequently, that it is precisely at this time of day that the body-subject's phenomenal sense of separation from its environment is at its weakest.[87]

The ambiguous nature of appearances is also captured by the oblique and indirect, apparently artless disposition toward the motif posited in some of the veld fragment paintings. The isolated trees in paintings like *Winter in the Transvaal* (see color plate 29), *Moon and Shadow* (see color plate 32), *Morning Tree*, and *Wag-'n-bietjies* in particular allude to another register in which Everard's ambiguous subjectivity might have shaped the coming into being of appearances. These haunting arboreal figures may, as we have seen, have stood in for the self-erasing colonial gaze, but it is also possible that for someone as religious as Everard they had meanings akin to what Freud called the *unheimlich*.[88] Most landscape painters report a sense of their subject confronting them, or "looking back"—as Cézanne described it, "the landscape thinks itself in me, and I am its consciousness"—and in the Highveld, where trees are rare, their standing, rising figures are easily anthropomorphized and assigned character. One suspects, however, that Everard's solitary trees were quite different from those in Pierneef's Transvaal paintings, which were meant to be symbols denoting the life of the cosmos and expressing the essence of Africanness.[89] Everard's strong religious beliefs, the enigmatic motifs of her paintings (heightened by the mythical names she gave some of them, such as *Twantwani* (ca. 1916) (see color plate 25) and *Land of Luthany* (1917), and her descriptions of her feelings when alone in the veld, all suggest that she saw the noumenal as an integral part of this landscape.[90]

It is possible, then, to argue that *what* Everard painted and *how* she painted it were tightly bound up with the desire for some kind of exchange with an enigmatic hinterland that was not just existential but also in some sense spiritual. Depicting the sense of some imaginary spirit, African or otherwise, in the landscape required finding equivalent—but never "realistic"—marks on the canvas, precisely what modern nonnaturalistic European painting permitted. In Everard's contingent, indirect, and ambiguous depictions of the coming into being of appearances, then, the landscape-subject becomes a metonymic symbol, not so much as an icon *of* God, but of a world where (a?) God might appear and speak. The Berg and the Komati valley are figured as a world that encouraged the inwardness necessary for the soul to find God. The invisible, the unrepresentable, the transcendent is connoted by a topography that, emptied of history, is infused instead with a compensatory, displaced corporeality. Foreground and background become blurred, and, as in the vision of unspoiled wilderness, the idol becomes the empty landscape itself.[91]

Delville Wood, Lekkerdraai, and the Transformation of the Pastoral

There are many reasons, then, to believe that Everard's painted explorations of the appearances of the Komati valley became a displaced representation of her own ambivalent, evolving relationship with that landscape. Together, the valley prospect and veld fragment paintings trace an ambiguous, unfolding, and dialectical inhabitation of a landscape that combined corporeal introjection and nostalgic memory, and encouraged these two forms of place-attachment to play off each other. Over time, Everard's paintings matured from exercises in finding a point of view in an unknown world into unapologetic representations of a mode of existence in it, and this evolution was mediated by a parallel evolution in relationship between the cognitive and noncognitive content of her paintings.

The tensions between these two aspects of artistic representation in Everard's earlier work became more resolved when she returned from her sojourn in Europe from 1922 to 1926 and once more immersed herself in life in the Carolina district. Everard's four years in Europe exposed her to the profound social and cultural changes that had occurred there since World War I and recharged her interest in modern art. While supervising her daughters' studies in London and Paris, she saw the work of many of the modern Post-Impressionist and Fauvist painters herself and experimented with some of their techniques in many landscapes she painted in Britain and France. At the same time, this sojourn also made her realize how attached she had become to her home in the Berg and the self-sufficient active, outdoor South African way of life.

The convergence between biographical, artistic, and ideological dimensions of her identity seems to have been powerfully precipitated by the experience, shortly before she returned to South Africa in 1926, of visiting Delville Wood, the World War I battlefield in northern France where an entire battalion of South Africans had been wiped out ten years before. Everard became obsessed with the site; she saw the devastated, cratered landscape, blasted trees, and deep pools of water reflecting the sky above "as a magnificent monument in itself, far more searing and permanent" than Baker's memorial, which "hovered like a ghost on the horizon."[92] Spending two weeks in Picardy and painting every day, she explored the battlefield from many different points of view and eventually produced ten paintings of it (see color plate 33).[93] While some of these paintings verge on rendering Delville Wood as a calvary (an obvious response for a devout Christian),[94] it also seems that the making of these paintings, more than any others up to this point, contributed to her reflexive sense of herself as a colonial national, South African artist. Although the Delville Wood paintings engaged a broader revisioning of landscape meaning that the war had brought about in Europe, her preoccupation with the site was also bound up with an important shift in her relationship with what she was painting. For the first time, she was painting a European subject for an imaginary African audience, rather than African subjects for an imaginary European audience. Paradoxically, her encounter with this devastated site thousands of miles from the Berg, on land ceded to Britain by a third, European nation, renewed her sense of what it meant to be South African.[95]

Delville Wood, like the rest of the Western Front, inverted long-standing European visions of landscape as a realm of pastoral tranquility and a nurturing source of life, turning it into an uncertain and unstable terrain devoid of shelter or rest.[96] The Western Front destroyed, once and for all, the illusion that European civilization was grounded in an ontological continuity between human intelligence and nature.[97] For European war artists, depicting this apocalyptic landscape had required a transformation in seeing and technique. Although some attempted to interpret the battlefields in terms of historic-academic conventions of spectacular ruination, others saw that this denatured, disorienting landscape with its peculiar light and vaporous weather conditions invited the use of the new, abstract language that was the currency of modernism.[98] Ironically, the blasted landscapes of the battlefields posed challenges for British painters similar to those posed by the empty subcontinental interior for their colonial national counterparts. Among the artistic themes that emerged in paintings of the Western Front were an interest in the fragmentation of time and place, the transformation of the spectacle of ruination into the aesthetics of transience and becoming, and the use of paint as an analogy for the deliquescent battlefield.[99]

Everard had already seen some of these war paintings before she visited Delville Wood, but her response was nevertheless intensely personal. It was as if the chaotic appearance of this man-made wilderness, and the terrible underlying order of things it symbolized, could only be depicted by means that were thoroughly modern. In her Delville Wood canvases, Everard used paint as a physical substance, moving it sculpturally on the canvas to establish abruptly simplified forms. The expressive shapes and strong, nonnaturalistic colors that first appeared in other landscapes she painted in France were applied almost exclusively with the palette knife. The violent forms and somber colors of these paintings referred to no known literary or religious subjects.[100] This was, ultimately, a kind of landscape that had never been seen before; the emotional content the paintings conveyed was the kind that attaches itself to any piece of land that has been manipulated and exposed by powerful technological forces, an effect that draws not on recognizable forms or historic associations, but upon raw, noncognitive somatic knowledge.

Everard's encounter with this with this dystopian, human-made wilderness that was the only trace of South Africa's involvement in World War I seems to have transformed her perception of the South African landscape itself. The canvases she painted after returning to Bonnefoi in 1927 display a new directness and abstraction and an interest in the consequences of human agency in the landscape. Both in their subject and their subjectivity, these late paintings represented a rejuvenated relationship with the Komati valley: as a "place where the self (could) remake itself in direct, unalienated labour."[101] The central motif in this lifeworld was the strong, simple form of the life-giving watercourse that nevertheless constantly changed according to locale and time of year or day. All these late paintings depict a riverine motif, either the Komati itself, or one of the water furrows that Everard helped dig to irrigate the lands on Lekkerdraai (see color plate 34).[102] A new relationship between motif, subjectivity, and technique reveals a reconstructed attitude toward home. The earlier paintings' ambiguous, reverie-like explorations of the appearances of the veld give way to the clear, almost graphic shapes and insistent lines that explicitly construct the landscape. The limpid color palette and flickering brush strokes that previously invited the eye to construct the landscape for itself are replaced by decisive brushstrokes, and a dark, almost monochromatic palette presents an unambiguous reading of the underlying topography, rendered as monumental, sculptural form.

Everard's earlier paintings of the lower Komati valley had posited an indirect, ambiguous, and nostalgic relationship between the notional viewer and a landscape in which signs of human inhabitation were largely invisible. Now, the toponymic content of the farm name became reflected in these late paintings: as Bunn has observed, the word "Lekkerdraai" not only denotes "both a pleasant prospect and the pleasure associated with a river loop," it also implies "a place where a private exchange between self and landscape can occur." In these late paintings, Everard mediated this exchange between the notional subject and landscape either by positioning herself at the bend in the river, or by emphasizing how the terse line of life-giving water flowing in the furrow is mirrored (and made possible by) the geometric line of soil she herself had helped excavate. The serpentine figure of the river or furrow functions in a similar fashion to the roads disappearing into the distance or the solitary trees seen in earlier paintings, only here they serve as witness for full presence; the viewer is drawn in by the promise of fulfillment and possible closure. This gestural movement is prevented from overcoming the wildness of the larger landscape by the fact that the river or furrow is a line that can never, strictly speaking, be *followed*.[103]

Everard's final vision of the Komati valley, then, like Smuts's recharged admiration for the Cape Dutch houses during the 1920s, challenged the catastrophic linkage between human agency and nature posited by the European battlefields. Instead, it emphasized the constitutedness and materiality of landscape, and how this was contingent on productive work and human stewardship. At the same time, it signaled that earlier connotations of the hidden valley had become less sustainable. By the 1920s, white fears of racial swamping as well as the challenges to Anglophone South Africanism meant that, for many colonial national whites, the prospects of empty, verdant valleys had come to mediate a complicated nostalgia. Satisfying associations and topographical memories previously evoked by pristine, hidden valleys were clouded by the growing sense that such topographies were threatened by the poor farming methods of a dispossessed tenantry ruined by the capitalization of agriculture.[104] *The New Furrow*, in particular, offered an optimistic resolution of this dilemma, as well as the fundamental contradictions that lay at the heart of earlier, nostalgic pastoralist visions of the landscape. This was that, to morally justify colonization, satisfy criticism of rural retreat, and guard against European degeneration, the landscape imagined as wilderness had to also show signs of physical labor, labor that moreover was performed by whites.[105] This was precisely what *The New Furrow* did. In it, a newfound sense of belonging abandoned the oblique, nostalgic subjectivity of the pastoral and embraced the pragmatic, embodied realism of the georgic.[106] Thus, while Everard might have given up painting because she found it too demanding as she aged, we could also argue that by the mid-1930s, it had served its purpose of helping her place herself in a white man's country.

Reception, Ideological Contradiction, and National Sentiment

Works of art that acquire significance for a broad range of people provide some kind of vision that is reciprocal to, and compensates for, the realities of their daily lives. Art that achieves this is not so much good art as art that shapes people's lives to the time and space in front of them and shows them how they might be.[107] The discursive persuasiveness of art, good or bad, to transform the shared structure of seeing depends on its ability to engage a perceptual economy created by a broad array of social practices and cultural discourses.[108] The processes whereby art does this are complex, ongoing, and iterative. What a painting represents goes beyond the totality outside of which, and in relation to which, viewers orient themselves; it also encompasses the means by which they decide their cognitive being in the world. When paintings make the problem of seeing palpable as a condition of their own effects, they "keep the viewer . . . at work in [their] actual presence," and sustain (rather than solve, elide, or obscure) the problematic "relations between making and seeing that are the practical conditions of all painting."[109]

Everard's work reveals much about the perceptual economy prevailing in interwar South Africa. The apathy toward her work was not unlike that encountered by other colonial national cultural producers during the same period who tried to interpret the South African experience using representational techniques and theories borrowed from Europe that were complex, ambiguous, and subtle. It did not help that Everard was a woman who lived in a region relatively isolated from urban centers and cultural life, in a male-dominated society. She was also an uncompromising, outspoken person who put high prices on her work and had limited personal connections with those who controlled galleries and commissions. But her paintings' initial lack of popularity was ultimately ascribable to the unresolved relations between making and seeing they mediated. In other words, it was not so much a matter of what they depicted as how they depicted it that made her paintings inaccessible to most urban white South Africans in the 1920s and 1930s. The paintings sought to synthesize a contingent aesthetic sensibility, advanced theories of optics and representation, and a knowledge about landscape inaccessible to most artists.

In many respects, the representational negotiations of Everard's paintings reflected her own subjective negotiations with the imaginary white man's country, as an educated white woman living on the margins of South Africa and the British Empire. Initially, her paintings mediated an inward-turning subjective identification with an experiential world whose chief frame of signification was a different continent. Depicting a remote corner of the national territory apparently untouched by urban capitalism, her paintings were acutely focused on the character of the land and rejected the grand narratives of nationhood and identity fixated on narrow ideas of sovereignty. The contrapuntal relationship between her backcountry life and her internationalist traveling subjectivity also exposed her to the tensions between possibility and loss wrought by modernity.[110] Consequently, her mature work depicted the South African landscape neither as an idealized *paysage* in which benign landowners supervised contented peasants (as Roworth's and Smithard's had earlier), nor as a fondly remembered farm-*werf* or icon of imaginary, collectively owned territory (as Pierneef did in the 1930s).[111] Instead, her paintings represented one small part of the Highveld as a place poised between the oppressiveness of a new order and the imprisonments of tradition, in which "the split between material and spiritual planes was temporarily resolved in a positive manner."[112]

The unresolved problem of seeing mediated by Everard's paintings can be more readily understood by comparing them to Pierneef's. Almost as much of an outsider in white society as Everard (he was the son of impecunious Dutch émigré parents), Pierneef was also an ambitious individual who, once he saw how the South African political climate was shifting in the 1920s, assiduously cultivated the emerging Afrikaner establishment. And although he is often thought of as "the first local painter whose style was entirely conditioned by the character of the indigenous environment," in fact, Pierneef, like Everard, used contemporary European ways of seeing in his work, though he drew upon the less familiar (and less ambiguous) Dutch monumental-decorative style.[113] Although Pierneef's self-promotion played its part, the popularity of his formalistic and eventually formulaic renditions of the South African landscape can be ascribed to the tendency for art that simplifies and idealizes to be embraced by societies seeking to avoid ideological contradictions in their makeup.[114] In such societies, any icon of nationhood must not only meet the approval of the artistic community but must mediate a broadly populist, discursive structure of seeing.[115] Images that do this tend to be ones that are forward-looking (that is, modern) in style and technique, but in which the play between making and seeing is, seemingly, already resolved. Chauvinism, it has been argued, is best conveyed through the hard edges and simple forms of illustration, posters, and advertisements than through high art.[116]

In the same way that a map's symbolic vocabulary defines and regularizes the territory it depicts, Pierneef's distinctive but consistent stylistic vocabulary and color palette regularized the many different regional landscapes of South Africa and assimilated them into a single, overarching, representational imagined geography. Not coincidentally, this vocabulary also translated easily into the medium of the woodcut, which was readily reproducible, easily published in magazines, and much cheaper to buy than a painting. The graphic accessibility and populist appeal of these black and white images, combined with Pierneef's active promotion of his work and overt support of Afrikaner nationalism, helped his work become widely recognized and discussed.[117] The Johannesburg Station panels, it turned out, had rehearsed a discursive vision of South Africa that Pierneef would almost single-handedly create during the 1940s and 1950s (see color plate 35). Together, his paintings of South African terrain were tailored to meet the tastes of the growing urban middle class, and his more populist woodcuts that appealed to impoverished newly urbanized Afrikaners became a screen on which the racist-environmentalist construction of Afrikaner history and identity could be projected during this period.

By contrast, Everard's paintings were less frequently exhibited and reproduced,[118] and offered little of the clarity, simplicity, and broad appeal that Pierneef's did; they depicted ambiguous subjects and little-known landscapes and employed techniques that resisted easy recognition and were constantly evolving. Although acutely attuned to the unique qualities of the South African landscape, Everard never aspired to paint landscapes that were typical, iconic, or symbolic of nationhood. Instead, she explored the problematic relations between making and seeing that resulted from bringing European modernism to bear on an intimately known portion of an African "white man's land." Although they depicted the Transvaal landscape as empty of prior inhabitation, her paintings did not convey a sense of distance from it, because the struggle to reconcile the imaginative and representational consequences of imperialism and modernity with local attachment was embedded in their *making*. It was only in the second half of the twentieth century, when the facility of Pierneef's work came to be too closely associated with the inhuman rationalism of the modern apartheid state and narrow Afrikaner-based white identity, that the more nuanced, contingent, and local exchange between self and landscape posited by Everard's work came to be appreciated.[119]

Images of specific landscapes only come to be read as shared and universal once the economic and political order creates the possibility of a shared sentiment cognate, if not identical, to that which led to their creation.[120] Everard's depictions of the Komati valley ultimately came to do this because, by simultaneously embracing and containing the effects of modernity, they mediated its ideological contradictions. If modernity sets up a tension between the local, private, and subjective temporality of the self, on one hand, and the objectified, socially measurable, intersubjective temporality of capitalist "progress," on the other, then nostalgia is an attempt to connect the two.[121] Nostalgia is also, fundamentally, a longing for an *imagined* place, one that sustains the sense of continuity that is a key to identity. By invoking a noncognitive, somatic knowledge of the landscape that was innately nostalgic, Everard represented the landscape as an active and still-unresolved site of memory. Although the Komati valley was a geographical space removed from urban progress, her paintings, through their subject, point of view, and painterly vocabulary, depicted it as a place where a resolution between the organic and the planned might be achieved, or, in other words, where modernity might be reconciled with memory. Taken as a whole, her oeuvre embodied a deepening of—literally, a descent into—the imperial, continental prospects that had so entranced Buchan, Baker, and others. Permanently marked by the displacement of ambivalent, involuntary corporeal experience, Everard's paintings evoked a subjectivity characterized by hybridity and informality at the same time as they promoted an aesthetic of individual, contemplative retreat.

MODERNITY, MEMORY, AND THE
SOUTH AFRICAN RAILWAYS
The Iconography of Emptiness

> The scope of the organic becomes broader than that assimilable by instantaneous
> perception, since increased speed condenses space. . . . "Transcendence" becomes
> a function of a certain loss of immanence, a certain loss of innocence. As every
> increase in technology entails a corresponding increase in anxiety about the loss
> of the natural, so too does every such increase in speed transform the perceptual
> apparatus so as to overcompensate for such a loss.
>
> —Allen S. Weiss, "No Man's Garden: New England Transcendentalism and
>   the Invention of Virgin Nature"

We begin with a scene that could not have been photographed at the time it occurred, but was sketched later, from memory. At its center, a campfire carves out a space from the all-encompassing blackness of the African night. In the firelight, travelers gather around the bulky shape of an upright piano, and behind, the side of a train looms, distinguishable by the regular reflections of firelight in its compartment windows. The scene takes place some 120 kilometers north of the Komati valley, in the Lowveld, and, although it is midwinter, the night is balmy. The fire's appeal, for those gathered around, derives not so much from its warmth or light but from the fact that they are in the middle of the wilderness. In the surrounding veld, the calls of lions and hyenas are distinctly audible in the intervals between melodies emanating from the piano, but the engine's searchlight playing in circles over the dark veld beyond the campfire helps reduce their fears to a frisson. One of those gathered around the fire finds himself looking up at "the purple South African sky out of which the stars look down on us in amazement, for we are here alone, not any other human being for fifty miles"; his (or her) thoughts "wing their way across the veld and mountains of this wild and impressive district to far away England."[1]

This highly orchestrated scene was an integral part of the "Round-in-Nine" package tours of the Transvaal run by the South African Railways in the 1920s. The setting for the campfire was the Sabie Game Reserve, a two-and-a-half-million-acre

Campfire scene in the Sabie Game Reserve. *South Africa Railways & Harbours Magazine*, April 1928, p. 545; Transnet Heritage Museum Library.

tract set aside earlier in the century to protect game populations, later to become the world-famous Kruger National Park. At a time when there were neither roads nor accommodations in this reserve (or in much of the rest of the Transvaal, for that matter), the otherwise little-used Selati railway line that passed through it allowed South Africans and overseas tourists to penetrate to the heart of the wilderness, where they stopped intermittently to view game and eat meals, and slept at night on the train.[2] These trains were virtually self-sufficient hotels on wheels, specially designed for the long distances of travel in South Africa (see color plate 36). The contrast between the interiors of these trains, which were carefully crafted from South African materials, and the raw bush just beyond the window was dramatic; nobody traveling in South Africa at this time could have been untouched by the juxtapositioning of civilization and wildness that was such a memorable and characteristic aspect of the country.

As this episode suggests, the frontier of civilization that John Buchan had felt to be such a distinctive quality of South Africa and that Bertha Everard had striven to capture in her paintings of the Komati valley was still alive in the 1920s and had not necessarily been displaced by the infrastructure of the modern state. The coming of the railways had broadly the same effects in South Africa as it had in other countries, but it also transformed white South Africans' imaginative relationship with their national territory in unexpected and sometimes poetic ways. Although the railways weakened the contemplative, solitary, and local experience of an unspoiled landscape that lay at the heart of the cult of the veld, they fashioned instead a new subjectivity toward the landscape that was reflexive, collective, and national. The railways vastly increased the accessibility of the nation's territory, set up new ways of experiencing it, and led to new ways of representing and discussing it. Because this synergistic relationship between experience and discourse was the work of an organization that directly or indirectly affected most peoples' lives, it was far more influential in shaping the discursive landscape of the new nation than the work of any individual writer, artist, or even photographer. Fusing topographical materiality, representational effect, and collective memory, the policies and practices of the railways encouraged a shared white identification with the geographical place of the nation.

The government corporation of the South African Railways (SAR) was created by fiat from the Central South African Railways (CSAR) after the South African War, as part of the 1909 South Africa Act that led to union. The CSAR, itself a fusion of the prewar Cape Government Railways, Natal Government Railways, and Netherlands South Africa Railway Company (NZASM), had been created by Milner immediately after the South Africa War as a key instrument of reconstruction. Milner was especially interested in the railroad's ability to promote agriculture and rural settlement, and he initiated a comprehensive program of branch line construction. After 1910, this use of the railways as an instrument of social change continued as the Union government quickly saw that the SAR could bring about the economic and social integration of what had previously been four separate countries. As the largest single corporation in South Africa during the country's first decades of existence, the South African Railways' practices and policies influenced every aspect of its development. It helped transform the economy from an import-dependent, pastoral-based one into an export-oriented one, and forged the disparate regions of the subcontinent into a single modern, urbanized, and economically self-sufficient nation. After World War I, a comprehensive program of port expansion, grain silo and cold storage facility construction, and the acquisition of a fledgling merchant fleet were all reflected in the addition of "Harbours" to the corporation's name in 1922. The South African Railways & Harbours (hereafter, SAR&H) not only made possible the rapid expansion of the Witwatersrand industrial and mining complex, it also facilitated the mass migration of workers such expansion required. It was also instrumental in laying the foundations of South African forestry, broadcasting, road-haulage, electrification, manufacturing, filmmaking, and commercial air travel.[3]

Despite the fact that the decades after union were marked by drought, economic depression, and internal political unrest, by the mid-1920s the SAR&H had become the most powerful single corporation in the subcontinent and the second largest state-owned railway system in the world. By this time, it employed around 7 percent of the white population (many of them Afrikaners displaced from rural areas), and provided 10 percent of the country's population with their livelihood.[4] Moreover, the SAR&H's policies and practices had become all but indistinguishable from those of the Union government on education, labor, welfare, housing, and segregation.[5] Given that it was the largest, most ubiquitous corporation in what was still only a partly industrial society, it is understandable that the SAR&H came to be seen as a "government within a government." As a corporation that embodied modernity and technological progress, the SAR&H was the ideal means for transcending the crosscurrents of ethnically based politics that the colonial national state wished to overcome. At a time when any social change easily became construed as a confrontation between offshore capitalist imperialism and indigenous settler society, the apparently neutral technocratic objectivity and rationalism of the SAR&H allowed the government to indirectly use it to enact innovations that would have been difficult through direct legislation.

The same intertwining of imperialism, modernity, nation building, and technical know-how that underpinned the SAR&H's social agency was reflected in its administrators. Early railway culture in South Africa was chauvinistically Anglophile.[6] Most of the SAR&H's first generation of administrators had previously worked on railways in Britain or elsewhere in the empire and were generally in sympathy with the Botha and Smuts colonial national politics. If the minister of railways was one of the most important members of the Union government, then the SAR&H's general manager from 1910 to 1928, William Hoy, was one of the Union's most important civil servants.[7] Knighted in 1916, he accompanied Botha and Smuts to the Versailles Peace Conference in 1919, coordinated South Africa's contribution to the Empire Exhibition, and represented the Union at the Imperial Conference in London in 1924.[8] Throughout his career, Hoy cast himself as the paternalistic head of the big family of the SAR&H and exploited his nominally apolitical position to enact initiatives that were in the larger (that is, colonial national) interest.[9]

The SAR&H's power and authority were reinforced by the penetration of its seemingly synchronized, efficient, and reliable practices into many different aspects of social and economic life, as well as the ubiquitous reach of its infrastructure. In remote parts of South Africa, the railways' twin ribbons of steel and attendant structures were often the only visible signs of modern governance and civilization in the landscape; even the smallest wayside halt had exactly the same standardized place name board as the largest city, complete with elevation above sea level. Similarly, in an era when few could afford a car or telephone, the daily train was the only link many remote dorps had with the rest of the country and the outside world. Under these circumstances, it is easy to imagine how the railways became an iconographic symbol of the progressive white state during the early twentieth century, and how they were effective in overcoming practical and ideological opposition to modernization in backcountry areas. The national importance of railways was reflected in the establishment of the SAR&H headquarters in Johannesburg in the 1920s. This location avoided the historical associations that had bedeviled the choice of the Union's capital and emphasized the fact that by this time, thanks in part to the railways themselves, the Witwatersrand had become the economic heart of the country. It also mediated a remapping of the imagined national territory, in which the Rand with its mines and industries began to vie for cultural importance with the older colonial port cities with their cultivated, metropole-oriented societies.

This shift was confirmed by the massive new Park Station erected in the center of Johannesburg at the end of the 1920s. As Johannesburg's economic importance increased, its station became a significant point of embarkation for everyone who traveled in South Africa, whether they were ordinary travelers, tourists, or businessmen, and the station building needed to project the image of a successful and progressive corporation, while simultaneously accommodating and promoting local and national tourism.[10] Designed by Gerard Moerdijk and Baker-disciple Gordon Leith, the Park Station included long-distance and suburban platforms, the SAR&H

administration's offices, and a central concourse surrounded by Pierneef's murals (see color plate 37). From its main street entrance (see color plate 38), initially intended to be flanked by two elephants rampant, to the portals of its platforms, which hinted at the romance of long-distance travel to the nation's far-flung regions, this modern complex, like the London termini of the great English railway companies, announced the nation-building power of the SAR&H.[11] Pierneef's murals, which were eventually installed in 1932, heightened the effect of the station as a gateway to "the glorious and the unknown."[12] Compared to the three panels Smithard had executed for Pretoria Station some two decades earlier,[13] Pierneef's twenty-eight offered a greatly expanded vision of the national territory within a single, centrally located public space that all long-distance travelers had to pass through. The murals included twelve landscapes from Transvaal, nine from Cape Province, three from Natal; one from Orange Free State, two from South West Africa, and one from Basutoland.

Like most railway systems, however, the SAR&H constantly struggled to make money. Quite apart from the fact that few railway systems turn a profit on operational turnover, the SAR&H had inherited large overseas debts incurred in the original period of construction, and it urgently needed to recoup these costs.[14] Its primary means of repaying this debt was through increasing traffic. As we have seen, the introduction of railways into the South African subcontinent had been solely driven by the need to connect the mines to the coastal ports, with little thought given to the huge stretches of thinly populated country that lay in between, which had little incentive to generate agricultural surpluses until incorporated into the time-space of the national economy. Creating and tapping this potential market became an ongoing concern for the SAR&H and the Union government. Amending tariffs and transportation legislation helped increase traffic somewhat, but the chief means of doing so was a comprehensive program of branch line construction that fed traffic from remote districts into the main trunk routes. By the end of the 1920s, the mileage of the SAR&H's network was three times what it had been in 1902. Together with the construction of grain elevators at their termini and the state's increasing intervention in agriculture, these new lines played an important part in bringing about the capitalization of rural South Africa and the so-called grain revolution, which consolidated white commercial agriculture and destroyed black peasant subsistence pastoralism. The railways also helped effect this capitalization of agriculture during the 1910s and 1920s by facilitating the movement of Afrikaners ruined by war, drought, and depression to the cities and providing them with employment once they got there.

The connection of cities to rural areas, and backcountry producers to national and international markets, was not the only form of time-space commodification the railways used to increase their revenue. They also actively promoted noncommercial, passenger use of their network. At first, this had to be encouraged: as one *SAR&H Magazine* author argued in 1924: "What do they know of Africa who rust forever in their own particular town or farm or district? There is a crying need for what the French call *va et vient*, the coming and going."[15] Although such "coming and going" would obviously increase network usage and revenue, it had an added, quite political, dimension: the Union government's desire to get white South Africans from the different parts of the country, who quite recently had been opponents in what had effectively been a civil war, to identify with or at least understand each other. It was also an echo of—or perhaps an attempt to achieve by different means—one of the goals of Milnerite Reconstruction: to settle English-speaking immigrants in thinly populated rural areas. The encouragement of white South Africans to see their country and get to know their fellow citizens converged with the Union government's desire to attract overseas investment, immigration, and tourism to the country. All three were urgently needed if the envisaged "white man's country" was to become a reality, and, until 1938, the SAR&H was the government's designated instrument for promoting them.[16] The overt promotion of white immigration, especially immigration to rural areas, was, however, politically problematic for the imperially identified Botha and Smuts governments during the 1910s and 1920s, when many non-English-speaking whites were losing their land and sinking into poverty.[17] As a result, attracting the white middle-class settlers it was thought South Africa needed became subsumed into coded publicity emphasizing attractions such as opportunities for land ownership, the healthy climate, the relaxed outdoor way of life, and the beauty of the country's landscapes.[18]

Hoy was not only a politically astute visionary, but also a born publicist, who had worked earlier in his life as a journalist. He realized that ideals often need to be imagined and projected before they could be practically achieved: "it is not so much a question as to whether or not overseas people desire to see our country, as it is that we wish to create the desire."[19] In 1914, he successfully persuaded the Union Parliament that a properly funded publicity agency was needed to meet this broadened responsibility. The SAR&H Publicity Department only became functional in 1919, due to World War I, but under the direction of A. H. Tatlow it expanded quickly, setting up its first overseas offices in London in 1921 and others in New York and elsewhere a few years later. The department's mission fell into two broad categories: the marketing, organization, and running of actual tours, and the design, production, and dissemination of publications about South Africa that would encourage tourism, investment, and (hopefully) settlement. The railways' dominance in this regard was absolute: it took on the responsibility of coordinating all arrangements for visitors to the new National Park created in 1926, and by the early 1930s, it had entered into agreements with 130 separate overseas companies promoting tourism to the Union on a commission basis.[20]

One of the Publicity Department's most important organs was the *South African Railways & Harbours Magazine*. Edited by Tatlow with assistance from Hoy, the corporation's monthly journal was one of the most widely read periodicals in South Africa at this time.[21] It published a great diversity of illustrated articles about all aspects of the Union's national development, written by a wide spectrum of individuals, South African and otherwise, including some well-known authors. Despite this authorial diversity, the consistency of the *Magazine*'s editorial tone is such that one can speak of a corporate narrative in which the values and workings of the SAR&H, as well as the government of the day, can be traced.[22] In this corporate narrative, the SAR&H followed many European railway companies that used rhetoric and metaphor to augment their technological and administrative authority, bind that authority up with nation building, and cast themselves as makers of history.[23] In addition, both through its choice of topics and the way these were treated, the *Magazine* also encouraged in its readers a sensibility of "seeing through other's eyes" similar to that which permeated other colonial national discourse about South Africa's future at this time.[24] Deploying a rhetoric of synecdochic nationalism,[25] it published many travel impressions, some written by overseas visitors, which compared well-known landscapes within South Africa to each other as well as to those in other countries.

Before turning to the abundance of print and visual culture created by the Publicity Department, however, we need to consider other less discursive though equally important ways in which the SAR&H helped to transform the imaginary territory of the nation in the 1920s. Changes in cultural values are invariably mediated by changes in spatial practice, and concomitantly, in the way the world is encountered. The expanded railway network not only increased and accelerated the circulation of goods and people through the country, it also altered the experience of geographical space. At the same time as the policies and initiatives of the SAR&H were helping to shape the social, economic, and political life of the new country, the railways were also having a profound impact on how its citizens encountered and interpreted the national territory, both imaginatively and as "corporeal subjects moving through material landscapes."[26] These encounters with the national territory played a powerful, albeit unintended, role in encouraging whites to see and celebrate the nominally united nation.

Traveling by Train, Transforming Lived Space

In early twentieth-century South Africa, as elsewhere, the transformation of the imaginary space of the nation by railways gave rise to a whole array of phenomenological effects that can be categorized as either infrastructural or "traveling." The former derived from the railways apparatus itself: where lines began and ended; how they were laid out in the landscape; the speed, duration, frequency, and cost of the journey; even the design of the carriages in which the traveler journeyed. The latter had to do with the corporeal experience of space, place, and territory engendered by this infrastructural apparatus. Both effects played a role in the railways' framing of the South African landscape.

Like Baker's rock-hewn buildings that helped mediate an understanding of the subcontinent as a landscape of rock and stone, the construction of the railways became a tectonic delving into the subcontinent's nature that transformed imperialistic visual appropriation into something more substantive. And like the multivalent orientation of Baker's houses on Parktown Ridge, the alignment of the railway helped to topographically characterize a previously unknown terrain. This incorporation of the terrain through engineering is, of course, latent in all railway construction, but in South Africa it was heightened by historical circumstances. Because railway construction in the subcontinent preceded industrialization and even settlement in many areas, the lines often stood in stark contrast to the terrain they traversed.[27] As in the United States, the contrast between modern infrastructure and wilderness lent the early South African railways a phenomenological presence and intensity that was unavoidable for anyone who encountered them.[28] This effect was heightened by the lack of detailed topographical knowledge about the interior, which combined with the unusually narrow gauge (adopted to speed construction of the lines into the interior) produced lines that emphasized, even exaggerated, the topographical character of the terrain they traversed.[29] The 3' 6" gauge allowed alignments to follow the terrain more

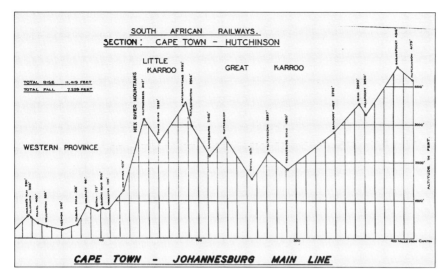

Elevations, Cape Town–Hutchinson section of the SAR. From *South African Railways: History, Scope and Organization* (Johannesburg: SAR&H Public Relations Dept., 1947), opp. p. 76; Transnet Heritage Museum Library.

closely, saved construction time and money by minimizing blasting and embanking, and permitted the exploitation of narrower mountain defiles.[30] But it also meant that lines frequently passed through totally unpopulated areas, following extravagantly serpentine alignments in mountainous terrain or arrow-straight vectors many miles long in the open interior, and that South African trains traveled more slowly than trains in other countries. All of these facts affected how South Africa's national territory came to be perceived, once these lines began to carry passenger trains.

Along with the local, topographical effects brought about by railway construction came the transformation of lived space wrought by train travel itself. Although Milner's schemes failed to eradicate the geographical and cultural separation between English- and Dutch-speaking whites, the railways brought about some of the same effects by expanding the horizons of the average white South African from the local to the regional and national, and by cutting across historic regional differences at a number of different levels. Railways not only incorporated distant places into the national economy, they also made it possible for citizens to visit those distant places. Although slow in modern terms, early South African trains dramatically shrank journeys that had previously taken days, or even weeks.[31] In any case, the railways' ability to draw together the different parts of South Africa was as much a consequence of their reliability as their speed. This ability to integrate the country within a single imaginary was exemplified by the coordinated national timetable, which linked all stations from the Cape to the Limpopo.

The experience of traveling by train also brought about a commonality of geographical experience unthinkable today. In a country of South Africa's size, where proper roads were rare outside urban areas and cars expensive, the train was the only affordable long-distance transportation until the 1950s.[32] Train travel forced everyone who traveled to do so at the same speed and between the same termini. To the extent that it divided these travelers into different classes, it also reflected and strengthened social divisions already inherent in the wider society.[33] The commonality of experience imposed by train travel was grounded in the fixity of railway infrastructure, unlike car travel, for instance, with its invitation to freedom, adventure, and opportu-

Kaaimans River bridge construction. MuseumAfrica Photographic Collection, file ref. Neave Collection; reproduced with permission.

nity for individualized experience.[34] All travelers between the same destinations saw the same landscape every time. The prescribed yet evanescent view from the train window not only framed the territory it passed through as something primarily seen (that is, as landscape), but it did so for more people than had been possible before in a regularized way.

This evanescent view from the train—the perception of what was out there—was not only determined by where the tracks went in the landscape but also by the design of the train itself, that is, where one was sitting. The SAR&H developed a hybrid of American and European carriage design for its long-distance trains that allowed travelers to move about and visit lounges and dining cars during journeys of more than a few hours, which they usually were in South Africa.[35] (The design and manufacture of these cars, which used South African woods and hides wherever possible, was a source of some pride to the SAR&H and the subject of frequent articles in the *Magazine*.)[36]

"Entrance to the Karoo" (railway with figures). Cape Archives, Jeffreys Collection #J866; reproduced with permission.

These train-sets were also designed to go for long periods without replenishment of food and water supplies (even, on the remote Kimberley to Bulawayo route, to make the return journey), a necessity when traveling through country with few facilities along the way. The experience of traveling in these self-contained, autonomous long-distance trains echoed the dramatic juxtaposing of modern infrastructural technology and wild environing terrain set up by the railway line itself. This effect was as dramatic for overseas visitors as it was for white South Africans, for whom, until very recently, travel had involved a close dependency on the terrain through which they were passing. Given this pervasive sense of contrast, it is not surprising that journeys on the SAR&H's long-distance trains were vividly experienced as "ventures into the unknown," connected back to civilization only by an umbilical cord of steel track.[37]

The detached view from the moving train also encouraged the viewer to see the landscape with something akin to panoramic perception. Always undergirded by the self-effacing apparatus that moves the viewer through the world, panoramic perception distances the viewer from the perceived object, and places him or her in a reflective relationship toward it. At the same time, it promotes a transformation of consciousness cognate with the transformation of the locally attached individual into a citizen of an imaginary nation. In South Africa, panoramic perception not only removed the traveler from direct bodily engagement with the terrain, it also unveiled a topography in which the relational qualities of the whole emerged as a product of effortless, uninterrupted movement. Key to this new vision was the fact, frequently

View from the summit of Hex River Pass. Transnet Heritage Museum Library Photographic Collection, neg. #1433; reproduced with permission.

remarked upon at the time, that the expansive scale of South African landscape had previously been incomprehensible because it unfolded too slowly. The train traveling at 30 mph made it possible to grasp, for the first time, South African territory as a coherent and characterful landscape. As one article in the *Magazine* asserted: "it is no inconsiderable thing to have an entrancing panorama unrolling itself minute by minute through the glass panels at your window, never so fast as to be obscured, and never so slow as to forfeit the tantalizing element which is so important to artistic pleasure."[38] "In any 50 miles in Europe, the traveler goes through endless changes of scene, with a fresh landmark at every turn [but in] South Africa, a mere 50 miles hardly takes you from one geological formation to another, let alone to a new type of vegetation or scenery"—observations like this would, quite simply, have been impossible without the synoptic, unfolding vision afforded by train travel.[39] Thus, the railway journey "choreographed" (to borrow Schivelbusch's term) the parts of the subcontinent characterized by monotony, size, and light into a continuous imaginary whole: "The velocity and linearity with which the train traversed the landscape did not destroy it. . . . [Instead] the motion of the train . . . displayed in immediate succession objects and pieces of scenery that in their original spatiality belonged in separate realms."[40]

From the early 1920s onward, a variety of initiatives began to make these effects accessible to increasing numbers of white South Africans. Improvements to rolling stock and rights-of-way improved the comfort and speed of trains, and seasonal excursion fares were reduced between the Witwatersrand and Cape Town and Port

Elizabeth in the summer, Durban and the South Coast during the winter. By the end of the decade, these advantageous fares were being offered on dedicated holiday excursion trains to a variety of destinations, including Lourenço Marques in Portuguese East Africa. The model for these long-distance trains were the Union Limited and the Union Express, the first-class express service introduced in 1923 between Cape Town and Pretoria, which soon became popular with Rand magnates, government officials, and other members of the white establishment, as well as overseas visitors. These Cape-to-Rand express trains were scheduled to connect with the weekly arrival and departure of the Union Castle mail boats that linked Cape Town and Southampton, events that became defining rituals of colonial national social life and reinforced the synchronization of national and imperial time-space.[41] (These trains also became an important part of another peculiarly South African phenomenon: the government's twice-yearly migration between its legislative and administrative capitals of Cape Town and Pretoria.)[42] The Cape-to-Rand and other long-distance services began to establish seasonal migrations and patterns of leisure time usage, and encouraged the development of coastal resorts within reach of the train lines, promoted by SAR&H publicity material. The emergence of fashionable resorts such as Sea Point, Muizenberg, Mossel Bay, Port Elizabeth, East London, and Port St. Johns during this period exemplified how railways concentrate cultural attention on the places they render accessible.

Because of these improvements, passenger miles rose consistently during the 1920s, as not only South Africans but also overseas visitors started traveling more and exploring previously unvisited parts of the country in greater numbers. Railways had been used for tourism in South Africa as early as 1901, when Thomas Cook organized tours to the battlefields.[43] Tourism planned by the railways themselves started in 1906, with a tour organized by the Central South African Railways from the Cape to Victoria Falls. After World War I, the Publicity Department started organizing several tours each season, using scheduled train services. From 1923 onward, these were supplemented by dedicated train tours, the so-called "Round-in-Seven" (or "Eight" or "Nine," depending on the region and itinerary) tours. On these tours, travelers slept, ate, and traveled on a train and were taken on bus drives to visit farms, factories, mountains, or coastal bays. The tours took advantage of the remote regions the railway lines passed through and provided travelers with experiences of landscapes like the Lowveld, which were otherwise completely inaccessible. Promotional material about these tours assured the traveler that some omniscient agent of civilization had gone before them into the unknown. The SAR&H was the only corporation able to run such tours, because its trains could substitute for modern hotels, which were still rare or nonexistent in remote areas at this time. The primary overseas clients for these tours were groups of British and American cruise passengers, who started arriving in South Africa from 1925 onward.[44]

Constructing a Structure of Seeing

Inseparable from this promotion of *va et vient* was the most ubiquitous and lasting aspect of the SAR&H Publicity Department's work: the array of publications it produced to describe life in South Africa and provide information for potential tourists, investors, and settlers, both local and overseas.[45] These publications, printed in runs of up to thirty thousand, included regional guides, as well as booklets, guides, and brochures on investment, farming, travel, game reserves, history, and various forms of recreation.[46] Dozens of these were commissioned during the 1920s for circulation at home and overseas, and many of them were collaborations with local authorities. Covering both popular tourist resorts and regions newly accessible via branch lines, these publications were often the first systematic descriptions of many parts of the country.[47]

An essential component of all the Publicity Department's publications were pictures of the South African landscape. In addition to its many other nation building operations, the SAR&H was the primary commissioner, publisher, and purveyor of images of the country at this time. It produced dozens of lantern slide sets hired out for use in public lectures in South Africa and overseas, and financed and collaborated in the production of the first films about South Africa, which were screened in passenger liners on the transatlantic and Australian runs.[48] Realizing that South Africa faced increasingly sophisticated competition overseas, the department turned to watercolors, woodcuts, and other forms of artwork, commissioning posters from some of the better-known artists of the day.[49] Some of this artwork was used for the railways posters that were printed in limited runs; others were placed as double-page spreads in popular metropolitan magazines with an imperial circulation, like the *Illustrated London News* and the *Sketch*. The expense of commissioning and reproducing these color images was justified in an era before color photography, because they made it possible to represent, in one image, two aspects of the South African landscape that, it was increasingly realized, were its chief attractions for overseas visitors: the sensual effects of the country's dry sunny climate, and the diversity of its terrain.[50] Like Pierneef's panels for the Johannesburg Station, these posters helped promote a synecdochic vision of the national landscape.

However, by far the most ubiquitous and important form of landscape imagery put out by the SAR&H Publicity Department was black-and-white photography. Taken at first for use in SAR&H's own publications, photographs also appeared in the compartments of its passenger trains, on posters in the windows of publicity offices in South Africa and overseas,[51] and eventually on other national railways, in foreign magazines and newspapers, and books about South Africa. In time, these photographs depicting both well-known resorts and out-of-the-way parts of the country began to form a substantial archive: in 1921, this archive already comprised twenty thousand negatives, and by 1928 around three thousand more were being added every year.[52] Although the quality of the images was extremely variable, the SAR&H's photographic archive was also extremely comprehensive, and it became the definitive source for images of the country, used by publicists, publishers, and editors in South Africa and the rest of the world.[53] Few photographs of South Africa published during the 1920s do not carry a credit to the "SAR&H Publicity Department."[54] These ubiquitous black-and-white images (color photographs only began to be taken and reproduced in the 1940s), often of anonymous authorship, were ultimately the most significant representations shaping the imaginative geography of nationhood during the interwar period.

The SAR&H's enthusiastic embrace of photography was no accident: during the second half of the nineteenth century, a powerful synergy had arisen between rail-

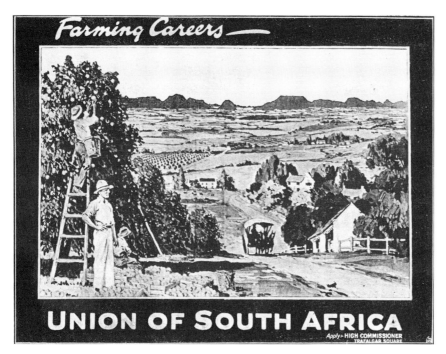

Advertising South
Africa in Great Britain.
*South African Railways
& Harbours Magazine*,
May 1923, p. 461;
Transnet Heritage
Museum Library.

ways and photography. Both were new technologies that regulated and ordered time
and space; natural allies in the creation and definition of new political territories,
they lent themselves to modern governance and nation building.[55] Photography's apparent transparency, clarity, and precision made it the ideal medium for corporations
like railway companies, whose authority was founded on technology, rationality, and
modernity.[56] This synergy was especially potent in overseas colonies, where connections between photography and railways as icons of modernity and European technology were repeatedly underscored by photographs of trains, stations, and dramatic
sections of lines that spoke of imperialism's benign progress.[57] The incentive to travel
created by railways' speed and reliability was complemented by photography's ability
to bring place to wherever an audience happened to be, and to engage their desire to
travel to places where they were not.[58] This joint conquering of space by photography
and railways not only encouraged circulation but mapped out the imaginary space
of circulation. In South Africa, this synergistic relationship between photography
and railways was heightened by the railways' establishment shortly after reproducible photographic imagery had entered everyday life. The development of collotype
and photolithography processes at the end of the nineteenth century, along with the
South African War, inaugurated a golden age of postcards that would last until the
beginning of World War I, during which time postcards were the primary form of
day-to-day communication and the main source of cheap, readily available images.[59]

Like other large railway companies, the SAR initially used photography as a
means of documenting its own operations, but it soon realized that the same kinds
of pictures could also allay misconceptions about train travel and attract potential
travelers.[60] Between 1910 and 1920, it reproduced many photographs depicting
newly completed lines as well as scenes of their previous survey and construction—
photographs that valorized the quite literal effects of nation building mentioned ear-

lier. The prospect of the railway line "[winding] away . . . in the distance, unfenced and unembanked, a light streak in a barren land" (as one early twentieth-century traveler described it) was a recurring and powerful motif at this time.[61] The railway line itself acted as a kind of prosthesis by which viewing subjects could insert themselves into an otherwise forbiddingly empty and arid landscape, transposing metaphysical longings for union with nature and embodying an imaginative synthesis of the nation and landscape. These kinds of connotations were especially potent in photographs that depicted the man-made line's sleek, unencumbered ("unfenced and unembanked") passage through wild, irregular terrain, or where the viewpoint of the photograph was manipulated so as to balance the dynamic movement of the railway with the resistant elements of the landscape.

The iconographic power of these passages through the landscape was augmented by later photographs of the same stretches of line in use: a typical SAR&H image depicts an express passenger train under full steam, winding its way dramatically through the scrubby *krantzes* (rocky outcrops or defiles) of the coastal mountains. Another frequently reproduced image, that of an SAR&H train crossing the Karoo, shows that this imaginary was equally vivid in the flat, open landscape of the interior: the ensemble of train and track allowed the landscape to be scaled and read, while simultaneously emphasizing its expansive, minimally differentiated topography. Images like these, in which unimproved landscape and railway simultaneously resisted and gave form to each other, suggested a "dissonant concordance" between technology and geology. Characterizing the terrain as topography, they naturalized the railway as an instrument of modernization. This naturalization, however, was qualitatively different from that which occurred in nineteenth-century Europe, where the introduction of the railway into long-inhabited landscapes had given rise to a phenomenal dialectic between modernity and history. In early twentieth-century South Africa, by contrast, it produced a dialectic between modernity and wilderness.[62]

As they proliferated and were reproduced, these various images discursively helped incorporate the entire country in one overarching narrative of time and space, an imaginary geography based on topographic figuration. They mediated an imaginative mapping of the subcontinent that was simultaneously about elevation and distance—precisely the phenomena that all railway construction seeks to overcome—and it is no accident that many descriptions of train travel in South Africa at this time figure the coastal mountains as something to overcome on the way to the elevated, open interior.[63] The most telling (and commonly experienced) example of this was the northward, upward journey from Cape Town across the Karoo to the Rand. This journey, which in the 1920s took two nights and a day, simultaneously invoked the lingering romance of great northward imperial trunk routes, and rhetorically cast the interior as a landscape of the future, toward which national progress directed

itself.[64] As South Africa's economic center of gravity shifted to a city that was "higher up than Zermatt," such narratives became key representations that synecdochically integrated space and time of an emerging imaginary geography with the corporeal experience of the traveler.[65]

There is little doubt that photographs commissioned and disseminated by SAR&H simultaneously promoted and confirmed the transformation of time-space occurring in South Africa during this period. At the turn of the twentieth century,

"Union Limited in Tulbagh Kloof." Transnet Heritage Museum Library Photographic Collection, neg. #46383; reproduced with permission.

little of South African territory appears to have been, in itself, considered picturable, that is, worth transfixing and reproducing for detailed appreciation, in part because people were not used to seeing it pictured. By the 1930s, however, a wide range of landscape motifs, effects, and points of views had acquired cultural currency in an emergent structure of seeing that mirrored white South Africans' familiarization and identification with the national territory. The SAR&H was intimately involved in this process of familiarization through picturing, both intentionally (through the aesthetics of travel promotion) and unintentionally (through the apparently objective use of photography that expanded the contexts and discourses in which landscape imagery played a role).[66] The evolving nature of the SAR&H photographs' subjects allows us to trace the parallel visualization of the national territory in early twentieth-century South Africa. Tracing the construction of this imagistic landscape is a complex process, because it is at once heuristic, iterative, and always ongoing. Although photographs become active in shaping the ways landscapes are viewed and valued when placed in circulation, their capacity to mediate a modernization of collective vision is by no means instrumental or unlimited.[67] In addition to the changing economic, political, and material factors shaping the use of the landscape, all territories have an inherent material aspect, for which a way of looking needs to be found. As in the United States a few decades earlier, it took time for South African photographers to accept the actual physical reality around them and find effective ways of capturing it. The photographer's scope for composition is more limited than that of the painter,

"A Passenger Train Crossing the Karoo." Transnet Heritage Museum Library Photographic Collection, neg. #24918, reproduced with permission.

restricted by the need to aim the camera at one particular piece of reality as well as by the alchemic transformation of the motif by technology, first when the photograph is taken, and then when it is reproduced and captioned.

The *SAR&H Magazine*'s assiduous promotion of photography itself suggests that those who ran the Publicity Department were not unaware of this subtle, imagistic aspect of nation building. The *Magazine* ran annual competitions for photographs that depicted "South African scenic features of general or unusual interest." It also frequently published articles on "photographers' adventures" that suggested how one should see the landscape, and highlighted the photogenic qualities and best viewpoints of specific parts of South Africa. The structure of seeing mediated by these articles was, initially at least, marked by the subjectivity of the colonial national administrators who commissioned and published them, which could best be described as ambivalent. As we have repeatedly seen, landscape vision is never innocent of cultural memory: landscapes engage the imagination through connections between the here and now of the site and some other there and then.[68] And, as we have also seen, the intensity of this coupling of seeing and remembering is always heightened for those who travel between cultures. This heightened tension between seeing and remembering would have been especially strong for functionaries of a government consciously trying to forge a new identity grounded in personal, subjective communing with an unimproved landscape.[69] Even at the same time as they were working to bring the railways to previously inaccessible regions, the "borrowed vision" of those who commissioned and disseminated the SAR&H's early photographs was also, paradoxically, one in which railways were far too reminiscent of contemporary Britain to be "the permanent interest in South Africa."[70]

The beginnings of what white South Africans found worth transfixing and reproducing for detailed appreciation can be traced in postcard scenes taken during the first decade of the twentieth century.[71] As in other colonial countries, the photographer's attention was drawn not so much by the landscape per se, but by the mines, civic buildings, or railways that were the agents of early settlement, or locales associated with significant events such as births, deaths, treaties, or battles.[72] Images of the general or ambient terrain are confined to occasional town overviews; other than this, the

MODERNITY, MEMORY, AND THE SOUTH AFRICAN RAILWAYS

"Mountain, Wood & Stream," scene on the Groote River, 1920s. Transnet Heritage Museum Library Photographic Collection, neg. #29370; reproduced with permission.

only images that could be described as landscapes were tightly framed street scenes, or distinctive local water features like dams, lakes, rivers, bridges, or waterfalls, sometimes enframing recognizable referents such as human figures, pleasure boats, vehicles, or livestock.[73] These subjects suggest both an audience that was, for the most part, European-born, and a decidedly sentimental, picturesque sensibility. In these early photographs, it impossible to separate the newly arrived immigrant's structure of seeing from the mentality of seeing through others' eyes that permeated colonial nationalists' search for cultural legitimacy. The picturability of these scenes stemmed not from their typicality or South Africanness, but from the fact that they were recognizable motifs in an otherwise undeveloped and possibly overwhelmingly empty territory. Reproducible images of signs of civilization (whether mines, civic buildings, and railways, or historic sites) not only made these seem more substantial and numerous than they were, but also served as certifications of civic responsibility. They provided a visual record of the urban settlements that structured overseas visitors' itineraries, and confirmed that metropolitan standards of governance—evidenced by orderly streets, flourishing commerce, and prominent government buildings—were to be found in the colony. These photographs' captions suggest that they were largely seen (and bought) as icons of local pride and identity, something that is not surprising since this was a time when the different parts of South Africa had not yet begun to operate as a unified society. Nevertheless, this structure of seeing attuned to recognizable signs of modern governance and civic progress played into the SAR&H and its predecessors' perceptions of themselves as makers of the nation and history, and images of their own stations and rolling stock were frequent subjects for postcards.[74]

During the decade following 1910, however, other kinds of subjects began to draw the eye and the camera, as immigrant memories began to fade and became overlaid by experiences of traveling to different parts of South Africa. Towns, factories, and mines were no longer remarkable phenomena, but familiar fixtures in an increasing number of white South Africans' lifeworlds. Trains, stations, and railway infrastructure became less common as subjects, and depictions of factories and mines disappear almost completely; landscape images as a whole became more frequent and varied in their subject matter. They depicted not only identifiable and peopled towns, streets, buildings, and gardens but also, for the first time, unpeopled stretches of country, landscapes that no longer needed the enframing or scaling device of trains, buildings, or people, but stood alone, as subjects in themselves. Initially, these images had a clear visual motif that invited recognition: either a scene that had already acquired iconic quality through constant repetition by painters—the view of Table Mountain rising out of the ocean to welcome the shipboard traveler, for instance—or ones that could be characterized through likeness. In the *Magazine*, the latter genre of image first appeared to illustrate travel accounts and regional descriptions that proposed various out-of-the way vacation places as South African equivalents of (or substitutes for) landscapes already reified in Britain. Thus, Port Alfred is cast as "the Dartmouth of South Africa," the Garden Route is described as having "the quiet serenity of Cumberland or Westmoreland," and Hermanus is rendered as the centerpiece of an expanded "South African Riviera" that radiated out from Cape Town.[75]

Winding through this use of English or European places and pasts to interpret the South African landscape of the present, however, there was a growing awareness that this approach might be inadequate for construing some of the country then being opened up by the SAR&H's branch lines. Here as before, earlier, imperial readings of the landscape in terms of a European citationary structure were challenged not only by the physical aspect of the country, but also by an ongoing restructuring of vision in those who actually inhabited it. Thus, during the 1920s, there was a growing interest in identifying, defining, and depicting "typically South African" (as opposed to local) landscape subjects. A whole array of places and regions never depicted before were proposed as landscape, and it is during this period that the circuit of tourist sights familiar to us today from decades of photography, started to become codified and reinscribed through recurring tourist practice. Some of these subjects one would expect: Kaaimans River and the beaches at Wilderness on the Garden Route, both of which had recently been made accessible by train, the Garden of Desolation near Graaf-Reinet, or Giant's Castle in the Drakensberg. Others echo Buchan's fascination with topographical boundaries and passages: the passes through the mountains, such as Magoebaskloof and Kowyns Pass in the northern and eastern Transvaal, the gorge where the Crocodile River carves its way into the Transvaal Escarpment near Waterval-Onder, and the Swartberg Pass between the Little and Great Karoo. Others still suggested an increasing recognition of regional difference in the landscape and were not so predictable: the winelands of the Cape, the mountain-enclosed Little Karoo near Oudtshoorn, the arid expanses of the Great Karoo, the endless, rolling hills of the Transkei, even occasionally the Rand mine dumps.[76]

This growing array of depictions revealed that, in fact, South Africa had many unusual landscape sights, and toward the end of the 1920s, SAR&H publicity material began, for the first time, to use a trope that would become a fixture of South African tourist promotion: that of South Africa as a land of contrasts. Even this apparent

218

MODERNITY,
MEMORY, AND THE
SOUTH AFRICAN
RAILWAYS

Blaauwberg Strand, Cape Town. Transnet Heritage Museum Library Photographic Collection, neg. #46843; reproduced with permission.

shift toward a more indigenous structure of seeing, however, remained conditioned by the landscape disposition of the SAR&H's publications, which for the most part were identical for local and overseas markets. Thus promotion of South Africa as a country one visited for the diversity of its landscapes could not be separated from the reality that, whatever their local significance or appeal, South Africa's towns and cities were but pale imitations of places Northern Hemisphere visitors were familiar with, and that for these visitors, the *general landscape* was a "setting which outshone its stone."[77] This formulation of South Africa as a land of contrasts also served to reassure tourists unsure whether to invest the considerable amounts of time and money required to visit the country.[78] Thus, the constitutive intertwining of indigenous and offshore imaginings even shaped the cultural appropriation of landscapes that apparently could not be found anywhere else.

The best example of this was the declaration of South Africa's first National Park, an event that marked an important threshold in white South Africans' growing familiarization and identification with their national territory landscape in the 1920s. As Jane Carruthers has argued, the establishment of Kruger National Park was a triumph for both nature conservation and national reconciliation.[79] It also enshrined outdoor life in an undomesticated terrain devoid of native inhabitants as an imaginary strand of a national identity. Like other milestones in the evolution of whites' structure of seeing, the first national park was the result of some debate. Initially, the editorial voice of the *Magazine* adopted a not unexpectedly European stance on this, inclining toward the most elevated ramparts of the Drakensberg, which rise to over eleven thousand feet, and which no doubt evoked strong associations with the Alps.[80] By the mid-1920s, however, the Drakensberg had been displaced in discourse by an utterly different landscape: the Sabie and Singwitsi Game Reserves, which had been

A Karoo farm. Transnet Heritage Museum Library Photographic Collection, neg. #3509; reproduced with permission.

Hermanus. Transnet Heritage Museum Library Photographic Collection, neg. #53135; reproduced with permission.

Near Oudtshoorn. Transnet Heritage Museum Library Photographic Collection, neg. #50946; reproduced with permission.

Kaaimans River in the 1920s. Transnet Heritage Museum Library Photographic Collection, neg. #509566; reproduced with permission.

Wilderness lagoon in the 1920s. Transnet Heritage Museum Library Photographic Collection, neg. #40940; reproduced with permission.

222

Swartberg Pass. Transnet Heritage Museum Library Photographic Collection, neg. #32304; reproduced with permission.

Transkei, general view. Transnet Heritage Museum Library Photographic Collection, neg. #48284; reproduced with permission.

God's Window, near Graskop, Transvaal. Transnet Heritage Museum Library Photographic Collection, neg. #20199; reproduced with permission.

View of Drakensberg (Giant's Castle). National Archives and Records Service of South Africa, file ref. #SAB 204; reproduced with permission.

created at the same time as Fitzpatrick had published his paean to the "mysterious veld." This territory, which eventually became Kruger Park in 1926, was located in the most un-European part of South Africa, the hot, humid, fever-ridden Lowveld.[81] Nevertheless, this decidedly African region tapped into Americans' fascination with South Africa's wildness, as well as imperial memories of the Lowveld as an exotic no-man's-land, familiar from the novels of Rider Haggard, Kipling, and Buchan.[82] Kruger Park was another expression of the cult of the veld and the broad shift in landscape taste in the 1920s away from landscapes of inhabitation and productive use and toward ones defined as both empty and external to society.[83] Game reserves reflected the growing psychological and physical necessity of setting aside land, as more rural districts started to be brought under commercial and scientific agriculture and subjected to scrutiny by prospectors, engineers, and geologists.[84]

As is often the case, the agents of tourism were implicated in the construction of the pristine wilderness subject to patriarchal stewardship: the SAR&H role in both the creation and the administration of this apparently nonpartisan icon of nationhood not only revealed its close connections with the Union government, but also its ambiguous role in mediating this nationalization of nature. Although railways are an unlikely component of any landscape construed as wilderness, as we have already seen, the underdevelopment of the South African interior developed surprisingly powerful synergies with the railways' practices. In fact, in South Africa, as in other colonial nations, railways were critical agents both in bringing visitors who appreciated remote and wild places and in creating the sensibility that led to their preservation in the first place. (Indeed, railways often depended on this appreciation and preservation to generate traffic.) During the early 1920s, the *Magazine* carried several articles extolling the delights of the Lowveld game reserves, illustrated by photographs taken by the specialist wildlife photographers, woodcuts, and pen sketches.[85]

MODERNITY, MEMORY, AND THE SOUTH AFRICAN RAILWAYS

First train entering Selati game reserve, 1912. South African National Parks Stevenson-Hamilton Collection, file ref. M3-7; reproduced with permission of James Stevenson-Hamilton.

(In these images, it is tempting to see the springbok, lion, or cheetah serving a similar role to the solitary tree in Everard's and Pierneef's paintings of the same period: a witness figure that simultaneously constructed and encouraged identification with an imaginary wilderness.) Several of these articles were written by game warden James Stevenson-Hamilton, the passionate promoter of the reserve since 1902, and illustrated by the painter and cultural critic Strat Caldecott. Caldecott, who had been commissioned by the SAR&H to design posters promoting tours to the Lowveld, and Stevenson-Hamilton, who became Kruger's first superintendent in 1926, soon struck up a friendship, and the two men's articles about the park, in the *Magazine* and elsewhere, were influential in rallying public opinion in its favor.

Once Kruger Park had been established, the SAR&H was responsible for its management before the fledgling National Parks Board was able to do so, and the park immediately became a centerpiece of its early package tours.[86] During these early years, a lack of funds abetted Stevenson-Hamilton's determination to keep the facilities of the park as primitive and minimal as possible, in order to sustain the experience of returning to the frontier or pioneering past.[87] Thus, a paradoxical synergy developed between the strategic and infrastructural operations of the state-run railways and the freedom and sense of adventure experienced by the park visitor.

The "Empty Veld" and the Reframing of History

The creation of Kruger Park both reminds us of the limits of photography in mediating collective vision and highlights the way its capacity to transform seeing is bound up with material practices and political ideologies. Political and social factors may have encouraged notions that the Lowveld was a landscape without precedent where white South Africans might understand their ancestors. However, it was not particularly photogenic, at least not when depicted in black-and-white photographs

MODERNITY, MEMORY, AND THE SOUTH AFRICAN RAILWAYS

Rest camp in the Kruger National Park, with ranger in foreground. South African National Parks Stevenson-Hamilton Collection, file ref. M4-36; reproduced with permission of James Stevenson-Hamilton.

Kruger National Park, 1932 (car and lions). MuseumAfrica Photographic Collection, file ref. MA590.72 Game Reserves; reproduced with permission.

subjected to the low-resolution reproduction processes common at this time, which were better suited to depicting spatially less complex environments. (Hence, most images the SAR&H used to promote Kruger Park did not illustrate its landscape but its wild animals, which were often best captured by pen sketches or woodcuts.)

At the same time, though, the declaration of Kruger Park confirmed how the white South African structure of seeing had become identified with the empty, unequivocally African landscape in the 1920s. (As we have already seen, wildness is invariably cognate with an absence of human inhabitation, or emptiness.) Perceptions of the subcontinent as empty had, of course been a constant refrain in travel writing by

Curios by the train, Victoria Falls station. Transnet Heritage Museum Library Photographic Collection neg. #35464; reproduced with permission

visiting Europeans since the early nineteenth century,[88] and they had been used to justify Boer expansion in the 1840s and British annexation in the early 1900s, two historic episodes in which there had been a coincidence between the colonizer's time of arrival and a temporary depopulation brought about by war.[89] And, as we have seen in preceding chapters, constructions of South Africa as "empty" had helped mediate a whole array of other cultural anxieties and fantasies during the first part of the twentieth century, the most significant of which was the imaginative erasure of prior African inhabitants from the landscape. It is probably fair to say that this erasure had become an integral part of the white worldview by the 1920s and 1930s, as successive acts of legislation emptied the South African interior using methods as effective as the earlier armies and commandos, sending African populations into reserves and poor whites into the industrializing cities. By this time, it had become hard to separate perceptions of the subcontinent's emptiness from the *desire* to see it as empty.

The policies and practices of the SAR&H had of course played their part in this emptying of the landscape, but railway travel itself fostered the perception that it *was* empty. The reserves to which Africans were increasingly confined during the 1920s and 1930s were usually far from the railway lines, and the diminishing likelihood that the train traveler would encounter them was reinforced by the tendency for people at the side of the track to appear, in the words of one traveler, as "mere picturesque phantoms with whom one is never destined to have any personal relations."[90] When travelers did encounter Africans in the landscape, it was for limited spells of time, as supplicants "clamoring for bonsellas [handouts]" at wayside stations, when the train was in some ambiguous realm, somewhere between the city and the rural landscape. This imaginative erasure of African rights to the land was echoed in SAR&H's publications, which depicted Africans as either harmless and exotically costumed anthropological curiosities or as "noble savages" who did not belong in cities and therefore

African women and South African Railways train, Transkei. Transnet Heritage Museum Library Photographic Collection, neg. #78227; reproduced with permission.

did not pose a challenge to white hegemony.[91] Railway travel's tendency to empty the land of its political complexities was alluded to by one train traveler, who observed that "a man becomes an optimist, in spite of himself, behind the window of a railway carriage."[92]

This imaginative emptying of the landscape reached an apotheosis during the 1920s in a new genre of photographs of the empty unimproved landscapes of the interior. While unsuitable for depicting the veiled complexity of the Lowveld, black-and-white photography's ability to condense and abstract landscapes with little visual detail made it an admirable medium to capture landscapes reduced to nothing more than earth and sky, and perhaps a few sheep. Here, we see how the constitutive dialectic between seeing and technique works in both directions. The recognition in the 1920s of the empty, unimproved landscape of the interior as "an anti-theatrical puzzle . . . a stage without a center," and the emergence of images of it in which "the apparently vacant center was revealed as part of a cohesive totality" derived in part from photography's capacity to restructure the way we see the world.[93] As South African War photographers had discovered, black-and-white photography develops a particular synergy with brightly lit and shadowed environments such as Southern Africa.[94] Images of unimproved landscape of the interior captured a part of South Africa never consciously depicted before and rendered it clean, uncluttered, and graphic (in other words, qualities we have come to associate with modernity).

These photographs epitomized the impulse to empty the landscape. In them, the brooding, austere landscape character that Buchan and others had remarked upon becomes manifest and tangible as a presence in its own right. Because these were

MODERNITY, MEMORY, AND THE SOUTH AFRICAN RAILWAYS

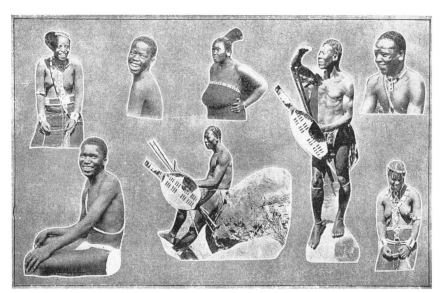

"Zulu Types." *South African Railways & Harbours Magazine,* December 1920, p. 1025; Transnet Heritage Museum Library.

not just representations of natural scenes, but "natural representations" of natural scenes—traces of icons of nature *in* nature itself—it seemed (to use Mitchell's formulation) as if nature had imprinted its essential structures on the perceptual apparatus of those who looked at the scenes.[95] The collective, unconscious orientation toward emptiness mediated by these photographs mirrored the collective colloquial usage, by all whites, of the Afrikaans word "veld." Deriving from the Dutch, the word had been popularized in Britain by the South African War and is usually defined in dictionaries as elevated, open landscape or grassland. In popular South African use, it acquires connotations of remoteness and lack of improvement, and even topographical featurelessness, all characteristics mostly to be found on the Highveld. It is in this connotative sense—as much an imaginary construct as a description of a specific terrain or region—that "the veld" came to be shorthand for a quintessential and universal South African landscape, one that in effect is everywhere and nowhere. As one visitor described this interior country: "To South Africa, the veld is more than topography; it is an environment, a milieu, a way of life."[96]

Images of the veld legitimized at the same time as they concealed the paradoxical ideology that gave rise to them. For those who took and reproduced them, images of the "empty," unimproved veld not only represented space waiting to be filled—by physical settlement as well as utopian imaginings—they also inaugurated a new imagined history for the territory they depicted. This was because these images both erased those recently displaced from the land and promoted a perception of timelessness. Spaces without artifacts such as buildings, railways, mines, and fences subvert conventional ways of relating to and perceiving landscape.[97] Emptiness not only makes ambiguous the time (period) of a landscape but also its ownership, a crucial connotation for a new nation seeking its own rootedness in a territory previously occupied. As we have seen, white South Africa's problematic recent history made it difficult to fall back on the narrative continuities in time and space that usually underpin the discursive construction of imagined communities.[98] (Thus, even the apparently solidly national iconography of the Cape Dutch farms was being ques-

Traditional ox-wagon on a country road. Transnet Heritage Museum Library Photographic Collection, neg. #45646/0; reproduced with permission.

tioned by the end of the 1920s.) Instead, in South Africa, as in Canada, representing national identity required positing "a subsisting component" that could be described "in terms of non-historical variables."[99] One of these nonhistorical variables was the landscape—not so much a physical space waiting to be filled as a particular spatiality and subjectivity engendered by inhabiting that landscape—that transcended ethnic roots, individual ownership, or historic period. Thus, the same author who described the veld as "a milieu, a way of life," also wrote: "There is and always will be a Boer psychology as long as there is a veld with wide horizons and fleets of galleon clouds passing overhead."[100]

Depictions of landscape as empty, then, allowed narratives to be inscribed into them that would otherwise have been impossible. The fact that they were easily reproducible images of recognizable concrete phenomena allowed these images of unowned landscapes to become vehicles for the collective imagination. As such, they encouraged a multiplicity of imaginary appropriations and mediated a place that a broad spectrum of whites could persuade themselves they had always known.[101] And it was precisely because they depicted the subcontinent's *interior*, in which the traces of agriculture and industry were most recent and least evident (and often seen to best advantage from a moving train), that these images of the empty veld came to exemplify this imagined "subsisting component."[102] We can see then that although the SAR&H Publicity Department carefully avoided depicting controversial sites after 1910, it could not avoid engaging the fluxes of historical consciousness. Ultimately, the imaginary nation that the Union government sought to promote was unrealizable without some recourse to the historical imagination; it was, after all, precisely (metropolitan) anxieties about the losses wrought by modernity and change that lent South Africa's landscapes such appeal at this time. This is why, as early as 1921, an article in the *Magazine* asserted that "South Africa should be seen before in the general transition its distinctiveness also is lost."[103] A few years later, another author wrote:

"South Africa is not a new country: she is in the happy possession of nearly 300 years of history."[104] But reconciling such a nostalgic and historicist mentality with a problematic history necessitated a form of landscape representation capable of selection, interpretation, and recuperation—precisely what photography did well, especially when complemented by the interpretive agency of captioning. Not only images of the veld but also generalized images of times and places that predated sharp divisions between whites, or referred to ubiquitous, distinctly South African practices, were ideal vehicles for this kind of impressionistic historicizing.

This elision of remembering and forgetting, this imaginary reconstruction of the time and space of the nation in the 1920s, was underscored by the discursive effects of photography. As we have already seen in the case of Arthur Elliot's images of the Old Cape, the camera's freezing of the visible world's factuality paradoxically "instigates history," turning "the past into an object of tender regard (and) disarming historical judgment."[105] According to Sontag, this creation of a past is common to all acts of photography, not just those that seek to fix forever aspects of the surrounding world that are disappearing.[106] Consequently, depictions of South African landscape as empty and awaiting improvement could, simultaneously, serve as records of an idealized imaginary past. Thus, the Railways Administration's ostensibly creative, future-oriented use of the modern medium of photography simultaneously helped construct a nostalgia for an imaginary, prelapsarian past that was, in effect, as new as the emerging nation, and no less real than the more European one conjured by images

Farmhouse near Franschoek. Transnet Heritage Museum Library Photographic Collection, neg #30605; reproduced with permission.

MODERNITY,
MEMORY, AND THE
SOUTH AFRICAN
RAILWAYS

Historic irrigation canal, Elsenburg, near Stellenbosch. Transnet Heritage Museum Library Photographic Collection, neg. #31869; reproduced with permission.

of the old Cape. Photographs of the empty veld became instant *memento mori* that offered a sense of stability in a changing world.[107]

The SAR&H's depictions of the empty, elevated interior landscape thus glossed over the contradictions of indigenous memory and citizenship in play during the 1920s and 1930s by invoking the same nonhistorical variables that fueled metropolitan visions of the subcontinent as an untamed frontier where Europeans could be rejuvenated by life on the land. As representations, they also powerfully mediated the cult of the veld by which the imaginary geography of white nationhood leapt the mountains and embraced the entire national territory.[108] It is no accident that these photographs of the empty, elevated interior landscape were taken at the same time as (and indeed, were sometimes used as illustrations for) articles published in the *Magazine* with titles like "The Call of South Africa," "The True Land of Hope and Glory," and "South Africa and the Lure of the Sun," all of which sought to define emergent South African identity.[109] As in the debates about South Africanism discussed earlier, these articles return repeatedly to the notion that this identity was grounded in a form of habitus, a sort of bodily alertness derived from living in wide-open spaces in a sparsely populated country. This usage of the photographs allows us to see how the equation of South Africanness with the empty veld refracted not only resolutely corporeal experience but also deep-seated cultural memories and starkly ideological anxieties.

Capturing and Losing the Lie of the Land

John Urry has argued that it is in the nature of sightseeing that travelers gaze upon new and unusual sights with a particular intensity and curiosity. Such sites/sights not only elicit pleasures and involve senses that are different from those experienced every day, they shape imaginary geographies that are of a different order from

"On the Rolling Highveld" (also known as "Jacobs Farm, Ermelo District"). Transnet Heritage Museum Library Photographic Collection, neg. #32976; reproduced with permission.

Landscape near Bethlehem, Orange Free State. Transnet Heritage Museum Library Photographic Collection, neg. #31744; reproduced with permission.

those associated with familiar or taken-for-granted lifeworlds.[110] These heightened landscape encounters are fused with public discourses of progress and nationhood through the work of photographers, travel writers, and tour operators. This alerts us to the fact that the kind of landscape valorized by the SAR&H during the 1920s and 1930s, which became part of the narrative of interaction binding whites to the national territory, was a highly touristic one conditioned by offshore visions of the subcontinent. The emergence of an array of landscapes that seemed to mediate quintessential South Africanness was in fact colored by a romantic "traveling subjectivity" and the marketing of the empty sun-struck landscape to a wider audience. The veld simultaneously came to be seen by visitors as the country's primary asset and the natural geographical correlative—a transitional object, perhaps—of South African identity.[111]

Not only the representations but also the practices and policies of SAR&H drove this construction of a South African imaginary geography. The cultural agency of all three derived from railways' supposed objectivity, rationalism, and efficiency, which, both metaphorically and operationally, exemplified the modern, progressive, nonpartisan governance that the new South African state was trying to establish. At the same time that the SAR&H's lines and services were transforming the time-space of South Africa's economic and social life, its photographic array was transforming the way it was imagined as geographical entity: the SAR&H was simultaneously responsible for imaging a national territory and the transformation of experiential time and space that made this construct conceivable. SAR&H provided not only the visual images that stimulated the desire to explore the national territory but also the infrastructural means to do so. These two phenomena are so interdependent that it is impossible to consider them separately. Photography's discursive power lay in the way it complemented travel and mobility: the erosion of closeness to the landscape (brought about by easier travel through the landscape) helped images of the landscape acquire a potency they had never had before.

Perhaps the most subtle example of how landscape images colluded with the citizen-travelers' experience in creating a continuously choreographed national territory occurs in a small but important genre of photography: the view of the empty landscape from the compartment of a moving train, or a locomotive's footplate.[112] These images, which at first seem to be straightforward depictions of the view from the carriage window so frequently remarked upon by many early train travelers, were in fact also closely related to the photographs in which the train itself provided the framing element that allowed the sweep of the landscape to be read. In the view from the carriage window, the landscape is framed first by the photograph's border, second by the train window, and third by the train itself. Together, the last two concatenate the enclosed, secure compartment with the great sweep of the landscape: the window frames the curving form of train, which in turn becomes a mediating device that affords the traveler a measure of the otherwise empty landscape. These photographs demonstrate how notions of South Africa as a land of contrasts were anchored in the most corporeal, taken-for-granted contrast of all—that between the train's interior and the landscape passing by the window. Significantly, this type of photograph emphasized the farthest visible portion of the landscape; as the blurred foregrounds of these photographs record, the middle ground and distant horizon are easier to look at

View from window
of moving train,
Aangenaamvallei,
Cape. MuseumAfrica
Photographic
Collection, file ref.
916.7; reproduced
with permission.

without discomfort from a moving train, because they pass more slowly. As we have seen, the horizon is precisely that part of the experiential realm where the terrain most characteristically displays itself, as silhouetted figure, and where the sky, that most distinctive aspect of the South African landscape, begins.[113]

These images demonstrate how railways, both practically and representationally, promoted an experience of landscape that encompassed modernity and romance and rehearsed how effects that an older, prenational mentality might have experienced as losses could in fact become sources of enrichment.[114] Here again we see the importance of the *framing of the landscape* in setting up the imaginary relationship between viewer and terrain. Deploying modern technology—that is, photography *and* railways, working in concert—to harness distance while keeping in play an elusive sense of incompletion and potential, these images encouraged the viewer to imagine the train journey as a trajectory that subjectively aligned them with the nation's territory and its historical destiny as a "frontier of civilization."

This constitutive interplay between railway travel, landscape representation, and cultural imagination was potent because of when it unfolded. The creation of the SAR&H's photographic archive—the first comprehensive representation of South Africa—coincided almost exactly with the first decades of the country's existence, when its future political, racial, and cultural character was still being formed. And if, as Raphael Samuel argued, "the idea of nationality belongs to the realm of the imaginary rather than—or as well as—the real,"[115] it is precisely during the period when a nation's future is most in balance that images testing the aesthetic character of its physical territory become most important in imagining that future. In South Africa, as elsewhere, this testing through imagery was grounded in remembrance and recollection, not so much to reproduce and perpetuate the past into the future, but as a schemata through which to imagine and project this future. This dialectical relationship between remembering and imagining, which is also one of the foundations of landscape aesthetics, was deeply embedded in the mentality of those who ran the railways in South Africa at this time.

This suggests that any reading of the effects of SAR&H images during the second two decades of the century needs to be alert to the biases of those who oversaw their commissioning and selection: civil servants of the colonial national state such as Hoy and Tatlow. There are some compelling reasons for arguing that the railways' use of photography was intended to perform ideological work. It was controlled by a small group of powerful administrators with close links to the colonial national state, precisely at a time when debates about national identity and the search among whites for a sense of belonging were at their most intense. It could also be argued that these debates were of particular significance to the railway administrators, whose liberal, inclusive, internationalist ideology was increasingly challenged by one emphasizing separatism and ethnic difference. However, it would probably be simplistic to overstate the role this group played in shaping SAR&H policies in general, and the vision of South Africa promoted by the Publicity Department in particular. Like all cultural discourses, the discourses that helped construct the imagined community and geography of white South Africa were improvisational processes of contestation that unfolded over time, on the ground. Images of South Africa did not so much construct the imagined community and geography of white South Africanism as mediate its emergence.

This simultaneous discursive construction of imagined geography and imagined community posited two visions of South Africa that were in constant tension with each other. The first of these, South Africa as a land of contrasts, valorized the wildness, heterogeneity, and newness of the country, the disparateness between the cultures of those who lived there, and most crucially of all, the juxtaposing of civilization and wildness that seemed so persistent and potent in the subcontinent. The second construction, that of the "home we have always known," rendered South Africa an imaginary territory that was a mnemonic and aesthetic extension of the metropole, a place of perpetual romance and rejuvenation. The inherent ambiguity of black-and-white photography allowed it to serve both visions simultaneously. With historical hindsight, we could argue that even more important than the imaginary geography mediated by the SAR&H practices and representations was the unified imagined community associated with it, and the way images of the South African landscape helped this community elide its radical contingency vis-à-vis that landscape.

When placed in circulation, these images refracted a peculiar convergence between seeing, experiencing, and remembering, and promoted a form of utopian communing with the world, in which the unimproved landscape became an extension of the self, and outer and inner states came to be seen as natural reciprocals of each other. South Africanness, in other words, was permeated by the (perpetual) quest for authentic experience. Needless to say, this communing was available to only a minority—those who were white and well-off. In addition to their legislative and economic banishment from the landscape, other South Africans were excluded from this audience or traveling community; they were banished, at several different levels, from the profoundly sovereign experience that lay at the heart of this environmental communing—the panoramic reverie induced by gazing from the train window as it passed through an empty landscape.

THE LIFE AND AFTERLIFE OF A
CONTRAPUNTAL SUBJECTIVITY

> The local and global are not set apart but seen as soliciting each other. The double
> geography of the global/local is not simply a matter of the global reaching into the
> local, but it is also a matter of the local needing that which is not local to constitute
> itself. The quest for a sense of identity is not simply a return to an autochthonous
> essence, it is always also about an "experience of division."
>
> —Jane M. Jacobs, *Edge of Empire: Postcolonialism and the City*[1]

The preceding account has traced the emergence of a geographically based white
identity during the period from 1900 to 1930, when South Africa was being transformed from a loose association of pastoral societies into a single modern, capitalist,
urban-industrial nation-state. At the beginning of the twentieth century, concepts
like "nations" and "national identities" were still relatively new in Europe, let alone in
colonial societies like South Africa, and a wide range of identities were to be found
in the tiny population of European-descended people living in the African subcontinent. One was that of the Boers living in virtual isolation in the interior, leading lives
not that dissimilar from the African pastoralists they had recently displaced from
the land. Another was that of traveled capitalists, politicians, administrators, and
"cultural producers" whose lives were divided between the cities of the subcontinent
and Britain and mainland Europe. In between was a spectrum of Europeans ranging
from those who had lived in the subcontinent for generations to those who had only
recently emigrated, and from those who only spoke English to those who only spoke
Dutch—all overlaid by differences in education, income, and class. These various
groups' geographical allegiances varied as widely as their cultural backgrounds. Some
saw themselves as Britons overseas, others saw themselves as unique kinds of Afro-
Europeans; for the most part, however, they did not really think about their identities
in national terms, feeling instead a sense of attachment to the region in which they

lived. Even these various overlapping categories and scales of identity didn't begin to take into account the diversity of the native, non-European population in South Africa.

That the cultural identity that emerged in this part of the world came to be imaginatively figured as "white" and was characterized by an overdetermined relationship to the land was not surprising. South Africa was an important part of the European imperium, and, like other ex-colonies, it had until recently been a *frontier* society, that is, one which lived close to the land yet could not strictly speaking construe that land as a "homeland." Moreover, struggle over land—between European groups and between Europeans and Africans—had long featured in the subcontinent's history. This incipient politics of territoriality had been deepened by the South African War, the political legacy of which further intensified the search for symbols that mediated a single, shared identity during the period of national formation. Initially, this search was shaped by a culturally and politically dominant group of white South Africans, whose imaginary geography was as much a product of a bifocal subjectivity as it was of actually inhabiting the land. This group used the subcontinent's landscape both as a symbol of and vehicle for South Africanism, a form of patriotism that tried to discursively foster reconciliation between the various elements of the white population, while simultaneously linking it with a worldwide association of English-speaking or English-influenced countries (see color plate 39).

This landscape subjectivity was initially nurtured and sustained by the same web of discourses, practices, and interactions through which most geographical places, regions, and identities are constructed and understood. The South African War brought the entire subcontinent under an avowedly imperialistic version of this web of knowledge, which figured the metropole as center and the colony as periphery, and already connected white administrators, soldiers, missionaries, and entrepreneurs in South Africa to their counterparts in the metropole.[2] This meant that, far from being self-contained, local, and reactive, the construction and territorialization of the white South African identity was powerfully conditioned by social and cultural conditions in the metropole that fostered dreams of personal freedom, autonomy, and success on the periphery.[3] While it is probably true that for much of the nineteenth and twentieth centuries, British identity was rehearsed and formulated in places outside Britain,[4] it has also been argued that the cultural relationship between Britain and South Africa during the first half of the twentieth century was especially intense, and that Britain's national identity was shaped almost as much by this relationship as was South Africa's. Certainly, during this period, South Africa was a recurring subject of discourse in Britain, used by politicians of all persuasions to position themselves on complex issues facing the British electorate.[5] Both during and after World War I, the country was a topic that helped minimize economic and class differences among the British population and generate a sense of national unity and support for imperialism. This geopolitical articulation of Britain and South Africa was reinforced by political and cultural figures who circulated between the two countries after the war and used each country as a physical and subjective viewpoint to critique what was happening in the other.

Thus, if the imaginative construal of any territory is always in some sense framed by some other world, the roots of white geographical imagination that emerged during the heyday of landscape in South Africa lay, crucially, in the encounter between British cultural memory and African terrain. Because this geographical encounter occurred at the end of the nineteenth century, it engaged two complementary strands of the pastoral imagination, both of which involved some kind spatiotemporal displacement. The first was perception of the margins of the British Empire as a countryside writ large—an idyllic retreat, an escape from the ills of civilization. The second reversed the traditional interplay between the present and past implicit in the form of the pastoral known as the georgic, and construed the region as a garden awaiting the hand of man in order to bloom (by contrast, that is, with the garden degenerating into wilderness).[6] Already latent in nineteenth-century geographical perceptions of the subcontinent, these strands of the pastoral imagination were brought into sharp focus by the creation of Crown Colonies in the old Transvaal and Orange Free State after the South African War, and the possibility of a "greater South Africa" that included Rhodesia, Kenya, and even possibly Tanganyika. Milner's Reconstruction encouraged many in Britain to see this dramatically rejuvenated Southern Africa as a background potentiality to be the foreground actuality of the metropole.[7] Countless visitors from Britain "attested to the capacity of the (South African) landscape to overwhelm them, inducing for many a life-long passion."[8] Compared to a gray, crowded, polluted, urbanized Britain, the newly pink-colored, temperate regions of the subcontinental map constituted an empty, sunlit south, a quintessential example of an imaginary realm containing what is felt to be lacking or lost, but not "other" (see color plate 40). This vision was romantic in the purest sense of the word: it was "a fictitious tale of wonderful and extraordinary events . . . characterized by . . . idealizing use of the imagination."[9] Like most dream spaces, too, imperial South Africa was some distance from most of the population for whom it held significance. Consequently, it became an ideal screen on which the contradictions and cleavages wrought by modern industrialization and urbanization in Britain might be projected without damage.[10]

This romanticization of South Africa as a dream space was not unrelated to the matter of personal aspiration. As we have seen, many of the figures who made their mark in early twentieth-century South Africa—Rhodes, Baker, Milner, Baden-Powell, Buchan, the Phillipses, William Hoy, even Bertha Everard—were individuals who used their work in the subcontinent to shape for themselves more meaningful lives than those they could ever have had in the metropole.[11] The opportunity for financial and class betterment was not the only impulse driving the working and middle classes to abandon the familiarity of Europe for the uncertainty of the colonies; so too was the desire for a life of adventure, agency, and significance. Lionel Phillips expressed the feelings of many when he wrote in his memoirs: "In a small community, every active man connected with large undertakings has recognized status. He can get things done. He can at times be a factor in leading public opinion and is able to see results of his efforts. In London, the . . . center of the world, he feels himself just a cipher."[12] As we have also seen, even common British soldiers subjected to the monotonous discipline of military life during the Boer War felt a similar sense of personal agency, which, when fused with the sense of freedom that arose from inhabiting an open landscape, was profoundly attractive. Seen from Britain, then, South Africa's "great spaces washed with sun" embodied potentiality above all else;

they constituted a territory in which the personal romance of pure adventure fused seamlessly with the modern romance of progress.[13]

Encouraged to live in this same image-world, white colonial national South Africans were no less affected by the romantic vision of their country as a realm of idealism and potentiality. Even if they had never been to Britain themselves, and some had, they lived in an unformed nation that was part of a "field of expanded loyalties" governed by British values and ideas that were subtly but consistently reinforced through hundreds of taken-for-granted symbols, practices, customs, and wares. During the early twentieth century, most white South Africans were immersed in a borrowed vision—or what one author described in the *State* in 1912 as "the distant glow from someone else's glowing imagination."[14] Future-oriented and nominally inclusive, the borrowed vision of loyalist South Africanism appealed not only to imperialists seeking a frontier for metropolitan rejuvenation and settlers looking for a sense of roots and identity, but also to autochthonous Europeans seeking a new start. This vision was continually recharged by the many British emigrants who filled professional, academic, and administrative positions in South Africa during the early decades of the twentieth century, due to the simplified nature of white society and the shortage of qualified local people. Because the borrowed vision and conciliatory politics associated with it ultimately disappeared, loyalist South Africanism has often been overlooked by historians, but during its four-decade life span it was an important factor in white identity formation.[15]

Ongoing ties between Britain and South Africa meant that perceptions of subcontinent continued to be conditioned by metropolitan disenchantment and by responses to the iron cage of rationalization, secularization, and capitalism in which the modern world seemed to becoming increasingly imprisoned.[16] Thus, for all its engagement of invented tradition, Graeco-Roman antiquarianism, and Hegelian historicism, the imaginary geography of South Africanism was in fact a displaced response to modernity. Its emergence coincided with the subcontinent's transition to a modern urban capitalist society, characterized by perpetual innovation and the struggle between universal progress and localism. Still, it is important to realize that this imaginary geography was not simply an exportation of modernity from the center to the periphery, but, following Miles Ogborn, a moment in the making of (global) modernities.[17] Even at the same time as the "white man's country" of South Africa served as an imaginary lost South to metropolitan Britain, it also confirmed one of the central ideas of Western modernity, that of Europe as a "point of departure for discovery, invention, and colonization."[18] For a time, the reciprocity between the borrowed vision of South Africanism and the metropolitan vision of the subcontinent as a lost, but not other, South was a potent one, exemplifying Bhabha's argument that the geography of the global/local is always a matter of the local needing that which is not local to constitute itself.

It is no surprise, then, that the imaginary geography of South Africanism mediated the two seemingly contradictory (but in fact mutually constitutive) impulses present in all landscapes of modernity: nostalgia and exploitation. For all its aspirations toward political and cultural inclusiveness, colonial national South Africanism remained a class-driven point of view, and its imaginary geography was an urban-based one of vision and contemplation rather than inhabitation and work.[19] The colonial national love for two soils that was the subjective counterpart of the field of expanded loyalties could never escape its origins in a borrowed, fundamentally imperialist subjectivity. It was ultimately founded on practices, values, and experiences of the "one half of the English population of South Africa that seem always to be either in Europe or on the sea" rather than a working class who lived face to face with the colonial territory.[20]

This unresolved tension between contemplation and inhabitation manifested itself in two major contradictions that funded romanticized visions of South Africa's landscape. The first of these was the question of labor. Ruskin, whose semifeudal idealism underpinned colonial national perceptions of the South African landscape, and were latent even in Milner's most pragmatic policies, held exalted views on the dignity and importance of manual labor. The yeoman farmers intended to become the backbone of the future white man's country were rural landowners who worked the soil themselves. As we have seen, it was precisely this vision that led to the Closer Settlement movement and the pre-Union colonial governments' support for white agriculture, as well as Milner's somewhat reluctant reestablishment of Boers on their farms. The possibility that white settlers in South Africa would degenerate into idleness was no peripheral matter to those in the metropole, in that it threatened one of the most fundamental justifications of expansive imperialism: that those inherit the earth who make the best use of it. As J. M. Coetzee has argued, the playing out of the pastoral ideal in South Africa not only had to involve labor to satisfy critics of rural retreat, but this labor had to be white, to satisfy the critics of colonialism.[21]

What actually occurred in South Africa after self-government bore only a passing resemblance to such rearguard views of the relationship between labor, land, and culture. Although initially conditioned by the aspirations of Reconstruction, the land policies of early Union governments soon began to be shaped by local realities. These governments found their power to create a new class of small-scale rural white landowners extremely limited, and from 1910 onward, they began to encourage settler accumulation through an array of policies that either turned Africans into pliable, cheap labor for white farmers or relegated them to crowded, easily forgotten reserves or urban townships. By the 1920s, white capitalists with close links to the urban mercantile world in South Africa or Britain outnumbered Milner's "yeoman gentry," who worked the land themselves as the dominant rural landowners, and the landscape of rural South Africa became a "white man's land" in terms of ownership rather than labor (or, as some of Milner's opponents had argued it would, a black man's country ruled by a white aristocracy).[22] This evolution heightened the aesthetics of nostalgic pastoralism in South Africa, even as it revealed the naiveté of its original operative calculus, which was replaced by an increasingly technological pastoralism that relied on a combination of cheap labor and state-sponsored scientific agriculture. Increasing numbers of landowners were individuals who acquired their farms as speculative investments rather than as properties on which to live and work. This reinforced an age-old pattern in which those most preoccupied with the land as landscape are usually those who make money out it but seldom inhabit it for very long. In early twentieth-century South Africa, this pattern led to the emergence of an English-speaking landed gentry and established a complex relationship between mines, state, white agriculture, and African peasants.

"View from the stoep of retired civil servant, Robertson." Transnet Heritage Museum Library Photographic Collection, neg. #32378; reproduced with permission.

Here we come to the second important lacuna that lay at the heart of and nurtured borrowed visions of the South African landscape: language, usually a key medium and mediator by which intersubjective meanings are shared and amended. All Anglophone colonial nationalist presence in the subcontinent was predicated on the economic and technological hegemony of imperialism—a project based on naming and controlling—yet in many ways they inhabited a landscape that challenged their own language's ability to name and control. This was especially true for members of the urban white establishment who dominated political and economic life in South Africa during the first three decades of the twentieth century and retained close connections to Britain. For them, living in a white man's country both invoked cultural memory and highlighted its inadequacy. In part this was a consequence of a political view that maintained, as in Canada, that the true soul of the nation was to be found not in the European settler languages but in the land itself. But the inadequacy of English as a mediator of subjective meanings in South Africa was of a different order from that in Canada, where both English and French were foreign. Afrikaans, based on eighteenth-century Dutch, had developed on African soil and incorporated words from most of the languages of those who had passed through the subcontinent in the previous two centuries, including French, German, Malay, and Arabic, as well as indigenous African languages. Few colonial nationalists were bilingual to the degree that Smuts was, and their own language was naggingly foreign when compared to Afrikaans, a unique language as indigenous as the terrain it so colorfully described.[23] Perceptions of this unique bond between land and language, of modes of knowledge that transcended simple naming and tapped into generations-old narration of the terrain, were mediated, for instance, by the mystical reverence Buchan accorded in novels to characters who, in addition to English and African languages, also spoke "the *Taal*."

While towns named after well-known centers in Britain or obscure colonial worthies enacted a limited and localized form of Anglicization, commonplace Afrikaans words like *kloof, veld, vlakte, koppie, kraal, nek, vlei, kuil, opstal,* and *krans* described ubiquitous features of the South African landscape, which quite simply had no direct equivalents, either in Britain or in English, and thus seemed to strengthen the moral right of those who used them to that territory.[24] It is easy to see how this pervasive toponymic incommensurateness encouraged Anglophone discourses of patriotic (rather than national) identity to reify precisely those dimensions of landscape difficult to express in words: the experiential and the adjectival. Here we see a powerful convergence between political exigency and a *mentalité* inclined to see culture as deriving from nature. The sense that being South African derived from both "sunshine and distance" and from being of European descent meant that this identity had to be mediated by something other than words, which of course betrayed an allegiance to language, and by extension, partisan political ideology. It is easy to see that for those who traveled, physically and mentally, between the metropole and the subcontinent, this sense of contingency transcended ideology and even the grid of language; it had to do with a perceptual thinness that was at once material and phenomenological, cultural and mnemonic.

Preoccupations with the South African landscape's "emptiness" alluded to the fact that there was so little there, not only physically but also discursively. As one white South African remembers growing up on the veld in the 1930s: "Everything around us was without confirmation, without background, without credentials; there was something unreliable, left out, about the whole place, and hence about all of us too."[25] This suggests that Anglophile South Africanism was grounded in incompletion and desire, a perpetual cycle of reach and withdrawal, and a displaced yearning for some kind of substantive exchange with the land. For some, the emptiness and "uncompromising clarity and hard beauty of the sunlight on the veld" was insurmountable and debilitating; for others, it was—like Buchan's "green summit against the unclouded blue"—an environmental image that served as a perpetual "summons to action."[26] This recurring valorization of the stimulating (in both senses of the word) effects of the austere, empty veld had a number of cultural and discursive consequences. It naturalized as a strand of emergent white South African identity a psychospatial disposition cognate with a landscape in which there is no middle ground, where everything is either distant horizon or right up close.[27] It also posited the idea that South Africanness was characterized by the poetic, unmediated juxtaposition of the unimproved and the urbane. In both these senses, it was therefore a peculiarly poignant confirmation of Derrida's argument that identity is constituted out of moments where difference remains gathered.[28]

The social construction of cultural imaginaries is always iterative, contingent, and ongoing; existing in the realms of discourse, they are never satisfactorily resolved or finalized. The arc of South Africanism was also quite short, due to rapidly changing political circumstances in South Africa and overseas, which brought to an end the

Man seated on rock,
Pilgrim's Rest District.
MuseumAfrica
Photographic Collec-
tion, file ref. #916.82;
reproduced with
permission.

period of intensive exchange between metropole and Dominion and marginalized proponents of patriotic or loyalist South Africanism. This meant that South Africanism never really evolved beyond a subjectivity of potentiality and possibility and was, arguably, always understood as a nonmonolithic identity, both in place and out of place at the same time.[29] (Smuts, as some have pointed out, was more effective as a cultural figure than a practical politician.) As language-based nationalism grew in the 1920s and 1930s, English-speaking South Africans who felt the "love of two soils" found it increasingly hard to sustain a deep sense of attachment to an autonomous nation of South Africa. These whites were caught in a trap; instead of saving them from a sense of territorial contingency, their borrowed cultural vision increased it, and simultaneously rejuvenated the romantic construal of South Africa as a realm of unrealized possibility. This was not, ultimately, a matter of the un-European physical character of much of South Africa; as we have seen, as many Anglophone colonial nationalists were drawn to the Karoo and the Highveld as to the Cape or Natal. Rather, it was because the attachment to place promoted by South Africanism was always predicated on a relatively narrow set of criteria and was undermined by its own distance from the terrain it claimed. This distancing was both practical (South Africanism was always strongest among urban dwellers) and cultural (emphasized by a language without historical or topographical fit to the terrain).

We have already seen how this complicated relationship to the South African landscape manifested itself in the work of Anglophone colonial nationalist artists, for whom its evocative muteness invited an energetic displacement of self into place. However, the poetic characterization of the land as pregnant with some meaning best understood and revealed through individual, direct experience, was probably most tellingly reflected in white Anglophone South African literature.[30] According to J. M. Coetzee, the central problem of South African literature during the first half of the twentieth century was whether a European language (and by extension, culture) could find a home in Africa—in other words, the need to "make the landscape speak, to give a voice to the landscape, to interpret it." This way of relating to landscape, through what Coetzee calls the "hermeneutic gaze," was constantly fueled by the sense that the longed-for sense of belonging—set up, as it were, by "nostalgic pastoralism"—might in fact be killed off by the "ascent into language," the sense that in South Africa, attempts to return to a "state of grace through art were foredoomed."[31] Behind the notion that the land was pregnant with meaning lurked the fear that it might, in the final analysis, have no meaning at all.[32] As Coetzee has argued, this idea reached its apotheosis in post–World War II white South African English writing, in which the imaginary relationship between writer and landscape becomes more and more antagonistic, the silence of the landscape absorbing the imagination and reflecting nothing.[33]

This account has been framed by two premises or intellectual wagers. The first is that topographical character, collective memory, corporeal experience, and cultural subjectivity play off each other in dialectical ways. The second premise is that in colonial nations, place identification tends to revolve around the notion that ultimately, nature determines culture rather than the other way around, and that the most powerful landscapes of identity are unimproved and uninhabited ones. We can now begin to tease out how these two socio-spatial processes might have played off and reinforced each other in early twentieth-century South Africa.

For Anglophone colonial nationalists, the notion that nature, specifically unimproved nature, determined culture reflexively freighted actions in and responses to the empty, unimproved landscape, precisely because it was deployed in terrain that, in a larger, more abstract sense, could not be inhabited. The expansive South African terrain turned a taken-for-granted European way of thinking about landscape into an overdetermined sense of contemplative selfhood and corporeal agency. Like the cultural vision that framed it, the subjectivity provoked by this refusal of the land to admit a substantial and satisfactory exchange emphasized potentiality and incompletion. Transformed into a different register, that of individual bodily experience, this sense of potentiality and incompletion became a perpetual invitation to action. This imaginative making a trial of the land by the body-subject in turn became a kind of surrogate labor whereby a new hybrid culture would, in the spirit of the naturalized nation, emerge from the native landscape. The product of this phenomenological labor was a disposition that combined contemplative inwardness with a reflexive corporeality and a broad-based, omni-competent way of being or habitus—an identity most vividly (or, following Bachelard, intimately) felt in (and therefore symbolized by) the immensity of the open veld.[34] As a discursive landscape, then, the veld was not only a resolutely un-European geographical interior, and the home of displaced autochthons that needed to be incorporated into a unitary nation. It was also a topography within which the mental and bodily dimensions of dramatic possibility of movement became fused.

Needless to say, this empowered habitus of possibility and action always had its

dark side, presupposing as it did a level of power and autonomy that cut across and devalued other ways of being. Under ideal circumstances, an empowered, distanced subject-position can encourage altruistic and benevolent practices. More often, it leads to benign tyrants, who see themselves as attended by fiercely loyal subjects, their expansive gestures unquestioned.[35] If having space is a fundamental condition of being, then being bred to have considerable space can often lead to a disproportionate sense of entitlement. Many have commented on the way the unchecked sense of agency and autonomy in settler societies invests individuals with license to lord over whole sections of society. Often, though, this overweening sense of autonomy and agency is haunted by the common day-to-day realities of colonial existence, the underlying dis-ease of those who do not fully understand their environment and are trying by force to control it. It is precisely as a compensation for this background dis-ease of day-to-day colonial existence that a subjectivity combining a heady mixture of the corporeal challenges of living in an uninhabited terrain and a discursively cultivated bifocal romanticism developed its affective, ideological charge. Although this is not quite the same charge as that which stems from being in transit—that is, a subjectivity that perpetually avoids the stagnation of being homebound and the alienation of homelessness—the two are similar and can easily become blurred.

Here, though, we begin to see how a habitus characterized by possibility, action, and potentiality might have been naturalized for reasons other than pure power relations. It is being increasingly recognized today that in modern societies, marginalized identities can develop around a sense of never wholly being in a place or experience, of always having a part of the self kept in reserve, as a kind of vantage point on the world. This suggests that a way of being characterized by incompletion and potentiality can in fact be permanent and normal. A marginal subjectivity such as this is cognate (and comfortable) with living with irreconcilable conflicts and is at home in places that are simultaneously at the edge and center of things, because, ultimately, it locates the pleasure of things in the (potential) losing of them. Such a subjectivity is a product of situations where feelings of difference that arise as a defense against the insidious sense of being somehow defective are transposed into feelings of being special, rarified, or elite. This kind of paradoxical subjectivity, which embraces the contradictions of history and celebrates a miraculous symbiosis between things usually thought to be opposite, is closely related to the cultural-geographical subjectivity of white Anglophone South Africanism and is perhaps its most profound and lasting contribution to South African national identity.[36]

This reminds us that the subjectivity of loyalist colonial nationalism that permeated cultural-geographical discourse in South Africa during the 1910s and 1920s was not entirely hegemonic. The effects of modernization—urbanization, the depopulation of the *platteland*, industrialization, and the restructuring of everyday life by agents such as the railways—were not only uneven, but were experienced differently by different groups in different parts of the country. For all its reconciliatory, patriotic aspirations, few ordinary Afrikaners, even staunch supporters of Botha and Smuts, could be expected to share modernization's ambiguous aesthetics and the "love for two soils." Before World War II, most Afrikaners still belonged to a different class and had quite different life experiences than their Anglophile or colonial national compatriots. But by 1930, an increasing middle ground of other, usually poorer, white South Africans simply identified themselves as citizens of an autonomous nation rather than a commonwealth of British-influenced states; their identity became national rather than colonial. This was already evident in the public response to that high point of bifocal South Africanism, the 1926 inauguration of the Delville Wood Memorial in France. The dedication of the memorial evoked limited interest in South Africa, and attempts to erect replicas in South Africa's cities in the 1930s met with apathy and even downright hostility.[37] The memorial never engaged the imagination of a broad spectrum of the nation's citizens in the way Australian and Canadian memorials did; the identity it embodied was essentially a transnational, "Zivilizationist" one that emphasized the (southern, marginal) nation's cultural maturity as a way of confirming its intimate relationship with the (northern, central) hearth of Western civilization. For a growing number of white South Africans in the early 1930s, these kinds of ideas about place and cultural identity, mediated by a site six thousand miles away, were either hard to relate to or irrelevant.

There is more than a grain of truth in Saul Dubow's description of the Delville Wood Memorial as the "dying monument of South Africanism."[38] Despite idealistic projects like the South Africa House in London's Trafalgar Square ("the hub of Empire"), with its stylized iconography of all things South African,[39] and publications like the *South African Nation* (a self-consciously bilingual successor to the *State*, published from 1924 to 1929), the dream of a unified, white loyalist-Anglophile South Africa had begun to lose its attraction by 1930. Many of the political, economic, social, and cultural props of autonomous nationhood had been successfully put in place, and some form of rapprochement had begun to emerge between English and Afrikaner, albeit founded on a mutual fear of a growing nonwhite proletariat. Post-1902 hopes in Britain for the subcontinent that had helped fuel the borrowed vision of South Afri-

South Africa House,
London, 1935.
National Archives and
Records Service of
South Africa, file ref.
SAB 3899; reproduced
with permission.

canism were waning, too. Although South Africa benefited from the desire of some
to flee exhausted, blighted post–World War I Britain for hotter climates, the appeal of
the Dominions declined between the world wars in the face of a countervailing sense
of England as an idealized home, a place of retreat and memory.[40] This imaginary
geography, latent in Britain since 1880, mirrored the decline of the British Empire

Springbok rampant, South Africa House, London, 1930s.
National Archives and Records Service of South Africa,
file ref. SAB 3764; reproduced with permission.

and focused on rural England: its
green peacefulness contrasted with
the tropical or arid places of actual
work and its sense of belonging
and community contrasted with
the tensions of colonial rule and
isolated alien settlement.[41] At the
same time, the British establishment was becoming less enchanted
with the subcontinent. It had become clear by the mid-1920s that
the grand expansionary project of
a greater South Africa was not going to materialize, and memories
of the South African War had
been overshadowed by memories
of World War I, in which some
of South Africa's strongest advocates in the British establishment
had died.[42] Many in Britain, too,
were alarmed and alienated by
the increasingly racist, republican
rhetoric of Afrikaner nationalists.

249

THE LIFE AND
AFTERLIFE OF A
CONTRAPUNTAL
SUBJECTIVITY

The Prince of Wales's extensive tour of South Africa in 1925 did not boost the popularity of Crown and Empire nearly as much as it was hoped.[43]

Weakening imperial links in turn affected those whites who before World War II were simply known as British South Africans—that is, South Africans who felt a strong sense of belonging to the Union as well as a larger imperial diaspora of transplanted British emigrant societies, with whom they shared an intense pride in being British. (The term "English-speaking South Africans" only really became a definitive and commonly used description in the early 1950s when a white identity evolved based on common language.)[44] In any case, notwithstanding the rhetoric of colonial nationalism and the background discursive effects of inhabiting a borrowed vision, English-speaking South Africans were a politically less homogeneous group than Afrikaners. Made up of those who had lived in the subcontinent for generations as well as those who had just immigrated, English-speaking white South Africans exhibited a greater diversity of opinion and allegiance, and being more individualistic, were less susceptible to being whipped into a unitary position by political rhetoric than their Afrikaner counterparts.[45] By 1930, some Anglophone white South Africans, increasingly buoyed by the country's ongoing development, began to cast their cultural and political lot with their Afrikaner compatriots. Others clung to British cultural values, feeling threatened by the Afrikaner nationalists' recurring threats of secession in their political rhetoric, as well as the flag controversy of 1926–27, both of which suggested that South Africa's future in the British Empire was less certain than they had thought.[46] The assertion of imperial rather than settler identity in response to the changing political landscape only fueled nationalists' accusations that these compatriots—whom they called *die Britte* or *die Engelse*—were not true South Africans.[47] With the passing of the 1931 Statute of Westminster (drafted in part by Hertzog, who had become prime minister of the Nationalist-led Pact government in 1924), which brought full independent status for all the Dominions, loyalist Anglophone white South Africans began to think of themselves as a cultural and political, if not ethnic, minority within their own country.

Given these political and cultural crosscurrents of the late 1920s and early 1930s, it is no surprise that the ambiguous dream of a nonpartisan, Anglophile South Africa did not survive the emergence of articulate, unambiguous Afrikaner nationalism. In the early 1930s, a new generation of urbanized Afrikaner middle-class cultural leaders and politicians began insisting on ever more starkly drawn expressions of white identity. For this group, who formed the Purified National Party (PNP) in 1935, the divided and complicated allegiances of colonial national South Africans were not significantly different than those of the British imperialists who had defeated the Boer republics some thirty years earlier. Founded by a core of republicanists within the older National Party, the PNP set out to unite a broad constituency of Afrikaans speakers, who up to that point had been divided along class, political, and regional lines, by promoting a strain of nationalist Afrikanerdom that rejected even General Hertzog's political and economic succor for Afrikaners as too ameliorative. Whereas both Smuts and Hertzog had wanted to keep South Africa in the Commonwealth, the PNP argued that Afrikaner nationalism could only be sustained in an independent republic under Afrikaner leadership divorced from the British Crown and Commonwealth.[48] This political movement was underpinned by Afrikaner academics who reworked segregationist ideas of the previous twenty years into a coherent ideology called apartheid, which claimed to not only guarantee the cultural identity of Afrikaners but also the supposedly threatened tribal heritage of Africans.

Initially, this political and cultural movement made use of popular media, extending Gustav Preller's earlier mobilization of folk memories about the South African War, which directed Afrikaner resentment not just at British imperialism but against all English-speaking South Africans, who were retrospectively lumped with Britain and blamed for what happened during that war.[49] This reworked and elaborated Afrikaner historiography also reached back into the nineteenth century to include the original Great Trek, whose centenary was celebrated in 1938 by a reenactment that culminated in the laying of foundations for a Voortrekker Monument outside Pretoria. A spate of popular books on the war appeared in the 1930s and 1940s, and biographies, poems, novels, essays, and popular magazines of the 1930s turned war generals like Christiaan de Wet and Jacobus de La Rey into household names, and the sites of battles like Spioenkop and Magersfontein and the concentration camps into sacred cultural places.[50] As in the first awakenings of Afrikaner consciousness after the South African War, the overtly ideological character of this alternative vision of nationhood masked its origins in changing economic relations brought about by modernization and industrialization.[51] First the extended drought of the late 1920s and then the Depression of the early 1930s affected small farmers and rural communities—still largely Dutch- and Afrikaans-speaking—particularly severely. In the 1930s, many Afrikaners lost their farms to debtors and had to take up menial jobs as workers on the mines, roads, and railways. A large proportion of these so-called poor whites were forced to migrate to the cities, where they felt exploited by a British-rooted capitalism and alienated by the values of a modern urban world.[52] Decades after the South African War, the loss of a country and a significant proportion of the ex-republics population once again became potent facts in the minds of impoverished, disoriented Afrikaners. It was in the 1930s that Afrikanerdom finally developed into a tribal identity that laid the foundations for the civil religion of post–World War II Afrikaner nationalism.[53]

This transformation of Hertzog's relatively mild Little South Africanism into the assertive ethnolinguistic nationalism of the 1930s caught liberal-minded, colonial national whites unprepared. Inhabiting as they did a *mentalité* characterized by potentiality and becoming, this largely urban, largely English-speaking group had been relatively optimistic about the country's future. They had believed that black "backwardness" was due to historic circumstances rather than racial inferiority, and that the market forces that increasingly drove the country's economy would eventually fuse together all the peoples of the country—black and white, English-speaking and Afrikaans-speaking.[54] By the end of the 1930s, some English-speaking South Africans began to have reservations about whether this process would ever happen, and some started to believe Afrikaner arguments that segregation needed to be permanently inscribed into the structure of South African society. Thus, although Afrikaner nationalism was founded on partisan memories of the war, and was therefore a fundamentally exclusive cultural ideology, it managed to supplant South Africanism as a force in white politics in 1948 by playing on the underlying and intertwined racial and economic fears of all whites. Although the traveling practices and imperial

Mining landscape
south of Johannes-
burg, 1930s. Transnet
Heritage Museum
Library Photographic
Collection, neg.
#43452; reproduced
with permission.

networks that underpinned it declined, the colonial national *mentalité* remained alive between 1930 and 1948, albeit increasingly overlaid by the cultural values encouraged by urbanization and nationalism.

The cognate transformation in geographical imagination associated with this new, more nationalistic cultural identity would take several decades to evolve. Although the creation of Kruger National Park in 1926 is often seen as a key episode in the construction of a single white South African identity because it revolved around a common valorization of the same landscape, the park was probably more a milestone in the construction of political-discursive détente than it was one in the construction for a shared imaginary geography, for which it should instead be seen as a precursor (and possible vehicle). Thus, emerging Afrikaner nationalism could still claim in the 1930s that Afrikaans- and Dutch-speaking whites were more authentic South Africans because they had a unique bond with the landscape of the subcontinent forged through generations of continuous inhabitation and husbandry. This was a claim that no apologists for English-speaking colonial national South Africanism could make or challenge. If social formations as ill-defined as nations derive their cohesive strength from their narrative of interaction with a defined territory—that is, through their territorial narrative—then Afrikaner nationalism simply constructed a more plausible and persuasive version of this than South Africanism after the mid-1920s.

During the interwar period, Afrikaners' growing sense of themselves as a chosen people was strengthened through the discursive construction of a territorial narrative that harnessed a series of historical episodes to appropriate the geography of the subcontinent as their own imaginative territory. This alternative narration of the historical time-space of the subcontinent—which began with the *trekboers* during the

THE LIFE AND
AFTERLIFE OF A
CONTRAPUNTAL
SUBJECTIVITY

Dutch East India Company period, continued with the Voortrekkers' journey from
the Eastern Cape into the Highveld interior, and included the Battle of Blood River
in the Natal Midlands—was triumphantly reinscribed in 1938 by the re-creation of
the Great Trek. The spatial story of Afrikanerdom delineated an imagined territory
similar in extent to that of colonial nationalism but with its own imaginative topography. Its heartland, as both Pierneef's Johannesburg Station panels and the Voortrekker Monument outside Pretoria signaled, was the subcontinent's interior, the land
that had been appropriated by the Boers in the 1840s during their Great Trek. This
self-representation of the Afrikaners as the true inheritors of the subcontinent grew
stronger as the possibility of political domination seemed more realizable and the
right to govern seemed to be indistinguishable from a cultural destiny or duty.[55]

Within this largely unassailable Afrikaner territorial narrative, two slightly
different attitudes toward landscape emerged. One important strand of Afrikaner
nationalist rhetoric drew upon Old Testament Calvinist principles[56] and equated the
destiny of Afrikaners continually displaced by Dutch and then British imperialism
with that of the Israelites searching for the promised, and therefore implicitly *empty*,
land where they could live closer to God.[57] The Battle of Blood River in particular
was seen as evidence of God's will that South Africa was indeed their *Gelofde Land*,
an image which Nico Coetzee argues functioned for many Afrikaners in the first
part of the twentieth century as an abstract yet manifest idea, corresponding to the
Calvinist idea of God: omnipresent yet intangible, austere yet just. An alternative
interpretation of Afrikaner landscape subjectivity, offered by J. M Coetzee, is that
Afrikaners saw themselves as farm people (*plaasmense*) rather than people of nature
(*natuurmense*). Noting the striking absence in pre-1930 Afrikaans literature of the

preoccupation with the silent landscape found so often in English colonial writing, Coetzee argues that the relationship between subject and landscape in Afrikaans literature during this period was mediated through narratives set in the georgic "little kingdom" (*klein koningrykie*) of the family farm.[58] As a group that had only very recently been expelled from the land and retained strong family ties to particular districts, it made sense that it was the working, inhabited *pays* rather than uninhabited wilderness that provided the imaginative pole of Afrikaner existence. J. M. Coetzee argues that the Afrikaners developed their own particular version of the pastoral, looking to the calm and stability of the long-inhabited farm as "a still point mediate between the wilderness of lawless nature and the wilderness of new cities," and a bastion of unchanging verities and collective forms of consciousness.[59]

Deciding which of these landscape subjectivities was more important in shaping emerging Afrikaner nationalist consciousness is beyond the scope of this book, though it certainly constitutes an interesting question for further study. Nevertheless, it raises questions about the continuities and differences between the landscape *mentalité* of patriotic Anglophone colonial nationalism and that of republican nationalism, and to what degree the former might have laid the foundations for the latter. Although the territorial narrative of Afrikaner nationalism valorized a different set of places and regions from that of colonial nationalism, much of the earlier, borrowed subjective attitude toward landscape survived in it (indeed, it could be argued that Afrikaner nationalism took the model of naturalization of the nation to its most extreme limits). Like colonial national South Africanism, Afrikaner nationalism invested *rural* rather than urban locales as loci of white belonging and cultural identity, and both the "white man's land" of the colonial nationalists and the Afrikaners' "promised land" drew on constructed cultural memory to mediate feelings of potentiality and idealism and the sense that the (home)land was "evermore about to be."[60] Similarly, one could argue that for the Afrikaner as *natuurmens*, or person of nature, the land becomes a deistic abstraction, an austere phenomenon whose eidetic meaning is best understood through direct, contemplative experience, very much like that alluded to in the work of John Buchan and Bertha Everard.

This last trope was perhaps most tellingly incorporated into the new national anthem, "Die Stem" ("The Voice"), written shortly after union and adopted in the early 1930s:[61]

> Uit die blou van onse hemel
> Uit die diepte van ons see
> Oor die ver verlate vlaktes
> Waar die kranse antwoord gee.

> (From the blue of our heavens
> From the depths of our oceans
> Across the far lonely plains
> Where the crags give answer.)

In these words we see the consummation of the idea that took hold during the apartheid era, that there was no distinction between the "land"—individually owned and known acreage—and the "Land" of a united, unequivocally white nation. As Peter

Henshaw has pointed out, after 1948 the National Party would make highly effective use of such imaginary connections between landscape and identity, first to rally Afrikaners to the apartheid republican cause, and then, once the goals of the republic and the end of the Commonwealth connection had been achieved, to unite whites under Afrikaner leadership. In so doing, they appropriated and perpetuated the same nation-building imaginary centered on nature that colonial nationalism had hoped would serve imperial British ends, and turned it to serve isolationist, Afrikaner ones.[62] Thus, beneath the contestation between colonial and nationalist ideologies, there was an underlying continuity in the progression toward nationhood in South Africa similar to that of other countries. First, national identity became bound up with territory that helped define it; second, this identity emerged as something more or less distinct from the state, a set of cultural attributes that became bundled with a succession of political objectives; and third, this identity encompassed a cluster of geographically based identities that coexisted and sometimes competed with it.[63]

If we accept that the cultural attributes of emergent white South African identity coalesced around a reflexive, self-sufficient disposition engendered by inhabiting an empty landscape, then what factors might have promoted this continuity? Even if we leave aside the propensity for all discourses about place and space, which are central to conceptions of self and identity, to reify the subject of contestation, there are a number of other possible factors for this landscape subjectivity that transcended political and ethnic divisions. The first of these was that the process was nurtured by the logic of the naturalization of the nation, a way of thinking about landscape and identity that was especially applicable to a country as unimproved as early twentieth-century South Africa. Another reason might be the growing convergence of the socioeconomic situation of all whites living in South Africa after 1930. If the construct of landscape was (and is) fundamentally a product of the empowered, distanced subject, then it is clear that this subjectivity started to become part of Afrikaner experience in the 1930s, when, for growing numbers of Afrikaners, the land ceased to be a practical, exploitable phenomenon and took on cultural, ideological connotations. In addition to J. M. Coetzee, several historians have noted that Afrikaners paid little attention to landscape until their ties with the land were being severed and the end of the rural *boere-nasie* (farmer nation) seemed likely. Thus, it could be argued that South Africanist landscape subjectivity remained alive because white South Africans who were neither colonial nationalists nor English speakers started to experience for themselves the transition to the disenchanted landscape of urbanization and industrialization.[64] Indeed, displacement from the land became one of the key tropes used by nationalist ideologues to construct an Afrikaner mythology during the 1920s and 1930s. According to this historiography, being ejected from a previously owned and cultivated domain was a defining experience of being an Afrikaner.[65]

There is little doubt, though, that this convergence between Afrikaner nationalist preoccupations with displacement from the land and Anglophone colonial national preoccupations with "making the land speak" was underwritten by the urgency of the question of how (and where) to place Africans in the landscape. Schwarz has argued that that the possibility of a shared white South African identity grew in direct proportion to the perception of a shared threat from the black population, and it is likely that this same awareness promoted a convergence of landscape vision in the

1930s.[66] All landscape visions are myths that nominally exclude the presence of some unspoken other(s), yet are seldom unmarked by this other. South Africa, like most ex-colonies, had come into being as a nation with an educated (and generally wealthier) colonial national elite oriented toward Europe who accepted natives as in some romantic, historical sense to be the owners of the land, and a relatively uneducated working class who lived face-to-face with the colonial territory and consequently had more pragmatic, less generous attitudes toward the native population. Initially, differences between these two groups in early twentieth-century South Africa expressed themselves largely through debates concerning Africans' rights to land within a unitary national territory.

In the end though, the colonial nationalists, for all their subscription to modern, liberal constitutionalist metropolitan values, ultimately found it impossible to imagine a white man's country without imagining the mechanics of segregation.[67] A structure of feeling that valorized a solitary, contemplative, aesthetic disposition toward the land simply could not accommodate Africans, other than as denizens of small, remote, and picturesque communities.[68] (This same contradiction had of course also been implicit in the problematic nostalgic pastoralist notions of farms owned and worked by whites, where black labor had no place.) These contradictions led some liberal-thinking whites to resolve the question of where African population belonged in this national territory by assigning them the role of a romanticized peasantry that needed paternalistic guidance and benevolent protection from the corrosive forces of modernization.[69] The wishful dimensions of this vision, which was only sustainable as long as Africans remained content to live in rural reserves, missions, and farms, were clear from the outset. It was a landscape vision that could not be reconciled with either the growing size of the African population or its economic, cultural, and political aspirations. Once those whites who had always had a less romantic view of the African population gained political power, they responded swiftly to these growing aspirations through an increasingly rational and bureaucratic organization of national territory and control of who could occupy and own it. Nevertheless, even these instrumentally racist policies were haunted by the longing for direct, unmediated contemplative exchange with a landscape that, in the final analysis, needed to be empty.

While these ideological dimensions of the social spatialization of South African national territory help explain the evolution of white landscape subjectivity, they tell us relatively little about the qualitative nature of that subjectivity. By this I mean the environmental predisposition or structure of feeling developed by any group of people sharing the same lifeworld, a *mentalité* that is soon apparent to outsiders but is often taken for granted by its habitués. This textured, affective, and interpretive web of meaning constructed through interactions with the material world returns us to questions posed in chapter 3 concerning the relative roles of discourse, practice, and experience in the dissemination and perpetuation of cultural attitudes toward landscape.

I have argued that an important basis for place-based identification was the landscape encounter, in which subject (person) and object (terrain) are conjointly characterized through situated human praxis. While such participatory undergoing *theoretically* opens onto an infinite array of subjective interpretations, associations,

and meanings, in practice it usually tends to converge toward a more or less somatic schema created by bodily competence and senses, a matrix of likely experiences that constitute some kind of continuity in a given lifeworld. (In this category we can place constructions like "a simple life in a genial climate," and "great spaces washed with sun.") Countering this approach is one that marshals sociological and cultural evidence to argue that there is no universality of human subjectivity and experience and that such intersubjective agreement—what I have earlier called the existential and cognitive dimensions of place—is nothing more than the function of normative socialization, which structures and frames experience. In this analysis, apparently subjective, experiential dimensions of place are set up by, and constructed through, discourse, especially the collective weight of images that distill the world as landscape and fix its meaning.

Such distinctions between individual subjectivity and socially constructed intersubjectivity are probably more useful as platforms for theoretical discussion than as descriptions of everyday life. Merleau-Ponty's prereflective body-subject was not only the "key to all those transpositions and equivalences which keep the world constant," it also synthesized in a single, thick horizon of meaning the phenomenal and the socially constructed. Involuntary and yet nonarbitrary, intensely felt yet beyond conscious retrieval, this bodily subjectivity reveals itself largely through our reactions to events, spaces, and things, as invitations to action. This gestural and expressive subjectivity is best alluded to through metaphor, analogue, allegory, and symbols—in other words, through images of every kind. The means by which this body subjectivity is mediated, and therefore also the means whereby the private and subjective is transposed into the social and cultural, and vice versa, is praxis.[70] Ubiquitous, but largely invisible, habitual ways of making use of the world (traveling, building, farming, surveying, cultivating, painting) create a protocultural operative syntax that simultaneously descries a body schema and a horizon of meaning. Seldom if ever defined, yet always implicit, these rules are transmitted through the tacit agreement of synchronized behavior within a given time and place, rather than through overt representation. Like Bourdieu's habitus, such praxis does not so much regulate subjectivity as constitute that subjectivity through the articulation of corporeal time and space. Because it is worked out through joint action in lived time and space, it is always to some degree collective, while remaining open-ended and contingent.[71]

Praxis is imaginatively displaced and bodied forth in places, which acquire their character and meaning as "sites within a potential whole."[72] It is largely through such imaginative displacement and bodying forth—exemplification—that places (locales that stand for larger worlds) invite intersubjective appropriation and become a focus and receptacle for collective ideas. To this degree, places distill, synthesize, and represent experience and praxis, making ways of being legible.[73] The physical configuration of places suggests what could or should take place in them. If the environing world is a realm in which imagination is constantly translated into use, and use into being, place is the vehicle of this translation and transposition. Places are, in the final analysis, intersubjective constructs in which individual imagination ("what might *I* do here?") slips into collective potentiality ("what might *anyone* do here?"); thus, they are primarily projections of consciousness, self, and identity.[74] The larger world comes into focus in places precisely *because* they privilege difference and singularity.

Places, then, are metaphorical constructions the meanings of which derive from their capacity to encode and exemplify not only ideological values but also preconscious corporeal undergoing. Our experience of them is almost by definition prereflective, registered deeply within involuntary bodily knowledge while we are preoccupied by other, more conscious agendas. Place *images* extend this homologous agency by standing between socially produced bodily subjectivity and the corporeally enacted material world, and bringing their (metaphoric) overlap into visibility. This encoding can draw upon the full spectrum of associations, feelings, ideas, constructs, and memories that attach themselves to the world and can be both mnemonic and anticipatory. While place representation might stabilize and propagate the meaning of the physical world, and indeed may be essential to our understanding of that world, it cannot escape the underlying order of things posited by body-subjectivity. All landscape representations are, potentially, embodiments, not only because they are usually attempts to recuperate corporeal experience but because each mode of representation is itself a form of praxis.[75] (Each encodes and discloses the praxis of the landscape encounter that gave rise to it in a slightly different way; the same locale or event will also be interpreted differently according to whether it is represented verbally, textually, or pictorially.) Places, then, are intersubjective simulacra whose polysemic powers of evocation are rooted in ineluctably quotidian practicalities worked upon—extended, diverted, inverted, transformed, supplemented, elaborated, refused—by representation.

The polysemic nature of place representation in mediating bodily and discursively constructed meaning is particularly apposite in early twentieth-century South Africa, where white seeing and talking about landscape repressed a skepticism about the recuperative powers of representation and mediated a deflection of attention away from identifiable locales onto unconfigured bodily experience. This evolving body-subjectivity was shaped by a number of social and cultural factors: transnational lives, traveling practices, and cultural memories that threw the environment's sensory and spatial qualities into high relief; the inability to acknowledge aboriginal presence; and the unfulfilled desire for a working reciprocity with an extensive, spacious terrain always experienced in passing. It was also shaped by the linguistic and historical difficulties of narrating this topography, something that was heightened by the inadequacy of the representational grid borrowed from Europe—writing, painting, photography—to capture its reflexive corporeality. For some, this representational incommensurateness drained the South African landscape of existential weight and meaning, to the extent that it was no longer, in the fullest sense of the word, a topography.[76] For others such as Kipling, Baden-Powell, Buchan, Baker, and Everard, this incommensurateness lent that corporeal experience an uncanny excess that disavowed the metropolitan, bourgeois economy of the body with its critical distance between reflection and corporeal participation,[77] and descried instead an unimagined, utopian potentiality. (Both of these sensibilities, of course, figure the land itself as a central problematic of existence.) Here we see how landscape representation helped create the corporeal subjectivity associated with the cult of the veld, precisely because it failed to adequately evoke the terrain that was its primary motif.

In the preceding account, I have traced both the intentional and unintentional ways in which this corporeal subjectivity coevolved with an imaginary geography that incorporated the South African territory as part of an imagined white identity. While it is probably true to say that the landscape subjectivity of colonial nationalism has left fewer physical traces in the South African terrain than has Afrikaner nationalism, in each of my handful of soundings I believe this incommensurability between representation and praxis escaped its usual fate—disappearance—and constitutively entered white cultural discourse. Baden-Powell's wartime chorographic conspectus of Mafeking, Buchan's prosopopoeic description of the Highveld as a realm of sensory revitalization, Baker's architectonic framing of the veld and the intercontinental view at Parktown, Everard's painterly descent into the Komati River valley, as well as photographs of a modern, "national" terrain seen from the moving train were all moments in the articulation of an evolving subjectivity toward space and place. Each of these representational places bodied forth some aspect of an immanent but otherwise inarticulable subjectivity, affording a process of recognition that was also, in a subliminal way, one of identification. To the degree that each episode of inhabitation imbued the landscape with meaning through a form of activation, each can be seen as contemporary, discursive equivalents of the genius loci, a locale that gathers, distills, and represents forms of life or action that are immanent and sensed but not easily described.

These connotations are only faintly accessible today, when both the practices and the physical environments that generated the original encounter have changed, and South African notions of space, place, and identity have been transformed by history. At the turn of the twenty-first century, Mafeking has become a bustling African border town. Still a place of meeting between two worlds, its streets are jammed with buses and sprawling markets, and the few remaining memorials to the siege are all but invisible and unnoticed in the colorful disorder. In the Woodbush, traces of Buchan's Hesperides can be seen in the rambling, evocatively named colonial period estates of Milner settlers looking out from the cloud-hung escarpment and the faded, high-ceilinged, lichen-streaked grandeur of the older parts of Tzaneen, but the region as a whole has embraced development and industrial-scale farming in the face of atavistic, seemingly random violence that stalks the forested valleys. Parktown Ridge has all but disappeared under highways and monolithic corporate and institutional buildings, and the continental view has filled with urban sprawl that today stretches virtually all the way to the once-fabled Magaliesberg. Bertha Everard's world is still largely intact, though some of the undulating grass valleys and thorn trees of the lower Komati have given way to conifer plantations and large dams. And only a few South Africans see their country from the train window today, when the preferred form of transportation is either the car or the airplane.[78]

Discussing the five subjective topographies as faded geographic icons obscures the fact that it was as discursive topographies—mediative, intersubjective cultural formations—that they originally functioned. These discursive topographies helped configure a national landscape because they indexed a matrix of social and physical praxis that was everywhere immanent in it. They certified and gave weight to a growing repertoire of cognate places throughout South Africa: "ordinary-looking places" that became symbolic centers, "gardens on the edge of wild," "hidden valleys," and houses that grew out of their topography. These discursive topographies did more than place individuals and groups in particular locales at particular moments; once absorbed into the web of daily life they became part of the shared "narrative of interaction" by which white, colonial national South Africans oriented and placed themselves within an imagined national territory.[79] As the first, tentative embodiments of a new nation, these discursive topographies initiated the process whereby successive generations of white South Africans absorbed the perceptions of the past, adapted them to the imperatives of their own time, and fed them back into the (re)making of the landscape.

Landscape representation's recursive potential to bring into consciousness otherwise inaccessible aspects of landscape and embed them in the lived world operates at both the perceptual and concrete level; it transforms "structures of seeing" as well as practices that physically make use of the world. Place representation functions both as an aid to memory and a framework for reconstructing an encounter, and as a guide to future encounters with or use of a given place.[80] (As we saw in the case of photographs of the empty veld, representations taken to represent one idea can represent something slightly different at a different time for a different audience.) It is largely through the discursive interplay between remembering and imagining that the traveling subjectivity of imperialism prepared the way for South Africanism, and South Africanism in turn prepared the way for white nationalist landscape subjectivity. Black and white photographs that represented the empty veld as simultaneously modern and archaic posited a territory that was a transitional object for Afrikanerdom's modern, rational appeals to historicist ideas of racial purity.

The power of landscape representation to take up lived experience and authenticate it as a vehicle of cultural continuity is epitomized by Pierre Nora's notion of the *lieu de mémoire* or "realm of memory," a cultural locus that compensates for modern society's loss of a shared *milieux de mémoire* as a result of the erosion of spontaneous memory. Although they are sometimes physical places, *lieux de mémoire* are also often icons, persons, stories, idioms, or events; in other words, they embody latent forms of praxis. Crucially, *lieux de mémoire* accommodate different readings over time; they are imaginaries in which culturally constructed narratives are protected and saved. *Lieux de mémoire* suggest that the polysemic capacity of place derives from certain intersubjective effects to engage and mediate shifting interpretations over time. Thus, although Buchan was among the first to be captivated by the distinctive character of the Highveld, he was not the last. A famous South African writer, an internationally recognized foe of the white apartheid government, described the same region (also the heartland of Afrikanerdom) some seventy-five years later: "The upland serenity of high altitude; the openness of grassland without indigenous bush or trees; the greening, yellowing or silver-browning that prevailed according to season. A landscape without theatricals except when it became an arena for summer storms, a landscape without any picture-postcard features; . . . (one that) you either find dull and low-keyed, or prefer to all others."[81]

Such apparently discursive continuities remind us that all place representations are to some degree memory traces, and as such, mediate a sense of what Proust called "something beyond the reach of the intellect, and [yet] unmistakably present in some material object."[82] The significance of this is deepened by Walter Benjamin, who, discussing Freud's argument that "consciousness comes into being at the site of a memory-trace," emphasizes Proust's distinction between voluntary memory (conscious memory of known facts and cultural narratives) and involuntary memory (protective remembrance of sensory impressions). Benjamin cites this distinction to suggest that, crucially, sensory impressions are powerful and enduring precisely because "the incident which left them behind was one that never entered consciousness."

Here, we have once again returned to Charles Harrison's arguments that the most profound effects of landscape are cognate with irreducibly metaphoric appeals to bodily experience, and that it is precisely in the automatism and involuntariness of such effects that we find "the signs of the body's resistance to ideology."[83] Harrison goes further, arguing that it is precisely at those moments when distinctions between the technical and the metaphoric dimensions of landscape representation become hardest to sustain that the effects of landscape are most vivid, and the legacies of landscape most pertinent. In these terms, we see that the legacy of landscape that became incorporated in white South African subjectivity through representation was the memory trace of involuntary and incommensurable bodily experience, and that the territorial interaction of white nationhood during the early twentieth century gave rise not only to a cultural consciousness but also to a shared somatic disposition.[84] The quintessential South African landscape was *empty* because in it a corporeal, participatory reciprocity was not only possible, but also most vividly and *reflexively* experienced. The cognate disposition to this empty landscape was characterized by nostalgic reverie and oriented toward improvement and potentiality, but also always enlivened, like all marginal subjectivities, by the aesthetics of eminent loss.

Thus, if white South African consciousness *was* discursively initiated by such early topographical negotiations with the subcontinent's terrain, then the memory traces that became incorporated as part of that consciousness were impressions that never entered consciousness. These encompassed not only the pure impressions of empty, architectonic space (with its intimations of agency and autonomy) but also the ineluctably fleeting, sensory ones: both the familiarly visual ones of light and color (the bleached color and shimmering mirages of the veld at midday, or its achromatic muteness just before the sun drops below the horizon) and the less familiar ones of smell (of the earth after rain, or burning veld grass) and sound (the trilling of the cicadas in a kloof, or the depthlessness of a shout in a landscape that is all horizon). It was ultimately in the image of the empty veld that this memory trace was most visible as a legacy that transcended political allegiance and became naturalized as a kind of birthright. Here, lived corporeal space and culturally haunted, imaginary space started to converge and create a paradoxical sense of home in which the pleasures of a simple life in a genial climate and a sense of living on the frontier of civilization were conjointly preserved.

NOTES

Chapter 1: Introduction

1. See, for instance, Beinart, "Soil Erosion, Conservationism and Ideas about Development" and "Empire, Hunting and Ecological Change"; Beinart and Coates, *Environment and History*; Beinart, Delius, and Trapido, *Putting a Plough to the Ground*; Bonner, *Holding Their Ground*; Christopher, *South Africa* and *Southern Africa*; Carruthers, "Nationhood and National Parks"; Grove, "Scotland in South Africa"; Hall, *The Changing Past*; and Murray, *Black Mountain*. A recent overview of this work is offered by Christopher, *The Atlas of Apartheid*, and Lester, *From Colonization to Democracy*. Dodson, "Dismantling Dystopia," 143.

2. See, for instance, Guelke, "Ideology and the Landscape of Settler Colonialism," and "Freehold Farmers and Frontier Settlers."

3. The most prolific exponent of this approach is David Bunn, whose work includes: "Whited Sepulchres"; "The Sleep of the Brave"; "Comparative Barbarism"; "'Our Wattled Cot'"; and "Relocations." See also Barnard, "Encountering Adamastor"; and Hall, "The Legend of the Lost City." Since this book went to press, two significant contributions to this field have appeared in print: Jennifer Beningfield, *The Frightened Land: Land, Landscape and Politics in South Africa in the 20th Century* (London: Routledge, 2006); and Nicholas Coetzer, "Between Bird's Nests and Manor Houses: Edwardian Cape Town and the Political Nature of Building Materials," in Katie Lloyd Thomas, ed., *Material Matters: Architecture and Material Practice* (London: Routledge, 2007).

4. Coetzee, *White Writing*, 2.

5. Coetzee, *White Writing*, 2.

6. Parker, "Fertile Land," 202.

7. Parker, "Fertile Land," 204–16. On this episode, see Lester, "Historical Geographies of Imperialism"; and Winer, "Landscapes, Fear and Land Loss."

8. For a discussion of the frequent conflation and elision of the construct "landscape" in the phrase "the land," see Bunn, "Relocations."

9. See, for instance, Foucault, *Power/Knowledge* and *The Archaeology of Knowledge*; and Said, *Orientalism* and *Culture and Imperialism*.

10. See Cosgrove, *Social Formation and Symbolic Landscape*, "The Picturesque City," and "Habitable Earth"; Daniels, *Fields of Vision* and "The Making of Constable Country"; Green, *The Spectacle of Nature*; Hyde, *American Vision*; Lowenthal, "European and English Landscapes as National Symbols," "British National Identity and the English Landscape," and "European Landscapes as National Emblems"; Matless, *Landscape and Englishness*; Bishop, *An Archetypal Constable* and *The Myth of Shangri-la*; and Shields, *Places on the Margin*.

11. On Australia, see Carter, *The Road to Botany Bay* and *Living in a New Country*; and Jacobs, "Earth Honoring" and *Edge of Empire*. On Ireland, see Nash, "Remapping the Body/Land," "'Em-

bodying the Nation,'" and "Visionary Geographies"; and N. Johnson, "Historical Geographies of the Present" and "Cast in Stone." On Israel/Palestine, see Mitchell, "Holy Landscape." On Canada, see Bordo, "Jack Pine"; and Osborne, "Warscapes, Landscape, Inscapes."

12. The argument for cultural analysis grounded in context and interpretation is made in Geertz, "Thick Description."

13. Said argued that while theories develop in response to specific historical and social reasons, the power and rebelliousness attached to them dissipates as they become domesticated and assimilated (often by an academic orthodoxy) into their new location. See Bayoumi and Rubin, *The Edward Said Reader*, 195.

14. Thrift, "Steps to an Ecology of Place," 297.

15. Bishop, "Rhetoric, Memory and Power," 115.

16. Yi-Fu Tuan, "Surface Phenomena and Aesthetic Experience," 233.

17. "Mood" is precisely the term used by the venerable American landscape architect Ed Bye to articulate landscapes' character and guide his interventions in them as a designer.

18. See for instance Appleton, *The Experience of Landscape* and *Symbolism of Habitat*; Bourassa, *The Aesthetics of Landscape*; Berleant, *Living in the Landscape*.

19. "The 'genius locii' was the 'spirit of the place', not just the the guardian deity of a particular locality but also the distinctive atmosphere or character of a place. Originally, this spirit was procreative: it did not hover around, nor had it been born of the place—it preceded the place and generated it, spoke in it and through it. The idea of 'genius locii' goes back to a polytheistic time when the air and earth seemed swarming with many deities, not yet pervaded by one single, ubiquitous immanent God. Each place had its own god, taking place in that place only, sovereign over that just that region." Miller, *Topographies*, 255–56.

20. On genius loci, see David Leatherbarrow, *The Roots of Architectural Invention*, 42. See also Kuttner, "Delight and Danger in Roman Water Gardens."

21. "Sacred presences" were evoked most notably in the animistic character assigned to fountains and in the capturing of views of singular natural features of the surrounding wilderness as an integral part of the garden's design. See Hunt, *Greater Perfections*.

22. Evernden, "The Ambiguous Landscape," 148. Early architectural treatises on the siting of towns and buildings, such as Alberti's *Ten Books of Architecture* and Vitruvius's *On Architecture*, performed a similar transition from this older mentality.

23. See Vesely, "Architecture and the Conflict of Representation" and "Architecture and the Poetics of Representation."

24. Leatherbarrow, "Character, Geometry and Perspective."

25. Anthony D. Smith, *National Identity*, 75.

26. On early landscape theorists, see Leatherbarrow, *Roots of Architectural Invention*, 53–55, and *Topographical Stories*. On the development of "natural theology," see, for instance, Fuller, *Theoria: Art and the Absence of Grace* and "The Geography of Mother Nature."

27. See Cosgrove, "Environmental Thought and Action" and "*Mappa mundi, anima mundi*."

28. Goethe, quoted in Sauer, *Land and Life*, 327.

29. E. Bunkse, "Humboldt and an Aesthetic Tradition in Geography."

30. Sauer, *Land and Life*, 323 (emphasis added).

31. See, for instance, Vesely, "Architecture and the Poetics of Representation" and "Architecture and the Conflict of Representation."

32. Kunze, "Sea-Food and Vampires," 114.

33. Kunze, "Cuisine, Frontality and the Infra-thin," 86.

34. In addition to those publications already mentioned, see Leatherbarrow, *Uncommon Ground*.

35. Another, earlier text that argues this point is Bloomer and Moore, *Body, Memory and Architecture*.

36. Kunze, "Sea-Food and Vampires," 105.

37. Kunze, "Cuisine, Frontality, and the Infra-thin," 106.

38. Kunze, "Cuisine, Frontality and the Infra-thin," 88 (emphasis added). Here, I use the term "analogical" in the sense of "the likening of something to another on the basis of some similarity between the two"; also a mode of imagination or representation that posits a relationship in a way that throws light on another, superficially different relationship.

39. For a discussion of this, see Leatherbarrow, *Roots of Architectural Invention*, 65–141.

40. According to Leatherbarrow, "the display of details in context" is the original meaning of the word "eurhythmy." See *Roots of Architectural Invention*, 90–99.

41. The close relationship between "character" and "type" is revealed by their dictionary definitions. "Character" is "the aggregate of features and traits that form the apparent individual nature of a person or thing"; "type" is "a kind, class or group distinguished by some particular characteristic"; both definitions are from *Webster's Encyclopedic Unabridged Dictionary* (New York: Gramercy Books, 1989).

42. Visser, *The Way We Are*, 288.

43. Aristotle, without the benefit of modern scientific research into cognition and memory, listed six different forms of representation. The following discussion draws heavily on Malcolm Heath's introduction to his translation of Aristotle's *Poetics*.

44. Harrison, "The Effects of Landscape," 227.

45. Kunze, "Cuisine, Frontality and the Infra-thin," 95.

46. See for instance Merleau-Ponty, "Eye and Mind," 129.

47. Kunze, "Cuisine, Frontality and the Infra-thin," 96.

48. See, for instance, Scully, *Architecture*.

49. Alexander, *John Dewey's Theory of Art, Experience and Nature*, 248.

50. Pollan, *A Place of My Own*, 37.

Chapter 2: From Imperialism to Nationalism

1. Pile and Thrift, *Mapping the Subject*, 9.

2. Leatherbarrow, *The Roots of Architectural Invention*, 58.

3. One dictionary defines the word "identity" as "the quality or condition of being a specified person or thing" and "the state of being the same in substance, nature, or qualities." *Concise Oxford Dictionary of Current English*, 8th ed. (Oxford: Oxford University Press, 1991).

4. Thus, subjectivity is seldom coterminous with personhood (any one individual participates in several different subjectivities at different times), and some commentators consider it more appropriate to use terms such as "subjectivities" or "subject-position" rather than "subjectivity." Because of the multiplicity of subject-positions possible in society, relations never form a single system, and an individual is never equal to his or her field of relations. See Beer, *Open Fields*, 1.

5. Green, *The Spectacle of Nature*, 129.

6. Kaplan and Herb, "Introduction: A Question of Identity," 2.

7. Kaplan and Herb, "Introduction," 3.

8. Kaplan and Herb, "Introduction," 3.

9. Anthony Smith, *National Identity*, 71.

10. Kaplan, "Territorial Identities and Geographic Scale," 33.

11. The nation has been seen as a product of structural change; a project of cultural elites; a discourse of domination; and a bounded community of exclusion and opposition. See Herb, "National Identity and Territory," 14.

12. See Anderson, *Imagined Nations*; Herb, "National Identity and Territory," 14.

13. Colquhon, "The Concept of Regionalism." The distinction between *Zivilization* and *Kultur* was first proposed by Norbert Elias.

14. See M. Bell, "'The Pestilence That Walketh in Darkness.'"

15. See Cosgrove, "Habitable Earth," 31–32; also Gradidge, *Dream Houses*, 37–46.

16. Anthony Smith, *National Identity*, 70.

17. J. Thomas, quoted in Bender and Winer, *Contested Landscapes*, 4.

18. The term "narrative of descent" is used by Prasenjit Duara in "Historicizing National Identity," 168.

19. Bender, *Contested Landscapes*, 4.

20. See Hutton, "The Art of Memory," 385–86.

21. South Africa was the last of Britain's major overseas colonies, except for India, to become an independent autonomous nation.

22. On white identity earlier than this, see for instance Lester, *Imperial Networks*.

23. The western two-thirds of South Africa is classified either as arid (i.e., receiving less than ten inches of annual precipitation) or semiarid.

24. Beinart, *Twentieth Century South Africa*, 58.

25. De Kiewiet, *History of South Africa*, 117.

26. The war was also known as the Anglo-Boer War. The terminology used here is more recent, adopted to reflect the fact that others besides British and Boers were involved in and affected by the war. Both sides used the indigenous population as scouts, runners, and spies, and the British put units of armed Africans into the field.

27. At the first census in 1896, only 15 percent of Johannesburg's population were ZAR citizens. See Shorten, *Johannesburg Saga*.

28. See for instance Schoeman, *Only an Anguish to Live Here*.

29. Pakenham, *The Boer War*, 494. For this reason, the forty-four concentration camps eventually established for Boer families were complemented by twenty-nine for Africans.

30. By contrast, only seven thousand burghers fighting in the field lost their lives. See Omissi and Thompson, "Introduction," 7. Altogether, nearly 20 percent of the prewar Boer republican population was lost.

31. After the war, it was not uncommon for Boer survivors to rebury family members who had died in the concentration camps on their own farms. See Buchan, *The Africa Colony*, 101.

32. On this, see Krikler, *Revolution from Above*; and Murray, *Black Mountain*.

33. This resonant phrase is taken from an essay written by Dr. J. M. Leighton, South African Cultural Attaché to London in the 1980s, titled "South Africa House in the Making" (n.d., probably reprint from *Lantern* magazine; South Africa House Library).

34. Milner's assistants would go on to play influential roles in public life in Britain and the Dominions. They included Lionel Curtis, John Buchan (later Lord Tweedsmuir and governor-general of Canada), Robert Brand, John Dove, Patrick Duncan (later governor-general of South Africa), Geoffrey Dawson (later editor of the *Times*), Lionel Hitchins, Richard Feetham, Phillip Kerr, and Leo Amery.

35. During the second half of the war, every time the Boers attacked British lines of communication, the British retaliated by burning and "clearing" the nearest farm, destroying all food, wagons, stock, and forage. Eventually, country within a ten-mile radius of the attack (i.e., an area of 340 square miles) was also "cleared." Milner estimated that thirty thousand farm buildings had been destroyed by the end of the war. See Spies, *Methods of Barbarism*.

36. On early mapping in South Africa, see Carruthers, "Friedrich Jeppe"; Lewis, "Topographical Mapping in the Union of South Africa"; Liebenberg, *Topografiese Kartering van Suid-Afrika* and "Mapping British South Africa"; and G. N. van den Bergh, "Voortrekker plaasbesetting op die Transvaalse Hoeveld."

37. Milner, like some of his Kindergarten, had been a student of Jowett at Balliol. See Pakenham, *The Boer War*, 13; also Saul Dubow, "Colonial Nationalism," 60. Nicholas Thomas writes: "In Milner's view, the 'gospel of creative imperialism' (which was more or less Rhodes' 'social imperialism') was not so much as continuation of British colonial policy, as a new and visionary departure." *Colonialism's Culture*, 150.

38. Tindall, *Countries of the Mind*.

39. Bishop, *The Myth of Shangri-La*, 140.

40. See for instance Howkins, "The Discovery of Rural England"; and Marsh, *Back to the Land*, 1–23.

41. Green, *The Spectacle of Nature*, 128–38.

42. See Katzenellenbogen, "Reconstruction in the Transvaal," 342–44. On the imaginative aspects of Milner's vision, see also Krikler, *Revolution from Above*, 76–77.

43. In a confidential letter to Percy FitzPatrick shortly after the beginning of the war, Milner wrote: "One thing is quite evident. The *ultimate* end is a self-governing White community, supported by well treated and justly governed black labour from Cape Town to Zambezi. . . . There must be one flag, the Union Jack, but under it equality of races and languages. Given *equality* all round English must prevail though I do not think, and do not wish, that Dutch should altogether die out." See A. P. Cartwright, *The First South African*, 111.

44. On Milner's "demographic engineering," see Katzenellenbogen, "Reconstruction in the Transvaal," 342–44. When the first census after the war was taken in 1904, it was found that, in the Transvaal at least, potential Boer voters roughly equaled the number of British voters. See Pakenham, *Boer War*, 575.

45. Henshaw, "John Buchan from the 'Borders' to the 'Berg,'" 10.

46. Even John Buchan, one of Milner's great admirers, admitted that Milner was "no countryman [and] unable to understand the tortuosities of the peasant mind." *Pilgrims' Way*, 96.

47. Morrell, "Competition and Cooperation in Middelburg," 377.

48. Christopher, *Southern Africa*, 148.

49. Beinart, *Twentieth Century South Africa*, 49.

50. Dubow, "Colonial Nationalism," 58

51. See Marks and Trapido, *The Politics of Race*; and Wilson and Thompson, *The Oxford History of South Africa*.

52. See Eddy and Schreuder, "The Edwardian Empire."

53. At the 1907 Colonial Conference, Australia, Canada, New Zealand, and South Africa were all accorded the status of "self-governing Dominions."

54. Schreuder, "The Making of the Idea of Colonial Nationalism."

55. S. Dubow, "Colonial Nationalism," 17.

56. See for instance Morag Bell, "'Citizenship Not Charity.'"

57. Chipkin, *Johannesburg Style*, 132.

58. S. Dubow, "Imagining the New South Africa," 81.

59. See, for instance, Schreuder, "Colonial Nationalism and 'Tribal Nationalism.'"

60. See Douglas Oakes, ed., *The Illustrated History of South Africa*, 280–95; and Krikler, "Social Neurosis and Hysterical Pre-cognition in South Africa," quoted in Schwarz, "The Romance of the Veld," 83.

61. For instance, Europeans and Africans had enjoyed something approaching legal parity in the Transvaal during the period of direct government, from 1902 to 1907.

62. For a thorough account of the path to Union, see S. Dubow, "Colonial Nationalism."

63. S. Dubow, "Colonial Nationalism," 58.

64. As S. Dubow observes, "the receptiveness of the Kindergarten to local South African perspectives was crucial to their subsequent political influence." See "Colonial Nationalism," 65.

65. These included the Onderstepoort Veterinary Institute (1908), the Department of Agriculture (1911), the Geological Survey of South Africa (1910), the National Statistic Survey (1911), the Metereological Office (1912), and the National Botanic Garden (1913). See Saul Dubow, "A Commonwealth of Science," 77.

66. De Kiewiet, *History of South Africa*, 151.

67. R. W. Johnson, "Jingoes," 30.

68. The main opposition party, the Union Party, was associated with mining and business interests.

69. The Union Buildings were begun in 1909, completed in 1912, and designed by Herbert Baker. A larger dome on the hill behind the complex, as well as a partly open Council Place, where African tribal leaders could be received, was planned but never built. See S. Dubow, "Colonial Nationalism," 55.

70. Gruffudd, "Landscape and Nationhood," 153–54.

71. Barnard, "Encountering Adamastor."

72. See, for instance, M. Bell, "'Citizenship Not Charity.'"

73. See Beinart, *Twentieth Century South Africa*, 77–78; and Giliomee, "Beginnings of Afrikaner Nationalism," 119. See also Shula Marks and Stanley Trapido, *The Politics of Race, Class and Nationalism*, 1–70.

74. S. Dubow, "Colonial Nationalism," 62.

75. Wheatcroft, *Randlords*, x.

76. Included in "British overseas" would be the significant number of English civil servants and army officers who had served in India and retired to the Cape since the nineteenth century.

77. S. Dubow, "Colonial Nationalism," 62.

78. P. Smith, *Mafeking Memories*, 69. Rhodes and Jameson had orchestrated the ill-fated Jameson Raid, an attempt to overthrow the ZAR government in 1895.

79. Lambert, "South African British, or Dominion South Africans?" 202.

80. It is estimated that in the twenty years after the discovery of gold (i.e., 1886 to 1906), 350,000 people immigrated to South Africa, including 75,000 from Britain and an estimated 40,000 Eastern European Jews who arrived in Southern Africa between 1880 and 1914 (see Beinart, *Twentieth Century South Africa*, 71).

81. See Kannemeyer, *History of Afrikaans Literature*, 5–8.

82. This took place in the period between the South African War and First World War. See Christopher, *Southern Africa*, 116–51.

83. See Hexham, "Afrikaner Nationalism, 1902–1914"; and Hofmeyr, "Building a Nation from Words." See also Kannemeyer, *History of Afrikaans Literature*, 9–27.

84. Giliomee, "Beginnings of Afrikaner Nationalism," 138–39. Hertzog was not explicitly republican (Beinart, *Twentieth Century South Africa*, 76). For him, the term "Afrikaner" simply meant any whites who accepted South Africa as their "fatherland," regardless of what language they spoke.

85. For a general description of this process, see A. Smith, *National Identity*, 139–41.

86. See Anderson, *Imagined Communities*.

87. From 1906 to 1931, only nine books about the South African War were published, and these were largely diaries or reminiscences of participants. See Grundlingh, "The War in 20th Century Afrikaner Consciousness."

88. These include *Die Volkstem* (1905), *Die Brandwag* (1910), and *Die Huisgenoot* (1916). On Preller, see Hofmeyr, "Popularizing History."

89. Hofmeyr, "Popularizing History," 529.

90. See, for instance, the first Afrikaans women's magazines, *Die Boervrou* (1919) and *Die Landbouweekblad* (1922). On the beginnings of Afrikaans publishing, see Muller, *Sonop in die Suide*; and Fisher and LeRoux, *Die Afrikaanse Woning*.

91. One of General Hertzog's more rousing statements was that "*die Engelse*" were "fortune-hunters" who had no intentions in South Africa other than getting rich; see D. Oakes, *Illustrated History of South Africa*, 296–97.

92. The colonial Dutch families included the Cloetes, Schoenegevels, van der Bijls, van der Spuys, van der Poels, Hofmeyrs, Malherbes, and Villets.

93. Gruffudd, *Landscape and Nationhood*, 161–62.

94. See Nasson, "A Great Divide," 51. Unlike the other rebel leaders, Fourie neglected to resign his commission in the Union forces before he joined the uprising.

95. In 1914, the governor-general made an urgent plea to Westminster not to call for conscription in South Africa, lest the political reconciliation achieved since Union be lost. Robert Holland, "The British Empire and the Great War."

96. This represented about one-tenth of the total white population at the time. In addition, eighty-three thousand Africans and two thousand "Coloureds" volunteered to serve in a noncombatant capacity. See Oakes, *Illustrated History of South Africa*, 303.

97. The proportion of white South African troops who were Afrikaner varied from 15 percent in 1916 to around 30 percent in 1918.

98. Nasson, "South Africans in Flanders," 299.

99. Nasson, "A Great Divide," 49.

100. On the participation of black South Africans in the war, see Grundlingh, *Fighting Their Own War*.

101. Grundlingh, *Fighting Their Own War*, 139.

102. See Morrell, *White but Poor*.

103. Key pieces of legislation were the Native (Urban Areas) Act, which extended segregation to towns (1923), the Labour Reservation Act (1926), and the Native Administration Act (1927).

104. This political process has been extensively covered by many different authors. See, for instance, Marks and Rathbone, *The Politics of Race, Class and Nationalism*; Keegan, *Rural Transformations in Industrializing South Africa*; S. Dubow, *Racial Segregation and the Origins of Apartheid*.

105. Chipkin, *Johannesburg Style*, 196. During the interwar years, earlier, broadly assimilation-

ist Native Affairs policies became much more rigidly segregationalist. Not only was the rural land set aside for Africans insufficient, but these reserves were subjected to ever tighter legislative and physical control. This confinement made it harder for Africans to make a living off the land, accelerated the degradation of land inside the reserves, and encouraged migration to the cities. See Hofmeyr, "The Spoken Word and the Barbed Wire."

106. See Keegan, *Rural Transformations in Industrializing South Africa*; also Morrell, "Competition and Cooperation in Middelburg." The transformation of South African farming from a stock-based operation to a grain-based one was significant, both economically and environmentally. It was begun by the reduction of railway tariffs in 1907, which made it possible to profitably transport maize from the interior to the coast. See Pirie, "Aspects of the Political Economy of Railways in South Africa," 19. Other factors promoting this transformation were the 1907 Co-operative Agricultural Societies Act and the establishment of a National and Agricultural Land Bank in 1912.

107. Beinart, *Twentieth Century South Africa*, 110.

108. The South African university system was created in 1916 by a series of laws passed by the Union parliament. Initially, it provided for three universities: Cape Town, Stellenbosch, and federated University of South Africa with its six constitutive university colleges. Barnard, "Encountering Admastor," 194.

109. See S. Dubow, "Commonwealth of Science."

110. S. Dubow, "Human Origins," 7.

111. Prognoses of environmental degradation in the early twentieth century were partly the result of unusually high rainfall in the 1880s and 1890s. Farming practices that evolved during these earlier decades could not be sustained after normal conditions returned in 1905 and were then perceived as "drought." An influential government agency in this regard was the Drought Investigation Commission, whose 1922 report was to shape land policy and perceptions of rural South Africa for several decades.

112. This began with the establishment of the Land Bank in 1913 and continued in the 1920s (especially after Hertzog came to power in 1924) with agricultural research, irrigation scheme construction, price support, and control of various agricultural industries to increase production and encourage exports.

113. See Barnard, "Encountering Admastor," 195–97. Coverage of the Union on a scale of 1:500,000 did not become available until 1937, and although reliable climatic figures for coastal cities dated back to 1841, rainfall measurements in the Transvaal only *began* in 1918, and first wind data were published in 1918. South Africa's first census was taken in 1904 (and subsequently in 1911 and 1921), but the black population was not estimated until after World War II. The first comprehensive mapping of South Africa's vegetation types, by I. Pole-Evans, was only completed in the mid-1930s.

114. Since the 1870s, geological and mineralogical knowledge about South Africa had always been more advanced than topographical knowledge; see for instance Carruthers, "Mapping the Transvaal."

115. Hofmeyr, *Tale That Is Told*, 72.

116. Indeed, in 1891, Afrikaner Bond had made national currency part of its political platform. See Gilbert, "National Currency Formation and National Identity."

117. Williams and Smith, "The National Construction of Space," 511–12.

118. S. Dubow, "Commonwealth of Science," 83.

119. Smuts's inclusion was unprecedented because he was neither a British citizen nor a member of Parliament. After the war, he went on to play an important role in the peace negotiations at Versailles, where he, along with Botha and Milner, used the example of South Africa over the previous seventeen years to support a plea for clemency toward the Germans. See Aldaheff, *South Africa in Two World Wars*, 27, 44.

120. The full description was "autonomous communities within the British Empire equal in status, in no way subordinate to one another in any aspect of their domestic or external affairs, though united in their common allegiance, and freely associated as members of the British Commonwealth of Nations."

121. *South African Nation*, 12 April 1924.

122. This concept might have emerged even earlier, with Sir George Grey, high commissioner to the Cape in the 1850s, who envisaged a united subcontinent in which the Dutch would identify with "Britishness." See Lambert, "South African British, or Dominion South Africans?" 200.

123. Its allegiances were severely tested by the South African War. Bondsmen subscribed to an inclusivist vision "in which Cape Afrikaner ethnicity, white Cape colonialism, pan-Afrikaner solidarity, and British imperialism lived side by side, not without tension, but on the whole quite happily." B. Tamarkin, quoted in S. Dubow, "Colonial Nationalism," 62.

124. Henshaw, "John Buchan from the 'Borders' to the 'Berg,'" 5.

125. On this group, see Wheatcroft, *Randlords*; and Stevenson, *Art and Aspirations*. Stevenson quotes a 1904 letter that Smuts wrote to Emily Hobhouse, in which Smuts stated that the Randlords "never loved their country or felt a passion for it in any shape or form. . . . They regarded (South Africa) with unconcealed contempt—a black man's country, good enough to make money or a name in, but not good enough to be born or die in" (176).

126. As one turn-of-the-century observer commented: "This is virtually one society, though dispersed in spots hundreds of miles from one another. . . . The five most important places are, for social purposes, almost one city. . . . There is a sort of unity to the upper society (here) which finds few parallels in any other parts of the world." Bryce, *Impressions of South Africa*, 490. Between 1910 and 1920, South Africa's white population was around 1.5 million, its black population around 5 million.

Two examples of English-Afrikaner reconciliation will have to suffice. Edward Roworth, English-born and -trained artist-academician, was a good friend of J. H. Pierneef, the Transvaal-born Dutchman whose paintings later became icons of Afrikaner nationalism. Gordon Leith was an architect who had studied in London, assisted Baker on the Union Buildings, been a scholar at the British School in Rome, fought in Flanders, and worked with Baker on the war graves in France; he went on to become "the principal heir to Baker's legacy in South Africa" and was a frequent contributor to the Afrikaans magazine *Die Boervrou* during the 1920s. See Chipkin, *Johannesburg Style*, 132.

127. Nasson, "A Great Divide," 47–48.

128. S. Dubow, "Imagining a New South Africa," 89. The most explicit expression of this was Rhodes's doctrine of ransom: "that those who defaced the fair face of nature by extracting her wealth should make due restoration by the creation of works of art and the preservation of natural beauty." Baker, *Cecil Rhodes by His Architect*, 10.

129. For discussion of the *State*, see Merrington, "'The State' and the Invention of Heritage"; and "Pageantry and Primitivism," 654. See also S. Dubow, "Colonial Nationalism," 70–71, and "Imagining the New South Africa," 84–86.

130. Nasson, "The South African War/Anglo-Boer War," 118.

131. Harvey, *The Condition of Post-Modernity*, 272.

132. See Nora, "General Introduction: Between Memory and History."

133. In some instances, this limited commonality is bolstered by a shared desire to break away from the colonizing power.

134. Bouchard, "The Formation of Cultures and Nations in the 'New World.'"

135. Bouchard suggests a number of alternate ways in which colonial societies address the challenge of creating a long memory from a short history. These include the suppression of contemporary differences through emphasis on common origins far back in the remote past; the valorization and commemoration of selected ancestors and antecedents; and setting the historical clock to zero at the date of nation's founding.

136. Quoted in Harvey, *Condition of Post-Modernity*, 86.

137. See Rosaldo, "Imperialist Nostalgia." On colonial elites, see Hobsbawm and Ranger, *The Invention of Tradition*.

138. On this topic, see Merrington, "'The State' and the Invention of Heritage," and "Heritage, Pageantry and Archivism."

139. See, for instance, Bunn, "Relocations," and McGregor, "The Victoria Falls 1900–1940."

140. This is well captured in Bunn, "Comparative Barbarism," 45.

141. To this list can be added the imposing Honoured Dead Memorial in Kimberley, the head-

quarters of Rhodes's de Beers mining empire, commissioned by him shortly before his death, as well as Rhodes's own grave in the Matopo Hills in Rhodesia.

142. See Merrington, "Carrying the Torch."

143. Other models might have been the Dutch Vereniging Natuurmonumenten (Society for the Preservation of National Monuments), also founded in 1905, and the German Bund für Heimatshutz, which provided historical monuments as well as natural areas, founded in 1904.

144. See Leibrandt, *Précis of the Archives of the Cape of Good Hope*; and Theal, *Records of the Cape Colony*.

145. Merrington, "Carrying the Torch."

146. The French Huguenots who came to South Africa in the 1680s and subsequently became assimilated into South Africa's white population had of course been Protestants.

147. Barnard, "Encountering Adamastor," 197.

148. Dodson, "Dismantling Dystopia," 145.

149. Fairbridge edited the letters of both women. Fairbridge, *Lady Anne Barnard at the Cape of Good Hope* and *Letters from the Cape by Lady Duff-Gordon*.

150. See Fraser and Jeeves, *All That Glittered*, 5–6.

151. Baker, *Architecture and Personalities*, 54. On the Phillipses at Vergelegen, see Fraser, *The Story of Two Cape Farms*.

152. Cran, *The Gardens of Good Hope*; Boddam-Whetham, *A Garden in the Veld*; and Fairbridge, *Gardens of South Africa*.

153. Although this was broadly true, many of the Dominion forces were men who had emigrated from Britain in the decades preceding the war. By the end of the war, when Britain's own manpower was exhausted, colonial soldiers formed around 40 percent of British forces.

154. The South African Brigade brought to Europe a springbok doe named Nancy, who traveled with them, marched ahead of them in parades, and was buried in France with full military honors when she died in 1917. See *Report from South Africa*.

155. Nasson, "South Africans in Flanders," 301–2.

156. Herb, "National Identity and Territory," 16.

157. The South African government itself seems to have initially shown little interest in an overseas war memorial. A 1918 proposal to build one above the Union Buildings in Pretoria was blocked by political rivalry. See Baker, *Architecture and Personalities*, 61. It was only in 1919 that the overseas project gained momentum, when Sir Percy Fitzpatrick took over the option on the devastated site, which had initially been secured by the South African military attaché in London, and broached the matter with Prime Minister Smuts. See Uys, *Delville Wood*, 232–33. On the politics of commemoration at Delville Wood, see Nasson, "Delville Wood."

Chapter 3: Visual Representation, Discursive Landscape, and "A Simple Life in a Genial Climate"

1. On the origins of the landscape idea, see Andrews, *Landscape and Western Art*, 25–67; Cosgrove, *Social Formation and Symbolic Landscape*, 69–101; Crandell, *Nature Pictorialized*, 59–82; and Ernst Gombrich, "The Renaissance Theory of Art."

2. See Bender, "Introduction," 3. Recently, these sociological arguments have been supplemented by ecological arguments that the landscape idea also obscures the natural processes whereby the terrain itself evolves over time.

3. Maunu Häyrinen, "National Landscapes and Their Making in Finland," 9.

4. See, for instance, Daniels, *Fields of Vision*.

5. See, for instance, Ryan and Schwartz, *Picturing Place*.

6. Anderson, *Imagined Communities*. See also Brennan, "The National Longing for Form."

7. Hirsch, "Introduction: Landscape, between Place and Space," 3–4. Augustin Berque explores the implications of "mediation" in *Médiance: De Milieux en paysages*.

8. Mitchell, "Holy Landscape," 195.

9. See Herb, "National Identity and Territory," 17.

10. See David Harvey on De la Blache's *Géographie de l'Est*, in *The Condition of Post-Modernity*, 85.

11. See Kaufmann, "Naturalizing the Nation."

12. See Crandell, *Nature Pictorialized*, 142–60; and Creese, "Yosemite National Park."

13. Zimmer, "In Search of Natural Identity."

14. Kaufmann, "Naturalizing the Nation," 667–68.

15. Kaufmann, "Naturalizing the Nation," 668.

16. Häyrinen, "National Landscapes," 9.

17. Herb, "National Identity and Territory," 24.

18. See Häkli, "Territoriality and the Rise of the Modern State."

19. Green, *The Spectacle of Nature*, 102. The term "synecdochic nationalism" is from Mels, "Nature, Home and Scenery."

20. See, for instance, McMillan, "'La France Profonde'"; and Brace, "Finding England Everywhere."

21. See Gregory, "Geographical Imagination," 217. Calling this phenomenon a "cultural topography," Said argues that it manifests itself through "structures of location and geographical reference that appear in the cultural languages of literature, history, or ethnography, sometimes allusively and sometimes carefully plotted, across [multiple] works that are not otherwise connected to one another, or to an official ideology." Said, *Culture and Imperialism*, 52.

22. See Dumas, "The Public Face of Landscape."

23. See R. Williams, *The City and the Country*.

24. McCaughey, "Likeness and Unlikeness."

25. Johns, "Landscape Painting in America and Australia."

26. See Sayers, "The Shaping of Australian Landscape Painting." The rise of public interest in distinctly Australian landscape painting in the 1880s and 1890s was reflected in the first purchase of a painting with an Australian subject by the Art Gallery of Southern Australia in 1880, and the organization of competitions for depictions of authentic Australian landscapes.

27. On this group's influence on South African artistic life, see Stevenson, *Art and Aspirations*.

28. Stevenson, *Art and Aspirations*, 23. Unlike some of his business associates, Lionel Phillips lived in Johannesburg and had survived an assassination attempt in 1913. See N. Green, *Florence, Lady Phillips*, Parktown & Westcliff Trust, September 1986.

29. Merrington, "Pageantry and Primitivism," 653.

30. Quoted in Stevenson, *Art and Aspirations*, 94.

31. Roworth, "Towards a National Art," 13.

32. Stevenson, *Art and Aspirations*, 90.

33. See E. Berman, *Art and Artists of South Africa*, 2; and Hillebrand, "The Background Story."

34. Harmsen, *Looking at South African Art*, 11–14.

35. Hillebrand, "Background Story," 67.

36. Merrington, "Pageantry and Primitivism," 654.

37. Thompson, "Art in South Africa," 186.

38. On the importance of historical associations to the discursive effects of landscape painting, see, for instance, Lowenthal, "European and English Landscapes as National Symbols"; and Claval, "From Michelet to Braudel."

39. Thompson, "Art in South Africa," 186.

40. Early immigrant artists included Frans Oerder (1867–1944, born in Rotterdam, emigrated to the ZAR in 1890) and Erich Mayer (born 1876 in Karlsruhe, emigrated to Orange Free State in 1898). In most cases, these individuals initially emigrated to work for the colonial or republican governments but, finding an audience for their artistic talent, they turned to painting.

Later immigrants included Allerley Glossop (1870–1955, born Twickenham, emigrated to South Africa in 1900), C. P. Canitz (1874–1959, born in Leipzig), George Smithard (1873–1920, born in Ireland, first came to South Africa in 1902), William Timlin (1896–1943, born in Britain, first came to South Africa in 1913), Pieter Wenning (1873–1921, born in Holland, emigrated to Transvaal in 1914), John Wheatley (1892–1955, born Abergavenny), and Gwelo Goodman (1871–1939, born in Britain, settled in South Africa in 1905).

Best known among native-born South Africans were Jan Volschenk (1853–1936), Jan Juta (1897–1972), Hugo Naude (1869–1941), Strat Caldecott (1886–1929), J. H. Pierneef (1886–1957), Irma Stern (1894–1966), and Bertha Everard (see chapter 8).

41. Gwelo Goodman, in *Our Art* 2 (Johannesburg: Lantern/SABC, 1961).

42. Sartwell, "Representation," 365–66, quoting Gombrich, 1983.

43. E. Berman, *Art and Artists of South Africa*, 7.

44. John X. Merriman, *The Natal Mercury*, 17 January 1913, 7.

45. E. Berman, *Art and Artists of South Africa*, 3–5. During the first quarter of the twentieth century, not more than one hundred professional or semiprofessional artists worked in South Africa.

46. Even though 50 percent of the painters whose paintings were selected by Lane for Johannesburg were still living, and the collection was lauded for its modernity when it was unveiled in 1910, it had few pictures painted after 1870 and only 10 percent that could be described as Impressionist. See Stevenson, *Art and Aspirations*, 84.

47. An example of this was Strat Caldecott, who, upon returning to South Africa from Paris in 1924, attempted to introduce Impressionism.

48. Textbook examples of this were the writers William Plomer, Roy Campbell, and Laurens van der Post, who, after the 1927 failure of their magazine *Voorslag*, a short-lived experiment in indigenous modernism, left to live and work in Europe. See Gardner and Chapman, *Voorslag*. On the struggle to be modern, see Cartwright, "South African Stories," 296. For a similar pattern in another Dominion, see J. Williams, *The Quarantined Culture*.

49. See Iziko s. a. National Gallery, www.iziko.org.za/sang.

50. Hillebrand, "Background Story," 68, 69.

51. Roworth was given the prestigious commission to paint the group portrait of the 1909 National Convention that led to union, and in 1935, he was awarded the King's Silver Jubilee Medal.

52. "Landscape Art in South Africa," published in a special issue of the *Studio* (C. Holm, ed.) entitled "Art of the British Empire Overseas," October 1917. In 1926, however, Roworth admitted that a South African art might be possible in an essay entitled "Towards a South African Art," published in the first issue of *Voorslag*. The origins of this sentiment are probably revealed elsewhere in the article: "There is no sale whatsoever for work which cannot be labelled 'South African.'" See Gardner and Chapman, *Voorslag*, 13.

53. See, for instance, Hillebrand, "Background Story," 73.

54. On this earlier episode of architectural hybridization, see Lewcock, *Early Nineteenth Century Architecture in South Africa*.

55. Men like John X. Merriman and Cecil Rhodes, who not only had an interest in history, but an interest in making money. Many of these ravaged vineyards, being close to Cape Town, were ideally suited for replanting with deciduous fruit trees, to take advantage of the new export markets opened by the introduction of refrigerated holds in ships. See D. Oakes, *Illustrated History of South Africa*, 229.

56. Letter, Olive Schreiner to Herbert Baker, in Greig, *Herbert Baker in South Africa*, 266.

57. Bierman, "The Sources of Designs for Historic Buildings at the Cape."

58. See Merrington, "Carrying the Torch." Trotter's book is *Old Colonial Houses and the Cape of Good Hope*.

59. For example, at Rhodes House in Oxford (1928), and South Africa House in Trafalgar Square, London (1933).

60. Baker wrote a chapter entitled "The Origin of Old Cape Architecture" in Trotter's book. On Baker's various activities, see Merrington, "'The State' and the Invention of Heritage," 130–31.

61. Baker, "The Architectural Needs of South Africa," *State*, May 1909, 512–24. In the July 1910 edition of the *State*, J. M. Solomon's article "The Union Buildings and Their Architect" stressed both the South Africanness and the modernity of Baker's work.

62. Of Fairbridge, Peter Merrington has written: "All her writing is, in various ways, dedicated to the idea of a unified South Africa, and further, to the supposed ideal of the Union of South Africa located within a unified British empire. Her imperialism is not of the jingoistic variety, but rather that of a colonial who desired the idea of a broader context—political, moral, cultural—for her own place, and who saw the empire (inevitably) as affording this context." "Writing for Empire," unpublished lecture, Institute for Commonwealth Studies, London, March 1996.

63. Bensusan, *Silver Images*, 101. Elliot's exhibitions included *Our History in Pictures* (1910), *The Story of South Africa* (1913), *The Old Cape Colony* (1926), *South Africa through the Centuries* (1930), and *The Cape, Quaint and Beautiful* (1938). Elliot died in 1938.

64. For a discussion of Elliot's photography of Cape Dutch buildings, see Fransen, *A Cape Camera*, 7–16. For an overview of Elliot's life, see Jaff, *They Came to South Africa*, 115–23.

65. See Sontag, *On Photography*, 71.

66. The prime ministers were Botha, Smuts, Hertzog, and Malan. Other public figures included the Phillipses, de Waal, Rissik, and Janssens; see Bensusan, *Silver Images*, 101.

67. Merrington, "Pageantry and Primitivism," 647.

68. Baker, *Architecture and Personalities*, 23.

69. Merrington, "'The State' and the Invention of Heritage," 131.

70. Fransen, *A Cape Camera*, 13.

71. In his introduction to Fairbridge's *Historic Houses of South Africa*, Smuts wrote: "those who have seen the awful destruction of the Great War and the absolute obliteration of everything in what were some beautiful districts of Europe will appreciate the necessity of recording by pen and pencil the works of the period in South Africa while they remain to us. . . . From the tragedy which has convulsed the older world, we look with thankfulness at our own South Africa, with her mysterious compelling attraction, her peace, and the great gifts that Providence has showered upon her" (x).

72. See, for instance, Herbert, *Martienssen and the International Style*, 37–41. Today, public appreciation of Cape Dutch buildings encourages their use as sites for revisionist historic interpretation, which emphasizes the lives of the slaves rather than their owners. See, for example, the recently restored outbuildings at Vergelegen.

73. Merrington, "Carrying the Torch."

74. Merrington, "Staggered Orientalism," 332.

75. The Western Cape is the only part of Southern Africa that has hot, dry summers and cool, rainy winters.

76. S. Dubow, "Imagining the New South Africa," 87. Books like Alys Trotter's *Old Cape Colony* extended this imaginary back to the time of first white settlement.

77. Dodson, "Dismantling Dystopia," 147. On this history, see, for example, D. McCracken and P. McCracken, *Natal: The Garden Colony*; and Lighton, *Sisters of the South*, 155–81.

78. Sending specimens to England was made possible by the discovery of the Wardian case, which allowed live plant specimens to be transported over long distances. Plants from the Cape were already well known in Britain by this time because they demanded little water and therefore traveled well. See McCracken and McCracken, *The Way to Kirstenbosch*.

79. S. Dubow, "Commonwealth of Science," 79.

80. See S. Dubow, "Commonwealth of Science," 78–82.

81. On the discourse of botanical nativism and floral preservation, see Van Sittert, "Making the Cape Floral Kingdom." According to Van Sittert, Cape botany had been a metropolitan science since the seventeenth century, patronized by European royalty and practiced by scientists who used the field observations of professional collectors, expatriate officials, and dilettante settlers, but it had been shaped as a discipline by dedicated amateurs like Harry Bolus and Rudolf Marloth, who arrived in South Africa in 1876 and 1883, respectively.

82. Van Sittert, "Making the Cape Floral Kingdom," 120.

83. Lighton, *Cape Floral Kingdom*, 44.

84. Lighton, *Cape Floral Kingdom*, 123–41.

85. On this, see Van Sittert, "Making the Cape Floral Kingdom," 117; S. Dubow, "Commonwealth of Science," 81; and Lighton, *Cape Floral Kingdom*, 108–13.

86. This construction was neatly reinforced by the fact that Cape Town, the so-called Mother City, was situated "strategically midway along the Kingdom's coastal curve from Port Nolloth to Port Elizabeth"; Lighton, *Floral Kingdom*, 6.

87. *Times* (London), 24 June 1926. On the battle and memorial at Delville Wood, see Uys, *Rollcall* and *Delville Wood*; and *Report from South Africa*.

88. The association was telling. Along with his son, Willem Adriaan (a later governor), Simon van der Stel had laid the foundations of South African viticulture and introduced European tree species like the oak to the Cape landscape (R. MacNab, *The Story of South Africa House*, 59).

89. For a discussion of some of the cultural meanings embedded in the Delville Wood memorial, see Foster, "Creating a *Temenos*."

90. Stevenson, "Art and Aspirations," 92–113.

91. S. Dubow, "Imagining the New South Africa," 90.

92. Van Sittert, "Making the Cape Floral Kingdom," 121.

93. According to Merrington, one of the main proponents of this idea was Dorothea Fairbridge ("Pageantry and Primitivism," 648). See, for instance, her somewhat wistful meditation on how South Africa's gardens would have been planned "if the Cape had originally been occupied by Italy or Spain." Fairbridge, *Gardens of South Africa*, 39–40.

94. See Vance, "California and the Search for the Ideal."

95. The only other comparable region is the central California coast around Santa Barbara.

96. It was precisely the last two decades of the nineteenth century that saw the colonization and "invention" of the French and Italian Rivieras by the English and other Europeans. See, for instance, Blume, *Cote d'Azur*.

97. See, for instance, Pemble, *Mediterranean Passion*, and Chard, *Pleasure and Guilt on the Grand Tour*.

98. Merrington, "Staggered Orientalism," 343.

99. See Merrington, "Staggered Orientalism," especially 341–50.

100. On this, see Chipkin, *Johannesburg Style*, 65–66.

101. Young, *In South Africa*, 16–17.

102. Peattie, *Struggle on the Veld*, 28.

103. This formulation, probably coined by Edward Roworth in his 1917 article "Landscape Art in South Africa," was subsequently much used.

104. Thus, "The South African sky is much higher than that in most parts of Europe, the horizons much wider, and consequently her perspective differs because of the wider angle view. Though at first sight the untilled land seems to lack color, more exact observations shows that it has many colors but with finer color differences. The shadows are much sharper and darker, but in the wide landscape glowing under the sun they are usually more concentrated in smaller areas than those of Europe. South African clouds seem firmer and the distances between individual summer clouds forming a layer in the sky are usually much greater than those in Europe. The shadows of clouds moving on a summer's day over the landscape are consequently so very thinly spread over the whole wide field that they cannot be used to organize a landscape picture as the Dutch painters did with alternating stripes of light and shadowed land." This comprehensive version of what was a common argument comes from F. L. Alexander, *Art in South Africa since 1900*, 42.

105. See N. J. Coetzee, *Pierneef, Land, and Landscape*, 2, 24.

106. S. Dubow, "Imagining the New South Africa," 87.

107. I borrow this notion of complementary discursive landscapes from S. Dubow, "Imagining the New South Africa," 91.

108. As Gérard Bouchard has argued, this strategy leads to the "memory trap" in which a significant proportion of the population cannot name themselves other than as non-Aboriginals. See Bouchard, "Formation of Cultures and Nations."

109. This perceptual emptiness is reinforced by the fact that in South Africa, unlike in the United States, for instance, farm buildings were seldom located within sight of public roads.

110. For a comprehensive account of this history, see Carruthers, *Kruger National Park*.

111. Assorted wildlife were featured on the Union's postage stamps, and the springbok's head became a watermark soon after union. The springbok displaced the King's head on South African money in 1926, the same year that Kruger Park was declared. See Beinart and Coates, *Environment and History*, 77. South African sports teams traveling overseas were being called "Springboks" by the 1920s.

112. Henshaw, "John Buchan from the 'Borders' to the 'Berg,'" 13.

113. Thus, the park's first supervisor was adamant that rest camps in the park should be functional, but spartan. See Carruthers, *Kruger National Park*, 78.

114. Lambert, "South African British, Or Dominion South Africans?"

115. *African Monthly* 3 (1908): 32, quoted in Dubow, "Imagining the New South Africa," 87–88.

116. Mels, "Nature, Home and Scenery." South Africa's game reserves were located in areas that had neither agricultural nor mining potential; see Carruthers, "Creating a National Park," 191.

117. See Carruthers, "Nationhood and National Parks," 127.

118. On this, see also Bunn, "Bushveld Golgotha."

119. Carruthers, *Kruger National Park*, 65.

120. The same animal imagery was implicit in the next two national parks established: the Kalahari Gemsbok (1930) and Addo (1931).

121. Deacon, "Place and Space of Illness." Parker, "Fertile Land, Romantic Spaces, Uncivilized Peoples," 202.

122. The most famous of these was Cecil John Rhodes, who initially came to South Africa for health reasons. Olive Schreiner was another influential South African figure whose life and career were shaped by an extreme susceptibility to climate.

123. See Schwarz, "Romance of the Veld," 76.

124. Beinart and Coates, *Environment and History*, 80.

125. This is tellingly reflected in the thirty-five pages devoted to climate and topography in Brown and Brown, *Guide to South Africa*.

126. Thus, as late as the 1920s, Lionel Phillips wrote: "Living at a high altitude imposes extra work on the heart and everyone so situated benefits from a periodical sojourn at sea-level. . . . The generation born in Johannesburg is vigorous and well-knit; thus a height of 6,000 feet is not necessarily injurious. . . . [However] the question of longevity cannot yet be confidently settled." *Some Reminiscences*, 90–91. On the debates concerning the healthfulness (or otherwise) of different parts of South Africa in the early twentieth century, see also M. Bell, "'Pestilence That Walketh in Darkness.'"

127. Barnard, "Encountering Adamastor," 194–95.

128. See Kennedy, "Perils of the Midday Sun."

129. Barnard, "Encountering Adamastor," 196.

130. For example, they finally felt able to dismiss the argument of one American geographer that the root of South Africa's "poor white" problem was the monotony of its temperatures; see Barnard, "Encountering Adamastor," 197.

131. Barnard, "Encountering Adamastor," 198.

132. These included Mary Byron (*Voice from the Veld*, 1913); Mary Boyd (*The Veld: A Bardic Poem*, 1921); Francis Carey Slater (*Footpaths thro' the Veld, and Other Songs and Idylls of South Africa*, 1905; *Calls Across the Sea*, 1917; *Settlers and Sunbirds*, 1919; *The Karroo and Other Poems*, 1924; *The Shining River*, 1925; and *Drought: A South African Parable*, 1929); Pauline Smith (*The Beadle*, 1926; and *The Little Karoo*, 1925); Leonard Flemming (*Settler Scribblings in South Africa*, 1911; *The Call of the Veld*, 1924; and *A Fool on the Veld*, 1923); and Sarah Getrude Millin (*Adam's Rest*, 1922; *The Coming of the Lord*, 1928; and *The Fiddler*, 1929). The works of William Plomer and Roy Campbell could also be included here. Olive Schreiner's writings—previously thought too radical or eccentric—began to find a wider audience in the 1920s; her influential *Thoughts on South Africa* was published posthumously in 1923.

133. See Bolitho, "South African."

134. L. Phillips, *Some Reminiscences*, 90.

135. "Introduction," *Picturesque Eastern Transvaal*.

136. *Lure of South Africa*, 61.

137. Bennion, "Call of South Africa," 1187–88.

138. Nasson, "South Africans in Flanders," 299.

139. Nasson, "South African War," 115.

140. Buchan, *History of the South African Forces in France*, 259–60.

141. Lambert, "South African British, or Dominion South Africans?" 200.

142. See Marlowe, *Cecil Rhodes*, 287–94.

143. Lambert, "South African British, or Dominion South Africans?" 210.

144. Reitz claimed that King George V kept a copy of his personal account of the South African War, titled *Commando*, permanently on his bedside table. (See *Adrift on the Open Veld*, 483.) For his part, Smuts earned himself a statue, prominently situated in Whitehall, after his death.

145. Marks and Dubow, "Patriotism of Place and Race," 164.

146. In this section, I draw heavily on Marks and Dubow's discussion in "Patriotism of Place and Race," 162–63.

147. The most famous of Smuts's hikes on Table Mountain was the one he made with King George V, memorialized in a photograph seen by millions over the years at the Table Mountain Cable Car Station.

148. Said, *Representations of the Intellectual*, 44; emphasis added. Said's term for this subjectivity is "contrapuntal," a construction he derived from musical polyphony: "In the counterpoint of Western music, various themes play off one another, with only a provisional privilege being given to any particular one, yet in the resulting polyphony, there is concert and order, an organized interplay that derives from the themes, not from a rigorous melodic or formal principle outside the work." Said, *Culture and Imperialism*, 51.

149. Clark, "*Travel Writing and Empire*," 10–13.

150. See Said, "Reflections on Exile," 171–72, and "Third World Intellectuals and Metropolitan Culture," 48–50.

151. Younghusband, "Natural Beauty and Geographical Science," 7.

152. Jill Ker Conway, *True North*, 137.

153. Schwartz, "Romance of the Veld," 74

154. Merrington, "Staggered Orientalism," 344n26.

155. Schwartz, "Romance of the Veld," 92. Rhodes commissioned Baker to build a "poets house," which he called The Woolsack, for Kipling to live in, half a mile from Groote Schuur. See Baker, *Architecture and Personalities*, 27–30, 34–35; *Cecil Rhodes*, 44–45.

156. See Irving, *Indian Summer*, 277.

157. Schwartz, "Romance of the Veld," 92.

158. On this ambivalent attitude toward new and old, see Merrington, "Pageantry and Primitivism," 644.

159. The Phillipses, for instance, traveled frequently between South Africa and Britain and lived in Britain from 1900 to 1906.

Chapter 4: Between Corporeality and Representation

1. Zimmer, "In Search of Natural Identity," 661.

2. A wide range of writing refers to this more subjective, corporeal dimension of landscape appropriation. This includes Bois, "Picturesque Stroll around Clara-Clara"; Corner, "Representation and Landscape"; Smithson, "Frederick Law Olmsted and the Dialectical Landscape"; Tilley, *Phenomenology of Landscape*; Van den Berg, "Human Body and the Significance of Movement"; and Weiss, *Mirrors of Infinity*.

3. Ingold, "Temporality of Landscape," 161.

4. Bender, "Introduction," 4.

5. See, for instance, Thrift and Dewsberry, "Dead Geographies—and How to Make Them Live."

6. Nora, "Between Memory and History," 13.

7. The term "corpselike" is Terry Eagleton's.

8. For instance, see Lang, "The Body in the Garden."

9. See Nash, "Reclaiming Vision."

10. Merleau-Ponty, quoted in Seamon, "Body-subject."

11. Merleau-Ponty, *Phenomenology of Perception*, 311.

12. Merleau-Ponty, *Phenomenology of Perception*, 320.

13. See Thrift, "Still Point."

14. Merleau-Ponty, *Phenomenology of Perception*, 243.

15. Norberg-Schulz, *Genius Loci*, 20–21. Norberg-Schulz's two criteria are conflated in Kevin Lynch's construct of "imageability." Lynch argues that the basic requirement for a good environmental "image"—a powerfully structured, clearly identifiable mental construct—and feelings of psychological well-being and security is a spatial structure that facilitates orientation and is made up of concrete objects of identification.

16. Pallasmaa, *Eyes of the Skin*, 26–51. Here, one is reminded of Edward Casey's assertion that place is primarily a refraction of consciousness, self, and identity. Casey, "Body, Self and Landscape," 404–6.

17. Here, I borrow Melanie Klein's notion of "projective identification," which holds that all human interaction implies projection of fragments of the self onto the other person. Pallasmaa, *Eyes of the Skin*, 46.

18. Leatherbarrow, *Roots of Architectural Invention*, 218.

19. See Weiss, "Vaux-le-Vicomte" 35.

20. See, for instance, "The Mapping Impulse," in Alpers, *The Art of Describing*, 119–68.

21. See, for instance, Goethe, *Italian Journey*; and Bunkse, "Humboldt and an Aesthetic Tradition in Geography."

22. See Hirschfeld, *Theory of Garden Art*.

23. According to Bois, "theoreticians of the picturesque have never been able to extract themselves from a veritable malaise engendered by a contradiction in their theory, by their stubborn determination to treat the scenic garden (promenade, temporal experience) and landscape painting as though they were one and the same things." "Picturesque Stroll," 353.

24. Ingold, "Temporality of Landscape," 156.

25. Here, it is helpful to remember that the etymological root of the word "experience" is "making a trial of" the world (Casey, *Getting Back into Place*, 30), as well as to note our habitual tendency to grasp "the present in terms of possibilities and histories." T. Alexander, *John Dewey's Theory of Art, Experience and Nature*, 202.

26. Gaston Bachelard, quoted in Kearney, *Poetics of Imagining*, 96.

27. Pallasmaa, *Eyes of the Skin*, 44–47. For an exploration of the idea of human society conforming to material environment, traceable to Halbwachs, see Sébastien Marot, *Sub-Urbanism and the Art of Memory*, 30.

28. See for instance Hiss, *Experience of Place*, 4–9, 27–36; and Rasmussen, "Rhythm in Architecture," in *Experiencing Architecture*, 127–58.

29. O'Niell, "Marxism and Philosophy," 180; emphasis added.

30. Olin, "What I Do When I Can Do It," 102.

31. Casey, "Body, Self and Landscape," 409.

32. Shields, *Places on the Margin*, 13.

33. See, for instance, Sennett, *Flesh and Stone*.

34. Higson, quoted in Shields, *Places on the Margin*, 216.

35. Tilley, *Phenomenology of Landscape*, 33.

36. See Tilley, *Phenomenology of Landscape*, 15–17.

37. For an excellent example of such a reading, see Glassie, *Passing the Time in Ballymenone*.

38. Bender, "Introduction," *Contested Landscapes*, 7.

39. Shields, *Places on the Margin*, 8.

40. Thrift and Dewsberry, "Dead Geographies," 425.

41. Scott, *Spoken Image*, 12.

42. As Henri Lefebvre argued: "There is no oeuvre without a regulated succession of acts and actions, of decisions and conducts, messages and codes. Nor can any oeuvre exist without things, without something to shape, without practico-material reality, without a site, without a 'nature', a countryside, an environment." See Lefebvre, "Right to the City," in *Writings on Cities*, 103.

43. J. Clark, "Social Ecology," 352.

44. Bishop, "Rhetoric, Memory and Power," 16.

45. Bishop, "Rhetoric, Memory and Power," 13.

46. An example of this occurred during the second half of the nineteenth century, when geography's aspirations to become a quasi-positivist science were greatly enhanced by the supposedly objective representational capacity of photography. This prompted some travelers to argue that the truest form of geographical knowledge was not the indexical truth captured on photographic plate or film, but rather that gained from the firsthand encounter with the terrain. While some travelers were entranced by photography's accuracy and ability to accumulate empirical detail and minutiae, others commented on how poorly it captured the experiential dimensions of a given terrain. What is of interest here is not so much which side in this debate was right as the fact that it was precisely photography as a medium that first threw such bodily dimensions of geographical knowledge into reflexive prominence. See Carter, *Living in a New Country*, 24.

47. Corner, "Representation and Landscape," 247.

48. Bender, "Introduction," in *Contested Landscapes*, 6.

49. Tilley, *Phenomenology of Landscape*, 33.

50. Corner, "Agency of Mapping," 229.

51. Here, I use the word "performative" in the sense of "usage," rather than the alternate that refers to the interplay of seeing and being seen.

52. Miller, *Topographies*, 157.

53. Indeed, topography, like character, exemplifies the fundamentally aporistic nature of all landscape description, the impossibility of deciding whether what one discerns is "imposed super-ficially on the earth, laid over the earth's skin," or "a hidden design already there but covered over." J. Hillis Miller associates this fundamentally undecidable question with Heidegger. See Miller, *Topographies*, 15.

54. See De Certeau, *Practice of Everyday Life*.

55. Miller, *Topographies*, 16.

56. Bender, *Contested Landscapes*, 6.

57. This phenomenon, which the behaviorist Edith Cobb argues is rooted in the "genius of child-hood," is discussed in her book *Ecology of Imagination in Childhood*.

58. Duncan and Gregory, *Writes of Passage*, 5.

Chapter 5: Baden-Powell and the Siege of Mafeking

1. See Pakenham, *Boer War*, 396–417.

2. See Blanch, "British Society and the War," 217.

3. P. Smith, *Mafeking Memories*, 10.

4. Wilfred Blunt, quoted in Pakenham, *Boer War*, 416.

5. Baden-Powell, *Sketches in Mafeking and East Africa*, 25.

6. Pakenham, *Boer War*, 397.

7. The population of the *stadt* of Mafeking ("the place of stones"), one of the few native urban settlements in the interior of South Africa at this time, was greatly swelled by those who took ref-uge there during the siege.

8. Milner considered the town expendable. The Boers had besieged both Mafeking and Kimber-ley on October 14, believing that attack was the best form of defense and would provoke a quick settlement.

9. MacDonald, *Sons of Empire*, 13.

10. Blanch, "British Society and the War," 216.

11. MacDonald, *Sons of Empire*, 90.

12. Those who had been part of the siege found on returning to Britain that no amount of denial could convince metropolitan Britons that their experience had been anything other than harrowing and heroic. Smith, *Mafeking Memories*, 127.

13. The slouch hat, which became common headgear for all the colonial irregulars in Baden-Powell's South African Constabulary formed later, was in fact Australian in origin.

14. Bourke, *Dismembering the Male*, 141.

15. Schwarz, "Romance of the Veld," 72.

16. Jeal, *Boy-Man*, xii.

17. On this, see MacDonald, *Sons of Empire*, 27.

18. The close relationship between the two aspects of his fame was reflected in the fact that he used the improvised cadet corps he organized during the siege as the prototype for the Boy Scout troop. See Pakenham, *Boer War*, 403.

19. These distinctive geological formations were the traditional aeries from which the Boers launched ambushes and to which they retreated when on the defensive (a use not available to the large and cumbersome British platoons). The Boers were eventually forced to abandon their kopjes when the British became aware of this use and took to bombarding them with their modern field guns. Pakenham, *Boer War*, 193. The kopje's iconic Africanness also made it a favorite landscape feature of war artists and photographers.

20. Pakenham, *Boer War*, 164. Although there is disagreement over exact figures, the sizes of the two armies are usually given as around 85,000 Boers and 450,000 British and colonial troops.

21. See Lee, *To the Bitter End*, 37–45.

22. The Boer general De Wet even fought one battle on his own farm in the Free State. Lee, *To the Bitter End*.

23. The bulk of maps supplied to the British forces by the Intelligence Division of the War Office were cadastral compilations made up from farm and mining surveys. Although these maps showed farm boundaries, roads, railways, telegraphs, and homesteads, they provided minimal physiographic and hydrological information. See Liebenberg, "Mapping British South Africa." Buller, when fighting in Natal, had to rely on a map compiled by his Field Intelligence Department, which, "like an explorer's map, . . . bore the legend 'Vacant spaces indicate that data . . . is wanting rather than that the ground is flat.'" Pakenham, *Boer War*, 208. See also Martin Marix-Evans, *Boer War*, 15.

24. Pakenham, *Boer War*, 164. In the interior, British infantry could not move much beyond eight miles from a railway line. Pakenham, *Boer War*, 252. The size of the British columns meant that their movements were often announced by huge clouds of dust.

25. The railways had been crucial to the exploitation of these minerals (which of course was overwhelmingly undertaken by British-controlled companies). The importation of equipment and people required by the mining towns of Johannesburg and Kimberley would have been impossible with the stagecoaches and ox wagons hitherto used, which were distinguished by their slowness, limited payload, and high cost. See Christopher, *Southern Africa*, 140.

26. De Certeau, *Practice of Everyday Life*, xix.

27. De Certeau, *Practice of Everyday Life*, xix.

28. Indeed, when Baden-Powell *did* try to use conventional military strategies, to capture Game Tree Fort just outside the town on what became known as Black Boxing Day, he was disastrously repulsed.

29. Baden-Powell couched these exchanges in sporting terms: replying to an ambiguous demand from Boer commander Eloff, he wrote, "just now we are having our own innings and have so far scored 200 days not out."

30. Pakenham, *Boer War*, 406–7. The later-famous African author, Sol Plaatje, who was in the town during the siege, records that despite repeated assertions that this was a "white man's war," a vital source of food for whites were the cattle lifted from behind Boer lines by African raiding parties. Oakes, *Illustrated History*, 248.

31. If not European capitalism: the BFF were in Rhodesia to protect the interests of Rhodes's British South Africa Company, which had the Royal Charter to administer the territory at this time.

32. Baden-Powell later transformed these dispatches into *Matabele Campaign* (1897). See MacDonald, *Sons of Empire*, 68.

33. The Matabele Campaign was unfolding only a few years after the dramatic last stands of the embattled Native American Indians on the North America plains, and almost exactly contemporaneously with the publication of Frederick Jackson Turner's 1893 essay, "The Significance of the Frontier in American History."

34. MacDonald, *Sons of Empire*, 6.

35. MacDonald, *Sons of Empire*, 64.

36. See O'Sullivan and Miller, *Geography of Warfare*, 20–21.

37. See Warnke, *Political Landscape*, 60.

38. MacDonald, *Sons of Empire*, 72.

39. The centrality to scouting of the ability to read local conditions is highlighted by the fact that Lord Lovat Scouts, a regiment formed to fight in the South African War, were recruited almost exclusively from Highland deer stalkers and gillies.

40. Baden-Powell himself learned most of his skills from Burnham and an Ndebele man, Jan Grootboom, who had previously also taught Selous (another great Rhodesian pioneer) and Burnham the secrets of the Matabeleland savanna.

41. As de Certeau himself observed, the geographical space of the map—universal and geometrically structured—"transforms action into legibility, but in doing so . . . causes a way of being in the world to be forgotten." See *Practice of Everyday Life*, 97.

42. Jeal, *Boy-Man*, 571.

43. MacDonald, *Sons of Empire*, 73–74.

44. Schwarz, "Romance of the Veld," 81; MacDonald, *Sons of Empire*, 85.

45. MacDonald, *Sons of Empire*, 19–25.

46. See Ploszajska, "Constructing the Subject" and "Down to Earth."

47. MacDonald, *Sons of Empire*, 97.

48. On imperialist propaganda in British schools, see Blanch, "British Society and the War," 211–13.

49. Out of the 11,000 volunteers who initially presented themselves in Manchester, 8,000 men were rejected outright and only 1,220 were accepted as fit in all respects. See Bourke, *Dismembering the Male*, 13.

50. Omissi and Thompson, "Investigating the Impact of the War," 9.

51. MacDonald, *Sons of Empire*, 77. This realization stemmed from the fact that of the nominally British Army in South Africa, 49,000 soldiers were colonial.

52. Harding, "South Africa in Word and Images."

53. This term was coined by John Buchan, *Memory Hold-the-Door*, 112.

54. Schwarz, "Romance of the Veld," 68.

55. Omissi and Thompson, "Investigating the Impact of the War," 11. Approximately 90 percent of men and 75 percent of women in Britain could read by this time. See R. Phillips, *Mapping Men and Empire*, 11.

56. Blanch, "British Society and the War," 216.

57. Blanch, "British Society and the War," 235.

58. Bryden, Guy, and Harding, *Ashes and Blood*, 429. On these press corps, see also Beaumont, "Making of a War Correspondent."

59. Bryden, Guy, and Harding, *Ashes and Blood*, 429.

60. The most famous instance of this was Winston Churchill, who was taken prisoner by the Boers when they ambushed the train on which he was traveling, and later escaped from imprisonment in the Transvaal. See Pakenham, *Boer War*, 171.

61. Schwarz, "Romance of the Veld," 72.

62. See Jaff, *They Came to South Africa*, 75.

63. Oakes, *Illustrated History*, 248. The popular association of Baden-Powell with Mafeking began during the war, when sales of his earlier book *Aids to Scouting* increased in Britain. On his personal use of the siege story, see for example *Scouting for Boys* (1932), 5–6. In this passage, Baden-Powell invokes the very ordinariness of Mafeking—the fact that "nobody expected it to be attacked"—in support of the need for constant preparedness.

64. Jaff, *They Came to South Africa*, 70.

65. A map of the actual defenses at the end of the siege shows that these were largely fictitious. See Marix-Evans, *Boer War*, 70.

66. To the south lay unconquered telegraph and railway lines leading to Cape Town, the primary point of entry and departure in British South Africa.

67. See Daniels and Cosgrove, "Spectacle and Text," 58.

68. Daniels and Cosgrove, "Spectacle and Text," 58.

69. Blanch, "British Society and the War," 230–36. Schwarz, "Romance of the Veld," 81.

70. In the following section, I draw heavily on Huston, *Actor's Instrument*.

71. Huston, *Actor's Instrument*, 77.

72. Huston, *Actor's Instrument*, 78. This is captured by Paul Ricouer's argument that "Action is the union of the inside and the outside of an event." *Aquinas Lecture*, 7.

73. Huston, *Actor's Instrument*, 14, 75.

74. In the Renaissance, the circus was the lowest form of theater, "mere visual spectacle" that originated in the arena for gladiators and animals. See Daniels and Cosgrove, "Spectacle and Text," 66.

75. See Baden-Powell, *Sketches in Mafeking and East Africa*, 35.

76. Lord Somers, Baden-Powell's successor as Chief Scout, wrote: "B-P's . . . most exciting adventures happened in Africa, when he had to match his wits against native warriors and trackers; one

slip and they would have caught him and shown no mercy. They called him 'Impeesa', which means 'the Wolf that does not sleep', because they recognized his courage and skill." See "Introduction," in *Scouting for Boys*, v.

77. Thus, Baden-Powell wrote: "I knew an old Boer who, after the South African War, said that he could not live in the country with the British because . . . they were so utterly stupid when living on the veld that they could not take care of themselves. . . . Being brought up in a civilized country, men had no training whatsoever in looking after themselves out in the veld." *Scouting for Boys*, 33.

78. Many local newspapers in Britain reserved a page for "Letters From the Front." On this phenomenon, see Emery, *Marching over Africa*.

79. De Certeau, *Practice of Everyday Life*, 119.

80. "The story is a discursive articulation of a spatializing practice, a bodily itinerary and routine. Spatial stories are about the operations and practices which constitute places and locales." Tilley, *Phenomenology of Landscape*, 32.

81. De Certeau, *Practice of Everyday Life*, 125.

82. MacDonald, *Sons of Empire*, 14.

83. Lee, *To the Bitter End*, 1–5.

84. Stereoscopic photography involved two almost identical photographs that, when viewed through an instrument called a stereoscope, appeared as a three-dimensional tableau. The largest publisher of these was Underwood & Underwood, a U.S.-based company with offices throughout the Anglophone world. It is estimated that around 190 different publishers were printing and distributing images of South Africa during the war. See Norwich, *Johannesburg Album*.

85. Bensusan, *Silver Images*, 44–52.

86. Lee, *To the Bitter End*, 5. Often the same image was used with a different caption, attributing the scene to one or another regiment.

87. Many photographs were not even taken in South Africa but were faked in Britain, with appropriately painted backdrops to provide a South African context. One British photographer used the same backdrop for scenes supposedly showing such topographically different battlefields as Elandslaagte, Colenso, Graspan, and Ladysmith. See Cowan, "Photographs." A survey of the Royal Commonwealth Society's photographic holdings for Southern Africa until the end of the nineteenth century (now stored in Cambridge University Library) suggests that around 70 percent of the images are groups or individual portraits of British Army officers.

88. This is de Certeau's definition of the "strategic."

89. For a discussion of how changes in photographic technology affected photographs taken during the war, see Lee, *To the Bitter End*, 5–12.

90. It is hard to know how many of the British and colonial troops in South Africa during the war had personal cameras, but it must have run into thousands. Lee, *To the Bitter End*, 10. Several commentators remarked on the number of troops who had cameras. In her memoirs, Lady Sarah Wilson, who was in Mafeking during the siege, writes of "newly arrived officers, nearly all carrying the inevitable Kodak." *South African Memories*, 247.

91. See P. Berman, "Body and Body Politic," 72.

92. Hatt, "Athlete and Aesthete." On Baden-Powell's attitudes towards male nudity, see Jeal, *Boy-Man*, 92–93.

93. During the Renaissance, the human figure in painting conveyed ideas about conduct, character, knowledge, and gender, and the notion that character was closely related to *praxis*—i.e., that "the movement of the body is the voice of the spirit"—was taken seriously. Sixteenth-century doctrines conventionalized gender according to *bodily movement*; conduct was conveyed through societal sanction and learned through practice of certain activities such as dancing, fencing, athletics. Feminine bodies were ideally upright, modest, and contained (to constrain women's "natural" volatility), while masculine bodies were expected to be vigorous, hard, and alert. See Fermor, "Movement and Gender," 131–34.

94. Schwarz, "Romance of the Veld," 97.

95. Bryeden, Guy, and Harding, *Ashes and Blood*, 85.

96. Blanch, "British Society and the War," 210.

97. *Royal Commission Report on the War in South Africa* (1904) quoted in Omissi and Thompson, "Investigating the Impact of the War," 8.

98. Blanch, "British Society and the War," 229.

99. Huston, *Actor's Instrument*, 84–85.

100. Schwarz, "Romance of the Veld," 72.

101. Blanch, "British Society and the War," 219.

102. I borrow this construction from Rob Shields's discussion about the geographical character of marginal places. See "Introduction," in *Places on the Margin*.

103. Schwarz, "Romance of the Veld," 73. Interest in the implications and outcome of the war was not limited to those immediately involved in the fighting. As a war in which the most powerful nation in the world was being challenged by one of the smallest, both sides drew in combatants of other nationalities sympathetic to their cause.

104. Omissi and Thompson, "Investigating the Impact of the War," 9.

105. For example, *Defence of Duffer's Drift*, by "Backright Forethought" (Capt. E. D. Swinton), first published in 1904, and reprinted many times up to 1914. See Bryden, Guy, and Harding, *Ashes and Blood*, 487.

106. Bryden, Guy, and Harding, *Ashes and Blood*, 83.

107. Bryden, Guy, and Harding, *Ashes and Blood*, 173.

108. The South African Constabulary that Milner asked Baden-Powell to form in 1901 recruited New Zealanders, Canadians, and Australians, as well as colonial South Africans.

109. Bourke, *Dismembering the Male*. Fabian Ware, the head of the IWGC, worked with Milner in South Africa after the war and retained lifelong links with colonial national South Africans such as Percy Fitzpatrick.

110. Schwarz, "Romance of the Veld," 72.

111. Schwarz, "Romance of the Veld," 65.

112. The somewhat bathetic pair of blockhouse lines that Kitchener established to try and prevent the free movement of Boers seemed to confirm that this was a terrain that was simply too large to be controlled by human occupation. A recurring feature in histories and memoirs of the war are maps that overlay, to the same scale, the part of South Africa under discussion with part of Britain.

113. Kunze, *Thought and Place*, 127.

114. Kunze, *Thought and Place*, 180.

115. Kunze, *Thought and Place*, 192.

116. "It is hard work out there—hard sweaty work, with arms tanned, sunbrowned faces with cheekbones showing . . . drinking in life with the breath of the veld, there is joy in it. It's a man's life." Robert Baden Powell, letter to Boy MacClaren, 1900, quoted in Jeal, *Boy-Man*, 92.

117. Many of the administrators and officials had been involved in the conflict. Baden-Powell's semimilitary South African Constabulary maintained law and order in captured Boer territory until after the war, when it assisted in Milner's resettlement schemes. It was eventually merged with the police force of the new Transvaal Colony.

118. Thus, notwithstanding its latent agenda of inculcating allegiance to the Union Jack, Crown, and Empire, we find that scouting proved equally popular with both English-speaking and Afrikaans/Dutch-speaking youth, to the extent that Afrikaans cultural leaders later felt the need to develop their own version. See Lambert, "South African British, or Dominion South Africans?" 211.

Chapter 6: John Buchan's Hesperides

1. Apart from his prolific literary output of popular novels, poems, biography, essays, and journalism, Buchan went on to become director of information during WWI, a director of Reuters, member of parliament for Scottish Universities, high commissioner of the Church of Scotland and chancellor of the University of Edinburgh. Created Baron Tweedsmuir in 1929, he was governor-general of Canada from 1935 to 1940. Two recent biographies are J. A. Smith, *John Buchan*, and Lownie, *Presbyterian Cavalier*.

2. Buchan, *Africa Colony*, 119.

3. Buchan also wrote about his South African experiences in his autobiographical *Memory Hold-the-Door*.

4. Milner had moved to the Transvaal when Johannesburg and Pretoria fell to the British in mid-1900. The guerrilla phase of the war was to continue for another twenty months in the more remote parts of the republics.

5. On his Woodbush trip, he covered 1,100 miles in five days by train, wagon, and horseback (Lownie, *Presbyterian Cavalier*, 77). During some of his early expeditions, Buchan had to avoid Boer commandos still active in field.

6. Some previous accounts of the Transvaal are Anderson, *25 Years in a Waggon* (1888); Balfour, *1200 Miles in a Wagon* (1895); McNab, *On Veldt and Farm* (1897); and Bryce, *Impressions of South Africa* (1898).

7. Books extolling the worthiness of British colonization of South Africa were something of a genre during the first decade of this century; Buchan's was one of the first into print after the war.

8. Schwarz, "Romance of the Veld."

9. Schwarz, "Romance of the Veld," 70.

10. See Rich, "Milnerism and a Ripping Yarn."

11. This was recognized even the time of the book's first publication. *Oxford Magazine*'s reviewer wrote: "*The Africa Colony* is the work of an artist in words, not of an artist in administration." Lownie, *Presbyterian Cavalier*, 85. In some respects, Buchan's book transcended the genre of the imperialist promotional tract, and belonged alongside the some two hundred works of fiction set in South Africa that were written in the first decade of the twentieth century. See Rice, "Fictional Strategies and the Transvaal Landscape," 1.

12. Gruffudd, *Landscape and Nationhood*, 156.

13. Schwarz, "Romance of the Veld," 75. As Michael Ignatieff has observed: "Right up to the First World War, the very idea of being a citizen, of belonging to a society or a nation would have seemed a distant abstraction to the peasants who made up the majority of the European population. Such belonging as a peasant felt was bounded by the distances his legs could walk and his cart could roll." See Ignatieff, *The Needs of Strangers*, 138. Quote from Cosgrove, "Habitable Earth," 32.

14. Buchan, *Africa Colony*, 86.

15. Schwarz, "Romance of the Veld," 99.

16. Buchan, *Africa Colony*, 86. Encountering a railway under construction in the veld, he remarked, "if there is an uglier thing than the raw scar made by earthworks and excavations and uncompleted culverts, I do not know it" (130).

17. On conditions in the Transvaal immediately after the war, see Krikler, *Revolution from Above, Rebellion from Below*, 73–74.

18. Keegan, "Making of the Rural Economy," 44–46.

19. Stanley Trapido estimates that one-fifth of the total land area of the Transvaal Republic belonged to land companies and absentee landlords in 1900. See "Putting a Plough to the Ground," 337.

20. See Hofmeyr, "Spoken Word and the Barbed Wire," 72.

21. Christopher, *Southern Africa*, 148–51.

22. Lownie, *Presbyterian Cavalier*, 80. Buchan does note that Boers and Africans farmed in different ways and used different parts of the same landscape.

23. See Parker, "Fertile Land, Romantic Spaces," 221.

24. For a discussion of the longstanding European notion that the truest inhabitants of a landscape were its cultivators, see Cosgrove, "Habitable Earth," 33.

25. Buchan, *Africa Colony*, 86.

26. See for instance Pratt, *Imperial Eyes*, 7.

27. Gregory, "Book and Lamp," 51, referencing Said, *Orientalism*.

28. R. Phillips, *Mapping Men and Empire*, 13.

29. M. Bell, "'Pestilence that Walketh in Darkness,'" 332–37. In Burton, *Land Settlement in the Transvaal* (1902), it was stated that "the climate is healthy, in winter decidedly bracing, and eminently suitable for European immigrants . . . the highveld in particular being delightfully fresh and invigorating."

30. Buchan, *Africa Colony*, 129.

31. Malaria remained a scourge in the Transvaal Lowveld until well into the 1950s (personal communication, Jurgen Witt, Tzaneen Museum, February 1996).

32. See J. A. Smith, *John Buchan*, 7–21; Lownie, *Presbyterian Cavalier*, 18–25.

33. *Pilgrim's Way*, 3. Buchan's later account of the growth of his environmental consciousness is extraordinarily perceptive, exemplifying Edith Cobb's notion of "genius of childhood."

34. The grasses are predominantly *Themeda triandra*. Acocks, *Veld Types of South Africa*, 100.

35. Lowenthal and Prince, "English Landscape," 314.

36. Lownie, *Presbyterian Cavalier*, 81. Lownie contends that "as a Scot, [Buchan] understood the Boers in a way that was impossible to many of his English colleagues." A similar argument is made by Henshaw, "John Buchan from the 'Borders' to 'the Berg,'" 4.

37. Saxons and Gaels, Calvinists and Catholics; see Henshaw, "John Buchan from the 'Borders' to the 'Berg,'" 17.

38. Saul, quoted in Kaufmann, "Naturalizing the Nation," 689.

39. Duncan and Gregory, *Writes of Passage*, 5.

40. *Africa Colony*, 80. Buchan's previous writings, which consisted of short stories, poems and two novels (*Sir Quixote of the Moors*, 1895; *John Burnet of Barns*, 1898), were heavily influenced by the work of Walter Scott, and always included poetic, detailed descriptions of the landscape. See J. A. Smith, *John Buchan*, 19–21.

41. Buchan, *Africa Colony*, 81.

42. Buchan, *Africa Colony*, 83.

43. *Africa Colony*, 80. Here, Buchan seems to be rhetorically invoking Ruskin's remarks on the associational dimension of natural beauty, discussed in chapter 6 of *Seven Lamps of Architecture*. See Clark, *John Ruskin*, 94–96.

44. Buchan, *Africa Colony*, 85.

45. Buchan, *Pilgrim's Way*, 114–15.

46. Bordo, "Terra Nullius of Wilderness."

47. Ciceronean rhetoric was divided into five basic subjects: invention, disposition, elocution, memory, and delivery. See Bowen, "Rhetoric of *The Essays*."

48. Buchan, *Pilgrim's Way*, 7.

49. See Leach, *Rhetoric of Space*, 8.

50. For a discussion of walking as an "ennobling and culturally enriching" pastime, see Wittenberg, "Ruwenzori."

51. Buchan probably wrote up each of his expeditions on his return to the Rand; the book was published a mere two months after his return to England.

52. His traveling companions typically included a guide, a cook, two Cape carts, a supply wagon and spare mules (Lownie, *Presbyterian Cavalier*, 77).

53. Buchan, *Memory Hold-the-Door*, 115. Faced with the prospect of leaving South Africa, he wrote in a letter: "A sedentary London life with clubs and parties and books—all that once seemed so attractive—seems to me now rather in the nature of the husks of which the swine do eat. I daresay I shall recover perspective when I get home." Quoted in Smith, *John Buchan*, 36.

54. Buchan, *Memory Hold-the-Door*, 120.

55. Miller, *Topographies*, 265.

56. See Kern, *Culture of Time and Space, 1880–1918*, 176–79. At the beginning of the twentieth century, the reflexive sense of subjective feelings and responses generated by this collapse had yet to find its quasi-scientific explanation in psychoanalytical theory.

57. William Gilpin, *Observations on Cumberland and Westmoreland*, 182–83.

58. Outram, "Enlightenment Journeys." See also, for instance, Gregory "Between the Book and the Lamp"; and Daniels, "On the Road With Humphrey Repton."

59. Carter, *Road to Botany Bay* and *Living in a New Country*.

60. Kunze, "Cuisine, Frontality and the Infra-thin," 86. On the evolution of the representational connotations of physical form, see Vesely, "Architecture and the Conflict of Representation," and "Architecture and the Poetics of Representation."

61. This term is Merleau-Ponty's.

62. Kunze, "Cuisine, Frontality and the Infrathin," 88.

63. Buchan, *Pilgrim's Way*, 8.

64. Buchan, *Africa Colony*, 129.

65. Langer, *Merleau-Ponty's Phenomenology of Perception*, 84.

66. Buchan, *Africa Colony*, 83, 131.

67. Buchan, *Africa Colony*, 157.

68. Buchan, *Africa Colony*, 131.

69. Tindall, *Countries of the Mind*, 188.

70. "First the miniature world of nooks and playgrounds; then the middle distance, the adjacent hills and neighbouring glens; and last, as we grew older and stronger, the high places and explorations." Buchan, *Pilgrim's Way*, 14.

71. "Horizons, since they are relative to place and move as people move, do not cut the land into pieces. Hence they mark the limits of perception, but they do not enclose." See Ingold, "Picture Is Not the Terrain," 29–31.

72. Buchan, *Africa Colony*, 85.

73. Rodaway, *Sensuous Geographies*, 124.

74. "Space is not encountered as an empty void of co-ordinates, but as a dramatic possibility of movement." John Dewey, quoted in T. Alexander, *John Dewey's Theory*, 196–97.

75. Buchan, *Africa Colony*, 81, emphasis added.

76. Rodaway, *Sensuous Geographies*, 96.

77. Buchan, *Africa Colony*, 87.

78. This insight comes from Jacobson, *Time and Time Again*, 10.

79. Buchan, *Africa Colony*, 110.

80. Although there is a considerable literature on the similarities between the "uncanny" and the Freudian "unheimlich"—a mode of fear of anxiety associated with repressed experience and memory—here I use the word "uncanny" in the sense of "the over accentuation of psychical reality in comparison with material reality"; see J. Diski, *London Review of Books*, 15 November 2001, 16.

81. Enzensberger, "Theory of Tourism," 126.

82. Dewey, *Art as Experience*.

83. Dewey, quoted in Alexander, *John Dewey's Theory*, 174.

84. Alexander, *John Dewey's Theory*, 202.

85. In fact, his South African sojourn did act as a catalyst for this. While he was there, Buchan was offered various positions in publishing, business, administration, and justice, in South Africa and Britain. Lownie, *Presbyterian Cavalier*, 70–85. In the end, Buchan returned to Britain in July 1903 and only visited South Africa once again, briefly, in 1905.

86. Buchan, *Memory Hold-the-Door*, 120.

87. Alexander, *John Dewey's Theory*, 234.

88. Dewey, quoted in Alexander, *John Dewey's Theory*, 234.

89. L. Phillips, *Some Reminiscences*, 74

90. Buchan, *Africa Colony*, 114.

91. For a discussion of how this head for heights played out in colonial imagination of Africa, see Wittenberg, "Ruwenzori."

92. See, for instance, Scully, *Architecture*, 1–21.

93. Buchan, *Africa Colony*, 127.

94. Buchan, *Africa Colony*, 118.

95. Buchan, *Africa Colony*, 127.

96. Buchan, *Africa Colony*, 118.

97. An intensified form of the Greek imaginary that imbued the physical landscape with the noumenal presence, a *temenos* was a space delimited against public and private land. See Hornblower and Spawforth, *Oxford Classical Dictionary* (Oxford: Oxford University Press, 2000), 1481.

98. The god Eurystheus sent Heracles as his eleventh labor to the Hesperides, a remote place far away in the west, nowadays thought to be the High Atlas Mountains, where he had to steal the golden apples growing on a sacred grove of trees. See Harvey, *Oxford Companion to Classical Literature*.

99. De Certeau, *Practice of Everyday Life*, 109.

100. Tindall, *Countries of the Mind*, 116.

101. Buchan, *Pilgrim's Way*, 17.

102. Green, *Spectacle of Nature*, 135.

103. He used the phrase "kindly soothing pastoral" in a poem he wrote some years earlier (Smith, *John Buchan and His World*, 7).

104. *Prester John* (1910) was set in South Africa, and the hero of *Thirty-nine Steps* (1915) and *Greenmantle* (1916), Richard Hannay, was based on various figures Buchan had met in South Africa and could talk the *taal*.

105. Tilley, *Phenomenology of Landscape*, 15.

106. At this stage in his career, Buchan still occupied a social position cognate with most of those who considered emigrating to the colonies at this time; unlike those who were comfortably established and had nothing to gain by leaving the metropole, these were individuals outside of the inner sanctum of the establishment and uncertain whether they would ever be granted entry to it.

107. Adorno, *Aesthetic Theory*, 108–9. See Said, *Culture and Imperialism*, 132–62.

108. Baden-Powell, too, had been in the same position. He was sent overseas in 1888 when his family realized that they could not afford to keep him with his regiment in England. Jeal, *Man-Boy*, 75. "Colonial sublime" is from "Romance of the Veld," 67.

109. Buchan, *Memory Hold-the-Door*, 124–25.

110. Henshaw, "John Buchan from the 'Borders' to the 'Berg,'" 14.

111. R. Phillips, *Mapping Men and Empire*, 72.

112. Buchan also wrote *History of the South African Forces in France*.

113. *Pace* V. S. Naipaul: "No . . . landscape is truly rich until it has been given the quality of myth by writer, painter or its association with great events." Quoted in Tindall, *Countries of the Mind*, 135.

114. Henshaw, "John Buchan from the 'Borders' to the 'Berg,'" 16.

115. Keegan, "Making of the Rural Economy," 47.

116. As De Kiewiet wrote, "When the British command decided to break Boer resistance by laying waste the land, it destroyed much that Reconstruction could never replace." See *History of South Africa*, 196.

117. Milton, "Transvaal Beef Frontier," 201.

118. De Kiewiet argued that the size of the six-thousand–acre loan farm, common during the Dutch period and later reinforced by the British after annexation, "became deeply ingrained habit in frontier society" and was a fundamental factor driving the history of white expansion into interior. See De Kiewiet, *History of South Africa*, 15–17.

119. For example, Lionel Phillips, Abe Bailey, Percy Fitzpatrick, George Smartt, and the Duke of Westminster; see Keegan, "Making of the Rural Economy," 46. Lionel Phillips was an ardent supporter of progressive agriculture and was a founder and active president for many years of the Witwatersrand Agricultural Society (Fraser and Jeeves, *All That Glittered*, introduction). A key contributing factor here might have been that the Highveld's aspect varies relatively little whether it is farmed as pasturage or left in its natural state. The *Concise Oxford English Dictionary* definition of the word "veld" is "open country neither cultivated nor true forest" (5th ed., 1972).

120. Keegan has argued that there was little spontaneous generation of capital within the farming economy during the early decades of the century, and agricultural expansion was primarily driven by English-speaking politicians, lawyers, auctioneers, and businessmen whose capital came from other sources. Keegan, "The Making of the Rural Economy," 46.

121. See Stevenson, *Art and Aspirations*, 67.

122. On the Phillipses' endeavors in the Woodbush, see Phillips, *Some Reminiscences*, 74, 83–84. See also Gutsche, *No Ordinary Woman*; and Wongtschowski, *Between Woodbush and Wolkberg*.

123. See N. J. Coetzee, *Pierneef, Land, and Landscape*.

124. The attractiveness of these topographical situations may have been enhanced by the relative ease with which cattle could be moved up and down the escarpment to provide year-round grazing, as the Phillips did on their Woodbush properties.

125. Barnard, "Encountering Adamastor," 193. In Smuts's vision, it was assumed that the adjacent lowlands would allow sufficient space for African communities to maintain their traditional way of life.

126. See, for instance, Bunn, "Comparative Barbarism," 40–42.

127. Rich, "Milnerism and a Ripping Yarn," quoted in Milton, "Transvaal Beef Frontier," 200.

128. Milton, "Transvaal Beef Frontier," 200–201.

129. The Afrikaans word *bodem* is closely related to the German *boden*, as in the Nazi phrase *Blut und Boden* (blood and soil), where it was intended to convey a sense of spiritual bond with the land of one's birth.

130. See for instance De Kiewiet, *History of South Africa*, 259–61.

131. During the 1930s, two-thirds of the Afrikaner population was deemed poor or desperately poor, largely due to the bankruptcy of small farmers. See Lester, *From Colonization to Democracy*, 96–97.

132. J. M. Coetzee, *White Writing*, 76.

133. Henshaw, "John Buchan from the 'Borders' to the 'Berg,'" 19.

134. Hofmeyr, *Tale That Is Told*, 68–77.

Chapter 7: Prospect, Materiality, and the Horizons of Potentiality on Parktown Ridge

1. Aron et al., *Parktown*, 15.

2. Shorten, *Johannesburg Saga*.

3. Or, as De Kiewiet put it: "This frontier of money and machines leapt into the Boer midst, bringing with it an aggressive and incompatible population." See *A History of South Africa*, 120.

4. Wentzel, *View from the Ridge*, 10.

5. Christopher, *Southern Africa*, 172.

6. Ebenezer Howard's book *Garden Cities of Tomorrow* was published in 1898.

7. See Cosgrove, "Habitable Earth," 32.

8. Chipkin, *Johannesburg Style*, 93–95. Over the next thirty years, many newer Parktowns were developed in the veld, all with smaller lots and less dramatic situations.

9. This wealth was based on huge investment profits, which in turn were due to the rapid economic expansion made possible by substantial Imperial Guarantee Loans introduced to support Reconstruction. In the early 1900s, mining investors were being paid annual dividends of anywhere from 100 to 200 percent, at a time when mineworkers received around fifty-five shillings per month. (Aron et al., *Parktown*, 55).

10. See M. Bell, "'Pestilence that Walketh in Darkness,'" 327–41.

11. See Cosgrove, "Picturesque City," 51–53. For a parallel French version of metropolitan utopianism deflected into colonial urban design, see Wright, *Politics of Design in French Colonial Urbanism*.

12. Other than Hohenheim (built in 1895 by Hermann Eckstein for Lionel Phillips) the only other significant house built before the war was Dolobran. See Wentzel, *View from the Ridge*, 12. The trees in the plantation probably came from Natal, where the Pietermaritzburg Botanical Garden, set up as a collecting and experimental station for Kew, cultivated trees species from elsewhere in the empire for use in the tree-poor South African landscape. See McCracken and McCracken, *Way to Kirstenbosch*. The lumber from the plantation proved unsuitable for its intended purpose, but the plantation functioned as a recreational forest until it was finally cut down in the 1920s. See Wentzel, *View from the Ridge*, 12.

13. The guerrilla phase of the war would drag on in remoter rural areas for another eighteen months before peace was formally signed in May 1902. In 1902–3, an estimated forty-five thousand *uitlanders* moved to the Witwatersrand.

14. By 1910, gold mines employed over two-hundred thousand people, and by 1913 the Rand produced 40 percent of the world's gold. In a matter of decades, gold mining had become the most important sector of the South African economy.

15. Before the war, only 36 houses had been built on the estate; by 1904, there were 170. See Aron et al., *Parktown*, 21.

16. Wentzel, *View from the Ridge*, 25. Pretoria was the government seat of the Transvaal Colony and, after union, it became the administrative capital of the Union.

17. Parktown's residents included Lord and Lady Phillips, Lord and Lady Dalrymple, Patrick Duncan (who became the first South African governor-general), Sir George and Lady Albu, Sir Drummond Chaplin, Prince Arthur of Connaught (governor-general in the 1920s), Sir Thomas

Cullinan, Sir George Farrar, Sir Percy Fitzpatrick (author of *Jock of the Bushveld*), the Dale Laces, and Judge Philip and Sarah Gertrude Millin.

18. For the administrators at least, their anticipated sojourn in the Transvaal was tied to the period necessary to ready the region for self-government, which happened sooner than expected, in 1907.

19. The German presence was reflected in house names such as Hohenheim, as well as the name of the plantation itself, Sachsenwald, supposedly after the Potsdam origins of its first forester.

20. See Baker, *Architecture and Personalities*, 52.

21. Stevenson, *Art and Aspirations*, 75.

22. Dorothea Fairbridge, *Pilgrim's Way in South Africa* (1928), illustrated with photographs by Lancelot Ussher and a frontispiece of a reproduction of a Gwelo Goodman painting.

23. For an expanded exploration of this journey, see Foster, "'Northward, Upward.'"

24. Fairbridge, *Pilgrim's Way*, 71.

25. The Renaissance architectural theoretician Alberti argued that the ideal location for a gentleman's country house was not "in the most fruitful Part of the Estate, but rather in the most honorable, where he can uncontrolled enjoy all the Pleasures and Conveniences of Air, Sun and fine Prospects, go down easily at any Time into his Estate, receive Strangers handsomely and spaciously, be seen by Passers-by for a good Way round, and have a View of some City, Towns, the Sea an open Plain and the Tops of some known Hills or Mountains." See Alberti, *Ten Books of Architecture*, book 5, chap. 18, p. 104.

26. Leatherbarrow, *Roots of Architectural Invention*, 34.

27. On this topic, see Constant, "From the Virgilian Dream to Chandigarh."

28. Leatherbarrow, *Roots of Architectural Invention*, 37.

29. See Vesely, *Architecture and Continuity*, 13.

30. Not all the Ridge houses were on north-facing slopes; some of the earliest houses, designed by British architects who had never visited South Africa, were south-facing. Nevertheless, I would argue that a majority of Baker's houses were oriented to the north, and perhaps more importantly, it was invariably these houses that became icons of the white South African imagination in subsequent decades, not only in representations such as Fairbridge's, but also through architectural imitation. This seems to emphasize the capacity of these houses to capture and articulate the spatial imagination that evolved on the Ridge, as well as its ability to transcend representational frames.

31. The emptiness of this landscape was of course highly dependent on who was observing it. In a curious coincidence, British South Africans were repeating the self-deception of the Boers, who had justified their own annexation of the same landscape fifty years earlier by the fact that they too had found it "empty." See Marks, "Myth of the Empty Land."

32. "The first in a series of recurring mountain horizons, series of wild and lapping land-locked tide-lines that extend like transverse barriers to the Matopos and beyond." See Chipkin, in Aron et al., *Parktown*, 54.

33. Landscape as horizon is landscape reduced to its most elemental expression, probably the original prompt for classical genius loci, and the implied co-relative of literary prosopopoeia.

34. Norberg-Schulz, *Genius Loci*, 24–25.

35. Africa has for several centuries been associated in Western minds with the primordial "inner darkness" of the unconscious. See Bishop, *Myth of Shangri-La*, 8. Even Olive Schreiner, never an unquestioning imperialist, was struck by the fact that gazing north, one felt "as if there were no civilization for thousands of miles." See Chipkin, *Johannesburg Style*, 30.

36. See, for instance, Hunt, "Idea of a Garden"; and Crandell, *Nature Pictorialized*, 59–93.

37. See Steenbergen and Reh, *Architecture and Landscape*, 34–46, 122–35.

38. See Bunn, "Whited Sepulchres," 99.

39. Baker, *Architecture and Personalities*, 60. Unlike the Parktown houses, which were built some years earlier, the Union Buildings faced south, over the country they administered.

40. The romantic pull of the route northward is ubiquitous in early twentieth-century representations of South Africa, from John Buchan's evocation of the Great North Road in *Africa Colony* and Violet Markham's contemplation on Rhodes's life in her book *South African Scene* to the masonic glyph that Baker used on the title page of his biography of Rhodes and the walls of South Africa

and Rhodes Houses in Britain. On this last symbol, see Merrington, "Pageantry and Primitivism," 650.

41. Egypt had been occupied by Britain since 1882, and several administrators and military figures who played important roles in South Africa from 1895 to 1910 had previously served in Egypt. Merrington, "Pageantry and Primitivism," 650–51.

42. Sometime Slade Professor at Oxford and a prolific author, Ruskin's ideas retained currency well into the twentieth century. As Kenneth Clark argued: "For almost fifty years, to read Ruskin was accepted as proof of a possession of a soul." See Clark, *John Ruskin*, xi.

43. Although Ruskin turned against imperialism in later life, Said cites as evidence of his initial enthusiasm for it his 1870 Slade Lecture at Oxford (a lecture that Rhodes attended). Said, *Culture and Imperialism*, 79.

44. Cosgrove, "Mappa mundi," 95. Ruskin's *axis mundi* placed the city of Venice at its epicenter, somewhat confusingly (Cosgrove, "Mappa mundi," 88). It is revealing to compare Ruskin's psychogeography with Derrida's doubled perception of the constitution of Europe, that is, either as the "point of departure for discovery, invention and colonization" or "the middle coiled up, indeed compressed along, a Greco-Germanic axis, at the very center of the cape." See Derrida, *Other Heading*, 20, quoted in Jacobs, *Edge of Empire*, 58.

45. The three climatic zones were "the Gothic from the frigid zone, the classical from the temperate, and the Arab from the torrid." Cosgrove, "Mappa mundi," 95.

46. See Merrington, "Staggered Orientalism."

47. "Built places in which humans dwell may be said to constitute intermediate entities in the tale of *topogenesis*; that is, they exist midway between oriented bodies and the wilderness. . . . Buildings in places, buildings *as* places, serve as the mediatrix between the artless earth and the skillful body. Every building is in this respect a compromise formation, a middle ground between nature and culture, given that its material constituents are taken (directly or ultimately) from the natural world, while its exact shape and actual use stem from the world of human purposes." See Casey, *Getting Back into Place*, 112.

48. Leatherbarrow, *Roots of Architectural Invention*.

49. Aron et al., *Parktown*, 22. Doreen Greig argued that it was more accurate to describe Baker's work as an eclectic amalgam of Cape Dutch, English, and Italian architectures; see her *Herbert Baker in South Africa*, 140.

50. Chipkin, *Johannesburg Style*, 31.

51. In his memoirs, Baker cites Rhodes's notion that it was "the duty of the wealthy in the raw, undeveloped country and cities of South Africa to build beautiful homes wherein to exercise the most excellent gift of hospitality. Thus . . . strangers, pioneers and farmers would see and hear the best of the country and its people." Baker, *Architecture and Personalities*, 52.

52. Gradidge, *Dream Houses*, 139.

53. Metcalf, "Architecture and Empire," 8.

54. See Cosgrove, "Ruskin and the Geographical Imagination," 47.

55. Cosgrove, "Ruskin and the Geographical Imagination," 58.

56. Cosgrove, "Ruskin and the Geographical Imagination," 54.

57. Baker emphasizes this through a rather curious interpretation of Ruskin's ideas in his biography of Rhodes: "Ruskin pictured in his imagination a beloved scene in the mountains of Switzerland transported to 'some aboriginal forest in the New Continent' and felt in his inner being that its beauty would seem to vanish there without the villages, fields and pastures of their valleys and foothills of their Alps. Rhodes must have absorbed this sentiment from Ruskin, and no doubt it inspired his cry for 'more homes, more homes.'" See Baker, *Cecil Rhodes*, 59. The friendship between Baker and Rhodes may also have been based on the fact that they were both émigrés who found their métier in South Africa.

58. In this account it is hard to decide whether the ideas expressed are Baker's or Rhodes's, but given the nature of their relationship it can probably be safely assumed that Baker often—retrospectively—used Rhodes as a mouthpiece for ideas that were in fact shared, or even his alone.

59. This imaginative conflation goes some way to explaining what some see as an apparent contradiction in Baker's South African work: that it was an essentially "socialist" architectural ideas

290

NOTES TO
PAGES 156–158

used to propagate imperialism. While I would argue that this supports a reading of Baker's work in other than stylistic terms, Baker's experience in South Africa mirrored that of his metropolitan peers, who found that the only people who could afford handmade houses were the wealthy.

60. See for instance Baker, *Cecil Rhodes*, 39–40.

61. Baker, *Architecture and Personalities*, 48.

62. Metcalf, "Architecture and Empire," 9.

63. See Baker, "Architectural Needs of South Africa." For a list of all Baker's publications, see Keath, *Herbert Baker*.

64. Greig, *Herbert Baker in South Africa*, 116.

65. Sometimes, this rapid growth led to three successive buildings being erected on the same site over a period of twenty years. See Chipkin, *Johannesburg Style*, 11

66. Chipkin, *Johannesburg Style*, 75.

67. Greig, *Herbert Baker in South Africa*, 100.

68. Thus Baker argued, "the education of a South African architect cannot be completed without a long study in Italy and Greece, where art flourished in countries and climates more similar to his own." From Baker's lecture notes on "Architectural Needs of South Africa," quoted in *Groote Schuur*, 22.

69. Metcalf, "Herbert Baker and New Delhi," 398, 392. Metcalf underscores this point by arguing that Baker's buildings cannot be seen in isolation, in terms of the colony in question, or even in terms of the relationship between that colony and London.

70. Baker's awareness of such sites could only have been deepened by the knowledge that Rhodes had planned to build himself a house on the Ridge when the war was over.

71. What the influential British Arts and Crafts architect T. H. Unwin called the "house place."

72. Baker may also have remembered that Ruskin had once labeled Classical architecture as the "architecture of slavery." See Cosgrove, "Ruskin and the Geographical Imagination," 61.

73. Baker, *Architecture and Personalities*, 47, 48. The words are virtually indistinguishable from Ruskin's.

74. Rhodes had originally emigrated to South Africa for health reasons, while Baker was devoted all aspects of outdoor life—not only horseback riding, but also gardens, nature, and sketching. Irving, *Indian Summer*, 277.

75. Gradidge, *Dream Houses*, 138.

76. Quoted in Greig, *Herbert Baker in South Africa*, 225.

77. Quoted in Chipkin, *Johannesburg Style*, 39. The supreme example of these outdoor rooms, which are sometimes seen as the weak point of his Transvaal buildings and described as wasteful and chilly, was the loggia at Villa Arcadia, which exceeded the length of the house itself.

78. Baker borrowed this memorable phrase from Kipling's poem on Rhodes death, "The Burial" (S. Dubow, "Colonial Nationalism," 83n95).

79. The quotation is taken from a 1911 enjoinder to local architects to study the work of San Michaeli of Verona, quoted in Greig, *Herbert Baker in South Africa*, 225.

80. From Baker's lecture notes on "Architectural Needs of South Africa," quoted in *Groote Schuur*, 22.

81. Quoted in Greig, *Herbert Baker in South Africa*, 225. On craft, see, for instance, Hurley, "About Making."

82. Buchan, *Africa Colony; History of the South African Forces*.

83. Stevenson, *Art and Aspirations*, 79.

84. Amazingly, Johannesburg had no functioning brickyards when Baker arrived, and one of the first things Baker did was help set one up. His antipathy toward some of the mining-camp construction materials mellowed with time, and he was later to expound the simplicity and honesty of corrugated iron when used appropriately, as he himself was forced to do on his large-scale projects for the mines. See Greig, *Herbert Baker*, 117.

85. Leatherbarrow, *Roots of Architectural Invention*, 158.

86. Greig, *Herbert Baker*, 118. Villa Arcadia (1909), Marienhof (now Brenthurst, 1904), and Towie (1903) were all built from plastered brick.

87. *Which* material is selected for use, *where* it is taken from, even *when* (how and when a piece of

timber or stone is cut greatly affects its longevity, for instance) are integral to imaginative constructions of that "nature."

88. Leatherbarrow, *Roots of Architectural Invention*, 159.

89. Although the appropriation and incorporation of the materials of the site into a building is one of the oldest methods of construction, it was not one much practiced anymore at this time in Europe.

90. Baker, *Architecture and Personalities*, 48.

91. Bunn, "Whited Sepulchres," 96.

92. There were other resonances to this in Johannesburg in the early 1900s. Terence Ranger has observed how revived and invented rituals of craft unionism were used by white workers to exclude Africans from participation in miners' unions at this time. See "Invention of Tradition in Colonial Africa." Part of the appeal of finding an application for European crafts in Africa may have been that many of these crafts were becoming redundant in the industrializing metropole at this time.

93. Bunn, "Whited Sepulchres," 96. For a comprehensive discussion about the reciprocity between technique, knowledge, and identity, see Fischer, *Necessity of Art*.

94. Greig, *Herbert Baker*, 118.

95. Chipkin, *Johannesburg Style*, 54.

96. Bunn, "Whited Sepulchres," 96.

97. On the implications of reading the South African landscape as one of rock and stone, see "Landscape Iconography" in Wagner, *Rereading Nadine Gordimer*, 166–216. Another resonance of Baker's use of local stone can be found in the intense geological research with which nineteenth-century imperialism drew the landscape's *past* (that is, its existence before the coming of the Europeans) into the contemporary web of imperial knowledge and control. See, for instance, Stafford, "Annexing the Landscapes of the Past."

98. In his memoirs, Lionel Phillips gives a detailed geological description of the Ridge. See *Some Reminiscences*, 100.

99. As Dorothea Fairbridge put it in her *History of South Africa* (1918), "a garden was the *fons et origo* of the country." Quoted in Merrington, "Carrying the Torch," n.p.

100. Helmreich, "Re-presenting Nature."

101. A broadly similarly nativist horticultural movement was emerging in the United States at this time, under the influence of Charles Eliot and Frederick Law Olmsted.

102. See Hunt, "'Come into the Garden, Maud.'"

103. Fairbridge described the view from Government House in Pretoria as "orange groves and gardens that grow peacefully on lands that were once the Black Man's and may be the Black Man's again if the White Folk of South Africa let themselves forget the necessity for standing together, shoulder to shoulder, to hold the land for civilization." *Gardens of South Africa*, 37.

104. Van Sittert, "Making the Cape Floral Kingdom," 119.

105. Fairbridge, *Gardens of South Africa*, 31.

106. Sims, *Tree Planting in South Africa*.

107. Schama, *Landscape and Memory*, 6.

108. Sims, *Flowering Trees and Shrubs for Use in South Africa*.

109. See, for instance, Lighton, *Sisters of the South*.

110. By 1910, at least 140 exotic plants had naturalized themselves in South Africa. See Van Sittert, "Making the Cape Floral Kingdom," 125.

111. See, for instance, Fagan, *Old Roses at the Cape of Good Hope*.

112. Fairbridge, *Gardens of South Africa*, 49–50.

113. For a discussion of the Parktown gardens, see Sklar, "Garden Suburb."

114. See, for instance, Fairbridge, *Gardens of South Africa*, 31–34.

115. Sklar, "Garden Suburb," 86, 89.

116. Fairbridge wrote that Villa Arcadia was "built on the lines of an Italian villa . . . breaking away from the tradition which has hitherto ordained that a South African house should be wholly English or wholly Dutch, or unsatisfactory hybrids. Here on the contrary is the spirit of Southern Europe, brought into South Africa, with triumphant success." *Garden of South Africa*, 33.

117. Helmreich, "Re-presenting Nature," 89–91.

118. For an exploration of how this phenomenon is mediated by places embedded within the city, see Johnson, "Cast in Stone."

119. Elaine Scarry argues that the more the object conforms to the projection, the more "it will seem to have been generated by the interior state itself and considered a visionary solution." See *Body in Pain*, 168.

120. That is, objects brought forth for the precise purpose of being objects of the imaginary state. Scarry, *Body in Pain*, 168.

121. For instance, there are strong parallels between Parktown Ridge and the Hogsback area near Guildford, where many large houses were built in the 1890s looking out over the South Downs. See Gradidge, *Dream Houses*, 43.

122. These two aspects are epitomized by the mythical figures of *Hera* and *Hermes*, which Casey associates, respectively, with the mobile, geometric, and conceptual ("the world"); and the stationary, topological, and participatory ("the earth"). See *Getting Back into Place*, 139.

123. Alexandre Chemetoff, "Des paysages," *L'Architecture d'Aujourd'hui* 303 (February 1997): 52.

124. The photographs are credited to "Alan Yates, lent by the architect, Sir Herbert Baker." Although they are not dated, the development that can be made out in the photograph includes what appears to be the Murray Gordon Mansion, which was completed in 1919 on Westcliff Ridge.

125. In architectural theory, the vertical opening (Perret's *la porte fenêtre*, the frame of these photographs) usually suggests the bringing into alignment with each other in a pre-modernist, perspectival relationship of the erect person, standing and looking, and the impression of *complete* landscape. See Colomina, "Split Wall," 112.

126. As Dalibor Vesely has observed, the vitality of metaphor stems precisely from complexities that cannot be solved and are instead given *room to occur.*

127. Renamed "Saxonwold" during World War I, when there were violent anti-German protests in Johannesburg.

128. The university program was supported by donations from Lady Phillips. See Herbert, *Martienssen and the International Style*, 9.

129. On South Africa House, see Baker, *Architecture and Personalities*, 131–34, and R. MacNab, *Story of South Africa House.*

130. Although Leith grew up in Pretoria (and attended school with Pierneef), he studied at the Architectural Association in London. After working with Baker on the Union Buildings, he won the first Baker Prize, a scholarship to study in Italy for one year, before serving with distinction in France during World War I, and he subsequently worked with Baker on the war graves in France. See Keath, "Baker School."

131. G. E. Pearse, the first professor of architecture at the University of the Witwatersrand, had worked in Baker's office and had been overseas from 1915 to 1920. The second professor of architecture, A. S. Furner, appointed in 1925, was English.

132. For a discussion of nationalism in South African architecture, see Chipkin, *Johannesburg Style*, 132–34, 280–81.

133. Herbert, *Martienssen and the International Style*, 40.

Chapter 8: Mrs. Everard's Lonely Career

1. Quoted in Harmsen, *Women of Bonnefoi*, 141. Harmsen provides a comprehensive overview of the life and work of Bertha Everard and her sister and two daughters, who together formed the so-called Everard Group of painters. This book also provides the most complete catalog available of Bertha Everard's work.

2. For many years this painting was assumed to be the one called *Peace of Winter*, in the Johannesburg Art Gallery, but it now seems that the original has disappeared, and that *Peace of Winter* was a close copy of it.

3. Harmsen, *Women of Bonnefoi*, 31.

4. Her work was shown in Bloemfontein in 1916, Durban in 1917, Cape Town in 1922, Johannesburg in 1927, and Cape Town in 1931.

5. For a comprehensive account of this project, see N. J. Coetzee, *Pierneef, Land, and Landscape*, 5–30.

6. His commissions included the murals for the new Herbert Baker–designed South Africa House in London (1933–35), murals depicting the Union Buildings in the new Union-Castle mail ship, the *Pretoria Castle* (launched in 1937), and the wall panels for the Johannesburg Magistrate's Court (1940). See N. J. Coetzee, *Pierneef, Land, and Landscape*, 3. For more on Pierneef's life and work, see Ferreira et al., *J. H. Pierneef*.

7. Frieda Harmsen, personal communication, February 1997. The "symphonic" size and rhetorical aspirations of these paintings were recognized by the Everard family, who called them "Beethovens."

8. See, for instance, Cope, "South Africa." On the flowering of the Modern Movement in Johannesburg, see Chipkin, *Johannesburg Style*, 155–92.

9. See T. J. Clark, *Painting of Modern Life*, 183–85.

10. Kern, *Culture of Time and Space*, 152.

11. Kern, *Culture of Time and Space*, 176, 160.

12. Carter, *Living in a New Country*, 63, 51.

13. Cosgrove, *Social Formation and Symbolic Landscape*, 26.

14. White South African women only received the vote in 1929, and before that they could only influence events as activists or pamphleteers (Olive Schreiner being the prime example). However, nobody living in the *platteland* and coming into daily contact with Afrikaners and Africans could have been unaware of the issues at stake during these decades.

15. Cornwall was one of the remoter parts of England, where artists' colonies started to emerge at the end of the nineteenth century. See Vaughan, "British Landscape Tradition."

16. Situated at a crossroads of the old wagon routes, Bonnefoi had long been a regional landmark, and "Everard's Store" is frequently noted on old maps of the ZAR period.

17. See Harmsen, *Women of Bonnefoi*, 39.

18. In the early twentieth century the winter migration to the Lowveld was an integral part of Highveld stock farming. It has lasted to the present day in some parts of South Africa. See Grosskopf, *Rural Impoverishment and Rural Exodus*, 1–43.

19. Harmsen, *Women of Bonnefoi*, 43.

20. Arnold, "Bertha Everard," 57.

21. John Buchan mentions Everard's store, the Machadodorp-Carolina railway line under construction, and the old stone bridge. See *Africa Colony*, 130.

22. Everard hired a Swedish stonemason to develop a quarry of the local stone for these later projects.

23. See M. Bell, "Woman's Place" and "'Pestilence That Walketh in Darkness.'"

24. For example, gardening, dairy work, beekeeping, poultry care, and fruit growing. See M. Bell, "Woman's Place," 140.

25. Before the coming of the railways to a district, local traders were enormously powerful figures because they controlled the marketing and sale of all agricultural surplus. See Keegan, *Rural Transformations in Industrializing South Africa*, 96–98. The single-line railway reached Bonnefoi around 1906.

26. Alston, *Heart of the Veld*. Although it does not give specific place-names, the book is clearly describing life somewhere in the Eastern Highveld sometime after union. Alston displays fiercely Milnerite sympathies. Although critical of the effects of "Liberal policy" in her district, she asserts that "loyalty to Empire soars above the arena of politics."

27. Harmsen, *Women of Bonnefoi* includes numerous examples of Everard's letters.

28. Alston, *Heart of the Veld*, 5.

29. Alston, *Heart of the Veld*, 47.

30. "I am living over again in my little way the life of my ancestors who whether they were great ladies or peasants . . . laid the foundations of our vast civilization. It is the joy in work which industrialism has killed. It is this joy, this spirit of play in work that Ruskin sought to recapture for us." See Alston, *Heart of the Veld*, 38.

31. Alston, *Heart of the Veld*, 45. For a masculine equivalent of Alston's book, see, for instance, *Call of the Veld* and other books by Leonard Flemming.

32. See Mills, "Gender and Colonial Space" and "Knowledge, Gender and Empire."

33. Alston, *Heart of the Veld*, 14.

34. Alston, *Heart of the Veld*, 219.

35. Everard passed this subjectivity on to her daughter Rosamund, who became a competent farmer, violinist, artist, and pilot, and spoke French and Swazi.

36. For a more thoroughly feminist reading of Everard's situation, see Arnold, "Bertha Everard."

37. Frieda Harmsen, personal communication, February 1997. On cars, Everard wrote: "Motors are nice retreats. . . . One just pulls down the blinds, shuts the doors and lives inside like a disagreeable snail." Unpublished letter, 1927; *Everard Phenomenon*, 96.

38. Shurmer-Smith, "Cixous' Space," 358.

39. Harrison, "Effects of Landscape," 215.

40. Mitchell, "Holy Landscape," 209.

41. Inglis, "Landscape as Popular Culture," 209.

42. Harrison, "Effects of Landscape," 216–17.

43. Bordo, "*Terra Nullius* of Wilderness."

44. Bordo, "Picture and Witness at the Site of the Wilderness."

45. Harrison, "Effects of Landscape," 228.

46. Harrison, "Effects of Landscape," 211–12.

47. Harmsen, *Women of Bonnefoi*, 11.

48. Inglis, "Landscape as Popular Culture," 206.

49. "The painter, like the poet, has to find within his paints and their actualization on paper the qualities which are equivalent to both what is in front of him, and what he wishes were in front of him." Inglis, "Landscape as Popular Culture," 206.

50. As Merleau-Ponty asserted: "Conception cannot precede execution. . . . Only the work itself, completed and understood, will prove there was *something* rather than *nothing* to be found there." See Merleau-Ponty, "Cezanne's Doubt," 69.

51. Conway, *True North*, 168.

52. On painterly conventions, see Mitchell, "Holy Landscape," 197.

53. Hence, Ingold's rhetorical question: "If to dwell means to live in the world, and if representation entails taking one *out* of it, then how can one represent *dwelling?*" Ingold, "Picture Is Not the Terrain," 30.

54. Sarah Mills argues that women "tend to see landscape in more relational ways: rather than seeking to subdue the landscape . . . they tend to see landscape in relation to domestic spaces and networks of interaction." See "Gender and Colonial Space," 132–35.

55. See Arnold, "Bertha Everard," 55–64.

56. Harmsen, *Women of Bonnefoi*, 39, 41, 45.

57. "Every expatriate longs to bring the two halves of life together, the world of birth and the world of here and now. The longing is an ache for continuity, as though our psyches were a Roman arch waiting for the last stone to join the curves into a symmetrical whole, able to frame a life completely, without disruption and continuity." See Conway, *True North*, 137.

58. See Bishop, *Archetypal Constable*, 53.

59. See Carter, *Living in a New Country*, 61–63.

60. For a geological and topographical description of this region, see King, *South African Scenery*, 222–52.

61. Quoted in Harmsen, *Women of Bonnefoi*, 99. The painting in question was *Asbestos Hills*.

62. Fuller, *Art and Psychoanalysis*, 188.

63. See Bordo, "*Terra Nullius* of Wilderness" and "Picture and Witness."

64. Everard's mother had taken her to England from South Africa when she was one year old, and she had grown up in the Lake District. On the character of upland landscapes in Britain, see Lowenthal and Prince, "English Landscape," 311–17.

65. R. Phillips, *Mapping Men and Empire*, 13.

66. Everard did not care for the typical lowland English landscape. When in Southern England in 1924, she wrote: "This is not my country and I shall never be moved by it as I am by my native land" (quoted in Harmsen, *Women of Bonnefoi*, 90); and in 1926, "Give me the wide new lands; let me leave this pretty pleasant land" (quoted in Arnold, "Bertha Everard," 56).

67. See, for instance, Matchotka, *Cézanne*; and Andrews, *Landscape and Western Art*, 197–99.

68. Bishop, *Archetypal Constable*, 124–28.

69. Bishop, *Archetypal Constable*, 119–22.

70. Bunn, "To the Valley Below," 13. This makes sense of an otherwise anomalous series of paintings, mostly dating from 1917, depicting the rock formations at the top of the Skurweberg Pass, where the family camped on their way between the two places.

71. Although such landscape acuity is hard to quantify or record, it is latent in the working relationships that all people develop over time with the object of their work. See, for instance, Stilgoe, "Salt Marshes"; and Leveson, "Geologic Clarity."

72. As a more contemporary South African landscape painter, Erik Laubscher, has argued, the challenge is to "create the illusion of the landscape having continuing vastness and the painting being part of the whole, instead of something complete and contained." Quoted in E. Berman, *Story of South African Painting*.

73. Bordo, "Jack Pine." The rise of the Group of Seven as agents in the "naturalization of the nation" in Canada was more or less contemporaneous with the less-organized emergence of modernism in South African landscape painting. Although its members first met before World War I, they came together after 1920 to paint the rougher, rawer elements of the Canadian north, primarily the Laurentian Shield. They became advocates of Canadian cultural nationalism, proposing a Nordic vision of Canadian identity and destiny that, unlike that of the United States West, was rooted in a struggle against nature in a harsh, isolated region. See Kaufmann, "Naturalizing the Nation." See also Osborne, "Interpreting a Nation's Identity" and "Iconography of Canadian Art."

74. Bordo, "Picture and Witness at the Site of the Wilderness," 231.

75. Bordo, "Picture and Witness at the Site of the Wilderness," 229.

76. See, for instance, Bunn, "Relocations."

77. Thus, of the most rigorous Postimpressionist, Cézanne, it was written: "He did not want to separate the stable things which we see and the shifting way in which they appear; he wanted to depict matter as it takes on form, the birth of order through spontaneous organization. . . . [Like Balzac] he wanted to understand what inner force holds the world together and causes the proliferation of visible forms." See Merleau-Ponty, "Cézanne's Doubt," 63–64.

78. Postimpressionism was introduced to England by the December 1910 exhibition of paintings by Van Gogh, Cézanne, Picasso, and Matisse mounted at the Grafton Galleries in London by Roger Fry. Fry's writings established English-language interpretation of French modern art, and his *Essay in Aesthetics* (1909) was an influential statement of modernist principles. See Harrison and Wood, *Art in Theory*, 78. Everard read Bell and Fry's articles in the *Studio*, then one of the more widely read art journals in the English-speaking world, as well as Bell's influential *Art*, published in 1914. It is unlikely that she saw the paintings they referred to, though, other than as reproductions when she visited England in 1911.

79. Harmsen, *Women of Bonnefoi*, 49, 41.

80. As one midcentury South African art historian wrote: "No European country demands so much architecture for its scenic art as South Africa. No country offers so little opportunity for fanatic romanticism, while demanding so much relentless clear-sightedness as the Transvaal and the Karoo." Bouman and De Bussy, *Painters of South Africa*. Similarly, Esme Berman argues that on the Highveld, "space and structure are the commanding features, color as such plays a subordinate role." *Art and Artists of South Africa*, 6.

81. E. Berman, *Art and Artists of South Africa*, 148. As any landscape painter will avow, tall grass is one of the hardest things to depict.

82. Here I am borrowing James Corner's argument that "landscape experience is received in moments, glances and accidental detours, kinesthetically unfolding through rambling and habitual encounters over time. . . . The subject in the landscape is a fully enveloped and integral part of spatial, temporal and material relations." See Corner, "Representation and Landscape," 251.

83. Bishop, *Archetypal Constable*, 110.

84. Hofmeyr, "Spoken Word and the Barbed Wire," 72.

85. For example, *Morning Tree* (1913), *Evening Voluntary* (1916), *Cypresses* (ca. 1916), *Rocks and Thunderheads, Skurweberg* (ca. 1916), *Veld-fire* (ca. 1913?), *Moonrise* (ca. 1910), *Pale Hillside* (ca. 1913), and *Moon and Shadow* (ca. 1917).

86. Pierneef argued that the South African landscape was devoid of color from 10 a.m. to 4 p.m. See Roos, *Kuns in Suid-Wes Afrika/Art in South West Africa*, chapter 4.

87. Straus, *Primary World of the Senses*. The influential English aesthete and painter Adrian Stokes was much preoccupied by the atmospheric, phenomenological, and existential consequences of the light on the cusp between night and day, especially in southern countries. See for instance Gowing, *Critical Writings of Adrian Stokes*, 24, 36, 55, 132–33.

88. That is, the overaccentuation of psychical reality in comparison with material reality.

89. N. J. Coetzee, *Pierneef, Land, and Landscape*, 21.

90. "Away beyond the now vivid green and the jagged blue hills of Swaziland, and on one side the nearer krantzes and headlands of the Highveld. The only noise is the noise we make ourselves. An overwhelming silence broods over this world when one sits alone. I like to sit alone for a few minutes, but I could not bear it for long." Undated letter by Bertha Everard, quoted in Leigh, "Dynamics of the Everard Paintings," 86.

91. I borrow this imaginative maneuver from Mitchell, who calls it "negative representation." See "Holy Landscape," 219.

92. Harmsen, *Women of Bonnefoi*, 124.

93. The large number of Delville Wood paintings, the fact that at least one of them bears a striking resemblance to a photograph in the Imperial War Museum, and the fact that Baker's restoration of the site would have been almost completed in early 1926, all suggest that some of Everard's Delville Wood paintings were not done *in situ*.

94. Harmsen, *Women of Bonnefoi*, 125.

95. The South African government declined Everard's offer of one of her Delville Wood paintings as a gift, though this may have had as much to do with the fact that they had already commissioned a more traditional depiction of the battlefield by William Orpen as it had to do with the style of Everard's painting. Nevertheless, Orpen's *Survivors of Delville Wood* is now in the Durban Art Gallery, and one of Everard's Delville Wood paintings is in South Africa House, a gift from the head of the Imperial War Graves Commission, Sir Fabian Ware. MacNab, *Story of South Africa House*, 51.

96. See Fussell, *Great War and Modern Memory*, especially chapter 2, "Troglodyte World."

97. See, for instance, Warnke, "From Battlefield to War Landscape," in *Political Landscape*, 53–62; Hynes, "Death of Landscape," in *War Imagined*, 189–202; Fussell, *Great War*; Gough, "Avenue at War"; and Howkins, "Discovery of Rural England."

98. Gough, "Epic of Mud," 409.

99. Gough, "Epic of Mud," 414.

100. Harmsen, *Women of Bonnefoi*, 122, 123.

101. Bunn, "To the Valley Below," 16. Although this paper was given to me by its author, I have been unable to date it accurately; its insights about Everard's work are too valuable to omit.

102. These paintings include *New Furrow* (ca. 1929), *Small Furrow* (ca. 1931), *Lekkerdraai 1* (1934), *Lekkerdraai 2* (1935), and *Dawn on the Komati* (1936–37).

103. Bunn, "To the Valley Below," 15.

104. Bunn, "To the Valley Below," 13.

105. J. M. Coetzee, *White Writing*, 3–5.

106. Bishop, *Archetypal Constable*, 58–59.

107. Inglis, "Landscape as Popular Culture," 203.

108. Green, *Spectacle of Nature*, 2–7.

109. Harrison, "Effects of Landscape," 228, 231, 229.

110. The 1920s were not only the period when the capitalization of South African agriculture was at its most intense, but also when modernist self-critique was most alive in Europe. See Bunn, "Relocations," 55.

111. This binary is well illustrated by the difference between the paintings Smithard executed for the Pretoria Station in 1912, and those Pierneef painted for the Johannesburg Station, ca. 1930. In the former, signs of inhabitation and productive use are omnipresent; in the latter they are confined to just a few images. For discussion of the Pretoria paintings, see N. J. Coetzee, *Pierneef, Land, and Landscape*, 11–13.

112. George Revill's definition of the "modernist pastoral." See "Lark Ascending," 29.

113. E. Berman, *Story of South African Painting*, 44. Like Everard, Pierneef traveled to Europe in the mid-1920s to familiarize himself with contemporary trends in art. His studies focused on the theories of the Dutch artist-philosopher Konijnenberg, nowadays a forgotten strand of European modernism. N. J. Coetzee, *Pierneef, Land, and Landscape*, 18–20.

114. Osborne, "Interpreting a Nation's Identity," 237.

115. As one South African art historian has written, "South Africans learnt to see their country through Pierneef's eyes." De Villiers, *J. H. Pierneef*, 12.

116. Osborne, "Interpreting a Nation's Identity," 243–44.

117. Pierneef published many articles in *Die Huisgenoot* and *Die Boervrou* calling for a national style in painting and architecture. This derived from a thoroughly modern desire to promote himself in the eyes of prospective patrons and gain entry to the emerging Afrikaner establishment, in which he, as a Dutchman, always felt an outsider. For a thoughtful overview of his relationship with emerging Afrikaner nationalism, see N. J. Coetzee, *Pierneef, Land, and Landscape*, 22–30.

118. The Medici Society in London printed *Peace of Winter* and *Moonrise* in 1924–25, *Delville Wood* in 1926, and *By the Banks of Komati* in 1932. Everard paid to have the first two printed (David Hardcastle, Medici Society, London, personal communication, August 2002). According to Harmsen, *Peace of Winter* was printed again ca. 1930 and was a common sight in Transvaal and Free State classrooms and homes from the 1930s onward (Frieda Harmsen, personal communication, February 1997).

119. Carter, "Living in a New Country," 65.

120. Inglis, "Landscape as Popular Culture," 209–10.

121. Bishop, *Archetypal Constable*, 121.

Chapter 9: Modernity, Memory, and the South African Railways

1. Visitor from England, "'Round in Nine,'" 710.

2. One traveler captured the experience of the railway safari: "The scenery was of the grandest and most magnificent nature. Yawning precipices on both sides with ravines and mountain torrents, so that it was a constant passing from one side to the other to look out. My admiration for the Engineering Dept. of the South African railways increases daily. The train was stopped halfway and we all alighted and walked the few yards to the edge of one of the precipices and looked straight down a sheer 2,000 feet to the Low Veld beneath. Even the engine drivers followed our example, one pointing out to me where the best photograph could be taken." Visitor from England, "'Round in Nine.'"

3. See Pirie, "Railway-Operated Road Transport and the South African Space Economy" and "Railway Plantations and Railway Sleepers in South Africa, 1910–1937."

4. See Pirie, "Railway-Operated Road Transport and the South African Space Economy" and "Aspects of the Political-Economy of the Railways in South Africa."

5. See Pirie, "White Railway Labour in South Africa," "Sleepers beside the Tracks," and "Racial Segregation on South African Trains."

6. Attempts at the end of the nineteenth century to introduce American locomotives, which were much better suited to South African conditions, met with resistance from operational staff. See Bigelow, *White Man's Africa*, 154.

7. Botha considered Henry Burton, minister of railways, along with Smuts, to be his strongest ally in the task of steering the SAP (South African Party) between ultra-loyalist and nationalist opposition between 1910 and 1920. See Fedorowich, "Weak Link in the Imperial Chain," 137–58.

8. There are strong parallels between Hoy and his counterpart Sir William van Horne, general manager of the Canadian Pacific Railways from 1882 onward. See Hart, *Selling of Canada*. On Hoy's life and career, see "Sir William Hoy, KCB: A Great South African," and "Forty Years of Railway Service in South Africa: The Career of Sir William Hoy, K.C.B.," as well as entries in *Who's Who of South Africa* (Johannesburg: Argus). Born in Scotland, Hoy worked for the Cape Railways before the South African War, the British Military Railway during the war, and the Central South African Railways after. He died in 1930.

9. It was during his tenure that strict directives were given that all passengers on the railways, regardless of color, were to be treated with equal respect and courtesy.

10. On this project, see N. J. Coetzee, *Pierneef, Land, and Landscape*.

11. See Revill, "Working the System," 712–13.

12. E. M. Forster on Kings Cross, quoted in Tindall, *Countries of the Mind*, 67.

13. These depicted the Woodbush, the Eastern Free State, and the (Cape Dutch) Tokai Manor House, near Cape Town.

14. Of South Africa's overseas debt after the South African War, 80 percent was related to railways, and, like most nonmanufacturing nations, South Africa's balance of payments was perpetually in deficit, and foreign exchange was in chronically short supply. See Henshaw, "Key to South Africa"; and Wilburn, "Engines of Empire and Independence."

15. The author continues in similar vein: "Send the Johannesburger to the coast, in order that he may cease, if only for a few days, his nervous, anxious endeavour to get rich quick. Those who live in *dorps* suffer like the farmer from apathy, their mental horizons as limited as their geographical boundaries are far flung." See Stent, "Holiday Hints," 231.

16. The individuals the SAR hoped to attract were, in order of priority: the "leisured tourist who has exhausted the novelties of travel in older countries"; potential farmers, "with not less than £2,000"; manufacturers and investors who might start industries in the Union; and university students or public schoolboys, on whose "mental horizon" South Africa should be when they came "to decide on a career." "Notes and Comments," *SAR&H Magazine*, February 1921.

17. On this, see Fedorowich, "Anglicization and the Politicization of British Immigration to South Africa."

18. See, for instance, "Advertising South Africa," and "Scenery as a National Asset," *SAR&H Magazine*, September 1921, 569–70.

19. 'O. B. J.', "Publicity That Pays," *SAR&H Magazine*, May 1929, 745.

20. N. J. Coetzee, *Pierneef, Land, and Landscape*, 7.

21. Personal communication, Eric Conradie, Transnet Heritage Museum Archives, 1997.

22. On the concept of corporate authorship, see Hones, "'Everything Hastens Where It Belongs,'" 36.

23. Revill, "Working the System," 710. Revill argues that the relationship between narrative and nationhood is grounded in the fact that "the act of narration is intrinsic to the ordering of experience for the individual and therefore to a sense of ontological security in the world of uncertainty."

24. See, for instance, "South Africa through Other Eyes," *SAR&H Magazine*, December 1922, 1134–35.

25. Mels, "Nature, Home and Scenery."

26. Introduction to Duncan and Gregory, *Writes of Passage*, 5.

27. In the 1940s, it could still be written that "the apparent endlessness of the Karoo and the Highveld has changed comparatively little with the passing decades, nor has the suddenness with which modern cities and the paraphernalia of industrialism leap out of the virgin land—the intensity of traffic which flows over the rails from these major centres of population bears no relation to the rawness of the landscape." See *South African Railways*.

28. See Marx, "Railroad in the Landscape," 194, and Monti, *Africa Then*, 131.

29. This was especially true in the early decades of the century, when the connection between the Rand and the outside world before and during the South African War was a mere single line. On the effects of a railway's gauge on its alignment in the landscape generally, see Schivelbusch, *The Railway Journey*, 96–103.

30. The construction of the first lines to the Rand was strongly determined by the need to build quickly, with expensive labor, across almost worthless land (as opposed to England, where labor was cheap and land expensive). On the task of building these railways in South Africa, see Bond, *They Were South Africans*, 170–87.

31. The average speed of South African long-distance trains in the early 1920s was only 30 mph, and the journey from the Cape to the Rand, a distance of 956 miles, originally took thirty-eight hours. By 1928, this has been cut down to twenty-nine hours. The landscape effects afforded by older modes of travel are discussed in J. Dubow, "Rites of Passage."

32. Even in the late 1920s, all-weather roads only extended some thirty or forty miles beyond the city limits of Johannesburg and Pretoria.

33. Faith, *World the Railways Made*, 235. This was especially true in South Africa, where non-whites automatically traveled third class. Under Hoy's regime, the SAR fought outright segregation on its trains. See Pirie, "Racial Segregation on South African Trains."

34. See Jussim and Lindquist-Cock, *Landscape as Photograph*, 105–6.

35. Reflecting the democratic self-image of its citizens (and the enormous distances most train journeys there covered), trains in the United States were, from the beginning, completely open cars. By contrast, in Europe, where journeys were much shorter, and people generally less outgoing, train carriages were made up of separate compartments, each with a separate door. See Schivelbusch, *Railway Journey*, 98–112.

36. One of these new "twin-diners" was shipped to London in 1924, where it was used as exhibit and refreshment facility at the Wembley Exhibition.

37. This quality was frequently mentioned by travelers from overseas at this time. For a typical paean to South African trains, see Holtby, "In Praise of Trains."

38. See R.A.W., "Travelling By Train."

39. Gardner, "Round in Three Thousand."

40. Schivelbusch, *Railway Journey*, 59–60.

41. Even after 1934, when the Union government assumed control of all commercial aviation in South Africa, the first intercity services of the newly created South African Airways were scheduled to connect with the arrival and departure of mail boats in Cape Town. At least one visitor noticed that the imaginative poignancy attached to the arrival and departure of the mail boats remained alive in the minds of some white South Africans until the 1950s: "To a people (living) at the tip of an unknown continent, 3,000 miles from a university or a great library or a fine dressmaker or a symphony orchestra or a Turkish bath, only the mail-boat brought the promise of support and sympathy." See Morris, *South African Winter*, 105–6.

42. One of the many compromises built into the original act of Union, this practice still survives today.

43. The tours used the same trains and lines that had so recently played a vital role in the action, to the irritation of English generals, who found that the presence of civilians near the theater of war complicated military operations.

44. Although the weekly Union-Castle mail service ships had long been the way most visitors got to South Africa, the 1920s saw the arrival of the first dedicated cruise ships at South African ports. The first of these was the *Saxon*, which brought 150 tourists in February 1925. After this, several ships, each bringing around 300 visitors, visited South Africa every year, but this ceased in 1930, due to the Depression.

45. Before the advent of the SAR&H brochures and guides, the chief source of information about the region had been "South African Guide," published by the Union-Castle Steamship Company, carriers of the Royal Mail to South Africa since 1895.

46. The SAR&H even published its own travel book, H. A. Chilvers's *Seven Wonders of South Africa*.

47. The places featured in these guides were not necessarily accessible by rail, but anyone visiting them had to use the railways to get there.

48. Lantern slide sets were also used in Britain by organizations such as the Victoria League to popularize their visions of a rejuvenated Empire. See Ryan, "Visualizing Imperial Geography." The first film about South African scenery had circulated "more or less continuously" since 1913. In 1928, it was replaced with "South Africa—Land of Novelty and Perpetual Sunshine," which was shown in England, Kenya, Australia, and the United States.

49. The artists included Canitz, Mason, Timlin, and Caldecott. These posters conformed to the so-called Double Royal format used on European railways at the time. Measuring 40 x 25 in., this format was not ideal for representing the spacious South African landscape, and the *SAR&H Magazine* intermittently ran competitions for the design of new posters.

50. Unlike a photograph, a painting could combine several dramatic landscape elements that in reality exist in different geographical locations.

51. These posters appeared in Great Britain, Austria, Norway, and Germany. Posters advertising South Africa also appeared in the London Underground (*Railways Administration General Manager's Annual Report*, 1926–27).

52. *Railways Administration General Manager's Annual Report*, 1928–29.

53. In 1927, the Imperial Tobacco Co. printed seventy-two "South African Scenes" on the backs of cards included in over four million cigarette packs sold worldwide. *Railways Administration General Manager's Annual Report*, 1927–28.

54. Some of these images were taken by in-house photographers, but many were furnished by regional professional and amateur photographers. Official SAR photographers were few and thinly spread; in 1927, only four covered the entire country. Their names (or any other information about them) remain unrecorded.

55. The contemporaneous emergence of railways and nation building occurred in Germany in the 1850s, Belgium in the 1830s, Italy in the 1860s, and in the United States from 1830 to 1860.

56. On the rhetorical effects of railway policies and practices, see Revill, "Working the System."

57. Ryan, "Visualizing Imperial Geography," 166.

58. On the relationship between photography and travel, see J. M. Schwartz, "'Geography Lesson.'"

59. See Lee, *To the Bitter End*. Although local newspapers had occasionally reproduced landscape photographs, before 1900 most South Africans would have encountered such images through expensive prints, framed on walls or hand-tipped into albums of "South African Scenes," which, despite their titles, only showed scenes of the Cape and Natal.

60. See Van Horne and Drelick, *Traveling the Pennsylvania Railroad*.

61. P. Kerr (Lord Lothian), quoted in S. Dubow, "Imagining the New South Africa," 83.

62. Schivelbusch, *Railway Journey*, 91–92.

63. This geographical trope appears a few years after the introduction of the railway into the interior; see for instance the Times Special Correspondent, *Letters from South Africa*, 1–5. It also found expression in paintings of SAR trains, with titles such as "From Sea Level to Nearly 6,000 Feet: 900 Miles in Twenty-Eight Hours," which appeared in illustrated magazines during the 1920s.

64. On this northward trajectory, see chapter 6, as well as Foster, "Northward, Upward."

65. Pevsner, "Foreword," in Harmsen, *Art and Articles*.

66. On this topic, see Scott, *Spoken Image*.

67. See John Stilgoe, "Popular Photography, Scenery Values and Visual Assessment."

68. Hunt, *Greater Perfections*.

69. In nineteenth-century France, for instance, it was deeply felt that the ease of railway communication would erode the individual character of the region. See Dumas, "Public Face of Landscape," 37. On the relationship between modern technology and tourism, see, for instance, Buzard, *Beaten Track*, 31–47.

70. Violet Markham, quoted in M. Bell, "'Citizenship, Not Charity,'" 206. Although William Hoy was a great devotee of the bucolic South Cape coastal resort of Hermanus (he and his wife were buried there, in the middle of the town, on Hoy's Koppie), he never permitted the railway to be built to the town.

71. Because many of these photographs were taken and printed on postcard backs by the local chemists/photographers, it is plausible to claim that these images represented what was of local interest. Karel Schoeman, South African Library, Cape Town, personal communication, February 1997. Nicolas Monti has observed: "For the commercial photographer, the growing cities and commercial centres not only offered the largest market for their his work . . . but also supplied a readily available subject matter: photographs illustrating the spread of cities, notable new buildings and other indicators of civil pride found a ready sale to visiting travellers and to settlers to send back to Europe." See *Africa Then*, 125.

72. D. Wolf, *American Space*, 4.

73. On the persistence of rivers and river crossings in South African landscape representation, see Kloppers, "Crossing Rivers," 64–68.

74. On the relationship between railways and postcards, see Rhind and Walker, *Historical Railway Postcard Journeys in Southern Africa*.

75. *SAR&H Magazine*, March 1920. See also Cox, "South Africa's Riviera."

76. Some of these examples are given in a fictional conversation between three travelers, discussing precisely this problem. See S. Kirkland, "From the Carriage Window."

77. F. Bell, "South Africa and the Lure of the Sun."

78. A constant challenge to South African tourism has been the fact that most of the visitors the country hopes to attract need to travel great distances to get there in the first place. In the mid-1920s the voyage from Southampton to Cape Town took seventeen days and cost £140 first class. See Markham, "South African Riviera."

79. The politics surrounding the establishment of the park are comprehensively covered by Jane Carruthers in "Dissecting the Myth," "Creating a National Park, 1910 to 1926," and *Kruger National Park*. Although Kruger Park was the culmination of decades of work by conservationists and administrators who were broadly colonial national in their allegiances, some of its greatest opponents were Johannesburg-based English-speaking farmers and landowners. Its naming, on the other hand, was a conciliatory gesture toward increasingly powerful Afrikaner Nationalist sensibilities.

80. See, for instance, Churchill, "South Africa's National Park"; and Hamilton, "A Holiday in Your Homeland." The Giant's Castle area was declared a game preserve in 1903. Early interest in the Drakensberg was clearly linked to the appeal of cool, elevated locations as retreats in a hot climate, as well as literary fascination with the transcendent isolation offered by the mountains of Africa; see, for instance, Wittenberg, "Ruwenzori." For an early account of the Drakensberg, see March, "Winter on the Drakensberg." The area only became generally accessible after the branch line to Bergville was completed in 1914. Hewitt, "25 Years of Development of Tourist Attractions in South Africa."

81. It was not until after World War II, when improved medicine and pesticides made the Lowveld safely habitable year round, that it was permanently inhabited by Europeans.

82. The *Eastern Province Herald*, Port Elizabeth, 21 February 1929, reported that "American tourists are not very much interested in South Africa's cities—they can see the finest cities in the world in the States, but they realize that South Africa has something unique to offer them. They are primarily interested in the scenery of this country, and the wilder it is the better." Carruthers argues that the declaration of Kruger Park was encouraged by the success of the first United States national parks in 1916 ("Creating a National Park," 207). For more on American tourism to South Africa during this period, see J. B. Wolf, "Grand Tour."

83. This shift was clearly signaled by the difference between the landscape murals in the Pretoria Station of 1912, and those in the Johannesburg Station, installed in 1932. In the former, signs of inhabitation and productive use are omnipresent; in the latter they are confined to few images. N. J. Coetzee, *Pierneef, Land, and Landscape*, 12.

84. Bunn, "Relocations."

85. See, for instance, Devitt, "Sabie Game Reserve in Fascinating Story." The most notable wildlife photographer was Paul Selby.

86. On early tourism to the park, see Carruthers, *Kruger National Park*, 74–79. Although the park was visited by only 180 cars in 1928, by the late 1930s it was attracting 30,000 visitors annually; see Beinart and Coates, *Environment and History*, 78.

87. Carruthers, *Kruger National Park*, 77–78.

88. See, for instance, J. M. Coetzee, "Picturesque and the South African Landscape," in *White Writing*, 36–62; and David Bunn, "'Our Wattled Cot.'"

89. See Marks, "Myth of the Empty Land."

90. R.A.W., "Travelling by Train," 1146. The distance of African settlements from railway lines not only erased Africans from white consciousness but also effectively made markets inaccessible to them. Pirie, "Racial Segregation on South African Trains," 8.

91. The depiction of Africans as exotics particularly appealed to overseas visitors. See Wolf, "A Grand Tour," 107; and "South Africa through American Spectacles." The tendency for train travel to encourage the imaginative erasure of the indigenous population from the landscape is captured in the account of one railway traveler elsewhere in Africa at this time: "The traveler is so carried away by his contemplation of nature's scenery that he can no longer bear human presence. Even the native may become a disturbing element, especially if he is 'bastardized'—in other words, when his poses and way of dress are more like the white man, so that he too becomes an alien element no longer harmony with nature." Quoted in Monti, *Africa Then*, 83.

92. R.A.W., "Travelling by Train," 1146.

93. D. Wolf, *American Space*, 7.

94. Lee, *To the Bitter End*, 12.

95. Mitchell, *Landscape and Power*, 15.

96. See Roderick Peattie, "Veld Is the Heartland," in *Struggle on the Veld*, 23–39.

97. As Said wrote of European appropriation of the Arabian Desert: "[It] appears as historically barren and retarded as it is geographically, [and is] thus considered to be a locale about which one can make statements regarding the past in exactly the same form [and with the same content] that one makes regarding the present." Said, *Orientalism*, 235.

98. For an alternative reading of settler cultural memory, see Bunn, "Whited Sepulchres."

99. Charles Maier, quoted in Osborne, "Interpreting a Nation's Identity," 251.

100. Peattie, *Struggle on the Veld*, 22. Peattie's observation was a response to Olive Schreiner's eulogy to "the Boer": "The little brown house on the plain, where the stranger met so stately and kindly a welcome, and the young South African grew up between his parents' knees, loving South African plains and kopjes dearer than life—will have passed away forever. It will have gone with the springbok and the koodoo and the eland and the lion, and with all the charm and poetry of this South Africa of ours, that we have loved so. The old krantzes will still look down from the flat mountain tops, and the blue sky stretch above all; but the Africa we have known will have gone forever. Men will not know then what it was we loved so." Schreiner, *Thoughts on South Africa*, 320.

101. Inglis, "Landscape as Popular Culture," 208.

102. On a similar relationship in the United States, see Weiss, "No Man's Garden."

103. *Travel in South Africa*, xviii.

104. Markham, "South African Riviera," 205.

105. See Sontag, *On Photography*, 71.

106. Although such conservationist agendas had been important in the early use of photography (see, for instance, Taylor, *Dream of England*) and found its equivalents in South Africa (for example, in the work of Arthur Elliot), there is little evidence of it in SAR&H publications until 1929, when a booklet entitled *Historic South Africa* was published, mostly for overseas distribution.

107. As Sontag argues, once something has entered into the world of images, "it has happened, and . . . will forever happen in that way." *On Photography*, 168.

108. This shifting valuation of the country's landscapes was echoed in 1929 by the introduction of excursion fares from the coast to the Transvaal (i.e., the "heart of the veld").

109. Bennion, "Call of South Africa"; Speight, "True Land of Hope and Glory"; F. Bell, "South Africa and the Lure of the Sun."

110. Urry, *Tourist Gaze*, 1, 11–12.

111. Here I use the term "transitional object" in Winnicott's definition, that is, an object outside of the self that is heavily used and therefore deeply familiar and invested as personal property, and through which the self differentiates itself from others.

112. For an expanded discussion of these photographs, see Foster, "Capturing and Losing the Lie of the Land."

113. As one article argues, "a railway carriage is nearly the only place where you can see, in perfect comfort, every kind of atmospheric effect over a broad expanse of changing country." R.A.W., "Travelling by Train," 1147.

114. Schivelbusch, *Railway Journey*, 59.

115. See Samuel, "Introduction," ix.

Chapter 10: The Life and Afterlife of a Contrapuntal Subjectivity

1. Jacobs, *Edge of Empire*, 40. Jacobs is paraphrasing Homi Bhabha's arguments in "Postcolonial Authority and Postcolonial Guilt."

2. See Lester, "Historical Geographies of Imperialism," 101.

3. Bender, "Introduction," 14.

4. See, for instance, Baucom, *Out of Place*.

5. Schwarz, "Romance of the Veld," 73. For a recent, comprehensive overview of twentieth-century relations between Britain and South Africa, see Hyams and Henshaw, *Lion and the Springbok*.

6. J. M. Coetzee, *White Writing*, 4.

7. Eric Hirsch argues that this dialectic is latent in all cultural appropriation of landscape. See "Landscape, Between Place and Space," 4.

8. Schwarz, "Romance of the Veld," 65.

9. *Webster's New World Dictionary*, 1997 edition.

10. Bunn, "Whited Sepulchres," 99.

11. Baker, for example, was one of eleven children, and his parents couldn't afford to send him to proper schools. He came to South Africa after apprenticing himself to an architect in Britain.

12. L. Phillips, *Some Reminiscences*, 182.

13. This frequently invoked phrase comes from Rudyard Kipling's elegy to Cecil John Rhodes, "The Burial," written to mark his interment in the Matopos in 1902, and part of which is inscribed on Rhodes Memorial in Cape Town.

14. Liebson, "South Africa of Fiction."

15. S. Dubow, "Colonial Nationalism," 76.

16. Colquhon, "Concept of Regionalism," 15.

17. According to Miles Ogborn, "Modernity's geographies are . . . made in relationship between places and across spaces. . . . This has tended to be understood as the 'exportation' of modernity from the center to the periphery, both for the metropole and the empire, and for the city and the country. This conceptualization, however, ignores the crucial ways in which these geographies of connection are moments in the making of modernities, rather than being matters of their transfer or imposition." See Ogborn, *Spaces of Modernity*, 19.

18. Derrida's formulation in *Other Heading*, 20, quoted in Jacobs, *Edge of Empire*, 58.

19. See, for instance, Lambert, "South African British, or Dominion South Africans?" 208–9.

20. Alston, *Heart of the Veld*, 220.

21. J. M. Coetzee, *White Writing*, 5.

22. Schwartz, "Romance of the Veld," 85.

23. On this politically debilitating thread in white society, see Butler, *Essays and Lectures, 1949–1991*; and Rich, *Hope and Despair*.

24. This effect was strengthened as Afrikaans became increasingly politicized, policed, and purified after 1930, when cultural functionaries sought to purge the language of "anglicisms" and suppress the fact that it was also the mother tongue of many South Africans of mixed ancestry.

25. Jacobson, *Time and Time Again*, 8.

26. Schwarz, "Romance of the Veld," 65. Buchan, *Pilgrim's Way*, 17.

27. See, for instance, Shepheard, *Cultivated Wilderness, or, What Is Landscape?* 139.

28. Derrida, *Other Heading*, 11, quoted in Jacobs, *Edge of Empire*, 58.

29. Indeed, South Africanism could be seen as a precursor to what David Kaplan describes as "modern trans-national, bi-focal identities that are not tied to specific places or regions, simultaneously referencing 'supranational' as well as 'sub-national' entities and institutions." See Kaplan, "Territorial Identities and Geographic Scale," 42–43.

30. For a discussion of the literary appropriation of the South African landscape, see J. M. Coetzee, *White Writing*; Gray, *Southern African Literature*; Boehmer, Chrisman, and Parker, *Altered State?*; Rich, "Romance and the Development of the South African Novel"; Watson, *Selected Essays, 1980–1990*; Butler, *Essays and Lectures, 1949–1991*.

31. J. M. Coetzee, *White Writing*, 176, 9, 170.

32. I am indebted to Jessica Dubow for this insight.

33. J. M. Coetzee, *White Writing*, 177.

34. Gaston Bachelard coined the term "intimate immensity" to describe the way the sweeping horizons of open landscapes give wing to thought, imagination, and dreams. See Bachelard, *Poetics of Space*, 183–210.

35. Bunn, "Whited Sepulchres," 98.

36. Here I draw on Daniel Mendelsohn's meditation on the intersection between place and gay identity, and his emphasis on the Greek roots of the word "paradoxical": *para* ("against") and *doxa* ("expectation"). See Mendelsohn, *Elusive Embrace*, 30–31.

37. Mindful that the memorial's location made it difficult for it to fulfill its intended function

of encouraging white South Africans to be inspired by the joint sacrifice made by English and Dutch South Africans at Delville Wood, the Memorial Committee proposed a number of projects to bring the "idea of Delville Wood" to the South Africa itself. On this topic, see Foster, "Creating a *Temenos.*"

38. S. Dubow, "Imagining the New South Africa," 78.

39. Designed by Baker in a style reminiscent of Delville Wood, and decorated by many South African artists. On this project, which was completed and opened in 1933; see Baker, *Architecture and Personalities*, 131–34; R. MacNab, *Story of South Africa House*; and Freschi, "Fine Art of Fusion."

40. For some, post–World War I Britain was a "sick, blighted land," uniquely cold, gray, and unsympathetic to the "life-force," and those who could fled England for hotter climates. See Tindall, *Countries of the Mind*, 182. On the interwar retreat into a "little England" mentality see for instance Bishop, *Archetypal Constable*, 115–40.

41. R. Williams, *City and the Country*, 98.

42. Schwarz, "Romance of the Veld," 87.

43. Lambert, "South African British, or Dominion South Africans?" 217–18.

44. Lambert, "South African British, or Dominion South Africans?" 203.

45. R. W. Johnson, "Jingoes," 30.

46. Although Hertzog abandoned the secession clause as part of his party's political platform after 1926 (the year of the Balfour Declaration), it returned in 1935 with the formation of the Purified National Party. On the flag controversy, some whites wanted to retain the Union Jack as the national flag, others to abandon it entirely. A compromise engineered by the governor-general that incorporated the Union Jack was the end result. By comparison, Canada and Australia continued to use the Union Jack without too much controversy until 1965 and 1950, respectively.

47. Lambert, "South African British, or Dominion South Africans?" 203.

48. Barnard, "Encountering Adamastor," 193.

49. Omissi and Thompson, "Investigating the Impact of the War," 6.

50. Nasson, "South African/Boer War," 115.

51. Grundlingh, "War in 20th Century Afrikaner Consciousness," 26.

52. The 1932 Carnegie Commission found one-third of Afrikaners "desperately poor" and another third "poor." In the 1930s, most unskilled, blue-collar jobs held by whites were held by Afrikaners. See Lester, *From Colonization to Democracy*, 96.

53. On the later development of Afrikaner identity, see February, *Afrikaners of South Africa*.

54. Barnard, "Encountering Adamastor," 199.

55. N. J. Coetzee, *Pierneef, Land, and Landscape*, 24.

56. N. J. Coetzee, *Pierneef, Land, and Landscape*, 24.

57. Mitchell, "Holy Landscape," 205.

58. J. M. Coetzee, *White Writing*, 175.

59. J. M. Coetzee, *White Writing*, 4. This of course collapses Coetzee's detailed analysis of the Afrikaners' imaginative relationship to the family farm, for which see "Farm Novel and Plaasroman," and "Farm Novels of C. M. Van den Heever," in the same book.

60. W. J. T. Mitchell uses this quote from Wordsworth to emphasize his point that the promised land is the greatest collective landscape mirage the human imagination has projected for itself ("Holy Landscape," 213).

61. I am indebted to Jessica Dubow for this insight.

62. Henshaw, "John Buchan from the 'Borders' to the 'Berg,'" 22.

63. See Kaplan, "Territorial Identities and Geographic Scale."

64. Urbanization and industrialization grew apace as the South African economy continued to be unusually dependent on foreign trade and on trade with Western Europe in particular. See Nattrass, *South African Economy*, 268.

65. This is echoed by Nico Coetzee, who argues that the idea that Afrikaners had some innate link to the land was very much an ideological construction, citing the fact that during the appalling rural poverty of the 1920s and 1930s, most poorer Afrikaner farmers remained indifferent to anything other than the land's potential as a speculative commodity. These attitudes led to severe soil erosion and environmental decline, further accelerating the exodus to cities. See *Pierneef, Land, and Landscape*, 28–29.

66. Schwarz, "Romance of the Veld," 77.

67. Schwarz, "Romance of the Veld," 100.

68. Thus, Africans were not permitted to walk the public roads in Kruger National Park in the 1920s. See Carruthers, "Nationhood and National Parks," 128.

69. See for instance Bunn, "Comparative Barbarism," 38–42.

70. Vesely defines praxis as "a situation where peoples are not only doing or experiencing something, but which also includes things which contribute to the fulfilment of human life." Vesely, "Architecture and the Poetics of Representation," 32.

71. Thus, "praxis is always situated between ideas and nature, and serves as a vehicle of their unity." See Vesely, "Architecture and the Poetics of Representation," 35.

72. Leatherbarrow, *Roots of Architectural Invention*, 33–41.

73. As Leatherbarrow argues, "action is primary. . . . The situation, not the object . . . is the underlying basis for human significance." *Roots of Architectural Invention*, 5.

74. Casey, "Body, Self and Landscape," 405–6.

75. As for instance in Barthes's description of a visit to Tokyo, in which the urban landscape's intense visual and corporeal qualities mediate a powerful "writability." See Duncan and Duncan, "Roland Barthes and the Secret History of Landscape," 33.

76. As one (ex-)South African author wrote: "As so many others had, in so many varying climates, I found it meant the reality of the countries from which the books and movies came that I was compelled to doubt; this undescribed and uncertifiable place where not a single thing, from the sand underfoot to the occasional savage thunderstorm overhead, was as other places were." See Jacobson, *Time and Time Again*, 8.

77. Bourdieu, quoted in Shields, *Places on the Margin*, 96.

78. Though the evanescent, distanced pleasures of early twentieth-century train travel have been recuperated by luxury train tourism aimed at international tourists. See, for instance, "La vie est un long train tranquille," *Le Figaro*, 27 July 2004, 24.

79. We cannot, as de Certeau insisted, truly inhabit places that are not in some way already "haunted." De Certeau, *Practice of Everyday Life*, 108.

80. Shields, *Places on the Margin*, 14.

81. Gordimer, *Conservationist*, 24–25.

82. Proust, quoted in Benjamin, "On Some Motifs in Baudelaire," 155.

83. Harrison, "Effects of Landscape," 221–27.

84. "With the appearance of the trace, of distance and mediation, we leave the realm of true memory and enter that of history." Nora, "Between Memory and History," 9.

BIBLIOGRAPHY

Acocks, J. P. H. *Veld Types of South Africa*. 3rd ed. Pretoria: South African Government Printer, 1988.

Addleson, Jill, ed. *The Everard Phenomenon: An Exhibition of Paintings by the Everard Family*. Durban: Durban Art Gallery, ca. 2002.

Adorno, T. W. *Aesthetic Theory*. Translated by C. Lenhardt. London: Routledge & Kegan Paul, 1984.

Alberti, Leonbattista. *The Ten Books of Architecture: 1755 Leoni Edition*. New York: Dover, 1986.

Aldaheff, V. *South Africa in Two World Wars: A Newspaper History*. Cape Town: Don Nelson, 1979.

Alexander, F. L. *Art in South Africa since 1900*. Cape Town: Balkema, 1972.

Alexander, Thomas. *John Dewey's Theory of Art, Experience, and Nature: The Horizons of Feeling*. Albany: State University of New York Press, 1987.

Alpers, Svetlana. *The Art of Describing: Dutch Painting in the Seventeenth Century*. London: John Murray, 1983.

Alston, Madeline. *From the Heart of the Veld*. London: John Lane, 1916.

Anderson, Andrew A. *25 Years in a Waggon*. Cape Town: C. Struik, 1974. First published 1888 by Chapman & Hall.

Anderson, Benedict. *Imagined Communities: Reflections of the Origins and Spread of Nationalism*. London: Verso, 1991.

Andrews, Malcolm. *Landscape and Western Art*. Oxford: Oxford University Press, 1999.

Appleton, Jay. *The Experience of Landscape*. Chichester: John Wiley, 1976.

———. *Symbolism of Habitat: An Interpretation of Landscape in the Arts*. Seattle: Washington University Press, 1990.

Arnold, Marion. "Bertha Everard: The Ties That Bind." In *The Everard Phenomenon: An Exhibition of Paintings by the Everard Family*, edited by J. Addleson, 55–66. Durban: Durban Art Gallery, 2000.

Aron, Helen, Arnold Benjamin, Clive M. Chipkin, and Shirley Zar. *Park Town, 1892–1972: A Social and Pictorial History*. Johannesburg: Studio Thirty Five, 1972.

Bachelard, Gaston. *The Poetics of Space*. Boston: Beacon Press, 1974.

Baden-Powell, R. S. S. *Scouting for Boys*. 29th ed. London: Pearson, 1955.

———. *Sketches in Mafeking and East Africa*. London: Smith, Elder & Co., 1907.

Baker, Herbert. "The Architectural Needs of South Africa." *State* 1 (May 1909): 512–24.

———. *Architecture and Personalities*. London: Country Life, 1944.

———. *Cecil Rhodes, by His Architect, Herbert Baker*. London: Oxford University Press/Humphrey Milford, 1934.

———. "The Origin of Old Cape Architecture." In *Old Colonial Houses and the Cape of Good Hope*, edited by Alys Fane Trotter, 1–7. London: B. T. Batsford, 1900.

307

Balfour, Alice. *1200 Miles in a Waggon*. London: E. Arnold, 1895.

Barnard, W. S. "Encountering Adamastor: Early 20th Century South African Regional Geographies and Their Writers." In *Text and Image: The Social Construction of Regional Knowledges*, edited by A. Buttimer, S. Brunn, and U. Wardenga, 192–204. Leipzig: Institut für Länderkunde, 1999.

Barnes, T. J., and J. S. Duncan, eds. *Writing Worlds: Discourse, Text and Metaphor in the Presentation of Landscape*. London: Routledge, 1992.

Baucom, Ian. *Out of Place: Englishness, Empire and the Locations of Identity*. New York: Princeton University Press, 1999.

Bayoumi, Moustafa, and Andrew Rubin, eds. *The Edward Said Reader*. New York: Vintage Books, 2000.

Beaumont, Jacqueline. "The Making of a War Correspondent: Lionel James of *The Times*." In *The Impact of the South African War*, edited by David Omissi and Andrew Thompson, 124–37. Basingstoke: Palgrave, 2002.

Beer, Gillian. *Open Fields: Science in Cultural Encounter*. Oxford: Clarendon Press, 1996.

Beinart, William. "Empire, Hunting and Ecological Change." *Past and Present* 128 (1990): 162–86.

———. "Soil Erosion, Conservationism and Ideas about Development: A Southern Africa Exploration, 1910–1960." *Journal of Southern African Studies* 11, no. 1 (October 1984): 52–83.

———. *Twentieth Century South Africa*. Cape Town: Oxford University Press, 1994.

Beinart, William, and Peter Coates. *Environment and History: The Taming of Nature in the USA and South Africa*. London: Oxford University Press, 1995.

Beinart, W., P. Delius, and S. Trapido, eds. *Putting a Plough to the Ground: Accumulation and Dispossession in Rural South Africa, 1850–1930*. Braamfontein: Ravan Press, 1986.

Bell, Fred. "South Africa and the Lure of the Sun." *SAR&H Magazine*, February 1928, 228–36.

Bell, Morag. "'Citizenship Not Charity': Violet Markham on Nature, Society and the State in Britain and South Africa." In *Geography and Imperialism, 1820–1940*, edited by M. Bell, R. Butlin, and M. Heffernan, 189–220. Manchester: Manchester University Press, 1995.

———. "'The Pestilence That Walketh in Darkness': Imperial Health, Gender and Images of South Africa." *Transactions of the Institute of British Geographers: New Series*. 18 (1993): 327–41.

———. "A Woman's Place in 'a White Man's Country': Rights, Duties and Citizenship for the 'New' South Africa, ca. 1902." *Ecumene* 2, no. 2 (1995): 129–48.

Bender, Barbara. "Introduction." In *Contested Landscapes: Movement, Exile and Place*, edited by B. Bender and M. Winer, 1–18. Oxford: Berg, 2001.

Bender, B., and M. Winer, eds. *Contested Landscapes: Movement, Exile and Place*. Oxford: Berg, 2001.

Benjamin, Walter. "On Some Motifs in Baudelaire." In *Illuminations*, edited by H. Arendt, translated by H. Zohn, 152–96. London: Fontana, 1992.

Bennion, B. "The Call of South Africa." *SAR&H Magazine*, December 1923, 1186–89.

Bensusan, A. D. *Silver Images: A History of Photography in Africa*. Cape Town: Howard Timmins, 1966.

Berleant, Arnold. *Living in the Landscape: Towards an Aesthetics of Environment*. Lawrence: University of Kansas Press, 1997.

Berman, Esme. *Art and Artists of South Africa: An Illustrated Biographical Dictionary and Historical Survey of Painters and Graphic Artists since 1875*. Cape Town: Balkema, 1983.

———. *The Story of South African Painting*. Cape Town: Balkema, 1975.

Berman, Patricia. "Body and Body Politic in Edvard Munch's *Bathing Men*." In *The Body Imaged: The Human Form and Visual Culture since the Renaissance*, edited by K. Adler and M. Pointon, 71–83. Cambridge: Cambridge University Press, 1993.

Berque, Augustin. *Médiance: De Milieux en paysages*. Montpellier: Documentation Francaise, 1990.

Bhabha, Homi. "Postcolonial Authority and Postcolonial Guilt." In *Cultural Studies*, edited by L. Grossberg, C. Nelson, and P. Treichler, 56–68. London: Routledge, 1992.

Bierman, Barrie. "The Sources of Designs for Historic Buildings at the Cape." In *The Preservation and Restoration of Historic Buildings in South Africa*, edited by R. F. Immelman and G. D. Quinn. Cape Town: Balkema/Cape Provincial Institute of Architects, 1968.

Bigelow, Poultney. *White Man's Africa*. New York: Harpers, 1898.

Bishop, Peter. *An Archetypal Constable: National Identity and the Geography of Nostalgia*. London: Athlone Press, 1995.

————. *The Myth of Shangri-La: Tibet, Travel Writing and the Western Creation of Sacred Landscape*. Berkeley: University of California Press, 1989.

————. "Rhetoric, Memory, and Power: Depth Psychology and Postmodern Geography." *Environment and Planning D: Society and Space* 10 (1992): 5–22.

Blanch, M. D. "British Society and the War." In *The South African War: The Anglo-Boer War, 1899–1903*, edited by P. Warwick and S. Spies, 210–38. Harlow: Longman, 1980.

Bloomer, Kent C., and Charles W. Moore. *Body, Memory, and Architecture*. New Haven: Yale University Press, 1977.

Blume, Mary. *Cote d'Azur: Inventing the French Riviera*. London: Thames & Hudson, 1992.

Boddam-Whetham, R. E. *A Garden in the Veld*. Wynberg: Speciality Press of South Africa, 1933.

Boehmer, E., L. Chrisman, and K. Parker, eds. *Altered State? Writing and South Africa*. Sydney: Dangaroo Press, 1994.

Bois, Yves-Alain. "A Picturesque Stroll around Clara-Clara." Translated by J. Shepley. In *October: The First Decade: 1976–1986*, edited by A. Michelson et al., 343–72. Cambridge, MA: MIT Press, 1987.

Bolitho, S. "The South African: Development of National Character." *The African World Annual*, 1926: 147.

Bond, John. *They Were South Africans*. Cape Town: Oxford University Press, 1956.

Bonner, Philip, ed. *Holding Their Ground: Class, Locality and Culture in 19th and 20th Century South Africa*. Johannesburg: University of Witwatersrand History Workshop, 1989.

Bordo, Jonathan. "Jack Pine: Wilderness Sublime or the Erasure of the Aboriginal Presence from the Landscape." *Journal of Canadian Studies/Revue d'études canadiennes* 27, no. 4 (Winter 1992–93): 98–128.

————. "Picture and Witness at the Site of the Wilderness." *Critical Inquiry* 26, no. 2 (Winter 2000): 224–47.

————. "The Terra Nullius of Wilderness: Colonialist Landscape Art and the So-Called American Exception.'" *International Journal of Canadian Studies* 15 (Spring 1997): 13–36.

Bouchard, Gérard. "The Formation of Cultures and Nations in the 'New World': A Comparative View." Plenary Paper, Eleventh International Conference of Historical Geographers, Quebec, August 2002.

Bouman, A. C., and J. H. De Bussy. *Painters of South Africa*. Cape Town: Haum, 1948.

Bourassa, Steven. *The Aesthetics of Landscape*. London: Belhaven, 1991.

Bourke, Joanna. *Dismembering the Male: Men's Bodies, Britain and the Great War*. London: Reaktion, 1996.

Bowen, Barbara C. "The Rhetoric of *The Essays*." In *Approaches to Teaching Montaigne's Essays*, edited by P. Henry, 41–47. New York: Modern Languages Association, 1994.

Brace, Catherine. "Finding England Everywhere: Regional Identity and the Construction of National Identity, 1890–1940." *Ecumene* 6, no. 1 (1996): 90–109.

Brennan, Timothy. "The National Longing for Form." In *Nation and Narration*, edited by H. Bhabha, 44–70. London: Routledge, 1990.

Brook, Peter. *The Empty Space*. Harmondsworth: Penguin, 1972.

Brown, A. S., and G. Gordon Brown, eds. *Guide to South Africa: For the Use of Tourists, Sportsmen, Invalids and Settlers*. London: Castle Mail Packets Co., 1896.

Brown, G. Gordon, ed. *South and Eastern African Year Book and Guide for 1938 with Atlas (44th issue)*. London: Sampson Low, Marston & Co., 1938.

Bryce, James. *Impressions of South Africa*. London: Macmillan, 1898.

Bryden, P., A. Guy, and M. Harding. *Ashes and Blood: The British Army in South Africa, 1795–1914*. London: National Army Museum, 1999.

Buchan, John. *The Africa Colony: Studies in Reconstruction*. London: Blackwell, 1903.

————. *Greenmantle*. London: Hodder & Stoughton, 1916.

————. *History of the South African Forces in France*. Cape Town: Maskew Miller, 1921.

————. *Memory Hold-the-Door*. London: Hodder & Stoughton, 1940.

————. *Pilgrim's Way: An Essay in Recollection*. Cambridge: Riverside Press, 1939.

————. *Prester John*. London: T. Nelson, 1910.

————. *The Thirty-Nine Steps*. London: W. Blackwood & Sons, 1915.

Bunkse, E. "Humboldt and an Aesthetic Tradition in Geography." *Geographical Review* 71, no. 2 (1981): 127–46.

Bunn, David. "A Bushveld Golgotha: Disease, Cattle and Permeable Borders in the South-western Kruger National Park." Unpublished paper, Historical Geographies of Southern Africa Symposium, University of Sussex, April 2002.

————. "Comparative Barbarism: Game Reserves, Sugar Plantations, and the Modernization of the South African Landscape." In *Text, Theory, Space*, edited by K. Darian-Smith, L. Gunner, and S. Nuttall, 37–52. London: Routledge, 1996.

————. "'Our Wattled Cot': Mercantile and Domestic Space in Thomas Pringle's African Landscapes." In *Landscape and Power*, edited by W. J. T. Mitchell, 127–73. Chicago: Chicago University Press, 1994.

————. "Relocations: Landscape Theory, South African Landscape Practice, and the Transmission of Political Value." *Pretexts* 4, no. 2 (Summer 1993): 44–67.

————. "The Sleep of the Brave: Graves as Sites and Signs in the Colonial Eastern Cape." In *Images and Empires*, edited by P. Landau and D. Kaspin, 56–89. Berkeley: University of California Press, 1998.

————. "To the Valley Below: Good Shepherds, Game Wardens and the Uses of Settler Landscape Prospect." Unpublished conference paper, ca. 1994.

————. "Whited Sepulchres: On the Reluctance of Monuments." In *Blank————: Architecture, Apartheid and After*, edited by H. Judin and I. Vladislavić, 92–117. Cape Town: David Philip; Rotterdam: NAi, 2000.

Burton, A. R. E., ed. *Land Settlement in the Transvaal: Handbook for Settlers*. Pretoria, 1902.

Butler, Guy. *Essays and Lectures, 1949–1991*. Edited by Stephen Watson. Cape Town: David Phillip, 1994.

Buzard, James. *The Beaten Track: European Tourism, Literature and the Ways to Culture, 1800–1918*. Oxford: Clarendon Press, 1993.

Carruthers, Jane. "Creating a National Park, 1910 to 1926." *Journal of Southern African Studies* 15, no. 2 (January 1989): 188–216.

————. "Dissecting the Myth: Paul Kruger and the National Park." *Journal of Southern African Studies* 20, no. 2 (June 1994): 263–84.

————. "Friedrich Jeppe: Mapping the Transvaal, ca. 1850–1899." *Journal of Southern African Studies* 29, no. 4 (2003): 955–75.

————. *The Kruger National Park: A Social and Political History*. Pietermaritzburg: University of Natal Press, 1995.

————. "Nationhood and National Parks: Comparative Examples from the Post-imperial Experience." In *Ecology and Empire: Environmental History of Settler Societies*, edited by T. Griffiths and L. Robbin, 125–38. Edinburgh: Keele University Press, 1997.

Carter, Paul. *Living in a New Country: History, Travelling, and Language*. London: Faber & Faber, 1992.

————. *The Road to Botany Bay: An Exploration of Landscape and History*. London/New York: Faber, 1987.

Cartwright, A. P. *The First South African: The Life and Times of Sir Percy Fitzpatrick*. Cape Town: Purnell, 1971.

Cartwright, Justin. "South African Stories." In *The Atlas of Literature*, edited by M. Bradbury, 294–97. London: De Agostini Editions, 1996.

Casey, Edward. "Body, Self and Landscape: A Geo-philosophical Inquiry into the Place-World." In *Textures of Place: Exploring Humanist Geographies*, edited by P. Adams, S. Hoelscher, and K. Till, 403–25. Minneapolis: University of Minnesota Press, 2001.

————. *Getting Back into Place: Toward a Renewed Understanding of the Place-World*. Bloomington: Indiana University Press, 1993.

Certeau, Michel de. *The Practice of Everyday Life*. Translated by S. Rendall. Berkeley: University of California Press, 1984.

Chard, Chloë. *Pleasure and Guilt on the Grand Tour: Travel Writing and Imaginative Geography, 1600–1830*. Manchester: Manchester University Press, 1999.

Chemetoff, Alexandre. "Des paysages." *L'Architecture d'Aujourd'hui* 303 (February 1997): 60–73.

Chilvers, H. A. *The Seven Wonders of South Africa*. Johannesburg: SAR&H Administration, 1929.

Chipkin, Clive. *Johannesburg Style: Architecture and Society, 1880s–1960s*. Cape Town: David Phillip, 1993.

Christopher, A. J. *The Atlas of Apartheid*. London: Routledge, 1994.

———. *South Africa: The World's Landscapes*. London: Longman, 1982.

———. *Southern Africa: Studies in Historical Geography Series*. Folkestone: Dawson, 1976.

Churchill, Frank. "South Africa's National Park: The Beauty and Attraction of the Drakensberg." *SAR&H Magazine,* December 1919, 854–63.

Clark, John. "Social Ecology: Introduction." In *Environmental Philosophy: From Animal Rights to Radical Ecology*, edited by M. Zimmerman et al., 345–53. Englewood Cliffs, NJ: Prentice Hall, 1993.

Clark, Kenneth, ed. *John Ruskin: Selected Writings*. Harmondsworth: Penguin, 1991.

Clark, Steve, ed. *Travel Writing and Empire: Postcolonial Theory in Transit*. London: Zed Books, 1999.

Clark, T. J. *The Painting of Modern Life: Paris in the Art of Manet and His Followers*. London: Thames & Hudson, 1985.

———. "Reservations of the Marvellous." *London Review of Books*, 22 June 2000, 3–9.

Claval, Paul. "From Michelet to Braudel: Personality, Identity and the Organization of France." In *Geography and National Identity*, edited by D. Hooson, 39–57. Oxford: Blackwell, 1994.

Cobb, Edith. *The Ecology of Imagination in Childhood*. New York: Columbia University Press, 1977.

Coetzee, J. M. *White Writing: On the Culture of Letters in South Africa*. New Haven: Yale University Press, 1988.

Coetzee, N. J. *Pierneef, Land, and Landscape/Land en Landskap: The Johannesburg Station Panels in Context*. Johannesburg: Johannesburg Art Gallery, 1992.

Colomina, Beatriz. "The Split Wall: Domestic Voyeurism." In *Sexuality and Space*, edited by B. Colomina, 73–130. New York: Princeton Architectural Press, 1992.

Colquhoun, Alan. "The Concept of Regionalism." In *Post Colonial Spaces*, edited by G. B. Nalbantoglu and C. T. Wong, 13–23. New York: Princeton Architectural Press, 1997.

Colquhoun, Archibald R. *The Africander Land*. London: John Murray, 1906.

Constant, Caroline. "From the Virgilian Dream to Chandigarh: Le Corbusier and the Modern Landscape." In *Denatured Visions: Landscape and Culture in the Twentieth Century*, edited by S. Wrede and W. H. Adams, 79–93. New York: MoMA, 1991.

Conway, Jill Ker. *True North: A Memoir*. London: Hutchinson, 1994.

Cope, R. K. "South Africa: Contemporary Painting and Sculpture." *Studio* 108, no. 499 (October 1934): 130–39.

Corner, James. "The Agency of Mapping: Speculation, Critique & Invention." In *Mappings*, edited by D. Cosgrove, 213–52. London: Reaktion, 1999.

———. "The Obscene (American) Landscape." In *Landscape Transformed*, edited by Michael Spens, 10–13. London: Academy Editions, 1996.

———. "Representation and Landscape: Drawing and Making in the Landscape Medium." *Word & Image* 8, no. 3 (July–September 1992): 243–73.

Cosgrove, Denis. "Environmental Thought and Action: Pre-modern and Post-modern." *Trans. Inst. of Br. Geog.*, n.s., 15 (1990): 344–58.

———. "Habitable Earth: Wilderness, Empire and Race in America." In *Wild Ideas*, edited by D. Rothenburg, 27–41. Minneapolis: University of Minnesota Press, 1995.

———. "John Ruskin and the Geographical Imagination." *Geographical Review* 69 (1979): 43–62.

———. "*Mappa mundi, anima mundi*: Imaginative Mapping and Environmental Representation." In *Ruskin and Environment*, edited by M. Wheeler, 76–101. Manchester: Manchester University Press, 1995.

———. "The Picturesque City: Nature, Nations and the Urban since the 18th Century." In *City and Nature: Changing Relations in Space and Time*, ed. T. Kristensen et al., 45–58. Odense: Odense University Press, 1993.

———. *Social Formation and Symbolic Landscape*. Madison: University of Wisconsin Press, 1998.

Cosgrove, D., and S. Rycroft. "Regional Knowledge for Pedagogy and Planning: Dudley Stamp and the Land Utilization Survey." In *Text and Image: Social Construction of Regional Knowledges*, edited by A. Buttimer, S. Brunn, and U. Wardenga, 122–29. Leipzig: Institut für Länderkunde, 1999.

Couzens, Tim, and Landeg White, eds. *Literature and Society in South Africa*. Harlow: Longmans, 1984.

Cowan, N. "Photographs: Their History and Their Place in South African History." In *Africana Byways*, edited by Anna Smith, 9–24. Johannesburg: AD Donker, 1976.

Cox, Leslie. "South Africa's Riviera: An Unspoilt Coast of Enchantment." *SAR&H Magazine*, December 1924, 1234–38.

Cran, Marion. *The Gardens of Good Hope*. London: Herbert Jenkins, 1926.

Crandell, Gina. *Nature Pictorialized: The View in Landscape History*. Baltimore: The Johns Hopkins University Press, 1993.

Creese, Walter. "Yosemite National Park." In *The Crowning of the American Landscape: Eight Great Spaces and Their Buildings*, 99–134. New York: Princeton University Press, 1985.

Daniels, Stephen. *Fields of Vision: Landscape Imagery and National Identity in England and the United States*. Cambridge: Polity Press, 1992.

———. "The Making of Constable Country, 1880–1940." *Landscape Research* 16, no. 2 (1991): 9–17.

———. "On the Road with Humphrey Repton." *Journal of Garden History* 16, no. 4 (Autumn 1996): 170–91.

Daniels, Stephen, and Denis Cosgrove. "Spectacle and Text: Landscape Metaphors in Cultural Geography." In *Place/Culture/Representation*, edited by J. Duncan and D. Ley, 57–77. London: Routledge, 1993.

Deacon, Harriet. "The Place and Space of Illness: Climate and Garden as Metaphors in the Robben Island Medical Institutions." Institute for Historical Research, London, 29 July 1997. http://www.history.ac.uk/ihr/Focus/Medical/articles2.html.

De Kiewiet, C. W. *History of South Africa, Social and Economic*. London: Oxford University Press, 1946.

Derrida, Jacques. *The Other Heading: Reflections on Today's Europe*. Bloomington: Indiana University Press, 1992.

De Villiers, Rina. *J. H. Pierneef: Pretorian, Transvaler, South African*. Pretoria: Pretoria Art Museum/ City Council, 1986.

Devitt, Napier. "The Sabie Game Reserve in Fascinating Story," with sketches by Joyce Rutherfoord. *SAR&H Magazine*, October 1926, 1495–501.

Dewey, John. *Art as Experience*. London: Allen & Unwin, 1934.

Dodson, Belinda. "Dismantling Dystopia: New Cultural Geography for a New South Africa." In *The Geography of South Africa in a Changing World*, edited by R. Fox and K. Rowntree, 138–57. Oxford: Oxford University Press, 2000.

Domosh, Mona. *Invented Cities: The Creation of Landscape in Nineteenth-Century New York and Boston*. New York/London: Routledge, 1996.

———. "Those 'Gorgeous Incongruities': Polite Politics and Public Space on the Streets of Nineteenth-Century New York City." *Annals of the Association of American Geographers* 88, no. 2 (1998): 209–26.

Duara, Prasenjit. "Historicizing National Identity, Or Who Imagines What and When." In *Becoming National: A Reader*, edited by G. Eley and R. G. Suny, 151–77. Oxford: Oxford University Press, 1996.

Dubow, Jessica. "Rites of Passage: Travel and the Materiality of Vision at the Cape of Good Hope." In *Contested Landscapes: Movement, Exile and Place*, edited by B. Bender and M. Winer, 241–55. Oxford: Berg, 2001.

Dubow, Saul. "Colonial Nationalism, the Milner Kindergarten and the Rise of 'South Africanism', 1902–1910." *History Workshop Journal* 43 (Spring 1997): 53–86.

———. "A Commonwealth of Science: The British Association in South Africa, 1905 and 1929." In *Science and Society in Southern Africa*, edited by S. Dubow, 66–99. Manchester: Manchester University Press, 2000.

———. "Human Origins, Race Typology and the other Raymond Dart." *African Studies* 55, no. 1 (1996): 1–30.

———. "Imagining the New South Africa in the Era of Reconstruction." In *The Impact of the South African War*, edited by D. Omissi and A. Thompson, 76–95. Basingstoke: Palgrave, 2002.

———. *Racial Segregation and the Origins of Apartheid in South Africa, 1919–1936*. Basingstoke: Macmillan, 1989.

Dumas, Ann. "The Public Face of Landscape." In *Landscape of France: Impressionism and Its Rivals*, edited by J. House, 30–39. London: Hayward Gallery, 1995.

Duncan, James, and Nancy Duncan. "Ideology and Bliss: Roland Barthes and the Secret History of Landscape." In *Writing Worlds: Discourse, Text and Metaphor in the Presentation of Landscape*, edited by T. J. Barnes and J. S. Duncan, 18–37. London: Routledge, 1992.

Duncan, J., and D. Gregory, eds. *Writes of Passage: Reading Travel Writing*. London: Routledge, 1999.

Eddy, John, and Deryck Schreuder. "The Edwardian Empire." In *The Rise of Colonial Nationalism: Australia, New Zealand, Canada and South Africa First Assert Their Nationalities, 1880–1914*, edited by J. Eddy and D. Schreuder, 19–62. Sydney: Allen & Unwin, 1988.

Emery, Frank. *Marching Over Africa*. London: Hodder & Stoughton, 1986.

Enzensberger, H. M. "A Theory of Tourism." *New German Critique* 68 (Spring/Summer 1996): 117–35.

Evernden, Neil. "The Ambiguous Landscape." *Geographical Review* 71, no. 2 (1981): 147–57.

Fagan, Gwen. *Old Roses at the Cape of Good Hope*. Cape Town: Brëestraat-publikasies, 1989.

Fairbridge, Dorothea. *Along Cape Roads*. Cape Town: Maskew Miller, 1928.

———. *Gardens of South Africa*. London: A. & C. Black, 1924.

———. *Historic Houses of South Africa*. London: Oxford University Press; Cape Town: Maskew Miller, 1922.

———. *Lady Anne Barnard at the Cape of Good Hope, 1797–1802*. Oxford: Clarendon Press, 1924.

———. *Letters from the Cape by Lady Duff-Gordon*. Oxford: Oxford University Press, 1927.

———. *A Pilgrim's Way in South Africa*. London: Oxford University Press, 1928.

Faith, Nicholas. *The World the Railways Made*. London: Bodley Head, 1990.

Farinelli, Franco. "L'arguzia del paesaggio/The Wit of the Landscape." *Casabella* 575–6: *The Design of the Italian Landscape* (January/February 1991): 110–11.

February, Vernon. *The Afrikaners of South Africa*. London: Kegan Paul, 1991.

Fedorowich, Kent. "Anglicization and the Politicization of British Immigration to South Africa, 1899–1929." *Journal of Imperial and Commonwealth History* 19, no. 2 (1990): 222–46.

———. "The Weak Link in the Imperial Chain: South Africa, the Round Table and World War One." In *The Round Table: The Empire/Commonwealth and British Foreign Policy*, edited by A. Bosco and A. May, 137–58. London: Lothian Foundation Press, 1997.

Fermor, Sharon. "Movement and Gender in 16th Century Italian Painting." In *The Body Imaged: The Human Form and Visual Culture since the Renaissance*, edited by K. Adler and M. Pointon, 129–45. Cambridge: Cambridge University Press, 1993.

Ferreira, O. J. O., and E. Pretorius, et al., eds. *J. H. Pierneef: His Life and His Work*. Johannesburg: Perskor, 1990.

Fischer, Ernst. *The Necessity of Art: A Marxist Approach*. Translated by A. Bostock. Harmondsworth: Penguin, 1963.

Fisher, Roger, and Schalk Le Roux. *Die Afrikaanse Woning: Herdrukke uit 'Die Boervrou.'* Hammanskraal: Unibook, 1989.

Flemming, Leonard. *The Call of the Veld*. London: Hutchinson, 1924.

"Forty Years of Railway Service in South Africa: The Career of Sir William Hoy, K.C.B." *SAR&H Magazine*, March 1930.

Foster, Jeremy. "Capturing and Losing the Lie of the Land: Railway Photography and Colonial Nationalism in Early 20th Century South Africa." In *Picturing Place: Photography and the Geographical Imagination*, edited by J. Ryan and J. Schwartz, 141–61. London: I. B. Tauris, 2003.

———. "Creating a *Temenos*, Positing 'South Africanism': Material Memory, Landscape Practice, and the Circulation of Identity at Delville Wood." *Cultural Geographies* 11, no. 3 (2004): 259–90.

———. "'Land of Contrasts', or 'Home We Have Always Known'? The SAR&H Publicity Dept. and the Imaginary Geography of South African Nationhood, 1900–1930." *Journal of Southern African Studies* 29, no. 3 (2003): 657–80.

―――. "'Northward, Upward': The Cape-to-Rand Railway Journey as *lieu de memoire*, 1895–1945." *Journal of Historical Geography* 31 (2005): 296–315.

Foucault, Michel. *The Archaeology of Knowledge*. New York: Harper & Row, 1972.

―――. *Power/Knowledge: Selected Interviews and Other Writings*. Edited and translated by C. Gordon. New York: Pantheon, 1972.

Fransen, Hans. *A Cape Camera: Photographs from the Arthur Elliot Collection in the Cape Archives*. Parklands: AD Donker/Jonathan Ball, 1993.

Fraser, Maryna. *The Story of Two Cape Farms*. Johannesburg: Barlow Rand, 1981.

Fraser, M., and A. Jeeves. *All That Glittered: Selected Correspondence of Sir Lionel Phillips 1890–1924*. Cape Town/Oxford: Oxford University Press, 1977.

Freschi, Federico. "The Fine Art of Fusion: Race, Gender and the Politics of South Africanism as Reflected in the Decorative Program of South Africa House, London (1933)." *De Arte* 71 (2005): 14–34.

Fuller, Peter. *Art and Psychoanalysis*. London: Hogarth, 1980.

―――. "The Geography of Mother Nature." In *The Iconography of Landscape: Essays on the Symbolic Representation, Design and Use of Past Environments*, edited by D. Cosgrove and S. Daniels, 11–31. Cambridge: Cambridge University Press, 1988.

―――. *Theoria: Art and the Absence of Grace*. London: Chatto & Windus, 1988.

Fussell, Paul. *The Great War and Modern Memory*. New York: Oxford University Press, 1975.

Gardner, C., and M. Chapman. *Voorslag: A Magazine of South African Life and Art*, edited by R. Campbell, W. Plomer, and L. van der Post, Facsimile Reprint of nos. 1, 2, and 3. Pietermaritzburg: University of Natal Pres, 1985.

Gardner, Guy. "Round in Three Thousand." *SAR&H Magazine*, December 1926, 1949.

Geertz, Clifford. "Thick Description: Toward an Interpretive Theory of Culture." In *The Interpretation of Cultures: Selected Essays*, 3–30. New York: Basic Books, 1973.

Gilbert, Emily. "National Currency Formation and National Identity: The Rise of Colonial Nationalism in Australia, South Africa and Canada." Paper presented at the Eleventh International Conference of Historical Geographers, Quebec, August 2002.

Giliomee, Hermann. "The Beginnings of Afrikaner Nationalism, 1870–1915." *South African Historical Journal* 19 (1987): 115–42.

Gilpin, William. *Observations on Cumberland and Westmoreland, 1786*. Poole: Woodstock Facsimile Editions, 1996.

Glassie, Henry. *Passing the Time in Ballymenone: Culture and History of an Ulster Community*. Philadelphia: University of Pennsylvania Press, 1982.

Goethe, J. W. *Italian Journey: 1786–1788*. Translated by W. H. Auden and E. Mayer. Harmondsworth: Penguin, 1970.

Gombrich, Ernst. "The Renaissance Theory of Art and the Rise of Landscape." In *Norm and Form: Studies in the Art of the Renaissance*, 107–21. London: Phaidon, 1966.

Gordimer, Nadine. *The Conservationist*. London: Cape, 1976.

Gough, Paul. "The Avenue at War." *Landscape Research* 18, no. 2 (1993): 66–77.

―――. "'An Epic of Mud': Artistic Interpretations of Third Ypres." In *Passchendaele in Perspective: The Third Battle of Ypres*, edited by P. H. Liddle, 409–21. London: Leo Cooper, 1997.

Gowing, Lawrence, ed. *The Critical Writings of Adrian Stokes: Vol. 2, 1937–1958*. London: Thames & Hudson, 1978.

Gradidge, Roderick. *Dream Houses: The Edwardian Ideal*. London: Constable, 1980.

Graham, Brian, and Catherine Nash. *Modern Historical Geographies*. Harlow: Longman, 2000.

Gray, Stephen. *Southern African Literature: An Introduction*. Cape Town: David Phillip, 1979.

Green, Nicholas. *The Spectacle of Nature: Landscape and Bourgeois Culture in 19th Century France*. Manchester: Manchester University Press, 1990.

Gregory, Derek. "Between the Book and the Lamp: Imaginative Geographies of Egypt, 1849–50." *Trans. Inst. Br. Geogr.*, N.S. 20 (1995): 29–57.

―――. "Geographical Imagination." In *The Dictionary of Human Geography*, edited by R. J. Johnston, D. Gregory, and D. M. Smith. Oxford: Blackwell, 1994.

Greig, Doreen. *Herbert Baker in South Africa*. London/Cape Town: Purnell, 1970.

Groote Schuur, Residence of South Africa's Prime Minister. Pretoria: SA Government Printer, 1970.

Grosskopf, J. F. W. *Rural Impoverishment and Rural Exodus: Carnegie Commission of Investigation on the Poor White Question in South Africa*. Vol. 1. Stellenbosch: Pro Ecclesia Drukkery, 1932.

Grove, Richard. "Scotland in South Africa: John Croumbie Brown and the Roots of Settler Environmentalism." In *Ecology and Empire: Environmental History of Settler Societies*, edited by T. Griffiths and L. Robbin, 139–53. Edinburgh: Keele University Press, 1997.

Gruffudd, Pyrs. *Landscape and Nationhood: Tradition and Modernity in Rural Wales, 1900–1950*. Doctoral thesis, Loughborough University of Technology, 1989.

Grundlingh, Albert. *Fighting Their Own War: South African Blacks and the First World War*. Johannesburg: Ravan Press, 1987.

———. "The War in 20th Century Afrikaner Consciousness." In *The Impact of the South African War*, edited by D. Omissi and A. Thompson, 23–37. Basingstoke: Palgrave, 2002.

Guelke, Leonard. "Freehold Farmers and Frontier Settlers, 1657–1679." In *The Shaping of South African Society, 1652–1840*, edited by H. Giliomee, 66–108. Middletown, CT: Wesleyan University Press, 1989.

———. "Ideology and the Landscape of Settler Colonialism in Virginia and Dutch South Africa." In *Ideology and Landscape in Historical Perspective: Essays on the Meaning of Some Places in the Past*, edited by A. R. Baker and G. Biger, 137–47. Cambridge: Cambridge University Press, 1992.

Gutsche, Thelma. *No Ordinary Woman: The Life and Times of Florence Phillips*. Cape Town: Howard Timmins, 1966.

Häkli, Jouni. "Territoriality and the Rise of the Modern State." *Fennia* 172 (1994): 1–82.

Hall, Martin. *The Changing Past: Farmers, Kings and Traders in Southern Africa, 200–1860*. Cape Town: David Phillip, 1987.

———. "The Legend of the Lost City; Or, the Man with Golden Balls." *Journal of Southern African Studies* 21, no. 2 (June 1995): 179–99.

Hamilton, C. H. "A Holiday in Your Homeland: The Drakensberg, an Alpine Arcadia." *SAR&H Magazine*, December 1925, 1246–54.

Harding, Marion. "South Africa in Word and Images: Study Collections at the National Army Museum." In *Ashes & Blood: The British Army in South Africa, 1795–1914*, edited by P. Bryden, A. Guy, and M. Harding, 131–77. London: National Army Museum, 1999.

Harmsen, Frieda. *Looking at South African Art*. Pretoria: Van Schaik, 1988.

———. *The Women of Bonnefoi: The Story of the Everard Group*. Pretoria: Van Schaik, 1980.

Harrison, Charles. "The Effects of Landscape." In *Landscape and Power*, edited by W. J. T. Mitchell, 203–39. Chicago: University of Chicago Press, 1994.

Harrison, Charles, and Paul Wood. *Art in Theory: An Anthology of Changing Ideas*. Oxford: Blackwell, 1992.

Hart, E. J. *The Selling of Canada: The Canadian Pacific Railway and the Beginnings of Canadian Tourism*. Banff: Altitude, 1983.

Harvey, David. *The Condition of Post-Modernity: An Enquiry into the Origins of Cultural Change*. Oxford: Blackwell, 1989.

Harvey, Sir Paul, ed. *The Oxford Companion to Classical Literature*. Oxford: Oxford University Press, 1984.

Hatt, Michael. "Athlete and Aesthete: Beauty and the Male Body in the 1890s." Unpublished paper, Twenty-fourth Annual Conference of the Association of Art Historians (AAH), Exeter, April 1998.

Häyrinen, Maunu. "National Landscapes and Their Making in Finland." *Topos 8: Landscapes of Remembrance* (1994): 6–15.

Heath, Malcolm. Introduction to *The Poetics*, by Aristotle. Harmondsworth: Penguin, 1996.

Helmreich, Anne. "Re-presenting Nature: Ideology, Art and Science in William Robinson's 'Wild Garden.'" In *Nature and Ideology: Natural Garden Design in the 20th Century*, edited by J. Wolschke-Buhlmann, 81–130. Washington, DC: Dumbarton Oaks, 1997.

Henshaw, Peter. "John Buchan from the 'Borders' to the 'Berg': Nature, Empire and White South African Identity, 1901–1910." *Journal of African Studies* 62, no. 1 (2003): 3–32.

———. "The Key to South Africa: Delagoa Bay and the Origins of the South African War." *Journal of Southern Africa Studies* 24, no. 3 (September 1998): 527–43.

Herb, Guntram. "National Identity and Territory." In *Nested Identities: Nationalism, Territory and Scale*, edited by G. Herb and D. H. Kaplan, 9–30. Oxford: Rowman & Littlefield, 2001.

Herb, Guntram, and David H. Kaplan, eds. *Nested Identities: Nationalism, Territory and Scale*. Oxford: Rowman & Littlefield, 2001.

Herbert, Gilbert. *Martienssen and the International Style: The Modern Movement in South African Architecture*. Cape Town/Rotterdam: C. Struik, 1975.

Hewitt, N. B. "25 Years of Development of Tourist Attractions in South Africa." *SAR&H Magazine*, October 1930.

Hexham, Irving. "Afrikaner Nationalism, 1902–1914." In *The South African War: The Anglo-Boer War, 1899–1903*, edited by P. Warwick and S. Spies, 386–403. Harlow: Longmans, 1980.

Hillebrand, Melanie. "The Background Story: Working as an Artist in 20th Century South Africa." In *The Everard Phenomenon*, edited by J. Addleson, 67–77. Durban: Durban Art Gallery, 2000.

Hirsch, Eric. "Introduction: Landscape, Between Place and Space." In *The Anthropology of Landscape: Perspectives in Place and Space*, edited by E. Hirsch and M. O'Hanlon, 1–30. Oxford: Oxford University Press, 1995.

Hirschfeld, C. C. L. *Theory of Garden Art*. Edited and translated by Linda Parshall. Philadelphia: University of Pennsylvania Press, 2001.

Hiss, Tony. *The Experience of Place*. New York: Knopf, 1991.

Hobsbawm, Eric, and Terence Ranger. *The Invention of Tradition*. Cambridge: Cambridge University Press, 1994.

Hofmeyr, Isabel. "Building a Nation from Words: Afrikaans Language, Literature and Ethnic Identity." In *The Politics of Race, Class and Nationalism*, edited by S. Marks and S. Trapido, 95–123. London: Longman, 1987.

———. "Popularizing History: The Case of Gustav Preller." *Journal of African History* 29, no. 3 (1988): 521–35.

———. "The Spoken Word and the Barbed Wire." In *We Spend Our Years as a Tale That Is Told: Oral Historic Narrative in a South African Chiefdom*, 59–77. Portsmouth, NH: Heinemann; Johannesburg: Witwatersrand University Press, 1994.

———. *We Spend Our Years as a Tale That Is Told: Oral Historic Narrative in a South African Chiefdom*. Portsmouth, NH: Heinemann; Johannesburg: Witwatersrand University Press, 1994.

Holland, Robert. "The British Empire and the Great War." Institute for Commonwealth Studies seminar paper, London, 12 March 1997.

Holtby, Winifred. "In Praise of Trains." *Manchester Guardian*, 12 August 1926; reprinted in *Testament of a Friendship: The Journalism of Vera Brittain and Winifred Holtby*, edited by P. Berry and A. Bishop, 276–78. London: Fontana/Virago, 1985.

Hones, Sheila. "'Everything Hastens Where It Belongs': Nature and Narrative Structure in *The Atlantic Monthly*, 1880–84." *Japanese Journal of American Studies*, no. 8 (1997): 35–62.

Howkins, Alun. "The Discovery of Rural England." In *Englishness: Culture and Politics, 1880–1920*, edited by R. Colls and P. Dodd, 62–80. Beckenham: Croom Helm, 1980.

Hunt, John Dixon. "'Come into the Garden, Maud': Garden Art as Privileged Mode of Commemoration and Identity." In *Places of Commemoration: Search for Identity and Landscape Design*, edited by J. Wolschke-Bulmahn, 9–24. Washington, DC: Dumbarton Oaks, 2001.

———. *Greater Perfections: The Practice of Garden Theory*. Philadelphia: University of Pennsylvania Press, 2000.

———. "The Idea of a Garden and the Three Natures." In *Greater Perfections: The Practice of Garden Theory*, 32–75. Philadelphia: University of Pennsylvania Press, 2000.

Hurley, Denzil. "About Making." *Perspecta: The Yale Architectural Journal* 19 (1982): 83–86.

Huston, Hollis. *The Actor's Instrument: Body, Theory, Stage*. Ann Arbor: University of Michigan Press, 1992.

Hutton, Patrick H. "The Art of Memory Reconceived: From Rhetoric to Psychoanalysis." *Journal of the History of Ideas* 48, no 3 (1987): 371–92.

Hyams, R., and P. Henshaw. *The Lion and the Springbok: Britain and South Africa since the Boer War*. Cambridge: Cambridge University Press, 2003.

Hyde, Anne Farrar. *American Vision: Far Western Landscape and National Culture, 1820–1920*. New York: New York University Press, 1990.

Hynes, Samuel. *A War Imagined: The First World War and English Culture.* London: Bodley Head, 1990.

Ignatieff, Michael. *The Needs of Strangers.* London: Hogarth, 1994.

In the Picturesque Eastern Transvaal: Barberton, Carolina and Lake Chrissie. Johannesburg: SAR&H Publicity Dept., 1928.

Inglis, Fred. "Landscape as Popular Culture." In *Reading Landscape: Country, City, Capital*, edited by Simon Pugh, 197–213. Manchester: Manchester University Press, 1990.

Ingold, Timothy. "The Picture Is Not the Terrain: Maps, Paintings and the Dwelt-in World." *Archaeological Dialogues* 1 (1997): 29–31.

——. "The Temporality of Landscape." *World Archaeology* 25, no. 2 (1993): 152–74.

Irving, Robert. *Indian Summer: Lutyens and Imperial Delhi.* New Haven: Yale University Press, 1981.

Jacobs, Jane M. "Earth Honoring: Western Desires and Indigenous Knowledges." In *Writing Women and Space: Colonial and Postcolonial Geographies*, edited by A. Blunt and G. Rose, 169–96. New York/London: Guilford, 1994.

——. *Edge of Empire: Post-colonialism and the City.* London: Routledge, 1996.

Jacobson, Dan. *Time and Time Again: Autobiographies.* London: Fontana, 1986.

Jaff, Fay. *They Came to South Africa.* Cape Town: Howard Timmins, 1963.

Jeal, Timothy. *The Boy-Man: The Life of Lord Baden-Powell.* New York: William Morrow, 1990.

Johns, Elizabeth. "Landscape Painting in America and Australia in an Urban Century." In *New Worlds from Old: 19th Century Australian and American Landscapes*, edited by E. Johns et al., 23–52. Canberra: National Gallery of Australia; Hartford: Wadsworth Athenaeum, 1999.

Johnson, Nuala. "Cast in Stone: Monuments, Geography and Nationalism." *Environment and Planning D: Society and Space* 13 (1995): 51–65.

——. "Historical Geographies of the Present." In *Modern Historical Geographies*, edited by B. Graham and C. Nash, 251–71. Harlow: Longmans, 2000.

Johnson, R. W. "Jingoes." *London Review of Books*, 6 May 2004, 30–31.

Jussim, Estelle, and Elizabeth Lindquist-Cock. *Landscape as Photograph.* New Haven: Yale University Press, 1985.

Kannemeyer, J. C. *A History of Afrikaans Literature.* Pietermaritzburg: Shuter & Shooter, 1993.

Kaplan, David. "Territorial Identities and Geographic Scale." In *Nested Identities: Nationalism, Territory, and Scale*, edited by G. Herb and D. Kaplan, 31–49. Oxford: Rowman & Littlefield, 2001.

Kaplan, David, and Guntram Herb. "Introduction: A Question of Identity." In G. Herb & D. Kaplan, eds. *Nested Identities: Nationalism, Territory, and Scale*, edited by G. Herb and D. Kaplan, 1–8. Oxford: Rowman & Littlefield, 2001.

Katzenellenbogen, S. E. "Reconstruction in the Transvaal." In *The South African War: The Anglo Boer War, 1899–1902*, edited by P. Warwick and S. Spies, 342–44. Harlow: Longmans, 1980.

Kaufmann, Eric. "Naturalizing the Nation: The Rise of Naturalistic Nationalism in the United States and Canada." *Comparative Studies in Society and History* 40, no. 4 (1998): 666–95.

Kearney, Richard. *The Poetics of Imagining: From Husserl to Lyotard.* London: HarperCollins, 1993.

Keath, Michael. "The Baker School." In *Architecture of the Transvaal*, edited by R. Fisher, S. le Roux, and E. Maré, 79–98. Pretoria: UNISA Press, 2002.

——. *Herbert Baker: Architecture and Idealism, 1892–1923; The South African Years.* Gibraltar, 1992.

Keegan, Timothy. "The Making of the Rural Economy: From 1850 to the Present." In *Studies in the Economic History of Southern Africa*, Vol. II, edited by Z. Konczacki, J. Parpart, and T. Shaw, 36–63. London: F. Cass, 1991.

——. *Rural Transformations in Industrializing South Africa: The Southern Highveld to 1914.* Braamfontein: Ravan, 1986.

——. "The Share-Cropping Economy, African Class Formation and the 1913 Native's Land Act." In *Industrialization and Social Change in South Africa: African Class Formation, Culture and Consciousness, 1870–1930*, edited by S. Marks and R. Rathbone, 195–211. New York: Longmans, 1982.

Kemal, S., and I. Gaskell, eds. *Landscape: Natural Beauty and the Arts.* Cambridge: Cambridge University Press, 1993.

Kennedy, Dane. "The Perils of the Midday Sun: Climatic Anxieties in the Colonial Tropics." In *Imperialism and the Natural World*, edited by J. Mackenzie, 118–40. Manchester: Manchester University Press, 1990.

Kern, Stephen. *The Culture of Time and Space, 1880–1918.* London: Weidenfeld & Nicolson, 1983.

King, L. C. *South African Scenery: A Textbook of Geomorphology.* Edinburgh: Oliver & Boyd, 1963.

Kirkland, S. "From the Carriage Window: Scenic Pageantry Beside the Line." *SAR&H Magazine,* October 1930, 1445–48.

Kloppers, Sandra. "Crossing Rivers, or Exploring the Interior of Southern Africa." In *Diversity and Interaction, Proceedings of the 5th Annual South African Association of Art Historians Conference,* 64–68. Durban: University of Natal, 1989.

Krikler, Jeremy. *Revolution from Above, Rebellion from Below: The Agrarian Transvaal at the Turn of the Century.* Oxford: Clarendon Press, 1993.

———. "Social Neurosis and Hysterical Pre-cognition in South Africa." *Journal of Social History,* 28, no. 3 (1995): 491–520.

Kunze, Donald. "Architecture as a Site of Reception, Part 1: Cuisine, Frontality, and the Infra-thin." In *Chora* 1, 83–108. Montreal: McGill University Press, 1994.

———. "Architecture as a Site of Reception, Part 2: Sea-Food and Vampires," In *Chora* 2, 109–34. Montreal: McGill University Press, 1996.

———. *Thought and Place: The Architecture of Eternal Places in the Philosophy of Giambattista Vico.* New York: P. Lang, 1987.

Kuttner, Ann. "Delight and Danger in Roman Water Gardens: Sperlonga and Tivoli." In *Landscape Design and the Experience of Motion,* edited by M. Conan, 103–57. Washington, DC: Dumbarton Oaks, 2003.

Lambert, John. "South African British, or Dominion South Africans? The Evolution of an Identity in the 1910s and 1920s." *South African Historical Journal* 43 (November 2000): 197–222.

Lang, Karen. "The Body in the Garden." In *Landscape of Memory and Experience,* edited by J. Birksted, 107–21. London: Spon, 2002.

Langer, Monika. *Merleau-Ponty's Phenomenology of Perception: A Guide and Commentary.* Basingstoke: Macmillan, 1988.

Leach, Eleanor. *The Rhetoric of Space: Literary and Artistic Representations of Landscape in Republican and Augustan Rome.* Princeton: Princeton University Press, 1988.

Leatherbarrow, David. "Character, Geometry and Perspective: The Third Earl of Shaftesbury's Principles of Garden Design." *Journal of Garden History* 4, no. 4 (1984): 332–58.

———. *The Roots of Architectural Invention: Site, Enclosure, Materials.* Cambridge: Cambridge University Press, 1993.

———. *Topographical Stories.* Philadelphia: University of Pennsylvania Press, 2004.

———. *Uncommon Ground: Architecture, Technology and Topography.* Cambridge, MA: MIT Press, 2000.

Lee, Emanoel. *To the Bitter End: A Photographic History of the Boer War, 1899–1902.* Harmondsworth: Penguin, 1985.

Lefebvre, Henri. *Writings on Cities.* Oxford: Blackwell, 1996.

Leibrandt, Rev. H. C. V. *Précis of the Archives of the Cape of Good Hope.* Cape Town: W. A. Richards & Sons, 1896–99.

Leigh, Valerie. "The Dynamics of the Everard Paintings." In *The Everard Phenomenon: An Exhibition of Paintings by the Everard Family,* edited by Jill Addleson, 78–97. Durban: Durban Art Gallery, ca. 2002.

Leighton, J. M. "South Africa House in the Making." N.d., probably reprint from *Lantern* magazine; South Africa House Library, London.

Lester, Alan. *From Colonization to Democracy: A New Historical Geography of South Africa.* London: I. B. Tauris, 1998.

———. "Historical Geographies of Imperialism." In *Modern Historical Geographies,* edited by B. Graham and C. Nash, 100–120. Harlow: Longmans, 2000.

———. *Imperial Networks: Creating Identities in 19th Century South Africa and Britain.* London: Routledge, 2001.

Leveson, David. "Geologic Clarity: A Geologist's Perspective On Landscape Aesthetics." *Landscape Journal* 7, no. 2 (1988): 85–94.

Lewcock, Ronald B. *Early Nineteenth Century Architecture in South Africa: A Study of the Interaction of Two Cultures, 1795–1837.* Cape Town: Balkema, 1963.

Lewis, A. D. "Topographical Mapping in the Union of South Africa." *South African Geographical Journal* 20 (1938): 3–11.

Liebenberg, E. "Mapping British South Africa: The Case of GSGS 2230." *Imago Mundi* 49 (1997): 132–33.

———. *Topografiese Kartering van Suid-Afrika, 1879–1972: 'n histories-geografiese ontleding.* Pretoria: UNISA, 1973.

Liebson, S. G. "The South Africa of Fiction." *State* 7, no. 2 (1912).

Lighton, Conrad. *The Cape Floral Kingdom.* Cape Town: Juta & Co., 1960.

———. *Sisters of the South.* London: Hodder & Stoughton, 1952.

Lowenthal, David. "British National Identity and the English Landscape." *Rural History* 2 (1991): 205–30.

———. "European and English Landscapes as National Symbols." In *Geography and National Identity*, edited by D. Hooson, 15–38. Oxford: Blackwell, 1994.

———. "European Landscapes as National Emblems." *Landscape Research* 21 (1992): 14–23.

Lowenthal, David, and Hugh C. Prince. "The English Landscape." *Geographical Review* 54, no. 3 (July 1964): 309–46.

———. "English Landscape Tastes." *Geographical Review* 55, no. 2 (April 1965): 186–222.

Lownie, Andrew. *John Buchan: The Presbyterian Cavalier.* London: Thames & Hudson, 1995.

The Lure of South Africa. Johannesburg: SAR&H Administration, 1928.

MacDonald, Robert H. *Sons of Empire: The Frontier and the Boys Scouts Movement, 1890–1918.* Toronto: University of Toronto Press, 1993.

MacNab, Frances (pseud.). *On Veldt and Farm: In Bechuanaland, the Cape Colony, the Transvaal and Natal.* London: Edward Arnold, 1897.

MacNab, Roy. *The Story of South Africa House: South Africa in Britain, the Changing Pattern.* Johannesburg: Jonathan Ball, 1983.

March, B. O. "Winter on the Drakensberg." *State*, March 1912, 203–11.

Marix-Evans, Martin. *The Boer War: South Africa, 1899–1902.* Oxford: Osprey Press, 1999.

Markham, Violet. "The South African Riviera." *SAR&H Magazine*, March 1925, 201–8.

———. *The South African Scene.* London: Smith, Elder & Co., 1913.

Marks, Shula. "The Myth of the Empty Land." *History Today* 30, no. 1 (1980): 7–12.

Marks, Shula, and Saul Dubow. "Patriotism of Place and Race: Hancock on South Africa." In *Keith Hancock: Legacies of a Historian*, edited by D. A. Low, 162–63. Melbourne: Melbourne University Press, 2001.

Marks, Shula, and Richard Rathbone, eds. *Industrialization and Social Change: African Class Formation, Culture and Consciousness, 1870–1930.* New York: Longmans, 1982.

Marks, Shula, and Stanley Trapido. *The Politics of Race, Class and Nationalism in 20th Century South Africa.* London: Longmans, 1987.

Marlowe, John. *Cecil Rhodes: The Anatomy of Empire.* London: Paul Elek, 1972.

Marot, Sébastien. *Sub-Urbanism and the Art of Memory.* London: Architectural Association, 2003.

Marsh, Jan. *Back to the Land: The Pastoral Impulse in England from 1880 to 1914.* London: Quartet Books, 1982.

Martin, E. "The South African: Development of National Character." *The African World Annual*, 1926–27: 147.

Marx, Leo. "The Railroad in the Landscape: An Iconological Reading of a Theme in American Art." In *The Railroad in American Art: Representations of Technological Change*, edited by S. Danly and L. Marx, 183–208. Cambridge, MA: MIT Press, 1990.

Matchotka, Pavel. *Cézanne: Landscape into Art.* New Haven: Yale University Press, 1996.

Matless, David. *Landscape and Englishness.* London: Reaktion, 2000.

McCaughey, Patrick. "Likeness and Unlikeness: The American-Australian Experience." In *New Worlds from Old: 19th Century Australian and American Landscapes*, edited by E. Johns et al., 15–22. Canberra: National Gallery of Australia; Hartford: Wadsworth Athenaeum, 1999.

McCracken, D., and E. McCracken. *The Way to Kirstenbosch.* Cape Town: South African National Botanic Garden, 1988.

McCracken, D., and P. McCracken. *Natal: The Garden Colony; Victorian Natal and the Royal Botanic Gardens Kew.* Sandton: Frandsen Publishers, 1990.

319

McGregor, JoAnn. "The Victoria Falls 1900–1940: Landscape Tourism and the Geographical Imagination in Southern Africa." *Journal of South African Studies* 29, no. 3 (2003): 717–37.

McMillan, James. "'La France Profonde' Modernity and National Identity." In *Landscape of France: Impressionism and Its Rivals*, edited by J. House, 52–59. London: Hayward Gallery, 1995.

Mels, Tom. "Nature, Home and Scenery: The Official Spatialities of Swedish National Parks." *Environment and Planning D: Society and Space* 20 (2002): 135–54.

Mendelsohn, Daniel. *The Elusive Embrace: Desire and the Riddle of Identity*. New York: Vintage, 2000.

Merleau-Ponty, Maurice. "Cezanne's Doubt." In *The Merleau-Ponty Aesthetics Reader: Philosophy and Painting*, edited by G. Johnson and M. Smith, 59–75. Evanston, IL: Northwestern University Press, 1993.

———. "Eye and Mind." In *The Merleau-Ponty Aesthetics Reader: Philosophy and Painting*, edited by G. Johnson and M. Smith, 121–49. Evanston, IL: Northwestern University Press, 1993.

———. *The Phenomenology of Perception*. Translated by C. Smith. London: Routledge, 1986.

Merrington, Peter. "Carrying the Torch: Dorothea Fairbridge and the Cape Loyalist Imagination." Paper presented at University of Pretoria, 2002. www.childlit.org.za/KonfBoerMerrington.html.

———. "Heritage, Pageantry and Archivism: Creed Systems and Tropes of Public History in Imperial South Africa, ca. 1910." *Kronos* (1998–99): 129–51.

———. "Pageantry and Primitivism: Dorothea Fairbridge and the 'Aesthetics of Union.'" *Journal of Southern African Studies* 21, no. 4 (1995): 643–56.

———. "A Staggered Orientalism: The Cape-to-Cairo Imaginary." *Poetics Today* 22, no. 2 (2001): 323–64.

———. "The State and the Invention of Heritage in Edwardian South Africa." In *The Round Table, the Empire/Commonwealth and British Foreign Policy*, edited by A. Bosco and A. Mays, 127–33. London: Lothian Foundation Press, 1997.

Metcalf, Thomas. "Architecture and Empire." *History Today* 30, no. 12 (1980): 7–12.

———. "Herbert Baker and New Delhi." In *New Delhi through the Ages: Essays in Urban History, Culture and Society*, edited by R. Frykenberg, 391–400. New Delhi: Oxford University Press, 1986.

Miller, J. Hillis. *Topographies*. Stanford: Stanford Press, 1995.

Mills, Sara. "Gender and Colonial Space." *Gender, Place and Culture* 3, no. 2 (1996): 125–48.

———. "Knowledge, Gender and Empire." In *Writing Women and Space: Colonial and Postcolonial Geographies*, edited by A. Blunt and G. Rose, 29–50. New York/London: Guilford, 1994.

Milton, Shaun. "The Transvaal Beef Frontier: Environment, Markets and the Ideology of Development, 1902–1942." In *Ecology and Empire: Environmental History of Settler Societies*, edited by T. Griffiths and L. Robbin, 199–212. Edinburgh: Keele University Press, 1997.

Mitchell, W. J. T. "Holy Landscape: Israel, Palestine and the American Wilderness." *Critical Inquiry* 26, no. 2 (2000): 193–223.

———, ed. *Landscape and Power*. 2nd ed. Chicago: University of Chicago Press, 2002.

Monti, Nicolas. *Africa Then: Photographs, 1840–1918*. London: Thames & Hudson, 1987.

Morrell, Robert. "Competition and Cooperation in Middelburg, 1900–1930." In *Putting a Plough to the Ground: Accumulation and Dispossession in Rural South Africa, 1850–1930*, edited by W. Beinart, P. Delius, and S. Trapido, 373–419. Braamfontein: Ravan, 1986.

———, ed. *White But Poor: Essays on the History of Poor Whites in Southern Africa, 1880–1940*. Pretoria: UNISA Press, 1992.

Morris, James. *South African Winter*. London: Faber & Faber, 1958.

Muller, C. F. J. *Sonop in die Suide: Geboorte en Groei van die Nasionale Pers*. Cape Town: Nasionale Boekhandel, 1990.

Murray, Colin. *Black Mountain: Land, Class and Power in the Eastern OFS, 1880–1980*. Edinburgh: Edinburgh University Press, 1992.

Nash, Catherine. "'Embodying the Nation': The West of Ireland Landscape and Irish Identity." In *Tourism in Ireland: A Critical Analysis*, edited by B. O'Connor and M. Cronin, 86–114. Cork: Cork University Press, 1993.

———. "Reclaiming Vision: Looking at Landscape and the Body." *Gender, Place & Culture* 3, no. 2 (1996): 149–70.

————. "Remapping the Body/Land: New Cartographies of Identity, Gender and Landscape in Ireland." In *Writing Women and Space: Colonial and Postcolonial Geographies*, edited by A. Blunt and G. Rose, 227–50. New York/London: Guilford, 1994.

————. "Visionary Geographies: Designs for Developing Ireland." *History Workshop Journal* 45 (1998): 49–78.

Nasson, Bill. "Delville Wood and the South African Great War Commemoration." *English Historical Review* 480 (2004): 57–85.

————. "A Great Divide: Popular Responses to the Great War in South Africa." *War and Society* 12, no. 1 (1994): 47–64.

————. "The South African War/Anglo-Boer War, 1899–1902, and Political Memory in South Africa." In *The Politics of War Memory and Commemoration*, edited by T. G. Ashplant, Graham Dawson, and Michael Roper, 111–27. London: Routledge, 2000.

————. "South Africans in Flanders: *Le Zulu Blanc*." In *Passchendaele in Perspective: The Third Battle of Ypres*, edited by P. H. Liddle, 292–304. London: Leo Cooper, 1997.

Nattrass, J. *The South African Economy: Its Growth and Change*. Cape Town: Oxford University Press, 1981.

Neumann, Roderick P. "Ways of Seeing Africa: Colonial Recasting of African Society and Landscape in Serengeti National Park." *Ecumene* 2, no. 2 (1995): 149–69.

Nora, Pierre. "Between Memory and History: Les Lieux de Mémoire." *Representations* 26 (Spring 1989): 7–25.

————. "General Introduction: Between Memory and History." In *The Realms of Memory: Rethinking the French Past, Vol 1*, edited by L. Kritzman, 1–20. New York: Columbia University Press, 1996.

Norberg-Schulz, Christian. *Genius Loci: Towards a Phenomenology of Architecture*. New York: Rizzoli, 1980.

Norwich, Oscar. *A Johannesburg Album: Historical Postcards*. Craighall: Ad Donker, 1986.

Oakes, Douglas, ed. *The Illustrated History of South Africa: The Real Story*. Pleasantville, NY: Reader's Digest, 1992.

Oakes, Timothy. "Place and the Paradox of Modernity." *Annals of the Association of American Geographers* 87, no. 3 (September 1997): 509–31.

Ogborn, Miles. *Spaces of Modernity: London's Geographies 1680–1780*. London: Guilford, 1998.

Olin, Laurie. "What I Do When I Can Do It: Representation in Recent Work." *Studies in the History of Gardens and Designed Landscapes* 19, no. 1 (Spring 1999): 102–21.

Omissi, David, and Andrew Thompson. "Introduction: Investigating the Impact of the War." In *The Impact of the South African War*, edited by D. Omissi and A. Thompson, 1–22. Basingstoke: Palgrave, 2002.

O'Neill, John. "Marxism and Philosophy." In *Phenomenology, Language and Sociology: Selected Essays of Maurice Merleau-Ponty*, edited by John O'Neill. London: Heinemann, 1974.

Osborne, Brian S. "The Iconography of Canadian Art." In *The Iconography of Landscape: Essays on the Symbolic Representation, Design, and Use of Past Environments*, edited by D. Cosgrove and S. Daniels, 162–78. Cambridge: Cambridge University Press, 1988.

————. "Interpreting a Nation's Identity: Artists as Creators of National Consciousness." In *Ideology and Landscape in Historical Perspective: Essays on the Meanings of Some Places in the Past*, edited by A. Baker and G. Biger, 230–53. Cambridge: Cambridge University Press, 1995.

————. "Warscapes, Landscape, Inscapes: France, War and Canadian National Identity." In *Place, Culture and Identity*, edited by A. Black and R. Butlin, 311–34. Quebec: Les Presses de l'Université Laval, 2001.

O'Sullivan, Patrick, and Jesse Miller. *The Geography of Warfare*. London: Croom Helm, 1983.

Outram, Dorinda. "Enlightenment Journeys: From Cosmic Travel to Inner Space." GIRG Colloquium *Centres/Networks/Margins*, Royal Holloway-University of London, September 1996.

Pakenham, Thomas. *The Boer War*. London: Weidenfeld & Nicholson, 1979.

Pallasmaa, Juhani. *The Eyes of the Skin: Architecture and the Senses*. London: Academy Editions, 1996.

Parker, Kenneth. "Fertile Land, Romantic Spaces, Uncivilized Peoples: English Travel Writing about the Cape of Good Hope, 1800–1850." In *The Expansion of England: Race, Ethnicity and Cultural History,* edited by B. Schwarz, 198–231. London: Routledge, 2000.

Peattie, Roderick. *Struggle on the Veld.* New York: Vanguard Press, 1947.

———. "The Veld Is the Heartland." In *Struggle on the Veld,* 23–39. New York: Vanguard Press, 1947.

Pemble, John. *The Mediterranean Passion: Victorians and Edwardians in the South.* Oxford: Clarendon Press, 1987.

Pevsner, Nikolaus. Foreword to *Art and Articles: A Festschrift in Honour of Heather Martienssen,* edited by F. Harmsen. Cape Town: Balkema, 1972.

Phillips, Sir Lionel. *Some Reminiscences.* London: Hutchinson, ca. 1924.

Phillips, Richard. *Mapping Men and Empire: A Geography of Adventure.* London: Routledge, 1997.

Pile, Steve, and Nigel Thrift, eds. *Mapping the Subject: Geographies of Cultural Transformation.* London: Routledge 1995.

Pirie, G. H. "Aspects of the Political-Economy of the Railways in South Africa." *University of Witwatersrand Dept. of Geography & Environmental Studies Occasional Paper,* no. 24, Johannesburg, 1982.

———. "Racial Segregation on South African Trains, 1910–1927: Entrenchment and Resistance." *South African Historical Journal* 20 (1988): 75–93.

———. "Railway-Operated Road Transport and the South African Space Economy." *South African Geographer* 13 (1985): 39–50.

———. "Railway Plantations and Railway Sleepers in South Africa, 1910–1937." *South African Forestry Journal* 122 (1982): 59–62.

———. "Sleepers Beside the Tracks: Housing in South Africa's State Railway Corporation, 1910–1980." *South African Geographical Journal* 64, no. 2 (1982): 144–54.

———. "White Railway Labour in South Africa, 1873–1924." In *White But Poor: Essays on the History of Poor Whites in Southern Africa, 1880–1940,* edited by R. Morrell, 101–14. Pretoria: UNISA Press, 1992.

Ploszajska, Teresa. "Constructing the Subject: Geographical Models in English Schools, 1870–1944." *Journal of Historical Geography* 22, no. 4 (1996): 388–98.

———. "Down to Earth: Geography Fieldwork in English Schools, 1870–1944." *Environment and Planning D: Society and Space* 16, no. 5 (1998): 757–74.

Pollan, Michael. *A Place of My Own: The Education of an Amateur Builder.* London: Bloomsbury, 1998.

Pratt, Mary Louise. *Imperial Eyes: Travel Writing and Transculturation.* New York: Routledge, 1992.

Pred, Alan. "Place as Historically Contingent Process: Structuration and the Time-Geography of Becoming Places." *Annals of American Assoiation of Geographers* 74, no. 2 (1984): 279–97.

Ranger, Terence. "The Invention of Tradition in Colonial Africa." In *The Invention of Tradition,* edited by E. Hobsbawm and T. Ranger, 211–62. Cambridge: Cambridge University Press, 1983.

Rasmusssen, Steen Eiler. *Experiencing Architecture.* New Haven: Yale University Press, 1951.

R.A.W. "Travelling By Train: Veldside Vignettes in Variety." *SAR&H Magazine,* July 1929, 1146.

Reitz, Deneys. *Adrift on the Open Veld: The Anglo-Boer War and Its Aftermath, 1899–1943.* Cape Town: Stormberg, 1999.

Report from South Africa—Commemorative Issue: Battle of Delville Wood, 15–20 July 1916. London: SA Govt. Dept. of Information, July 1966.

Revill, George. "The Lark Ascending: Monument to a Radical Pastoral." *Landscape Research* 16, no. 2 (1991): 25–30.

———. "Working the System: Journeys through Corporate Culture in the 'Railway Age.'" *Environment and Planning D: Society and Space* 12 (1994): 705–26.

Rhind, David, and Michael Walker. *Historical Railway Postcard Journeys in Southern Africa.* St. James: M. Walker Publishing, 1996.

Rice, Michael. "Fictional Strategies and the Transvaal Landscape." University of the Witwatersrand History workshop paper, Johannesburg, 1981.

Rich, Paul. *Hope and Despair: English-Speaking Intellectuals and South African Politics, 1896–1976.* London: British Academic Press, 1993.

———. "Milnerism and a Ripping Yarn: Transvaal Land Settlement and John Buchan's Novel *Pre-*

ster John, 1901–1910." In *Town and Countryside in the Transvaal: Capitalist Penetrations and Popular Response*, edited by B. Bozzoli, 412–33. Johannesburg: Ravan Press, 1983.

———. "Romance and the Development of the South African Novel." In *Literature and Society in South Africa*, edited by T. Couzens and Landeg White, 120–37. Harlow: Longmans, 1984.

Ricoeur, Paul. *The Aquinas Lecture: The Reality of the Historical Past*. Milwaukee: Marquette University Press, 1984.

Rodaway, Paul. *Sensuous Geographies: Body, Sense and Place*. London: Routledge, 1994.

Roos, Nico. *Kuns in Suid-Wes Afrika/Art in South West Africa*. Pretoria: J. P. van der Walt, 1978.

Rosaldo, Renato. "Imperialist Nostalgia." *Representations* 26 (Spring 1989): 107–22.

Roworth, Edward. "Landscape Art in South Africa." In *Art of the British Empire Overseas*, edited by C. Holme. Special issue of *The International Studio*. London: The Studio, 1917.

———. "Towards a National Art." In *Voorslag: A Magazine of South African Life and Art*, edited by C. Gardner and M. Chapman (1985): 13–18.

Ryan, James. "Visualizing Imperial Geography: Halford Mackinder and the Colonial Office Visual Instruction Committee, 1902–11." *Ecumene* 1, no. 2 (1994): 157–76.

Ryan, James, and Joan Schwartz, eds. *Picturing Place: Photographs in the Construction of Imaginative Geographies*. London: I. B. Tauris, 2003.

Said, Edward. *Culture and Imperialism*. New York: Knopf, 1993.

———. *Orientalism*. New York: Pantheon, 1978.

———. "Reflections on Exile." *Granta* 13 (1984): 157–72.

———. *Representations of the Intellectual: The 1993 Reith Lectures*. London: Virago, 1994.

———. "Third World Intellectuals and Metropolitan Culture." *Raritan* 9, no. 3 (1990): 27–50.

Samuel, Raphael. Introduction to *Patriotism*, edited by R. Samuel, xviii–lvii. Andover: Routledge, Chapman & Hall, 1989.

Sartwell, Crispin. "Representation." In *A Companion to Aesthetics*, edited by David E. Cooper, 364–69. Oxford: Blackwell, 1995.

Sauer, Carl O. *Land and Life: A Selection from the Writings of Carl Ortwin Sauer*. Edited by J. Leighly. Berkeley: University of California Press, 1963.

Sayers, Andrew. "The Shaping of Australian Landscape Painting." In *New Worlds from Old: 19th Century Australian and American Landscapes*, edited by E. Johns et al., 53–70. Canberra: National Gallery of Australia; Hartford: Wadsworth Athenaeum, 1999.

Scarry, Elaine. *The Body in Pain: The Making and Unmaking of the World*. Oxford: Oxford University Press, 1985.

Schama, Simon. *Landscape and Memory*. London: Collins, 1996.

Schivelbusch, Wolfgang. *The Railway Journey: The Industrialization of Time and Space in the 19th Century*. Leamington Spa: Berg, 1986.

Schoeman, Karel. *Only an Anguish to Live Here: Olive Schreiner and the Anglo-Boer War, 1899–1902*. Cape Town: Human & Rousseau, 1992.

Schreiner, Olive. *Thoughts on South Africa*. London: T. F. Unwin Ltd., 1923

Schreuder, Deryck. "'Colonial Nationalism' and 'Tribal Nationalism': Making the White South African State, 1899–1910." In *The Rise of Colonial Nationalism: Australia, New Zealand, Canada and South Africa First Assert Their Nationalities, 1880–1914*, edited by J. Eddy and D. Schreuder, 192–226. Sydney: Allen & Unwin, 1988.

———. "The Making of the Idea of Colonial Nationalism." In *The Rise of Colonial Nationalism: Australia, New Zealand, Canada and South Africa First Assert Their Nationalities, 1880–1914*, edited by J. Eddy & D. Schreuder, 63–93. Sydney: Allen & Unwin, 1988.

Schwartz, Joan M. "'The Geography Lesson': Photographs and the Construction of Imaginative Geographies." *Journal of Historical Geography* 22 (1996): 16–45.

Schwarz, Bill. "The Romance of the Veld: Projections of South Africa, 1899–1910." In *The Round Table Movement: The Empire/Commonwealth and British Foreign Policy*, edited by Alex May and Andrea Bosco, 65–125. London: Lothian Foundation Press, 1997.

Scott, Clive. *The Spoken Image: Photography and Language*. London: Reaktion, 1999.

Scully, Vincent. *Architecture: The Natural and the Man-Made*. New York: St. Martins Press, 1991.

Seamon, David. "Body-subject, Time-Space Routines and Place Ballets." In *The Human Experience of Space and Place*, edited by A. Buttimer and D. Seamon, 148–65. New York: St. Martins Press, 1980.

Sennett, Richard. *Flesh and Stone: The Body and the City in Western Civilization.* London: Faber, 1994.

Shepheard, Paul. *The Cultivated Wilderness, or, What is Landscape?* Cambridge, MA: MIT Press, 1997.

Shields, Rob. *Places on the Margin: Alternative Geographies of Modernity.* London: Routledge, 1991.

Shorten, J. *The Johannesburg Saga.* Johannesburg: Johannesburg City Council, 1970.

Shurmer-Smith, Pamela. "Cixous' Space: Sensuous Space in Women's Writing." *Ecumene* 1, no. 4 (1994): 349–62.

Sims, T. R. *Flowering Trees and Shrubs for Use in South Africa.* Johannesburg: Speciality Press of South Africa, 1919.

———. *Tree Planting in South Africa.* Pietermaritzburg: Shuter & Shooter, 1927.

"Sir William Hoy, KCB: A Great South African." *SAR&H Magazine*, October 1926.

Sklar, Shirley. "The Garden Suburb: The Victorian Garden in Parktown." In *Parktown 1892–1972*, edited by H. Aron, A. Benjamin, C. Chipkin, and S. Zar, 79–90. Johannesburg: Studio Thirty Five, 1972.

Smith, Anthony. *National Identity.* Harmondsworth: Penguin, 1991.

Smith, Janet Adam. *John Buchan and His World.* London: Constable, 1979.

Smith, Phillip Thurmond, ed. *Mafeking Memories, by Frederick Saunders, 1883–1964.* Madison, NJ: Fairleigh Dickinson University Press, 1996.

Smithson, Robert. "Frederick Law Olmsted and the Dialectical Landscape" and "A Tour of the Monuments of New Jersey." In *Robert Smithson: The Collected Writings*, edited by Jack Flam, 157–71. Berkeley: University of California Press, 1996.

Solomon, J. M. "The Union Buildings and Their Architect." *State*, July 1910.

Sontag, Susan. *On Photography.* Harmondsworth: Penguin, 1976.

"South Africa through American Spectacles." *SAR&H Magazine*, May 1926, 630–31.

"South Africa through Other Eyes." *SAR&H Magazine*, December 1922, 1134–35.

The South African Railways: History, Scope and Organization. Johannesburg: SAR&H Public Relations Dept., 1947.

Speight, W. L. "Land of Hope and Glory." *SAR&H Magazine*, July 1925, 703–10.

Spies, Stephanus. *Methods of Barbarism: Roberts, Kitchener and Civilians in the Boer Republics, January 1900–May 1902.* Cape Town: Human & Rousseau, 1977.

Stafford, Robert. "Annexing the Landscapes of the Past: British Imperial Geology in the 19th Century." In *Imperialism and the Natural World*, edited by John McKenzie, 67–89. Manchester: Manchester University Press, 1990.

Steenbergen, Clemens, and Wouter Reh. *Architecture and Landscape: The Design Experiment of the Great European Gardens and Landscapes.* Bussum: Thoth, 1996.

Stent, Vere. "Holiday Hints." *SAR&H Magazine*, March 1924, 231.

Stevenson, Michael. *Art and Aspirations: The Randlords of South Africa and Their Collections.* Vlaeberg: Fernwood Press, 2002.

Stilgoe, John. "Popular Photography, Scenery Values and Visual Assessment." *Landscape Journal* 3, no. 2 (1984): 111–21.

———. "Salt Marshes." In *Alongshore*, 101–30. New Haven: Yale University Press, 1994.

Straus, Erwin. *The Primary World of the Senses.* Translated by J. Needleman. New York: Free Press of Glencoe, 1963.

Taylor, John. *A Dream of England: Landscape, Photography and the Tourist Imagination.* Manchester: Manchester University Press, 1994.

Theal, G. M. *Records of the Cape Colony.* Vols. 1–35. London: Clowes, 1897–1905.

Thomas, Nicholas. *Colonialism's Culture: Anthropology, Travel and Culture.* London: Routledge, 1995.

Thompson, Mudie. "Art in South Africa." *State* 2 (August 1909): 181–88.

Thrift, Nigel. "Steps to an Ecology of Place." In *Human Geography Today*, edited by D. Massey, J. Allen, and P. Sarre, 295–322. Cambridge: Polity Press, 1999.

———. "The Still Point: Resistance, Expressive Embodiment and Dance." In *Geographies of Resistance*, edited by S. Pile and M. Keith, 124–51. London: Routledge, 1997.

Thrift, Nigel, and John-David Dewsberry. "Dead Geographies—and How to Make Them Live." *Environment and Planning D: Society and Space* 18 (2000): 411–32.

Tilley, Christopher. *A Phenomenology of Landscape: Places, Paths and Monuments*. Oxford: Berg, 1994.

Times Special Correspondent. *Letters from South Africa*. London: Macmillan, 1893.

Tindall, Gillian. *Countries of the Mind: The Meaning of Place to Writers*. London: Hogarth Press, 1991.

Trapido, Stanley. "Putting a Plough to the Ground: A History of Tenant Production on the Vereeniging Estates, 1896–1920." In *Putting a Plough to the Ground: Accumulation and Dispossession in Rural South Africa, 1850–1930*, edited by W. Beinart, P. Delius, and S. Trapido, 336–72. Braamfontein: Ravan Press, 1986.

Travel in South Africa. Johannesburg: SAR&H Publicity Dept., 1921.

Tripp, Edward, ed. *Dictionary of Classical Mythology*. London: HarperCollins, 1988.

Trotter, Alys Fane. *Old Cape Colony: A Chronicle of Her Men and Houses, from 1652 to 1806*. London: Selwyn & Blount, 1903.

———. *Old Colonial Houses and the Cape of Good Hope*. London: B. T. Batsford, 1900.

Tuan, Yi-Fu. "Surface Phenomena and Aesthetic Experience." *Annals of the Association of American Geographers* 79, no. 2 (1989): 233–41.

Urry, John. *The Tourist Gaze: Leisure and Travel in Contemporary Societies*. London: Sage, 1990.

Uys, Ian. *Delville Wood*. Johannesburg: Uys Publishers, 1983.

———. *Rollcall: The Delville Wood Story*. Johannesburg: Uys Publishers, 1991.

Van den Berg, J. H. "The Human Body and the Significance of Movement: A Phenomenological Study." *Philosophy and Phenomenological Research* 13, no. 2 (December 1952): 159–83.

Van den Bergh, G. N. "Voortrekker plaasbesetting op die Transvaalse Hoeveld: 'n versteurde beeld." *Suid Afrikaanse Tydskrif vir Landmeetkunde en Kartering* (December 1990).

Van Horne, John, and Eileen Drelick, eds. *Traveling the Pennsylvania Railroad: The Photographs of William H. Rau*. Philadelphia: University of Pennsylvania Press, 2002.

Van Sittert, Lance. "Making the Cape Floral Kingdom: The Discovery and Defense of Indigenous Flora at the Cape, ca. 1890–1939." *Landscape Research* 28, no. 1 (2003): 113–29.

Vance, James E., Jr. "California and the Search for the Ideal." *Annals of the Association of American Geographers* 62, no. 2 (1972): 185–210.

Vaughan, William. "The British Landscape Tradition." In *Towards a New Landscape*, 84–101. London: Bernard Jacobson, 1993.

Vesely, Dalibor. *Architecture and Continuity*. London: Architectural Association, 1982.

———. "Architecture and the Conflict of Representation." *Architectural Association Files* 8 (1985): 21–38.

———. "Architecture and the Poetics of Representation." *Daidalos* 25 (1987): 24–36.

Visitor from England. "'Round in Nine': Being the Record of a Trip through Northern and Eastern Transvaal." *SAR&H Magazine*, July 1924, 710.

Visser, Margaret. *The Way We Are*. Harmondsworth: Penguin, 1997.

Wagner, Kathrin. *Rereading Nadine Gordimer*. Bloomington: Indiana University Press, 1994.

Warnke, Martin. *Political Landscape: The Art History of Nature*. London: Reaktion, 1994.

Watson, Stephen. *Selected Essays, 1980–1990*. Cape Town: Carrefour Press, 1990.

Weiss, Allen S. *Mirrors of Infinity: The French Formal Garden*. New York: Princeton Architectural Press, 1995.

———. "No Man's Garden: New England Transcendentalism and the Invention of Virgin Nature." In *Unnatural Horizons: Paradox and Contradiction in Landscape Architecture*, 84–107. New York: Princeton Architectural Press, 1998.

———. "Vaux-le-Vicomte: Anamorphosis Abscondita." In *Mirrors of Infinity: The French Formal Garden*, 32–51. New York: Princeton Architectural Press, 1995.

Wentzel, John. *A View from the Ridge: Johannesburg Retrospect*. Johannesburg: David Phillip, 1975.

Wheatcroft, Geoffrey. *Randlords: The Men Who Made South Africa*. London: Weidenfeld & Nicholson, 1985.

White, Silvo. "On the Comparative Value of African Lands." *Scottish Geographic Magazine* 7 (1891): 191–95.

Wilburn, K. E. "Engines of Empire and Independence: Railways in South Africa, 1863–1916." In *Railway Imperialism*, edited by C. B. Davis and K. E. Wilburn, 25–40. Westport, CT: Greenwood Press, 1991.

Williams, Colin, and Anthony D. Smith. "The National Construction of Space." *Progress in Human Geography* 7 (1983): 502–18.

Williams, John. *The Quarantined Culture: Australian Reactions to Modernism, 1913–1939*. Cambridge: Cambridge University Press, 1995.

Williams, Raymond. *The City and the Country*. London: Paladin, 1975.

Wilson, M., and L. Thompson, eds. *The Oxford History of South Africa*. Vol. 2, *1870–1966*. Oxford: Oxford University Press, 1971.

Wilson, Lady Sarah. *South African Memories*. London: Edward Arnold, 1909.

Winer, Margot. "Landscapes, Fear and Land Loss on the 19th Century South African Colonial Frontier." In *Contested Landscapes: Movement, Exile and Place*, edited by B. Bender and M. Winer, 257–71. Oxford/New York: Berg, 2001.

Wittenberg, Herman. "Ruwenzori: Imperialism and Desire in African Alpinism." In *Spaces and Crossings: Essays on Literature and Culture in Africa and Beyond*, 235–58. New York: P. Lang, 2001.

Wolf, Daniel, ed. *The American Space: Meaning in Nineteenth-Century Landscape Photography*. Middletown, CT: Wesleyan University Press, 1983.

Wolf, James B. "A Grand Tour: South Africa and American Tourists between the Wars." *Journal of Popular Culture* 25, no. 2 (1991): 99–116.

Wongtschowski, B. *Between Woodbush and Wolkberg*. Haenertsburg: B. E. H. Wongschowski, 1990.

Wright, Gwendolyn. *The Politics of Design in French Colonial Urbanism*. Chicago: Chicago University Press, 1991.

Young, Francis Brett. *In South Africa*. London: Heinemann, 1952.

Younghusband, Frances. "Natural Beauty and Geographical Science." *Geographical Journal* 56, no. 1 (July 1920): 1–13.

Zimmer, Oliver. "In Search of Natural Identity: Alpine Landscape and the Reconstruction of the Swiss Nation." *Comparative Studies in Society and History* 40, no. 4 (1998): 637–65.

INDEX

Note: Illustrations are indicated by page numbers in italic type. Color plates are indicated by "*pl.*"

Addison, Joseph, 8
advertising, *213*
aesthetic feeling, 132–33
aesthetics, 7
Africa Colony, The (Buchan), 120–39
Africa, comparative land values of, *pl. 1*
African National Congress, 34
African population of South Africa, *228, 229;*
    apartheid and, 251; attitudes toward, 118;
    Buchan on, 143; displacement of, 19, 25, 34,
    71, 143; erasure of, from national landscape,
    227, 237, 255–56; and farming, 123, 193; land
    reclamation by, 20; and Mafeking siege, 97;
    narratives of descent and, 39–42, 68–69; politi-
    cal relations with, 23, 28, 29, 143; representation
    of, for tourists, 227; reserves for, 227; resistance
    by, 34; in urban areas, 34; and World War I, 33
Afrikaans, 29, 31–32, 36, 243–44, 304n24
Afrikaanse Taalgenootskap, 31
Afrikaner Bond, 37
Afrikaners: in cities, 34, 204, 251; definition
    of, 30; education of, 75; family farm as icon
    of, 142; identity and experience of, 248, and
    landscape, 252–55; and nationalism, 29–34, 36,
    39, 63, 198–99, 250–55; and Pierneef's painting,
    198–99; and railways, 202, 204
agency, personal, 240, 246–47
agriculture: advertising poster for, *213*; African
    versus European approaches to, 193; Afrikaners
    and, 253–54; Boers and, 122–24; and carrying
    capacity of land, 35–36; ideological function of,
    22–24, 155; land ownership and, 40, 140; land
    settlement and, 139–40; nineteenth-century,
    24–25; railways and, 204; Reconstruction and,
    25; technological developments in, 142; in
    Transvaal, 122–24; white settlement and, 242
Alston, Madeline, *From the Heart of the Veld*,
    184–85
analogical imagination, 9, 11, 12, 264n38

Anglo-Boer War, 266n26. *See also* South African
    War (1899–1902)
animals, 70–71
apartheid, 251, 254
appearance, and underlying order, 191–94
architecture: Baker and, 157–66; body and,
    8–10; Cape Dutch, 46, 56, 58, 60, 158, 159,
    177; construction methods in, 158–59;
    imperialism and, 157–60; of Johannesburg, 159;
    landscape and, 166–67; materials of, 158–59,
    163–65, 291n84, 291n87; meanings of, 157–58;
    modernist, 60, 177, 180; nationhood and, 58, 60,
    159–66, 176–77; of Parktown Ridge, 148, 152,
    157, 160–66, 289n30; Ruskin and, 158
Argentina, 24
Aristotle, 104; *Poetics*, 9–10
art: colonial, 181; and cultural identity, 53;
    modernist, 54, 56, 180; public collections of,
    52–53, 55, 63–64; public support for, 55, 179–80;
    reception of, 197. *See also* landscape painting
Arts and Crafts movement, 157–58, 162
Australia, 24, 26, 44, 49, 51

Bachelard, Gaston, 84, 129, 246
Baden-Powell, Robert, 240, 259; as Boy Scouts
    founder, 93–94; at Mafeking, 93, 96–97, *100,*
    101, 102–6, *104,* 116–18; in Matabeleland,
    97–98, 101; "Old Acquaintances," *106;* reportage
    of, 98, 102; and scouting, 99; *Scouting for Boys,*
    94; sketch of Mafeking, 103–5, *104,* 117
Baker, Herbert, 43, 52, 58, 60, 78, 140, 148, 150,
    155–68, 174, 176–77, 240, 259, 289n30, 290n57,
    291n84, 304n11; *Bosch en Dal, pl. 17;* Delville
    Wood Memorial, Longueval, France, *43,* 63,
    64, 195; Ednam, Parktown Ridge, *170, 172;*
    Glenshiel, Parktown Ridge, *145, 170, 171,*
    172; Government House, Pretoria, *172, 174;*
    Northwards, Parktown Ridge, *150, 151, 170,*
    172; Rhodes House, Oxford, 176; South Africa

House, London, *176*; Union Buildings, Pretoria, *28*, 28, 160, *161*, *257*; Villa Arcadia, Parktown Ridge, *162*, *163*, 170, 172, *pl. 18*

Balfour Declaration (1926), 37

Balzac, Honoré de, 88

Bambatha Rebellion (1906), 27

Barnard, Anne, 42

Basutoland, 28

Bechuanaland, 28

Bell, Clive, 191

Benjamin, Walter, 261

Berg, the, 140, 142, 183, 188–91, 194

Bergson, Henri, 84

Bethlehem, Orange Free State, landscape, *233*

Bhabha, Homi, 241

Bishop, Peter, 3, 5, 189–90, 192

Blaauwberg Strand, Cape Town, *219*

black nationalism, 33

Black Week, 93

Bloemfontein, 28

Blood River, Battle of, 253

Boddam-Whetham, Ruby, 43

body potential, 84

body/bodies: architecture and, 9–10; displacement of, 9–10; drama and, 104–5; landscape and, 10–12, 81–89, 129–32, 246, 256–59, 261; landscape painting and, 189; and movement, 83–84, 110; place-signification and, 81–82, 258–59; praxis and, 258; of soldiers, 110, 113; as subject, 82–84, 130, 135, 258–59

Boer farm house burning, *20*

Boer Republics, 19–20

Boerevrou, Der (magazine), 177

Boers, 19–21, 23, 25, 27, 30, 33, 39, 93, 95, 118, 123–25, 138, 253

Bonnefoi, 181–84, 188, 196, *pl. 24*

Bordo, Jonathan, 186, 189, 191

botany, 61–63, 274n81

Botha, Louis, 28, 32–34, 43, 75, 203

Bourdieu, Pierre, 84, 258

Boy Scout movement, 93–94, 116

Braamfontein Company, 146, 148, 149

Brink, Andre, 3

Britain: and character, 99–100; gardens in, 168; and gold, 19; imperialism of, 21–26, 92–93, 99–101, 149, 183–84; map of, *xvi*; and masculinity, 100; nature and nationhood in, 50; patriotism of, 91–93; social ideas in late nineteenth-century, 22–23; and South Africa, 2, 17, 21–23, 30, 33, 37, 239–41, 249–50; and South African War, 19–20, 93, 101–2, 113–16 (*see also* Mafeking)

British Settlement of South Africa Ltd., 141

Broederbond, 32

Brook, Peter, 91

Buchan, John, 71, 75, 85, 116, 163, 224, 240, 244, 254, 259; *The Africa Colony*, 120–39; *Greenmantle*, 138; and landscape, 122–43; life of, 133–34, 283n1; novels of, 138–39; *Prester John*,

138, 140; and Reconstruction, 120–24; and Scotland, 125, 138; subjectivity of, 132–38; and Woodbush, 119

Bulawayo Field Force (BFF), 98

Bunn, David, 155, 190

Bunyan, John, *The Pilgrim's Progress*, 127

Burnham, Frederick, 98

Caldecott, Strat, 225

calisthenics on beach, *74*

Calvinism, 253

Camoens, Luiz Vaz de, *The Lusiads*, 2

Canada, 24, 26, 44, 49, 243

Canberra, 147

Cape Colony: architecture of, 56–60; and nationhood, 40, 60–61; plants in, 61–63, 169; white settlement of, 2, 18–20, 156. *See also* Old Cape; Western Cape

Cape Dutch architecture, 46, 56, 58, 60, 158, 159, 177

Cape Floral Kingdom, 63

Cape Government Railways, 202

Cape Monthly Magazine, 41

Cape Times (newspaper), 58

Cape Town, 28

carriages, railway, 208–9

Carruthers, Jane, 219

Carter, Paul, 129, 181

Casey, Edward, 173

Catalans, 16

Celliers, Jan F. E., *Die Vlakte*, 32

Central South African Railways (CSAR), 202, 211

Cézanne, Paul, 192, 193

Chapman's Peak Drive, 65

character: of architecture, 9; drama and, 10; of landscape, 6, 11–13; personal, 99–100; type versus, 265n41

Childers, Erskine, 116

chorography, 103, 105

"Christmas in South Africa," *pl. 40*

Churchill, Winston, 116

cities: African population in, 34; antiurban attitudes, 22–24, 78, 80, 100–101, 118, 138, 147, 241; colonial artists' relation to, 180–81; imaginings in British, 85, 93, 98, 101–6, 113–18, 121; intelligentsia in, 35; migration to, 50; planning of, 146–47; rural landscapes versus, 51, 78, 80, 137, 240, 254; strategy and tactics in, 106–7

civilizationist model of society, 16

Clark, T. J., 1

class, 114, 147

climate: and cultural essence, 16; geniality of South African, 73, 80, 81; map of South African, *pl. 9*; Mediterranean, 64, 160; Ruskin on importance of, 158, 160; suitability of, for Europeans, 72–73, 98, 161; of Woodbush, 119

Closer Settlement movement, 184, 242

Closer Union movement, 27, 37, 38

Coetzee, J. M., 3, 242, 246, 253–55
Coetzee, Nico, 253
collective memory. *See* memory
colonial art, 181, 186, 189
colonial nationalism: Afrikaner nationalism and, 254–55; and art, 52; and collective memory, 39–42; concept of, 26–27; and cultural activism, 42–43; dual allegiances of, 26–27, 30, 37; and landscape, 50; and language, 243; and local-imperialism relation, 185; Parktown Ridge and, 149; and patriotism, 37–40; promotion of, 37–44; and segregation, 256; and World War I, 43–44. *See also* South Africanism
colonial societies: landscapes of, 50–51, 68; and modernity, 39–40; narratives of descent in, 39–40
colonialism. *See* imperialism
communication media, 101–2
communitas, 114, 116
"Comparative Value of African Lands," *pl. 1*
Conan Doyle, Arthur, 116
concentration camps, 19–20, *21*, 31, 251
Cook, Thomas, 116, 211
Cosgrove, Denis, 3, 181
crafts, local, 164
Cran, Marion, 43
cult of the veld, 66–71, 140, 224, 232
cultural activism, 38, 42–43, 150, 170
cultural identity: activism and, 38, 42–43, 150, 170; apartheid and, 251; art and, 53; Buchan and, 122; discourse and, 46; in early white South Africa, 238–39; gardens and, 168; landscape and, 2–5, 12–13, 17–18, 45–46, 158–59, 244; of nations, 16; nature and, 16. *See also* nations and nationhood
culturalist model of society, 16, 22, 48
curio sellers, 227
currency, 36
Curtis, Lionel, 38

Daily Mail (newspaper), 101
Dalrymple, Lady, 145
Daniels, Stephen, 3
Dart, Raymond, 35, 72
Daughters of the Empire (Canada), 41
dawn, 193
De Certeau, Michel, 88, 95–96, 99, 106–7, 117, 136
De Wet, Christiaan, 251
De Wet, Marie Koopmans, 42
"Deep sabbatical calm, A," *pl. 14*
Delville Wood, Longueval, France, 194–95, 297n93, 297n95
Delville Wood Memorial, Longueval, France (Baker), 43, 63, 64, 195, 248
depth, 130–31
Dewey, John, *Art as Experience*, 132–34
discourse, 46–49, 81
Dominions, 26, 33, 37, 40, 44, 250

Drakensberg, 219, *224*
drama: body and, 104–5; character and, 10; setting for, 105. *See also* theater
Dubow, Saul, 77, 248
Duncan, James, 3
dusk, 193
Dutch East India Company, 2, 18, 52, 168, 253

East London, 211
Eckstein, Hermann, Hohenheim house, Parktown Ridge, 144, 288n12
economy: industrialization and, 35; post–World War I, 33–34; railways and, 35, 202
"The Edge of Beyond," 135
Ednam, Parktown Ridge (Baker), 170, *172*
Education Act (Britain, 1870), 101
elevated landscapes, 45, 134–35, 151–52, 188
Elliot, Arthur, 57, 58, 59, 60
emotion, nature and, 132–33
Empire Exhibition (Wembley), 37, 203
empty landscapes, 44, 66, 68–69, 73, 75, 80, 85–86, 94, 107, 130, 152, 169, 188, 226–32, 244, 253, 262. *See also* wilderness
English-speaking South Africans, 250–51
Enlightenment, 7–9, 15, 16, 83
"Entrance to Karoo," *209*
environment. *See* landscape; nature; place
environmental determinism, 72
environmental imagination, 6, 7, 11, 12
Ermelo District, *247*
escarpment near Harrismith, *141*
escarpment near Letsitele, *pl. 15*
Eskom, 34
"Eventide—when the smoke of battle clears" (Underwood and Underwood), *109*
Everard, Bertha, 178–99, 240, 254, 259, 260; appearance and underlying order in work of, 191–94; *Asbestos Hills*, 188; *Baboon Valley*, 188, *pl. 26*; critical reception of, 178–79, 197–99; Delville Wood paintings by, 194–95, 297n93, 297n95; European travels of, 180, 183, 194; *Evening Voluntary*, 188; as farmer, 179, 182–83, 192–93; *Green Hills*, 188; *The Krantz*, 190; *Land of Luthany*, 188, 194; landscape subjects of, 188–97, 199; life of, 181–83; *Looking towards Swaziland* (also known as *Opal Valley*), 188, 192, *pl. 27*; *Masimoni Vale*, 190; *Mid-winter on the Komati*, 178, 188; and modernity, 199; *Moon and Shadow*, 190, 193, *pl. 32*; *Moonrise*, 188; *Morning Tree*, 190, 193; *The New Furrow*, 197, *pl. 34*; *Pale Hillside*, 189, 190, *pl. 28*; *Peace of Winter*, 181, 188, *pl. 19*; and religion, 182, 194, 195; *Spring, Eastern Transvaal*, 189, *pl. 30*; subjectivity of, 185, 187, 190, 192–99; technique of, 191–96; training of, 180, 181; *Trees and Trenches, Delville Wood*, *pl. 33*; *Twantwani*, 188, 194, *pl. 25*; *Wag-'n-bietjies*, 190, 193; *Winter in the Lowveld*, 190, *pl. 31*; *Winter in the Transvaal*, 190, 193, *pl. 29*

Everard, Charles, 181, 184
Everard Group of painters, 293n1
experience, of nature, 127–32

Fairbridge, Dorothea, 42, 43, 78, 170, 174, 273n62;
    Along Cape Roads, 58; *Historic Farms of South
    Africa*, 58; *Historic Houses of South Africa*, 58; *A
    Pilgrim's Way in South Africa*, 58, 151
False Bay coast, St. James, 65
Farinelli, Franco, 80
farmhouse near Franschoek, *231*
farming. *See* agriculture
Faulkner, William, 88
fauna. *See* animals
Fauvism, 194
Finns, 16
First Afrikaans Language Movement, 31
Fitzpatrick, Percy, 42, 140, 224; *Jock of the
    Bushveld*, 71
flora. *See* plants
Foucault, Michel, 3
Fourie, Jopie, 33
France, 50
Freud, Sigmund, 193
Fripp, C. E., *The City's Own in Action near Pretoria*,
    115
From Sea Level to 6,000 Feet, pl. 36
frontality, 10
frontier, 98, 201, 235, 239
Fry, Roger, 191, 296n78

Garden Route, 218
gardens: Buchan and, 119, 135–36; cultural activ-
    ism and, 43; on estates, 142; meanings of, 157;
    national botanical garden, 61–62; nationhood
    and, 168; of Parktown houses, 160, 167–72; rural
    landscapes and, 168
Garrett, Edmund, 58
Gems from a Floral Paradise, pl. 7
gender roles, 100, 183–84
genius, 117
genius loci, 7–8, 126, 191, 260, 264n19
genre de vie, 48, 81, 122, 123
geographical territory: imaginary, discursive
    construction of, 46–49; nations and, 15–17;
    South Africa and, 29. *See also* landscape; place
geography: landscape and, 8; photography and,
    278n46; in South Africa, 36, 71–73
George, Prince, *78*
German South West Africa, 33, 37
Gilpin, William, 128
Girl Guides, 94
Glenshiel house, Parktown Ridge (Baker), *145*,
    170, *171*, 172
God, 194, 253
God's Window, near Graskop, Transvaal, *223*
Goethe, Johann von, 8, 11, 83
gold, 19, 21, 145
Gombrich, Ernst, 54

Gondwanaland, 63
Goodman, Gwelo, 42, 56, 60; *The Hex River Valley*,
    pl. 4; *The Paarl Church*, pl. 6
Gordimer, Nadine, 3
Gordon, Lucy Duff, 42
Government House, Pretoria (Baker), *172*, *174*
grain revolution, 204
Graphic (magazine), 98, 101
Great Trek, 18, 34, 251, 253, 253
Greater South African identity, 29–30, 37, 240
Green, Nicholas, 3
Gregory, Derek, 3
Grocott & Sherry, plan of Johannesburg, *147*
Group of Seven (Canada), 191, 296n73
guerrilla warfare, 19, 98
Guild of Loyal Women, 40–41, 42, 116, 168

habitus, 84
Haenertsburg, *120*
Häkli, Jouni, 49
Hardy, Thomas, 88
Harrismith, escarpment near, *141*
Harrison, Charles, 186, 261
Häyrinen, Maunu, 49
health, 51, 80, 99–100, 124, 184
hearing, sense of, 131–32
Henshaw, Peter, 255
Herder, Johann Gottfried von, 7
Hermanus, 218, 220
hermeneutics, 86
Hertzog, Barry, 31, 33, 34, 37, 250
Hertzog Prize, 31
Hex River Pass, view from, *210*
Highveld, 66–71, *68–69*, 73, 124–25, 130–37,
    139–40, 169, 182–84, 188, 190, 261, pl. 13, pl. 14
Hirschfeld, C. L. L., 83
historical revivalism, 39, 56, 58
history, reframing of, 229–32, 251
Hofmeyr, Isabel, 193
Hohenheim house, Parktown Ridge (Eckstein),
    144, 288n12
Hopkins, Gerard Manley, 8
horizons, 130–31, 153–56
Hoy, William, 203, 205, 240
Hyde, Ann, 3

identification, 11, 82–83
identity: constructed, 40; landscape and,
    81–82, 84–85; memory and, 39; origins of, 14;
    place and, 14–15. *See also* cultural identity;
    subjectivity
Illustrated London News (magazine), 101, 212
images: bodily subjectivity and, 258; hermeneutic
    role of, 86–87
immigration: Milnerite Reconstruction and,
    23–24; poster advertising, 24; significance of,
    30; suitability of land for, 72–73
Imperial Conference (London, 1924), 203
Imperial Exhibition (1927), 56

Imperial War Graves Commission, 44, 116
imperialism: architecture and, 157–60; and gender roles, 183–84; and moral character, 99–101; Parktown Ridge and, 149; popular support for, 92–93; and Reconstruction, 21–26; South Africanism and, 241–42; and subjectivity, 137–38
Impressionism, 180, 191
improvement, landscape as locus for, 51, 123, 139–42, 155
inauguration ceremony, Rhodes Memorial, Cape Town, 156
indigenous population. *See* African population of South Africa
Industrial and Commercial Workers Union, 34
Ingold, Tim, 84, 187
intelligentsia, 35
interdisciplinarity, 4–5
Ireland, 25
Irish, 16
irrigation canal, 232
Iscor, 34

Jacobs, Jane M., 238
Jameson, Leander Starr, 30
Jameson Raid (1895), 93, 150
Jebb, Richard, *Studies in Colonial Nationalism*, 26
Jekyll, Gertrude, 168
Jock of the Bushveld (Fitzpatrick), 71
Johannesburg: architecture of, 159; growth of, 144–46; mining landscape to south of, 252; and national identity, 144–45; panoramic view of, 146; plan of, 147; railway station in, 203–4, *pl. 37, pl. 38. See also* Parktown Ridge
Johannesburg Art Gallery, 52, 164
journey, 136–37
Juta, Jan, 42

Kaaimans River, 208, 221
Karoo farm, 220
Kaufmann, Eric, 48–49
Kendall, Franklin, 42
Kenya, 240
Kerr, Phillip, 38
Kindergarten, 21, 22, 26, 27, 38, 120, 148–49, 156–57, 266n34
Kipling, Rudyard, 38, 78, 116, 224, 259
Kirstenbosch Botanical Gardens, 61–62, 62
Kitchener, Horatio Herbert, 19, 114
Kodak, 108, 110
Komati River and valley, 182, 182–83, 188–94, 196, 199, 260, *pl. 20–23*
kopjes, 94, 279n19
Kruger National Park, 70, 70–71, 201, 219, 224–26, 226, 252, 302n79
Kruger, Paul, 69, 91, 114
Kunze, Donald, 9–11

La Rey, Jacobus de, 251
labor, 242
Labor Party, 34
land. *See* geographical territory; landscape; nature; rural landscapes
Land Act (1913), 34
Land Survey Act (1927), 36
landscape: Afrikaners and, 252–55; architecture and, 166–67; body and, 10–12, 81–89, 129–32, 246, 256–59, 261; Buchan and, 122–43; character of, 6–8, 11–13; cultural significance of, 2–6, 12–13, 17–18, 49, 158–59, 244; emptiness of, 44, 66, 68–69, 73, 75, 80, 85–86, 94, 107, 130, 152, 169, 188, 226–32, 244, 253, 262; European versus South African, 52–53; identity and, 81–82, 84–85; ideological function of, 45–46; intersubjective versus subjective relation to, 88–89, 256–58; language and, 243–44; as locus of improvement, 51, 123, 139–42, 155; mood of, 6; and movement, 83–84; nationhood and, 17–18, 45–50, 139, 239, 255; phenomenological experience of, 193; photography of, 215–19, 225–26, 228–32; pictorial-visualist approach to, 67, 86; political significance of, 1–3; presence of, 6–8; railways and, 206–7; representations of, 86–88, 258–62; responses to, 3, 6, 11–12, 126; scouting and, 98–99; Smuts and, 77; social transformation and, 2; South African War and, 20, 72, 113; spatial qualities of, 67–69, 73, 75; suitability of, for Europeans, 72–73, 124–25, 159; symbolic, 49–50; textual representations of, 88, 127; World War I and, 195. *See also* geographical territory; nature; place; rural landscapes
landscape painting: in Australia, 51; famous practitioners of, 272n40; history of, 185; Impressionist, 180, 191; institutional aspects of, 54; meanings of, 51; methods of, 53–54; nationhood and, 50–56, 179, 197–99; origins of South African, 53–54, 272n40; styles of, 54; subjects of, 54, 56, 186–88; and technique, 191–96; viewer and, 185–91, 196–97; and ways of seeing, 197–99; and wilderness, 189, 191; World War I and, 195–96. *See also* Everard, Bertha
Lane, Hugh, 52
Langenhoven, C. J., 39
language, 28–32, 36, 243–46, 250, 304n24
Laubser, Maggie, 180
Le Corbusier, 177
League of Nations, 37
Leatherbarrow, David, 8–10, 83
Lefebvre, Henri, 81
Leibrandt, C. V., 41–42, 73
leisure, 211
Leith, Gordon, 176, 203–4, 293n130; "The Huts," Riviera, Killarney, 177
Lessing, Doris, 3
Letsitele, escarpment near, *pl. 15*
lieux de mémoire, 261

literacy, 101, 107
literature, 246, 253–54
Little South African identity, 29–31, 251
"Lord Roberts' Irresistibles on the way to Pretoria" (Underwood and Underwood), *109*
Lovat, Lord, 141
Lowenthal, David, 3
Lowveld, 135, 200, 224
Lutyens, Edward, 52, 63, 168

Macmillan, W. M., 35
Mafeking: contemporary, 260; defense of, 96–97, *97*, 102–6; meaning of, for Britain, 116–18; relief of, 91–93, *pl. 10*; sketch of, 102–5, *104*, 117; town of, 92, 107
Magaliesberg mountains, 153, 260
maps and mapping: of Boer Republics, 21; chorography, 103, 105; lack of, 36; nationhood and, 49; in South African War, 95
Marais, Eugene, *Winternag*, 32
Markham, Violet, 38
Marks, Shula, 77
Marloth, Rudolf, 43, 63
Martienssen, Rex, 177
masculinity: British, 100; outdoor life and, 71, 73, 75, 100, 117–18; soldiers and, 110; and thinking, 131
Masey, Francis, 42, 58
Matabeleland, 97–98
Matabeles, 97–98
materials: in architecture, 158–59, 163–65, 291n84, 291n87; in nature, 158–59, 164–65
Matless, David, 3
Mediterranean, the, 64, 66, 157, 159–60, 163–64
memorials, public, 40, 43, 44, 116
memory: identity and, 39; nationhood and, 17; realm of, 261; representation and, 261; South Africa and, 39–42, 262; voluntary versus involuntary, 261
Merrington, Peter, 66, 273n62
merchant class: artistic tastes of, 53, 56; farms bought by, 140
Merleau-Ponty, Maurice, 82, 130, 258
metaphor, 10, 96, 128, 174, 186, 258, 261
metaxy, 86
Metcalf, Thomas, 160
metis, 117
metropole. *See* cities
Michaelis Collection, 52, 63
Michaelis, Max, 52
Miller, J. Hillis, 45, 88
Millin, Sarah Gertrude, 66
Milner, Alfred, 14, 20–21, 22, 23–27, 92, 115, 120–22, 139, 145, 148, 149, 157, 159, 202, 240, 242
mimesis, 9–11
mining landscape, south of Johannesburg, 252
modernism: in architecture, 60, 177, 180; in art, 54, 56, 180

modernity: colonial societies and, 39–40; diverse effects of, 248; Everard's painting and, 199; photography and, 213; railways and, 202–3, 213–14, 235; South Africanism and, 241; and wilderness, 214
Moerdijk, Gerard, 177, 203–4
Montesquieu, Charles-Louis de Secondat, Baron de La Brède et de, 7
monuments. *See* memorials, public
Morris, William, 8, 158, 164
Mossel Bay, 211
"Mountain, Wood & Stream," 217
movement, 83–84, 110, 131
Muizenberg, 211

narratives of descent, 17, 18, 29, 39–42, 68–69, 168
Nasionale Pers, 32
Natal Colony, 18–19
Natal Government Railways, 202
national anthem, 254
National Flag Act (1926), 36
National Gallery, Cape Town, 55, *55*–56, 63
National Monuments Council, 36, 41
national parks, 69–71. *See also* Kruger National Park
National Parks Act (1926), 36
National Parks Board, 225
National Party, 33, 34, 255; Afrikaner, 33
National Society for the Preservation of Objects of Historic Interest and Natural Beauty in South Africa, 41, 42, 43
National Union of South African Arts and Crafts, 164, 178
nationalism: Afrikaner, 29–34, 39, 63, 198–99, 250–55; black, 33; colonial, 26–27, 30, 37–44, 50, 52, 149, 185, 254–55; language-based, 245; South Africanism, 37–44, 67, 73, 85, 145, 170, 177, 241–42, 244–45, 248
nationalization of nature, 48–49
nations and nationhood: architecture and, 58, 60, 159–66, 176–77; flora and, 61–63; gardens and, 168; geographical territory and, 15–17; identity of, 16; landscape and, 17–18, 45–50, 139, 239, 255; landscape painting and, 50–56, 179, 197–99; and memory, 17; nature and, 48–49, 80; photography and, 215–18, 228–37; place and, 15; railways and, 201–2, 204–7, 234–36; SAR&H publications and, 212, 215–18, 224–27, 234–36; as social construction, 15–16; states and, 15; tourism and, 234. *See also* cultural identity; nationalism
Native Land Areas Act, 139
natural monuments, 48
naturalization of the nation, 48–49, 68, 254, 255
nature: cultural identity and, 16; masculinity and, 71, 73, 75, 100, 117–18; materials in, 158–59, 164–65; nationhood and, 48–49, 80; Parktown Ridge and, 172–73; and personal character, 99–100. *See also* landscape; rural landscapes

Naude, Hugo, 56
Netherlands, 2
Netherlands South Africa Railway Company
   (NZASM), 202
New Delhi, 147
New Zealand, 24, 26, 44
newspapers, 101–2
Nguni people, 19
noncognitive process, art and, 186, 194, 196
Nora, Pierre, 261
Norberg-Schulz, Christian, 82–83
northward route, 156, 289n40
Northwards, Parktown Ridge (Baker), 150, 151,
   170, 172
Norval's Pont Concentration Camp, 21
nostalgia, 3, 5, 39–40, 48, 60, 66, 77, 121, 147, 155,
   168, 172, 189, 191, 193, 194, 196, 197, 199, 231, 242,
   256

Ogborn, Miles, 241
Old Cape, 60, 63
Old Town House, Cape Town, 52
"On the Rolling Highveld," 233
"On the Stoep," pl. 39
Orange River Colony, 20–21, 26–27
Oranje Vrijstaat (Orange Free State), 18–19, 32, 66
orientation, 152
Oudtshoorn, near, 221
outspan, Ermelo District, 247
ox-wagon, 230

painting. See landscape painting
Palladio, Andrea, 164
panoptical vision, 99
panoramas, 209–10
Park Station, Johannesburg, 203–4, pl. 37, pl. 38
Parktown Ridge: architecture of, 148, 152, 157,
   160–66, 289n30; climate of, 160; contemporary,
   260; creation of, 144, 146–48; gardens of,
   160, 167–72; inhabitants of, 148–51, 288n17;
   layout of, 146–47; and nature, 172–73; physical
   attributes of, 151; and politics, 175; prospect
   from, 157, 173–76; views from/of, 150, 152–57,
   153, 154, 176
"Passenger Train Crossing the Karoo," 216
pastoral body, 189
pastoralism, 22, 39, 48, 121, 142, 147, 155, 168,
   189–91, 193, 197, 240, 242, 254, 256
patriotism, 37–40
Peace of Winter (Everard), pl. 19
performatives, 88
phenomenology, 82, 193
Phillips family, 42
Phillips, Florence, 42–43, 52–53, 61, 78, 140, 144,
   149–50, 164, 170, 172, 178, 240
Phillips, Lionel, 43, 46, 52, 61, 78, 140, 144, 150,
   172, 240
photography: black-and-white, 212, 228, 236;
   geography and, 278n46; and history, 231–32;

landscape, 215–19, 225–26, 228–32; modernity
   and, 213; nationhood and, 215–18, 228–37; from
   Parktown Ridge, 174; railways and, 234–36; in
   SAR&H publications, 212–19; of South African
   War, 92, 108, 109, 110, 111, 112, 113; space and,
   213; tourism and, 218
phylloxera epidemic, 56
Picturesque, 83–84, 141–42
Pierneef, Jan Hendrik, 177, 179–80, 192, 194,
   198–99, 204, 253, 298n117; Amajuba, pl. 35
Pilgrim's Rest District, 245
Pilrig, Parktown Ridge, 165
place: bodily experience of, 81–89, 129–32,
   258–59; identification with, 82–83, 129, 256–57;
   identity and, 14–15; representations of, 258–61.
   See also geographical territory; landscape;
   nature; space
plants, 61–63, 168–70, 172, pl. 7
politics, landscape and, 1–3
Pollan, Michael, 11
polo meet, 74
Pope, Alexander, 8
popular culture, 101–2, 114
Port Alfred, 218
Port Elizabeth, 74, 211
Port St. Johns, 211
Portugal, 2
postcards, 107, 213, 216–17
posters, 212, 213
Post-Impressionism, 191–92, 194, 296n78
poststructuralism, 82
praxis, 258–59, 306n70
precognitive knowledge, 128, 132, 134
Pred, Alan, 119
Preller, Gustav, 31–32, 39, 251
Pretoria, 28
print media, 101–2
prospect, 45, 94, 157, 173–76, 188–90. See also views
Proust, Marcel, 88, 261
Purified National Party (PNP), 250

race, white unity and, 34, 36–37
racism, 2, 40, 256. See also apartheid
railways: carriage design, 208–9; construction
   of, 206–7, 208; and development, 35, 202, 204;
   economic development and, 35; elevations,
   Cape Town-Hutchinson section, 207;
   modernity and, 202–3, 213–14, 235; national
   parks and, 224–25; nationhood and, 201–2,
   204–7, 234–36; passenger use of, 204–5, 210–11,
   260; photography and, 212–19, 234–36; social
   impact of, 203; and South African War, 95, 102;
   spatial transformation by, 206–11, 213; tourism
   and, 37, 200–201, 201, 205, 211, 218–19; travelers' experience on, 207–9; and wilderness, 201,
   206, 209, 214, 224–25. See also South African
   Railways & Harbours
Randlords, 38, 52
reality. See underlying order, and appearance

recognition, 9–11
reconciliation, of white settlers, 27–28, 34, 38, 39, 60, 75, 118, 138, 219, 239
Reconstruction, Milnerite, 20–26, 34, 39, 48, 67, 120–22, 139–40, 149, 202, 205, 240, 242
Reitz, Deneys, 75
"Relief of Mafeking," newspaper placard, *pl. 10*
Renaissance Italy, cities and countryside in, 154
representation, 8–10, 86–88, 187, 258–62
republicanism, 31–33, 39
rhetoric, 127
Rhodes, Cecil John, 20–21, 30, 40, 41, 58, 61, 75, 76, 93, 102, 145, 148, 149, 156–59, 240, 290n57
Rhodes House, Oxford (Baker), 176
Rhodes Memorial, Cape Town, *156*, 156
Rhodesia, 28, 37, 240
Rider Haggard, Henry, 224
Roberts, Lord, 102, *103*
Robinson, William, 172; *The Wild Garden*, 168
Romanticism, 16, 48
romanticization of South Africa, 240–42
Rousseau, Jean-Jacques, 7, 129
Roworth, Edward, 42, 55–56, 198; *A Farm on the Hills, Kuils River*, pl. 5
rural landscapes: gardens and, 168; landscape painting and, 50–56; metropole versus, 51, 78, 80, 137, 240, 254; nationhood and, 18, 48; and social ideals, 22–24
Ruskin, John, 8, 56, 58, 102, 156–58, 160, 164, 242

Sabie Game Reserve, 69, *70*, *71*, 200–201, *201*, 219
Said, Edward, 3, 4, 124, 137, 277n148
Salisbury, 147
Samuel, Raphael, 144, 235
SAR&H. *See* South African Railways & Harbours
Sauer, Carl O., 8, 11
Schreiner, Olive, 158
Schwarz, Bill, 114, 137, 255
Scotland, 23, 125–26, 138
scouting, 98–99, 105–6, *106*
Scouting for Boys (Baden-Powell), 94
sculpture. *See* memorials, public
Sea Point, 211
Second Afrikaans Language Movement, 31
Selati Game Reserve, *225*
Selbourne, Lord, 26
senses, 131–32, 262
Serton, Piet, 72
Shaftesbury, Anthony Ashley Cooper, Third Earl of, 7–8, 11
Shields, Rob, 3
Shonas, 97
Shurmer-Smith, Pamela, 178
sightseeing, 232
Singwitsi Game Reserve, 69, 71, 219
Sketch (magazine), 101, 212
Smithard, George, 42, 198, 204; *Summer in the Soutpansberg*, 140, *pl. 16*
Smuts family, *42*

Smuts, Jan Christiaan, 32–34, 37, 43, 52, 75–78, *78*, 141, 203, 243, 245, 250
soldiers: bodies of, 110, 113; casualties of, 114; correspondence of, 107; images of, *92*, *109*, *111*, *112*; and photography, 108, 110; South Africa as experienced by, 115
Solomon, J. M., 42
Sontag, Susan, 231
sound, 131–32
South Africa: Boers in, 19–20; Britain and, 2, 17, 21–23, 30, 33, 37, 239–41, 249–50; British, *xvi*, 25, 250; capital cities of, 28; climatological map of, *pl. 9*; colonial, 18–28; Dutch in, 18; Europe and, 2; geographical study of, 36; government of, 27–28; imaginary views of, 2; as land of contrasts, 218–19, 234, 236; landscape's role in, 1–6; productivity of, 4; rainfall in, 18; as state, 15, 18, 27–28. *See also* African population of South Africa; nationalism; nations and nationhood; white South Africa
South Africa Act (1909), 27–28, 202
South Africa House, London (Baker), 176, 248, 249
South African Academy of Art, 180
South African Association of Science Journal, 61
South African Brigade, 44
South African Constabulary, 25
South African Institute of Art, 180
South Africanism: and collective memory, 39–42; and cult of the veld, 67; decline of, 244–45, 248, 251–52; Delville Wood Memorial and, 248; imperialism and, 241–42; Johannesburg and, 145; and landscape, 73, 85; loyalist, 241, 248; and modernity, 241; Old Cape and, 177; and patriotism, 37–39; plants and, 170; women and, 42–43; World War I and, 43–44. *See also* colonial nationalism
South African Labour Corps, 33
South African National Union, 41
South African Nation (journal), 248
South African Natives National Council, 34
South African Party, 28, 32, 33
South African Railways & Harbours Magazine, 204–6, 208, 210, 216, 218, 219, 224–25, 230, 232
South African Railways & Harbours (SAR&H): administration of, 203; creation of, 202; economic impact of, 35, 202, 204; finances of, 204; journal of, 204–6; and nationhood, 212, 215–18, 224–27, 234–36; Park Station for, 203–4; political impact of, 202–3, 224; publications of, 211–19, 224–27, 230; Publicity Department, 205–6, 211–12, 216, 230, 236; and tourism, 37. *See also* railways
South African Railways (SAR), 200, 202, *207*
South African Republic. *See* Zuid Afrikaansche Republiek
South African Society of Artists, 54
South African War (1899–1902): Afrikaner historiography of, 251; Afrikaner nationalism and, 251; Boer army in, 94–95; Boer field map,

96; Britain and, 19–20, 113–16; British army in, 94–95, 114; British responses to, 93, 114–16; images of, *92, 108, 109, 110, 111, 112*, 113; landscape and, 20, 72, 113; map of, *pl. 11*; name of, 266n26; overview of, 19–20; print media and, 101–2; soldiers of, 107–13; tourism connected with, 116; white South Africa and, 19, 72, 239. *See also* Mafeking

space: Impressionist painting and, 180; intersubjective versus subjective relation to, 86; phenomenology of, 82; photography and, 213; railways and transformation of, 206–11, 213; of South African landscape, 67–69, 73, 75, 85–86; subjectivity and, 246–47. *See also* place

spatial stories, 88, 107–8, 113

Spectator (magazine), 121

speed, 210

springbok rampant, South Africa House, London, *249*

SS Mendi, 33

State (journal), 38, 39, 53, 58, 61, 66, 159, 241

states, 15. *See also* nations and nationhood

statues. *See* memorials, public

Statute of Westminster (1931), 250

"Stem, Die" ("The Voice") (national anthem), 254

Stern, Irma, 180

Stevenson-Hamilton, James, 225

Stone House, Parktown Ridge, *165, 166*, 171

strategy, versus tactics, 95–96, 98–99, 106–7

structures of seeing, 215–19, 225–29, 260

subcontinent: Afrikaner nationalism and, 252–53; British imagination and, 114, 116; British settlement of, 23–25, 28–30, 40, 120–22, 139–40, 205; Buchan and, 121; South African War and, 19–21; suitability of, for Europeans, 71–73, 124–25

subjectivity: body and, 82–84, 130, 135, 258–59; Buchan and, 132–38; contrapuntal, 77–78, 184–85, 277n148 (*see also* traveling); defined, 14, 265n4; of Everard, 185, 187, 190, 192–99; imperialism and, 137–38; and intersubjectivity, 86, 88–89, 256–58; marginal, 247–48; of painters, 186–87; of scouts, 98–99, 105–6; space and, 246–47; traveling, 77–79, 138, 174, 177, 192, 234, 277n148 (*see also* contrapuntal). *See also* identity

Sublime, 188

suburbs, 147

Suid Afrikaanse Akademie for Wetenskap en Kuns (South African Academy of Science and Arts), 179

Summer in the Soutpansberg (Smithard), 140, *pl. 16*

Swartberg Pass, 222

Swaziland, 28

Switzerland, 48–49, 81

synoptical vision, 99, 210

tactics, versus strategy, 95–99, 106–7, 117

Tanganyika, 240

Tatlow, A. H., 205

technological pastoralism, 142, 242

temenos, 134, 136, 286n97

territory. *See* geographical territory

texts, landscape and, 88

"The Huts," Riviera, Killarney (Leith), *177*

Theal, George McCall, 41–42, 73

theater, 103–6. *See also* drama

Thrift, Nigel, 82

Tilley, Christopher, 85, 87, 137

Times History of the War in South Africa, 115

Times (London) (newspaper), 102

Timewell, Parktown Ridge, *167, 175*

Tongaat-Hulett Sugar Estates, 60

tourism: British, to South Africa, 37; medical, 72; nationhood and, 234; nature and, 71; photography and, 218; railways and, 37, 200–201, *201*, 205, 211, 218–19; and South African War, 116; in Western Cape, 64, 66

Transkei, *223*

Transvaal, 20–21, 23, 25–27, 32, 66, 119–37, *133, 135, pl. 12. See also* Highveld

Transvaal Game Protection Society, 69

travel, 127–29. *See also* tourism

travel writing, 124, 126

trees, 169, 190–91, 193–94

Trotter, Alys Fane, 42, 58

Tuan, Yi-Fu, 5, 12

Tucker, Kidger, "Rhodes Over Africa," 155

Turner, E. S.: *In an Old Dutch Garden at the Cape, pl. 3; Zimbabwe Ruins at Midnight, pl. 2*

type. *See* character

underlying order, and appearance, 191–94

Underwood and Underwood, *109*, 282n84

Union Buildings, Pretoria (Baker), *28*, 28, 160, *161*, 257

Union Department of Agriculture, 142

"Union Limited in Tulbagh Kloof," *215*

United States, 48–49

University of Witwatersrand, 35, 176, 180

urban areas. *See* cities

Urry, John, 232

utopian visions of South Africa, 78, 139, 259

Van der Stel, Simon, 41, 63

Van der Stel, Willem Adriaan, 43, 61

Van Riebeeck, Jan, 40, 61

Van Riebeeck Society, 41

Van Sittert, Lance, 62

veld, 66–71, *68–69*, 73, 126, 229–30, 234, 244, 246, 253. *See also* Highveld

Versailles Peace Conference (1919), 203

Vesely, Dalibor, 306n70

Victoria League (Britain), 41, 116

Victoria, Queen, 102

"View from the stoep of retired civil servant, Robertson," *243* viewer, landscape painting and the, 185–91, 196–97

views: from/of Parktown Ridge, 152–57, 176; on landscape, 45; from trains, 208–9. *See also* prospect

Villa Arcadia, Parktown Ridge (Baker), *162, 163, 170, 172, pl. 18*

Volksblad, Die, 14

Volschenk, Jan, 56

Von Humboldt, Alexander, 8, 83

Voortrekker Monument, 251, 253

Vrouemonument, 31

wagons across the veld, 253

Wales, 23

Wallace, Edgar, 116

war correspondents, 102, *103*

War Graves Commission, 63

Ware, Fabian, 38

Weiss, Allen S., 200

Wellington, John, 72

Wembley Empire Exhibition (1924), 37, 56

Wenning, Pieter, 56

Wernher, Beit & Company, 150

Western Cape: climate of, 274n75; European character of, 61; flora of, 62–63; landscape painting in, 54, 56; Mediterranean character of, 64, 66, 157, 159–60

Westminster, Duke of, 141

"Where Good Sport Is Followed by Good Appetite," *pl. 8*

Whistler, James Abbott McNeill, 193

white South Africa: British settlement of, 205; Cape Dutch architecture and, 60; cult of the veld and, 66–71; empty landscape and, 226–32; establishment of, 28–37, 64, 239; landscape and, 3–4; and national identity, 28–37, 255; and

patriotism, 37–40; photography and, 215–16, 236; railways and, 201–7, 210–11; reconciliation in, 27–28, 34, 38, 39, 60, 75, 118, 138, 219, 239; settlement of, 23–26, 139–40; South African War and, 19, 72, 239; and statehood, 27–28; suitability of land for, 72–73, 124–25, 159. *See also* nationalism; nations and nationhood

wilderness: landscape painting and, 189, 191; meaning of, 48; modernity and, 214; nationhood and, 48; preservation of, 69–71; railways and, 201, 206, 209, 214, 224–25; veld and, 66–69. *See also* empty landscapes

Wilderness lagoon, 222

Williams, Raymond, 50

Witwatersrand, 203

Witwatersrand gold mines, 21

women: in cultural movements, 42–43; and gender roles, 100, 183–84; on the veld, 184; voting rights of, 294n14

Woodbush, 119, *120*, 134–40, 260

"Worcesters charging a kopje" (Underwood and Underwood), *109*

working classes, 114

World War I, 33–34, 43–44, 63, 75, 195–96, 249

Wren, Christopher, 162, 164

Yates, Alan, 293n124; view from Northwards, Parktown Ridge, *150*

Younghusband, Francis, 77

Zionism, 15

Zuid Afrikaansche Republiek (ZAR, South African Republic), 18–19, 120, 145

Zuid-Afrikaansche Akademie voor Taal, Letteren en Kunst, 31

"Zulu Types," 229